Adolescent Psychology

ADOLESCENT PSYCHOLOGY

A Developmental View

Norman A. Sprinthall
North Carolina State University

W. Andrew Collins
University of Minnesota

ADDISON-WESLEY PUBLISHING CO.

Reading, Massachusetts
Menlo Park, California
London
Amsterdam
Don Mills, Ontario
Sydney

Library of Congress Cataloging in Publication Data

Sprinthall, Norman A., 1931–
  Adolescent psychology.

  Includes bibliographical references and index.
  1. Adolescent psychology. I. Collins, W. Andrew,
1944–   . II. Title. [DNLM: 1. Adolescent psychology.
WS 462 S769a]
BF724.S67 1984   155.5   82-18397
ISBN 0–201–16301–2

ISBN 0–201–16301–2
ABCDEFGHIJ–HA–89876543

To
Douglas, Jayne, and Carolyn Sprinthall
and
Caroline and Drew Collins

Preface

.This volume on adolescent psychology, like all efforts to encapsulate a field of knowledge, is a product of the history of the field, but it is also an attempt to frame the knowledge more coherently and helpfully than its precursors. The history of psychology indicates that as late as the 1950s the psychology of adolescence was usually not viewed as a distinct field of study. Adolescence was commonly treated either as simply a recapitulation of earlier stages of development or as a sociocultural phenomenon that existed only when the organization of a society fostered or required it. In the latter case the study of adolescence was largely a derivative of sociology. This ambivalent history has generally left adolescent psychology as a field of study without a strong central focus. Commonly, texts are relativistic and eclectic, without a coherent set of theories concerning adolescence. As a result, knowledge of adolescent development has seemed rather like an encyclopedia of findings, loosely fitted together.

A major shortcoming results from this approach: The bits and pieces of information about adolescence can rarely be applied to gain a better understanding of the experiences and behaviors of youth. Philosophers such as Ryle and Scheffler distinguish between knowledge *about* and knowledge *how to*. Most information currently available on adolescent development is of the first type. A usual approach in texts on adolescent development is to present information and descriptions gleaned from numerous research studies that are themselves largely atheoretical. Such descriptive information is interesting; but often little thought is given to its usefulness, either by the researchers who produced the information or by the persons who work with adolescents everyday.

In our view the information that has now accumulated about adolescent development is potentially useful to such persons. Consequently, this volume attempts to present both knowledge about adolescents and knowledge about how to work with them. By adopting an emergent and promising framework, one outlining the multiple domains in which adolescent development occurs, we can address both aspects of the study of adolescent development. Whether you are simply a person who has a general interest in and curiosity about the nature of adolescence or are someone who is looking forward to or is currently filling a helping role, we think you will find this dual focus helpful.

Just a few examples make the point. Often in a helping role it becomes obvious that a teenager may be experiencing emotional difficulty. In Chapter 11 you will be given descriptive information about the basic psychological defenses commonly employed in such cases and some clues about how to "read" the common significance of certain behaviors, particularly how to distinguish between normal developmental difficulties and more serious problems. Then you will be given some how-to information—in this case how to refer a teenager for needed help. In our view both perspectives are of value; it is important to understand general principles and concepts about adolescents and also to consider how the ideas might be applied.

In another section of the book you will find further material to help you understand the common stages of value development of adolescents, as well as suggestions on how to lead discussion groups focused on value dilemmas faced by teenagers. Similarly, on the sensitive issues of sexual development we present some basic facts on sexuality and its emergence around puberty, and then we offer examples of sex education approaches particularly appropriate to teenagers at different stages of growth. There is also a section outlining major ideas about interpersonal development during adolescence, followed by a detailed curriculum guide on peer counseling as a technique for facilitating interpersonal and self-awareness. You will find other examples throughout the text linking theory and research to practice.

We have tried to present current information on adolescent development in a format that will broaden your appreciation for the connection between the world of psychology and the worlds of teenagers and their families as described in anecdote and in the great accounts of youth in literature. We have included special topics throughout the book to highlight the parallels. For example, we compare Sylvia Plath's tragic suicide with the account from the novel *I Never Promised You a Rose Garden* to illustrate both the despair and the hope in treatment for extreme forms of mental illness. We quote some excerpts from Dostoevski—from *Crime and Punishment* to illustrate a stage of Kohlberg's theory of moral development and from *The Brothers Karamazov* to illustrate the link between the Grand

Inquisitor as an earlier version of cult power and the Jonestown tragedy. Throughout, we draw from cases of adolescents—troubled, floundering, coping—that illustrate the principles of social and personal change that characterize the second decade of life.

Finally, we have selected a few outstanding figures in the study of adolescent development for whom we provide biographies. We tried to do more than just give facts about leading theorists and practitioners such as Erik Erikson, Gisela Konopka, David Elkind, and Lawrence Kohlberg; we also tried to reveal something about the significant events in their own lives. For example, we recount Erikson's moment of truth when Freud asked him to give up his moratorium and join Freud's institute; Konopka's almost unbelievable life on the run from the Nazis; Elkind's autonomy in rejecting the common psychological theories of his graduate professors; and Kohlberg's moral stand as a graduate trainee in opposing indiscriminate electroshock therapy. These biographies should help you understand the human side of the enterprise of psychology. Behind every theory is a fully human being, a person who is the product of interesting and formative interactions.

There are a number of persons we wish to thank for their assistance. Reviews from Dale Blyth, Larry Shelton, Frederick Schwants, and Elizabeth Henry provided us with needed perspective and helpful feedback. Less formal but nonetheless real help was provided by our colleagues, such as Lawrence Kohlberg, William Perry, and Ralph Mosher from the banks of the Charles River in Boston; James Mackey, James Rest, William Bart, Robert Beck, Willard Hartup, and Megan Gunnar from the banks of the Mississippi River in Minneapolis. Lonnie Behrendt performed the crucial task of translating often hurried, sometimes cryptic, and frequently misspelled phrases into polished product with grace and speed. For that help we are indeed grateful.

Our final thought is one that often comes with closure on a project. As writers, we are prone to feel at this moment a bit like Ed McMahon in his classic routine with Johnny Carson. McMahon says, "And here in my hand is all there is to know about———. Everything is right here!" Carson usually turns and, with clever rhetoric and obvious nonverbal demurrer, says, "Not quite," and he then proceeds to add new and intriguing information. To forestall that possibility in our own case, we will resort to Gordon Allport's dictum. Our closure is temporary. We will remain open to new ideas and evidence. For the present we have taken a stand, thus being in Allport's words "whole-hearted yet half-sure" or in William Perry's terms "committed relativists."

Minneapolis, Minnesota   N.A.S.
April 1983   W.A.C.

Contents

CHAPTER 6
Moral Judgment and Value Development   175

CHAPTER 7
Family Relations and Influences 215

CHAPTER 8
Peer Relations and Influences
in Adolescence 259

CHAPTER 9
Adolescent Sexuality   293

Adolescents and Secondary Schools   407

CHAPTER 13
Career Development During Adolescence

CHAPTER 14
College Students: A New Phase of Adolescence?

APPENDIX
A High School Course: Peer Counseling— A Curriculum Guide

Adolescent Psychology

CHAPTER 1

History and Directing Concepts

"Those who ignore history are doomed to repeat it."
SANTAYANA

INTRODUCTION

In this chapter we will attempt to honor the philosopher Santayana by providing you with a brief history of adolescence. The question that is almost always asked is simple: Is adolescence real, a genuine stage; or is it merely an artificial invention by a few societies or cultures? Obviously, this question is an important one. If adolescence is a cultural invention, then we must look to sociology rather than psychology for information, since the existence of adolescence as a concept in that case depends totally on each particular culture. On the other hand, adolescence may be a genuine stage of human development, or it may represent the situational responses of individuals to the transition to adulthood in a given society or culture. If these perspectives are more nearly accurate, then ignorance of adolescent psychology will doom us, just as the lack of historical knowledge would doom the diplomat.

A second objective of the chapter is to provide you with some basic concepts. The assumptions, or presuppositions, of any particular field of study are important. Often, however, these assumptions are not shared with the new student of a subject. Since the overall framework for the study of adolescence is based on several fundamental elements, we think it is important to give you those concepts at the outset. We are aware of the dangers of this approach, namely, that you may not understand how all of these pieces fit together until you have finished the book. As a result, we have tried to do more than just give you some definitions and assumptions. Relevant connections are provided so that you may anticipate the *gestalt*—the whole picture—while learning about some of the parts. Now to history.

ADOLESCENCE: A GENUINE STAGE OR AN ARTIFICIAL CULTURAL INVENTION?

There is a theory, sometimes called historical inevitability, that says that great persons would have been created if they had not, in fact, existed. In other words, during certain periods historical forces create the atmosphere that allows individuals to emerge and achieve recognition. Thus in Germany in the 1930s, unemployment, inflation, the elimination of the monarchy, the harsh terms of the Versailles Treaty, and other factors created the conditions that produced a "strong man," Hitler. The times in Germany were ripe for a dictator in 1933, although just ten years before, Hitler's attempted coup d'etat had failed miserably. It is possible to make similar cases for George Washington's emergence as a brilliant general or for Joan of Arc's success in galvanizing French nationalism.

In a similar vein, particular cultural and societal events seem to have fostered the emergence of adolescence as a distinct period of human development—and as a legitimate field of study. Although the fundamental psychological and physiological components have always existed in each young person regardless of historical period, the culture—the adult society—has not always recognized the unique characteristics of adolescence. There is an old philosophical chestnut that asks, "Does a falling tree in Siberia make any noise if there is no one around to hear it?" An updated version would be, "What if we gave a war and nobody came?" Can something like a tree falling—or a war, or an adolescent—exist if it is not acknowledged?

In other words, can an adult society ignore something that is as real as adolescence? That idea may strike you as odd, but such has been the case for adolescence—and for other developmental periods as well. For example, until adults recognized and allowed childhood to emerge, it hardly existed. For long centuries it was thought that as soon as a child reached the age of six or seven, the child was ready to be trained as an adult. Children were considered as little more than midget-sized adults [1]. Except for a tiny proportion of the rich and the well-born, they worked alongside adults in the fields, they fought adult wars, they worked in the mines, and with the coming of industrialization they worked from dawn to dusk in the factories. They also died in those work places and in those wars.

Schooling for children, over the 4000–5000-year span of written history, is only a recent phenomenon. Even in this country, free public primary schools did not come into being until the reforms of Horace Mann in the 1850s. So only in the past 150 years or so have adult Western societies even recognized childhood, the juvenile years from 6 or 7 to 12 or 13, as a special stage of growth. The children, of course, have been there all along. But adult recognition was required before childhood could be discovered.

Once childhood was discovered, a whole series of changes followed. Laws were passed protecting children's health and welfare. The practice in England of harnessing young children like dogs to haul coal-filled sleds out of the mines ended. Sending children to war in crusades was largely abandoned, although there were some gruesome exceptions during the waning days of World War II. New school programs were set up to help nurture the special abilities of juveniles; gone was the mindless repetition, the endless copying of assignments.

What was true for the discovery of childhood in the last century has been the case for adolescence in this century. Only recently have adults in industrialized nations and cultures begun to perceive adolescents' physiological and psychological needs and capabilities as unique, and this perception has created the opportunity to recognize a stage of human growth. As a result, our understanding of the nature of persons in that stage has increased. In the last half of the twentieth century we are beginning to witness some changes in how adolescents are treated by adult society, similar to the changes experienced by juveniles in the nineteenth century. The extension of public education beyond eighth grade in this country is the most obvious difference. In western Europe this change has not yet occurred; there apprenticeships are still the rule for the majority of adolescents.* Similarly, school-age adolescents no longer go to war, as they once did. The accompanying illustration is a copy of the enlistment papers of William Wellman as a Seaman in the U.S. Navy just prior to the War of 1812. He was just over 4 feet tall and 13 years old at the time. He was following the family tradition. His older brother Jeddadiah had fought against the British in the Revolutionary War in 1786; Jeddadiah at the time was also an early adolescent.

Whether society acknowledges adolescence as a special time between childhood and adulthood determines the distinct recognition of this life period; but acknowledgment alone does not necessarily solve the problems of adolescents. Without recognition, as discussed above, young persons in their early teens were simply rushed into adulthood in the past. As described in the chapter on secondary schools, this definition of adulthood was assigned to all teenagers who did not continue schooling beyond grammar school. That is, if you did not stay in school past grade 7 or 8, you became an adult. If you were one of the few who did stay in school, you

---

* One author's father was bound at the age of 13 as a dry goods clerk in England—a contract that was broken when he left work one day to join his family migrating to America.

No. 6727

I, DAVID GELSTON, Collector of the District of New-York, *do hereby certify, That* William W Wellman —— *an American Seaman, aged* thirteen —— *Years, or thereabouts, of the Height of* four *Feet* 1 1/2 *Inches,* light —— *Hair,* light *Complexion,* is very much freckled in the face & has a large scar on the back of his right hand born in Fairfield County State of Connecticut —— *has this Day produced to me Proof, in the Manner directed by the Act, entitled, " An Act for the Relief and Protection of American Seamen;" and, pursuant to the said Act, I do hereby certify, That the said* William W Wellman *is a Citizen of the United States of America.* In Witness whereof *I have hereunto set my Hand and Seal of Office, this* twenty first *Day of* June 1806.

David Gelston Collector.

William Wellman's enlistment papers for the U.S. Navy in 1806 at age 13 years

were not an adolescent; you were a "large boy." If you were a girl in the 1850s, you finished schooling and childhood at about 12 or 13 and then went into the mills or to the farms [2].

Despite the obviously critical importance of social definition, much of what we usually recognize as unique about the adolescent experiences clearly is not new to this century. Norman Kiell's highly acclaimed work, *The Universal Experience of Adolescence,* clearly shows that teenage issues and concerns have existed down through the centuries [3]. In fact, passages from Saint Augustine (fourth century A.D.), John Milton (seventeenth century), and Beatrice Webb (nineteenth century), for example, contain themes relevant to the contemporary scene. Augustine's dislike for schooling at age 15 sounds highly similar to that of Salinger's modern Holden Caulfield, the twentieth century's prototypical adolescent. John Milton's use of put-downs and nicknames is simply an earlier version of the epithets scribbled on high school walls and the name-calling common in the corridors today. Beatrice Webb, a social reformer, wrote an adolescent diary (1874) containing references to a preoccupation with morbidity and suicide, her tone not too dissimilar to the tone of poet Sylvia Plath (see p. 396) in the past decade.

In a sense the adolescents of earlier times were both exceptions to and a means of validation for our current psychological perspectives on adolescence. Since such adolescents represented, in their historical period, such a tiny minority of youth—most of whom became adults at age 13 or 14— they were clearly exceptions and not the norm. Those few instances in which a person—because of birth, an unusual set of parents, or other social and economic reasons—was allowed a period of growth between childhood and adulthood also help to validate the existence of a ground plan for adolescence as an identifiable stage of human growth. Now as a result of scientific investigation, we know more about the meaningfulness and genuine nature of adolescence. But the early case studies presented by Kiell foreshadowed what is common for many today and attest to the distinctiveness and generality of this stage of growth.

However, it is still possible to find societies and subcultures within societies that do not recognize adolescence. For example, prior to the uprising on Mainland China in the 1960s, the period of the famous teenage Red Guards, there was no official phrase in the Chinese language for adolescence. And certainly, there are still countries where children move directly into adulthood at age 13 or 14, complete with arranged marriages, but such practices are becoming the exception. Closer to home, there is a paucity of information about the nature of adolescence within subcultures, as we will point out later in the text. In general, however, there is a clear and continuing trend. As societies become industrialized and increasingly depend on an educated work force, and as governments decide that an educated populace is important for stability and growth, then the period between childhood and adulthood will continue to be recognized in countries around the world.

In the following subsections we discuss several views of adolescence as they have evolved in this century.

Hall: The Columbus of Adolescence

The conditions from a social and economic standpoint—the historical forces at work in this country at the turn of the twentieth century—created the context in which adolescence could be discovered. America had largely completed its internal geographical expansion. Industrialization and urbanization were in full swing. A national identity had been formed in the aftermath of the Civil War; the nation was even ready to enter the international scene in its own right, after a century of isolation and protection. All of these events, in addition to the continuing waves of immigration, almost exclusively from Europe, created the conditions that made the emergence of adolescence inescapable.

The reasons for its emergence, incidentally, were not always altruistic. For example, as the adult labor force grew—with the birth of trade unions following the creation of large-scale industries—Congress enacted the child labor laws, which carried with them at least some sense of protecting adult jobs. Keeping young teenagers in public schools did keep them off the job rolls, as possible low-wage competitors.* Also, the increasing technological sophistication of industrialization created a need for a more adequately educated work force.

In addition to these economic reasons for the emergence of adolescence, there was also a social one—a growing awareness of some fundamental democratic goals. Much of the nineteenth-century rhetoric of Horace Mann and other educational reformers had found a more responsive audience by 1900. Congress by that time had passed a major land-grant legislation creating a public system of higher education, and states were busily expanding secondary education. Thus the theories of the common school and America as a melting pot joined forces to further the opportunities for public education beyond grammar school.

Upon this scene came G. Stanley Hall. As noted in his biography (see pp. 8–10), he was soon the single most important theorist concerned with adolescence. His own personality as well as his academic position gave him the platform he needed to make his point: Adolescence should be denoted as a special stage of human development. Psychologists and educators could no longer distinguish children and teenagers only in terms of size differences from small to large. Hall built the framework. He erred in specifying some of the content, but the overall structure of his theory was a major breakthrough for psychology.

Part of the difficulty in reading Hall today comes from his use of Victorian (and overblown) rhetoric, but Hall proclaimed the significance and established the epiclike terminology of adolescent psychology as a field of study. With Charles Darwin's evolutionary theories as a clear influence, Hall deduced that adolescence was an evolutionary stage of develop-

---

* Such issues are by no means totally resolved. A recent (1981) proposal by the Reagan administration to allow teenagers to work at wages below the federal minimum standards was opposed in some quarters because such a change would create unfair competition. Companies could hire cheap teenagers rather than expensive adults.

ment—thus unique and deserving of special study. He went further by announcing that adolescence was a stage in which a person actually experienced all the earlier stages of development for a second time, only at a more complex level. Furthermore, each of these stages recaptured a phase in human history.

Individual development, then, represented a *recapitulation* of the evolution of the species. For example, Hall viewed the grammar school period (7–13 years) as one of barbarism. The child was simply not capable of higher-order functions such as reason, morality, religion, love, and sympathy. Childhood was a mere collection of barbaric associations, a period of development reminiscent of "some remote, perhaps pigmoid, stage of human evolution" [4]. With the onset of adolescence at approximately age 14, a completely new order was possible. He called it "a second birth." The adolescent could work through all previous stages during the rebirth and achieve new heights of development. Children functioning as no more than pigs could now become transformed into a higher nature during adolescence: "the birth of love in the largest Christian sense, psychologically free from all selfish motives" [5]. Adolescence was a difficult period because it recapitulated a historical period of rapid and chaotic civilizing changes.

Hall had an optimistic view of the importance of education. Adolescents were extremely malleable: "No age is so responsive to all the best and the wisest adult endeavor. In no physic soil, too, does seed, bad as well as good, strike such deep root, grow so rankly or bear fruit so quickly or so surely" [6]. It was this optimism, however, that led him to such an extreme view that his theory lost credence.

Hall believed that no less than the salvation of the human race depended on how adult societies responded to the needs of adolescents. For the human race, not the individual self, to become supreme, he advocated a completely elitist and sexist position: A society could become fully actualized and civilized through the careful education of selected teenage males. Adolescence "is the only point of departure for the super anthropoid that man is to become." The selected males were to be trained for citizenship and leadership. The remaining males were to be relegated to manual labor, while females were to be readied for marriage and child rearing. In a passage that may send chills down the spines of those who recall the 1930s and speeches about a master race, Hall said:

> Many gather at the foot of the mount, some ascend a little way, but only a chosen few can scale the summit above the clouds. . . . The few hundred picked and ripened adolescents who could and would live solely for research and the advancement of the kingdom of man and of truth in the world are too often lost in the growing academic circles. [7]

G. STANLEY HALL (1846–1924)

An early turning point in the career of G. Stanley Hall occurred in the 1860s. After a period of study at the Union Theological Seminary, Hall found himself thoroughly confused about career goals. He enjoyed the social action theme of the pre–Civil War and distinctly northern pulpits. Other dimensions of the ministry seemed meaningless, however. He floundered. His early brilliance, though, had come to the attention of the famed clergyman Henry Ward Beecher (whose daughter was to achieve even greater fame). Beecher, as a mentor, raised funds and pointed Hall to Berlin University for the intensive study of philosophy.

Returning from the continent filled with ideas of the philosopher Johann Fichte, who championed a nineteenth-century version of Plato's *Republic* and governance by an elite class, Hall enrolled at Harvard. In 1878 at the age of 34, he received the first Ph.D. in psychology awarded in this country. Psychology as an academic discipline had just barely been founded by William James, who in the same year began to write the first textbook for psychology. In fact, Hall joined James as a lecturer in psychology at Harvard for a time before moving to a professorship at Johns Hopkins.

As this country's first Ph.D. in psychology, the spirit of innovation and challenge burned fiercely in Hall. Early in his career he had departed from orthodox theology and risked study in an entirely new field. Even after he was established as a professor at the prestigious Johns Hopkins University, he still sought more challenge. He literally jumped at the opportunity in 1902 to become the first president of Clark University in Worcester, Massachusetts, all the while maintaining his commitment to psychology. Thus it comes as no surprise that Hall, also at the turn of the century, became a primary force in founding the American Psychological Association.

His talents and abilities were not limited to teaching, administrating, or professional leadership, though. His academic scholarship, by any standard, was prolific. A steady stream of articles, papers, and books poured from his pen, numbering over three hundred before his retirement. His work attracted large numbers of graduate students. Clark became the center for the child study movement. His major contribution through all this work was, of course, his single-handed efforts in—and perhaps single-minded devotion to—the psychology of adolescence. Adolescence he viewed as a major, new stage of human evolution, and his scope was as broad as his monumental two-volume title, *Adolescence: Its*

G. Stanley Hall (1846–1924)

Photograph from Clark University Archives

Psychology and Its Relation to Physiology, Anthropology, Sociology, Sex, Crime, Religion and Education [1].

Unfortunately, one of Hall's characteristics eventually caused his views to decline in influence. As an innovator and a breaker of tradition, he possessed great personal strength and inner-directedness. This characteristic allowed him to challenge the prevailing views of the time, which had essentially dismissed adolescence as a legitimate field of inquiry. This same dedication and commitment, however, prevented Hall from modifying his views to any major degree. His very enthusiasm and his skills as a speaker seemed to convince him of the correctness of his interpretations. And it was his interpretations that became the problem. He seemingly went overboard in presenting the rationale for adolescence as a stage. This stance led him to the excesses noted in the text: for example, the claim of a super race composed of a few male leaders, the overvaluing of educational impact, a somewhat distorted view of Darwin's evolutionary theory applied to humans, a claim that all adolescents experience monumental stress and storm, and similar overstatements.

(Continued)

G. STANLEY HALL (Continued)

His excesses left him an easy target for critics. Psychology at the turn of this century had an ample supply of such critics just waiting for targets. Hall led with his chin; the counterpunchers battered away. The empiricists attacked his research methods as inadequate. Cultural relativists refuted his storm-and-stress hypothesis. Psychologists in general were upset with his super-race concepts. The attacks continued and seemed to drive Hall to further and more extreme claims. In the last decade of his life he went to even greater lengths to speak on the need for the kingdom of supermen and the inability of the masses to rule the world. His psychology of adolescence became an ideology and thus could be quite easily attacked and then dismissed. Leta Hollingworth, a major author on the psychology of adolescence in the post-Hall era, commented concerning her own omission of any significant reference to his work: "Students of Dr. G. Stanley Hall will miss extensive reference to his voluminous pioneer works. . . . such reference would seem of historic value primarily, rather than of scientific or practical value today" [2].

Robert Grinder, a major contemporary theorist, with the benefit of perspective, offers a more balanced view. His provocative comment: "Had G. Stanley Hall studied adolescence to test recapitulation theory rather than to justify it, he might never have lost stature in the field he did so much to establish" [3].

In 1980 the American Psychological Association, founded by Hall some eighty years earlier, officially established the G. Stanley Hall Lecture Series. The child has finally honored its father, his excesses as well as innovations.

REFERENCES

1. G. S. Hall, *Adolescence,* vols. 1 and 2 (New York: Appleton, 1904).
2. L. S. Hollingworth, *The psychology of adolescence* (New York: Appleton, 1928), p. ix.
3. R. E. Grinder, *Studies in adolescence* (New York: Macmillan, 1963), p. 16.

Hall's excessive claims led to a reaction during which many of his positions were challenged, but Hall remains the most important pioneer in the field of adolescence. We now realize that many of his views were overstated. The intervening years of study, however, have shown that many of his concepts were sound: Adolescence *is* a unique stage of growth, previously ignored by psychology and by society. Major psychological and physiological changes occur that transform the quality of cognitive and emotional processes. Growth tends to be uneven during the transition period. And adolescence can be a period of some stress, although nowhere near the period of enormous "sturm und drang" (storm and stress) that Hall claimed. Drained of the overstatements and the excesses of prophecy, his basic view is still highly relevant.

Hall created a place for adolescence as an important period in human development. Adolescence is not a mindless interlude between two stages, nor is it simply preparation. That these views are important today results from Hall's willingness to break with the traditions of his day.

Another issue Hall bequeathed to later students of adolescence was whether the unique characteristics of adolescence as an age period reflected something inevitable and characteristic of human beings. Hall was, in one sense, merely echoing a frequently suggested, commonsense view of development—namely, that what emerges in the course of development is merely what is wired into each organism as a result of human nature or the evolutionary history of our species. This *maturationist* point of view emphasized development as the emergence of particular psychological and behavioral patterns according to a predetermined biological timetable.

It was not Hall, however, who clarified the significance of a maturationist view. A Viennese physician, Sigmund Freud, thinking deeply about the causes of adult emotional problems, began to construct a theory that added credence to both the maturationist view and the storm-and-stress hypothesis.

Freud's View of Adolescence

Sigmund Freud also saw adolescence as a necessarily difficult, turbulent period. His ideas are maturationist as well [8]. In fact, Freud built his whole view of human nature on the idea that certain strong psychological pressures—*instinctual drives*—were inborn in each individual. These drives determined the most important human experiences throughout one's life. Although drives are psychological rather than physical, Freud nevertheless felt they were sources of energy that stimulated individuals to engage in many different types of behavior. Some of these behaviors were socially acceptable and even beneficial to the person and to others as well; some were less desirable behaviors and potentially brought a person momentary pleasure but did not lead to long-term satisfaction or social approval. It was the role of socialization in childhood and adolescence to direct and channel instinctual drives into socially acceptable forms. The ultimate goal, in Freud's view, was an important one: to enable children to develop into adults who were capable of forming stable heterosexual relationships.

Sigmund Freud (1856–1939)

Photograph from Pictorial Parade

These relationships, he thought, were necessary for perpetuating the society and the culture into future generations.

In Freud's view the turbulence of adolescence grows out of necessary changes in psychological patterns that facilitate the establishment of healthy, mature heterosexual relations in adulthood. Such changes take place throughout life, and they present critical difficulties in each successive period of development. Freud described development as a series of *psychosexual stages*. For example, during infancy most of the child's needs are met through feeding and sucking; Freud calls this period the *oral stage* of psychosexual development. In the toddler years the focus is on the experiences of toilet training and learning control over unacceptable impulses; this period is referred to as the *anal stage* of psychosexual development. Finally, between ages 3 and 6 the *phallic stage* begins. In this psychosexual stage individuals learn to deal with sexual feelings and to strengthen their identification with male and female sex roles. The basic groundwork for mature heterosexuality, then, is laid by age 6, according to Freud. He would have agreed with six-year-old Susan, who remarked to her parents on her sixth birthday: "Well, I'm six years old now. I must be a people."

Psychosexual development between the age of six and the time of puberty, Freud thought, was relatively calm, psychologically. This *latency stage* is an important time for learning about the culture and about social roles and relationships. Compared with adolescence, as well as with the psychosexual stages that occur before age 6, latency is an island of quiet in the midst of a raging storm. The storm becomes particularly violent, in Freud's view, in adolescence.

In fact, like Hall, Freud saw adolescence as turbulent and adolescents as unpredictable, mercurial, and tormented. The period is turbulent because the physical changes of puberty increase sexual desires, and it becomes necessary for adolescents to find appropriate objects for their sexuality. Before adolescence, most adolescents' major relationships were with their parents or with friends of the same sex. Sexual relationships with a family member or with same-sexed friends are socially disapproved, however. So in Freud's view the turbulence of adolescence comes largely from the stresses of finding a satisfactory focus for the heterosexual feelings for which the stages of psychosexual development have prepared them. At the same time, adolescents are facing the need to become independent of parents, with whom many of the important experiences of psychosexual development have occurred in childhood. The necessity of facing these social transitions at a time when there are strong internal impulses resulting from the changes of puberty is responsible for the turmoil of adolescence, according to Freud. Young people can only bring this stormy, stressful period under control by developing patterns of coping with the strong sexual feelings of puberty and at the same time learning patterns of behavior that keep family and peers—both males and females—in proper, socially acceptable balance with each other.

Like Hall, Freud saw the turmoil of adolescence as an inevitable experience for every human being. The difficulties were wired in biologically. They emerged according to a timetable over which the individuals themselves had no control. Of course, environmental changes, such as transitions in social relationships, certainly contribute to the difficulties of adolescence. But Freud would even argue that those social relationships developed under the control of the biological timetable.

Maturational views of adolescence appeal to many adults because they seem to capture some of the inner feelings of adolescence and some of the perplexing problems adolescents often pose for their elders. Even parents who have unusually calm, positive relationships with their children during childhood are likely to say that adolescence presents special problems and difficulties for them and their youngsters. But these common observations do not necessarily mean that the turbulence and turmoil of adolescence are predetermined and inescapable for everyone. What raises serious doubts about the maturationist viewpoint is the work of cultural anthropologists who have observed the nature of adolescence in cultures different from our own. They have concluded that the storm-and-stress hypothesis of maturationists like Freud and Hall is not necessarily valid. In other cultures the transition between childhood and adulthood may be smooth rather than turbulent.

We must point out that the cataclysmic view of storm and stress even at the time it was announced had some rather obvious, unique cultural elements. Both Freud as an Austrian and Hall as a student at Berlin University had witnessed firsthand what happened to upper-class German adolescents in schools and colleges. The academic program was so rooted in the classics that it was said that the Kaiser himself complained quite bitterly that such study taught Germans to become good Greeks and Romans but not good Germans. Beyond the content, however, was an atmosphere of intense academic competition. Also, there were no outlets for student energies except the goal of academic excellence. The German youth of the period were tense and overburdened, almost to the point of being crushed by the requirements. Suicide often accompanied academic failure [9]. Yet it was not a careful examination of the German experience that cast doubt on the storm-and-stress hypothesis. Instead, it was the work of a young American female, barely out of graduate school and studying in a remote Pacific island, that provided a different view.

The Legacy of Cultural Anthropology

In the 1920s anthropology student Margaret Mead visited the island of Samoa in order to study adolescent development among the natives [10]. She found an experience of growing up that was remarkably smooth and free of conflict and distress.* In the Samoan culture the main events of life, including birth, death, and sex, were handled frankly and openly. The mundane aspects of life were also organized in such a way that the transition from childhood to adolescence was smooth and gradual. Responsibility for carrying out necessary tasks in the community began when children

---

* Very recently Mead's research has been called into question. This instance is not the first time her methods and findings have been criticized. Basically, anthropological research always has a subjective element. How much did Mead find what she wanted to find, and to what extent did the teenagers in her interviews mislead her as to the nature of adolescent development? Such questions, of course, can never be totally resolved. On the other hand, as we note in this volume, much recent work in psychology has substantiated Mead's conclusion that adolescence is not necessarily a time of deep and intense storm and stress. There are problems during adolescence to be sure, but not to the extent suggested by the original Hall and Freud theories. Thus Mead's work was a first step in correcting the imbalance from prior theory.

Margaret Mead (1901–1978)
Photograph from Edward Rice—Photo Trends

were very young. Their assigned duties were part of the essential tasks of island life but were appropriate to the abilities of children their age. Each contribution was taken seriously and rewarded and praised equally regardless of age. Furthermore, there were institutionalized ways for dealing with interpersonal conflicts, including those between adolescents and their parents. In short, far from being a time of storm and stress, adolescence in the Samoan society in the 1920s was obviously a pleasant time of life.

Not all primitive cultures manage the transition to adulthood as smoothly as the 1920s Samoans. LeVine and LeVine describe a Kenyan tribe in which the transition is much less gradual—and presumably much more traumatic [11]. In this tribe the tasks and responsibilities of children and those of adults are rigidly differentiated. The tasks assigned to children are "children's tasks" and have very low status. Only after being admitted to the ranks of adults may children be assigned the tasks and privileges reserved for adult society. Thus very little training takes place during childhood for the responsibilities of adulthood. The transition to adulthood is strictly marked by a ritual ceremony—a *rite de passage,* or right of passage. In Kenya this ceremony consists of genital operations for both males and females. In spite of their lack of training for adulthood, young people in the society are understandably eager to be permitted to undergo this rite in order to enjoy adult status. Once they have undergone the ceremony, only a brief, intensive period of indoctrination prepares them for their new roles.

These two contrasting cultures are examples of the range of adolescent experiences documented by cultural anthropologists. Furthermore, compared with the experience of adolescence in Western industrialized societies such as the United States, the experience of adolescence in Samoa and Kenya is also very different. Obviously, the nature of adolescence as a period of life is less rigid, fixed, and biologically determined than the maturationists' storm-and-stress hypothesis indicates. How stormy and stressful adolescence is depends largely on demands and expectations of the culture in which an adolescent lives.

What are the cultural differences that make adolescence a more or less generally difficult experience for young persons in our society? Anthropologist Ruth Benedict surveyed information from a large number of societies to answer this question [12]. She concluded that the major determinant of the difficulty of adolescence was the extent to which socialization for adulthood was *discontinuous* in a society. By *discontinuous* Benedict refers to the necessity for an individual to learn a different set of behaviors, roles, and attitudes for adulthood from the set learned in childhood. In the Kenyan society discontinuity was obviously great, since a different set of expectations and status rules governed the behavior of children and adults. In the Samoan society described by Margaret Mead, discontinuity was minimal. Rather, the progression of responsibilities and expectations built up smoothly and gradually from childhood to adolescence; socialization was far more *continuous*.

Benedict found that three dimensions of discontinuity were especially important in determining the nature of adolescence. These three dimensions are responsibility-nonresponsibility, dominance-submissiveness, and sexual activity–inactivity.

1. *Responsibility-nonresponsibility:* In societies that achieve continuity during socialization, children are involved in essential tasks for the society that are suited to their capacities and abilities. In discontinuous socialization, childhood activities are considered distinctive from the activities of others in the society, and responsibility is not specifically expected of them.

2. *Dominance-submissiveness:* Under patterns of continuity some societies encourage the young to develop dominance in limited areas such as leadership in hunting and fishing activities. In societies where socialization is discontinuous, children are expected to be submissive to a range of other persons, but they are not given an opportunity to practice dominance.

Thus when they reach adulthood, they have had little experience in dominant behavior, which is often a significant aspect of adult social roles.

3. *Sexual activity–inactivity:* Under conditions of continuity some societies permit a wide range of sexual activity during adolescence. In discontinuous socialization, children are expected to behave as though they were nonsexual, usually until marriage or at least until such an age when society approves of their sexual activity. Thus there is little teaching about or experimentation in sexual activity that is approved prior to a certain age. Yet mature, well-functioning sexual behavior is expected of adults.

Benedict's point is that adolescence is a difficult, stressful time when adolescents are required to become responsible, dominant, sexually active individuals within a very short period of time, after having been taught and encouraged in patterns of directly opposite behavior during childhood. Although Western societies, particularly the United States, do not approach the extremities of societies in which children's and adults' lives are rigidly segregated, a considerable amount of discontinuity obviously does exist. Furthermore, while in primitive societies the transition from childhood to adolescence is intense, it is often restricted to a short period during which initiation into adulthood takes place. The transition to adolescence in Western society, however, generally takes place over a very long period of time. Thus in contrast to adolescents in many other societies, adolescents in the United States and Europe by and large experience relatively discontinuous socialization to adulthood; their assumption of adult status and responsibilities is delayed for very long periods of time.

This circumstance has led psychologist Kurt Lewin to describe adolescents as *marginal* persons [13]. Since they belong clearly to neither the child nor the adult social groups, he sees them as facing ambiguous expectations and unclear rights and privileges. This marginality, as well as the discontinuity involved in making the transition from childhood to adulthood, contributes to the difficulties—the personal storm and stress—of adolescents' experiences. However, the lesson of cultural anthropology is that the extent to which adolescence is stormy and stressful depends not just on the maturation of the individual to a certain age but also on the changing expectations and demands of the culture in which that individual lives.

Social Learning View of Adolescence

The cultural anthropologists emphasize an environmentalist view of adolescence rather than a maturationist one. As they see it, the difficulties of adolescence reflect the nature of learning the childhood role before adolescence and also how well that learning equips adolescents to face the demands and changing roles of the second decade of life. For them *social learning* is the basis of whatever stresses and difficulties occur in adolescence.

The basic assumption of social learning is that the behaviors of individuals are acquired through experiences. Links between situations and circumstances (stimuli) and behaviors, attitudes, and values (responses) are built up gradually from the beginning of life. The links are forged and strengthened through the rewards, punishments, and observations of others' behaviors that each person experiences. If these experiences lead to behavior patterns that equip adolescents to meet the demands and expectations of adolescence and adulthood, then the stresses of adolescence are not likely to be excessive or unusual.

For example, if parents have rewarded youngsters for being appropriately independent in childhood and for continuing that pattern in adolescence, learned patterns are preparing them to accept increased independence as they move out of adolescence and into adulthood. But if social learning experiences have reinforced dependence in children and young adolescents, the transition to an independent life-style will be much more difficult. Similarly, if sexual activity and even expressions of sexual interest in childhood are punished, as they often are by American parents, then the transition to healthy sexual development during adulthood may be difficult and awkward. But in societies where sexual interest is treated more positively, the transition to sexual activity in late adolescence and young adulthood seems to be accomplished more smoothly. In other words, the transitions from dependence to independence and from sexual inactivity to sexual activity that Benedict described depend partly on the social learning that prepares an individual to accomplish the transitions.

One of the best-known social learning theorists, Albert Bandura, has spelled this point out in more detail [14]. Bandura was interested in the problems of antisocial, aggressive boys. He argued that antisocial behavior is a learned pattern, probably stemming from childhood experiences in the family and the community. Once a child reaches adolescence, the problem *appears* to become more pronounced only because, as adolescents, the boys have obtained adult size and strength. Thus their antisocial aggression is more fearsome to the people around them, because the people feel that they can potentially be overpowered by these stronger, bigger youths.

Bandura argued that these kinds of illusory changes govern many of our reactions to adolescents—and our assumptions about the nature of adolescence. For example, he argues that we tend to *overgeneralize* from isolated instances of unusual behavior by adolescents. Consequently, when we read of some act of violence or vandalism committed by a young person, we are likely to overgeneralize from that isolated instance to say that young people in general have a tendency to behave badly. No doubt the tendency is enhanced by mass media sensationalism. Furthermore, we are inclined to overinterpret superficial signs of nonconformity. The dress fads of adolescents, for example, are often taken by adults as signs of how different adolescents are from other age groups. Of course, within adult society there is a huge variation in dress style, and some of these styles are as distasteful to many adults as are the nonconformist fads of adolescents. Bandura's point is that adults often attribute adolescent fashion to the peculiar nature of adolescents. Finally, Bandura says that our impressions of adolescents often reflect our own expectations that adolescents will behave differently. Thus we create *self-fulfilling prophecies* in which our expectations become suggestions to adolescents about how they are expected to behave. Furthermore, our own impressions of their behavior are colored by our stereotypes.

Like the cultural anthropologists, Bandura does not think adolescence is inevitably a time of storm and stress. Whatever difficulties there are—and there may be real ones—should be seen as the result of environmental experiences, not as the result of an inevitably difficult period of human development.

Maturation and Social Conditioning: A Cognitive-Developmental Synthesis

In a sense the maturationist view of adolescence and the social conditioning position mark two extreme points on a theoretical continuum containing explanations about the nature of adolescence. Recent work in cognitive-developmental theory has attempted to incorporate elements of both views into a synthesis, that is, to combine the apparently diverse positions into a comprehensive theory.

It is obvious that both maturation and culture affect human development. No amount of maturation by itself could produce a fully developed human being. Studies of children reared in isolation tragically demonstrate that fact. On the other hand, no amount of social conditioning could transform a midget into a basketball center or a retarded child into a genius. Thus the cognitive-developmental theory incorporates elements of both theories, namely, that human growth is determined by the interaction of maturation and social conditioning.

We will now describe the main elements of cognitive-developmental theory in general. In succeeding chapters we will present various domains of development as they relate to aspects of the growth of adolescents.

BASIC CONCEPTS: STAGES AND DOMAINS OF GROWTH

In contemporary developmental psychology the concept of *stage* has an important and special meaning. A stage of growth is a system of human functioning that is distinctive, unique, and consistent as a whole. The differences between an earlier and later stage are qualitative, not quantitative. The stages are sequential, with each building on the prior stages. Growth from stage to stage is not automatic but depends on a combination of physiological maturation and appropriate interaction with the environment. In this section we will take up these assumptions one at a time.

Stage: A Distinctive, Unique, and Consistent System of Human Functioning

Developmental psychologists assume that all human beings actively process experience, that is, that the human mind seeks to attach meaning to experience. As humans we possess the capacity to think, to reflect, to consider and reason. When we experience events, we try to process them in the sense of actively seeking to arrive at some meaning. In other words, we are not empty vessels, or passive objects, as behaviorists have often implied. Rather, we are active participants in life, seeking to make sense of experience. Our reflective capacity is intrinsic to our human condition; we have a strong urge to seek meaning from experience.

How an individual actually processes experience constitutes the stage, the system of mental operations that the person will generally employ. Within rather broad age groupings cognitive operations tend to share a set of similar characteristics. Also, the person will tend to use the same general system of thought in a generalized and consistent manner. Various phrases are used to denote the conception of a cognitive-developmental stage: schema, cognitive structure, mental structure, internal mediating system, or problem-solving strategy, that is, the amount of weighing of pros and cons a person employs in decision making [15].

Cognition, the act of thinking—or, more broadly, the processing of experience—is an inherently human capacity. At particular points in development the system that a person employs will have characteristics that are readily identifiable as a coherent and internally consistent cognitive-developmental stage. For a developmentalist or an educator it is most

Stages of development: Conformity to different models

Photograph from Charles Gatewood

important to be able to identify the system of reasoning and processing the person actually uses, since to do so enables the person to start where the learner is currently functioning.

Stages: Systems of Processing That Are Qualitatively Different

A second distinctive feature of cognitive-developmental theory is that stages are qualitatively different [16]. The differences between one stage and the next are differences in kind. This view contrasts with the general view of humans held in the late nineteenth century, namely, that childhood, adolescence, and adulthood were points on a continuum. Thus, for example, children were considered physically smaller, mentally slower, and capable of memorizing fewer lines and writing shorter sentences than adolescents or adults. Children were just like adults, only smaller versions. There were no essential *characteristics*, with the possible exception of reproductive capacity, that were different. The differences were all in degree, with adults having more of a characteristic and the child or teenager less.

In cognitive-developmental theory the changes from stage to stage are transformations. An appropriate analogy comes from entomology: the process of change from an egg to a caterpillar to a butterfly. Each stage of human development ideally represents such a metamorphosis. Another analogy comes from physics: When there is a radical new discovery—a new method of understanding some aspect of the universe, such as Newton's discovery of gravity—the new law is described as a quantum leap. In the same manner, a shift in stage functioning is a quantum leap to a new level of processing experience. The new stage is more complex than the earlier stage and represents a new mode, or new system, of thought.

Stages of Development Are Sequential

Stages are ordered according to levels of complexity. All, or nearly all, persons start at approximately the same level of development, and growth, almost by definition, proceeds from the less complex to the more complex. Since each new stage builds directly on experiences of the prior one, the growth is sequential, from one stage to the next, in order of complexity. We noted in the previous section that the stages are qualitatively different; therefore they represent a hierarchy. The hierarchy of stages and the sequential nature of growth mean that the order is directional and stepwise. A person cannot skip the prior stages [17].

There is another equally important aspect of this assumption. Generally, if a person achieves a particular level of stage functioning in its fullest sense, the person will not return to a less complex level. Technically, this phenomenon is referred to as the inability for *structural regression* to occur. In this view, once a person leaves childhood, that person cannot fully return to the naivete of a child's world view (assuming that the faculties remain intact). This observation does not mean that an adult could never be childlike, but the experience could not be qualitatively the same.

Stages Represent Different Domains of Human Processing

One of the most troublesome aspects of cognitive-developmental theory, due to its recency, has been a misunderstanding of the content definition of the stages. There has been a tendency to assume that when we referred to a stage of development, we were generalizing to the entire realm of human processing. Although it is easy to slip into this overgeneralization, current research indicates that we need to be quite careful in specifying what particular aspect or domain of processing we are referring to.

Stage theorists themselves have focused their efforts on distinctively different arenas of functioning. In fact, in this book we have chosen to present the information on particular areas in different chapters. Thus you will find a description of Piaget's work focused on the domain of how children and adolescents process their experience in a particular area—the physical world of time, space, and causality, as Piaget would say. Thus when we refer to Piaget's stages, we are also, and only, referring to how individuals process their experience in that domain. Similarly, when we refer to the domain of value development, we are focusing only on the question of the stage of processing in that area. The same holds for the other areas such as self-development stages, stages of interpersonal functioning, and stages of concept formation. You might think of these domains as different strands of development. By looking at the chapter headings, you can see how we are presenting the separate domains—and that each domain has an identifiable content sequence.

Stage Growth Depends on Interaction

The final and in some ways most important assumption is that growth depends on interaction, as we have noted earlier. Some early developmentalists unfortunately had suggested almost the opposite, namely, that development was largely internally directed, a maturationist view sometimes called the "immaculate unfolding hypothesis." Growth, however, is not unilateral. The ground plan (as Erik Erikson calls it), or the organic determinant, is only one element in the process. Whether growth occurs depends on both the kind and the quality of environmental stimulation that interacts with the capacity of the person to benefit from experiences. The constant sequences of stages offers a broad outline of the way growth proceeds as a result of the person-environment interaction.

The dangers here are essentially twofold. We can shut down growth either by preventing interaction or by overmatching the person with the environment. In the first somewhat extreme case, for example, keeping retarded children in closets, garages, and attics ensured that they would not develop, even within their somewhat limited potential. Another example involves hearing-impaired children. For some reason the official educational policy some years ago was that such children were to be taught only to lip-read. But this environmental stimulation was not optimal for the children. As a result, they generally exhibited developmental lags. Minimizing interaction of the hearing-impaired reduced their opportunity for growth [18]. Fortunately, we have wisely discarded the old policy.

Other examples of the effect of lack of stimulation come from the classroom. A study in New York City elementary schools showed that minority children's intellectual skills decline as a result of the schooling itself [19]. Their achievement scores, reading scores, and self-concepts fell during the elementary years. An analysis of the actual classroom interactions indicated the children were in a dull, listless environment where they were basically ignored.

There are also studies that tragically indicate that too much stimulation, in the form of premature adulthood, can be devastating to children. For example, a study was conducted of white children from disorganized families in the Boston area [20]. Those preschool-age children had to manage their younger siblings; four- and five-year-olds were taking care of newborns. They learned to shop, to dodge traffic, and often to care for alcoholic parents. They demonstrated advanced social skills. Such premature development, however, inflicted serious lags on their emotional and personal stages of growth. They were excessively fearful. They exhibited a marked inability to learn basic skills as early as the first grade. The costs of premature adulthood foreclosed their future before formal schooling began.

Other studies have shown the positive effects of just the right amount of stimulation and support. Effective preschool programs for economically disadvantaged children provide very convincing evidence that positive and appropriate interaction promotes healthy psychological development. And what is true for schools is also true for homes. A study by Sandra Scarr and Richard Weinberg documented the dramatic effects of placing young adopted children from economically deprived backgrounds into homes where the children received adequate stimulation [21]. Under such conditions the facilitating environment nurtured the children's growth. Astonishingly, not only did their general functioning improve, but also their IQ scores averaged some 20 points higher than those of controls. In Chapter 4 we explain why such an outcome is plausible. Even intellectual skill is modifiable during childhood with appropriate environmental interaction. Intellectual capacity is not entirely fixed at birth but very much depends on the quality of interaction.

The importance of interaction goes beyond childhood. For example, as shown in Chapter 6, the developmental curves and base rates for the adolescent years indicate that in many instances growth levels off, or stabilizes. This result indicates that appropriate interaction in schools or homes may no longer occur. For instance, the majority of adolescents do not approach their schoolwork at the level of abstract reasoning. Theoretically, at least, the majority are clearly capable of developing reasoning and thinking skills at this level. The educational programs, however, do not provide adequate stimulation. Consequently, less than a third of adults achieve the intellectual level of which they are capable. That domain of growth has apparently been prematurely stabilized through the lack of appropriate stimulation. Similar findings indicate that what is true for formal reasoning is also true for value development, self-development, and interpersonal relations. From a developmental view this set of circumstances is not inevitable. There is evidence that particular types of educational programs can make a difference. In other words, growth during adolescence can occur not only physiologically but psychologically as well. We must keep in mind the *interaction process* as the key for stimulating such development.

To summarize, then, the key developmental assumptions are as follows:

1. Humans process experience according to their *stage* of development. A stage is a cognitive structure with a relatively homogeneous set of mental operations (the mental operations hypothesis).

2. Stages are qualitatively distinct. Differences in the quality of mental operations from stage to stage are differences in kind rather than degree (the egg-caterpillar-butterfly hypothesis, or the metamorphosis dictum as exemplified in a famous novel by Franz Kafka).

3. Stages are sequential and directional. Each stage builds on the previous one. Development proceeds from the less complex to the more complex. Once a person fully achieves the mental operations of a stage—a structural change—the person rarely goes back to a previous stage (the "you can't go home again" view, to quote from Thomas Wolfe's novel).

4. Stage descriptions are specific to different domains of functioning. We have no single superstage theory but, rather, evidence that supports a theory of a series of strands of growth. The tapestry of development is composed of separate strands that may gradually be woven together.

5. Growth from stage to stage depends on appropriate stimulation through interaction. *Developmental education* broadly defined means just the right balance in stimulating and supporting growth—as opposed to the dictum of growth as an automatic unfolding.

6. One final point about basic assumptions: No individual is totally in one stage at any particular instance. Thus it is not accurate to say that an individual is at stage one, two, or three in a particular theory or system. Generally, it is more accurate to say that a person's usual method of processing experience in a specific domain may be in a particular stage. For that person, that stage would be modal. Some of the time the person might perform at a higher stage (one stage up) and sometimes at a lower stage. In other words, persons show variation, both higher and lower, around their current modes. This observation also means that a person is not in one stage permanently. Rather, the modal stage represents the person's current and preferred style, not a fixed state that must endure forever.

SUMMARY

We have attempted in this chapter to provide you with both the history of and the contemporary framework for the study of adolescence from a developmental view. As we note in the Preface, the factors that contribute to the nature of adolescents' experiences are not simple. They include physiological, cognitive, social, and cultural influences. We have chosen to place these complex, interacting forces within a developmental framework. By focusing on the developing individual, we hope to show how the interacting influences of adolescents have an impact on the personal adjustments and experiences of individual adolescents.

A Framework for Understanding Adolescent Development

A useful framework for organizing the information about this complex period of life has been suggested by John P. Hill [22]. In Hill's view, which is outlined in Table 1.1, adolescence is seen in terms of a set of primary changes operating through certain social contexts to produce important secondary changes in the developing person.

The *primary changes* include changes in *social definition*, or the expectations that others form of adolescents as a result of the physiological transformations of puberty; *physical changes* themselves, including the alterations in body size and shape that put stress on an individual's self-image; and *cognitive changes*, including the ability required for more complex and inclusive reasoning processes. These changes occur within important *contexts*, including family, peer relationships, and school settings. Finally, the interacting influences of primary changes and contexts produce a set of changes that raise many psychological issues for adolescents. Hill refers to these changes as *secondary changes*. Table 1.1 shows some especially significant secondary changes: the transformation of family relations, an increase in individual autonomy, or independence; an accruing sense of identity, or self; an altered view of achievement, including new goals for the future and views of how such goals might be achieved; and a transformation in personal and social outlook on sexuality.

TABLE 1.1   John Hill's model of adolescent development

Primary changes	occur within and have impact on ⟶	Contexts
Social definition		Family
Physical		Peer
Cognitive		School

Secondary changes	And psychological issues surrounding the changes during adolescence
Issue	**Adolescent change**
Family relations	Transforming childhood social bonds to parents to bonds acceptable between parents and their adult children
Autonomy	Extending self-initiated activity and confidence in it to wider behavioral realms
Identity	Transforming images to self to accommodate primary and secondary change; coordinating images to attain a self-theory that incorporates uniqueness and continuity through time
Achievement	Focusing industry and ambition into channels that are future-oriented and realistic
Sexuality	Transforming acquaintanceships into friendships; deepening and broadening capacities for self-disclosure, affective perspective taking, altruism

Adapted from J. P. Hill, *Understanding early adolescence: A framework* (Chapel Hill, N.C.: Center for Early Adolescence, 1980).

The Plan for the Book

In the chapters to come, as you learn about the various domains or strands of development, you will see how these secondary changes emerge from the primary changes and the contexts of adolescents' lives. You will always see the potential effects of the changes themselves on people and the situations around them. Accordingly, we have mixed a discussion of secondary changes in with the treatment of primary changes and contexts. In Chapters 2 through 6 we discuss the important primary changes of the second decade of life and attempt to show their importance for secondary changes in adolescence. In Chapters 7 through 11 our focus is on the contexts of adolescence—the social-psychological milieu within which primary changes occur and upon which they act. These contextual factors include family influences, peer relationships, and the secondary changes associated with sexuality, alienation and behavior problems, and individual psychological difficulties. Finally, in the last three chapters we elaborate some contexts and secondary changes that are of particular interest from the standpoint of education. Thus we consider the influence of the interaction between primary changes and context on adolescents' experiences in school, in choosing a career, and in moving out of adolescence proper into the college years.

Throughout, our emphasis is on the importance of interactions among individual and contextual factors in adolescent development. Furthermore, we attempt to provide a dual focus on theory and practice. Even though our knowledge of adolescent development is still incomplete and much more research is needed, we think there is a basis in what we do know for suggesting actions that will improve the lives and maximize the developmental potential of adolescents. In our view the material we present in this book is applicable to work with adolescents in many different settings.

Reading through and thinking about the assumptions is never easy. You will find, however, that the skeletal framework will gather the needed flesh as you proceed. In the meantime, Table 1.1 provides an outline of Hill's framework for understanding adolescent development. It can also serve as a helpful guide to you as you integrate for yourself the knowledge presented in the remainder of this book.

KEY POINTS AND NAMES

Adolescence: a stage or an invention?

Norman Kiell

G. Stanley Hall

Recapitulation

Storm and stress

Maturation

Sigmund Freud's stages

Margaret Mead: anthropology

Ruth Benedict

Albert Bandura: social conditioning

Stages of growth

Qualitative differences

Sequence

Domains of human processing

Interaction

John P. Hill: primary and secondary changes

REFERENCES

1. L. K. Frank, The fundamental needs of the child, *Mental Hygiene* 22(1938):353–379.

2. R. L. Church and M. W. Sedlack, *Education in the United States* (New York: Free Press, 1976).

3. N. Kiell, *The universal experience of adolescence* (Boston: Beacon Press, 1967).

4. G. S. Hall, *Adolescence*, vols. 1 and 2 (New York: Appleton, 1904), pp. ix–x.

5. *Ibid.*, p. 193.

6. *Ibid.*, pp. xviii–xix.

7. *Ibid.*, p. 559.

8. S. Freud, *General introduction to psychoanalysis* (New York: Washington Square Press, 1960).

9. Kiell, p. 718.

10. M. Mead, *Coming of age in Samoa* (New York: New American Library, 1950).

11. R. LeVine and B. LeVine, *Nyansongo: A Gusii community in Kenya* (New York: Wiley, 1966), p. 196.

12. R. Benedict, Continuities and discontinuities in cultural conditioning, *Psychiatry* 1(1938):161–167.

13. K. Lewin, *Field theory and social science* (New York: Harper & Row, 1951).

14. A. Bandura, *Principles of behavior modification* (New York: Holt, Rinehart and Winston, 1969).

15. H. J. Flavell, Stage-related properties of cognitive development, *Cognitive Psychology* 2(1971):421–453.

16. H. Werner, The concept of development from a comparative and organismic point of view, in *The concept of development*, ed. D. Harris (Minneapolis: University of Minnesota Press, 1957).

17. J. Rest, Morality, in *Cognitive development*, ed. J. Flavell and E. Markman, a volume in the series *Handbook of child psychology*, ed. P. Mussen (New York: Wiley, 1983).

18. H. Schlesinger and K. Meadow, *Sound and sign: Childhood deafness and mental health* (Berkeley: University of California Press, 1972).

19. E. Leacock, *Teaching and learning in city schools* (New York: Basic Books, 1969).

20. E. Pavenstadt, *The drifters* (Boston: Little, Brown, 1967).

21. S. Scarr and R. Weinberg, I.Q. tests performance of black children adopted by white families, *American Psychologist* 31,10(1976):726–739.

22. J. P. Hill, *Understanding early adolescence: A framework* (Chapel Hill, N.C.: Center for Early Adolescence, 1980).

CHAPTER 2

Adolescence and Identity Formation

INTRODUCTION

If there is any single concept that is ascribed almost universally to the process of personal growth during adolescence, it is identity development. And if there is a single theorist that is mentioned almost universally on the topic, it is Erik Erikson. In fact, he has been referred to as "the man who gave adolescents an identity crisis!" Certainly, within the modern era Erikson has been the single most important contributor to our knowledge of adolescence. What Freud was to emotional aspects of childhood, and what Piaget was to intellectual development for children and adolescents, Erikson is to adolescents and identity formation.

Prior to his work, as we noted in Chapter 1, theory for adolescents had been remarkably outdated or somewhat contrived. G. Stanley Hall's views were timely at the turn of the century, but they are not adequate for today's youth. Similarly, the official theory for adolescence derived from psychoanalytic psychology is inadequate. In this view adolescence is really not a stage of development at all but, rather, a recapitulation of earlier developmental periods. The process of adolescent growth is essentially working through, for the second time, the childhood stages defined by Freud—oral, anal, and phallic.*

---

* As strange as it may seem, there were few bona fide academic courses at the higher education level at the time. Theory and practice for adolescent psychology was not an academic discipline. Ironically, at Harvard in the early 1960s, with Erikson himself literally just around the corner, the official program for teachers and counselors included only the recapitulationist theory—studying the phases of development in the first six years—as a basis for adolescent development. Such a reworking was the precursor to the adult genital stage.

29

ERIK ERIKSON (1902–)

Erik Erikson spent his early years in Europe. As a son of well-to-do parents, his education was both formal and informal. Like other upper-class children, when he finished his regular school work, he traveled the continent. He described this period as his own "moratorium." Later in his professional career he developed a theory of human development in stages across the entire span of the life cycle. For adolescents and young adults he noted the importance of a moratorium, a temporary life space between the completion of general academic education and the choice of a life career. He noted that at the time of his own young adulthood it was fashionable to travel through Europe, gaining a perspective on civilization and on one's own possible place in it. He chose the avocation of portrait painting as an activity during this time. It permitted maximum flexibility for travel and yielded some productive output as well. Obviously talented, he soon gained a reputation as a promising young artist, especially for his portraits of young children.

The turning point in his life came when he was invited to a villa in Austria to do a child's portrait. He entered the villa and was introduced to the child's father, Sigmund Freud. Then began a series of informal discussions while he completed his work. A few weeks later he received a written invitation from Freud to join the psychoanalytic institute of Vienna and study child analysis. Erikson has commented that at this point he confronted a momentous decision—the choice between a continued moratorium with more traveling and painting and a commitment to a life career. Fortunately for psychology, and particularly for our eventual understanding of children and adolescents, Erikson ended the moratorium.

After completing his training, he migrated to the United States and served from 1936 to 1939 as a research associate in psychiatry at Yale; he also worked with Henry Murray on the Thematic Apperception Test (TAT) at Harvard. From 1939 to 1951 he served as professor at the University of California, and from there he moved to the Austen Riggs Clinic in Pittsburgh.

With each move his reputation grew. His theoretical framework was adopted in toto by the White House Conference on Children in 1950. The conference report, a national charter for child and adolescent development in this country, was almost a literal repetition of his thoughts. In 1960 he was offered a university professorship at Harvard in recognition of his national and international stature in the field of human development. The career that started so informally that day at Freud's villa culminated with a professorship in America's oldest and most prestigious institution of higher education—all without the benefit of a single earned academic degree. In contrast, he was offered only associate status in the American Psychological Association—and the offer came as late as 1950. This oversight was partially rectified in 1955 when he was elected as a fellow of the Division of Developmental Psychology, even though he had never been a member.

His work, as we note in the text, made a major contribution to our understanding of healthy psychological growth during all aspects of the life cycle. In addition to having an unusually high quality of insight, Erikson possessed a genuine flair in linguistic expression, both spoken and written.

Erikson's genius was in his ability to see the threefold relationship among the person, the immediate environment, and historical forces. Thus each human is partially shaped by environmental and historical events, but each human in turn shapes the environment and can change the course of history. Erikson is equally at home describing the balance of individual strengths and problems for a single average child or teenager and analyzing major historical figures such as Martin Luther and Mahatma Gandhi. He shows through personal history how events and reactions during childhood and adolescence prepare humans to be adults. American essayist Ralph Waldo Emerson said that there is no history, only biography. Erikson's work attests to this wisdom.

If there is a criticism of his overall framework it is that he differentiated between the sexes. As might be expected, he was conditioned and shaped by the major historical and psychological forces of his own time, following in the tradition of a predominantly male-oriented theory for psychology. This issue reminds us of the limits set by historical circumstances, which impinge on all humans. He was able to break with many of the limiting traditions of his time, particularly in moving the concept of development from an exclusive pathological focus to a view that emphasized the positive and productive aspects of growth. He was not, however, successful in breaking with the cultural stereotypes regarding female growth.

In sum, Erikson personified his own theory of development in achieving a sense of personal and professional integrity, "an acceptance of his own responsibility for what life is and was and of its place in the flow of history." These factors include his limitations as well as his many successes.

Erik Erikson (1902–)
Photograph from Harvard
University News Office

Erikson, as noted in the accompanying biography, changed the common view of the nature of adolescence rather dramatically. His mastery of expression and depth of insight combined to form a new acknowledgment of adolescence as a stage in its own right. Gisela Konopka, whose views on adolescence we will present in Chapter 10 on delinquency, put it quite succinctly when she said:

> We reject the common conception that adolescence is solely preparation for adulthood. . . . Adolescents are persons with specific qualities and characteristics who have a participatory and responsible role to play, tasks to perform, skills to develop at that particular time of life. [1]

In this chapter we will outline the features of Erikson's contributions to the theory of adolescence and indicate the connection between identity formation and other aspects of the period.

ERIKSON: REVISING FREUD AND BEYOND

Erikson's first major departure from Freud was to create a system of emotional growth not based exclusively on pathology. Freud's contributions, as great and insightful as they were, were essentially an outline of phases of psychological disturbance. When it came to defining healthy adulthood, Freud simply spoke of "the ability to love and to work"—a characterization profound in its simplicity but quite inadequate as a framework for understanding growth. Erikson realized that each milestone of psychosocial growth could be characterized by specific bipolar dimensions. How the individual successfully resolved these bipolar crises at each stage would determine the process of healthy growth or its opposite. The framework defined the successful as well as the unsuccessful aspects of psychosocial growth. Normality was not defined as the absence of pathology, nor was it defined in so a glib a generality as "to love and to work." We should point out that what Erikson did for views of adolescence, he also did for views of childhood.

A key aspect of Eriksonian theory bears the label *epigenesis*. This term means that psychosocial growth goes through stages and phases according to a ground plan. Development is not random but, instead, proceeds according to the outline from the plan. Also, development is not automatic but, rather, depends on the interaction between the person and the environment. As we noted in Chapter 1, interaction is a cardinal principle in Erikson's view of development. From his studies with children and adolescents in a variety of cultures, he concluded that the epigenetic ground plan could be depicted as shown in Table 2.1.

The plan, then, represents a sequence of interconnected stages as well as a definition of content. For example, the initial, main bipolar struggle is the question of basic trust versus mistrust. Infants in the first year are

TABLE 2.1 Erikson's Ground Plan for Psychosocial Growth

Age	Bipolar crises at each stage (outlined)					
Birth to 12 months	Basic trust vs. mistrust	Earlier autonomy, etc.	Earlier initiative	Earlier mastery	Earlier identity	Earlier intimacy
2–3 years	Later forms of trust, etc.	Autonomy vs. shame	↓	↓	↓	↓
4–6 years	↓	Later forms of autonomy	Initiative vs. guilt	↓	↓	↓
6–12 years	↓	↓	Later forms	Mastery vs. inferiority	↓	↓
13–18 years	↓	↓	↓	Later forms	Identity vs. diffusion	↓
18 years to early adulthood	↓	↓	↓	↓	Later forms	Intimacy vs. isolation

maximally ready for developing trusting or mistrusting attitudes as a result of experiences with their care givers. Imprinting may be too strong a word for this experience, yet it does convey the power of the quality of interaction during year 1 in laying the foundation of trust or its opposite. In other words, there is an ascendant emotional process at each point as the ground plan unfolds. Erikson emphasizes the significance of each point by phrases like "critical alternative," "decisive encounter," and "a crisis." Each stage, then, is considered a potential turning point determining healthy versus unhealthy development. Of special importance is the adequacy of the resolution of each crisis. Thus healthy growth involves the process of finding an appropriate balance on the positive side of resolving the crisis. This resolution enables the ground plan to continue to unfold to the next stage. As the studies described in the special topics in this chapter indicate, Erikson's levels of development are related to several important components of human functioning.

We will now turn to the most salient single theme of personal development during adolescence: identity formation.

ADOLESCENCE AND THE CRISIS OF IDENTITY

Because adolescence represents such a major discontinuity in growth, Erikson has singled out one critical issue as the major task of this stage: resolving the crisis of personal identity. Our definition of self—how we see ourselves *and* how others see us—forms the foundation of our adult personality. If that foundation is firm and strong, a solid personal identity results; if it is not, the result is what Erikson calls a diffuse identity. *Identity diffusion* is something like suffering from amnesia or like perpetually wandering over a landscape trying to find a selfhood. With no sense of past or future, diffuse personalities are strangers in their own lands, with no roots and no history. The sense of personal alienation prevents the establishment of a stable core for the personality.

Western societies have made it extremely difficult for adolescents to come through this period with a firm sense of personal identity. Industrialized societies have exaggerated the marginal status of adolescents by overextending the period of dependency. They justify this prolonged period by pointing out the amount of special learning and training that is needed to survive in our complex world. However, it is easy to forget the negative personal effects of keeping a 21-year-old, or even an 18-year-old, in a position of dependency. To make matters worse, adults seem to be unable to decide just when a teenager becomes an adult. The age of legal adult responsibility is extremely inconsistent in this country: The legal age for marriage differs not only by sex (girls are permitted to marry without parental consent earlier than boys are) but also according to state residency, with some states permitting legal marriage as early as 14 years of age. And there are similar discrepancies in the legal age for going to work, driving a car, entering into a legal contract, voting in elections (for most of this nation's history adolescents were old enough to die for their country in war before they were old enough to vote in elections), drinking alcoholic beverages, and enlisting in the military services.

These few examples serve to highlight the problem of identity formation. Erikson notes that the teenager is caught between two major systems, both of which are in flux [2]. Adolescents have to cope with internal, cognitive, and glandular changes at the same time that they are confronting a series of inconsistent and changing external regulations. And they go through all this change while simultaneously discarding their identity from the previous stage, the age of mastery. Kick-the-can, bike riding (teenagers would rather walk than admit they aren't old enough to drive a car), Boy Scouts and Girl Scouts, the "Three Stooges" on TV, tomboys, and, most important, the view that adults are almost always correct because they are older and bigger—these dimensions of personal development during the elementary age all have to be discarded in adolescence.

As a result of massive changes, entering adolescence is almost like entering a foreign country without knowing the language, the customs, or the culture; only it's worse because the teenager doesn't have a guidebook. It is truly a shock during adolescence to find that adults are not always right and, in fact, are often working very hard to cover up their mistakes. The discovery of relativism, especially in the moral behavior of adults, further exaggerates the difficulties of personal development. In this context, relativism refers to the realization that people often follow quite different behavioral codes than the official norms and values society dictates, as though right and wrong were relative to transient circumstances. On the one hand, teenagers learn that some police officers take bribes, some professors plagiarize, some teachers copy others' lesson plans, some major corporations fix prices, some elected officials solicit bribes, some professional athletes play under the influence of drugs, and so on. On the other hand, these same adults lecture teenagers on the subject of responsibility, the importance of obeying rules, and above all, the importance of showing respect to adults. The resulting teenage overreaction is well known: Since you can't rely on some adults, don't trust anyone over thirty. Since some businesspersons are overly materialistic, all businesspersons are crass and exploitative. Since some adults are unfaithful, all marriages are institutionalized hypocrisy. The list is endless and serves as a poignant reminder of how difficult it is to understand the highly complicated problems of living and personal development in a modern society when so many values and mores are in flux.

SPECIAL TOPIC
Rebaptism During Adolescence: The Confirmation of a Delinquent?

In much of the literature on juvenile delinquency there is a theme indicating that adult caretakers too often are not sensitive to the legitimate needs of teenagers. Gisela Konopka (see p. 348) called it a faceless authority, remote and uncaring. This issue is particularly important. Adolescence, as we have noted, is the time for developing a mature identity in the Eriksonian sense—that is, of resolving the question of who am I as a person and what I stand for. Erikson, in fact, suggests that during adolescence a kind of rebaptism occurs. Because of the many changes of that life stage, an adolescent gradually sheds a childhood definition and becomes a different person. Adolescence, then, is a critical period for the maturation process. Since identity formation has not yet jelled, adult society has the opportunity to make a significant impact on an adolescent's development.

Erikson often quotes as an example an incident he witnessed: a brief encounter between a court judge and a teenager accused of bad driving [1]. The incident took place in the 1950s when youth exhibited their uniqueness in hairstyle and clothing, just as they do today, although the styles themselves are different, of course.

> A "smart alecky" youth who wore pegged trousers and a flattop haircut began six months on a road gang today for talking back to the wrong judge.

IDENTITY FORMATION

Erikson takes the position that adolescence is the process of identity formation. The exact course of the process depends on interaction. The ground plan depicts the polar opposites of formation versus diffusion and denotes the possible outcomes to the generic question of "Who am I?" As we noted, there are major changes both in the teenager personally and in society's expectations. *Identity formation* is viewed as a process of integrating these personal changes, societal demands, and expectations for the future. Erikson states that identity formation involves "the creation of a sense of sameness, a unity of personality now felt by the individual and recognized by others as having consistency in time—of being as it were an irreversible historical fact" [3].

Michael A. Jones, 20, of Wilmington, was fined $25 and costs. But he just didn't leave well enough alone.

"I understand how it was, with your pegged trousers and flattop hair cut," Roberts said in assessing the fine. "You go on like this and I predict in five years you'll be in prison."

When Jones walked over to pay his fine, he overheard Probation Officer Gideon Smith tell the judge how much trouble the "smart alecky" young offender had been.

"I just want you to know I'm not a thief," interrupted Jones to the judge.

The judge's voice boomed to the court clerk: "Change that judgment to six months on the roads." [2]

The young man, perhaps without awareness of consequences, chose to speak out for himself, to put his offense in a legitimate context. After all, his misdemeanor was simply that and not a crime. The judge overreacted. In sentencing the youth to six months in jail, he may have, in Erikson's words, "actually encouraged new identity." Erikson called it "the confirmation of a delinquent."

REFERENCES

1. E. H. Erikson and K. T. Erikson, The confirmation of a delinquent, *Chicago Review* 10(1957):15–23.

2. *Ibid.*, pp. 15–16.

Thus the process is positively reciprocal when it works. The key phrases in Erikson's definition are (1) the sense of sameness and unity of personality that the person truly feels and (2) the recognition of such unity by adults. There can be substantial tension, quite obviously, between what one feels is one's personality and what the adult community is willing to accept. Erikson likens this process to the process of a religious confirmation marking the passage between childhood and adulthood. In fact, in the special topic describing Michael Jones, Erikson uses the term *rebaptism*, to indicate the possible negative consequences that result from interaction. The youth sought some acknowledgment as a growing person; the judge decided he needed to be taught a lesson.

In this section we will discuss some of the issues surrounding identity formation for junior high, senior high, and college students.

Psychosocial Differences in Junior High School

Recently, a study was conducted by E. B. Chisholm to examine possible differences among junior high school pupils according to Erikson's stages [4]. Using a personality test designed to measure each person's resolution of the first six stages of psychosocial development, Chisholm compared two groups of junior high pupils. From teacher/counselor observation and participant-observer ratings of an expert developmental psychologist, the pupils were divided into two groups: (1) social isolates and (2) social leaders. The first group was identified as noninteractive: eating alone, walking the halls alone, not participating before or after class with peers, friendless, and generally never initiating activities in classes. The second group was the opposite: active, highly participative in class and outside class, and so on. There were no differences between the groups on IQ score, social class background, or age. Males and females were equally represented in both groups.

The results indicated that in almost every case the social isolates were less successful than the social leaders in resolving the bipolar psychosocial issues. The major difference was *not* that the interactives were so high on the positive side of each stage but, rather, that the noninteractives were high on the negative side. The isolates were much more mistrustful, ashamed, guilty, diffused in identity, and isolated than the interactives were. Only in industry and inferiority were differences not significant.

Overall, then, the study indicates that the noninteractives were functioning at a less complex level than the interactive adolescents. The former

Teenagers' hair and clothing styles are temporary attempts to form an identity that often result in adverse adult reactions

Photograph from Elizabeth Hamlin/Stock, Boston

were not necessarily disturbed; in Erikson's terms their emotional growth had not kept pace with the developmental ground plan.

What emerges from these findings is that the process of identity development probably occurs at different rates as a young person gradually resolves the psychosocial issues. Chisholm did not find evidence of a crisis in the literal meaning of that word, but she did find that the isolates were lagging behind. On the positive side she found correlates of identity formation. The students who were rated as indicating a higher level of identity development also had higher scores on a test of moral judgment (see Chapter 6) and were more competent socially. Those with more positive levels of identity formation could accurately identify emotions in other persons. This result may indicate that they were less egocentric—less likely to be overly focused on their own perspective of social interactions and events (see Chapter 5)—and could understand emotions in a more complex, differentiated way. In other words, in a variety of psychosocial domains students (both males and females) who were on the positive side of the bipolar identity formation–identity diffusion dimension exhibited greater maturity in other areas of social understanding.

The problem of identity for adolescents could be viewed as a question of psychosocial education rather than one of treatment for emotional disturbance. It does seem clear, as we will note elsewhere, that programs to promote psychosocial growth can be put into place in regular school classes. It also seems clear that there is a real need to do so. In her study Chisholm was quite careful in the selection of criteria to identify children who were markedly separate from peers and teachers. She raises a most challenging question to educators and youth workers at the end of her report:

> And what do we do with the silent one
> who walks the halls alone,
>   sits apart
>   and slips away
> when class time is done? [5]

She dedicated the study "to Charlie, one of the lonely ones, who died September 4, 1978, at age fifteen." He died in an accident without having known the meaning of positive relationships.

Adolescents in High School: Identity Crisis or Transformation?

Erikson's picture of identity struggles in adolescence is a dramatic one. He seems to see teenagers as being overwhelmed by the demands and ambiguities of adulthood. He even talks about a "moment of decision" in which an adolescent faces identity issues and resolves them—or fails to resolve them. Like Hall and Freud, whose ideas you read about in Chapter 1, Erikson sees adolescence as a time of storm and stress, of powerful, turbulent forces in a person's life. The eye of the storm is not hormonal—or sexual, or physical—change alone; it is the task of bringing all of these changes together with the uncertain expectations about, and hopes for, the future into a coherent self-concept—an identity.

Some recent studies of adolescents in the 1970s fit nicely with Erikson's ideas about identity during the secondary school years. They also raise some questions about the view he gives us of the identity crisis as a cataclysmic experience. Jerome Dusek and John Flaherty examined the self-concepts of more than 1600 middle school and high school students ranging in age from 10 to 18, in 1975, 1976, and 1977 [6]. All of the students in the study were asked to indicate how strongly certain adjectives applied to "my characteristic self." There were 21 adjective pairs, such as "relaxed-nervous," "happy-sad," "satisfied-dissatisfied," "smart-dumb," "friendly-unfriendly." The students could mark any one of seven points between each of the adjectives in a pair. In this way they could show, for example, *how* friendly or unfriendly they considered themselves to be. Dusek and Flaherty's research plan allowed them to test the self-concepts of 330 adolescents across the three-year period—a *longitudinal study*. In each year, however, they also tested groups of students at each age who had not been tested before and compared them with the longitudinal group. This technique permitted the researchers to see whether being repeatedly asked about self-concept affected the adolescents' typical responses. In addition, they were able to compare students of different ages in each year—a *cross-sectional study*.

Dusek and Flaherty found that four major factors can be identified in the self-concepts of adolescents. The first factor is one's sense of adjustment (how "relaxed," "steady," "refreshed," "stable," "healthy," "happy," and "satisfied" one feels). The second factor is the sense of achievement and leadership ability; this aspect includes self-rating on scales labeled "smart-dumb," "success-failure," "superior-inferior," "sharp-dull," "valuable-worthless," and "confident-unsure." The third dimension is congeniality, or sociability; this aspect refers to a sense of self in interactions with others (how "nice," "kind," "friendly," and "good" one considers oneself). The final factor is perception of relative masculinity/femininity (how one rates oneself on being "rugged," "hard," "strong," etc.). These clusters of descriptive terms were as much a part of the self-concepts of 10-year-olds as they were of 18-year-olds. The components of self-concept, or identity, seem surprisingly *continuous* over the adolescent years. It is not the case that some drop out and new ones replace them, although the storm-and-stress view of adolescence would have predicted more disruption and *discontinuity* in the factors that contribute to self-views.

Even though adolescents tend to include the same dimensions in their self-concepts from year to year, they do not always rate themselves the same way on those dimensions. Dusek and Flaherty found that adolescents gave themselves roughly the same ratings on achievement/leadership, adjustment, congeniality, and masculinity/femininity from year to year. But there was enough variation in the way they rated themselves to support Erikson's notion that adolescents' self-concepts do change. At any given time they may rate themselves more or less highly on a characteristic because of particular situations they are facing. For example, Dusek and Flaherty found that twelfth graders' ratings of adjustment were lower than they had been in previous years, probably because of the uncertainties and stresses introduced by graduation from high school. Similarly, changes in relationships with family or peers may influence how positively young persons see themselves. As discussed in Chapter 5, the ability to grasp the complexities and the significance of situations and relationships changes as adolescents mature cognitively, and these changing abilities may also affect self-concept, at least temporarily.

Dusek and Flaherty concluded that self-concept does indeed undergo change in adolescence but that the changes occur much more gradually than theorists like Erikson, Hall, and Freud have implied. Rather than meaning a "moment of decision," identity formation for most adolescents probably means successfully meeting a long series of small, relatively minor challenges. Of course, some adolescents do experience great difficulty in facing identity issues. In many of these cases the problem may be that several identity challenges must be faced simultaneously or that personal and situational stresses may make meeting ordinary challenges more difficult than usual.

As you will see in later discussions of adolescents' changing relationships, adolescent development—including the central development of identity—is increasingly being viewed as a series of important transitions in which the adolescent is an active, contributing participant. While Dusek and Flaherty's information gives us a clearer picture of the pace and intensity of identity formation, we still need to ask about the important transitions that are involved. For instance, how do particular experiences in adolescents' lives affect their emerging identities? And how does an emerging sense of identity contribute to adolescents' abilities to participate effectively in their own tasks and relationships?

Marcia: Phases of Identity Formation Among College Students

James Marcia has provided the most complete picture to date of systematic gaps in growth (horizontal *décalage*) during the identity formation stage [7]. Using open-ended interviews with college students, a research technique familiar and common to most researchers in cognitive-developmental work, he created a framework, or a taxonomy, of phases of psychosocial growth.

SPECIAL TOPIC
Identity Foreclosure: Dostoevski's Grand Inquisitor

Fëdor Dostoevski (1821–1881), whom many consider to be the first literary giant to apply psychological dimensions to the novel form, presented a telling description of the problem of identity foreclosure. We note in the text that during the process of identity formation there is one phase that adolescents may adopt that prevents further growth: It is almost as if the adolescent were opting out of the identity formation crisis. In foreclosure the teenager gives up fashioning an identity and accepts the identity that an adult authority figure proposes. The adolescent meekly obeys. To understand why this outcome might be possible, we turn to Dostoevski.

In a memorable scene in *The Brothers Karamazov*, Dostoevski presents a chilling description of what might have happened if Jesus of Nazareth had returned to earth at the height of the infamous Spanish Inquisition [1]. During that period and in the name of religion, thousands of humans were put to death as religious heretics. In charge of such mass execution was "the Grand Inquisitor," a tall 90-year-old cardinal with a withered face and sunken eyes. He confronts the returned Christ: "Why hast Thou come? . . . Didst Thou not often say, then, 'I will make you free'?"

Then the Inquisitor turns and boasts that the people have rejected the burden of such freedom: "They have brought their freedom to us and laid it humbly at our feet. . . . Was this Thy freedom?"

He continues to describe how the people have willingly traded their freedom for materialism. The people "will find us and cry to us, 'Feed us, for those who have promised us fire from heaven haven't given it.' . . . In the end they will lay their freedom at our feet and say to us, 'Make us your slaves but feed us.' "

The Inquisitor concludes his confrontation with a tormenting question: "Didst Thou forget that man prefers peace and even death to freedom of choice in the knowledge of good and evil?"

There is no guarantee that given the opportunity for self-directed freedom, humans will employ it wisely. In fact, in the view of the Grand Inquisitor such a hope is an illusion. Instead, he proclaims that there are three powers that control us: mystery, miracle, and authority.

A foreclosed identity is an illustration of the Grand Inquisitor's point. The person gives up the opportunity for self-development; the burden of individuality seems too great. In order to avoid either the dead-end of identity diffu-

Fedör Dostoevski (1821–1881)

Photograph from The Bettman Archive, Inc.

sion or the pain of fashioning an achieved identity, the individual presents himself or herself to the authority. Individual judgment and reasoning are also foreclosed. The person essentially disappears as a thinking and feeling human and reemerges as an obedient robot. The current epidemic of religious cults in the United States may remind us of the power of Dostoevski's insights and the dangers of a foreclosed identity.

Dostoevski demonstrated the power we have come to know all too well in this century—the power to dehumanize, to atomize individuality. The scene with the Grand Inquisitor closes as he solemnly puts Christ on notice: "Tomorrow, Thou shalt see that obedient flock who at a sign from me will hasten to keep up the hot cinders about the pile on where I shall burn Thee."

In 1979 over eight hundred persons obediently committed suicide in Jonestown. They too had given over their individuality to a self-proclaimed but demented religious prophet. The costs of a foreclosed identity can be high indeed.

REFERENCE

1. F. Dostoevski, *The brothers karamazov* (New York: Modern Library, 1950), pp. 292–313.

In the interview Marcia asked questions in three areas of concern common to college students: (a) occupation, (b) religious ideology, and (c) political ideology. The questions were in a "What is your world view on _____?" format to allow students to talk at length about their own thoughts. For example, he asked "How would you compare your own political ideas with those of your folks?" (political ideology). In religion he asked, "Is there any time you've doubted any of your religious beliefs?" In occupation he asked, "How have you become interested in _____ career?" Of course, whether such an approach yields informative data depends on the skill of the interviewer not to lead but to stimulate reflective thought. Fortunately, Marcia and his staff were highly skilled counselors who were comfortable with silences and could ask a wide variety of open-ended questions until they were convinced that they had a good sample of the students' world view in a particular area.

On the basis of a series of studies with this technique, Marcia found that he could group the students' thought according to four distinct aspects of identity formation. Essentially, he uncovered two intermediate phases between the bipolar identity and identity diffusion extremes. He labeled and described the phases as follows:

Identity diffusion A state of suspension from life is a predominant mode here. There are few, if any, commitments to anyone or to any set of beliefs or principles. Instead, there is a major emphasis on relativity and living for the moment. No area of personal gratification is relinquished; all things are possible. There seems to be no core to the person; social roles are tried on and abandoned quickly. The person seems egoless, directionless, and wandering.

Identity foreclosure The main theme here is the avoidance of autonomous choice. The person is other-directed rather than inner-directed. There is very little questioning; the person largely accepts whatever role authority figures or influential friends prescribe. There seems to be little dissonance. The person accepts somewhat fatalistically what adults say about career, religion, and politics. The struggle to establish the self as an independent and autonomous person is avoided. It is as if the person were fearful of the responsibility that goes with personal freedom (see the Special Topic, "Identity Foreclosure: Dostoevski's Grand Inquisitor").

Identity moratorium A moratorium is often a result of a painful and deliberate decision to take time off from the current press, such as school, college, or a first job. The goal is to create some breathing space in order to explore more fully both one's own psychological self and objective reality. The surface difference between moratorium and diffusion may appear sub-

Developing a sense of satisfaction in one's origins
is an important part of achieving an adult identity
Photograph from Charles Gatewood

tle; yet underneath, the difference is substantial. In moratorium there is a
genuine search for alternatives, not simply a biding of one's time. There is
a major need to test oneself in a variety of experiences to increase one's in-
depth knowledge of self. Commitments are temporarily avoided for legitimate reasons: "I need more time and experience before I can commit myself to a career such as medicine." Or "I am not ready to go for a Ph.D. in
history. There are too many unknowns I need to explore first." Thus a
moratorium is not simply a cop-out so that the person can drift aimlessly.
Instead, it is an active process of searching, with the major goal of preparing for commitment.* Erikson's own life, as the biography points out,
contained a very significant moratorium, as well as an even greater commitment. One flowed from the other, Erikson would say.

Identity achievement The final phase of identity formation results in an
achieved identity. Erikson's definition is the clearest: "the accrued confidence that one's ability to maintain inner sameness and continuity is
matched by the sameness and continuity of one's meaning for others" [8].
The person gradually incorporates each successive childhood identification, yet goes beyond those earlier forms. A new personal entity is formed
as a unique individual. The process, however, is reciprocal as we noted
earlier. The emergence of such individuality and self-direction on the part

---

* It is interesting historically to note that prior to Eriksonian theory practically all college
dropouts were viewed as cop-outs, as immature kids seeking to avoid adulthood. Now the
view has almost reversed. College policies today encourage stepping out and even go so
far as to admit students to the first year of college with a one-year proviso (e.g., "You may
enter one year from now if you wish.").

of the person (the core personality) is acknowledged by others. It is this latter aspect of identity formation that can be the most troubling and troublesome, since such recognition is neither automatic nor necessarily universal. In fact, now-recognized great persons often had a major crisis during which the individual's emergent achieved identity was not immediately recognized by adult society in general. Erikson's biography of Martin Luther (*Young Man Luther*) contains the most complete account of this phenomenon, and similar episodes can be found in the personal histories of major figures such as Malcolm X, George Bernard Shaw, and Marie Curie.

Marcia found, most importantly, that identity achievement almost always contained elements of personal crisis, confrontation, and thoughtful decision making. The person was aware of the variety of tough choices life offers: The choice selected was accompanied by commitment, that is, a personal pledge that the psychological resources that the individual possessed would be placed in the service of the goal.

Changes in Identity Status During College

Although we do not have national sample base rates for the proportion of young adults at the various points on the identity formation continuum, some studies with college males at a selective undergraduate college indicate findings in accord with expectations—and also some surprises [9]. In one study identity achievement increased substantially over the four-year period in the identity areas of occupation and ideology. Thus as shown in Table 2.2, by graduation 40% and 44% of the seniors had reached identity formation in the areas of occupation and ideology, respectively. Similarly, there was a sharp decline in moratorium. On the other hand, there was little change in foreclosure in the occupation area. From the table we see that almost 30% of the seniors had not seriously considered their own reasons for occupational choice but, rather, were just going along with family and authority expectations. Even more surprising was the finding of the high proportion of seniors in the longitudinal study who were still in diffusion—no change at all in four years. As the note in Table 2.2 indicates, a total of 46% of all seniors were in diffusion in one or both areas. If we consider students in foreclosure and diffusion as persons with inadequate solutions for the identity crisis, then we must conclude that a large proportion of the sample did not experience psychosocial development at all. Apparently, the general college environment was not a responsive educational atmosphere for students in the process of identity formation.

Also, it is important to note that the above findings were from college-age adults who were actually attending college. The percent of adults in general in that age period who reveal identity achievement may be significantly different from the figure from a college population. One study by L. K. Andersen did indicate that only 20% of an adult female sample (N =

TABLE 2.2 Eriksonian Identity Formation During College: Males

Identity area	Identity phase	Freshman year	Senior year	Change
Occupation	Achievement	7 (14%)	19 (40%)	+12
(N = 47)	Moratorium	8 (17%)	0 —	−8
	Foreclosure	17 (36%)	14 (29%)	−3
	Diffusion	15 (32%)	14 (29%)	−1
Ideology	Achievement	5 (11%)	20 (44%)	+15
(world view)	Moratorium	4 (8%)	1 (2%)	−3
(N = 45)	Foreclosure	19 (42%)	7 (15%)	−12
	Diffusion	17 (38%)	17 (38%)	0

Adapted from A. S. Waterman, P. S. Geary, and C. K. Waterman, Longitudinal study of changes in ego identity status from the freshman to senior year at college, *Developmental Psychology* 10(1974):390.

Note: Thirteen percent of the seniors were in diffusion on both occupation and ideology, and an additional 33% of the seniors were in diffusion in one of the two areas, for a total of 46% of all seniors.

70, median age 36) could be classified at identity achievement on Marcia's scheme [10]. However, when Andersen examined the profile across the entire sample, she found the distribution shown in Table 2.3.

Since Andersen's sample included women who had completed college as well as others who went directly into careers after high school, she was able to examine the relationship between college attendance and identity formation. She reported a correlation of +0.43 between identity status and educational level. This result was noteworthy because there were no positive correlations between identity status and a series of other variables

TABLE 2.3 Erikson Identity Status in the Andersen Study: Adult Females (N = 70)

Identity status	N	%
Achieved	15	21
Transition (achieved/moratorium)	21	30
Moratorium	21	30
Diffusion	13	19

Adapted from L. K. Andersen, Careers of adult women: Psychological profiles from a developmental perspective. (Ph.D. thesis, University of Minnesota, 1980).

Note: Since the sample was composed of mature women, the ratings were a modified version of Marcia's taxonomy. "Parents" as a category was replaced by "woman's role." Also, there was no evidence of identity foreclosure.

SPECIAL TOPIC
Eriksonian Differences in College: The Inability to Take Hold

Erikson makes the point of the critical importance of identity formation during middle and late adolescence. He sees diffusion as a major setback. He often uses Biff, the son in Arthur Miller's play *Death of a Salesman*, as an example. Caught in the midst of a series of confusing and contradictory expectations, Biff appears aimless and lost. "I just can't take hold, Mom, I can't take hold of some kind of life." Bewildered, he exemplifies a person who has no identity. His self-definition is diffused—indeed, almost atomized.

Recently, a major study was conducted of college students in teacher training. Training programs require both skill and commitment, since the student teacher must learn academic material and then be able to present it to either high school or elementary school students in coherent and concise procedures. Student teachers regularly report how demanding and how personally stretching such a role is. Student teaching, particularly in junior and Senior high schools, can often come close to the chaos described in William Golding's novel *Lord of the Flies* if the teenagers decide that it's time to challenge a beginning teacher. Thus the stress factor is a major component of the student teacher's role.

If Erikson's theory has validity, then college students might perform in such a demanding role in accordance with their stage of identity formation.

(age, income, socioeconomic status, and years married). Such a finding, then, would indicate a possible relationship of identity development and college attendance. Since this study was a correlational study, however, we cannot assume that college attendance produced identity achievement. Waterman, Geary, and Waterman's study with males (Table 2.2), which was longitudinal, provides firmer evidence on this question.

In both cases the results point in two directions. On the one hand, identity formation is associated with higher education. On the other hand, there are considerable numbers of students who complete college while still in Erikson's negative polar status of diffusion. These figures can be construed as indicating a genuine need for educational programming designed to help stimulate the resolution of the identity crisis during adoles-

To test that hypothesis, Shirley Walter and Eugene Stivers sorted a large sample of student teachers (N = 319) by Erikson's level of identity versus diffusion [1]. They next assessed the actual in-class teaching effectiveness on an important series of elements: responsiveness to pupil questions, open-ended questions, empathy, use of positive reinforcement, accuracy of content—in short, characteristics of what is often called higher-order teaching.

The results were almost exactly as we would predict from Erikson's theory. The teachers with the highest scores on identity resolution were the most effective in responsive teaching and classroom management. The student teachers with high scores on identity diffusion were the least effective. Such student teachers had difficulty accepting pupil ideas, asked rote questions, and exhibited uneven classroom management. In fact, the Erikson identity score was the single most important predictor variable. The study included variables such as college board score (SAT), the cumulative grade point average, and IQ. None of those cognitive elements were as powerful as the measure of identity status. The student teachers, particularly the males, who were the most confused in the process of identity formation (i.e., who had the highest diffusion index scores) had the greatest difficulty in teaching. In Erikson's sense they apparently were still so far from resolving their identity conflicts that "they couldn't take hold."

REFERENCE

1. S. A. Walter and E. Stivers, The relation of student teachers' classroom behavior and Eriksonian ego identity, *Journal of Teacher Education* 38,6(177):47–55.

cence. Also, these figures can be indicative that such problems are not necessarily pathological but, rather, are reasonably common attributes of general adolescent development.

As pointed out in the Special Topic titled "Eriksonian Differences in College: The Inability to Take Hold," there is evidence supporting the relationship between identity phase and performance. Other studies have confirmed these views. That is, men and women who reach identity achievement usually manifest high self-esteem and tolerance for stress, resist mindless conformity, and make thoughtful, committed decisions [11]. Those in diffusion, on the other hand, often manifest opposite characteristics, such as poor self-esteem, inability to tolerate stress, and tendency toward impulsive decisions.

INTIMACY VERSUS DISTANCE

Adolescence as a series of psychosocial tasks comes to a close with the achievement of a firm sense of one's own identity. The successful achievement of identity leads to the first task of adulthood: developing a sense of true intimacy. Failure to achieve identity leads to *distance*—Erikson's term is distantiation: "the readiness to repudiate, to isolate, and if necessary, to destroy those forces and people whose essence seems dangerous to one's own." Thus successful resolution of this developmental transition is obviously extremely important. In fact, in Chapter 9, "Adolescent Sexuality," we present an extensive discussion of this question.

The heart of the problem, according to Erikson, is that genuine intimacy only can follow after identity formation. That is, identity precedes the possibility of real intimacy with another person. Thus a sense of self is the requisite prior step to *intimacy*, which is defined as the ability for mutual psychological as well as physical relationships with another person. Mutuality is the key here, in the sense that both persons must simultaneously process their own needs, thoughts, and feelings as well as the needs, thoughts, and feelings of the other.

Much of this process involves true sexual intimacy, as we note in our discussion of goals for sex education in Chapter 9. However, Erikson means more than sexual intimacy by his concept. A broadened definition of intimacy includes adult friendships, leadership, and inspiration. A loving act in this form need not be overtly or covertly sexualized to fit the definition of intimacy. For instance, in the now-classic movie *Brian's Song*, two football players, Brian Piccolo (dying of cancer) and Gale Sayers, develop a genuinely intimate adult friendship. Unfortunately, in our society as a whole there is some discomfort with such a concept—in fact, we have no really good word to describe it. Certainly, adult friendship is a rather bland description of the genuine mutuality involved in this Eriksonian stage. Our discomfort with this concept may account for some of the newest findings from studies of adult development. For example, Levinson conducted a precedent-setting study of adult males, discussed in his book *The Seasons of a Man's Life*. He found almost no examples of genuine adult friendship: "We would say that a close friendship with a man or woman is rarely experienced by American men. . . . We need to understand why friendship is so rare, and what consequences that deprivation has for adult life" [12].

For Erikson the consequences of such deprivation are clear. Distantiation leads to polarized relationships. The person becomes absorbed totally within the self. The other, whether of the same sex or the opposite sex, becomes the object of exploitation and eventually may lead to "various forms of incisive combat." Rampant individualism, as exemplified by

Overcoming a sense of psychological isolation is a developmental task of young adulthood
Photograph from Rick Smolan/Stock, Boston

phrases like "I'd step on my grandmother to get ahead" or "our goal is to win at any cost," serves as a reminder of distantiation and self-absorption.

A positive solution to this first stage of adulthood bears an important relationship to identity formation. As the studies in the previous section have shown, there is a compelling need for programs that stimulate identity formation during late adolescence. Psychological maturity does not evolve automatically in young adulthood. Instead, development depends, as it does at all ages, on experiences that stimulate growth. Consequently, colleges and initial employers for noncollege youth need to understand both the importance of the problem and the need for new approaches to stimulate psychological maturity at this stage.

TIME PERSPECTIVE AND IDENTITY FORMATION

A study by Santanicola demonstrated important differences in time perspective among college students [13]. Those students in identity diffusion exhibited a much greater time restriction than other students did. For example, their thinking concerning both the present and the past was much less specific and detailed than the thinking employed by those in moratorium. The identity diffusion students seemed to be looking down the road to the future, all the while avoiding connecting those thoughts, plans, and feelings to their present or their past.

Remember that Erikson indicated that identity formation included incorporating one's past identities with one's present view. He suggested that those in diffusion apparently were attempting to short-circuit that process, to leap over their past and present directly into the future. College students in diffusion may be dwelling on the future as a means of avoiding the identity crisis of the present. Thus it may be most difficult for educators and counselors to communicate with students in diffusion, unless such people understand the mental processes that are characteristic of that phase.

Erikson's emphasis on the concept of time perspective reminds us that time is both abstract and relative. The maturing adolescent "learns to grasp the flux of time, to anticipate the future in a coherent way, to perceive ideals and to assent to ideals" [14].

IDENTITY FORMATION: ATTENDING COLLEGE VERSUS WORKING

Young people who attend college and those who don't may, of course, face different identity issues. At this point not much information is available about what those differences might be. In a study by Munro and Adams, however, college students were compared with individuals of the same ages who had taken jobs right after high school graduation [15]. On Marcia's identity measures more of the college youth were in the diffusion and moratorium statuses than in the foreclosure or identity achievement statuses. By contrast, more of the working youth were classified in the identity achievement category than in the diffusion or moratorium statuses. In particular, working youth tended to have reached a commitment (achievement or foreclosure) on religious and political ideologies, while college youth were more often in diffusion or moratorium with regard to political and religious issues. Interestingly, the two groups were equally likely to be reaching or approaching commitment on their occupational identities.

It may be that college environments are hospitable to questioning, relativistic political and religious attitudes, while the workaday world encourages well-defined views. These findings come from a fairly small group of college students and working youth, however. Much more information must be gathered before we have a clear picture of how these groups might meet identity challenges.

A study by James Rest also compared college students and working youth [16]. Rest focused on moral judgment, a domain somewhat akin to religious ideology in Marcia's work; his results indicate that young adults tend to reach a plateau of development after completing formal education.

In assessing levels of developmental reasoning on value issues, Rest found the college group continued to increase in complexity of reasoning not only between high school and college but also after college, as indicated in Table 2.4. The working youth sample leveled off during the same time period. Because of the small sample size, however, as was the case for the Munro and Adams study, generalization from this study must be cautious.

Piaget has suggested that the process of moving from school to work can have a major impact on the level of formal operations and identity (see Chapter 13). Certainly, from a cultural standpoint, leaving the status of student and taking full-time employment marks a transition. In Erikson's view the adult community will likely confirm or rebaptize the adolescent as a young adult.

The problem in this area of study is that we lack a solid research base from which to draw conclusions. From Munro and Adams we might draw an inference that moving from high school directly to a job promotes identity achievement. On the other hand, the results of Andersen and of Rest, as well as those from a study by Eugene Mischey, cast doubt on such a conclusion.

For example, the recent Mischey study indicated that college students were much more likely to exhibit higher identity achievement scores, higher moral-reasoning scores, and higher scores on a measure of complex religious faith reasoning [17]. The subjects at the higher score levels had a greater grasp of the issues of living. The subjects at the lower level exhibited a complacent and compliant acceptance of authority. There was a major lack of questioning on the part of the young adult workers. They seemingly ignored controversial issues. Instead, they exhibited contentment in following in the steps of their parents. In Chapter 6 we will discuss the concept of agency, or self-directed choosing, as an important aspect of mature development; the working youth in the Mischey study demonstrated very little agency.

TABLE 2.4   Moral judgment reasoning in Rest study: Percentages of principled thought

Group: Males	Time of testing		
	High school	**Two years later**	**Four years later**
College bound (N = 5)	32%	48%	52%
Working (N = 18)	29%	36%	35%

Adapted from J. R. Rest *Development in judging moral issues* (Minneapolis: University of Minnesota Press, 1979), pp. 133–135.

But again we must exercise caution in drawing conclusions. Since the study was not longitudinal, it cannot be considered definitive, even though the study method was quite intensive, with lengthy individual interviews, probes, and carefully coded and reliably derived score assignments. Logically, however, it would appear that identity formation as a process requires extensive personal inquiry, self-knowledge, and exploration. Thus from this viewpoint we can speculate that self-exploration as a means of promoting identity development would occur more frequently in a higher education setting than in a regular work environment.

SUMMARY: ERIKSON'S CONTRIBUTION

Overall, Erikson must be considered the single most important theorist for the contemporary psychological study of adolescence. His general ground plan moved the field of study toward a discipline in its own right. Before Erikson came along, adolescence was viewed in rather traditional psychoanalytic terms as a recapitulation of the first six years or, at the other extreme, as a relativistic invention of certain cultures and not others. Erikson's genius was to combine psychology and sociocultural issues. His idea of development as the interaction of individual personality with society during the unfolding of the epigenetic ground plan defined personality development in new ways.

Before Erikson's time, personal and emotional development was considered out of bounds for educators, being the exclusive province of child guidance clinics and of those specially trained to deal with pathological problems. Erikson's great contribution was to bring the problems of personal growth out of the shadows of pathology and to integrate them into an overall process of healthy personality development. Erikson spelled out the major personal issues for us so that we can understand much more about our pupils at each of the various stages. We hope that such insight will guide us to more effective ways of helping children and teenagers during important—indeed, critical—times.

Erikson's insights helped spur theorists and researchers to further specify aspects and domains of healthy psychological development. The sectors and segments that we will detail in subsequent chapters all owe at least part of their origin to his work. Thus when we outline aspects of development of interpersonal growth and self-growth (Selman and Loevinger), value and moral development (Kohlberg), college student development (Perry), and career development (Miller-Tiedeman and Tiedeman), we hope you will realize the links to Erik Erikson. It will be in those subsequent chapters that we will specify program implications. Here we have chosen to focus on the general framework for adolescent personality development. Erikson sums it up:

Each successive step, then, is a potential crisis because of a radical change in perspective. There is, at the beginning of life, the most radical change of all: from intrauterine to extrauterine life. But in postnatal existence, too, such radical adjustments of perspective as lying relaxed, sitting firmly, and running fast must all be accomplished in their own good time. With them, the interpersonal perspective, too, changes rapidly and often radically, as is testified by the proximity in time of such opposites as "not letting mother out of sight" and "wanting to be independent." Thus, different capacities use different opportunities to become full-grown components of the ever-new configuration that is the growing personality. [18]

KEY POINTS AND NAMES

Erik Erikson

Epigenetic growth

Bipolar stages
  Identity versus diffusion
  Intimacy versus isolation

Identity crisis

Identity formation

Psychosocial issues in junior high school

Identity struggles in high school

Jerome Dusek and John Flaherty

Longitudinal study

Cross-sectional study

Identity formation in college

James Marcia

Identity statuses
  Diffusion
  Foreclosure
  Moratorium
  Achievement

Time perspective

Differences between college students and young adult workers

REFERENCES

1. G. Konopka, Requirements for healthy development of adolescent youth, *Adolescence* 31(1973):291–316.

2. E. H. Erikson, *Identity: Youth and crisis* (New York: Norton, 1968), pp. 22–23.

3. E. H. Erikson, *Youth: Change and challenge* (New York: Basic Books, 1981), p. 11.

4. E. B. Chisholm, *Developmental differences between socially interactive and non-interactive junior high pupils*, Plan B Research Project (Minneapolis: University of Minnesota, 1980), pp. 5–6.

5. *Ibid.*, p. 28.

6. J. Dusek and J. Flaherty, The development of the self-concept during the adolescent years, Monograph of the Society for Research in Child Development 46(1981):4.

7. J. E. Marcia, Development and validation of ego identity status, *Journal of Personality and Social Psychology* 3(1966):551–558.

8. E. H. Erikson, Identity and the life cycle, *Psychological Issues* 1(1959):89.

9. A. S. Waterman, P. S. Geary, and C. K. Waterman, Longitudinal study of changes in ego identity status from the freshman to senior year at college, *Developmental Psychology* 10(1974):387–392.

10. L. K. Andersen, Careers of adult women: Psychological profiles from a developmental perspective (Ph.D. thesis, University of Minnesota, 1980), pp. 20–35.

11. For a review of studies specifying the behavioral relationship between developmental stage and adult performance, see N. A. Sprinthall and L. Thies-Sprinthall, The teacher as an adult learner: A cognitive developmental view, in *NSSE yearbook*, ed. G. Griffin (Chicago: University of Chicago Press, 1983).

12. D. Levinson, *The seasons of a man's life* (New York: Ballantine Books, 1978), p. 335.

13. A. Santanicola, Identity, decision making and time perspective in late adolescence (Ed.D. thesis, Harvard Graduate School of Education, 1970), pp. 13–50.

14. E. H. Erikson, The golden rule and the cycle of life, in *The study of lives*, ed. R. W. White (New York: Atherton Press, 1963), p. 417.

15. G. Munro and G. Adams, Ego-identity formation in college students and working youth, *Developmental Psychology* 13(1977):523–524.

16. J. R. Rest, *Development in judging moral issues* (Minneapolis: University of Minnesota Press, 1979), pp. 132–134.

17. E. J. Mischey, Faith, identity and morality in late adolescence, *Character Potential* 9,4(1981):175–191.

18. Erikson, Identity and life cycle, p. 55.

CHAPTER 3

Physical Changes and Their Psychological Effects

INTRODUCTION

We said in Chapter 1 that adolescence is partly a social invention, a response by adults to the characteristics of individuals during a certain period of their lives. Probably the most significant characteristic of adolescents for adults is the multitude of physical changes that occur with puberty. Of course, important cognitive and personality changes go along with these signs of physical growth. But if adolescence has a single defining characteristic, it is the dramatic bodily changes that occur in the second decade of life.

What are these physical changes? How do they occur? And how do adolescents, their parents, and others in the society react to them? These are the questions we will address in this chapter.

PUBESCENCE AND PUBERTY

From a physiological point of view the most fundamental biological change of adolescence is that of reaching reproductive or sexual maturity. But the physical changes that may affect adolescents psychologically involve far more than reproductive capacity; they include all of the changes in appearance and physical ability that cause others to have different expectations, different standards for performance of tasks, and different norms for behavior for adolescents than they had for the same individuals as children. Perhaps the pressures that accompany physical maturity explain the complaint of one teenage girl: "I can *bear* children. It's adults I can't bear."

In this section we will discuss the growth spurt and the changes in body size, shape, and physical capacity that occur during adolescence.

The Growth Spurt

The physical changes of adolescence begin when the hypothalamus, an area at the base of the brain, stimulates the pituitary gland to secrete certain hormones. The hormones, in turn, stimulate the ovaries, testes, and the adrenal glands to produce other hormones. These hormones then set in motion the rapid rate of increase in height and weight called the adolescent *growth spurt*. We will discuss these hormonal mechanisms in more detail later in the chapter; but for the time being let's consider the growth spurt itself and the many ways in which it affects the appearance and abilities of adolescents. Figure 3.1 shows the rapid increase in one aspect of physical growth, height, during the growth spurt. Notice that the rate of growth almost doubles for both sexes during the adolescent spurt, yet the onset occurs two years earlier for girls.

The growth spurt is a sign of *pubescence*, the period of physical changes that lead to reproductive maturity. *Puberty* marks the end of pubescence; it is the point at which reproductive maturity is reached. Before that point, however, adolescents' appearance and physical capacities have already begun to differ from what they were in childhood. We turn now to a description of the most dramatic physical changes in adolescence.

Changes in Body Size, Shape, and Physical Capacity

The adult's body is significantly different from the child's body, and the transition from one to the other can be a time of great uncertainty and concern for adolescents. Not only are their bodies growing very rapidly, but the proportions of their bodies are also changing and, with them, adolescents' capacities for physical activity and work. Although adolescents may feel that these changes in themselves are painfully unique, they are, of course, actually very predictable. Let's review the major changes in body size and shape.

Height   We have already seen (Fig. 3.1) that height changes dramatically as a result of the adolescent growth spurt. This increase in stature comes when the long bones in the body, such as those in the arms and legs, begin to grow quite rapidly at both ends. This dramatic bone growth continues until the open ends of the bones, called the epiphyses, close—an event brought about by changes in hormones during puberty. This closing does not happen suddenly; rather, the very rapid changes in height begin to slow down and gradually cease toward the end of the second decade of life [1].

Teenagers themselves, of course, are concerned both with their rapidly changing bodies and with the implications of these changes for what they will be like as adults. As it happens, the majority of individuals end up

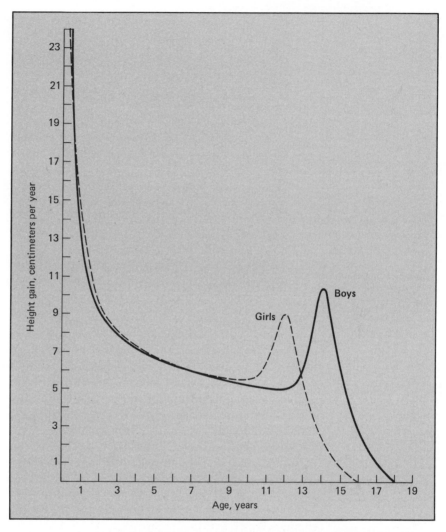

FIG. 3.1 Growth rates for height during adolescence

Redrawn from J. Tanner, R. Whitehouse, and M. Takaishi, Standards from birth to maturity for height, weight-height velocity and weight velocity; British children, 1965, *Archives of the Diseases of Childhood* 41(1966): 468. Reprinted by permission.

about the same size relative to their peers after the growth spurt as they were before. In other words, even after his own height changes dramatically, an adolescent boy is likely to be shorter than the boys who were taller than he was before they all experienced the growth spurt and taller than the boys who were shorter than he was [2].

Adolescent growth spurt occurs later, on the average, for boys than for girls
Photograph from Donald Dietz/Stock, Boston

Table 3.1 shows how well, on the average, mature adult height can be predicted from height in any of the first 19 years of life. As we can see from the table, growth from one year to the next in childhood tells more about how tall a person will be as an adult than do the year-to-year changes during pubescence. Thus for most adolescents the changes that occur in the growth spurt will not make as much of a difference for adult appearance as adolescents often fear. However, about 30% of the time the variation in height after the growth spurt is due not to preadolescent height but to the magnitude of the growth spurt itself. As one expert puts it, "Some adolescents get a nasty and unavoidable shock" when their period of rapid growth arrives [3]. These young people need sensitive understanding and support from adults to help them adjust to the especially dramatic physical changes they are experiencing.

Body shape Just as dramatic as the growth in height—and with even more profound implications for how adolescents will look as adults—are changes in the shape of the body. Infants' and young children's bodies are dominated by head and trunk; in fact, at all ages these parts of the body are closer to maturity in size and shape than are the extremities [4]. When the adolescent growth spurt begins, the extremities catch up in growth; the hips, the chest, and the shoulders change as well. By the end of adolescence the relative proportions of these body parts are quite different from what they were in childhood.

TABLE 3.1 Percentages of mature height attained at different ages

Chronological age, years	Percentage of average mature height		Chronological age, years	Percentage of average mature height	
	Boys	**Girls**		**Boys**	**Girls**
Birth	28.6	30.9	10	78.0	84.4
1	42.2	44.7	11	81.1	88.4
2	49.5	52.8	12	84.2	92.9
3	53.8	57.0	13	87.3	96.5
4	58.0	61.8	14	91.5	98.3
5	61.8	66.2	15	96.1	99.1
6	65.2	70.3	16	98.3	99.6
7	69.0	74.0	17	99.3	100.0
8	72.0	77.5	18	99.8	100.0
9	75.0	80.7	19	100.0	100.0

Adapted from N. Bayley, Growth curves of height and weight by age for boys and girls, scaled according to physical maturity. *Journal of Pediatrics* 48(1956):187–194. Reprinted by permission.

The proportions change differently for males and females, of course. Males' shoulders become broader, especially relative to the hips, and their legs are relatively long compared with trunk length. The typical female silhouette shows relatively narrow shoulders, broad hips, and short legs relative to trunk length [5]. One reason for the different body shapes for the sexes is the different distribution of body fat in males and females. During the growth spurt boys rapidly lose the subcutaneous fat that is characteristic of both male and female children. Teenage girls, however, lose less body fat as a result of physical changes in adolescence, and fat deposits in the regions of the pelvis, the breast, the upper back, and the backs of the upper arms give females' bodies a more rounded appearance [6]. Differences in musculature also affect body appearance. The muscles of males are more apparent than those of females because of the camouflage of subcutaneous fat carried by even quite muscular females [7].

One pronounced change in shape for both boys and girls is that of the face. In infancy and early childhood the face is shorter and broader than it is in adulthood. During pubescence the facial skeleton becomes longer, the profile becomes straighter, the nose projects more, and—perhaps most obviously—the jaw becomes a good deal more prominent [8]. Facial appearance is also affected by recession of the hairline, which occurs in both females and males, although much more distinctly in males. A comparison of a person's school pictures from, say, third grade through ninth or tenth grade shows these facial changes dramatically.

SPECIAL TOPIC
Physical Change and School Change: Too Much Too Soon?

Physical changes sometimes dominate our attention so that we forget that other dramatic changes also take place in adolescents' lives at about the same time they are undergoing puberty. One such change is the transition from elementary school to junior high school. In some locales the organization of school systems into middle schools and high schools makes it possible for young adolescents to remain separate from older teens; but not all young adolescents have the opportunity to attend middle schools. Instead, many adolescents are obliged to enter junior high or senior high school—and experience corresponding changes in social demands—when they are also coping with the physical and social changes of puberty.

In recent years this problem has been studied by sociologists Roberta Simmons, Dale Blyth, Edward Van Cleave, and Diane Bush [1]. In one of their studies they investigated the emotional effects of changing from elementary school to junior high school for adolescents who were experiencing pubertal changes. In particular, they studied the effects on adolescents' *self-esteem* of changing to junior high school rather than remaining in the elementary school through eighth grade (a K–8 school). They compared pubertal adolescents in these two types of school settings with adolescents who had not yet reached puberty.

The group that showed the lowest self-esteem was the seventh grade girls who were postpubertal, had begun to date, and had shifted to junior high school in the same year. The accompanying figure shows the change in self-esteem from sixth to seventh grades for this group. Girls who experienced only one or two of these changes were not as low in self-esteem. In other words, the achievement of a new physical status accompanied by changes in social demands and by the additional stress of shifting to a new school environment produced significant emotional effects for girls.

Boys showed less effect from the transition to junior high school, regardless of their pubertal status. Indeed, there was some tendency for more physically mature seventh grade boys in junior high school actually to have higher self-esteem than less mature boys.

What is the reason for this difference in adjustment for boys and girls? The researchers found that girls placed more importance on appearance and popularity than boys did during this age period—probably a result of typical sex role socialization patterns for females and males in our society. Thus girls may be more susceptible than boys to the uncertainties brought about both by

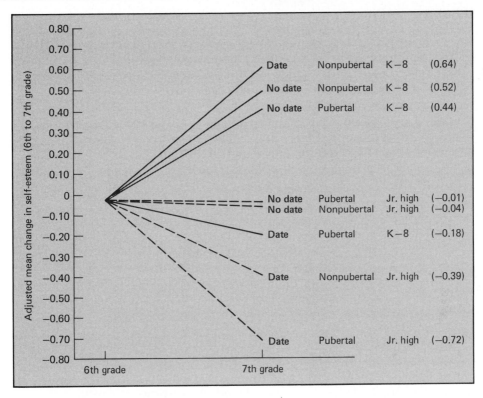

Changes in self-esteem between sixth and seventh grade by dating behavior, puberty, and school type (white girls in comparable schools)

Redrawn from R. Simmons, D. Blyth, E. Van Cleave, and D. Bush, Entry into early adolescence: The impact of school structure, puberty, and early dating on self-esteem, *American Sociological Review* 44(1979):961. Used with permission of the American Sociological Association.

pubertal changes and by a new social situation. Furthermore, physically mature girls who were dating also frequently reported feelings of sexual pressure—which were less often a problem for boys. Here's an example from one girl's account:

Interviewer: First of all, were you meeting boys or going out with boys at that age?

Girl: Yeah, I was meeting guys, and then going out roller skating and stuff. . . . I'd always go with a group. I find that I do

(Continued)

SPECIAL TOPIC (Continued)

feel more comfortable when I'm with a group. . . . My main reason is because, the reason I don't want to be with just one boy is because like I said, I don't know what to talk about. And I'm not the kind who likes to hold hands all the time. I've got to be free, you know? And there's some guy the other night that was wanting me to sit down and I wouldn't. I mean, not me, I mean I'm a happy person, I guess. I feel happy, and the only way I can keep feeling happy that way is if the guy doesn't want to hold my hand, and I don't really like to be kissed, you know.

Interviewer: You feel that's not where the boys are? They do want to hold hands and kiss you?

Girl: Yeah. That's what happened when, like I told you, [I went out with] my brother and his girlfriend [and a guy] and, well, they were kissing up in front, and he wanted to; I didn't. So I faked sleeping which I shouldn't of did cause he caught me. [2]

These findings are important reminders that drastically changing experiences and circumstances—both within adolescents and in the social world around them—can multiply to have profound effects on the psychological adjustment of young people during this period. Adolescence is a result not of internal changes only nor of external pressures only but of a unique combination of changes in both within a very short period of time.

REFERENCES

1. R. Simmons, D. Blyth, E. Van Cleave, and D. Bush, Entry into early adolescence: The impact of school structure, puberty, and early dating on self-esteem, *American Sociological Review* 44(1979):948–967.
2. *Ibid.*, p. 964. Used with permission of the American Sociological Association.

Strength and physical capacity   Changes in physical appearance during pubescence and puberty are accompanied by truly remarkable changes in the capacity of the body for physical exertion. One important reason for the increase in strength is the growth of the muscles—by a factor of 14 between the ages of 5 and 16 for males, a tenfold increase for females [9].

Size and capacity of the heart and lungs increase as well. The weight of the heart nearly doubles during the growth spurt, and systolic blood pressure increases dramatically [10]. There are also increases in the number of red corpuscles and in blood hemoglobin and blood volume, which permit more efficient distribution of oxygen so that the body recovers more rapidly following exertion [11]. Both the size of the lungs and respiratory capacity increase, so that in a given time more air can be taken in at a single breath. Heart and lung development make it increasingly possible for the body to function while incurring an oxygen debt, a significant advantage in physically demanding activity. Like other changes in physical capacity during adolescence, these improvements accrue to boys more than to girls [12].

Do sex differences in growth mean that the physical capacity of adolescent and adult males is greater than that of females? In terms of averages for large groups of people, the answer is yes. Nevertheless, experts are careful to point out that "there is much overlap between the two sexes" [13]. Thus many women are superior in physical capacity to many men. One expert has summarized what we know about sex differences in strength and physical capacity in this way:

> The various physiological differences that characterize the two sexes at the end of puberty add up to the generally superior ability of males for intense physical exertion and recovery from its effects. . . . The net effect is that, after puberty, males generally excel in activities like lifting, throwing, hitting, running, jumping, and so on. This advantage has tended to become generalized into a conception of all-encompassing male "physical superiority" which is quite unwarranted. In the last analysis, the ability to survive is the critical overall index of physical fitness and the death rate for women is lower than that for men in every decade of life.

> Even within the limits of acknowledged male physical superiority, social factors should not be disregarded. Physical prowess depends to a large measure on exercise and training, which in turn depend on personal motivation, social expectations, and practical opportunities. Males have received more encouragement in this regard, which has contributed greatly to the gap that exists in physical ability between the two sexes. [14]

There is considerable reason to doubt that physical capacity differences between males and females should be the basis for distinctions between the two sexes in their fitness for most of the occupations that are available in modern industrialized societies. The capacities of males and females overlap in many cases, and women are quite often as capable as men of carrying out even fairly physically demanding work. Thus there is little biological justification for sex discrimination in hiring. Both women and men should feel free to aspire to most occupations in our society.

SPECIAL TOPIC
Blooming Physically

Blooming, a recent novel by Susan Toth, a professor of English at Macalester College, provides in case study form at least some of the issues associated with physical growth, as adolescents experience them. The following excerpt from Toth's novel discusses her adolescent reactions to swimming pools.*

I always ask for a window seat so I can see the swimming pools. As we descend over the suburbs, I stare like a child with nose pressed to glass at the brilliant blue eyes that stare back at me from the ground. They blink in the sun with affluent pride. What would it be like, I wonder, to live in a neighborhood where every yard had its pool? When I was growing up, our town had ten thousand people and only three swimming pools for us all, so that on hot days we were packed like Vienna sausages into the water. The pools I see below me look empty and lonely, unable to convey the intense excitement and fear I remember. My own swimming pools were three enchanted places, each casting a different spell, and we girls growing up in Ames passed through certain rites there. . . .

Why we were so determined to swim would have mystified any outsider. The nearest lake of any size was a two-hour drive, far away in the corner of the state, and few of us knew anyone with a cabin there. We simply wanted to hold up our heads at Blaine's Pool, the town's only public swimming place, and to do that we had to know how. . . .

Even changing into a swimsuit was part of the physical education of swimming lessons. I wasn't all that shy; after all, I had a sister. But still it was unsettling to get undressed in a line of other freckled, tanned or pale bodies that looked so critically different from mine. Even though my best friend was famous for her golden hair, I was still surprised to see that the little fur of hair between her legs was blonde too, not brown like mine. I had thought everybody's was probably brown.

As I unfastened my cotton-knit band that masqueraded as a bra, I looked surreptitiously around at the other girls. Some of them had actual breasts. I looked away again quickly. I only wore my "bra" because recently one of the cruder boys in our seventh grade had told me he could see my titties through my sweater. I wasn't sure what he meant, until he pointed. Then I held back tears, and embarrassment, until I could get back home for lunch and demand that my mother take me out right away, that noon, to Younkers to buy a bra. I wondered why she hadn't seen that I needed one. As I pulled my swimsuit up to fasten it, I looked down at myself and felt once again that somehow all the bumps fell in the wrong places.

All this examination of bodies, furtive as it was, made me feel as though there were something faintly medical about the college pool. We had to splash through a footbath of gray, smelly disinfectant before we trooped down the inner stairs to the pool. This footbath, we were informed, was to guard against all kinds of fungi, like athlete's foot; I wasn't sure what that was but knew that it must be very personal, infectious, and unpleasant. I associated it in my mind with rumors I had heard about something called syphilis. Even today, when someone mentions v.d., I sometimes think of footbaths. . . .

I suppose there were women's swimming teams somewhere in those days, but I could never imagine them practicing in the college pool. Big Mike was the men's coach, and I always thought of his precincts as a man's pool. Later in the day boys we knew would come to take their swimming lessons. We knew, because one of them had told one of us, that they swam naked. Without any suits at all. I never thought much about male bodies: I had no brothers, I had not yet been exposed to art, and I simply could not picture all those boys in the pool. I would shudder a bit and feel very cold. I was glad I wore a suit.

Sometimes after lessons we could stay and watch the advanced class, older high-school girls who practiced diving and fancy strokes. Once I was very late in getting dressed, and on an impulse I climbed up the back upper stairs to the tiny gallery overlooking the pool. There I could see six girls, dressed in identical one-piece striped suits, all with dolphin insignia, performing a sort of water ballet. They were Big Mike's synchronized swimmers, special protegees, and he even occasionally smiled at them as they dipped and dove, turned and flipped, kicked in unison like submerged cancan dancers. I stared, entranced, until Big Mike glanced up and saw me. He frowned, waved his hand, called something, and I backed away. But I carried home with me the vision of those lovely, beautiful bodies, all grace and precision, moving in the water as though they were sleek fish.

When summer finally came and I was ready to go with my friends down to Blaine's Pool, how I longed to be able to swim like a fish. My lessons always seemed to leave me half-finished, almost passing advanced beginners, or just a few backstroke lengths short of moving on from intermediate. It wasn't so much that I wanted to *swim* like Big Mike's special girls, I just wanted to *look* like them in the water. As I tried on swimsuits at Younkers, sucking in my stomach, I looked in the mirror and saw nothing there but plump discouragement in a bright shirred Hawaiian print. All the elastic in the world wouldn't transform me into a dolphin.

* S. A. Toth, *Blooming: A small-town girlhood* (Boston: Little, Brown, 1978), pp. 23–27. © 1978, 1981 by Susan Allen Toth. Reprinted by permission of Little, Brown and Company.

PRIMARY AND SECONDARY SEX CHARACTERISTICS

It has been said that the only way in which males and females are truly distinct is in their reproductive roles. Thus despite the changes in physical size and shape and physical capacity as a result of the adolescent growth spurt, the changes in adolescents' bodies that enable them to procreate are the most dramatic changes of pubescence and puberty. Let's examine those changes in detail, along with the associated changes in the appearances of males and females.

The changes in *primary sex characteristics,* which are the characteristics that permit reproduction per se, are not the most obvious sex-related changes of adolescence. Rather, it is the emergence of secondary sex characteristics that produces the most apparent changes—the changes that are the source of most concern to adolescents. *Secondary sex characteristics* are aspects of appearance or function that are important to the distinction between males and females but are not essential to basic reproductive functions; for example, axillary and pubic hair (and facial hair for males), female breasts, and so on are secondary sex characteristics. Table 3.2 outlines changes in both primary and secondary sex characteristics in boys and in girls during pubescence and puberty. Although the timing of pubescent physical changes varies from person to person, the changes seem to occur in the same sequence across individuals. The table shows the order in which some standard physical signs of pubescence can be expected to appear for both boys and girls. Because the changes are so fundamentally different for the two sexes, we will discuss the course of sexual maturation separately for boys and for girls.

Female Development

In females the sign that full reproductive maturity has been reached is the beginning of menstruation, called the *menarche.* This event occurs, on the average, at about 13½ years, although its timing varies greatly. It signifies the maturing of one or more ova, or eggs, which, if fertilized by the male sperm, could result in pregnancy. At whatever age it occurs, menarche tends to be personally significant.

Before menarche occurs, a number of important secondary sex characteristics develop. These characteristics affect the way many adolescent girls regard themselves and the way they are regarded by others in the society. The changes begin with the appearance of the breast buds, an event that can occur as early as eight years. Several stages of breast development are shown in Fig. 3.2. Knowing about this sequence of changes can often be reassuring to adolescent girls who are concerned about whether they are developing normally. The second most obvious secondary sex characteristic to appear is pubic hair; later, underarm, or axillary, hair appears. In addition, the vulva, or external covering of the female genitals, becomes enlarged and more sensitive [15]. Although the external genitals are not

TABLE 3.2 Sequence of pubescent changes

Girls	Boys
Initial enlargement of breasts	Beginning growth of testes
Straight, pigmented pubic hair	Straight, pigmented pubic hair
Kinky pubic hair	Early voice changes
Age of maximum growth	First ejaculation of semen
Menarche	Kinky pubic hair
Growth of axillary hair	Age of maximum growth
	Growth of axillary hair
	Marked voice changes
	Development of the beard

Adapted from D. Ausubel, *Theory and problems of adolescent development* (New York: Grune & Stratton, 1954), p. 94.

nearly so obvious or readily used as an index of sexual maturity for females as they are for males, many teenage girls may feel self-conscious about the genitals' appearance and what they are assumed to indicate about femininity as well as maturity.

The important characteristics for reproductivity per se are, of course, the internal sexual organs. These organs—the two ovaries, which produce ova, the fallopian tubes, the uterus, the vagina—increase rapidly in weight and size during adolescence. Changes in the lining of the vagina, called the epithelium, begin to take place very early in pubescence, even before the development of breasts or pubic hair [16]. Interestingly, though, the ovaries, the organs that actually produce the ova, change little during adolescence. In fact, at birth ovaries are already well-developed organs and contain all of the eggs a female will ever develop. After puberty these eggs mature according to the monthly cycles [17].

There is usually a lag between the beginning of menstruation and full fertility for an adolescent girl. However, contrary to widespread belief, girls are not always sterile for some period of time after menarche, nor can the period during which there is relative sterility be reliably estimated [18]. Therefore, no teenager can rely on natural infertility as a guarantee that sexual intercourse will not result in pregnancy. The current high rate of pregnancies among unmarried adolescent girls, some of them very young, is urgent testimony to the fact that conception can and does occur quite early. This problem will be discussed in more detail in Chapter 9.

Male Development

In males the first sign of pubescent changes is initial growth of the testes and penis. Testes parallel the ovaries in the female; they produce the sperm and the male hormones that make possible the development of

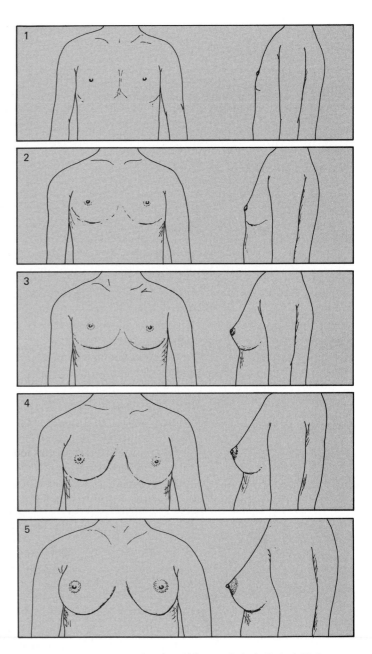

FIG. 3.2 Stages of breast development in adolescent girls: (1) prepubertal flat appearance like that of a child; (2) small, raised breast bud; (3) general enlargement and raising of breast and areola; (4) areola and papilla (nipple) form contour separate from that of breast; (5) adult breast—areola is in same contour as breast

Redrawn from J. M. Tanner, *Growth at Adolescence*, 2nd ed. (Oxford: Blackwell, 1962), p. 37. Reprinted by permission.

other secondary sex characteristics. Along with changes in these organs, a complex network of tubes develops to convey the sperm from the testes through the penis during ejaculation. Other glands associated with mature sexual function, such as the prostate glands and the seminal vesicles, also enlarge during puberty. Ejaculation of semen, which comes from the prostate gland and carries the sperm produced by the testes, is an event that can only occur following the primary sexual changes of pubescence. (In contrast, the capacity for orgasm, the event that accompanies ejaculation, is present at birth [19].) Thus ejaculation can be one indicator of sexual maturity for males. Reports of first ejaculations are rarely used as criteria for pubertal stage in research on adolescent physical changes, however, largely because such reports tend to be very unreliable. One of the most reliable indicators must be derived from laboratory tests: whether or not live spermatozoa are present in the urine [20]. Like the beginning of menstruation for girls, first ejaculations, which often occur as nocturnal emissions, or "wet dreams," sometimes create shock and fear. In the following excerpt G. Stanley Hall describes his reaction to his own early-adolescent nocturnal emissions.

Nocturnal Emissions

So great was my dread of natural phenomena that in the earliest teens I rigged an apparatus and applied bandages to prevent erethism while I slept, which very likely only augmented the trouble. If I yielded to any kind of temptation to experimentation upon myself I suffered intense remorse and fear, and sent up many a secret and most fervent prayer that I might never again break my resolve. At one time I feared I was abnormal and found occasion to consult a physician in a neighboring town who did not know me. He examined me and took my dollar, and laughed at me, but also told me what consequences would ensue if I became unchaste. What an untold anguish of soul would have been saved me if some one had told me that certain experiences while I slept were as normal for boys in their teens as are the monthly phenomena for girls. I did not know that even in college and thought myself secretly and exceptionally corrupt and not quite worthy to associate with girls. This had probably much, if not most, to do with my abstention from them and was, I think, the chief factor that brought about my "conversion" in my sophomore year, although this made the struggle for purity far more intense, though I fear but little more successful.

I fear the good Lord on whom I was told, and tried, to cast my burden did not help me much here. Indeed, perhaps in transferring and committing all to Him I trusted my own powers less. Perhaps, again, my profound sense of inferiority here prompted me to compensate by striving all the harder for excellence in other lines, although there was always a haunting sense that if

I succeeded in making anything of myself it would be despite this private handicap. I should certainly never dare to marry and have children. It was ineffable relief, therefore, to learn, as I did only far too late, that my life in this sphere had, on the whole, been in no sense abnormal or even exceptional [21].

Changes in the penis continue throughout pubescent development. In the later stages of development the testes become larger, the penis lengthens, and the scrotum becomes coarser, eventually darkening with pigmentation. Sometime after the initial changes in external genitalia, pubic hair begins to appear; and later facial and axillary hair develop. The growth of the beard is widely valued as a sign of maturity—one that is more apparent than genital changes. Changing of the voice is another pubertal event by which the world at large judges males' physical maturity [22].

Skin Changes

Skin changes occur in pubescence for both sexes. The most important of these changes is the growth of sebaceous glands, which are associated with hair follicles. These glands excrete oil that, when combined with dirt from the air, often creates comedones, or blackheads [23]. This condition is the basis of acne, a disease that causes physical and social discomfort for many adolescents. The acne problem will be discussed later in the chapter along with other health problems of adolescents.

INDIVIDUAL DIFFERENCES IN DEVELOPMENT

Pubertal events are a great leveler. All teenagers go through events in the same sequence, although often at quite different ages. The variation across adolescents is summarized in Fig. 3.3. Girls (shown in the top chart) mature earlier than boys do, on the average; but both boys and girls show wide variability around the averages for their sex. For example, according to Fig. 3.3, breast development accelerates at about age 11 for most girls, and growth is ordinarily completed by age 15. But breast development may begin as early as age 8, and in some few girls changes begin as late as age 13 and are not complete until age 18. James Tanner, who based these averages on his studies of British adolescents, says: "At age thirteen, fourteen, and fifteen there is an enormous variability among any group of boys, who range all the way from practically complete maturity to absolute preadolescence. The same is true of girls aged eleven, twelve, and thirteen" [24].

Let's consider some of the influences on the timing of puberty from one adolescent to another.

Heredity

Physical characteristics, the timing of puberty itself, and the rate at which pubertal changes occur are largely determined genetically [25]. For exam-

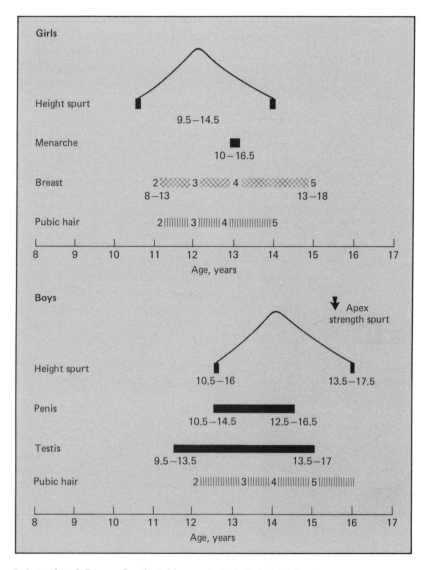

FIG. 3.3. Indicators of sexual maturity

Redrawn from J. Tanner, *Growth at adolescence*, 2nd ed. (Oxford: Blackwell, 1962), p. 13. Reprinted by permission.

ple, identical twin girls—who share the same genetic inheritance—experience menarche within 2.8 months of each other, on the average. By comparison, nonidentical twins, who are less similar genetically, differ by 10 months, on the average; and nontwin siblings differ by an average of 13 months in time of menarche.

Why should genetic similarity affect timing of puberty? One factor may be body build, which also tends to be similar within families. Girls who are tall and thin tend to mature later than girls who are short and stocky. A similar pattern occurs for boys who differ in body type. Body weight in particular has been found to affect timing of puberty [26].

Racial and Ethnic Differences

Racial and ethnic differences in puberty are minor. Differences between individuals are impressive, but average differences between groups are small. Subcultural differences within countries probably have less to do with race and ethnic inheritance than with the living conditions, including nutrition, of adolescents in these groups [27].

THE PROBLEM OF ASYNCHRONY IN GROWTH

As mentioned earlier, adolescent physical growth varies greatly in its timing from person to person. Furthermore, pubescent changes are not even synchronized within individuals. This *asynchrony* means that different body parts show rapid growth at different times. In Fig. 3.3 we can see how variable pubertal events are. They emerge across virtually the entire second decade of life. Keep in mind, however, that the *sequence* of pubertal events, if not their timing or coordination, is fairly regular, as we saw in Table 3.2.

The asynchrony of physical growth is especially dramatic in the case of height. Growth in height involves growth of two constituents: leg length and trunk length. Leg growth accelerates first; then about a year later, on the average, trunk growth accelerates. As we have already noted, in the adolescent growth spurt feet and hands grow larger first, and parts of the trunk and the head change somewhat later. The general principle seems to be that during the changes of puberty "the more distal part of the limb grows faster first" [28]. Hands and feet may seem outsized for a time until the rest of the limbs grow into proportion with them.

Asynchrony in physical development probably accounts for several popular stereotypes about adolescents. One of the most common is that rapid periods of growth during adolescence are often followed by periods of decline and then further advancement. Experts agree that growth during adolescence is characterized by steady advance, not advance and decline. For example, although physical strength lags behind the growth spurt for height and musculature, there is no truth to the belief that individuals are weakened by rapid growth in adolescence [29]. Neither are adolescents especially poorly coordinated and awkward, despite the fact that some body parts grow at different rates from others. Coordination and balance may improve more slowly than the body is growing—another instance of asynchrony—but they do not deteriorate. If adolescents are more awkward than other individuals, it is probably because of self-consciousness or the characteristics of the individual rather than of pubescent growth per se [30].

Before we begin to discuss some of the psychological implications of relatively early or relatively late pubertal growth, we turn briefly to a discussion of how these fundamental events are regulated—a topic that takes us into a discussion of hormonal mechanisms in the human body.

REGULATION OF PUBERTAL CHANGES

How are the events of pubescence set into motion? This is the question we will examine in this section. Knowing the controlling mechanisms helps us to understand what is happening to adolescents in the precipitous changes of pubescence and puberty.

The Role of Hormones

The story of physical and physiological changes in the second decade of life is in many ways simply a continuation of the story of growth generally. The leading actors are *hormones,* chemical substances secreted by glands directly into the bloodstream that affect the body's metabolism and, therefore, its growth.

The gonadal hormones   The changes of puberty are brought about primarily by the gonads (testes and ovaries) and the cortex of the adrenal gland. These glands secrete hormones called *progesterone,* which produces the primary and secondary sex characteristics.

Although the gonads themselves directly affect these changes, the process is initiated by a complex series of events in the endocrine system and the brain. The control center for these events is the hypothalamus, an area at the base of the brain. By releasing special hormones of its own, the hypothalamus triggers the activity of the anterior pituitary gland just below it. The anterior pituitary then secretes a group of hormones that affect the development and hormone-producing activities of the gonads and the adrenal cortex. The pituitary hormones that seek out the gonadal tissues are called *gonadotropic* (the Greek word *tropic* means "seeking out"); those that affect the adrenal cortex are called *adrenocorticotropic* hormones (ACTH) [31].

Once the anterior pituitary hormones begin to work, the changes of puberty are set in motion. As the gonads and adrenal cortex enlarge and begin to secrete their own hormones, they stimulate growth generally. The growth spurt itself results from increased androgen in both males and females; the growth spurt is believed to slow when androgen reaches certain concentrations and triggers the closing of the epiphyses, the growing ends of long bones. Similarly, the growth of pubic and axillary hair in both sexes is enhanced by androgens. Normal development in both sexes results from the same hormones [32].

Sex differences result from different concentrations of the gonadal hormones. Males have much higher concentrations of the androgens (testosterone) than do females; these higher concentrations produce the internal and external changes that cause the male reproductive system to develop differently from the female system. Testosterone causes the enlargement of testes and penis and the structural changes that make sperm production possible, as well as the deepening of the voice and the development of facial and body hair that are characteristic of males.

Estrogens and progesterones from the ovaries cause development of the female reproductive organs—the ovaries, uterus, and vagina. They also affect development of the breasts and the distribution of fat that makes the female body generally more rounded than the male body. Although, like androgen, these gonadal hormones are present even before puberty, during adolescence they become more cyclical and thus regulate the monthly menstrual cycle. During this cycle levels of estrogen and progesterone fluctuate and control the complex combination of changes in the uterus, cervix, and vagina that produce ovulation. If the egg is not fertilized, estrogen and progesterone decrease dramatically, and the uterine lining formed to sustain a developing fetus sloughs away, producing the menstrual flow.

Facial hair appears fairly late in pubescent changes
Photograph from Charles Gatewood

Just as females produce androgens, males produce some female gonadal hormones. Their effects on male development and functioning are not known, however [33].

Hormonal feedback   Exactly how puberty begins and ends is still a mystery, but scientists now think that this universal experience of adolescence is set into motion and controlled by a complex system in which the parts provide feedback to each other. The system itself is apparently present at birth; as we have already noted, the important puberty-controlling hormones are present in small amounts in children and in some cases even in fetuses. The sensor for the feedback system seems to be the hypothalamus. Its hormones are withheld when necessary to keep the other hormones at the proper level in the bloodstream. Apparently, at puberty the hypothalamus becomes more sensitive to gonadal hormones, so the hypothalamus produces more to stimulate more production of gonadotropic hormones by the anterior pituitary, and so forth [34].

But why does this change in sensitivity occur? No one knows. One hypothesis is that the hypothalamus is sensitive to the total weight of the body; when body weight reaches a critical point, the hypothalamus raises its threshold of sensitivity to gonadal hormones. In one study of adolescent girls, for example, menarche and other pubertal events were found to occur at the same average weights for girls who matured at a very early age and for those who matured at a much older age [35]. Thus the feedback system controls the time at which puberty occurs. Knowing the effects of hormones on different aspects of growth in males and females and the systematic way in which the hormones and brain regulate pubertal events is a major help to physicians whose adolescent patients, for one reason or another, don't experience pubertal changes as they should.

Environmental Effects on Puberty

The beginning and the course of puberty are also affected by environmental conditions. In industrialized North America, variations in environment are, by and large, not sizable ones, either in terms of climatic and seasonal variations or in terms of living standards. However, data from other countries and cultures have given us information about the effect of environment on pubertal changes.

Several aspects of the environment are implicated. For example, although climate appears to have virtually no effect on the time at which adolescents experience the beginning of puberty, the season of the year does markedly affect the rate of pubertal change. Height, for instance, has been found to increase twice as fast in the spring, and weight increases four or five times as fast in the autumn. In girls, menarche is most likely to occur either in the summer months or in December or January and is relatively unlikely in the spring. Exactly why season should effect pubertal growth is not clear; the best guess is that there are some subtle, but important, changes in hormone production from season to season [36].

The effects of nutrition on puberty are somewhat less surprising. We noted above that body weight seems to be correlated with the onset of puberty and with other significant events of adolescent physical change. Adolescence is a time when calorie requirements, in absolute terms, are higher than they are in any other period of life; thus adolescents are probably especially sensitive to variations in how much and what kind of food they have. If adolescents are malnourished, pubescent events can be slowed down noticeably or even delayed. For example, children whose nutrition has been affected by famine or by severe poverty have been stunted in their growth generally. Malnutrition tends to slow growth overall; during puberty the parts of the body that change most in all adolescents continue to change even in malnourished individuals but at a slower rate. The differences in the age at which significant pubertal events like menarche occur in different countries probably reflect the differences in the nutritional adequacy of the diets in those countries. Thus in poor areas of the world puberty is likely to be delayed somewhat more than it is in countries where diet is more adequate [37].

Nutrition may also contribute to differences among social classes in the rate of growth and the onset of puberty. In many instances during this century differences of several months for the average age at which puberty begins have been found for different socioeconomic groups. For example, one scientist reports that Chinese adolescents in Hong Kong experienced menarche much earlier if they came from well-to-do families than if they came from poor families [38].

Another environmental characteristic may also help to explain some of the differences among members of different social classes. According to recent research, children who grow up in an adverse environment, in which adults are harsh toward them or in which they lack the nurturance that appears to benefit psychosocial development generally, show a stunting of growth [39]. The physical effects of these psychological conditions are difficult to explain. It may well be that hormonal changes during puberty intensify emotional reactions to being treated badly; conversely, emotional states may affect production of hormones.

Finally, severe or chronic injury or disease often affects pubescence and puberty. Chronic heart and kidney diseases have been shown to retard growth, in particular, as do other diseases that keep children confined for long periods of time. If diseases disrupt hormone production, of course, puberty would doubtless be affected. Fortunately, most diseases of childhood and adolescence do not significantly retard pubertal development, possibly because they are relatively transient and less traumatic for the system [40].

**The Secular
Trend**

Perhaps because of environmental changes over the past hundred years, the average age at which puberty and peak growth in height occur has changed considerably. This trend to earlier physical maturation is called the *secular trend*, meaning that it is a change that has occurred for many different populations of people.

Since 1900 children of all ages have increased significantly in size, but the increase is most pronounced in adolescents. In fact, average height has increased 2–3 centimeters for each of the intervening decades; thus adolescents in the 1980s are 16–24 centimeters taller on the average than their 1900 counterparts were [41]. Better nutrition, including more protein in their diets, and better control over illness and disease have contributed to this change in adolescents.

By and large, however, the psychologically significant change in physical growth is not in the adult height that individuals can expect to reach but in the earlier time at which physical maturation occurs for today's adolescents as compared with their forebears. For example, age at menarche has increased by three to four months per decade since 1850 in western Europe [42]. Because of the secular trend, adolescence is now a longer period of time in Western industrialized society than it once was. When we consider the lengthening effect of college education for many adolescents—a period during which they remain dependent and somewhat insulated from the full responsibilities of adulthood—we see that the average time of adolescence has stretched beyond the boundaries of the second decade of life.

PSYCHOLOGICAL EFFECTS OF PHYSICAL CHANGES

Even though pubescence is the universal biological experience of adolescence, the changes it brings nevertheless underlie many of the psychological adjustments that individual teenagers must make during the second decade of life. Why do biological changes have such far-reaching effects? It does not appear that changes in the biological system directly produce psychological changes. Despite the impressive change in hormones during adolescence, for example, there is little evidence that hormonal changes as such account totally for psychological effects of puberty. Instead, biological changes seem to influence psychological development through the subjective meanings that the changes have for adolescents themselves and for adults and peers around them.

Figure 3.4 suggests that the effects of the primary physical changes of adolescence are *socially mediated* by the reactions of self and others. In this view one's self-image and self-esteem reflect one's own and others' subjective reactions to biological maturation. And these reactions are determined by sociocultural standards, norms, and expectations about physical characteristics that are widely held in a society or culture.

SPECIAL TOPIC
The Tyranny of Body Type

It may not be widely recognized, but most Americans—indeed, most participants in American culture—hold very definite standards for personal attractiveness. One of the most subtle aspects of those standards is body type, or the shape of the physique. Generally speaking, physical shape can be characterized by one of three very general categories:

- Endomorphs, who are relatively heavy individuals.

- Mesomorphs, who are ideally proportioned—for males, slim hips and broad shoulders; for females, a typical hourglass shape.

- Ectomorphs, who are thin, relatively tall individuals.

These body types were suggested many years ago by Sheldon along with the suggestion that they correspond to different types of physical constitutions that produce distinctly different behavior patterns [1]. In recent years another possibility has been strongly considered: Maybe it's not the constitutions of persons who have these body types that create the differences in their personalities. Instead, it may be strong expectations, or stereotypes, about the behavior of people who are shaped a particular way that produce personality differences. Those expectations or stereotypes may result in social experiences that reinforce different types of behavior patterns for individuals whose body types are different.

There is no question that there are widely held expectations about what sorts of personality characteristics go along with different body types. Even in studies with both boys and girls at very young ages, knowledge of those stereotypes is apparent [2]. By showing silhouettes of figures to children and asking them to describe what sorts of people look like those silhouettes, researchers found that endomorphs are considered jolly or offensive; ectomorphs are considered retiring, nervous, or shy; and mesomorphs are considered attractively aggressive, outgoing, or active. In addition, nursery school and young elementary school children indicated that they would prefer to have a friend who looked like the mesomorphic silhouette and would chose persons who looked like that silhouette for social relationships and honors. In addition to understanding the stereotypes very well, these children also knew their own body type. They could select the silhouette among the ones presented to them that corresponded most closely to their own body shape.

What effects does knowledge of strong social stereotypes have on the emerging notion of self in childhood and adolescence? It is difficult to answer that question, because expectations about the sorts of personality characteristics that inhabit particular types of bodies are strong but subtle. However, there are some indications that self-concepts—persons' views of what they are like—show remarkable correspondence to culturally held expectations about what people who fit certain body type categories are supposed to be like.

In one study conducted by Cortes and Gatti, a group of high school boys and girls rated themselves on an adjective scale that included the terms with which ideal body types have typically been described [3]. Adjectives like "dominant," "loves risk," "self-assured," and so forth were listed along with many other adjectives that might be descriptive. Independently, these adolescents were rated for body types by a group of raters who judged them from their pictures. Cortes and Gatti were interested in discovering whether individuals who fell physically into the mesomorph, endomorph, and ectomorph categories rated themselves as having the personal characteristics that are usually included in stereotyped descriptions of different body types. Their results clearly showed that that was indeed the case. For example, mesomorphic adolescents described themselves in terms that were similar to the terms used by people who were asked to describe a typical mesomorph; ectomorphs described themselves in terms similar to those used in typical descriptions of ectomorphs. By late adolescence, then, people have incorporated cultural stereotypes of themselves, perhaps because throughout their lives they have been responded to by others as though the stereotype represented the kind of person they indeed were.

It is possible, of course, that people were giving accurate self-descriptions. We are not suggesting that they have distorted notions of what they are like. The question is whether their self-concepts reflect actual inborn, genetically determined behavioral tendencies, or whether their behavior patterns and self-concepts have been shaped and channeled in the experiences of growing up by a set of socially and culturally held expectations associated with their physical appearance.

REFERENCES

1. W. Sheldon, S. Stevens, and W. Tucker, *The varieties of human physique* (New York: Harper & Row, 1940).

2. R. Lerner, "Richness" analyses of body build stereotype development, *Developmental Psychology 7,* 2(1972):219; J. R. Staffieri, Body build and behavioral expectancies in young females, *Developmental Psychology* 6(1972):125–127.

3. J. Cortes and F. Gatti, Physique and self-description of temperament, *Journal of Consulting Psychology* 29(1965):432–439.

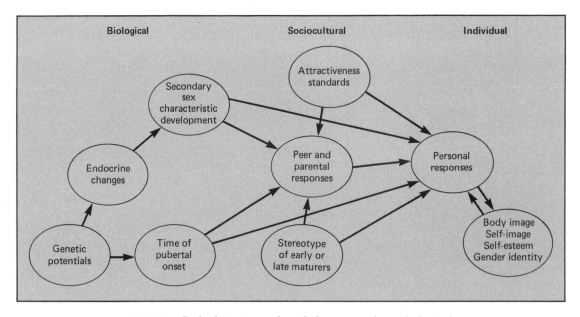

FIG. 3.4 Paths between pubertal changes and psychological responses

Redrawn from A. Peterson and B. Taylor, The biological approach to adolescence, *Handbook of adolescent psychology*, ed. J. Adelson (New York: Wiley, 1980), p. 147. Reprinted by permission.

From one culture to another very different expectations are associated with the physical changes of puberty. These expectations influence how pubertal changes are noticed and interpreted by persons within the culture, including individual adolescents themselves. In cultures where a great deal of significance and anxiety are attached to pubertal changes, adolescents will probably feel anxiety and conflict over pubertal changes in themselves. By contrast, in societies like Margaret Mead's Samoa, pubertal changes are little noticed, and little social significance is attached to them. Perhaps this societal attitude explains why Mead found so little stress associated with adolescence among the Samoans [43].

In our society, which does emphasize physical development, the important intermediate influences on pubescence are sociocultural norms and expectations, conveyed through parents' and peers' responses to biological changes (see Fig. 3.4). These influences, in turn, affect adolescents' own personal responses to the changes in their bodies, which determine body image, self-image, self-esteem, and gender identity [44].

The personal and emotional responses to the physical changes of adolescence will be discussed in further detail in later chapters. For now, let's consider two particular examples of physical changes in adolescence that illustrate the ways in which primary physical changes interact with sociocultural influences to produce psychological effects. The first example comes from studies of adolescents who experience puberty either markedly early or markedly late. We will examine the effects of early and late maturation both for the adolescent years and for later adult functioning. In the second example we will consider the possible effects of adolescent physical changes on body image and self-concept.

Early and Late Maturation

Studies of early- and late-maturing adolescents have been some of the most important sources of information on the psychological effects of pubertal changes. The idea behind these studies is that adolescents who are either very early or very late in experiencing puberty may show the effects of sociocultural reactions to physical changes in an especially pronounced way. For example, reaching adult size and appearance earlier than the average might mean that adolescent boys or girls would experience fewer difficulties in adolescence because they would be more easily accepted in the adult world than would boys and girls who matured physically at a much later time. Another possibility, however, is that reaching adult physical status early may lead to adolescents being pressured into adult roles and responsibilities before they are psychologically ready. Both possibilities seem to be true to a certain extent, judging from studies of adolescents conducted over the past 50 years. The patterns of effects are somewhat different for boys and for girls, as we discuss below. Moreover, some effects are more pronounced in adolescence and others in adulthood.

Cultural standards of physical attractiveness help to determine teenagers' reactions to their own pubertal changes

Photograph from Cary Wolinsky/Stock, Boston

Effects on boys Early-maturing boys are those who, in their age group, are among the first 20% to reach puberty. These boys seem to have considerable advantage over boys of the same age who mature at a slower-than-average rate. This information comes from a longitudinal study in which children were followed from preadolescence to adulthood [45]. Early-maturing boys were consistently judged by adults and peers to be more attractive and competent than late maturers during adolescence. Late maturers—those who were among the last 20% to reach puberty—were rated as more tense, eager, active, bossy, talkative, and uninhibited. Late maturers clearly do not enjoy the social advantage and prestige that early maturers enjoy in the adolescent society. To some extent, the early maturers' advantage persists into adulthood. Follow-up studies of these adolescents at ages 33 and 38 indicate that early maturers were more successful in their social life and in their occupations than late maturers were. In other words, long after the physical maturation differences had passed, certain social-status advantages were still apparent for early maturers.

But there is another side to the psychological effects of early and late maturation in males. While early-maturing males were more successful than late-maturing males in adulthood, they were also more rigid, moralistic, humorless, and conforming. By contrast, late maturers were more flexible in the face of new problems, more insightful and perceptive, and better able to cope with the ambiguities of new situations. Thus in terms of many important personal-coping skills, late maturers seemed to have an advantage over early maturers.

Psychologist Harvey Peskin has suggested that these differences between early and late maturers may result from differences in the amount of psychological preparation for adulthood that early and late maturers have. For example, early maturers often experience early acceptance by the adult world. As a result, they may adapt to social conventions without trying out different alternatives or possibilities for handling situations and problems. Late maturers, however, are less likely to be able to rely on the conventions of the adult world for their success in adolescence. Thus they may become more flexible in finding ways of responding to social situations and other types of problem solving. In Freud's terms late maturers may benefit from a longer latency period because puberty occurs so late. Early maturers, by constrast, have a foreshortened latency. Thus early maturers may be more likely to experience identity foreclosure because they have a shorter time for consolidating the adolescent ego development in preparation for identity achievement during adolescence. Peskin's results make clear that physical changes alone do not determine effects of puberty from psychological adjustment. Acceptance by adult society and the experience of coping with the ambiguous social definitions of adolescence contribute to the psychological effects of puberty [46].

Early physical maturation is often a social advantage in adolescence

Photograph from Abigail Heyman/Archive Pictures, Inc.

Effects on girls The advantages of early maturing are less clear-cut in adolescence for girls than for boys. At first, girls who develop breasts and curvaceous figures earlier than their age-mates may well be *less* popular than girls who have not yet reached puberty. In fact, early-maturing girls often seem to be more introspective, more unsure, less poised, less expressive, and more submissive and withdrawn than their age-mates. Late-maturing girls appear to be higher in expressiveness, activity, sociability, leadership, prestige, and popularity than early-maturing girls at the time pubertal changes are just beginning. But by the time the majority of girls in an age group have matured physically, girls who mature early are often among the most popular members of the girls' crowd. And in adulthood early-maturing girls are clearly more coping, self-possessed, and self-directed persons than girls who were noticeably late in reaching puberty. Perhaps because early-maturing girls can turn to social convention less readily than early-maturing boys can, they are obliged to develop some of the self-awareness and flexibility in problem solving that characterize late-maturing boys. By contrast, the social prestige of late-maturing girls before puberty and the loss of prestige as puberty is delayed may be a difficult psychological experience in adolescence that contributes to less adaptive behavior for these girls in adulthood.

With girls, as with boys, the effects of very early and very late physical maturation interact with the demands and rewards of adults and peers so that these adolescents develop very different patterns of psychological responses. These patterns characterize not only their behavior as adolescents but also their adjustment as adults. In Fig. 3.4 the sociocultural influences on the reactions of others and of adolescents themselves are clearly shown.

Body Image and Pubertal Change

A second example of the psychological effects of pubertal changes is adolescents' satisfaction with their body and changes in body image at puberty. Many adolescents indicate that physical characteristics and appearance are among the problems that concern them most. In general, these concerns do *not* arise because adolescents are inaccurate in their perceptions of themselves. For the most part they are well able to identify, from a group of body profiles, the profile that is most similar to their own [47]. What is significant are the value judgments that adolescents tend to make about their characteristics and appearance.

Like stereotypes of early and late maturers, stereotypes of body image and cultural norms of attractiveness strongly influence adolescents' perceptions of their bodies. These attractiveness standards are communicated by family, peers, and the society at large, often in very subtle ways. Society and culture condition each of us to view certain physical characteristics and personality traits as more or less attractive.

In Western society, generally speaking, the slim-hipped, broad-shouldered male and the female with an hourglass figure represent the cultural ideals of physical attractiveness. Even young nursery school children know and abide by this norm. With so well-defined a standard, it is not surprising that Western adolescents should be aware of their own appearance and concerned about their deviations from the ideal. And adolescents from families that place a high degree of value on physical attractiveness are especially likely to feel anxious and dissatisfied about their appearance [48]. The accompanying special topic, "The Tyranny of Body Type," shows how cultural norms and expectations of appearance may affect adolescents' images of themselves.

The appearance changes of pubescence often include some painful conditions that illustrate the psychological impact of physical growth. One notorious example is the acne problem. During pubescence the sebaceous glands of the skin secrete excess oil that sometimes clogs pores, causing them to become inflamed. This condition is aggravated by the eating habits of teenagers and the social anxieties and tensions of adolescence, and disfiguring blemishes that are difficult to control can result [49]. To a self-conscious boy or girl the acne problem can intensify the social anxieties of adolescence. Unfortunately, those tensions often further compound the tensions that aggravate acne in the first place, creating a vicious circle of self-consciousness leading to skin problems leading, in turn, to continued self-consciousness.

Adolescent awkwardness may be another example of an apparently physical problem that is the result of physical change and social factors working together. As we noted earlier, the legendary clumsiness of adolescents, particularly boys, probably does not result from uneven growth rates of different body parts. Rather, it probably shows a general uncertainty that teenagers feel during this transitional age period, especially in new and unusual situations.

Problems of body image and special difficulties resulting from acne, awkwardness, and other physical conditions offer additional examples of the way in which even the most fundamental biological factors are subject to the standards and expectations of the social world in which adolescents live. Since adolescents are facing the task of becoming adult inhabitants of that world, the reactions and expectations of others take on new and compelling importance. In the next chapter we will discuss changes in adolescents' skills for reasoning and solving problems in the widening world of the teen years.

SUMMARY

The physical changes associated with puberty are the most dramatic primary changes of adolescence. In this chapter we discussed pubescence—the period of physical changes leading to reproductive maturity—and puberty—the point at which reproductive maturity is reached. Pubescent changes include alterations in body size, shape, and physical capacity. Many of these changes appear during the so-called adolescent growth spurt, during which height changes more rapidly than at any other period of time except the first year of life. With this physical growth comes dramatic changes in strength and physical capacity, which render adolescents more capable of adult physical activity.

Although patterns of growth are often strikingly different in males and females during adolescence, the only way in which males and females are truly distinct is in their reproductive roles. At puberty the capacity for sexual reproduction has been obtained. Consequently, pubescent changes include many alterations in the appearance and function of primary sex characteristics. More obvious, however, are secondary sex characteristics, including enlargement of breasts in girls, voice changes and facial hair in boys, and the growth of pubic and axillary hair in both sexes.

The timing of puberty varies greatly and is influenced by genetic factors and environmental influences, including nutrition and disease. The *sequence* of pubertal changes is the same for all individuals. However, growth tends to be *asynchronous,* meaning that different body parts show rapid growth at different times. This asynchrony may be one of the sources of the discomfort many adolescents feel during pubertal changes.

Puberty is regulated by hormones secreted by the testes and ovaries (gonads) and the cortex of the adrenal gland. The various hormones appear to be regulated by a complex system in which the parts provide feedback to each other. Central to the system is the hypothalamus, an area at the base of the brain, which acts as a sensor for the hormonal feedback system. The physical changes of puberty do not directly affect the psychological states of adolescents. Rather, psychological effects are mediated by responses to the physical changes of puberty from parents, peers, and adolescents themselves. These sociocultural influences can be readily seen in adolescents who reach puberty either much earlier or much later than usual. Psychological effects of early and late maturing clearly reflect the impact of acceptance in the adult world and experiences in coping with the ambiguous social definitions of adolescents. In addition, the difficulties faced by many adolescents in adjusting to bodily changes partly illustrate the strong influence of sociocultural norms of physical attractiveness on adolescents' self-concepts. The psychological effects of puberty thus reflect both the pressure of social norms and expectations and the self-evaluative responses to bodily changes that are influenced by them.

KEY POINTS AND NAMES

Pubescence	Hormones
Puberty	Gonadal hormones
Hypothalamus	Hormonal feedback
Growth spurt	Environmental effects on puberty
Physical changes in adolescence	Secular trend
Primary and secondary sex characteristics	Psychological effects of adolescence
Menarche	Early versus late maturers
Asynchrony	Body image
	Sociocultural influences

REFERENCES

1. J. M. Tanner, Sequence, tempo, and individual variation in the growth and development of boys and girls aged twelve to sixteen, *Daedalus,* Fall 1971, pp. 907–930; H. Katchadourian, *The biology of adolescence* (San Francisco: Freeman, 1977), p. 35.

2. Tanner, Sequence, tempo, and individual variation, pp. 907–930.

3. J. Tanner, R. Whitehouse, and M. Takaishi, Standards from birth to matu-

rity for height, weight-height velocity and weight velocity; British children, 1965, *Archives of the Diseases of Childhood* 41(1966):455–471. p. 466.

4. Katchadourian, p. 44.

5. J. M. Tanner, *Fetus into man: Physical growth from conception to maturity* (Cambridge, Mass.: Harvard University Press, 1978), pp. 70–74.

6. D. Sinclair, *Human growth after birth* (London: Oxford University Press, 1973), pp. 90–92.

7. Katchadourian, p. 29.

8. *Ibid.*, p. 44.

9. D. B. Cheek, *Human growth, body composition, cell growth, energy and intelligence* (Philadelphia: Lea & Febiger, 1968), p. 112.

10. M. M. Maresh, Growth of the heart related to bodily growth during childhood and adolescence, *Pediatrics* 2(1948):382–404.

11. Katchadourian, pp. 46–47.

12. *Ibid.*

13. *Ibid.*, p. 49.

14. *Ibid.*

15. J. Tanner, *Growth at adolescence*, 2nd ed. (Oxford: Blackwell, 1962), pp. 28–39.

16. Katchadourian, p. 59; W. A. Marshall and J. M. Tanner, Puberty, in *Scientific foundations of pediatrics*, ed. J. A. Douvis and J. Dobbing (London: William Heinemann Medical Books, 1974), pp. 124–152.

17. Katchadourian, p. 59.

18. *Ibid.*, p. 62.

19. H. A. Katchadourian and D. T. Lunde, *Fundamentals of human sexuality*, 2nd ed. (New York: Holt, Rinehart and Winston, 1975).

20. Tanner, Sequence, tempo, and individual variation, pp. 907–930.

21. G. Stanley Hall, *Life and confessions of a psychologist* (New York: D. Appleton, 1924), p. 47.

22. Tanner, Sequence, tempo, and individual variation, pp. 907–930.

23. Katchadourian, p. 71.

24. Tanner, Sequence, tempo, and individual variation, pp. 914–915.

25. Tanner, *Growth at adolescence*, pp. 113–121; Katchadourian, pp. 75, 78.

26. Katchadourian, p. 78; R. E. Frisch and R. Revelle, Height and weight at menarche and a hypothesis of critical body weights and adolescent events, *Science* 169(1970):397–399.

27. Katchadourian, pp. 77–78.

28. *Ibid.*, p. 37.

29. J. M. Tanner, Physical growth, in *Carmichael's manual of child psychology*, vol. 1, ed. P. Mussen (New York: Wiley, 1970), p. 96.

30. W. A. Marshall, The body, in *The seven ages of man*, ed. R. S. Sears and S. S. Feldman (Los Altos, Calif.: Kaufman, 1973), p. 47.

31. Katchadourian, pp. 104–111.

32. *Ibid.*, pp. 97–100.

33. *Ibid.*

34. *Ibid.*, pp. 119–120.

35. Frisch and Revelle, pp. 397–399.

36. L. Zacharias, W. M. Rand, and R. J. Wurtman, A prospective study of sexual development and growth in American girls: The statistics of menarche, *Obstetric and Gynecological Survey* (supplement) 31(1976):325–337; Katchadourian, pp. 79–80.

37. Katchadourian, pp. 80–82.

38. Tanner, Sequence, tempo, and individual variation, p. 928.

39. Katchadourian, p. 84.

40. Tanner, *Fetus into man*, pp. 142–143.

41. Tanner, Sequence, tempo, and individual variation, p. 928.

42. *Ibid.*

43. M. Mead, *Coming of age in Samoa* (New York: Dell, 1928).

44. A. Petersen and B. Taylor, *The biological approach to adolescence*, in *Handbook of adolescent psychology*, ed. J. Adelson (New York: Wiley, 1980), pp. 145–149.

45. M. C. Jones, The later careers of boys who were early or late maturing, *Child Development* 28(1957):113–128.

46. H. Peskin, Pubertal onset and ego functioning, *Journal of Abnormal Psychology* 72(1967):1–15.

47. F. Arnhoff and E. Damianopoulos, Self-body recognition: An empirical approach to the body image, *Merrill-Palmer Quarterly* 8(1962):143–148; A. Frazier and L. Lisonbee, Adolescent concerns with physique, *School Review* 58(1950):397–405; E. Clifford, Body satisfaction in adolescence, *Perceptual and Motor Skills* 33(1971):119–125.

48. Petersen and Taylor, pp. 144–145; R. Lerner and S. Korn, The development of body-build stereotypes in males, *Child Development* 43(1972):908–920.

49. Katchadourian, pp. 156–158.

CHAPTER 4

Cognitive Growth in Adolescence

INTRODUCTION

To most observers, physical changes are the most apparent transformations of adolescence. As we saw in Chapter 3, changes in physique accompany altered physical and reproductive capacities. They also often serve as an important sign to family and community that a child is becoming an adult. Equally dramatic—but less obvious to the world at large—are changes in abilities for thinking, reasoning, and solving problems. These cognitive changes are the focus of this chapter.

We will begin with a discussion of some important contrasts between the cognitive characteristics of adolescents and those of younger children. Next, we will examine how these transitions might take place and some implications of newly emerging cognitive abilities for adolescents' adjustments in school and other life tasks. Since there are varied ways of understanding the developing thinking and reasoning abilities of adolescents, we will sample a range of problems to which such skills might be relevant. For example, school consumes a great deal of adolescents' time and energy; the ability to perform well in academic tasks is one aspect of the intellectual changes that are important to adolescent cognitive development. But intellectual changes affect how we get along in the world in a number of ways. Thus it is important to ask how adolescents solve problems more generally, even if those problems seem only incidentally relevant to school learning. Later, in Chapter 5, we will consider some of the aspects of social and emotional development that involve thinking and reasoning abilities as well.

ADOLESCENT THOUGHT

Our first step in understanding adolescent thought is to specify some ways in which the thinking of, say, a junior high school or high school student is different from that of a younger child. In this section we will look at a few of these differences.

The Las Vegas Game

Imagine the following situation: An adult is offering children and adolescents an opportunity to play a new game. In many ways the game resembles slot machines, so we'll call it the Las Vegas Game. It involves an apparatus with three buttons, red, yellow, and blue. When the correct button (red) is pressed, a reward or prize drops into a small chute. The catch is that the machine is adjusted so that it pays off only 66% of the time. Thus the most efficient strategy is to push the red button repeatedly. Children and adolescents of all ages try the game, and after a time it becomes apparent that there are marked differences from age to age in how they approach the game.

In one study conducted with this game, elementary school children were puzzled by the fact that no matter which of the three buttons they pushed, the prize came out only part of the time [1]. For example, Lisa, age 9, concluded that the best strategy was shifting from button to button—for example, "If you win you shift, and if you lose you shift." Once she and other nine-year-olds had settled on a strategy, they stuck with it, even when it was apparent that their strategy did always lead to success. As a result, they received many fewer prizes than they would have had they simply pushed the red button repeatedly.

Fifteen-year-old Angie also entertained the idea that the strategy might be a complex one. But once Angie saw that the strategies she tried were not successful, she abandoned them and fairly quickly came to the conclusion that the most efficient way to play the game was to push the red button repeatedly. Her score was much higher than Lisa's score.

It was not better, however, than four-year-old Jenny's score. Jenny, like other young children, was quite happy to continue pushing the red button once she discovered it was the one that gave prizes. More than either Lisa or Angie, Jenny stayed with the winning solution!

Childhood Versus Adolescent Thought

The different strategies on the Las Vegas Game show us some of the differences between the characteristic thought of adolescents and of school-aged children. After many years of studying these differences, psychologists have identified five contrasts that seem to be especially important [2]. These contrasts are outlined in Table 4.1; we discuss them in detail below.

TABLE 4.1 Comparison of childhood and adolescent thought

Childhood	Adolescent
Thought limited to here and now	Thought extended to possibilities
Problem solving dictated by details of the problem	Problem solving governed by planned hypothesis testing
Thought limited to concrete objects and situations	Thought expanded to ideas as well as concrete reality
Thought focused on one's own perspective	Thought enlarged to perspective of others

Thinking about possibilities The thought of school-aged children is limited largely to objects and situations that they are experiencing or have encountered in the here and now. They focus on what they can directly experience. When they are solving problems like the Las Vegas Game, elementary school children jump right into the particulars or details of the problem, without considering the possible ways in which these details might be arranged. For example, in the Las Vegas Game Lisa behaved as though she were overwhelmed by the fact that there were three buttons on the machine. Instead of considering that two of the buttons might have been irrelevant, she seemed to feel that feature of the game had to be incorporated into her way of solving the problem.

Adolescents, by contrast, are much more likely to recognize that there are many logically possible ways in which a given situation or problem might be put together. While Angie recognized the possibility that more than one button might be involved in the solution, she was also quite aware that there were other possibilities, and her performance on the game reflected this awareness. To put it another way, school-age children tend to think about what *is;* adolescents are likely also to consider what *might be*.

Thinking through hypotheses Adolescents' abilities to think about different possibilities enable them to test hypotheses as a part of solving problems—much as scientists test hypotheses in conducting research. The tendency of elementary school children to be overwhelmed by the concrete details of the situation interferes with hypothesis testing. For example, when Lisa's hypothesis about the complex sequence of button pushing that would win the Las Vegas Game seemed not to be true, she was unable to shift her strategy to others that might be more satisfactory. Angie, on the other hand, was able to test a number of hypotheses about possible ways of winning and to do so quickly and efficiently. As a result, she was able to arrive at an effective strategy far sooner than Lisa was.

One further point to note is that Lisa was perfectly able to form hypotheses and to begin to test them in a haphazard way. The difference between Lisa and an adolescent thinker is that her approach is more rigid. She sticks with one or two hypotheses instead of thinking more extensively about all the possible solutions that might exist. Compared with problem solving in school-aged children, adolescent problem solving includes the ability to test hypotheses that seem impossible as well as those that seem to be a likely solution at the moment.

Another example of the difference between childhood and adolescent thought involving hypotheses is apparent in the following classroom experiment:

Stonehenge: A Fort or a Religious Temple?

David Elkind, a leading Piagetian scholar, teaches a discovery unit in elementary school social studies to illustrate the inability of concrete-thinking pupils to distinguish between facts and theories [3]. He shows a series of pictures of Stonehenge. He points out a large number of facts—the huge size of the stones, their placement in an open field, the circular trenches of outer and inner defense lines, and similar bits and pieces of information from which it is possible to conclude that Stonehenge was a prehistoric fort. He is careful to list a very large number of facts to back up the conclusion. He then presents just a few facts such as the open field and the two stones (the heel and the altar) that line up perfectly with the sunrise on June 21 each year, thereby suggesting that the site was really a religious temple. This second conclusion has fewer facts behind it yet essentially is more logical. The children, however, will not change their minds. To them the large number of concrete facts, a quantitative difference, is more important than the smaller number of facts that "prove" the religious nature of the site. Essentially, for children at this age there is no difference between theories and facts. What is important is how many. Thus the basis for complex scientific and logical reasoning is not yet available to elementary-age children.

Stonehenge

Thinking ahead The thought of adolescents, including their use of hypotheses and problem solving, is also more planful than the thought of school-aged children. When Angie attacked the Las Vegas Game, she seemed to be working through a set of possible ways of solving the problem in a fairly systematic, organized way. Lisa, in contrast, tried one solution and then another without considering the systematic way in which one solution might be related to another.

A classic demonstration of this characteristic of thought involved the following task: Find the combination of five colorless chemicals that would produce a solution of a particular color [4]. Most adolescents know immediately that the right answer is one of the logically possible combinations of the colorless chemicals. Most of them proceed to solve the problem by simply trying each possible combination in turn until the right color shows up. Younger children, however, are less likely to conceive the possible combinations of so many liquids, nor can they proceed systematically through the possible combinations in search of the correct ones.

These three characteristics—thinking about possibilities, hypothesis testing, and planfulness—generally mean that adolescents think and reason *more abstractly, speculatively,* and *flexibly* than most children do. They are not limited by what they can see or what they have seen in the past. Formal thinkers recognize that what they perceive is only one possibility among many; things *might* be different than they seem.

Thinking about thought Adolescents do not simply think more flexibly and speculatively about objects and situations around them. They also actually think about their own thoughts and the thoughts of other persons. For example, psychologists Daniel Osherson and Ellen Markman tested school-aged children and adolescents in a guessing game [5]. They extended their hands, which were closed into fists, and explained that they were holding a poker chip. They then asked the children and adolescents, one by one, to say whether certain statements were true or false. One statement was, "The chip in my hand is green *and* it is not green." Later, the same statement was made while a red or a green chip was held up for the participants to see. School-aged children usually say that they "can't tell" whether the statement is true or false when the fist is closed; when the chip is visible, children answer the statement on the basis of what they see. For example, if the color of the chip matches the color mentioned in the statement, school-aged children are likely to say that the statement is true. They focus on the connection between the statement and what is visible; they overlook the fact that the statement cannot possibly be true in the first place. Adolescents and adults, however, are more likely to answer that the statement is not true because, logically, it cannot be true. The chip cannot be both green and not green. Thus adolescents are more likely to deal with the propositions themselves than with the connection between the propositions and the irrelevant visible reality.

This example makes it easier to understand how adolescents might think about thought. They are willing to focus on the abstract rather than the concrete. Thus abstract thoughts can become objects of thought, much as concrete situations and circumstances can be objects of thought.

The ability to think about thought has other implications as well. For example, adolescents are much more likely than children to have some understanding of how they know things and what is required for solving problems. While younger children may be capable of solving the same problems, they are less likely to be able to talk about how they did it or what would be needed for someone else to do the same task. Finally, because adolescents have the capability of thinking about thought, adolescents spend far more time than younger children in reflecting on their ideas and their imaginings about how problems might be resolved about the future. One result is that adolescents reflect on themselves and what they are like. For example, one high school student remarked:

> I am always anticipating—most of the time I am anticipating good things, but when it comes to other people I find that I tend to—other people or myself—I tend to anticipate bad things. I am afraid of being—I think I am more afraid than most people. . . . of getting involved and getting hurt.

Reflection like this about the self is rarely present before adolescence because it requires the ability to think about thoughts.

Perspectivistic thinking   Closely related to thinking about thoughts is the awareness that different people have different thoughts about the same situation or circumstance. This characteristic was demonstrated in some early studies by Swiss psychologist Jean Piaget [6]. Piaget demonstrated repeatedly that young children tend to think everyone views situations as they do. He described these young children as *egocentric* because they were centered or focused on their our view. Adolescents, however, are more likely to recognize that others' viewpoints are different from their own. It is as though they understand that others have different interests, knowledge, and ways of understanding than they have. In a sense they recognize that their own viewpoint is only one possible view of a situation and that there are as many other viewpoints as there are persons. Perspectivistic-thinking ability is obviously related to a number of other characteristics of adolescent thought that we have described above. It is a particularly important aspect of an adolescent's ability for reasoning and for considering social relationships, as we will see in Chapter 5.

The Question of Change

We have examined several differences between the typical thought of school-aged children and the typical thought of adolescents. We have primarily focused on *descriptions* of these differences. So far, we have not considered *how* the change from childhood thought to adolescent thought might take place. The question of change is an important one for several reasons. First, knowing about the process by which cognitive growth occurs will enable us to understand better the struggles of adolescents as they undergo the transition from childhood to adolescence. Second, it may be possible to facilitate or stimulate cognitive change for adolescents whose thinking and reasoning abilities are not adequate for the situations they encounter every day. Only by understanding how change takes place can we provide help, however.

We now turn to an explanation of adolescent thought that has been provided by Jean Piaget. Our focus will be on Piaget's explanation of the nature of differences in the thought of children of different ages and his ideas about how the changes from one age to another take place.

PIAGET'S STAGE THEORY OF COGNITIVE DEVELOPMENT

Jean Piaget devoted most of his long career to the painstaking study of children and adolescents, many of whom he followed over long periods of time. Piaget's goal was to chart the course of cognitive growth. He wanted to be able to explain why infants and young children seem *not* to possess certain intellectual skills while older children and adults do. Piaget concluded that the cognitive abilities of adolescents described earlier in this chapter *develop* from the reasoning and thinking abilities that are typical of younger children [7]. He believed that each new thinking skill represents an elaboration and an integration of previous thinking skills. Furthermore, he thought that development follows a logical pattern that characterizes everyone—a pattern he described in terms of the series of stages of intellectual growth for which he is now famous.

In this section we will examine Piaget's theory of cognitive development, the stages he described, and the process of cognitive change.

Psychological Structure and Developmental Stages

Piaget's stages are actually descriptions of different thinking and reasoning abilities that result from qualitatively different psychological structures. These structures become more elaborate and more widely applicable in the course of development. Two examples of Piagetian structure may make this point clear.

First, infants show rather overt patterns of motor skill that Piaget calls *schemes*. These patterns of sensory and motor actions are children's intelligence—their ways of experiencing and understanding the world. One example of schemes is the act of grasping. Children know a great many items as things to be grasped—fingers, rattles, models, and, later, cups, blocks, saucers, balls, boxes, and so on. The grasped things have different shapes, textures, and dimensions, but the action pattern of grasping has a certain sameness. It is that sameness of action toward objects that is the visible evidence of a structure, a particular way of experiencing reality.

A second example shows the relative complexity of school-aged children's mental structures. One of Piaget's most famous descriptions concerns the child's awareness that changes in appearance do not always involve changes in the basic nature of some aspects of the world. This ability is referred to as *conservation*, because it involves conserving an awareness of the basic characteristics of objects even though their appearances change. The classic example involves two identical containers (A_1 and A_2) filled with water. The liquid in container A_2 is emptied into a shorter, wider container (B). Although the amount of liquid stays the same, most children up to the middle elementary school years will say that B contains less water than A_1 contains. Apparently, the child is confused by the lesser height of the liquid in container B. The child fails to consider that although height has been subtracted, width has been added.

Responses to the conservation task reflect certain underlying psycho-

"Which glass has more!" is a difficult cognitive problem for young children, but adolescents solve such problems quite easily.

Photograph from Sandra Johnson

logical structures, in Piaget's view. The child who focuses on height is working with a simple structure that dictates that judgments of quantity—how much or how little of something there is—are made on the basis of a single dimension: how tall the thing appears. More mature individuals are aware that size involves more than one dimension and that all the relevant dimensions must be taken into account in figuring out whether the quantity of material has actually changed when its appearance changed. The latter, more complex structure involves the *coordination* of two dimensions of the problem rather than *centration* on only one dimension.

Piaget argues that complex structures are, in fact, systems for thinking and reasoning. More mature children will not only say that containers A_1 and B hold the same amount of water. More importantly, they will also show that they have an organized set of reasons for giving that answer. They will note that (1) A_2 would look the same as A_1 if the liquid from B were put back into it, (2) the different width of B compensates for the difference in height between the liquids in A_1 and B, and (3) these facts would be true no matter how many different-shaped containers were used to hold the liquid from A_2. These are important, interrelated points, and they show that the children have cognitive *systems* for thinking and reasoning. Although their systems are still applied primarily to concrete objects and perceptions, school-age children are doing something much more sophisticated and elaborate than children whose psychological structures do not permit them to understand conservation.

Stages of Cognitive Development

Piaget describes four major periods of cognitive development. These stages are outlined in Table 4.2. Each stage represents a time in the child's life when the psychological structures that make thinking and reasoning abilities possible have become increasingly complex and abstract [8]. The changes are *qualitative,* meaning that the qualities of thought change from one period to the next. Let's turn now to a discussion of these stages.

Infancy and early childhood The cognitive life of infants consists mostly of the overt actions they are able to carry out on objects around them. Consequently, Piaget calls the earliest period of development the *sensorimotor period* because he believes that infant intelligence is largely reflected in what the infant is able to do by virtue of senses and motor abilities. Gradually, these external action schemes became *interiorized,* in Piaget's terms. Then thought consists of *mental actions* that the sensorimotor child first carries out overtly. This period, which includes most of the preschool years, is called the *preoperational period* because it is a period of transition and preparation for the relatively mature cognitive skills that Piaget calls operational thought.

TABLE 4.2 Piaget's stages of cognitive growth

Age	Stage
0–2	Sensorimotor
2–7	Intuitive or preoperational
7–12	Concrete operations
12–adult	Formal operations

At more advanced levels, cognitive structures become more than mental simulations of particular action sequences. More mature thought involves generalized logical patterns that apply to many different kinds of relations among people and objects in the child's world. Piaget calls these more generalized principles *operations.* Operations are higher-order mental actions that "enter into all coordinations of particular actions" [9]. For example, objects and persons—and, later, ideas and propositions—can be united, arranged in order, and subjected to all the other operations that are a part of the logic of sets. Generally, operations refer to the ways in which the things one thinks about are mentally arranged and rearranged in the process of thinking. The most important characteristic of operations is that they are *reversible.* For example, we can combine the class of "fathers" and the class of "mothers" to form a new class, "parents"; and we can reverse that operation by taking away the "father" class and leaving the "mother" class as it was before. The intuition that these sorts of rearrangements are possible underlies the greater flexibility of older children's thought.

School age and adolescence Piaget characterizes the thought of school-aged children and adolescents in terms of operations. He refers to school-aged children's thought as *concrete operational,* and he refers to adolescents' thought as *formal operational.* Thus different operations are Piaget's way of characterizing the differences between the school-aged child's thought and the adolescent's thought. We described those differences in the first part of this chapter.

In both cases children have abstract schemes of logically possible relations among the objects and people around them. Consequently, they think about their experiences and environments more systematically and solve problems more deliberately and planfully than they did as preschool children. Thinking becomes less a matter of step-by-step action and more a matter of abstract, logical reasoning and problem solving.

These abstract schemes also make possible the simultaneous coordination of more cognitive elements (e.g., objects, persons, or events) than the preoperational child typically uses. In Piaget's view cognitive development takes place as the child applies schemes to more and more elements and—

on the plane of mental, rather than motor, action—considers relationships among them. As we saw in the section on adolescent thought, the main differences between concrete-operational and formal-operational thought concern the greater use that adolescents can make of abstractions—abstract possibilities and abstract thoughts—and the greater flexibility with which they can reason about both the real and the possible. The contrast between the concrete-operational thought of childhood and the formal-operational skills required of adolescents is illustrated in Fig. 4.1.

An example of formal-operational skill   One of Piaget's experiments shows how the formal-operational thinker may be advanced over the concrete-operational thinker [10]. He and his colleague, Barbel Inhelder, presented adolescents and school-aged children with a scale balance (see

---

The Pendulum Problem   (a Piaget test of formal operations)

Materials: A length of string
A series of different-size weights

1. Demonstrate the swing of a pendulum by attaching one weight to the string and letting it swing.
2. Ask the class to predict which is more important in determining how fast or slow the pendulum swings—the *length* of the string or the size of the *weight*.
3. Demonstrate different lengths and different weights and repeat question 2.

Even though it will be clear that the size of the weight has no influence on how fast or slow the pendulum swings, many pupils will still insist that weight does make a difference.

© 1965 United Feature Syndicate, Inc. Reprinted by permission.

FIG. 4.1   Piaget's pendulum problem and Sallys' math problem: Both require formal thought

Piaget's INRC Set: What Does That Mean?

We describe in the text aspects of formal operations as a method of logical and abstract thinking and contrast the elements of such formal thought with the method of the prior stage, concrete operations. Piaget, in an attempt to provide a totally comprehensive definition of formal operations, uses an acronym, the INRC set, to represent his view. Understanding what this set means, however, may be quite difficult.

The set is comprised of four operations that represent a combinatorial system: I (identity), N (negation), R (reciprocity), and C (correlativity). The set essentially describes the process of either inductive or deductive reasoning. So far so good. Yet when we attempt to identify what is specifically meant by each element of the INRC set, the difficulty becomes apparent. Piaget says:

> Let us take, for example, the implication p > q; if it stays unchanged we can say it characterizes the identity transformation I. If this proposition is changed into its negation N (reversibility by negation or inversion) we obtain N = p and not q. The subject can change this same proposition into its reciprocal (reversibility by reciprocity), that is, R = q > p; and it is also possible to change the statement into its correlative (or dual), namely c = not p and q. Thus, we obtain a commutative 4 group such that CR = N, CN = R, RN = C and CRN = I. [1]

At this point, unless you are a math major or have had advanced logic, you are likely to shrug and mutter to yourself, "What the heck does that mean?" Recently Everett Dulit, a Piagetian scholar, decided that there must be a better way to describe the meaning of the combinatorial set. For exam-

Fig.4.2) to which extra weight had just been added to one pan. The exercise involves four variables: adding or subtracting weights and moving closer to or further from the fulcrum. The question to the participants was, "How can the scale be brought back into balance?" The simplest answer—and the one that school-aged children prefer—is to remove the weight that has made one pan sink lower than the other one. Adolescents are much more likely to generate several possibilities. Besides the possibility of taking away the added weight, they can also imagine compensating for the added weight by changing the distance of the weighted pan from the fulcrum on which the two pans are balanced. If the heavier pan is moved closer to the

ple, for the balance beam illustration (see Fig. 4.2), Dulit describes each operation in sequence [2]. Imagine yourself sitting in front of the beam, which is balanced. You now place a weight on one side, and the beam moves down on that side. *Identity* is the initial operation. You remove the weight and *negation* occurs, restoring the beam to balance. *Reciprocity* occurs when you do one of two things to restore the balance: add a new weight to the other side *or* move the pan. In either case the effect is reciprocal, and the beam again balances. For *corelativity* you simply undo the previous operation: Take away the new weight and/or move the pan back to its original position. At this point the beam moves once again back down on the initial side, so your procedure now correlates with the original I.

This concrete example of INRC describes the structure of formal reasoning. As we point out in the text, the process is most important—it is used to make hypotheses, arrive at logical outcomes, verify the accuracy of propositions, and consider all possible variations. Ralph Mosher sums it up well:

> The adolescent can think about thoughts, words, ideas, concepts, and hypotheses and can do so concerning a wide range of phenomena from the physical world to real and ideal concepts of self. [3]

REFERENCES

1. J. Piaget, Intellectual evolution from adolescence to adulthood, *Human Development* 15(1972):6. Reprinted by permission S Karger AG, Basel.
2. E. Dulit, Adolescent thinking ala Piaget: The formal stage, *Journal of Youth and Adolescence* 1, 4(1972):281–301.
3. R. Mosher, *Adolescents' development and education: A Janus knot* (Berkeley, Calif.: McCutchan, 1979), p. 18.

fulcrum, then the two pans may be brought back into balance again without removing the added weight. Both solutions are forms of reversibility, which is characteristic of psychological structures in the concrete-operational period. However, adolescents recognize more different forms of reversibility than school-aged children do.

Another example of the greater complexity and flexibility of formal operations is the colorless chemicals task described earlier. Adolescents, but not concrete-operational school-age children, are likely to construct all possible combinations of the colorless liquids and test them systematically to find which combination produces the desired result. Piaget's point is

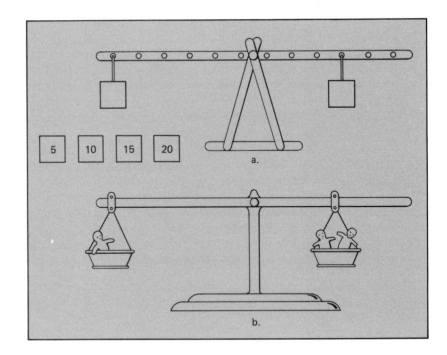

FIG. 4.2 The balance beam problem (testing formal operations)

that these abilities represent changes in underlying structures between the elementary school years and the adolescent years.

The Process of Change

Movement from stage to stage in Piaget's theory—including the change from concrete-operational to formal-operational thought—involves changes in the psychological structures that underlie thinking and reasoning in each successive stage. Changes in mental structures result from encountering new aspects of objects and situations. Piaget calls this change process *equilibration* because he thinks new experiences force a disequilibrium in the functioning of mental structures that motivates the person to make the structure more complex and more applicable to abstractions.

It may be helpful to think about equilibration by using a parallel between the biological processes through which food is ingested to the benefit of the body's organs and the growth of structures, which have been referred to as "psychological organs." In fact, Piaget says that individuals adapt psychologically to experience through the same processes that explain how the body makes use of food. Let's examine Piaget's explanation more closely.

Each time we encounter an intellectual problem—an object, situation, or other thing to be understood—we attempt to approach it in terms of our existing mental structures. This process, called *assimilation*, involves our trying to make the characteristics of the situation fit existing action patterns. At the same time we try to adjust those patterns to the unfamiliar characteristics of the new experience. This process involves *accommodation*, a bending of the existing structures in an attempt to take account of the characteristics of new persons, objects, or other aspects of the situation. Assimilation and accommodation are believed to work together in thinking and reasoning. They are also believed, in most cases, to be in balance; that is, the two occur to about the same extent in most successful intellectual acts.

However, if we encounter more complex experiences than we have been accustomed to, this equilibrium between the ongoing processes of assimilation and accommodation can be upset. Take the case of conservation. When children become aware that the short, wide container and the tall, thin container *do* contain the same amount of water, even though they make liquid columns of different height, the children are suddenly obliged to consider another dimension besides height. Their existing scheme, which involves judging an amount of liquid in terms of its height in a container, must be altered to consider other physical dimensions of the container and the coordination among the dimensions. How would Piaget explain it? He would say that the need to consider an additional dimension causes a disequilibrium between assimilation and accommodation. To reestablish equilibrium, the child's efforts to accommodate the existing structure to the additional dimension must become balanced with the assimilation of the problem to the existing scheme, in which only height is considered. This new equilibrium can be established only when the structure itself has been enlarged. Thus equilibration is a process of reestablishing an equilibrium between assimilation and accommodation because of a new and more complex structure.

Piaget's theory of psychological change emphasizes the gradual elaboration of mental structures, or patterns for intellectual actions, through equilibrating experiences. Others, like learning theorists, think of cognitive change in terms of a quantitative buildup of skills rather than the qualitative change that Piaget implies. However, both learning theorists and cognitive developmentalists like Piaget affirm that a variety of experiences in many settings affect cognitive development.

Training formal-operational reasoning Piaget assumes that the transitions from stage to stage occur as the result of ordinary, everyday experiences in the lives of children and adolescents. Using these ideas, several researchers have attempted to improve adolescents' reasoning abilities by inducing equilibration. Let's consider one of these training programs.

In one study psychologist Barnaby Barratt wanted to improve adolescents' ability to solve problems in which one has to consider a number of aspects simultaneously [11]. Here's an example of the type of reasoning he was interested in:

> At a party there were only four bowls of food. The first contained rice, the second chicken, the third tomatoes, and the fourth mushrooms. Everybody took some food. Some people took just one kind of food, some took two kinds, some took three, and one person had some of all four kinds. Everybody at the party took a different mixture of foods. What is the maximum number of people that could have attended the party, and what did they eat?

This may sound more like a riddle than a serious problem, but in its complexity, at least, it is similar to many practical problems in everyday life.

Barratt undertook to train 80 early adolescents chosen from the top math tracks of a secondary school in Great Britain. The adolescents were 12, 13, and 14 years old. Barratt carefully assessed their reasoning abilities on several problems that required considering several elements simultaneously. He found that their performance was generally poor, rarely showing the flexibility and complexity of thought characteristic of formal operations. Afterward, he trained some of them in two phases. In the first phase he trained them on problems in which they were required to consider only part of the elements at one time. For example, in the food problem described above he would have asked them to consider how many people could have eaten if each person took two of the four foods rather than combinations of three or more. In the second session he moved to the more demanding task of considering all possible combinations of elements. He was interested not only in whether the adolescents could give correct answers to the problems but also in what they thought was necessary for solving the problems and how other persons could go about solving them.

After the two training sessions he again tested the adolescents on their abilities to solve these problems. He compared their performance with the performance of adolescents of the same ages who had not received training. The training was most effective for the 14-year-olds. Their Piagetian stage scores were almost three times the scores of 14-year-olds who did not undergo training. Perhaps 14-year-olds showed this improvement because their general level of cognitive development was higher than the younger participants'. It may be that they could better take advantage of the training and could more readily incorporate the effects of such training into their existing way of solving problems.

Studies like Barratt's provide some support for using training to try to stimulate cognitive growth. It could be, of course, that the effects of training are not due to a reorganization in psychological structures such as

Piaget proposed. Many cognitive developmentalists contend, however, that it would be impossible to achieve the improvements that are achieved through the use of training programs simply through practice or additional learning about particular problems [12]. They argue that a cognitive reorganization is necessary to explain the dramatic shifts that take place in effective training programs—and in the course of normal cognitive development, as well.

Some qualifications   The shift from concrete to formal operations is a dramatic one. But much of the information we have about the usefulness of Piaget's ideas for describing adolescent thinking suggests that we should keep in mind two important qualifications.

One qualification is that the change from concrete-operational thinking to formal-operational thinking does not come abruptly. Rather, the transition is a gradual one. For quite long periods a young person may show many instances of mature thought, accompanied by just as many instances of relatively immature thought. Indeed, Piaget recognizes that at each stage of cognitive development we will also see thinking and reasoning that seem more characteristic of earlier stages and—sometimes—later stages. When Piaget refers to a formal-operational thinker, he merely means that in most instances that person shows a level of intellectual performance that seems to reflect the abstract, complex, and flexible qualities of formal operations.

In early adolescence, in particular, thinking and reasoning abilities may seem highly variable. Young adolescents sometimes show the reliance on immediate reality that characterizes concrete-operational thinkers; at other times they show the capacity for abstract reflection that is more characteristic of formal-operational thought. The ambiguity is sometimes very difficult for teachers and parents to accept. In fact, the tendency is probably to either overestimate or underestimate the level of cognitive functioning of which a young adolescent is capable.

The second important qualification is that individuals may show more maturity in some areas of their functioning than in others. For example, some adolescents may be quite skilled socially and may think in very complex ways about the nature of interpersonal relationships and interactions, but they may or may not show evidence of advanced cognitive skills in academic subjects. Conversely, skilled academic thinkers may be less skilled socially.

This point is especially important because of the relatively narrow way in which formal-operational thought has typically been studied. Piaget developed his ideas in terms of formal logical principles. But he himself recognized that individuals who are relatively unfamiliar with academic areas of achievement may still be at the formal-operational level, although

Adolescents develop formal patterns of thinking and are able to attain logical, rational strategies
Photograph from Frank Siteman/Stock, Boston

we may only observe it in particular areas [13]. For example, he argues that primitive tribes may show a great deal of cognitive sophistication in the hunting and tracking methods that they use in the jungle. If you understand the complexities of their task, you can see how complex their thinking processes are. However, they would probably not perform well on a colorless chemicals task or a balance beam problem. By the same token, adolescents who live in inner-city environments may be extraordinarily skillful at negotiating the complexities of street life, but they may not do well in academic subjects.

It is important to remember that formal-operational thought refers to the abstractness, flexibility, and complexity with which ideas, objects, and situations are understood and approached. Piaget makes it possible for us to see the intelligence of adolescents as involving a broad range of specific thinking and reasoning skills that vary in complexity and applicability. Later in this chapter we will discuss some of the ways in which adolescents differ from each other in their intellectual skills.

COGNITIVE DEVELOPMENT AND ADOLESCENT COGNITIVE PERFORMANCE

One test of Piaget's view of differences between childhood and adolescent thought is whether the distinction helps us understand teenagers' behavior in the ordinary tasks they are called upon to perform. In recent years two types of intellectual problems common to the lives of adolescents have been examined: decision making and school achievement. In this section we turn briefly to the information available on these two types of tasks.

Decision Making

One of the issues in the definition of adolescence, as we discussed in Chapter 1, is the competence of young people to make legally regulated decisions, such as decisions involving marriage, consent to medical treatment, volunteering for experimentation, and choice of custodial parent when parents divorce. Piaget's notion of formal thought suggests that adolescents are far more competent than school-aged children to consider the often complex aspects of such decisions. However, since formal thought is gradually, rather than suddenly, acquired, we still need to know how adolescent decision making changes over the course of the second decade of life.

In a recent study Catherine Lewis examined the decision making of adolescents between the ages of 12 and 18 (grades 7 through 12) [14]. She told the adolescents that each one would hear tape-recorded statements of other young people, and she asked them to give advice to each of these people. For example, she presented the following statement from a young woman:

> I have been thinking about having this operation. It won't make me healthier or anything, but I'd like to have it because it would make me look better, since I've always had this ugly thing like a bump on my cheek. I could have an operation to remove it. I'm trying to decide whether to have the operation, and I can't decide. Do you think I should have the operation? [15]

Another dilemma involved questioning the trustworthiness of an adult:

> Professor Johnson is a scientist who is pretty famous for his studies of how people think. I mean he has been on TV and his research has helped a lot of people. . . . Professor Johnson spoke at a school assembly, and afterwards a lot of kids went to his laboratory to help him with research, and I went to it and it was really interesting, and also we got paid a lot by Professor Johnson. So I was really surprised to hear someone in my class say that Professor Johnson had lied to him about his research . . . told him that lots of kids his age had done it when they really hadn't. So I don't know whether to trust Professor Johnson or to believe the person in my class. What would you think of Professor Johnson now? Who would you trust if it were you? [16]

Afterward, Lewis carefully analyzed the advice that the adolescents had given in response to the tape-recorded problems. She found that the advice given by adolescents of different ages differed in how much the following considerations were taken into account:

- Awareness of risk and an assessment of risk taking.

- Orientation to the future.

- Advice seeking and compliance to advice.

- Treatment of negative information about adults.

- Recognition that some person involved in the problem had a vested interest in particular actions or outcomes.

There was a marked increase from grades 7 to 12 in the extent to which adolescents noted the potential risk involved in various decisions and talked about the future consequences of decisions in giving advice. As they grew older, adolescents also were more likely to recognize vested interests and to treat them with caution in making decisions. And, finally, the older the adolescents, the more likely they were to recommend consultation with a knowledgeable professional who could give independent advice. Surprisingly, Lewis did not find that adolescents increasingly distrusted adults. Rather, the major shift in adolescents' advice about decisions was to an increasing awareness of relatively abstract considerations like the motives or vested interests of other parties and awareness of the importance of an independent, unbiased perspective on personal problems. Just as our information on formal-operational thought indicates, older adolescents' approach to problems seemed more complete and well balanced in their consideration of the relevant issues for making decisions.

Lewis's study is one of the few studies available of adolescent thinking and reasoning about real life problems. As you will see later in this text, such decision making is pertinent to issues of adolescent sexual involvement and the risk of unmarried pregnancies among adolescents (Chapter 9) and to issues relating to career choice (Chapter 13). Undoubtedly, many other decisions that affect adolescents and society also involve the extent to which adolescents have reached a level of cognitive reasoning and thinking that permits adequate reasoning and thinking about complex, problematic situations. Lewis concludes that early adolescents, even those as old as tenth graders, lack the full complement of cognitive skills that are necessary for many of the decisions that are now denied to them by law. In particular, they are less likely than, say, most 18-year-olds to imagine risks and future consequences, to recognize the need for independent professional opinions in certain situations, and to recognize the potential vested interest of other parties. Younger adolescents may not depend on cognitive factors alone, of course. Compared with older adolescents, they have simply had less experience in making decisions that affect their own lives and the lives of others and less opportunity to learn decision-making skills from others. However, many aspects of the development of formal thought are also involved in the change in decision-making abilities across the years of adolescence.

School Achievement

The emergence of formal-operational abilities also has a number of implications for adolescents' performance in traditional school subjects. For example, their attainment of logical, rational, abstract strategies means that symbolic meanings, metaphors, and similes can now be understood. Stories with a moral can be generalized. Games and simulations can be presented so that pupils understand their implications. For example, if we want to teach something about economic theories and principles, we can use a game like Monopoly, asking questions that point to general principles. At the elementary age, children could understand the game only as a game; they could not see the general issues it addresses. Adolescents are also more likely to respond to the abstract notions embedded in movies and film clips and in art forms such as painting, drama, dance, and music. The more active the symbolic process, the more it enhances cognitive growth. For example, during this stage, writing poems is more effective than reading poems, making films more effective than viewing them, taking part in an improvisational drama more effective than observing one.

In recent years a number of attempts have been made to examine typical school experiences and their appropriateness for young people who are engaged in the transition to formal-operational thought. John Renner and his associates at the University of Oklahoma have conducted the most extensive series of studies examining the match (or mismatch) between adolescents' level of cognitive development and components of the secondary school curriculum [17]. They also rated the complexity of readings and assignments in each subject area (e.g., English, biology, sciences, etc.). They found a discrepancy between teenagers' cognitive stages, as assessed through Piagetian tasks, and the curriculum subjects of their schools. For example, an English curriculum could be difficult yet quite concrete in structure—for example, "All right class, the assignment is to memorize exactly the first 100 lines of 'Snow-Bound' by John Greenleaf Whittier."

In Renner's study students from a large sample (588) representing 25 different secondary schools (junior and senior high schools) were tested individually on nine of Piaget's tasks of formal operations. Only a minority of pupils at all grade levels had attained formal operations (see Table 4.3). However, most of the curriculum materials assumed a formal-operational level of cognitive abilities. For example, the biology course included concepts such as genetic bases for physical characteristics and the meaning of ecosystem, which represent difficult, abstract intellectual tasks for young

TABLE 4.3 Secondary pupils and formal operations

Level	Sample size	Percent of formal operations
Junior high		
Grade 7	96	17
Grade 8	108	23
Grade 9	94	18
Senior high		
Grade 10	94	27
Grade 11	99	29
Grade 12	97	33

Adapted from J. W. Renner, *Research, teaching, and learning with the Piaget model* (Norman: University of Oklahoma Press, 1976), p. 97.

teenagers. Furthermore, Renner found that the more a student showed formal-operational abilities, the more likely he or she was to do well on tests of basic concepts in senior courses such as physics and chemistry. Cognitive skills apparently do matter in adolescents' school performance.

Renner's results imply that the majority of students do not understand what a class is all about, what they are supposed to do on their assignments, or what the concepts mean. The students, it is true, sit in class and go through the motions—at least, they did for the most part in Renner's study. Yet little in the way of genuine learning appears to take place. This result is consistent with Piaget's contention that individuals will not comprehend the complexities of problems that demand reasoning beyond the cognitive level at which they are functioning. The same circumstance was apparently true in a now-classic example cited by the first American psychologist, William James:

> A friend of mine, visiting a school, was asked to examine a young class in geography. Glancing at the book, she said, "Suppose you should dig a hole in the ground, hundreds of feet deep, how should you find it at the bottom—warmer or cooler than on top?" None of the class replying, the teacher said: "I'm sure they know, but I think you don't ask the question quite rightly. Let me try." So, taking the book, she said: "In what condition is the interior of the globe?" and received the immediate answer from half of the class at once: "The interior of the globe is in a condition of ingenious fusion." [18]

The discussion above suggests that if pupils are not helped to develop their potential for formal thought, they will remain rather like concrete robots, dutifully repeating phrases on call at the behest of teachers. Perhaps most distressing of all are the results shown in Table 4.3, which indicate that there is very small change in the level of functioning over the 3 years of junior high school. Similarly, the educational experience in high school yielded a gain of 6% in formal thought; after 3 years of 180 days per year, at 5 or 6 hours per day, that amount of change is not impressive. The vast majority (two-thirds) of the pupils still function at the concrete level. Perhaps if there were a better match between students' cognitive level and the subject matter presented in school, there would be more opportunity for intellectual stimulation to facilitate cognitive development. The evidence that there are major discrepancies between the curriculum materials—teaching methods, on the one hand, and the complexity of reasoning, on the other—raises the need to reemphasize the developmental assumptions discussed in earlier chapters.

Growth to more complex stages depends on matching the learning environment to a young person's present level of functioning and then *gradually* raising the complexity of the teaching. This process can go wrong in either direction: We can teach ineffectively either by overmatching or by undermatching the task to the pupil. For example, we could ask third graders to read *Moby Dick* and interpret the meaning of Ahab's obsession— a clear case of overmatching. Third graders could not grasp the symbolic meaning of the white whale and the pursuit. We do not mean that we could not get them to memorize the right answers. We could certainly get them to recite all the proper phrases, much as children did in the nineteenth-century school curriculum in this country; but there would be no genuine comprehension. To know by heart, Piaget would say, is *not* to know. Undermatching obviously goes in the opposite direction. For example, having high school students (or, indeed, college students) memorize long lists of facts is a case of negative mismatch. Another example is a homework problem in which the student adds a column of ten to fifteen digits and then does another twenty problems that are exactly the same.

The developmental problem for education is not simple: How can we create educational conditions to stimulate growth in formal operations? How can we nurture the potential for abstract and symbolic reasoning during adolescence? Note that this question is not the so-called American question of how do we speed up growth. We are not trying to rush pupils through cognitive stages so that first graders will be formal thinkers. In the first place, such acceleration is not possible. Remember Piaget's assumption that stages must be passed sequentially; each advance requires considerable experience in order for full acquisition and consolidation of cognitive skills to occur. The question for schools, then, is not how to accelerate but rather how to prevent stagnation—how to provide stimulating interaction to nurture growth.

SPECIAL TOPIC
Promoting Formal Operations: The Renner Method

John Renner and his associates have examined, in a preliminary way, the potential of educational programs to promote cognitive development [1]. In one study they compared regular junior high science courses with classes organized around Piaget's ideas.

The regular classes employed standard texts; the teaching was done through expository lectures. The pupils then read and recited from the text, learned such concepts as the meaning of the scientific method, and studied topics concerned with the matter formed on earth, geologic periods, and rock formations. Somewhat with tongue in cheek, Renner calls this method the "tell 'em, show 'em, ask 'em" method.

The experimental classes, in contrast, were set up to follow Piaget's dictum. Students in transition from concrete to formal operations were exposed to (1) substantial structure, such as explicit expectations and careful directions, (2) hands-on experience in solving laboratory problems, (3) the use of open inquiry and student-directed investigations, and (4) colleague support and direction by the teacher. Since the students were not yet at the formal level, abstractions and generalizations were minimal at the outset.

The students in both sets of classes were tested before and after on six Piaget tests individually administered. The classroom teachers had no knowledge of these tests or the experiment and so could not teach for the test. The results are reported in the accompanying table.

As the table indicates, the experimental classes emphasizing hands-on experience with manipulatives and problem solving on actual science projects promoted a marked increase in formal thinking. This result provides evidence on two important points: (1) teaching methods and materials can have an im-

INDIVIDUAL DIFFERENCES IN ADOLESCENT COGNITIVE SKILLS

Piaget's descriptions of thinking and reasoning show that adolescents' grasp of the world is *qualitatively* different from younger persons' understanding. Contrasts between stages capture the kinds of transitions that occur in cognitive functioning but mostly ignore differences in cognitive skills from one adolescent to another. An approach that gives us important

EFFECTS OF A PIAGET TYPE OF SCIENCE PROGRAM WITH JUNIOR HIGH PUPILS

Class	Concrete operations	Formal operations
Experimental[a] (N = 92; 72 at concrete operations on pretest)	35	57
Regular (N = 119; 92 at concrete operations on pretest)	91	28

[a] Highly similar results were derived in an independent project reported by J. Premo and G. Engstrom, Using Piaget's model in basic science instruction (Minneapolis Public Schools, 1978).

pact on cognitive development, and (2) the learners' developmental level is an effective entry point. This second result is particularly important. The use of concrete manipulative materials did not retard development but, rather, aided students to visualize the problems they were to solve and then became a basis for more complex reasoning.

Similar results in a different field of study, humanities, were reported at the college level in the pioneering work of Widick; Knefelkamp, and Parker (see Chapter 14). They were able to design curriculum materials and methods to stimulate growth from concrete to formal operations with college freshmen. Twenty-one of twenty-two students who started the class at the concrete level moved to formal thought by the end of the term. The details of the study are presented in Chapter 14. The point to note here is that it is possible to promote cognitive development rather than assume it.

REFERENCE

1. J. Renner, D. Stafford, A. Lawson, J. McKinnon, F. Friot, and D. Kellogg, *Research, teaching, and learning with the Piaget Model* (Norman: University of Oklahoma Press, 1976).

information about individual differences in reasoning and thinking is the well-known mental abilities, or IQ-testing, approach. In contrast to Piaget's qualitative descriptions, information from IQ tests during childhood, adolescence, and adulthood offers a *quantitative* approach to the important changes of this period and to individual variation in cognitive skills. In this section we will discuss the mental abilities tests and what they tell us about adolescent cognitive skills.

SPECIAL TOPIC
Adolescent Literature: Starting Where the Learners Are?

A question of continual controversy concerns secondary school English and adolescent literature: Are they compatible? Traditionally, the content of high school English has been the classics, from *Beowulf* to James Joyce, including a heavy dose of Shakespeare and the romantic poets, with lengthy excerpts from the works of Nathaniel Hawthorne, O'Henry, Edgar Allen Poe, and perhaps even Jack Kerouac. Whatever the specifics, the content is selected as representing some dimension of significant, written expression by adults for adults. The levels of abstraction are high and the plots are complex, complete with subtle interplays of recurring themes and dramatic irony. In short, all aspects of writer's license are explored, most of all the use of symbolic communication. The complexities of the human condition in the hands of skillful craftspersons and wordsmiths such as Jane Austen or Herman Melville are viewed as the foundation for secondary school courses in literature.

But what of the adolescents themselves? What are they reading if left to their own choice? Perhaps a few can be found browsing through Elizabeth Barrett Browning or *Twelfth Night*, but most are reading works of a totally different genre. Adolescent literature is just that: novels written with a deliberate appeal to teenagers. The plots are less complex by design. Good recent examples include Zindel's *My Darling, My Hamburger,* Klein's *Mom, the Wolfman and Me,* and Childress's *A Hero Ain't Nothing but a Sandwich.* The main characters clearly represent a variety of unambiguous values. Generally brief and to the point, the novel has a message that is clear from beginning to end.

Mental Abilities Tests

The IQ-testing approach is probably the most popular way to characterize cognitive abilities. Nevertheless, it may be helpful to review the concept of abilities tests here so that you understand what typical adolescent performance on them means—and does not mean.

Generally, mental abilities tests tell us how quickly, easily, and efficiently a person can solve age-appropriate intellectual problems. Scores from these tests must be compared with a standard, a norm of intellectual performance derived from the typical performance of many people. Usually, for children and adolescents the standard is the performance of a sample of people of their own age.

In a sense these writings are very similar in construction to daytime TV soap operas. If we borrow from our own framework in this volume, an analysis of the main themes would place most adolescent literature at a level at which appearance, peer group pressure, and conventionality are dominant values.

So the paradox. Teenagers avidly devour their own literature—the romantic mysteries and the Harlequin romances (which, recently, are only modernized versions of the Hardy Boys, Nancy Drew, and the "fabulous" Merriwell Brothers). Yet these works cannot be considered uplifting. They do little to deepen a person's understanding of life, and they can hardly be the means of increasing the majesty and mystery of humanity. In developmental terms there is almost too much of a match between adolescent literature and the adolescent. The literature mirrors almost exactly the point where most teenagers are developmentally. Yet, on the other hand, teenagers are clearly not ready to delve into the likes of Dostoevski's *Crime and Punishment*. That is, the traditional material is often too great a mismatch, as we have noted.

Solutions to such a dilemma are hard to come by, but it is clear that the need for them is great. Classic works of literature and adolescents are, to quote from a great work, "like ships passing in the night"—only in this case there is not even a hail in the night before darkness descends again. A developmental solution would require substantial research and trial, but we can, at least, outline a possible direction here. Starting where the learner is would require teaching adolescents how to analyze their own literature, as a beginning. To write off their own literature with a grand gesture of disgust is clearly not the way to proceed. After analysis could come the gradual introduction of works representing slightly greater levels of complexity. Comparative examination could then become the first step on the path to more complex readings, where the works no longer represent where the teenager is now but, rather, what the teenager is in the process of becoming.

What do such tests tell us? Mental abilities tests are simply a way of measuring average growth rate in one particular area of functioning—mainly, the kind of symbolic problem solving that is characteristic of traditional academic work. The tests are made up of a series of questions, grouped on the basis of their difficulty for particular age groups of children. For example, the items for 14-year-olds are those that can be solved by the majority of 14-year-olds, are too difficult for all but a small minority of 13-year-olds, and are solved by almost all 15-year-olds. The age-level problems that an adolescent can solve represent his or her score, or mental age (MA). Comparing mental age with chronological age (CA) theoretically gives an indication of the adolescent's rate of mental growth. So the standard formula for IQ has always been

$$\frac{MA}{CA} \times 100.$$

Thus for 13-year-olds who pass 14-year-old items, we have

$$\frac{14}{13} \times 100 = 108.$$

In current practice an adolescent's score is more often converted, by the use of norms for the test, into a relative standing in any one of a number of comparison groups (e.g., tenth graders nationwide, high school graduates, or Army recruits). Thus scores only have meaning relative to the scores of other persons. Instead of telling us how absolutely bright a child is, these tests tell us how an adolescent performs on symbolic problem-solving tasks compared with other adolescents in that age group. In general, mental abilities tests tell us about *differences among adolescents* rather than about age differences between children and adolescents or between adolescents and adults.

Such scores are limited, however, in two important ways. First, the test scores are relevant to very restricted problem-solving areas, best described by standard academic tasks. They are not good predictors of a wide range of problem-solving tasks that are not characteristic of school learn-

Mental abilities tests, widely used to assess adolescents' cognitive skills, are most appropriate for assessing achievement in standard academic tasks
Photograph from Arthur Grace/Stock, Boston

ing. They are also poor at predicting aptitude for creative activities, like art, music, and drama. Leona Tyler, one of the recognized experts of the abilities-testing field, points out that intelligence tests are "not an all-important index of intellectual capacity nor a measure of *amount* of anything." In fact, she says: "It would be well for all those who are using intelligence tests for one purpose or another to realize that what is measured by such tests is probably a more limited human trait than they are assuming" [19].

Second, and more generally, the tests are highly culture-specific. That is, the items on most mental abilities tests tap abilities that are characteristic of tasks facing white, middle-class individuals in Western countries. Several attempts to create tests appropriate for members of minority groups indicate that nonwhites perform better on them than whites. Clearly, the language and types of problems on most standardized tests may make it difficult for non-middle-class adolescents to perform well on them.

Mental Abilities Tests and Formal Operations

Both the qualitative tasks described in the early part of the chapter and the quantitative measurements taken in mental abilities tests are attempts to characterize thinking and reasoning. Do they, in fact, get at the same qualities of adolescents' thought? In a very general sense, they do. In some studies adolescents have been asked to do various Piagetian tasks, like the balance beam and the pendulum problems, and also to complete standard mental abilities measures. Compared with adolescents with average mental ability scores, adolescents who score quite high on quantitative tests also perform at a higher cognitive level on the tasks designed to measure qualitative aspects of thinking [20]. In contrast, some researchers have argued that qualitative and quantitative approaches each measure unique aspects of cognitive functioning [21]. The most reasonable interpretation of the information now available, however, is that the two approaches tap closely related aspects of thinking and reasoning but give different types of information about them.

Changes in Mental Abilities Performance in Adolescence

This description of the nature and use of intelligence tests gives us some background for understanding how mental abilities scores may change during the teen years. In the usual case, of course, mental age scores increase across age levels, while mental abilities scores (which are a ratio of mental age to chronological age) may remain relatively constant. Nevertheless, the mental abilities scores of adolescents predict their adult scores better than their childhood scores do. That is, an adolescent's test performance is more indicative of what that person will be able to do as an adult on similar tests than is that person's performance as a child. A child's score can tell us with only about 35% likelihood what the relative standing of that person is likely to be when he or she is an adult. In adolescence a mental abilities score predicts adult standing on a similar test with about a 65% likelihood of being correct [22].

Why this slippage from one age to another? For one thing, there is no mental abilities test that is appropriate for people of all ages. Therefore children, adolescents, and adults all take different mental abilities tests; the differences in the tests account for some of the variation in performance at different age levels. For another thing, the experiences of adolescents are especially appropriate to the kinds of skills measured on mental abilities tests. Much of adolescents' time is spent in school, and hence they are dealing with subject matter and skills that are typical of the abilities tested in most standard abilities instruments. Indeed, people's mental abilities scores actually increase overall between the ages of 16 and 21, particularly for people who go to college. Scores then tend to decline somewhat after age 21. This fluctuation from adolescence to adulthood reminds us of the importance of experience both in determining general competence and in fitting a test taker for specific skills needed to do well on the test.

Perhaps the most important point for consumers of mental abilities test information is that the variation in scores over the adolescent years and the relative inconstancy of scores across the whole life cycle mean that an individual's test scores must be handled with care. If children don't perform well, it doesn't mean they won't do better as adolescents or adults either on intelligence tests or on real world problems. We should not assume that because we have the results of mental abilities tests, we thereby have all the relevant information about a child's competence or prospects for the future.

Now let's turn to two aspects of change in mental abilities performance that are significant for adolescence: the age differentiation hypothesis and sex differences in scores.

The age differentiation hypothesis   A major change in the pattern of mental abilities scores during adolescence is that for that period it is possible to be more specific about particular intellectual strengths of persons than it previously was. This *age differentiation hypothesis* implies that over the adolescent years abilities become more differentiated and specific than they were in childhood. Thus not only should we be better able to predict adult standing on mental abilities test from adolescent performance, but we should also be able to say more specifically what the intellectual strengths—and weaknesses—of an individual are likely to be in facing the kinds of problem solving for which mental abilities test are relevant.

The hypothesis of differentiation with age comes partly from the technicalities of test and measurement. The developers of standard mental abilities tests believe that mental development may be described in terms of more and more refined and specific sets of abilities as children grow older. That is, testers think that we can only describe young children's mental abilities in quite general terms. Thus while we can say that a three-year-old is bright or dull, we usually can't say that the child's verbal skills are better or worse than the child's quantitative skills. But for ten-year-olds it becomes easier to say that a child is good at math or reads and writes well. As children move into adolescence, this two-way division is further broken down. Theoretically, we can describe a person's problem-solving abilities on a number of specific types of problems—for example, verbal ability, inductive reasoning, deductive reasoning, numerical facility, mathematics achievement, or arithmetic reasoning, depending on the particular test that is used. In short, instead of talking about a single general score as a description of an individual's intellectual ability, for adolescents we can talk far more specifically about the sorts of cognitive tasks on which individuals are particularly skilled.

Perhaps the most thorough test of the age differentiation hypothesis was undertaken by Dye and Very [23]. They gave standard mental abilities tests to more than 500 individuals in grades 9 and 11 and in college. They found that, indeed, they could tell more about particular abilities of individuals from test performance in eleventh grade and college than in ninth grade. That is, more specific abilities emerged at older ages. Dye and Very also found interesting patterns of sex differences in the extent of differentiation. Males and females showed similar *absolute* levels of brightness. However, males at all ages were more differentiated than females, meaning that we can more easily identify specific areas that are strong—and weak—for males' abilities than for females'. Female competence continues to be described in more general terms even during adolescence.

Sex differences in test scores   One of the unsurprising differences between males and females that emerged from Dye and Very's study is that in adolescence—and at other age levels—females show generally greater verbal facility than males, while males show some superiority in reasoning and arithmetic abilities. That is, in some of the specific mental abilities subtests, females are superior; in others males are superior.

How might such sex differences in mental abilities performance be explained? There is some indication that hormonal differences between males and females may contribute to different responses on various subtests. For example, psychologist Anne Petersen found that higher male performance on spatial abilities increases during the teen years, relative to females, and is more pronounced for individuals with higher levels of male hormones during and following pubescence [24].

However, a number of obvious environmental factors probably also contribute to sex differences in patterning of abilities. Consider that two decades ago, when Dye and Very's research was done, there were substantial, socially reinforced differences in expectations and experiences for males and females in most United States high schools. Females were generally reinforced for being relatively skilled in verbal areas and for maintaining a wider range of expertise than that of males. By contrast, males were reinforced largely for being interested in so-called male activities, such as mathematical reasoning and mechanical skill. So perhaps different available involvements, different patterns of reinforcement, and different social roles influence the performance shown on mental abilities tests, quite apart from the general overall level of brightness an adolescent's test scores indicate.

The age differentiation hypothesis and sex differences in differentiation in adolescence, like the findings on changes in test scores over the life cycle, point to the important role of experience in intellectual growth. The principle is similar to the point made in our discussion of formal-operational thought: Advanced cognitive ability may be manifested on types of tasks familiar to an adolescent, even though performance on standard tests of formal-operational thought is poor.

A note about test scores   The concern of many people about mental abilities tests is not so much their goals but the inappropriate uses to which test scores are often put. The use of these scores should be very restricted. For example, they are not supposed to be used as an index of an individual's total ability, because there are too few competences that the test purports to measure and too much slippage between what they purport to measure and what the scores actually mean. Properly interpreted, however, mental abilities test scores permit us to characterize adolescents' relative strengths on some types of tasks. They may be particularly helpful in our attempts to understand difficulties in school and in related situations.

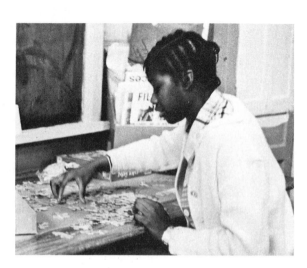

Standard mental abilities tests may not be appropriate measures for testing everyone's abilities nor for assessing abilities of every type
Photograph from Charles Gatewood

SPECIAL TOPIC
Sex Differences: Is Biology Destiny?

One of the most controversial current issues concerns the nature of differences between males and females. It is not a question of whether or not there are differences. Obviously, there are physical and physiological differences of major proportions. The controversy is over the dual question of causes and consequences. Because of years of reluctance by psychologists in general to examine the question, and because of a pervasive atmosphere of male-dominated sexism, the most common stance has been to accept the obvious sex differences as an indication of male superiority and female inferiority. The fact that women were so rarely represented in high-status careers was interpreted as an indicator of inferior genetic backgrounds. Feminine biology predetermined the outcome. Evolution, in a Darwinian sense, had proclaimed that a woman's place was in the home, since she was not equipped to interact in the complex world of adult males.

A series of recent studies, the most notable by psychologists Eleanor Maccoby and Carol Jacklin, has cast serious doubt on both aspects of the male superiority question [1]. There are certainly differences between the sexes, but the most important differences (those associated with successful performance in a complex Western society) can be explained by socialization. Maccoby and Jacklin say we have looked in the wrong place for causes. Rather than examine genetics, we should examine how boys and girls are raised. If we do, as they have done, we will find that a major determinant of differences is pattern of upbringing.

The differences in upbringing are subtle but pervasive—so strong, in fact, that even some of our most cherished differences, rooted in folk wisdom, can be questioned. For example, a commonly observed difference is in the area of aggressiveness. The authors found, from intense observation of three- and four-year-olds, that nursery school teachers were responding differentially. Boys received approval for initiative-aggressive acts (short of mayhem), while girls received censure. In parent interviews they found that parents often reward and punish in the same way—praise boys for initiating aggression and punish girls for such activity.

In other words, the pattern of differential socialization common throughout formal schooling starts very early and is based to a large degree on cultural stereotypes. In our culture males are expected to be independent, initiating, aggressive, and career-oriented; the culture supports these views. So, for

(Continued)

SPECIAL TOPIC (Continued)

example, if during high school males are commonly academic underachievers, the condition is accepted as temporary. They receive support and help to outgrow the problem of developmental lag, and they turn out to be successful in adult careers. If, on the other hand, females in junior high exhibit signs of so-called math anxiety, then the culture (and, unfortunately, some psychological researchers) supports the view of inferior female "math" genes.

Even previous research that established sex differences in certain abilities can be questioned. A careful reanalysis of more than seventy studies has shown that the reported differences are highly problematic. Janet Hyde reexamined studies of four major abilities: (1) verbal, (2) quantitative, (3) visual-spatial, and (4) visual analytic [2]. She found that the differences between males and females actually accounted for only 1%–5% of the overall variation. Essentially, this result means that the bell-shaped distribution curves for males and females overlap by more than 94% as a minimum, and it is important to remember at least three-fourths of the studies were conducted with middle to late adolescents. By that time the cultural stereotypes—such as those suggesting that females should avoid mathematics and science, subjects that heavily employ three of the four abilities studied—would have had maximum impact.

From our view, whether an individual develops certain skills and abilities depends on the quality of interaction between the person and the environment. So far, we can say, on the basis of the recent studies by Maccoby and Jacklin and others, that most (if not all) major psychological differences between males and females are due to differences in interaction, not to biological sex differences. Most important to note is that the observed performance differences generally appear during the later stages of development, when so-

Creativity: A Different Kind of Ability

One reaction to the limitations of mental abilities tests has been an effort to find ways to measure other aspects of cognitive functioning. In particular, many abilities testers have attempted to devise a way to measure *creativity*, the ability to create something new and unusual or the ability to find very ingenious or uncommon solutions to problems. Creativity refers to abilities that have many implications for the quality of life in a society. These creative abilities have not been the focus of the tests of abilities we have been discussing. And yet there are people who are strongest in just this kind of functioning.

J. P. Guilford, one of the psychologists interested in developing tests

cialization and culture would have the greatest impact. For mathematics learning, for example, researchers recently found that high school females exhibited a pattern of "learned helplessness" in attempting to solve math problems. That is one of the consistent findings of recent sex difference research, derived from the original fear-of-success syndrome documented by Matina Horner. In the math case females have come to accept and believe in the cultural stereotype—namely, that math is too tough for them [3]. This result is probably the most discouraging finding of all. The person victimized by the cultural stereotype ends up accepting it as truth.

Research may yet prove that there are important differences between the sexes beyond the obvious anatomical and skeletal-musculature differences. Thus far the evidence strongly supports the view that learning capacities in a wide variety of complex disciplines and careers are independent of gender. The problem at hand, as Maccoby and Jacklin note, is how to dismantle the myths of female inferiority and encourage socialization patterns that will provide females with an equitable chance at success in a broad range of careers.

REFERENCES

1. E. Maccoby and C. Jacklin, *The psychology of sex differences* (Stanford, Calif.: Stanford University Press, 1974), pp. 17–163.

2. J. S. Hyde, How large are cognitive gender differences? *American Psychologist* 36, 8(1981):892–901.

3. P. Wolleat, Sex differences in high school students' causal attribution of performance in mathematics, *Journal of Research in Mathematics Education* 11(1980):356–366.

of creativity, points to an especially important contrast between creative thinking and thinking as mental abilities tests measure it [25]. Guilford characterizes standard mental abilities tests as measuring *convergent thinking*, mental functioning devoted to arriving at a correct answer. For example, an arithmetic problem requires convergent thinking; one must marshall the correct steps to arrive at the correct arithmetic solution to the problem. Guilford thought that creativity was much more likely to include *divergent thinking*, which involves the generation of a variety of possibilities, since in creative thought there is no one correct answer. Certainly, this kind of thinking partly involves what might be rather than what is—a part of Piaget's definition of formal thought.

For example, consider the differences among the following opening sentences to teenage autobiographies:

- "In 1943 I was born. I have been living without interruption ever since."

- "I was transferred from another world or 'hatched,' as you might call it, at a very young age (0 for a fact)."

- "My family is not extraordinary except that my brother has two heads. . . ."

- "When my father saw me he ran away screaming into the hills. We followed. . . ."

In contrast, consider this opening:
- "I was born on November 10, 1942, in Chicago. I was the first of three children to be born to my mother and father."

The playfulness, imagination, and, uninhibited expressiveness of the first four examples are obvious when compared with the overtrained realism of the last example [26].

Guilford's aim, and that of others like him, has been to devise a way to assess an individual's creative potential—those aspects of a person's potential productivity that are not assessed on convergent-thinking tests. From a psychological tester's viewpoint this goal requires a test of divergent thinking, a test that is designed to assess abilities that are not measured on tests of convergent thinking (like standard mental abilities tests). They have succeeded at this task: The items they have devised to measure divergent thinking appear to be more closely related to each other than to items from mental abilities tests [27]. Some examples of these test items are shown in Table 4.4. Such a test might give school officials, parents, and the adolescents themselves a broader understanding of abilities than that given by mental abilities tests.

To isolate the differences between intelligence and creativity, Jacob Getzels and Philip Jackson studied two other groups of teenagers: a highly intelligent group and a highly creative group [28]. They concluded that highly intelligent students (with average IQ scores of 150) are not necessarily creative and that highly creative pupils do not necessarily have extraordinarily high IQ scores. The point is that the mental processes that produce high IQ scores do not necessarily produce high scores on creativity tests.

Michael Wallach and Nathan Kogan have shown the possible psychological implications of paying attention to creative abilities [29]. These psychologists studied preadolescents who were both above and below the average of their group on measures of both intelligence and creativity.

Thus there were four possible combinations of scores from the mental abilities and creativity tests: high IQ/high creativity, high IQ/low creativity, low IQ/high creativity, and low IQ/low creativity. Wallach and Kogan then examined personality tests scores of preadolescents who fell into these four groups.

Not surprisingly, in Wallach and Kogan's study the most successful and well-adjusted children in the school were those who were high in both creativity and intelligence. Their personality test scores showed that they

TABLE 4.4 Sample test items of creativity and problem-solving ability

Item	Answer
Verbal tests of creativity	
1. Flanagan's ingenuity test[a]	
As part of a manufacturing process, the inside lip of a deep, cup-shaped casting is machine-threaded. The company found that metal chips produced by the threading operation were difficult to remove from the bottom of the casting without scratching the sides. A design engineer was able to solve this problem by using one of the following. Can you determine which solution he chose?	The correct answer is (e), upside down, or uʍop ǝpısdn.
a) i————p h——h b) m————n c——e c) f————r w——i d) l————d b——k e) u————e d——n	
2. Guilford's sample insight problem[b]	
A man went out to hunt a bear one day. He left and hiked due south for ten miles, then due west for ten miles. At this point, he killed a bear. He dragged the bear back to his camp, a distance of exactly ten miles. What was the color of the bear? Why?	The correct answer is "white." Only at the North Pole are these directions possible. Is it creativity or a good convergent knowledge of geometry and geography that one employs in finding the correct answer?

[a] Adapted from F. Barron, *Creative person and creative process* (New York: Holt, Rinehart and Winston, 1969); p. 27. Reprinted by permission.

[b] Adapted from W. S. Ray, *The experimental psychology of original thinking* (New York: Macmillan, 1967). Reprinted by permission.

(Continued)

TABLE 4.4 (Continued)

Item	Answer	
Nonverbal tests of creativity[c]		
3. Pattern meanings	*Unique response*	*Common response*
Tell what each card looks like to you.		
a) b)	a) Lollipop bursting into pieces	Flower
	b) Foot and toes	Table with things on it
	c) Five worms hanging	Raindrops
c) d)	d) Three mice eating a piece of cheese	Three people sitting around a table
4. The line meaning test	*Unique response*	*Common response*
What does each incomplete drawing bring to your mind?	a) Squished paper	Mountain
a) b)	b) Squeezing paint out of a tube	Piece of string
c)	c) Fishing rod bending	Rising sun

[c] Adapted from M. A. Wallach and N. Kogan, *Modes of thinking in young children: A study of the creativity-intelligence distinction*, p. 34. Copyright © 1965 by Holt, Rinehart and Winston, Inc. Reproduced by permission of Holt, Rinehart and Winston, Inc.

balanced both control and freedom—both the ability to find the right answer and to find innovative approaches to problems for which a right answer is most obvious. High IQ/low creativity children also did well in school and were generally well rewarded for their performance. At least in their school years, relatively low divergent-thinking ability did not present problems for them. By contrast, children who were low in IQ and low in creativity had generally poor adjustment; they were bewildered and relatively low in self-esteem. Their confusion was manifested in excessive anxiety, timidity, or psychosomatic symptoms, although some turned to intensive social activities as a kind of compensation for their lack of success in other ways. The really unfortunate cases, in Wallach and Kogan's view, were the low IQ/high creativity children. Their personality scores showed them to be quite angry and conflicted both within themselves and within their environment. Not surprisingly, they had feelings of inadequacy and unworthiness. But in a stress-free context they blossomed cognitively.

The difficulties of these adolescents are underscored by some findings from Getzels and Jackson's study [30]. They found that the teachers in their study much preferred the students with high IQs to those with high creativity, despite the fact that the creative pupils produced significantly more imaginative and original writing samples. A further indication that teacher preference was determined by convergent versus divergent styles was that the researchers found no difference on outcome or amount learned by the two groups. That is, standard measures of academic achievement in various academic subjects revealed no difference between the two groups. Thus the highly creative adolescents who did not have the highest IQ scores were less well liked by the teachers, even though the pupils' standard achievement scores were substantial. Getzels and Jackson commented that highly creative pupils had somehow "learned" to get along without the support and encouragement of their teachers.

It may not be possible for most educational institutions to respond to the needs of adolescents in plights like this one. But the creativity-testing movement is potentially important for those of us who are concerned about adolescents, because it helps make us aware that not only relative brightness but also the qualities of thought are critical to adolescents' adjustment to both their intellectual and their social worlds. As we learn more about the distinctions between convergent and divergent thinking and the value of both, we may also produce more effective methods of stimulating both modes of thought. A number of programs designed to promote divergent thought have recently been developed. Yet much careful work remains to be done. We know that brief, one-shot games on a late Friday afternoon do not suffice as an approach to stimulating human creativity.

SUMMARY

In this chapter we presented a description, based largely on the work of Jean Piaget, of stages of cognitive development, focusing particularly on the differences between children and adolescents. Piaget believed that contrasts between cognitive abilities from one stage to another are the result of underlying psychological structures that increase in complexity, abstractness, and flexibility as individuals mature. These qualitative cognitive changes are the result of equilibration, Piaget's fundamental view of the nature of cognitive growth.

During adolescence, individuals develop an important potential for formal thought. In contrast to the characteristic thought of childhood, adolescent thought includes greater ability for thinking about possibilities, for thinking through hypotheses, for thinking ahead, for thinking about thoughts themselves, and for thinking about the perspectives of others.

Although adolescents in industrialized Western nations ordinarily have an opportunity to develop cognitively to the level of formal thought, there is no automatic guarantee that all individuals will develop that ability. However, as shown by the work of Barratt and Renner, thinking ability can be stimulated. Such stimulation will require substantial change from current achievement standards and the passive curricula of most public schools, though.

In this chapter we also focused on individual differences and quantitative, or IQ-testing, approaches to mental abilities. There is considerable variation in mental ability during adolescence, as there is during childhood. As a result, predictions of how well an adolescent will do in college or work or later in life, based on mental ability test scores, should be conservative. During adolescence it becomes possible to identify relative strengths and weaknesses in individuals' mental test performance. That is, adolescents' skills in a variety of intellectual tasks (e.g., verbal, arithmetic, or spatial abilities) can be differentiated, whereas in childhood only a general ability score can be derived from a mental abilities test. We also discussed the meaning of possible sex differences in scores on different types of problems included in mental abilities tests.

Finally, we presented a discussion of creativity. We noted that creativity and measured mental ability do not necessarily overlap. An adolescent may score either high or low on mental abilities tests and also either high or low on tests of creative thinking. The patterns of abilities young persons show have important implications for their adjustment to standard school settings, where the skills that serve well in mental abilities tests are demanded. At least one study demonstrated that teachers strongly preferred high-IQ students to high-creativity students.

Different ways of measuring the cognitive skills of adolescents have different implications for practical application to our understanding of individual adolescents. They also have different implications for how well adolescents may be expected to adjust to the typical challenges they face in our society.

KEY POINTS AND NAMES

Adolescent thought modes
  Thinking about possibilities
  Thinking through hypotheses
  Thinking ahead
  Thinking about thought
  Perspectivistic thinking

Daniel Osherson and Ellen Markman

Jean Piaget

Stages of cognitive development

Psychological structures

Schemes

Conservation, coordination, and centration

Sensorimotor period

Preoperational period

REFERENCES

1. M. W. Weir, Developmental changes in problem solving strategies, *Psychological Review* 71(1964):473–490.

2. D. Keating, Precocious cognitive development at the level of formal operations, *Child Development* 46(1975):276–280; J. Flavell, *Cognitive development* (Englewood Cliffs, N.J.: Prentice-Hall, 1976), pp. 101–148.

3. D. Elkind, *Children and adolescents* (New York: Oxford University Press, 1970), p. 54.

4. B. Inhelder and J. Piaget, *The growth of logical thinking from childhood to adolescence* (New York: Basic Books, 1958), p. 122.

5. D. Osherson and E. Markman, Language and the ability to evaluate contradictions and tautologies, *Cognition* 3(1975):213–226.

6. J. Piaget and B. Inhelder, *The child's conception of space* (London: Routledge & Kegan Paul, 1956).

7. J. Piaget and B. Inhelder, *The psychology of the child* (New York: Basic Books, 1969), pp. 132–151.

8. J. Flavell, *The developmental psychology of Jean Piaget* (Princeton, N.J.: Van Nostrand, 1963), pp. 41–84.

9. Piaget and Inhelder, *Psychology of the child*, pp. 93–94.

10. Piaget and Inhelder, *Growth of logical thinking*, pp. 168–181.

11. B. Barratt, Training and transfer in combinatorial problem-solving: The development of formal reasoning during early adolescence, *Developmental Psychology* 11, 6(1975):700–704.

12. Flavell.

13. J. Piaget, Intellectual evolution from adolescence to adulthood, *Human Development* 15(1972):1–12.

14. C. Lewis, How adolescents approach decisions: Changes over grades seven to twelve and policy implications, *Child Development* 52(1981):538–544. Published by University of Chicago Press.

15. *Ibid.*, p. 540.

16. *Ibid.*

17. J. W. Renner, D. Stafford, A. Lawson, J. McKinnon, F. Friot, and D. Kellog, *Research, teaching, and learning with the Piaget model* (Norman: University of Oklahoma Press, 1976).

18. W. James, *Talks with teachers* (New York: Norton, 1958), p. 106.

19. L. Tyler, *Tests and measurements* (Englewood Cliffs, N.J.: Prentice-Hall, 1963), p. 54.

20. Keating, pp. 276–280; D. Kuhn, Relation of two Piagetian stage transitions to IQ, *Developmental Psychology* 12(1976):157–161.

21. S. Martorano, The development of formal operations thought, *Dissertation Abstracts International* 35(1974):515B–516B. (University Microfilms No. 74–15, p. 486.)

22. N. Dye and P. Very, Developmental changes in adolescent mental structure, *Genetic Psychology Monographs* 78(1968):55–88.

23. *Ibid.*

24. A. Petersen, Physical androgyny and cognitive functioning in adolescence, *Developmental Psychology* 12(1976):524–533.

25. J. P. Guilford, *The nature of human intelligence* (New York: McGraw-Hill, 1967), pp. 312–341.

26. J. Getzels and P. Jackson, *Creativity and intelligence* (New York: Wiley, 1962), pp. 100–101.

27. M. Wallach and N. Kogan, *Modes of thinking in young children* (New York: Holt, Rinehart and Winston, 1965), pp. 25–65.

28. Getzels and Jackson, pp. 100–101.

29. Wallach and Kogan, pp. 286–332.

30. Getzels and Jackson, pp. 100–101.

CHAPTER 5

Social Reasoning in Adolescence

INTRODUCTION

For adolescents the task of achieving an identity, a topic we discussed in Chapter 2, may be largely a matter of reconciling their past and current experiences and characteristics with what they hope to be in the future. In Chapters 3 and 4 we considered some changes in adolescents that are relevant to this task. For example, physical maturity not only changes the capabilities of adolescents to occupy roles that require adult size and strength; it also raises the expectations of adults that those adolescents can fill certain types of roles in the future—football lineman, construction worker, business executive, affluent socialite. Similarly, cognitive changes make possible not only more adultlike reasoning and thinking but also the capacity for imagining future roles, choices, and possibilities. That is why we have referred to physical and cognitive changes as *primary*, or fundamental, aspects of adolescence. They are basic developmental changes that seem to precipitate many of the social and psychological challenges that adolescents face, and they probably partly underlie the different ways in which individual adolescents approach the problems of achieving an identity.

In this chapter we look backward to our discussions of these primary physical and cognitive changes, and we look forward to a group of chapters in which we discuss the effects of families, peers, and other social influences on adolescents. The task of establishing an identity takes place amidst the relationships and activities of adolescents' day-to-day lives. Families, friends, teachers, school, the mass media, the world of work—all are settings in which adolescents must find new roles and new under-standings of themselves. Consequently, we must consider how adoles-cents change in their reasoning and thinking about the personal world of self and others, much as we examined the changes in cognition for the impersonal world of logical problem solving and school tasks in Chapter 4.

The plan of the chapter is, first, to consider some of the characteristic changes in social reasoning and thinking during adolescence. Next, we will examine some implications of these changes for adolescents' understand-ing of interpersonal relationships. We will be especially concerned with the effect of developing notions about the self and social relationships on the development of identity.

COGNITIVE CHANGE AND SOCIAL COGNITION

In Chapter 4 we identified several marked qualitative changes in the nature of thinking and reasoning during the second decade of life. Although the nature of these changes emerged from studies of impersonal problems and skills, many of these characteristics of thinking and reasoning extend to adolescents' thinking about their social worlds. For example, the increas-ing complexity and abstractness of adolescents' thought generally means that adolescents are likely to notice and simultaneously consider more aspects of social situations and relationships than they did as children. Decisions may become more complicated and bothersome for them be-cause they recognize that choices often carry more ramifications than they previously had realized. Going to a movie with friends, for example, can be viewed simultaneously as an opportunity to see an amusing film, a chance to see and be seen by peers, an alternative to a planned family activity, and a competitor for time that should be spent studying. Elementary school youngsters are not likely to be troubled by these various possibilities, be-cause, as we saw in Chapter 4, they typically do not reason in terms of multiple conflicting possibilities.

CHARACTERISTICS OF ADOLESCENT'S SOCIAL COGNITION

Three characteristics of adolescent thinking about persons and social rela-tionships and situations seem especially important to development during this period. We discuss each characteristic in detail below.

Awareness of Discrepancies Between the Real and the Possible

Saying that the adolescent develops an awareness of discrepancies be-tween the real and the possible may make the adolescent sound more like a formal philosopher than is appropriate. However, adolescents do tend increasingly to perceive reality as only one of the many possibilities that might occur, and this tendency probably affects responses to many com-

Adolescents compare their own experiences and characteristics with those of others, often as seen in the mass media
Photograph from Christopher Brown/Stock, Boston

mon situations. This idea was first suggested by David Elkind, who points out that adolescents often experience a "grass is greener" reaction when they recognize that things *could* be different than they are [1].

Younger children are less likely to have this intuition. They are more likely to focus on what *is* rather than what *might be;* consequently, children are more likely simply to accept things as they are. For example, children may be unhappy about an authoritarian family structure, but they'd be more accepting of it than adolescents because they don't sense that there are other ways in which families might operate. Adolescents are more apt to recognize that families can be organized in different ways and to resent an unsatisfactory family situation—or at least to wish fervently that it were different. Elkind attributes some of the melancholia and rebelliousness of the stereotyped adolescent to the awareness that things might be different than they are.

Dispositional Concepts of Self and Others

In addition to understanding the possibilities inherent in real life situations, adolescents may have complex, abstract concepts of what other people—and they themselves—are like. Young children are likely to describe others exclusively in terms of their appearance or some characteristic activity: for example, "She has red hair," "He plays ball," or "They live next door." Children focus on external, observable characteristics. In contrast, adolescents are likely to talk about persons' *traits* or *dispositions* that summarize, or perhaps explain, the overt, observable things they do: for example, "She dresses very well," or "He is the athletic type, plays outdoors a lot." Quite often, such characterizations of others are based on inferences about personal traits that may lie behind a number of different instances of observed behavior. In cases like these adolescents may often show their more advanced cognitive abilities by offering more highly qualified, complex descriptions of themselves or others [2]. For example, in Lisa's description of her intelligent friend Anne, she might specifically exclude some potentially unattractive qualities: "She's really smart, but she's not a bookworm."

Finally, adolescents' descriptions of others are more *objective* than the descriptions of younger children [3]. Younger children often characterize people in terms of the activities they share—not a surprising tendency, since childhood friendships are often based on shared activities. However, even when describing close friends, adolescents are more likely than children to speak as though they were detached observers. For example, 16-year-old Deborah described her friend Carrie this way: "She's a very romantic person, likes to read novels about romance, dreams about being serenaded under her window. That's the kind of person she is." This kind of description may be possible because of adolescents' realizations that perspectives other than their own personal one exist and that describing from a neutral perspective makes the description more understandable—or credible—to others.

Role Taking and Perspectivistic Thinking

Understanding others' perspectives is important in most social interaction—and is certainly essential to mature relationships. Unfortunately, understanding others' perspectives on ambiguous social situations is often very complicated indeed. This social task has often been called *role taking*, a term that refers to the ability to infer another person's mental perspective on a social circumstance, usually for the purpose of adjusting one's own interaction with that person to make it more appropriate [4]. The ability to take account of others' thoughts and perspectives on social situations has been called the central element of adolescent cognitive growth; more than anything else, it distinguishes their social reasoning from that of younger children [5].

The development of role-taking abilities was first discussed in detail by Jean Piaget as an outgrowth of his studies of intellectual development. Piaget stimulated children to talk about their relationships with others. He concluded that children's understanding of their social worlds reflected cognitive skills similar to those they might employ to understand the behavior of physical objects [6]. For instance, part of what must be accomplished in cognitive development is gradually overcoming the tendency to center on too few aspects of problems. In childhood several problems of social understanding come from children's centering on their own experiences and perceptions. Piaget uses the term *egocentrism* for this failure to recognize that other people's experiences and perceptions are independent of their own.

A related problem is apparent in children's difficulties with conservation, which we discussed in Chapter 4. Just as children are centered on the height dimension before acquiring conservation of liquid volume, egocentric children are centered on their own points of view, failing to take account of others' viewpoints. Consequently, they tend to confuse their perspectives with others' point of view. Consider Piaget's famous three-mountain task, which is shown in Fig. 5.1 [7]. In this task a child is seated in the unnumbered chair, and a doll is placed in each of the numbered chairs, in sequence. The child is asked to describe how the mountains look from where the doll sits. Piaget found that young children always thought others' view of a model terrain was the same as their own. But with increasing age they recognized that others' views were different, and they improved at guessing what the perspectives were. This perceptual-perspective task shows the young child's egocentrism and how it is gradually overcome with age.

FIG. 5.1 Piaget's three-mountain task

Redrawn from *The origins of intellect: Piaget's theory,* by John L. Phillips Jr. W. H. Freeman and Company. Copyright © 1975.

Adolescents' Concepts of Others

Not only do adolescents seem more attuned to the opinions and reactions of others, they also appear to make more detailed and complex appraisals about the people around them. Take the situation where a person sometimes appears to be helpful and friendly but at other times seems less positive. Would an adolescent be more astute in grasping a discrepancy like that than a younger person? And if so, why?

Eugene Gollin sought answers to these questions by analyzing the descriptions of another person that 10-, 13-, and 16-year-olds provided [1]. The person they all described was an 11-year-old boy who appeared in a movie that Gollin made. In the first scene the boy was doing nothing in particular, but the viewers had an opportunity to become familiar with his appearance. Then four scenes followed showing the boy engaged in either "good" or "bad" actions. In two scenes he was being helpful toward and protective of younger children, but in two others he was being overbearing and destroying property of other children. The film was 3½ minutes long. Half the subjects at each age saw the good scenes first; half saw the bad scenes, then the good ones.

After the film the preadolescent and adolescent boys and girls were asked to "write down what you think of this boy and the things you saw him do." They were to "pretend you are telling someone about him" and were asked to give their opinion of him as well.

Gollin took these descriptions and had adult judges decide whether or not each one of the following characteristics was present in what each subject had written:

1. Does the subject go beyond what the character *did* to ascribe some motive or underlying condition for his action? That is, did the subject say something about *why* the boy did a good or bad action? If so, the judges noted that the subject had made an *inference* about what had been seen in the movie.

2. Does the subject try to explain why the character is sometimes good, sometimes bad? That is, does the subject try to explain the diverse actions portrayed in the movie? If so, the judges noted that the subject had tried to form a *concept* of the character as a person.

Most adolescents tried to explain the actions they saw (inference), while fewer than one-fourth of the preadolescents did. Even fewer 10-year-olds tried to explain the fact that the boy sometimes seemed good, sometimes bad

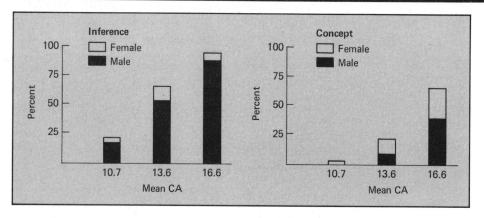

Percentage of subjects whose written statements included inference and concept statements
Redrawn from E. Gollin, Organizational characteristics of social judgment: A developmental investigation, Journal of Personality 26(1958):139–154.

(concept), although more than half of the 16-year-olds spontaneously did so in writing their descriptions. The graphs in the accompanying figure show how closely this pattern is tied to chronological age. They also show that adolescent girls are even more likely than adolescent boys to think about other people in terms of motives and causes for behaviors and the underlying traits that explain diverse actions.

The skills Gollin measured involve some of the intellectual assets that are described as formal-operational abilities. The adolescents who relied on their inferences about underlying motives and causes that explain diverse behaviors might have been reflecting the greater abstractness and complexity of formal thinking. They might also have been recognizing the possibility of realities that one can't see directly, a speculative dimension that the preadolescent subjects in the study may have possessed to a lesser degree. Another possibility is that the adolescent subjects had had more numerous opportunities to learn about the behaviors and motives of others, and their ways of describing the movie character may have simply reflected their greater knowledge. In any case, the kind of change in thinking about others that Gollin's study documents is probably a social skill that adds a dramatic new dimension to adolescents' dealings with others.

REFERENCE

1. E. Gollin, Organizational characteristics of social judgment: A developmental investigation, *Journal of Personality* 26(1958):139–154.

Michael Chandler and Stephen Greenspan recently demonstrated how perspectivistic thinking might work in everyday problem solving [8]. In their study frames from a cartoon sequence portrayed a child losing some money and reacting with great distress. In the last frame a stranger walked up and noticed the distress; the participants were asked to explain what the newcomer thought. The younger participants (preschool and elementary school children) often acted as though the stranger knew what had happened in the early frames of the cartoon sequence, although the task clearly required them to realize that the newcomer did not have this privileged information. In other words, they confused their knowledge of the situation with the newcomer's. From about age 11 on, however, participants clearly seemed aware of the difference between their knowledge of the situation and the newcomer's knowledge. These more cognitively mature preadolescents recognized the newcomer's different perspective and used that knowledge to answer Chandler and Greenspan's questions. In summary, then, one of the necessary accomplishments in the development of social reasoning skills is decentering from one's own perspective and coordinating it with other perspectives.

In the remainder of the chapter we will examine more closely the increasing awareness of discrepancies between the ideal and the real, the increasing abstractness of thought about self and others, and perspective-taking ability. And we will consider how these social cognitive changes affect the task of identity formation.

SOCIAL COGNITIVE DEVELOPMENT DURING ADOLESCENCE

Up to now, we have focused mainly on the difference between adolescents' and children's social cognitive skills. But it is also important to recognize that early adolescence is itself a time of change and transition in social-reasoning abilities. In fact, a number of psychologists today contend that many of the difficulties of adjustment and interpersonal relations that young adolescents experience partly reflect certain incomplete transitions to more mature patterns of social reasoning. In this section we will discuss two of these ideas: David Elkind's contention that a particular, socially significant kind of egocentrism occurs in the transition to formal operations, and Robert Selman's theory of the gradual emergence of mature understanding of self and others during adolescence. These views of adolescent social cognitive change will form the background for a consideration of the role of cognitive change in identity formation taken up later in the chapter.

Elkind:
Adolescent
Egocentrism

In a now-classic article, "Egocentrism in Adolescence," Elkind pointed out that the difficult process of cognitive growth continues in adolescence [9]. Following the general developmental model, he notes that growth occurs in two directions, up and sideways. Most important, Elkind makes the point that adolescents do not simply jump full-blown into the new stage. Instead, like Piaget, he believes that when adolescents move up to a higher stage in the developmental sequence, they start to function in that new stage in highly immature modes.

From a personal standpoint, with the rise of formal operations (see Chapter 4) the teenager can begin to conceive of the self in much more complex terms. During the process of identity formation teenagers have access to a new cognitive stage, a more sophisticated system to process experience. This access contributes to the gains, the growth up.

Upon entering the new stage, however, adolescents often move into a position of egocentrism. This shift may entail behavior that seems even more immature than usual. For example, Elkind has argued that although most adolescents realize that others' perspectives are different from their own, they still make the partial cognitive error of assuming that they themselves are the subject about whom others are thinking. In other words, Elkind believes that there may be a peculiar brand of *adolescent egocentrism* that leads adolescents to believe that they are the focus of everyone's attention, although others' attention is probably directed to a variety of other people or things. Elkind has likened this change to the now-discarded Ptolemaic view that the earth is the center of the universe. In terms of early formal thought the teenager often thinks that he or she is the center of the interpersonal world. If Elkind is right, he has indeed suggested a reasonable explanation for the self-consciousness that seems so pronounced in adolescence.

This phase of egocentrism reaches its peak in junior high school but also continues into middle adolescence for many young persons. It has two very noteworthy characteristics: (1) the personal fable and (2) the imaginary audience.

The personal fable This view comprises a deep-rooted belief in one's own personal uniqueness—the notion that no one else in the world can possibly understand how I really feel. As Elkind notes, the complex beliefs create an aura for adolescents: Only they can suffer with such agonized intensity or experience such exquisite rapture. To retain this image, an adolescent may create a personal fable, a story that one tells oneself (and others) that is not true.

One good example of personal fable is found in the novel *Catcher in the Rye* by J. D. Salinger. In the novel Holden Caulfield, every-person-as-adolescent, describes a classic dialogue about sexual prowess with one of his near friends, "Old Ackley." Holden narrates that he listened silently as Ackley described in monotonous detail how he "made it" with a girl friend last summer. Holden is patient to a point, but he has heard Ackley's story at least a hundred times—only each time it is different. In Elkind's terms

DAVID ELKIND (1931–)

If there is one theme that runs through David Elkind's career, it is his willingness to break with tradition and to promote a broad view of the nature of development. As a graduate student at UCLA he attempted to balance his study between learning theory and classical Freudian psychology. He said that it was "a bit schizophrenic. In the morning I would hear from the learning people how bad the Rorschach was. In the afternoon I was fortunate in having a very good teacher—Bruno Klopfer—for the Rorschach in the clinical program" [1].

This somewhat dialectical education in traditional theories probably convinced him that neither approach was sufficiently broad to suit his world view. As a result, his formal education continued, first as a postdoctoral student at the Austin Riggs Clinic working with Erik Erikson, and a few years later as an assistant in Geneva working for a year with Jean Piaget. Working directly with two giants of developmental psychology was enough to convince him to help establish the new field of cognitive-developmental psychology. As part of that effort he joined a new developmental psychology training program at the University of Rochester in the 1960s. At Rochester he also began a series of research investigations that led to such major new insights as the paradox of the emergence of formal operations during adolescence accompanied by egocentric thinking. He also was heavily involved in translating some of Piaget's rather difficult concepts into understandable ideas. Along this line he did a series of filmed interviews with children at different stages, which still stands today as the clearest example of the patterns of childhood and adolescent concept formation [2].

In the late 1970s he left Rochester to take a professorship at Tufts University in Medford, Massachusetts, and from Tufts he has continued to exert great leadership in theory and application for adolescent development. A prolific writer, he has produced hundreds of journal articles and numerous books. As a sign of his continued independence, he still

this is Ackley's personal fable—an untrue story repeated *ad infinitum* (and *ad nauseam*).

Another common fable concerns the adoption, or I-was-really-an-orphan, story. As teenagers begin to think about themselves from different perspectives, it is not at all unusual for them to become suspicious that their own parents are not their natural parents. Fantasies such as "I was a foundling" are created along with private stories about who their real

David Elkind (1913–)

refuses to seek large-scale funds for research—which he sees too often as a means of promoting traditional and conventional ideas, "writing what other people want." And he still feels strongly that psychology as the study of human behavior must remain broad in its viewpoint—and that it will as long as we focus very carefully on what children and adolescents actually say and do, not on what we think they will say or do.

REFERENCES

1. D. Elkind, Going beyond Piaget, *APA Monitor*, November 1980, p. 4.
2. *What do you think? David Elkind interviews children,* color film (New York: Appleton-Century-Crofts, 1967).

parents are. This story also may include some rather melodramatic circumstances about why they could not be raised by those mythic parents. Such stories are usually told to their closest friends and written about at some length in private diaries. Naturally, during the process of identity formation teenagers will make inquiries, both to themselves and to others, concerning family background. If a teenager finds even one characteristic, whether it be physical (such as hair and eye color, body build, gait) or psychological (such as temperamental traits), that is somewhat different, then such a difference can feed into the adoption fantasy. Or it may take only one story in a newspaper concerning the extremely rare circumstance of newborns being given to the wrong parents by a hospital to fuel the teenage fable.

A popular movie of many years ago, *The Secret Life of Walter Mitty*, is a good example of general fables. In this fictionalized account the main character, normally a quiet and unassuming young man (played by Danny Kaye in the movie), switches into a series of the wildest and most heroic fantasies: a captain of a ship in the throes of a major storm, a rescuer of a damsel in distress, a war hero, and others. Less extreme is 15-year-old Natalie Mitchell's sense of uniqueness in Hannah Green's short story "The Grey Bird" [10]. Vacationing with her family at the seashore, Natalie imagines that she is riding waves and diving beneath the water, free and self-contained as a wild grey bird. The personal fable is one extreme identification of adolescents' abilities to imagine what *might be*—and to notice the discrepancy between what is real and what is possible.

The imaginary audience   The second common feature of adolescent egocentrism involves the growing ability to take the perspective of others. While young adolescents generally recognize that others have different

The life of James Thurber's fictional daydreamer Walter Mitty (portrayed here in a 1940s film by Danny Kaye) was dominated by a series of personal fables that overwhelmed his real identity

Photograph from The Museum of Modern Art/Film Stills Archive perspectives from their own, they often fail to recognize that these perspectives can be focused on any number of different concerns. Because they themselves are increasingly preoccupied with their appearance and abilities, they mistakenly conclude that others are focused on them as well. And since others' perspectives are different from their own, adolescents are never sure how they're being viewed. Consequently, Elkind suggests that adolescents are often playing to an unseen audience in their own minds.

Extremes of self-admiration naturally follow apace, even though, as Elkind says, "a good deal of adolescent boorishness, loudness, and faddish dress is probably provoked . . . by a failure to differentiate between what the young person *believes* to be attractive and what others admire" [11]. For example, it was often felt during the 1970s, when teenage males dressed in tattered jeans and had lengthy, unkempt hairstyles (among other characteristics), that no change would occur until teenage females decided that such appearances were out. Major disapproval from adults not only failed to deter such dress but probably increased it. The teenage boys were not, after all, playing to the adult audience. Similarly, the 1980s fad of Valley Girl talk seems to imply both a preoccupation with the peer group that shares this idiosyncratic vocabulary and speech pattern and self-admiration that in adults would be called snobbery.

Probably the most common imagining during this period is teenagers' self-generated melodrama concerning their own demise: "Imagine how parents and other unfeeling adults will react to news of my death." The ability to play mentally with such fantasies is the heart of formal thought. As an example Elkind cites the classic scene from *Tom Sawyer*, with all its bittersweet and totally adolescent feeling, not to say poignancy. Tom and his friends had run away and presumably drowned. They stealthily crept back into town and began witnessing their own funeral.

> But this memory was too much for the old lady, and she broke entirely down. Tom was snuffling, now, himself—and more in pity of himself than anybody else. He could hear Mary crying and putting in a kindly word for him from time to time. He began to have a nobler opinion of himself than ever before. Still, he was sufficiently touched by his aunt's grief to long to rush out from under the bed and overwhelm her with joy—and the theatrical gorgeousness of the thing appealed strongly to his nature too—but he resisted and lay still. [12]

Another feature of such activities is that the acting is almost always overdone. These performances seem to arise from a conviction that no one has ever really suffered as much, ever been as downcast, as happy, or as tormented. Thus the combination of personal fable and imaginary audience leads the early adolescent to the conclusion that no one else can possibly really understand. Each teenager feels unique and special. Researchers interviewing eighth graders asked the question "What's the most important thing to you?" The unhesitating reply was, "Myself."

Gradually, Elkind believes, the preoccupation with both appearance and behavior subsides. For example, the movie *Breaking Away* presented a believable portrait of a young man at the height of a fantasy as a world-class Italian bike racer. Finally, though, the hero sets aside his "as-if" role and begins the painful process of establishing his own identity. His previously bewildered parents come out of shock. Similarly, one author remembers quite distinctly the audible sigh of relief in the family when at age 16 he gave up a month-long imitation of W. C. Fields. Elkind believes these characteristics of egocentrism are overcome by social experiences that stimulate further maturation of adolescents' cognitive structure. Among these experiences are interpersonal intimacy, in which adolescents learn about the thought and feelings of others and recognize that they are similar to their own. At the same time they see that there are differences between others' preoccupations and concerns and their own. In short, with maturity is acquired both the cognitive ability to see others' concerns as distinct from one's own and the emotional sensitivity to appreciate the feelings of others as well as one's own.

Elkind suggests that we never completely overcome either the fable or the audience, although both are gradually modified for the great majority of adolescents. On the other hand, it is certainly important that those elements be adjusted to conform to reality. Otherwise, there would be little chance to achieve a realistic sense of self—an identity—in adolescence. Neither could there be an improvement in the understanding of others and of social relationships within which identity is sought.

Selman: Levels of Social Cognition

Robert Selman has elaborated Piaget's and Elkind's ideas about social cognitive development to help explain the development of mature understanding of social relationships [13]. He started by asking open-ended questions to children and adolescents. His questions were structured so that there was no single right or wrong answer. Instead, like Piaget, Selman wanted to know *reasons* for social judgment and social decision making. You may understand his approach better by reading the following problem, which he presented to adolescents:

Mike and the Puppy—What Would You Do?

Tom is trying to decide what present to buy his friend Mike, who will be given a surprise birthday party the next day. Tom meets Mike by chance and learns that Mike is extremely upset that his dog, Pepper, has been lost for two weeks. In fact, Mike is so upset that he tells Tom, "I miss Pepper so much I never want to look at another dog again." Tom goes off, only to pass a store with a sale on puppies; one or two are left and these will soon be gone. What should Tom do? What would you do if you were Tom? Why?

Selman was especially interested in answers to the last question—in the reasons children gave for their choices. His next step was to examine the structure of the reasons. As we noted in Chapters 1 and 4, cognitive-developmental psychologists carefully distinguish between content and structure. *Content* refers to the surface-level characteristics of a statement. In the case of Mike and the puppy the content of an answer would be the decision itself: "Yes, I would buy another puppy," or "No, I would not." The content, then, is pretty much a factual description of what the person said. *Structure,* on the other hand, refers to the complexity of reasoning. The investigator has to listen carefully in order to classify the person's reasons according to levels of reasoning, from the simple to the complex. Structure, then, refers to the organized system of thought the person uses to reason about a problem. In Selman's research, answers were analyzed to see whether the children recognized that the two individuals in each story were aware of each other's perspectives and also for the probable effects of this awareness on their interaction. For example, knowing that Tom realizes that Mike is not ready to accept another puppy in place of the lost one is an indication of relatively complex reasoning. Remember that the levels Selman describes refer to the *structure*—the complexity—of thinking about social problems, not the *content*.

Levels of interpersonal understanding   Selman tried to establish a set of categories of responses based on the reasons children and adolescents gave for their solutions to interpersonal problems like "Mike and the Puppy." At each level he found evidence that two aspects of social reasoning had changed: (1) concepts of persons and (2) concepts of relations between persons. The levels are outlined in Table 5.1. If children said, "I'd get him the puppy—'cause *I* like dogs," Selman considered the structure of their thought to be simple, concrete, and *egocentric*. Compare that response with that of a child who says, "Well, I'm not sure. A new puppy might make Mike feel sad at first because he'd be reminded of the one he lost, but then he might feel better about it when he has the fun of playing with a new puppy. So I think I'll tell him that and give him a new puppy." (Lest you view this situation as somewhat juvenile, a recent episode on a major, award-winning, weekly television series, "The Lou Grant Show," presented exactly the same dilemma. The newspaper owner, Mrs. Pynchon, was a victim of dognappers. Lou Grant thought about getting her a new puppy. His reasoning at first was, unfortunately, at a simple level, so he ended up caring for the new puppy until Mrs. Pynchon was ready.)

During the preadolescent years, awareness of others' perspectives enters into increasingly complex social reasoning [14]. The first level of complexity is recognizing that individuals have different perspectives—that they are *subjective*. Unlike more mature children, a preadolescent at the subjective level fails to realize that those perspectives affect one another in

TABLE 5.1 Selman's levels of interpersonal understanding

Level	Concept of persons	Concept of relations
0: egocentric perspective taking (under 6 years)	Undifferentiated: confuses internal (feelings, intentions) with external (appearance, actions) characteristics of others	Egocentric: fails to recognize that self and others have different feelings and thoughts as well as external physical characteristics
1: subjective perspective taking (ages 5–9)	Differentiated: distinguishes feelings and intentions from actions and appearances	Subjective: recognizes that others may feel and think differently than self—that everyone is subjective but has limited conceptions of how these different persons may affect each other (e.g., gifts make people happy, regardless of how appropriate they are)
2: self-reflective or reciprocal perspective taking (ages 7–12)	Second-person: can reflect on own thoughts and realizes that others can do so as well (cf. recursive thought); realizes appearances may be deceptive about true feelings	Reciprocal: puts self in others' shoes *and* realizes others may do same; thus thoughts and feelings, not merely actions, become basis for interactions; however, the two subjective perspectives are not assumed to be influencing each other
3: Mutual perspective taking (ages 10–15)	Third-person: knows that self and others act *and* reflect on effects of their action on themselves; recognizes own immediate subjective perspective and also realizes that it fits into own more general attitudes and values	Mutual: can imagine another person's perspective on oneself and one's actions, coordinates other's inferred view with own view (i.e., sees self as others see one); thus comes to view relationships as ongoing mutual sharing of social satisfaction or understanding
4: In-depth and societal-symbolic perspective taking (ages 12–adult)	In-depth: recognizes that persons are unique, complex combinations of their own histories; furthermore, realizes that persons may not *always* understand their own motivations (i.e., that there may be unconscious psychological processes)	Societal-symbolic: individuals may form perspectives on each other at different levels, from shared superficial information or interests to common values or appreciation of very abstract moral, legal, or social notions

interactions. In the problem of Tom and Mike, Paul (age 9) recognized Mike's and Tom's different perspectives, but he did not appreciate that Mike's perspective might be affected by Tom's intentions in buying him a new puppy. His answer reflects this attitude: "If [Mike] says he doesn't want a dog, then he doesn't. He'll be angry [if Tom gives him a puppy]."

Gradually, adolescents come to recognize that persons are *self-reflective*. They recognize a fairly elaborate possibility: that Tom knows that Mike's perspective may be affected by his inferences about Tom's good intentions in buying him a new dog. Their comments on the dilemmas indicate that they realize that each of the two characters can base his actions on (1) inferences about the other's perspectives and (2) the knowledge that the other person is simultaneously making inferences about their perspectives. In 11-year-old Karen's words: "Mike says he doesn't want one now. But he'll change his mind later on. If I were in his place, I'd feel like he does; but I'd feel different later on."

Finally, Selman believes adolescents acquire the skill to recognize that two people can consider their interaction objectively (the *mutual level*). They are both aware of the simultaneous perspective taking of each other and the possible effects of this mutual activity. Selman sees evidence of this skill in the following comment made by Steve, age 15: "Mike will understand what Tom was trying to do, and even if he doesn't like the dog, he'll appreciate that Tom thought he would when he bought it." Steve imagines

Social relations often involve complex inferences about the experiences, feelings, and attitudes of others
Photograph by O'Neil/Editorial Photocolor Archives

Mike thinking that Tom was thinking about him and his perspective. Such complex reasoning is one of the underlying tasks in many instances of social reasoning, and its development is a major achievement in social cognitive growth.

Selman's approach to the development of social perspective taking focuses on one type of social experience in which this skill might be brought to play—namely, understanding the actions of others. It is not clear whether children's responses in these hypothetical dilemmas involving two other individuals also give us a full picture of what must take place when the adolescents themselves are the interactors. One possible difficulty is that the adolescent's own perspective might intrude more in his or her efforts to recognize and appreciate the interactive nature of both perspectives. However, Selman believes that adolescents' responses to his dilemmas reflect developing *concepts* of social interactions that should affect their own behavior as well as their understanding of others' behavior. We will see how Selman's view pertains to two important aspects of adolescents' social lives—family and peers—in Chapters 7 and 8.

One way to understand Selman's distinctions is to practice with everyday issues. You might try the example of birthday presents to illustrate stage reasoning for yourself. Simply list the most personally meaningful gifts you have received in the past year. This list may give you a clue about the social cognitive level of the senders. How many gifts show special concern for your interests or needs? On the other hand, how many presents are always the same, year after year, perhaps indicating that the senders still see you as you were five, ten, or twenty years ago? How many presents do you hide and have to bring out when some relatives visit? Or do you follow a safer path and publicize carefully what you want? After you have completed the exercise of assessing the role-taking ability of those who have selected presents for you, try it the other way. Reexamine some of the gifts you have selected for others. How many of those truly represented an attempt by you to place yourself in the others' shoes?

Interpersonal understanding: The process of change   At first glance the changes Selman documents may seem somewhat automatic. There are roughly five levels, starting with level 0, that describe social functioning from birth through adolescence. So do we simply find out the person's age, look on the chart, and then know what to expect? Does interpersonal reasoning simply unfold? Selman's work indicates that such is not the case. As was true for development on Piaget's cognitive tasks, development of complex interpersonal functioning occurs as a result of appropriate interaction with other persons. Without appropriate experience and reflection in social interaction, the child will not automatically proceed from one stage to the next. In fact, Selman has shown that children who have experienced inadequate interpersonal relations—for example, those whose environments were emotionally impoverished—function at lower levels of social cognition than do same-age children who were not emotionally impaired.

In one study 24 emotionally disturbed boys between the ages of 7 and 12 were compared with 24 relatively well-functioning peers [15]. Both groups were similar on Piaget's tests of logical and physical reasoning. The emotionally disturbed group, however, was at a lower level across the board on tests of social cognition. In other words, in the disturbed group, functioning was uneven: It was age-appropriate in general cognitive tasks but age-inappropriate in interpersonal relations. For example, a well-functioning 11-year-old usually is capable of simultaneous and mutual role taking (stage 3). He could see personal problems from his view, a friend's view, *and* an objective third party's view. An 11-year-old with emotional problems would most likely function at a lower stage, perhaps understanding problems only from his own viewpoint. This result is sometimes noted, as we have pointed out, as an example of *asynchrony*. Development in one area does not guarantee—nor should we so assume—development in other areas.

We should also not assume that progress through Selman's levels occurs precisely at the ages he lists. As the age norms in Table 5.2 show, there is age overlap across the levels. Thus not everyone automatically jumps up a level exactly on his or her birthday. For example, at the extremes of the age groups shown in Table 5.2, all 4-year-olds are either in level 0 or 1, and all 24-year-olds are in level 4. The most common (modal) level for 10-year-olds is level 2, and for 16-year-olds it is level 3. Note also that within each age grouping individuals usually fall either one level below or one level above the modal level. Thus growth seems to follow a regular sequence.

Selman also examined longitudinal data to see whether the same indi-

Table 5.2 Levels of interpersonal relations: Age norms

Age, years	Selman level				
	0	1	2	3	4
4 (N = 10)	8	2			
8 (N = 10)		4	5	1	
10 (N = 24)		4	18	2	
13 (N = 14)		1	7	5	1
16 (N = 14)			3	8	3
24 (N = 14)					14

From R. Selman, *The development of interpersonal understanding* (New York: Academic Press, 1980), pp. 42–43.

viduals over time show similar growth trends. With a sample of 10 persons interviewed five times over 3 years, he found that all the participants moved from level 2 at 10 years to level 4 at 22 years of age. There were no reversals of the sequence; each person moved from one level to the next higher level in the sequence.

One final point: Thus far, Selman has found that within age groups both males and females tend to function at approximately the same level of interpersonal relations. In a sample of 46 males and 46 females grouped into four age ranges, there were no differences in interpersonal maturity scores (IMS) within each age group. The subgroups of 15–18-year-old boys and girls (N = 22) were both clustered at level 3. In fact, most adolescents seem to reason about others and interpersonal relationships primarily at levels 3 and 4.

Interpersonal understanding and everyday behavior   As Selman's work continues, we will be able to document much more clearly the points during adolescence where interpersonal growth may be halted or stalled. Selman himself has already documented a number of cases of young adolescents undergoing treatment for behavior problems. For example, he reports the case of Tommy, age 14, a socially deprived youngster, abused by his parents. In early adolescence Tommy was very shy and was isolated from other members of his class in school. When he did make overtures, he tended to do so at a very low level of social development. In fact, he primarily sought out younger children, with whom he interacted mostly by sharing toys and games. He was awkward and ineffective in attempting to enter the activities of groups of young people his own age. Neither could he respond effectively when 14-year-olds made overtures to him. In Tommy's case Selman's levels of social cognitive development gave a perspective on his difficulties, upon which an effective mode of treatment could be built. Since it was possible to say how Tommy's own interpersonal cognitive skills were deficient, it was also possible to specify ways in which they might be improved.

By contrast, Selman tells about Raymond, age 11, who was a developmentally advanced youngster. At 11 he seemed a loner, friendless in the school setting. But when he was interviewed, it was discovered that his own interpersonal cognitive skills were advanced beyond those of other preadolescents in his age group. He felt his classmates were babyish, and had developed friendships with older adolescents outside school from which he derived a great deal of satisfaction. With Selman's approach it was possible to see that Raymond was out of phase with other 11-year-olds. Fortunately, he had found a satisfactory way of interacting with others who were at the same level of development he was.

It is clear that very few formal or informal educational experiences provide the necessary developmental match and mismatch to stimulate growth to higher stages. Thus a majority of adolescents probably remain at the early phases of symbolic role taking (abstract). Adolescents are clearly capable of developing and employing genuine empathy for self and others, understanding the subjective nature of experience, viewing social problems from a variety of perspectives, including an objective third party—in short, all aspects of advanced level 4 functioning. In general, however, they do not function at that level.

Research studies indicate that by far the majority of teenagers in secondary school remain at a level of significant social conformity. Similarly, studies of high school pupils (detailed in Chapter 12) indicate that there has been almost no change in the level of functioning in the past thirty years. The classic Coleman study in the 1950s and the Goodlad study in 1980, both discussed in Chapter 12, reached the same conclusion. Interpersonal relations in secondary schools are still ruled by a leading crowd that determines the social values. Teenagers are essentially functioning at the level of social conformity where good looks, clothes, cars, and athletics determine the quality of interpersonal relations. And the power of social conformity is strong enough to prevent the development of greater interpersonal independence—primarily the ability to view such situations from an objective, third-party perspective.

The prejudice against out-groups, nonconformists, or pupils from different backgrounds (social, religious, ethnic, or special education differences) partly reflects the lack of interpersonal development during secondary school. We do not yet know whether the same conclusion holds for college students. Some studies seem to indicate, however, that interpersonal growth is, in effect, random (see Chapter 12). In one instance researchers found that the majority of students they studied, even in a selective college, formed social groups designed to confirm their somewhat narrow-minded social values, as though to protect themselves against a liberating education.

We will concentrate on the educational issue later in the chapter. For now, we simply emphasize that from a developmental view the growth of complex interpersonal functioning does not always develop automatically. Therefore without deliberate attention to this area during adolescence, educators may be guilty of benign neglect and may be missing an opportunity for important interpersonal development.

Selman believes that social perspective taking is the most important ingredient in understanding interpersonal relations. Perspective taking is necessary for a person to realize that a relationship is not something concrete, nor can it exist only in the view of one person. A relationship is an abstraction, a special kind of interaction between two people, and both have to understand it as an interactive process. A person thus needs to reason about self and about the other person in the pair. The development of formal thought is essential to such complex reasoning.

SPECIAL TOPIC
Ego Development and Self-Concept: The Same Side of the Coin?

Past traditions in psychological research have tended to regard developmental stage and self-concept as separate worlds. Developmental theorists view the process of growth as a sequence of milestones, of qualitative changes (e.g., the egg-caterpillar-butterfly analogy). Self-concept theory, on the other hand, is rooted in existential or phenomenological psychology. The theory of self-concept seems incompatible with developmental theory since it is based on the propositions that each person is unique and that individual differences are so strong that psychology can meaningfully study only individuals one at a time, or idiographically. In other words, each person makes meaning from his or her experience in absolutely unique systems; the job of the psychologist is to aid that single individual in understanding all of the special components of his or her personality. Such assumptions contrast with stage theory, which is based on the ideas that there are regularities across individuals and that the individuals clustered at a particular stage tend to process experience in terms of similar thought structures.

Recently, a study was conducted to investigate the possible relationships between stage theory and self-concept theory. The idea was to assess, for early, middle, and late adolescents, both their stages of development and their self-concepts, then to examine linkages if any. Charlotte Rogers conducted the study with three groups of young women: 30 junior high students, 30 high school students, and 30 college juniors [1]. The sample was controlled for social and economic class. She used Loevinger's test for the estimate of ego stage. For self-concept she used the Q-sort technique. This method enabled each person to decide how she wished to describe herself by arranging individual descriptive statements into piles or clusters of attributes made up by mental health experts. Each person completed two *sorts*: (1) how I see myself and (2) my ideal self. The discrepancy between the actual self and the ideal self is usually an index of a positive or a negative self-concept, an index that is unique to each individual.

Rogers took this process one step further. Instead of presenting her students with the Q-sort adjectives from the standard list, she asked them to write out their own self-descriptions—for example, "List eighteen sentences which describe yourself, both positive and negative." In this way, through two sorts of Q-techniques, she had a set of unique idiographic descriptions of each person's self and ideal self, in accord with phenomenological theory. Both the Loevinger test answers and the Q-sort answers were then rated by expert judges to assess the level of complexity of reasoning, using Loevinger's scoring manual.

Were the students employing the same method or level of reasoning on both instruments? The results indicated quite clearly that they were. For example, the junior high girls clustered at Loevingers I–3 stage (conformist), with high levels of social desirability, a somewhat simple and banal system of characterizing one's inner life, a heavy emphasis on external characteristics, and a narrow definition of right and wrong. On the self-concept test their answers were somewhat similar. They were essentially processing the two tests through the same cognitive system for personal and interpersonal understanding. Their self-concepts were positive if they were in with the crowd, had nice clothes and friends, and so forth. The structural content of both positive and negative self-concepts was at the same level as the stage of ego development. Thus a poor self-concept at the junior high stage mostly reflected unhappiness with not being in, with having the wrong clothes, with having the wrong group of friends or no friends at all—that is, it had the same thought properties as positive self-concept, but with opposite surface content.

At the other end of her sample, the college juniors, a similar pattern was confirmed. The women (N = 14) who were rated at high levels of ego stage (I–4/5 and higher) used similarly complex thought structures to describe their self-concepts. The positive self-concepts used phrases like "I set difficult goals for myself, but generally achieve them," "The feelings, needs, aspirations and goals of my friends are important to me," and "I don't think I'm very pretty but sometimes, I'm self deceptive." Negative self-concepts were similarly complex in thought structure: "I hardly ever really feel satisfied with my school work or personal life," and "I find myself envying people who are assertive and self confident. It also leaves me feeling resentful."

These results seem to indicate that developmental stage and self-concept are not separate aspects of individual development. Self-concepts at successive age periods appear to be elaborations of ego development stages. In other words, we need not view self-concept merely as a positive versus a negative dimension. Rather, we can view the positive-negative aspect of self-concept within each stage of personal development. From Rogers's findings we can say that the structure of a healthy self-concept is clearly different for women at different stages of ego development, even though the positive or negative valence associated with them may be consistent from one stage to the next. There is every reason to believe the same findings would hold for men.

Reference

1. C. P. Rogers, An examination of the relationship between ego development and self esteem (Ph.D. thesis, University of Minnesota, 1980).

UNDERSTANDING OF THE EVERYDAY WORLD

The processes of perceiving and evaluating others are clearly fundamental to social reasoning. In addition, other aspects of social understanding and reasoning reflect many of the same developmental principles that we discussed in the earlier sections of this chapter. For example, adolescents develop in their understanding of larger social categories, like groups and societies, and the relations within them. In this section we will discuss three areas of social understanding in which adolescent thought shows important changes: reasoning about political concepts, understanding of problem behavior, and problem solving in general.

Political Concepts   One area in which developing social cognitive capabilities are manifested is that of concepts of society and societal entities like *community* and *law*. These subjects are very difficult to investigate, because adolescents simply know more than children about the particulars of government organization and the mundane meaning of words like *community* and *law*. However, Joseph Adelson partly overcame this difficulty by an ingenious method of interviewing children and adolescents about a hypothetical social organization [16]. He first explained that a group of people had inhabited a distant island; the group had no laws, rules, or procedures, and it was attempting to establish a new community from the ground up. The participants were asked a series of questions about what would be involved.

The results of these interviews indicate that there is a general shift between the ages of 13 and 15 in the complexity of reasoning and thinking about such matters. Before this age children's political and social concepts tend to be concrete, absolutistic, and authoritarian. They are true concrete-operational thinkers, focusing on the particular and the immediate rather than the inclusive and extensive. For example, preadolescents talk about laws in terms of effects on particular persons (vaccinations are required to "keep little children from getting sick"), while adolescents tend to see effects on large groups, even the whole society (vaccination against disease serves to protect the health of the community). Similarly, preadolescents think of government in personalistic terms—as the individuals who administer or represent it, like the president, mayor, police chief, or simply "them." More mature views are more abstract and inclusive; a sense of community emerges, in which social institutions, norms, and principles are the salient elements. The similarities between this shift and the transition from concrete-operational to formal-operational thinking are apparent [17].

In addition, preadolescents seem unable to grasp certain abstract ideas that are fundamental to the more mature thought of the adolescent political or moral thinker. For example, adolescents usually understand the idea of *rights*, including the idea that individuals might have legitimate wishes and needs that would go contrary to social norms or the demands of the state. Thus older adolescents, but not younger ones, were concerned that a law requiring vaccination might interfere with the rights of persons whose religious principles forbade it. A second cognitive difficulty for preadolescents is the notion that laws and institutions can be changed at the behest of the people they serve. They tend to think such instrumentalities are rigid, fixed, and immutable; they behave as though a law, once it has been made, cannot be changed. Furthermore, they are willing to be rather Draconian in enforcing laws, even unsatisfactory ones. Asked about an unpopular law prohibiting cigarette smoking, 9- and 11-year-olds were willing to use martial force to see that citizens did not use tobacco! In contrast, 15- and 18-year-olds saw the possibility and need for legislative action to change the law [18].

It appears that the political concepts of preadolescents are often contrary to the rather complex theoretical underpinnings of a political system like democracy. Adelson notes, for instance, that preadolescents are more likely to favor one-man rule over representative or direct democracy [19]. The decline in authoritarianism and the increasing abstractness of political reasoning in the early adolescent years is a dramatic development. Its major benefit is to make adolescents capable of appreciating the relativism involved in a democratic community.

Concepts of Deviance and Disorder

Increasingly complex thinking skills also affect children's notions of deviance and the possibility of personal maladjustment. As in their descriptions of others, younger children typically fail to go beyond the immediate details of another person's behavior to test it against behavioral norms and the needs and rights of others and, if necessary, to make inferences about the other person's motivations for action. These superficial social perceptions are noticeable when children are asked to describe others they consider different or to explain the behavior of hypothetical characters who are excessively aggressive or suspicious.

In a study by John Coie and Bruce Pennington grade school children were found to focus on the immediate consequences of others' actions and whether or not they violated established rules [20]. That is, they did not consider the actions in terms of a larger societal context. Teenagers, though, were likely to consider whether actions fit in with typical behavior by members of the social group. Furthermore, adolescents' responses clearly required more complicated role taking than younger children showed. For example, adolescents tended to talk in terms of psychological disorder or instability. These notions presuppose the recognition that others' different perspectives may lie outside the normal range of perceptions of reality—a judgment that involves relatively complex reasoning.

Although the behaviors the children were asked to explain—aggression, allegations that other persons are watching you—are perfectly under-standable and explainable in some situations, they were not warranted by the situations in the stories used by the researchers. Teenagers recognized that the behavior was inappropriate. They implicitly acknowledged that different situations demand different behaviors and thus were obliged to attribute the behavior of the story characters to something idiosyncratic to them rather than to the situation. In effect, they understood that persons sometimes "fail to match up to a social criterion for psychological stability" [21]. Grade school children tended to believe that the suspicious characters were the real victims of threat or some other straightforward circumstance, even though there was no apparent justification for this belief in the story.

Both the political concepts and the deviance/disorder studies are sus-ceptible to the charge that the age differences may reflect verbal sophistica-tion rather than cognitive change. However, the observed changes so closely parallel developing cognitive capabilities in other domains that it is reasonable to hypothesize that some fundamental transformations occur in reasoning and thinking about these social problems.

Social Problem Solving

Children also change in their awareness that alternatives exist in situa-tions. Probably because of the rigidity of immature thinking, individuals often think in terms of only one outcome or an otherwise limited number of outcomes for a given set of circumstances. It is possible that such indi-viduals may become prematurely frustrated by the failure of a single option in a situation, when trying alternative responses might result in a more successful outcome.

This point of view has been argued and investigated by George Spivack, Jerome Platt, and Myrna Shure [22]. They focused on adolescents' awareness of alternatives and its relationship to their actual social adjust-ment. Awareness of alternatives was assessed by asking participants to respond to a series of hypothetical stories or incidents. For example, in one study two groups of adolescents were compared. In the first group were 33 adolescents who were patients at a private psychiatric hospital. They had gone into the hospital for what was called "adjustment reactions to adoles-cence." In the second group were high school sophomores who were similar to the hospitalized group in age, race, and social and economic background. Both groups were tested on a number of problem-solving skills: ability to identify problem situations, ability to think of different alternative solutions to problems, awareness of the importance of consider-ing the causes of an event, awareness of consequences, and ability to reason from cause to consequence (means-ends thinking). The major dif-ferences between the adolescents who were having adjustment problems and the comparison group of high school students came from the abilities required for solving problems: generating alternative solutions, means-end thinking, and role-taking skills. The two groups were not different in recognizing problem situations or being aware that consequences are important to consider and that causes can and should be identified. Thus their difficulty was not in recognizing problems but in finding ways of solving them.

This comparison does not mean, of course, that there is a causal relationship between the contrasting social cognitive skills and the personality adjustment differences in these two groups. However, the relationship indicates that young people who are distressed and showing poor adjustment may also lack social cognitive skills that might be helpful in their reaching a more satisfactory sense of themselves.

Do social cognitive skills that develop in adolescence—although they may vary from person to person at any given age—underlie behavioral skills that make possible effective interactions in social relationships? Although relatively few researchers have investigated social reasoning and social behavior in the same studies, those who have done so report links between them [23]. For example, adolescents under treatment for personality adjustment problems performed more poorly on a range of social problem-solving tasks than a comparable group of adolescents who had not manifested these adjustment problems [24]. Similarly, Selman found that 7- to 12-year-old boys who had learning and peer relationship problems showed poorer social perspective-taking skills than a comparison group of better-adjusted boys [25].

Adolescents' view of community and social cooperation are more sophisticated than those of children
Photograph by Charles Gatewood

More dramatic, perhaps, is the finding that poor social cognitive abilities appear to characterize children and adolescents who behave antisocially. In experimental studies of cheating, for example, it was found that cheating is more likely if a child functions at a lower level of social cognitive development. The higher the level, the less is the likelihood of cheating. Furthermore, delinquents are often lower in role-taking skills than comparable groups of nondelinquent youngsters, as we will show in greater detail in Chapter 10.

Recently, psychologist Martin Ford has shown a connection between social cognitive skills and social competence in groups of ninth and twelfth graders [26]. Ford first assessed abilities of the adolescents in nine social cognitive tasks, including means-end thinking, awareness of consequences of actions, empathy, and ability to set and make plans to reach goals. He then compared overall performance on the nine tasks with ratings of each participant's general competence in six hypothetical social situations. The scale on which the ratings were made was anchored at one end with the words "very competent, smooth, poised" and at the other end by "ineffective, unresponsive, inappropriate emotions or behavior." Each participant was rated by teachers, peers, and an adult interviewer. The participant also gave a self-rating. After combining these ratings, Ford found that the social cognitive measures were a good basis for predicting accurately adolescents' standings on the social competence ratings.

In short, social cognitive abilities may often be an important foundation for social actions. However, we are only beginning to understand the nature of the relationship and how and under what conditions it is important.

SOCIAL REASONING AND IDENTITY

One area in which social reasoning skills may be especially important is in identity formation, the process we identified in Chapter 2 as the basic task of adolescence. In Erikson's view identity achievement in adolescence involves integrating past conceptions of self with present and future expectations. Erikson thinks of identity as a special emotional sense about the self (ego), a sense of well-being and of coherence of past, present, and future. Erikson's idea has been elaborated by Jane Loevinger, a psychologist who has devoted her research to understanding how the sense of self develops [27]. Let's briefly consider Loevinger's view, which she labels *ego development*.

Loevinger's Levels of Ego Development

Loevinger considers the self—identity—to mean the way in which a person has organized, or has found coherence in, the diverse experiences and feelings he or she has encountered. She believes that an important aspect of achieving identity is the cognitive structure that a person is capable of bringing to thoughts about the self. And she has suggested a sequence of stages of ego development that show how identity might emerge as social reasoning becomes more abstract, flexible, and speculative.

Following the cognitive-developmental tradition, Loevinger based her scheme on literally thousands of statements subjects made in response to her open-ended questions. She asked subjects to finish a series of incomplete sentences, eventually thirty-six items. In the tradition of semiprojective assessment she wanted to get at a person's private thoughts about the self and how they thought about other persons. Sentence stems included phrases like the following:

- When I think about my mother, . . .

- If I can't get what I want, . . .

- When I'm criticized, . . .

- When they avoided me, . . .

- When a child won't join in group activities, . . .

She then categorized the answers according to their level of structural complexity. In short, she was applying a general strategy of developmental psychologists by assessing the complexity of the thinking and reasoning behind the content of statements, rather than the content itself. For example, one person might respond to the item about mother by saying "she's nice." This response would be assessed as a rather concrete and simple level of reasoning. An answer such as "I feel sad to realize she never had the opportunities for college which I have" would be assessed as a more complex level of reasoning.

After over a decade of gathering responses from people of different ages and backgrounds, Loevinger looked for similar cognitive structures in the responses. She found that they could be classified into six levels, with three transition stages. Table 5.3 presents the descriptions for her first two domains, which she labeled "character development" and "interpersonal style."

Do Stages of Ego/Self-Development Make a Difference?

There is a rather consistent relation between a person's stage on Loevinger's tests and how that person behaves, although the connection is not exact. There is always some element of unpredictability in persons, as well as some slippage in the measuring instrument, so we will not find perfect correlations. On the other hand, findings from a variety of studies indicate both an empirical and a logical relation between ego level and a person's performance.

TABLE 5.3 Loevinger's stages of ego/self-development and interpersonal relations

Stage	Code	Character development	Interpersonal style
Presocial			Autistic
Symbiotic	I–1		Symbiotic
Impulsive	I–2	Impulsive, fear of retaliation	Receiving, dependent, exploitative
Self-protective	Δ	Fear of being caught, externalizing blame, opportunistic	Wary, manipulative, exploitative
Conformist	I–3	Conformity to external rules, shame, guilt for breaking rules	Belonging, superficial niceness
Conscientious-conformist	I–3/4	Differentiation of norms, goals	Aware of self in relation to group, helping
Conscientious	I–4	Self-evaluated standards, self-criticism, guilt for consequences, long-term goals and ideals	Intensive, responsible, mutual, concern for communication
Individualistic	I–4/5	*Add:* Respect for individuality	*Add:* Dependence perceived as an emotional problem, separate from physical or financial dependence
Autonomous	I–5	*Add:* Coping with conflicting inner needs, toleration	*Add:* Respect for autonomy, interdependence
Integrated	I–6	*Add:* Reconciling inner conflicts, renunciation of unattainable	*Add:* Cherishing of individuality

Adapted from Jane Loevinger, *Ego development* (San Francisco: Jossey-Bass, Inc. 1976), pp. 24–25. Reprinted by permission.

Note: ''*Add*'' means in addition to the description applying to the previous level.

With samples of junior high school to college students, there were consistent and predictable outcomes between stage and behavior. Teenagers rated at I–2 on Loevinger's tests manifested marked antisocial/delinquent behaviors. Teenagers at I–3 demonstrated significant social conformity in the eyes of their peers and in their school performance. College students rated at delta (between I–2 and I–3) were highly likely to become discipline problems, while none of the students at the I–4/5 level were placed on disciplinary probation. These studies, summarized by Ralph Mosher, indicate that important connections exist between behavior and the qualities of self described in Loevinger's stages [28]. In addition, several studies demonstrate relationships among adolescents' cognitive level, moral judgments, and ego development [29]. In the accompanying special topic the relation between stage and actual interaction between mothers and their children makes clear the substance beneath Loevinger's ideas about self and ego stage.

The general range of ego development stages for adolescents is presented in Table 5.4. In general, the great majority—80–85%—of all teenagers fall into these categories. Thus if you work with teenagers, the table gives you at least some general guidelines about initial expectations.

The study by Charlotte Rogers described in the special topic on pages 154–155 confirmed that there is a strong relationship between ego stage and self-concept. This result does not mean, however, that early adolescents all have poor self-concepts or that older adolescents have positive ones. A teenager can have a positive or negative self-concept at any stage. The structural content of the self-concept, however, will be highly reflective of the individual's stage of ego development. For this reason we have continually referred to ego development and self-development as virtually the same processes. When we apply this stage theory to interpersonal relations, we are attempting to show the connections between the work of Selman and Loevinger.

Now we will shift from theory to practice—school and community programs to stimulate interpersonal ego/self-development.

TABLE 5.4 Ego/self stage of development (Loevinger)

Age group	Predominant stage
Early adolescence, ages 12–15	Delta
	I–3
	I–3/4
Middle adolescence, ages 15–18	I–3
	I–3/4
	I–4
Late adolescence, ages 18–21	I–3/4
	I–4
	I–4/5

SPECIAL TOPIC
Ego/Self-Development and Interpersonal Relations: Young Mothers and Their Babies

As part of a large-scale investigation of patterns of mothering directed by Byron Egeland and Alan Sroufe of the University of Minnesota, Patricia Bielke studied the relation between the stage of ego development of young mothers and their interactions with their babies [1]. The purpose of the study was to identify possible factors and predictors of potential child abuse. In other words, were there any particular characteristics of these young mothers that might predispose them to inflict harmful physical punishments on the children?

The sample included over 140 women. The majority (60%) were on welfare, were white (81%), and were unwed (62%) at the time of delivery. Many of the mothers were in middle adolescence, with the average age of the entire sample being 21. Thus the sample provided a picture of patterns of mothering in a relatively young group of mothers (mostly between 17 and 24) with their first child. The subjects all took the Loevinger test, which was scored and rated "blind" by experts. Then their effectiveness as mothers was rated through a highly complex procedure that involved both home visits and videotapes of their interactions with their babies. The mothers were later debriefed, but at the time of the actual observations they did not know of the videotaping. Secrecy was maintained to ensure, as far as possible, that the mothers would not fake or put on a good show for the observer but, rather, would give natural and spontaneous responses to the needs of their children.

The results indicated that there were consistently positive relationships between ego level and effective parenting. Mothers at higher stages were more sensitive, more cooperative, and more flexible in their responses to the demands of the child. The actual correlations were modest but always consistent and positive: (+0.25, +0.24) at 6 months and (+0.34, +0.34) at 12 months.*

To give you a sense of what this result means, we present two paragraphs below taken from the actual observation guide; they describe

---

* The possible size of the correlation was reduced because of the restricted range of ego level scores. Of the 147 women, 104 were rated at I–3 and I–3/4, the conformist and transition stages. An analysis of variance technique confirmed the positive relationships between ego level and effective mothering ($F = 4.92$ at 6 months and $F = 4.11$ at 12 months). For details, see Bielke's report.

an extremely sensitive pattern of mothering and an extremely neglectful pattern:

Highly Sensitive   This mother is exquisitely attuned to B's signals, and responds to them promptly and appropriately. She is able to see things from B's point of view; her perceptions of his signals and communications are not distorted by her own needs and defenses. She "reads" B's signals and communications skillfully, and knows what the meaning is of even his subtle, minimal, and understated cues. She nearly always gives B what he indicates that he wants, although perhaps not invariably so. When she feels that it is best not to comply with his demands—for example, when he is too excited, over-imperious, or wants something he should not have—she is tactful in acknowledging his communication and in offering an acceptable alternative. She has "well-rounded" interactions with B, so that the transaction is smoothly completed and both she and B feel satisfied. Finally, she makes her responses temporally contingent upon B's signals and communications.

Highly Insensitive   The extremely insensitive mother seems geared almost exclusively to her own wishes, moods, and activity. That is, M's interventions and initiations of interaction are prompted or shaped largely by signals within herself; if they mesh with B's signals, this is often no more than coincidence. This is not to say that M never responds to B's signals; for sometimes she does if the signals are intense enough, prolonged enough or often enough repeated. The delay in response is in itself insensitive. Furthermore, since there is usually a disparity between M's own wishes and activity and B's signals, M who is geared largely to her own signals routinely ignores or distorts the meaning of B's behavior. Thus, when M responds to B's signals, her response is characteristically inappropriate in kind or fragmented and incomplete. [2]

The findings of the study indicated that 70% of the lower-stage mothers were rated as either mildly or severely neglectful. The ratings were exactly reversed for the higher-stage mothers—70% of them were rated as attentive and *not* neglectful. Also, the correlations indicated that the lower-stage mothers deteriorated in their mothering between 6 and 12 months. But consider that as babies grow and develop, there are, as we all know, dramatic changes, especially between 6 months and 1 year. The individuality of each child emerges. They are more active and more responsive, on the one hand, and they require more complex mothering, on the other. Their needs for interaction are greater. In everyday language, the task of caring for a child who is 12 months of age is more complicated than it is for a newborn. It calls for a greater ability, especially in terms of social cognition, to be able to read what the baby wants and legitimately needs. It is during this time that the baby ceases to be a doll to play with and becomes a human with whom interaction

(Continued)

SPECIAL TOPIC (Continued)

*Consistently positive relation-
ships exist between young
mothers' ego level and their interactions with their babies*
Photograph from Wide World Photo

is necessary in order to stimulate growth. Thus, and quite unfortunately, the direction of functioning of the lower-stage mothers was headed the wrong way. They gave signs of increasing incompetence in their roles as caretakers.

From the standpoint of social cognitive development, such a pessimistic result is at least understandable. At the less complex stages of ego/self-development (read the descriptions of functioning at the I–2 and Δ stages given in Table 5.3 of the text), it would be extremely difficult to understand the genuine needs of other humans, especially from their perspectives. It would be difficult, if not impossible, for a mother at this stage to be able to put herself in the baby's place and recognize the potential for self-direction. Yet the ability to use recursive loops is certainly central to effective parenting—for example, "This is how it seems to me, how might it seem to a baby?" Or "What's the best thing to do for the long run?" Or "Is that cry just fussy or real hunger?"

Probably the most unfortunate outcome of all in the study was the realization that there were basically no educational programs that might stimulate the ego/self-development level of the young mothers. The mothers as a whole were doing the best they could on their own. For some the results indicated reasonably effective interpersonal functioning. For others . . . ?

REFERENCES

1. P. A. W. Bielke, The relationship of maternal ego development to parenting behavior and attitudes (Ph.D. thesis, University of Minnesota, 1979).
2. *Ibid.*, pp. 85–87.

EDUCATIONAL PROGRAMS: WALKING IN ANOTHER'S SHOES

If we review for a moment the descriptions of complex interpersonal functioning given by Selman and Loevinger, we see certain similarities. Selman's level 4 suggests the ability to engage in simultaneous role taking, placing oneself *intellectually* and *emotionally* in the shoes of another. (The old American Indian proverb, "Don't judge another until you've walked a mile in his moccasins," asks us to experience, as genuinely as possible, the thoughts, feelings, and perceptions of the other.) The educational problem revolves around the question of how to stimulate the development of role-taking capacity. Selman's contention is quite clear: Perspective taking is a central ingredient in the growth of more complex social cognitive development. Loevinger, although more conservative on the question of planned educational programs, does suggest that a major difference between her I–3 conformist and I–4 conscientious stages has to do with the ability to recognize and process ideas and feelings in *self* and *others* at more complex levels. Many educators believe that since development depends on interaction, it is important to try methods that may improve or stimulate levels of psychological maturity—as long as such attempts include safeguards for the participants.

There has been a series of studies and experimental programs at the secondary school level in an attempt to construct such educational programs [30]. This work has gone on for the past ten years, and the results are promising. We will discuss some of these programs in this section.

Increasing Social Role-Taking Capacity in a High School Course

To provide a specific example, we describe here an actual high school course designed to stimulate the growth of interpersonal maturity. The class was called Peer Counseling, and in it the high school pupils actually learned some of the theory and techniques of counseling psychology. However, the goal was *not* to create a cadre of teenage therapists. Instead, the researchers chose the techniques of counseling as a means of improving students' own abilities to listen and respond to others.

Effective counseling demands an iron discipline—the ability to systematically set self aside. One must avoid interrupting, changing the topic, refocusing on self, one-upping the other person, and denying the accuracy of the other person's experience. Studies of communication indicate, romantic myths to the contrary notwithstanding, that teenagers are just as poor listeners as adults are. They cut each other off and up, pick up only shreds of content, and almost never recognize the emotions behind the message. They tend to be egocentric and systematically to tune-out the other person. So the purpose of Peer Counseling was to teach adolescents to listen in order to facilitate their abilities to place themselves in someone else's moccasins. The phases of the Peer Counseling class are described in the Appendix.

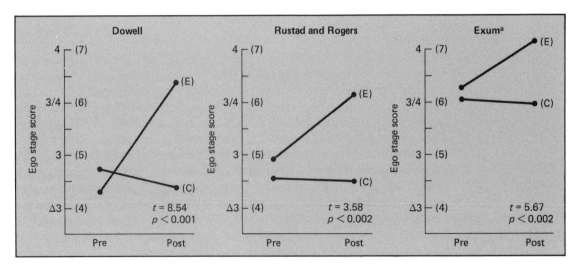

FIG. 5.2 Changes in students' ego development stages (Loevinger)

Note: Loevinger stage scores were converted to a 10-point scale for the statistical analyses. Numbers in parentheses represent the numerical score. All probabilities are reported for one tail. E = experimental; C = control. The studies cited above each graph are noted in reference 30 in the text.

[a] These programs were year-long classes. The other programs were from 12 to 14 weeks long.

The basic format for the course was tried and tested three times (twice with high school students and once with junior college pupils) before it was introduced into a high school curriculum. The results were positive, as expected [31]. On Loevinger's measure of ego/self-development, members of the counseling classes showed significant gains in maturity, while other classes showed no change. As Fig. 5.2 shows, before the counseling classes students were at stage 3, in which persons are dominated by what others think of them, tend to follow the crowd, do not recognize individual differences, and have limited ability to understand feelings. After the counseling course most students shifted upward to stage 3/4, meaning that they manifested more inner reliance, less egocentrism, and more differentiation of perception and feeling. In other words, the stage changes reflected the goals of the program.

Participants also improved greatly on measures of their communication skills. When their actual responses to others were coded and rated according to levels of accurate empathy, they were found to have made significant gains.

Finally, the pupils themselves reported very positive experiences. The students on questionnaires indicated that they learned the following activities or concepts from the class: "To express myself more clearly," "To evaluate myself," "To talk freely," "To be aware of other people," "To understand people different from myself," "To listen to others," "To see the effects others have upon me," and "To help other people." These responses were selected from a list of twelve possible activities and were noted by at least half of the students in the class. Perhaps most significant was another item. In one class ($N = 27$) all students listed "Students learn from each other, not just from the teacher" as their major perception of what they had learned in class.

Open-ended written assessments from pupils included comments like the following:

> "It was easy to listen and learn from others in the class, teachers and students. My group seemed together and powerful working toward a common goal, we achieved a lot."

> "A weird class but I think I learned a lot without the usual books, and just from other people. Also it's useful outside of school too and in the future."

> "The class was very helpful to me. In our small group we dealt with the real feelings and not *just* practicing the things we learned (empathy scale, Roger's article, etc.). Maybe that's why it was so good—because it was real and not *just* a learning experience. I enjoyed it." [32]

There are other school courses that achieve similar goals. For example, classes in Cross-Age Teaching have also been successful in stimulating interpersonal maturity [33]. Teenagers take course work that enables them to teach junior high and elementary children and to work in preschools. These courses, as was the case for the counseling course, are not designed as pre–vocational training but, rather, as a means for improving students' general abilities to instruct and respond to younger peers. Indeed, learning to teach someone else often benefits the tutor as much as the tutee.

One reason for the benefit in the Cross-Age Teaching course is that the process of organizing one's thoughts and material to teach someone, at least the first time through, can stimulate growth. But mostly it is the necessity for and practice in social perspective taking in teaching that generates developmental growth. Furthermore, experimental programs such as Peer Counseling and Cross-Age Teaching appear to provide a means of engaging adolescents in the process of learning. The programs may seem like a welcome change from the usual passivity, pendantry, and peer pressure that is almost endemic in the secondary schools of the country, as we will detail in Chapter 12.

Goals: Happiness or Interpersonal Complexity?

The ideas of Robert Selman and Jane Loevinger emphasize the potential of adolescents to function at higher levels of interpersonal understanding and interaction. The normative data, on the other hand, indicate that there is a gap between what is and what might be. In fact, Loevinger's studies with adults indicate that less than 33% function at her stage 4 or higher *during adulthood*. Perhaps the adolescent years represent an important educational opportunity to provide experiences that may enhance interpersonal growth.

Does establishing interpersonal growth as an educational objective mean that the goal is happiness? Will promoting personal development make people more satisfied with their lives? There is no guarantee, nor can there be, that such developmental goals are associated with happiness in the fantasy sense portrayed in tales like *Mary Poppins*. The goal is complexity—in the sense of more complete, comprehensive thinking. The goal is to make one more aware—in thought, feelings, and actions—of the relations between oneself and others to whom one relates. Such interpersonal maturity most likely will deepen rather than simplify the human condition.

As we will see in Chapters 7, 8, and 9, interpersonal relationships serve several important functions in adolescent development. In particular, the ideas of Harry Stack Sullivan discussed in Chapter 9 point to the emotional importance of relationships with others in achieving a sense of identity. Thus social cognitive growth, as it contributes to such relationships, is an aspect of adolescent development with clear implications for social and emotional maturity.

SUMMARY

In this chapter we focused on the nature and influence of social cognitive processes during adolescence. Jean Piaget's early work and some recent theory and research, such as that of David Elkind and Robert Selman, have indicated that major shifts take place during the second decade of life. These shifts correspond to the transition from concrete to formal thought described in Chapter 4. Three aspects of the transition are particularly important for adolescents' social development: (1) Adolescents become more capable of considering a variety of circumstances and events that *might* occur and are thus especially likely to recognize discrepancies between the real and the possible; (2) adolescents increasingly infer personal characteristics, motivations, and other causes that lie beneath the surface of social behaviors and events; and (3) adolescents develop an awareness that different individuals, including themselves, take differing perspectives on the same set of circumstances. These social cognitive changes typically take place over periods of months and even years. They include upward shifts in the complexity of social perceptions and reasoning and also sideways shifts to extend developing cognitive capabilities to new types of social relationships, circumstances, and events.

Before formal thought abilities are fully realized, however, adolescents often show a special form of egocentrism, according to the views of David

Elkind. One component of this adolescent egocentrism, the imaginary audience, refers to adolescents' apparent belief that although others' perspectives are different from their own, the focus of others' attention is the adolescent. Thus teenagers may adjust their behavior to please the audience they assume to be watching them. The second component, the personal fable, refers to adolescents' convictions that their feelings are unique and that no one else is capable of understanding them. As a transitional phase in cognitive development, adolescent egocentrism is overcome through social experiences with other adolescents that stimulate the maturation of social cognitive capabilities.

Particularly significant for development during adolescence is a series of changes in interpersonal understanding. Robert Selman has identified two primary ways in which adolescents change in their concepts of self and others: (1) in the recognition that others have different perspectives from oneself, and (2) in understanding the ways in which these different perspectives may affect each person's behavior toward the other. Although he is primarily concerned with the role of cognitive abilities involved in interpersonal understanding, Selman's own research and the findings of other scholars indicate that adolescents with more advanced social cognitive abilities generally show more successful social adjustment than teenagers whose social cognitive abilities are less advanced. In addition, the development of interpersonal understanding appears to parallel an increasing sophistication of several concepts that are fundamental to social life in a society such as the United States. For example, during adolescence there are significant changes in understanding of political concepts, such as community and the nature of law and individual rights, and in abilities for recognizing when the behavior of others is antisocial, deviant, or psychologically disturbed.

Social cognitive development appears to play an important role in the adolescent task of achieving an identity. According to Jane Loevinger, adolescent ego, or self, development involves a shift from a conformist stage, in which individuals are primarily concerned with superficial signs of social belonging and with avoidance of trouble or punishment, to conscientious or individualistic stages, in which ideas of self reflect concern for one's own standards and goals, a respect for individuality, and a desire for relationships characterized by mutual concern and communication. Teenagers' development of self, as Loevinger describes the process, is closely related to the development of social cognitive skills, to judgments about social problems and relationships, and to actual patterns of mature, socially appropriate behavior.

Social cognitive development may be stimulated through educational programs designed to help adolescents become less egocentric and more empathic in interactions with others. In programs such as the peer-counseling class described in this chapter, adolescents' empathy, their communication skills, and their responsibility to others were found to improve as a result of stimulation from other adolescents.

In Chapters 7, 8, and 9 we will examine the implication of social cognitive development for the relationships with others that form the social world of adolescents.

KEY POINTS AND NAMES

Social cognition
  Real and possible
  Dispositional concepts
  Role taking and perspective taking

Jean Piaget

Egocentrism

David Elkind

Adolescent egocentrism

The personal fable

The imaginary audience

Robert Selman

Stages of interpersonal understanding
  Egocentric

Subjective
Self-reflective
Mutual

Content and structure

Joseph Adelson

Political socialization

Concept of deviance

Social problem solving

Jane Loevinger

Social reasoning and identity

Stages of ego development

Ego stage and behavior

Educational programs: stimulating maturity

REFERENCES

1. D. Elkind, Egocentrism in adolescence, *Child Development* 38(1967):1025–1034.

2. W. Livesley and D. Bromley, *Person perception in childhood and adolescence,* (London: Wiley, 1973).

3. B. Peevers and P. Secord, Developmental changes in attribution of descriptive concepts to persons, *Journal of Personality and Social Psychology* 27(1973):120–128.

4. M. Feffer, The cognitive implications of role-taking behavior, *Journal of Personality* 27(1959):152–168; H. J. Flavell, The development of inferences about others, in *Understanding other persons,* ed. T. Mischel (Oxford: Blackwell, Basil, Mott, 1974), pp. 66–116.

5. Elkind.

6. J. Piaget, *The language and thought of the child* (Cleveland: Meridian Books, 1955).

7. J. Piaget and B. Inhelder, *The child's conception of space* (London: Routledge & Kegan Paul, 1956), pp. 209–213.

8. M. Chandler and S. Greenspan, Ersatz egocentrism: A reply to Borke, *Developmental Psychology* 7(1972):104–106.

9. Elkind.

10. H. Green, The grey bird, in *Adolescence in literature*, ed. T. Gregory (New York: Longman, 1978), pp. 380–389.

11. Elkind, p. 1030.

12. M. Twain, *The adventures of Tom Sawyer* (New York: Grosset & Dunlap, 1946), p. 142.

13. R. Selman, *The development of interpersonal understanding* (New York: Academic Press, 1980).

14. R. Selman and D. Byrne, A structural-developmental analysis of levels of role taking in middle childhood, *Child Development* 45, 2(1974):803–806.

15. R. Selman, D. Jaquette, and D. Lavin, Interpersonal awareness in children, *American Journal of Orthopsychiatry* 47, 1(1977):264–274.

16. J. Adelson, The political imagination of the young adolescent, *Daedalus* 100(1971):1013–1050.

17. J. Adelson and R. O'Neil, Growth of political ideas in adolescence: The sense of community, *Journal of Personality and Social Psychology* 4, 3(1966):295–306.

18. J. Adelson, B. Green, and R. O'Neil, The growth of the idea of law in adolescence, *Developmental Psychology* 1(1969):327–332.

19. Adelson, pp. 1022–1027.

20. J. Coie and B. Pennington, Children's perceptions of deviance and disorder, *Child Development* 47(1976):407–413.

21. Coie and Pennington, p. 412.

22. G. Spivack, J. Platt, and M. Shure, *The problem-solving approach to adjustment* (San Francisco: Jossey-Bass, 1976).

23. P. Grim, L. Kohlberg, and S. White, Some relationships between conscience and attentional processes, *Journal of Personality and Social Psychology* 8(1968):239–253.

24. J. Platt, G. Spivack, N. Altman, D. Altman, and S. Peizer, Adolescent problem-solving thinking, *Journal of Consulting and Clinical Psychology* 42, 6(1974):787–793.

25. R. L. Selman, Toward a structural developmental analysis of interpersonal relationship concepts, in *Minnesota symposia on child psychology*, vol. 10, ed. A. Pick (Minneapolis: University of Minnesota Press, 1976), pp. 156–200.

26. M. Ford, Social cognition and social competence in adolescence, *Developmental Psychology* 18(1982):323–340.

27. J. Loevinger, *Ego development: Conceptions and theories* (San Francisco: Jossey-Bass, 1976).

28. R. Mosher, *Adolescents' development and education: A Janus knot* (Berkeley, Calif.: McCutchan, 1979).

29. E. Sullivan, G. McCullough, and M. Stager, A developmental study of the relationship between conceptual, ego, and moral development, *Child Development* 41(1970):399–411.

30. C. Dowell, Adolescents as peer counselors (Ed.D. thesis, Graduate School of Education, Harvard University, 1971); K. Rustad and C. Rogers, Promoting psychological growth in a high school class, *Counselor Education and Supervision* 14, 4(1975):227–235; H. Exum, Cross-age and peer teaching (Ph.D. thesis, University of Minnesota, 1977).

31. N. A. Sprinthall, Learning psychology by doing psychology, in *Developmental education*, ed. G. D. Miller (St. Paul: Minnesota Department of Education, 1976), pp. 23–44.

32. Dowell, p. 124.

33. V. L. Allen, *Children as teachers: Theory and research on tutoring* (New York: Academic Press, 1976).

CHAPTER 6

Moral Judgment and Value Development

INTRODUCTION

Almost no single aspect of adolescent development is simultaneously as highly significant yet extremely perplexing as is that of values. Norman Kiell in his excellent set of readings concerning the universal experience of adolescence has no separate chapter title for value development. Instead, his chapter is headed "Gambling, Lying, Cheating and Stealing"; it is an account of adolescent values and antisocial behavior. Similarly, according to a recent set of clay tablets from a Sumerian dig, the following conversation was recorded some four thousand years ago between an adult and a teenager:

"Grow-up. Stop hanging around the public square and wandering up and down the street. Go to school. Night and day you torture me. Night and day you waste your time having fun." [1]

A collection of recently discovered memoirs of President Everett of Harvard College (1846–1849) indicated a similar distress with adolescents. As a scholar he was regarded as an equal to Pericles of Athens; as a college administrator he complained bitterly about the values of youth. From his library, while pondering the eternal questions of democracy and citizenship, his thoughts shifted:

Hateful duties in the morning to question three students about beckoning to loose women in the College Yard on Sunday afternoon; to two others about whistling in the passage; to another about smoking in the College Yard. Is this all I am fit for? . . . The life I am now leading must end, or it

will end me. . . . My time taken up all day with the most disgusting details of discipline, such as make the heart perfectly sick—fraud, deception,
falsehood, unhandsome conduct, parents and friends harassing me all the
time and foolishly believing the lies their children tell them. [2]

And today, one has only to read the letters-to-the-editor column of any
newspaper, or an Ann Landers or Erma Bombeck column, to find similar
sentiments and frustrations expressed by adults. Underneath all this upset
and concern is a poignant question: "Why can't we *do* anything about the
value systems teenagers employ?" This question may be followed by an
even more poignant (and a factually incorrect) comment, calling for a return to the old days for the inculcation of traditional values.

In this chapter we will explore some of the most recent theory and
research on the process of value development during adolescence. We will
outline a developmental stage model that helps to determine the different
systems teenagers actually use. Then we will describe actual educational
programs designed to stimulate value development.

A DEVELOPMENTAL FRAMEWORK: KOHLBERG'S THEORY

As we discussed earlier in Chapters 4 and 5, a series of highly significant
developmental shifts occur during and after puberty. The onset of formal
thinking, the ability to abstract, and the ability to distinguish between self
and other and between the subjective and the objective obviously affect
how teenagers view and understand themselves. Such new questioning, of
course, affects in a major way the value systems that are also undergoing
transformations during this period.

However, it is no longer accurate to describe value development in
either-or terms, in the old and somewhat simplistic view that held that
adolescence as a stage was simply oppositional to adulthood. That is,
whatever an adult valued, a teenager devalued. This view, of course, led to
some extremely complex interactions. Adults would say the opposite of
what they meant in order to trick the teenager into compliance. Teenagers,
of course, caught on fast to such double thinking. Soon the dialogue esca-
lated another notch—to the point of infinity. In fact, a naturalistic study of
communication patterns between teenagers and parents could find no systematic pattern of communication, using standard frameworks. The researcher could not fit the actual dialogues between adults and teenagers
into a design until she created a new category, "active noncommunication"
[3]. As a result, it was tempting in the past to view the process of value
development in extreme terms—that teenagers value just the opposite of
what adult society values. Now, however, it seems quite valid to view the
process as parallel to development in other domains, as the discussion in
this chapter will show.

Adolescence often seems like a stage of opposition
Photograph from Brody/Editorial Photocolor Archives

Without doubt the most significant and influential theory and research on value development derives from the work of Lawrence Kohlberg [4]. After conducting a long series of studies with children and adolescents, Kohlberg found that moral growth occurs in a specific sequence of developmental stages regardless of culture or subculture, continent or country. Thus we can no longer think of moral character in either-or terms or assume that character is something we do or do not have. Instead of existing as fixed traits, moral character occurs in a series of developmental stages. In other words, what Piaget identified as stages of cognitive development, and what Erikson suggested to be stages of personal development, Kohlberg described as stages of moral development.

Stages of moral and value judgment, then, are similar to the stages in the other domains. Each stage is qualitatively distinct. Development moves from the less complex to the more complex, and the sequence is invariant. Whether or not growth occurs depends on the interaction between the adolescent and the environment. Certain atmospheres and experiences will foster positive value development; others may not affect the process at all. Finally, still other environments and interactions may prevent or prematurely stabilize value growth. In this section we will examine Kohlberg's stages in detail.

The Stages Defined

In a manner very similar to the research procedures of Piaget, Kohlberg conducted an extensive series of interviews with children and adolescents. His studies were longitudinal: On a three-year cycle he and his associates interviewed the same persons. This process allowed him to chart the process of development over time, a procedure that provides in-depth information about the nature and direction of growth. Also, because the original sample was all male and had largely a working and middle-class background, Kohlberg and other researchers have since surveyed other populations. Their additional studies included female samples and cross-cultural groups. These new studies all tended to confirm the original findings, thus providing a highly reliable and valid research basis for Kohlberg's claim for stages of moral growth.

Table 6.1 presents the definitions of Kohlberg's six stages grouped by three global categories: *preconventional, conventional,* and *postconventional* systems. It is extremely important to note that these are thought systems, that is, systems describing how persons reason and process moral and value questions. Piaget asked children to think out loud and give reasons for their understandings of the physical world. Kohlberg, on the other hand, asked his subjects to take a position or a stand on a moral question (dilemma). The crucial part of the process, however, was not the choice of outcome but the reasons behind the decision. That is, what system of justification and support did a subject produce in defense of his or her decision? Thus in the Kohlberg system there are no right or wrong answers. Rather, there are levels of reasoning that represent the structure of a person's thought process. It is this structure—the type of reasoning—that he grouped into the six stages of moral development.

Moral Judgment: Content

Although it is beyond the scope of this book to engage in a long debate over the philosophical meaning of moral and value definitions, the point is important. Essentially, the content area of moral judgment involves questions of ethics and justice. Thus we are dealing with questions central to human existence. When and under what conditions, if ever, we are justified in taking another person's life, stealing someone else's property, refusing to help a person in distress? Such questions form the basis for this domain. How we respond to such issues of ethics and social justice in a democratic society is usually determined by our system of values.

In his studies Kohlberg constructed a series of such questions in the form of open-ended dilemmas. In the dilemma format there are no easy solutions. Conflict situations that are difficult to resolve are deliberately selected. Two of the original research dilemmas are presented below. In the first one there is a conflict between following the law and preserving a human life. In the second dilemma the issue concerns a parent who breaks his promise and a child who lies.

Dilemma 1: Heinz's Problem

In Europe a woman was near death from a special kind of cancer. There was one drug that the doctors thought might save her. It was a form of radium that a druggist in the same town had recently discovered. The drug

TABLE 6.1 Kohlberg's stages of moral growth

Basis of judgment	Stage of development	Characteristics of stage
Preconventional moral values reside in external, quasi-physical happenings, in bad acts, or in quasi-physical needs rather in persons and standards	Stage 1	Obedience and punishment orientation; egocentric deference to superior power or prestige, or a trouble-avoiding set; objective responsibility
	Stage 2	Naively egoistic orientation; right action is that instrumentally satisfying one's own and occasionally others' needs; awareness that value is relative to each person's needs and perspectives; naive egalitarianism and orientation to exchange and reciprocity
Conventional moral values reside in performing good or right roles, in maintaining the conventional order, and in meeting others' expectations	Stage 3	Orientation to approval and to pleasing and helping others; conformity to stereotypical images of majority or natural role behavior, and judgment by intentions
	Stage 4	Orientation to doing one's duty and to showing respect for authority and maintaining the given social order for its own sake; regard for earned expectations of others
Postconventional moral values are derived from principles that can be applied universally	Stage 5	Contractual-legalistic orientation; recognition of an arbitrary element in rules or expectations for the sake of agreement; duty defined in terms of contract, general avoidance of violation of the will or rights of others, or of the majority will and welfare
	Stage 6	Orientation to conscience or principles, not only to ordained social rules but to principles of choice appealing to logical universality and consistency; conscience is a directing agent, together with mutual respect and trust

was expensive to make, but the druggist was charging ten times what the drug cost him to make. He paid $200 for the radium and charged $2000 for a small dose of the drug. The sick woman's husband, Heinz, went to everyone he knew to borrow the money, but he could only get together about $1000, which is half of what it cost. He told the druggist that his wife was dying, and asked him to sell it cheaper or let him pay later. But the druggist said,"No, I discovered the drug and I'm going to make money from it." So Heinz got desperate and broke into the man's store to steal the drug for his wife.

1. Should Heinz have done that?

2. Was it actually wrong or right? Why?

Dilemma 2: Alex's Problem

Joe's father promised he could go to camp if he earned the $50.00 for it, and then changed his mind and asked Joe to give him the money he had earned. Joe lied and said he had only earned $10.00 and went to camp using the other $40.00 he had made. Before he went, he told his younger brother Alex about the money and about lying to their father. Should Alex tell their father?

1. What are the reasons to tell?

2. To not tell?

Thus the content of value judgments is represented by the reasoning process that the individual employs in attempting to resolve significant issues of social and personal justice.

Moral Judgment: A Sequence of Stages

After defining the content of each stage according to the predominant thought mode, Kohlberg was able to chart the path of development. In other words, the system of judgment was associated with particular ages and stages of growth. His studies were done not only in this country but also in other countries. Figures 6.1 and 6.2 indicate that the sequence of development is always the same, although the proportions may vary. In addition, individual analysis of the age trends indicated that none of the subjects in the longitudinal sample skipped stages. Each person progressed one stage at a time.

The figures show that there were some overall differences due to cultural and socioeconomic factors. For example, the subjects (age 13) from rural villages in Turkey and the Yucatan had a higher proportion of stage 1 responses than those from urban United States, Taiwan, or Mexican cities. At the other end the urban subjects had a greater proportion of stage 4 reasoning at age 16 than did the rural village teenagers. However, the overall trends were the same. The preconventional stages (1 and 2) were always higher at age 10 regardless of background. By age 16 the conventional stages (3 and 4) predominated. Lower-stage use declined systematically as higher-stage use increased—hence the phrase "moral judgment development as an invariant sequence." Development was stepwise from the less complex to the more complex.

These data were scored by using the original and somewhat intuitive scoring system. Recently, all of the responses from the longitudinal sample in this country have been rescored according to a more sophisticated manual for moral judgment assessment. The results of the rescoring have changed the percentage of use by age group and will be outlined in the next section. However, these changes are modifications only in terms of

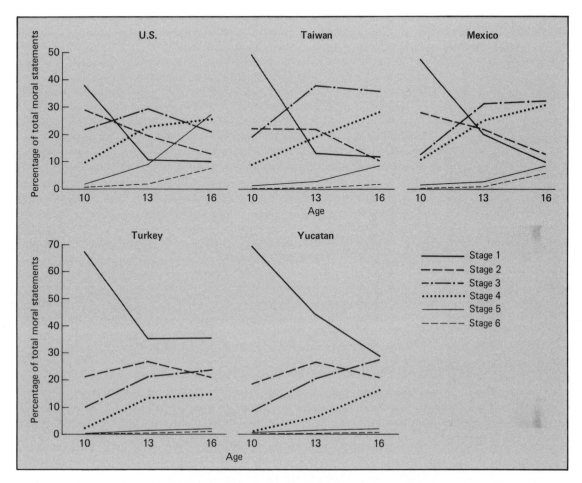

FIG. 6.1 Cross-cultural studies. (*a*) Middle-class urban boys in the U.S., Taiwan, and Mexico. At age 10 the stages are used according to difficulty. At age 13, stage 3 is most used by all three groups. At age 16 U.S. boys have reversed the order of age 10 stages (with the exception of 6). In Taiwan and Mexico, conventional (3–4) stages prevail at age 16, with stage 5 also little used. (*b*) Two isolated villages, one in Turkey, the other in Yucatan, show similar patterns in moral thinking. There is no reversal of order, and preconventional (1–2) thought does not gain a clear ascendancy over conventional stages at age 16.

Redrawn from *Handbook of Socialization Theory and Research* (ed.) Goslin, pp. 384–385. Copyright © 1969 by Houghton Mifflin Co. Used by permission.

the amount of moral judgment within the age groupings. The overall trends are still the same as an invariant sequence. As more of the old data are rescored, the norms for each age group will shift, yet the pattern of development will remain the same [5].

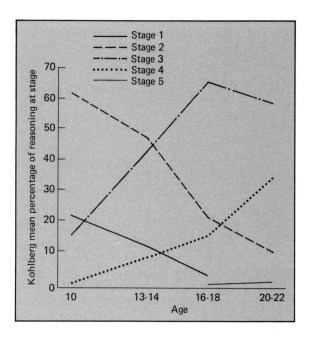

FIG. 6.2 Moral judgment according to age trends (Kohlberg's longitudinal subjects; re-scored 1979)

MORAL JUDGMENT STAGES DURING ADOLESCENCE

As Table 6.2 depicts, the content of value judgment during the junior high years (ages 13–14) is almost an equal balance between stages 2 and 3. At the junior high level well over 80% of the total moral/value reasoning is grouped at stages 3 and 2 almost equally. Thus, in general, pupils at this age will view moral questions from the standpoint of their own materialistic gain or of seeking approval from others. Such thinking is sometimes called *other-directed*. Instead of looking to self or to one's own standards and values, pupils at stage 3 generally will depend on another person's views.

However, research studies have shown that some pupils (15%) at the elementary level also employ this stage. There is a critical difference here. At the elementary level the students are interested in following and pleasing their parents when making moral judgments. At the junior high level there is a double shift. The percentage of thought increases to almost 50% at stage 3 *and* the reference group changes. Students now commonly seek approval from their peer group. In a sense stage 3 has two sides, like a coin. During childhood, parents and teachers represent the group that children may seek to please through social conformity. During junior high the peer group becomes the new—and stronger—reference group, the new source of value choice.

TABLE 6.2 Percentage of moral judgment use for ages 13–14 (longitudinal subjects; rescored 1979)

Stage	Percentage
1	7
2	45
3	42
4	3
5	—

Note: The total does not equal 100% since some scores are too mixed to assign to a single stage.

The findings above are not revolutionary. However, it is important to realize that stage 3 judgment is still stage 3 whether the reference group is the adult or the adolescent peer group. The individual is still not processing judgment according to rational and stable self-directed and democratic values. Thus the teenager could be directed by a variety of others: parents, peers, or perhaps some new cult leader. The great vulnerability of this level of moral and value judgment is the lack of stability of the reference group. A person without the ability to process important questions concerning self and ethics remains wide open to whatever fad comes along. Any new simplistic solution to the difficult problems of living will be attractive to thought at this stage as long as a specific reference group approves. It is also important to realize that such thinking is easily subject not only to relatively superficial aspects of life at this age, such as looks, hairstyle, and clothing, but also to much more significant value questions, such as racism and other forms of ethnocentrism.

In this section we will explore various facets of moral judgment stages during adolescence, including the types of reasoning involved, age differences, sex differences, and personal issues.

Stage Three: Perspective Taking and Empathy

Despite the concerns discussed above, stage 3 is adequate as a reasoning method. The system is more complex than thought at the less complex levels (stages 1 and 2). Reasoning at those simpler levels is almost exclusively concrete: Choices are made either to avoid physical punishment or to obtain materialistic gain. At stage 3 the reasoning is conducted at a more abstract level: How do other people view the question and, most importantly, how do other people feel about such issues? The person can now take the social perspective of others. Also, this stage marks the beginning of genuine *empathy*, the ability to place self emotionally in someone else's shoes.

LAWRENCE KOHLBERG (1927–)

Kohlberg spent three years as a junior engineer in the merchant marine before entering college. After those years at sea he was ready to buckle down and push through the rigorous program at Chicago in record time. He completed the four-year B.A. degree in 1949 after only two years' work. He clearly demonstrated a great capacity for academic scholarship, and it was natural for him to enroll as a doctoral candidate at the same university. He completed his doctorate in 1958: He took two years to complete his undergraduate studies, but he took nine years to complete his Ph.D. studies. He remarked wryly that it only proved you couldn't accurately predict human behavior in all cases.

One of the major reasons for the delay was his eventual topic: moral development in children and adolescents. A major portion of his doctoral work was in traditional areas of clinical psychology and child development, including a traineeship at Children's Hospital in Boston. But he found that while he was learning the traditional theories, including psychoanalytic views, he was becoming increasingly skeptical of them. He began to evolve an alternative set of ideas to explain how children develop moral reasoning. What started as a traditional thesis on the relationship between the superego (the Freudian term for conscience) and moral behavior was transformed into a remarkably original framework for moral development in stages. It is rare for a young doctoral candidate to produce new insights into human behavior theory. And it is truly unique that his thesis forced almost a complete revision of moral development theory.

With the completion of his thesis Kohlberg accepted an assistant professorship at the University of Chicago in 1962. Just six years later he was offered and accepted a full professorship at Harvard University; he joined that faculty to form an innovative graduate program in human development. He was also awarded a special five-year Research Career Award by the National Institute of Mental Health to promote his longitudinal study on stages of moral development in adults as well as in children and adolescents.

The significance of his work derives from its possible applications in promoting psychologically healthy human beings. And as if creating a new theory were not enough, Kohlberg has also been concerned with actions and programs in practice. An outspoken critic of the status quo, he has often confronted the psychological establishment, even early in his career. As a doctoral student assigned to a psychiatric ward, for in-

Lawrence Kohlberg
(1927–)
Boston Globe Photo

stance, he vigorously opposed the hospital's indiscriminate use of electroshock therapy. His supervisors criticized him for wearing mismatched socks; he countered by confronting them with their use of electric shock as an inhumane method of punishment. In doing so, and in standing up for his principles while still a probationary trainee, he showed not only a sense of justice but great courage as well.

Thus it is not surprising to find that he has been working as hard at applying his theories as at researching the concepts. This stance finds him in unusual places. For example, he spent three years (on a weekly basis) working directly with female prisoners and their guards in a Connecticut prison to create a more humane correctional environment. Also, as is noted in a special topic in this chapter, he designed and participated in the Just Community School—attending meetings, discussing plans, and using his one vote as a member of the community. Theory, without application, he would say, is nothing more than armchair abstraction. The test of a theory is whether it works. Few researchers are willing, as Kohlberg is, to subject their best work to such a test.

It is perhaps too facile to dismiss reasoning at stage 3 as inadequate. Instead, we should note that it represents a definite gain over the less complex stages. The person is able to view issues from a broader perspective than that of narrow self-interest. There is still significant reasoning occurring at the preconventional level (stages 1 and 2) during adolescence. However, the amount (45% at stage 2 and 8% at stage 1) represents a sharp decline from the amount at age 10. At age 10 almost 85% of moral reasoning is at the preconventional level.

Thus there is a significant overall decline in preconventional judgment by ages 13–14. However, there is still a substantial amount of stage 2 reasoning. In other words, major aspects of materialistic self-interest still govern much of the value choices of junior high pupils. But the system is in decline, and the stage 3 mode is assuming rising importance. This shift from the preconventional to the conventional, however, finds its completion during the high school years.

Stages of Judgment During the High School Years

By ages 16–18 the stage 3 process has become almost the exclusive mode. Reasoning at the stage 2 level drops sharply during this period, from 45% to 20%. Narrow self-interest does remain a theme for value choice, but in a much less significant way than during junior high. Approximately two-thirds of all reasoning about issues of justice, fair play, and major value choices is determined by social conformity with the leading crowd. To be in, liked, and respected and to have a good reputation are much more significant at this stage than at any other point in the scheme of development. However, as we noted, there is a positive side of such judgment when compared with stage 2 thought.

The emergence of some stage 4 process by high school, even though relatively small (14%), is highly important, as shown in Table 6.3. The advantages of such thinking over stage 3 thinking are perhaps obvious. A person begins to process value questions in accord with a broad set of rules and societal laws. Often, writers will suggest in an offhanded way that this stage is a narrow law-and-order version of value development—in other words, that the stage is a euphemism for oppression and the arbitrary application of power requiring compliance. But such a view does not accurately represent the thinking at stage 4. Central is the idea that a democratic society's laws represent at a given moment the distilled wisdom of experience. As a result, such laws and rules are considered more stable, more generalized, and less arbitrary and exclusionary than decisions made at the stage 3 level. What a leading crowd may think and feel would be much more subject to passions of the moment than an established code of laws would be. Thus persons, both adolescents and adults, at stage 3 might participate in a series of avowedly antidemocratic acts—for example, local censorship, discrimination in housing—for fear of ostracism. At the

TABLE 6.3   Percentage of moral judgment use
             for ages 16–18 (longitudinal
             subjects; rescored 1979)

Stage	Percentage
1	1
2	20
3	60
4	14
5	0

Note: Total does not equal 100% since some scores are too
mixed for a single assignment to one stage.

high school level this behavior often takes the form of an inner circle
arbitrarily excluding other teenagers from school clubs, extracurricular activities, and the like. Thus judgments based on the somewhat superficial
concerns of social popularity and conformity are clearly not as adequate as
decision making based on laws.

A further point is that the shift from stage 3 to stage 4 involves a
change in focus of reference. At stage 3 the reference is to the social group;
thinking is other-directed. At stage 4 thinking becomes inner-directed. A
person develops the ability to review questions in a rational manner. Planning, analyzing, and reviewing issues become the major differences in the
thought process when compared with stage 3. In other words, the higher
stage incorporates aspects of the prior level and adds new abilities and
judgment. With a new reference point—society's laws—the individual is
more likely to ponder and weigh questions at a more comprehensive and
less volatile level.

We do not mean, however, that the process necessarily stops at this
point. There will be value choices and decisions that cannot be processed at
the stage 4 level, particularly when the laws conflict. At that point it is
necessary to process questions in accord with stage 5: democratic principles. For example, in a recent case high school students were expelled for
wearing black armbands as a protest of our involvement in a war in South-
east Asia. The school justified its decision on the basis of the need to keep
good order in the school. Wearing armbands, the school said, was disrupt-
ing the learning process and thus breaking a law. Such a disruption in the
learning atmosphere violated the local and state laws that charge schools
with the responsibility to teach pupils. There are, of course, other state
laws that say that schools may not exclude pupils for arbitrary reasons such
as clothing or appearance. Resolving such a question cannot be accomplished with reference to existing law. Instead, it is necessary to analyze

the principles behind both laws and then decide when one is more just. That the court held for the students is not significant. What is significant is that the court justified the decision on the basis of principle: Wearing an armband was considered a symbolic and silent protest well within the constitutional provisions of a peaceful redress. The silent protest was not considered a disruption of the teaching-learning process. Such reasoning, however, is extremely rare on the part of high school pupils—and it is not all that common for adults, either, as Fig 6.2 indicates.

Variations Within Age Groupings

The cluster of judgment patterns at each age grouping does not hold for all individuals. Rather, these patterns are based on the mode, the most common system of thought. In other words, if a person employs stage 3 more than half the time, then he or she would be classed at that stage. There is, however, some variation within each person. Almost no one uses one stage exclusively. Instead, a person may use the equivalent of substages— some thought processes either slightly higher or slightly lower than the mode. Table 6.4 presents the variations by a global moral maturity score for students in the age ranges 13–14 and 16–18. The table indicates that during the junior high years there is some thinking at stages 1 and 2 (a mix), stage 2, stages 2 and 3 (a mix), stage 3, and stages 3 and 4 (mix). A similar pattern

Adolescents demonstrating for ecology show a concern for the greater good

Photograph from Charles Gatewood

TABLE 6.4 Variations in global moral judgment (longitudinal subjects; rescored 1979)

Stage	Percentage, ages 13–14	Percentage, ages 16–18
1 and 2 (mix)	8.1	2.2
2	16.2	11.1
2 and 3 (mix)	56.8	17.8
3	16.2	44.4
3 and 4 (mix)	2.7	24.4
4	0	0

of variation appears during the high school years but with an overall shift to a higher grouping of stage reasoning.

This reminder is important. We cannot assume that an individual reasons exclusively at one and only one stage. Thus any labeling of individuals is uncalled for and inaccurate. Yet there is an unfortunate tendency for humans to categorize each other. After one hears a person employ stage 2 process, for instance, it is not unusual for one to then say that that person is a stage 2 person. But this generalization is unwarranted. Rather, one should specify that the person does employ (say) stage 2 process in regard to the issue at hand, and this stage may be the mode. At the same time the person may employ more complex or less complex reasoning in other instances. In fact, two interesting aspects of adolescence as a stage are the modes or group trends *and* the variations. At both the 13–14 and 16–18 groupings five stages and substages are represented. During the previous age (10) four stages are represented. By age 36 (middle adulthood) only three stages represent the spread of scores. Thus the amount of variation of moral judgment process peaks during the two major adolescent age groupings. This result underscores the importance of avoiding labeling for any single individual even though there are significant modal trends.

Sex Differences   Since the members of the original Kohlberg sample were males, the question of sex differences naturally arises. Are preadolescent and adolescent females the same as or different from males on levels of moral development? Do they move through the stages in the same sequence and in the same proportion as males?

The most comprehensive study of this question was conducted at the Ontario Institute for the Study of Education (OISE) [6]. The researchers tested three groups of 12-, 14-, and 17-year-olds with equal numbers of males and females. The results indicated that there were no sex differences in moral stage score at any of the ages. All the 12-year-olds had scores clustering at a stage 2(3) mix. Similarly, both male and female 14-year-olds scored at stage 3; the 17-year-olds averaged a stage 3(4) mix. In other words, age was significant but sex was not. Also, the sequence of stage growth was the same for both groups. From this study, then, it seems safe to conclude that males and females are similar in moral development during early and middle adolescence.

There is some evidence, though, that there may be differences between males and females after college [7]. Such differences, however, may derive from differences in role-taking opportunities available to men and women at the time the study was conducted. In this study, conducted in 1972 (53 couples), all the males were college graduates with professional careers; almost all the females were college graduates, yet only three of them had careers. In other words, if adult women are systematically denied access to participation in career roles, they may not have the opportunities for responsibility and decision making that males have. This conclusion, however, is quite speculative. Research on possible stages of adult development in moral judgment is still in the very initial phases.

Moral Reasoning: Personal Issues and Sexual Dilemmas

All of the studies noted in this chapter have employed a standard set of dilemmas in order to assess differences according to age and stage, sex, and cross-cultural background. These dilemmas follow a format similar to that of "Heinz's Problem" and "Alex's Problem," the dilemmas presented earlier in the chapter. They typically ask the subjects to reason out loud on very general issues pertaining to questions of the value of life, freedom of expression, following the law, and similar somewhat personally removed and abstract questions of democratic justice. In fact, Kohlberg deliberately chose the original dilemma issues on the basis of personal and psychological distance in order to create a system to measure generalizations not involving the immediate personal experience of the subject. Such a method does raise questions. Would subjects use a different level of moral judgment if the dilemmas were closer to home, if the subjects could identify with the problem, and if they would reason through a problem that they might be confronting in real life?

To test these questions, Kohlberg and one of his professional colleagues, Carol Gilligan, conducted studies with teenage subjects [8]. They quite ingeniously rewrote the standard dilemmas in the form of sexual dilemmas quite commonly faced by teenagers in this country. One such dilemma is presented below.

A Teenage Sexual-Reasoning Dilemma

STORY A

A high school girl's parents are away for the weekend and she's alone in the house. Unexpectedly, on Friday evening, her boyfriend comes over.

They spend the evening together in the house and after a while they start necking and petting.

1. Is this right or wrong? Why? Are there any circumstances that would make it right (wrong)?

2. What if they had sexual intercourse? Is that right or wrong? Why?

3. (*If applicable:*) Why do you think petting is OK but sexual intercourse is wrong?

4. Are there any circumstances that would make sexual intercourse right (wrong)? (*If not elicited spontaneously:*) (a) Does the way they feel about each other make a difference? Why? (b) What if they are in love? What do you think love means and what is its relation to sex? (c) Suppose the couple was engaged, what difference would that make? (d) What about birth control? If they have a safe and foolproof method, would that make it all right for them to have intercourse? Why? (e) If they have sexual intercourse are they obligated to use birth control?

5. Suppose the girl is less willing than the boy to have sexual intercourse. The girls think sex before marriage is OK for boys but not for girls. What reasons does she have for thinking that? What is your thinking about this?

6. The girl's parents return and find out that the couple had sexual intercourse—what should the parents do? Why? (a) (*If says parents should talk to girl:*) What should parents say? What would that do? (b) (*If says parents should punish:*) What is the reason for punishing? What effect would punishment have? Should boy be punished, too?

7. Do you think these issues about sex have anything to do with morality and immorality? (a) What does the word moral mean? What is its relation to sex? (b) Can you tell me something that you think is immoral? Why? Immoral in sex? Why? (c) Is this immoral for all people everywhere? Why? (d) You think that ——— (*use example given in 7b*) is immoral in sex. It's immoral in our society. I wonder if you think it would be immoral to do it in a society that is very different, where it is accepted. Like in Sweden it is accepted to have premarital relations. I wonder if you think it would be immoral to do ——— in a society where it is accepted?*

After administering a series of three such dilemmas, the researchers then scored the level of reasoning of the teenagers according to the regular Kohlberg stage system. A comparison was made between the reasoning on the standard dilemmas and the sexual content dilemmas. The results are reported in Table 6.5.

On the average, the results indicate that for both boys and girls there is a noticeable drop in moral judgment reasoning when the dilemmas are

* From G. Gilligan, L. Kohlberg, M. Lerner, and M. Belenky, *Moral reasoning about sexual dilemmas. Technical report of the U.S. Commission on Obscenity and Pornography, VI* (Washington, D.C.: Government Printing Office, 1971), pp. 141–174.

TABLE 6.5 Moral judgment scores for high school students

	Boys (N = 24)	Girls (N = 24)
Score on standard Kohlberg dilemmas	351	340[a]
Score on sexual content dilemmas	314	318[b]

[a] The difference between the average scores for boys and girls (351 versus 340) was not statistically or theoretically significant.

[b] The difference between the average scores for boys and girls (314 versus 318) was not significant.

changed to have sexual content. Both groups were about halfway between stage 3 (300) and stage 4 (400) on the standard dilemmas. Thus they were in transition from social and peer group conformity to adherence to our laws as a basis for value judgment. Again, as in the OISE study discussed above, there were no major differences at the high school level between boys and girls. When the content was changed to issues closer to home—reasoning on issues of sexual experimentation—then the level of judgment *dropped* for both groups. Both boys and girls reasoned at one-half stage lower. Thus their thinking became less complex when the issue became more personal.

A drop of 40 points, as shown in Table 6.5, is statistically and theoretically significant. But even more significant are the reasoning characteristics of the next lower stage, in this case, stage 3. At this level decisions are based on external social pressures. Individuals make a decision not on the basis of their own best judgment or what they think is morally appropriate as individuals. Instead, individuals will tend to go along with the values of the leading crowd and make choices on the basis of what is currently socially popular. This characteristic does not mean, however, that at stage 3 both boys and girls will engage in sex. Instead, it means that they will make the decision in accord with other people's wishes and desires. Inner direction and the ability to withstand social pressures (either way) are lacking at stage 3. Choice is made to please others. And the real conflict at this stage comes from competing reference groups. A young woman at stage 3 may be caught between the social pressures of pleasing her parents by remaining chaste and of pleasing her boy friend by engaging in sex. Similarly, a boy at this stage may be trying to be sexually active and macho in order to measure up to others' expectations of what it takes to be a real man while also adhering to his parents warnings about young men who get captured by seductive girls.

The drop in scores was significant for both groups. On an individual basis 20 out of 24 boys reasoned at a lower level, while 19 out of 24 girls did. Such results point in two directions. First, the results indicate that in dealing with dilemmas that are personal and close to home, adolescents may use a level of reasoning that is lower than that used in the general case. Second, the results indicate what happens when students are asked to reason and judge in areas generally considered taboo or out of bounds. As we noted in Chapter 3, there is great discomfort in this culture in even discussing issues of sexual activity. The laws in many states and the cultural morals in general reflect a nineteenth-century, Victorian, hands-off position. In fact, this position is still the official position in most schools. Sex education, if allowed at all, is usually such a watered-down, fact-based approach that the pupils learn very little. One author's teenage daughter, for instance, reported recently on her experience. The health teacher, a coach, raced through a unit on reproduction. When the author asked what the daughter learned, she replied, "Well not much, really, except that the teacher blushed the whole time!" As a result of these attitudes, discussions of sex, if they take place at all, probably occur mostly among peers and are based on somewhat random information.

Summary of Stage Changes in Value Judgment

During ages 13–14 the following changes occur:

- There is a decline in stage 2 process from 65% to 45%.

- There is an increase in stage 3 process from 15% to 42%.

- There is a decline in stage 1 process from 22% to 7%.

- On an overall basis stages 2 and 3 account for almost all the moral judgment reasoning at this age.

- There is a shift in reference group at stage 3, with peers replacing parents as a source of value judgment.

During ages 16–18, the following changes take place:

- Stage 3 accounts for almost two-thirds of value reasoning.

- There is a further major decline in stage 2 process to 22%.

- There is an emergence of stage 4 process, from 3% to 14%.

It is important to note that these results are based on group trends. Thus there will always be single individuals in any classroom or group who depart from these age trends. There will still be some teenagers who continue to process at stage 1. Similarly, at the other extreme there will be some individual teenagers who process at a principled thought level, stage 5. These few will process difficult dilemmas on the basis of constitutional principles, such as equal right and protection, freedom of speech and press, and human dignity for all. However, such teenagers will be exceptions. Perhaps with more adequate educational experiences, though, we can stimulate the growth of higher, more complex democratic thought. It is to this issue that we now turn.

SPECIAL TOPIC
Family Influences on Value Autonomy: Holstein's Basic Research and Stanley's Application

How do families influence the development of value autonomy? One hint might come from the information discussed in this chapter about the kind of independent reasoning required for moral thinking. Kohlberg's levels of conventional and postconventional, or principled, moral reasoning require that the individual show evidence of having independently reasoned about judgments of right and wrong. By contrast, at Kohlberg's preconventional level of thinking, individuals rely heavily on external influences. Kohlberg's more mature and complex levels of moral reasoning correspond to what we call *value autonomy*—the tendency to reason for oneself rather than to adopt a position in response to external influences.

Psychologist Constance Holstein recently reported on a longitudinal study of adolescents over the period from age 13 to age 16 [1]. These young persons and their parents were examined for level of moral reasoning on Kohlberg's scale. In addition, parents were interviewed about child rearing and the family environment. Holstein predicted that adolescents whose parents showed the highest levels of moral judgment would change more than adolescents whose parents showed lower levels of judgment. In addition, she predicted that the degree to which parents were warm toward their children and actively involved them in discussions of decisions and judgments would affect the influence of the parents' level of moral reasoning on adolescents' development.

The accompanying table shows the results of Holstein's study. Clearly, the more complex the parents' moral-reasoning ability, the more likely it is that adolescents will be conventional, rather than preconventional, thinkers on Kohlberg's measure. When the parents do little to encourage discussion and debate about moral issues, however, adolescents are much more likely to be preconventional thinkers.

Partly as a result of this study, there have been some recent attempts to create educational applications of the Kohlberg theory to show families how to promote more complex moral reasoning. Sheila F. Stanley, one of Ralph Mosher's graduate students at Boston University, broke new ground in the late 1970s when she created a special educational program for parents and their adolescent offspring [2]. She wanted to examine whether or not parents could learn to educate their own children systematically in order to promote more complex moral reasoning. As we note in this chapter, levels of moral reasoning do make a difference in how humanely people behave in moral di-

ROLE OF PARENTAL ENCOURAGEMENT OF CHILD'S PARTICIPATION IN FAMILY DISCUSSIONS IN CHILD'S MORAL JUDGMENT DEVELOPMENT

Parents' Moral Judgment Level	Parental Encouragement	Child's Moral Judgment Level	
		Preconventional	Conventional
Both conventional	Low	75	25
	High	32	68
One or both principled	Low	—	—
	High	28	72

lemma situations. Holstein showed that parents already at more complex levels of moral development tended to induce such growth in their own children. Stanley wanted to take these implications a step further. If moral dilemma discussions led by sensitive teachers in school and college classrooms could promote growth, would they also work if parents used some of the same strategies?

Stanley put together a curriculum guide very similar in format to that of the high school programs. She selected a series of controversial dilemma (open-ended) topics for discussion groups of parents and their adolescents. She also taught them open-communication methods similar to the active-listening materials found in the Appendix. The combination of dilemma content and open communication basically forced both parents and their children to listen to each other's point of view and to gradually reason through difficult issues at more complex levels. Also, she taught the groups to employ democratically based methods of conflict resolution.

The statistical and clinical evaluations of Stanley's program both indicated that the process was successful. The experimental group demonstrated significant gains at the end of the course and continued to show growth in a follow-up study one year later. The control groups did not. Thus it seems that it is possible to provide educational help to families. Such groups can learn to communicate more effectively on questions that involve moral judgment. Stanley's research is another recent example that educational programs to promote developmental growth can make a difference.

REFERENCES

1. C. Holstein, The relation of children's moral judgment level to that of their parents and to communication patterns in the family, in *Readings in child development*, ed. R. Smart and M. Smart (New York: Macmillan, 1972), pp. 484–494.

2. S. Stanley, Family education: A means of enhancing the moral atmosphere of the family and the moral development of adolescents, *Journal of Counseling Psychology* 25(1978):110–118.

EDUCATIONAL PROGRAMS: CAN WE EDUCATE FOR VALUE DEVELOPMENT?

Given the framework presented above, an obvious question follows: Can adults create learning experiences that promote value growth? This is a continuation of the question asked of intellectual as well as interpersonal development. Since the heart of cognitive-developmental theory rests on the assumption of interaction, then the answer is obviously a yes, with qualifications. Like all areas of human development, value development is a slow and complex process. Brief and flashy single class periods, weekend retreats, or similar short-term learning approaches will not affect the system of cognitive processing in general. And what holds in the general case is even stronger in the instance of values. Of all the questions and subject matter disciplines that we struggle with as humans, none is so complex as the issue of values and ethical judgment. Thus as we consider and review possible approaches to value development in this section, it is well to remember these qualifications.

Classroom Moral Dilemma Discussions

By far the newest and most common technique for promoting value growth at both the junior and the senior high school level is to present a sequence of open-ended moral dilemmas for discussion and analysis. In this approach the instructor's role is critical. The instructor is to clarify and encourage the pupils to verbalize *their* reasons for choice. Especially during the initial periods of group discussion, it is extremely important for the instructor *not* to step in, take over, and start lecturing and correcting. The students need time and support in order to articulate their own reasoning. Also, the instructor needs to facilitate the process in order to clarify the different levels of reasoning within any class or group. Remember that, as the previous figures indicated, there is a modal stage for age groups, but there is also a range both above and below the mode.

There are a number of excellent books that detail the role of the teacher/adult discussion leader, so we will simply outline the format in brief [9].

First, the leader must be able to identify the variety of reasoning levels. To do so, the leader may have to ask clarifying questions. For example, suppose you are running a discussion on a dilemma like Heinz and the drug, and a pupil says, "Heinz should steal because I would." At this point you don't have enough information to assess the level of reasoning. So you go on and ask, "OK, but why would you?" This question might lead to another dead end, such as, "Well, I think it's OK to steal, sometimes." Then further clarification would be needed, such as, "Well, how do you decide when it's 'sometimes'?" At that point the pupil might present some reasons, such as, "Well a person's life is more important than. . . ." And then you could identify the judgment level.

A second phase of group discussion involves teaching the pupils to listen to each other's different levels—in other words, to have the pupils

Dilemma discussions in high school can promote value development
Photograph from James L. Shaffer

respond to one another. In the above example, for instance, one or two pupils might say that life is more important than property (stages 5 and 6); others might say it's against the law to go around ripping off stores (stage 4); and still others might say, "Well, it's OK to steal if he can figure out a way to pin it on someone else" (stage 2). Then it would be important to help the students listen and understand the different answers and different sets of reasons. Often a leader can use role reversal techniques at this point—asking a pupil who takes one position to discuss the question from someone else's view. Occasionally, this technique is called moral musical chairs since it involves changing positions in the discussion (without leaving someone out, however).

Role Reversal and Plus One

The role reversal technique is useful but it has limits. A series of studies have shown that, in general, people tend to process value issues a majority of the time at one particular level, their modal response. Through active listening and clarifying, that level can become evident. Also, people can comprehend the level of reasoning at all stages *below* their modal stage but at only *one* stage above it [10]. This point is crucial. Reasoning that is more than one stage above people's most common system is essentially beyond their comprehension. As a result, an individual might pay lip service to such reasoning, but it would not influence behavior.

With this qualification in mind, then, the instructional process becomes somewhat more complex. Besides open-ended discussion and role reversal techniques, discussion between the contiguous stages also is important. In a somewhat simplified format, then, promoting development for persons using stage 2 means helping them understand the reasoning at the next stage up, stage 3, rather than expecting them to understand, say, stage 5 principles. This process is sometimes called *jamming* or *plus one*, since it involves reasoning at the next highest stage. By asking a pupil to process issues at a slightly more complex level, the leader needs to realize that there is discomfort and probably some resistance on the part of pupils. As soon as people hear reasoning at a more complex level, they do not necessarily immediately agree. A person is attracted to but only partially appreciates the slightly more complex judgment. It's somewhat like turning the corner of the next page rather than the whole page all at once. This appreciation of and attraction to slightly more complex thought, then, forms a foundation on which to build a democratic system of value judgments.

Expanding Dilemma Content for the Classroom

A tendency in applying psychological understanding to actual situations is for the applications to become too narrow and singular. Such was the case with the Kohlberg materials. For example, his original research employed the fictitious case of Heinz and the drug. Since he published his report, this particular dilemma and others almost completely like it in content have been employed in the classrooms and small discussion groups in this country from kindergarten to graduate school. The narrow application of "Heinz," "The Return of Heinz," "The Son of Heinz," and "Heinz Part Two" is obviously not recommended. Pupils, particularly adolescents, will not long endure such repetition. Instead, we recommend that the application of the dilemma format involve much broader content areas.

An example of broad content areas for the dilemma format is found in a series of field-based projects currently in use, the Ethical Quest Project for junior and senior high schools [11]. In this project students and teachers employ the discussion format for issues of recent or current controversy. For example, in a high school social studies course the lesson plan is as follows:

Sample Lesson for Senior High School Students: Unit on Moral Action (Ethical Quest Project)

TOPIC OR THEME: CAINE MUTINY COURT MARTIAL

Dilemma Objective:	Explore the conflicts of duty, rules and concern for human life.
Mutiny Dilemma:	*Lieutenant Maryk* is the executive officer aboard the "USS Caine" during World War II. Maryk is conscientious, loyal and very capable. He is also very con-

cerned about the ship's captain. He feels *Captain Queeg* has consistently shown paranoid behavior in the unjust and irrational treatment of the men, and the bizarre running of the ship. Yet the "Caine" has never been in an endangered position before. *Lieutenant Keefer*, a writer, and the other ship's officers are also acutely aware of Captain Queeg's psychological problem. In fact, Maryk and Keefer at one time had almost reported the situation to the admiral of the fleet, but backed out because of the consequences, and lack of support from Keefer.

The "Caine" gets caught in a severe typhoon, in which Captain Queeg's irrational judgment is threatening the ship's safety. Lieutenant Maryk is torn between his sense of loyalty and duty and his realization that Queeg's behavior and poor judgment may sink the ship with the loss of many lives.

Discussion Questions:

a. What are Maryk's alternatives?

b. What are the consequences of each alternative?

c. Is there any way that Maryk and the other officers could help Queeg?

d. What is an act of mutiny?

e. What is the punishment for mutiny?

f. What would you do if you were Maryk?

g. Is what Maryk thinking of doing really mutiny?

h. Why is the punishment for mutiny so severe?

i. What is loyalty? Duty? Responsibility? Is there any conflict among these three?

j. What is justice? Fairness?

k. Is justice and fairness the same for each person or situation?

l. If Maryk took command of the "Caine," and later was brought before a court martial board on which you had the deciding vote, would you vote to convict or acquit him? Why? Is it ever right to break the law? Why, or why not?

m. If Maryk were found guilty, what punishment would you give to him? Why?

n. What is the purpose of punishing someone who breaks the law?

Read and View:

The Caine Mutiny Court Martial.

Follow-up Discussion:	(e.g., reconsider earlier answers to Discussion Questions.)
Writing Instruction and Assignment:	Discuss the concept of justice and fairness in terms of Queeg, Maryk and Keefer.
	Is justice and fairness the same for all three, or is it different for each one?
	Be specific with support from the play, and any other sources familiar to you.*

In a similar project at Carnegie-Mellon Secondary School, English classes discuss dilemma questions inherent in great works of literature, and social studies courses examine dilemma issues from the milestones of United States history [12]. In a high school English class, for instance, the following format is employed for a discussion of Huck Finn:

Examples of Written Dilemmas for English

GUIDE FOR A MORAL DISCUSSION BASED ON MARK TWAIN'S NOVEL *HUCKLEBERRY FINN*

The climax of the novel comes in Chapter Thirty One. To identify the dilemma which Huck must deal with, it is suggested that the teacher read, or have the students read, or have the chapter reproduced as a handout, to just slightly past mid-chapter when Huck says, "I studied a minute, sort of holding my breath, and then says to myself. . . ."

Now have the books closed, or the reading stopped, or the handout put aside, and rehearse the dilemma. You might make students aware at this point, too, that in spite of Huck's lack of education, he is still able to think his way through to a solution.

The "duke" and the "king" are arguing, as the chapter gets moving, and Huck runs off to the raft to find Jim to escape them. No Jim. Instead, Huck encounters a boy who describes the capture of a runaway slave for whom there is a reward. Now Huck thinks about writing to Miss Watson to tell her where Jim is. Notice how he sets up the reasons why Jim should be returned:

1. Miss Watson's dependence on Jim (but also, on the negative side, that she might punish Jim and/or resell him);

2. Jim's own family back in St. Petersburg, Missouri;

3. Huck's own reputation: "It would get all around, that Huck Finn helped a nigger to get his freedom . . .";

---

* Reprinted from *Character Potential: A Record of Research* VIII, no. 4 (August, 1978) p. 233. Used with permission.

4. The religious aspects of violating the law of slavery as "sinning." "I was stealing a poor old woman's nigger that hadn't (the woman) ever done me no harm, and now was showing me there's One that's always on the lookout . . . and something inside of me kept saying, 'There was the Sunday school . . . and if you'd a done it they'd a learnt you, there, that people acts as I'd been acting about that nigger goes to everlasting fire.' "

So Huck writes the note revealing Jim's whereabouts to Miss Watson. Then the other side of the question pops up:

5. The friendship me and Jim have shared, and several examples of the friendship:
   a. "I'd see him standing my watch on top of his'n, stead of calling me, so I could go on sleeping;
   b. and see him how glad he was when I come back out of the fog;
   c. when I come to him again in the swamp . . . and such-like times;
   d. and would always call me honey and pet me, and do everything he could think of for me;
   e. and how good he always was;
   f. and at last I struck the time I saved him by telling the men we had small-pox aboard, and he was so grateful, and said I was the best friend old Jim ever had in the world, and the *only* one he's got now. . . ."

This is Huck's dilemma. Ask the class what Huck should do. Divide the class accordingly, and proceed with the discussion and the probe questions, if necessary.

PROBE QUESTIONS FOR HUCK FINN'S DILEMMA

1. Is it ever right to break a law? When? How do you decide?

2. Should Huck consider the fact that protecting his friend may make him an outcast in society?

3. Which is more important, an obligation to a friend or to the law? Why?

4. Does Huck have any obligation to Miss Watson who depends on Jim? Why or why not?

5. Would it make a difference if Huck were sure Miss Watson would punish or resell Jim? Why or why not?

6. From the point of view of Jim's own family back home, what should Huck do?

7. Should Huck violate religious teachings to make his choice about Jim? Why or why not?*

* From *The Carnegie-Mellon Civic Education English Curriculum* (Pittsburgh: Carnegie-Mellon University, 1976), p. 42. Supported by the Danforth Foundation. Reprinted by permission.

SPECIAL TOPIC
A School Community Based on Justice?

By far the most ambitious attempt in promoting value education in schools has been conducted by Kohlberg and his colleague Elsa Wasserman in Cambridge, Massachusetts, and across the Charles River in Brookline by Ralph Mosher [1]. They went well beyond creating curriculum units for English and social studies classes. They organized an entire secondary school, the Just Community School—literally a school within a school—according to a Kohlbergian framework. Below is an excerpt of an article written by Wasserman that describes how the school, both pupils and staff, learned to function as a democratic (Stage 5) community.

The Structure of the School

The school's structure and procedures are derived from Kohlberg's research and from the collective experience of the community as its members strive to build and maintain a just school. School structure revolves around community meetings, small group meetings, advisor groups, the discipline committee, and the staff-student-consultant meetings.

In a participatory democracy the community meeting is the central institution of government; it is here that final agreement is reached about the policies and rules for the school. Its function is to promote the controlled conflict and open exchange of opinions about fairness that are essential to the moral development of the individuals in the community.

We opened our school with no rules or procedures of our own, but with an agreement to abide by the rules of the larger school. Our students quickly saw that if we did not make our own rules and develop our own procedures for handling them, we were no better off than we were in the traditional high school. As issues arose—as students created disturbances in classes, or were caught with drugs by school officials—we established rules, consequences for breaking rules, and decision-making procedures in our community meetings. The long-run result is a social contract established jointly by staff members and students. Each staff member and student has one vote in rule making and in the resolution of conflicts through fair decisions. The rules and disciplinary procedures cover disruptive behavior in the school, cutting classes, unexcused absence from school, the use of drugs, theft, and grading. The community also has held extended discussions about decision-making procedures, particularly on appeals to the community from decisions of the discipline committee. In addition, the community has discussed broader policy issues such as race relations within the school and student recruitment and enrollment.

The agenda for each weekly community meeting is planned in advance by staff and some students in a democracy class and in a weekly staff-consultant-student meeting. Issues coming before the community meeting are usually discussed in small groups the day before the meeting. Then, at the community meeting, a representative from each small group presents the group's position on a particular issue, and a general discussion follows which usually involves a comparison of various proposals. At this time, members of the small groups are called upon to defend their positions.

The first community meetings, chaired by staff members, were sometimes chaotic. Accordingly, a group of students and one faculty member decided to create a democracy class whose purpose was to train students to chair community meetings and to help develop fair and efficient procedures. This group has helped to develop a procedure in which a student or a pair of students chair the meeting. The chair recognizes students or staff members in the order in which they raise their hands. Still, much disorder can arise when the issue is "hot" and everyone wants to speak at once. The most difficult problem has been to determine when to call for votes. A premature call for a vote can cut off important discussion and lead to a poor decision, while lengthy discussions can be boring and frustrating to students and staff.

On major substantive motions a straw vote is taken to clarify whether there is substantial agreement or a need for further discussion. Finally, a "real" vote is taken on the motion with all approved amendments. If the proposal passes, the result is a policy or rule for the community.

The small groups (upper limit of 12) function like a small-scale community meeting. They precede the community meetings so that the issues and arguments around a specific problem can be clarified. The small groups encourage greater personal involvement in moral discussions, more role-taking, and more exposure to higher-stage reasoning. In addition, they lead to more widely discussed and carefully thought-out decisions in the community meeting. The small group meetings are essential for the creation of a viable governance structure and for an increased sense of community.

Advisor groups also play a vital role. Each student has a faculty advisor who takes over most guidance and counseling functions with supervision from a counselor. Staff members meet their advisees in advisor groups which meet at least once a week during school time. The advisor group functions as a support group where students can discuss problems of a personal or academic nature. It differs from the small group in its focus on personal concerns rather than on community issues. In one advisor group a student spoke of feeling hurt about what she perceived to be unfair and unequal treatment at home. The group helped her clarify her perceptions of the conflict, gave her its ideas about how it perceived the situ-

(Continued)

SPECIAL TOPIC (Continued)

ation, and offered her advice about how she might best present her feelings to her parents.

The discipline committee was formed to help enforce the school rules. The committee is composed of one student representative from each advising group. These representatives are randomly selected and rotate each term. One staff member also serves on the committee. The function of the discipline committee is to decide how to treat students or staff members who break school rules. Decisions of the discipline committee may be appealed to the community meeting. Many of our more fruitful community meetings have dealt with appeals which have resulted in reconsideration of rules over substantive issues of fairness.

The staff, interested students, and the consultants (Kohlberg and two associates) meet one evening each week. At these meetings, they review the preceding community meeting, analyze the current functioning of the school, suggest new ways to meet problems which have arisen, develop the skills of staff members, plan coming community meetings, and clarify the staff's understanding about moral issues which come before the community. Since the staff had no opportunity to study Kohlberg's research or to develop skills during the summer when the school was being planned, these staff meetings have played an indispensable role in the school. One of the consultants also conducts an afternoon curriculum workshop in which staff members learn to lead moral discussions and to integrate them into the curriculum.

The Cluster School in Operation

The early community meetings reflected the difficulties students and staff encountered as they tried to develop a successful democratic community process. Staff members tended to dominate discussions and to present reasoning which reflected their own concerns. They sometimes presented arguments based on Stage 5 reasoning which most students in the school could not understand. Students, not used to participating equally with staff, tested the one-person-one-vote system. The first community meeting, for example, ended with a vote reversed at the next meeting) that students could leave before the close of school if they did not like the courses offered. This incident led to the development of the straw vote as part of the decision-making process.

After several months, however, the school had developed a viable democracy. The conditions for moral growth—consideration of fairness, concern for the community, role-taking, and active participation in and a sense of responsibility for group decisions—are now directly observable in most community meetings. There is a greater awareness of and concern for the feelings of community members who are diverse ethnically, academically, and in life-styles.

This year a difficult issue of fairness focused on the admission of students for six remaining openings in the school. There were 47 white students in the school and 18 black students. The black students wanted more equal representation in the community. But there were already six students on the waiting list, only one of whom was black. The democracy class proposed that all six openings be filled by blacks.

A transcript of the community meeting which focused on this issue illustrates the conditions for moral development at work in the school. Students take the roles of others and give reasons which show understanding of opposing points of view. The issue is considered as one of fairness. Concern for the welfare of the community is manifested at different levels of moral reasoning, but it is this very concern which underlies the resolution of the competing viewpoints.

Two students chaired the meeting, one black and one white. One of the students stated the issue in the following words:

> All right, this is about admission of six new students to Cluster School. There's six openings and there's only one black person on the waiting list. And there's room for six more people. In democracy class a lot of people wanted all the rest of the people that would come to Cluster School to be black.

A white student immediately asked the implications for the white students on the waiting list:

> Does that mean that there's only one black on it now, but you want to get five more blacks to jump in front of the rest on the waiting line?

The students responded loudly, both supporting and opposing this reply. One chairperson stopped the commotion saying:

> Wait. I just want to stop this. I don't want no one jumping out of hand, because disturbances are going to be going like crazy, because I ain't in no mood for no one jumping out of hand in this meeting. I'm going to go around [and call on each in turn].

A black student presented a subjective point of view:

> I'm going to try to tell you how I feel about the situation. Because, you see, I'm one of the people that wants some black people to come in. . . . From what I see I feel I would be more comfortable with them here. I want them here. I want to let some new black people come in and experience the school.

A white student continued by elaborating on the issue of fairness to the white students already on the waiting list:

> Yesterday, right, you were talking in democracy, you were saying there's six openings, right. If they were all black people, it would be fair to let them in.

(Continued)

SPECIAL TOPIC (Continued)

I don't care if there were six black people on the waiting list, they could come in, but these five white people, they were first, right?

Other white students argued that fairness meant considering the discomfort of black students, now in the minority, who felt uncomfortable:

It doesn't matter to me whether they're black or white, they're people. But why can't everybody just accept the fact that the blacks would feel more comfortable and get a better education with more blacks in school? And why can't we just let the people that have signed up be black and come to the school, because that will improve all the blacks in the school.

In response to questions by some of the white students as to why more blacks had not volunteered to enter the school, a black student replied:

What would we say about how no black kids are signed up? One reason why they don't is they look at this school and see all these white people and they say this school is for whities. I don't want to go here 'cause there ain't going to be nobody here that I know. And no black people are ever going to sign up as long as they see there's only 18 black kids and 47 whites. Now how they going to feel signing up to go to this school?

Another black student added:

Can I ask all you white people something? I'm not prejudiced, but is it going to make that much difference if there's six more black people instead of white? Is it? There's 47 of you whities now. There's 18 blacks! Six more blacks isn't going to make one difference!

After some angry exchanges, a white student tried to pull together the feelings of the community:

All the people in this community right now are all saying in some way or another—usually they don't want to say it—but they're expressing feelings that they care about the other people and how their education goes and how their working with this community goes. And I feel that the blacks in this community can't work as well and feel as comfortable without more blacks in this community. It's not fair. Everybody knows that everybody in this school, no matter how it sounds now, cares about the other people. Then why can't you allow six more blacks in, so 20-whatever blacks will be able to get a good education in this school and a good sense of democracy and just everything. And you know, why can't we just let six more blacks in, it would help the whole thing. The whole community, the whole school would be helped by that.

A white student asked why the black students felt uncomfortable in the school. A black student responded:

Well, I'm going to tell you why I feel uncomfortable. Before I knew who was here, I phoned Cambridge Latin and I didn't want to sign up with Latin, so I heard about Cluster and I came down. This is my first year in this school and I don't know who's here. Never in my life have I seen as many of you who have outnumbered me and mine, anyway. OK, then I get to know them. I say, these whites are all right, you know. And my opinions changed, they changed just a little bit, all right? And then I go home and I look, I listen to the news and I see what the whities are doing to the blacks. For what? Because they want to learn. And then I come back here and I try to get some of my brothers and sisters into this school so they can be helped like I'm being helped. And what do I hear? No. Because they don't want to hear it. Why can't they just give us 18 blacks a little personal satisfaction within ourselves to have some more of us so we can be together?
All right! (*Applause*)

Another black student asked the white students to consider how they might feel if they were in the minority:

You know, if you all were in a class, one or two of you with 20 black kids, how would you feel?

After more discussion, a straw vote was taken which indicated that the majority of the community was in favor of the proposal. Most of those voting in opposition expressed concern for the white students on the waiting list.

The reason I voted against the proposal was that I wanted to hear more reasons from the black kids, but I'm also feeling a little guilty because I want six black kids to come in, but I don't know what to say about the five white kids on the waiting list. What are we going to tell them?

In response, these reasons were given:

All you have to do is explain to them that the community decided that it was the best idea to take all blacks this time for the community's sake and from now on, every time we're going to admit more kids, we'll admit half black and half white. By then, eventually it will be fairer and we can accept blacks and whites the same way.

Finally, the community voted almost unanimously to adopt the proposal from the democracy class. There was a feeling of elation among the strong supporters of the motion and some bitter feelings among the opposed. Small groups are continuing to discuss the issue and to suggest ways to incorporate the opposing views in a final resolution of the issue.*

---

* From E. Wasserman, Implementing Kohlberg's "Just Community concept" in an alternative high school, *Social Education* (April 1976):203–207. Reprinted with permission of the National Council for the Social Studies.

(*Continued*)

SPECIAL TOPIC (Continued)

In addition to comments by teachers and students about the effectiveness of the Just Community high school, there have been more formal and objective evaluations. Generally, the regular high school curriculum has had no impact on the level of moral judgment over the period of one year. Studies by a number of researchers have shown that students in their junior and senior years remain at stage 3. In other words, as we will show in Chapter 12, the school program in general does very little, if anything, to stimulate psychological maturity and the development of value judgments. In contrast, the Just Community high school approach, as described by Wasserman, does impact value development. In the carefully researched study by Ralph Mosher in the Brookline (Mass.) schools, he found important evidence of positive change. A random sample of students in the school within a school (the Kohlbergian school) showed improvement in moral reasoning as a result of the program. Their scores on the Kohlberg Moral Dilemma Test improved an average of 32 points—an increase of $+\frac{1}{3}$ stage from stage 3 toward stage 4. Regular school programs have no such positive effects.

The results of the studies really indicate two points: (1) Positive change is possible, and (2) it requires substantial time and effort on the part of the school staff to stimulate such growth. In an area as complicated and as important as value development, we cannot expect some quick fix. Effective change is, by definition, slow—but with carefully created school programs, it is also sure.

REFERENCES

1. E. Wasserman, Implementing Kohlberg's "Just Community concept" in an alternative high school, *Social Education* (April 1976):203–207; R. L. Mosher, A democratic high school: Damn it, your feet are always in the water, in *Adolescents' development and education: A Janus knot.* (Berkeley, Calif.: McCutchan, 1979), pp. 497–516.

For more informal settings such as youth group meetings, dormitory discussions, and the like, a series of excellent, brief (15-minute) excerpts from major motion pictures are available. For example, in a classic depiction of a person facing a dilemma, Marlon Brando as Terry Molloy in *On the Waterfront* struggles with issues of loyalty to his family and his union—and, indeed, his existence—versus telling the truth about who killed Joey Doyle [13]. In such an instance the general issue of a code of silence can become the overall dilemma. The trade unions call it D&D, deaf and dumb; however, other professional groups such as police, doctors, corporate executives, and government employees have similar codes, and they are much like the codes teenagers have. The stage 3 reasoning of never betraying a friend is, of course, a central and continuing dilemma that teenagers as well as adults face all the time, even though the content of such dilemmas may be different. To raise these issues during adolescence provides them with an opportunity not only to examine such positions in detail but also to discuss alternatives.

Writing Dilemmas

It is also appropriate for teenagers to write their own dilemmas. It is not recommended, however, that educational programs adopt this procedure as an initial phase. Adolescents generally need some experience with solving dilemmas at a general level first. Then they may be better prepared to write their own in accord with the general framework.

For this type of program both teachers and students should be aware of the following characteristics of dilemmas:

1. They should allow reasoning at each level.

2. They should be open-ended.

3. They should permit discussion of issues on either side of each reasoning stage.

Let's examine each of these characteristics. On the first point, sometimes there may be a tendency to rewrite the dilemma so that the issue disappears. Then differential reasoning vanishes. For example, in a sinking lifeboat dilemma, what happens if the crew suddenly discovers a secret compartment that contains material to patch the holes? The dilemma would be resolved, and the issue could not be reasoned through.

On the second point, it may be difficult at the outset for students to understand the concept of open-endedness. For a variety of reasons, perhaps even social conditioning, teenagers are more comfortable with one answer, or closure. After all, most films they see, most novels they read, and most stories we tell them reach specific conclusions. In fact, we commonly point out the moral of a story, implying that there is a single rule or outcome. So it is not unusual for adolescents to indicate some annoyance with open-endedness. It will take time and patience to gradually help them become comfortable with the divergent thought involved in open-ended discussions. O'Henry's "Lady or the Tiger" is, after all, the exception, not the rule.

On the third point, students should be able to argue and reason at different levels and on different sides of the same stage. For example, consider the case of Terry Molloy in *On the Waterfront* (Marlon Brando): He could refuse to rat on the boss because by doing so, he'd get a good job, easy work, and extra money—in other words, stage 2 reasoning, materialistic gain. Or he could turn his boss in because if he did so, the police or the FBI would pay him more money—but his reasoning is still at stage 2, a greater materialistic gain. If a person sells out to the highest bidder without distinguishing between principles and conformity, then the judgment process is the same even though outcomes may differ.

Value Development: A Review

The question of schooling and value development is obviously of great significance. A multitude of studies indicate that there is a clear functional relationship between a person's modal stage of judgment and his or her behavioral acts. These relationships are not precisely one to one, but the trends are extremely strong. For example, in a somewhat unique study students were asked to prepare a talk on the meaning of the parable of the good Samaritan [14]. Then, one by one, they were guided by an authority figure to a class across campus that was waiting to hear the talk. On the way a confederate of the research study, posed as a down-and-out drug addict, stopped the student and pleaded for help. The authority figure (a professor) urged the student, "Come along. We are in a hurry!" Table 6.6 presents the percentages of students who helped the victim in spite of the commands of the professor.

As the table shows, a large proportion of the students at stages 2, 3, and 4 refused to stop and aid the addict. Instead, they rushed past the victim in order to comply with the professor and give their prepared talk on the meaning of the good Samaritan parable. In contrast, a large proportion of the students at stage 5, and all the students at stage 6, gave help to the addict in spite of the directions from the authority figure.

Similar results have been reported in other studies. There was always a strong tendency for those subjects classified at the higher stage of moral judgment to act in a manner consistent with the principles of a democratic society. Thus the issues are highly significant since the systems of judgment do affect how we behave.

On an overall basis, then, the Kohlberg stage system presents an important framework with which to comprehend the structure of a person's reasoning process in the domain of value judgment. The stages are systems of judgment and impact how we behave. Each person tends to use a particular stage at specific ages; this stage is denoted the modal stage. In addition to this predominant mode there are submodes, usually thought process at the next highest and next lowest stages. Thus each person is a mix of stages, with one major modal system accompanied by some processing at levels on each side of the major one.

By asking open-ended questions, particularly on difficult issues that do not have pat solutions, one can identify the major system a person employs. It is also helpful for individuals to learn to hear and analyze their own system. In fact, the process of self-development requires that each

Table 6.6 Percentage of college students who
helped a person in distress (N = 110)

Kohlberg stage	Percentage
2	11
3	27
4	38
5	68
6	100

person learn to process, in an open way, his or her own methods of judgments. This procedure increases the likelihood that the person will develop greater self-reliance. By learning to think through difficult questions on the basis of rational rules and principles, each person will be less swayed by short-term considerations. Since adolescents as a group are particularly subject to value judgment based on social conformity rather than rational and principled thought, the issue is not irrelevant.

An optimistic point in this framework is the tendency for persons to be attracted to the next stage up in the sequence. Cognitive capacity for more complex thinking is ready for growth at particular points as long as stages are not skipped over [15]. Thus stage 3 is easily available to junior high pupils employing stage 2. Similarly, at the high school level stage 4 is within the range of the majority of pupils.

However, an upward movement in development does not happen automatically or quickly. We noted earlier in the Piaget discussion (Chapter 4) that growth can oscillate between new and old modes of thought. Persons are attracted to the new, the novel, and the slightly more complex. Yet they are creatures of habit. They desire stability almost as strongly as they desire growth. Thus a single exposure, a charismatic lecture, or any brief experience will not stimulate growth. We may get pupils to say the right words to fit higher stages, but their behavior will not be influenced. For example, a junior high debating team was taught to present their opening arguments at a stage 5 level. All went along fine until the off-the-cuff rebuttal. At that point the stage 2 and stage 3 thinking surfaced immediately. Thus it is important to remember that developmental growth occurs slowly. People will not part readily with old systems, or shed a method that has merit for a new and as yet untried system.

SUMMARY

Piaget has indicated the folly of attempting to artificially accelerate growth, and we should not fall into this trap in any area of development. But since the question of values is so central to a democratic society—and, indeed, to any system that rests on humane ethics—we may be tempted to rush the process.

As we noted at the beginning of the chapter, adults for centuries have alternately struggled with and despaired over the problem of values during adolescence. The Kohlberg system presented in this chapter is a framework that can help anyone who works with adolescents. As we noted in the chapter, the system provides information about the sequence and the content of moral judgment thought systems teenagers employ, especially during the junior and senior high school years. We have also shown that both boys and girls use similar stages of reasoning according to age. Also, we have indicated that the systems of reasoning may vary according to the content issues being discussed. Thus a teenager might reason at one level on an issue such as Heinz and the drug question but reason at a lower level on a more personal issue, such as a question of sexual involvement.

In addition to providing a framework for identification of reasoning levels, we also presented information on educational programs designed to promote reasoning at more complex and more thoughtful levels. Features of classroom moral dilemma discussions were outlined, and information was given on how to create dilemma situations for discussion. As we noted, works from literature, films, and similar sources can be employed as stimulus material for open-ended discussions. We also showed the importance of learning to listen to the actual levels in a discussion and the need to suggest or clarify issues at a slightly more complex level.

The basic point for the question of value development is essentially the same as that for the question of general cognitive development, as noted in Chapter 4. Growth to higher stages of reasoning is possible but not automatic. Adolescents need the opportunity to examine value dilemma questions both to understand the issues involved and to grow from the experience.

KEY POINTS AND NAMES

Lawrence Kohlberg

Stages of moral judgment
   Preconventional
   Conventional
   Postconventional

Dilemma

Stage sequence

Modal stages and changes during adolescence

Empathy

Variations in age groups

Sex differences in judgment

Moral judgment and sexual dilemma

Carol Gilligan

Educational programs
   Dilemma discussions
   Role reversal Plus one
   Expanded content
   Writing dilemmas

REFERENCES

1. Quoted in *Everyday life in bible times* (Washington, D.C.: National Geographic Society, 1968).

2. Quoted in *Harvard Alumni Bulletin*, May 1, 1965, p. 583.

3. E. Rogoff, Patterns of communication between parents and adolescents (Ph.D. thesis, Harvard Graduate School of Education, 1969).

4. L. Kohlberg, Collected papers, Harvard School of Education, Cambridge, Mass.

5. L. Kohlberg, *Measuring moral judgment* (Worcester, Mass.: Clark University Press, 1979).

6. E. Sullivan, G. McCullough, and M. Stager, A developmental study of the relationship between conceptual, ego, and moral development, *Child Development* 41(1970):399–411.

7. C. Holstein, Irreversible, stepwise sequence in the development of moral judgment: A longitudinal study of males and females, *Child Development* 47(1976):51–61. Also on this point, Carol Gilligan has recently suggested that some of the possible sex differences may result from a male scoring bias. See Martha Saxton, Are women more moral than men? An interview with Carol Gilligan, *Ms*, December 1981. A large number of studies by James Rest with his objective measure of moral judgment, however, have consistently indicated that there are no differences between male and females on the level of value development. See Rest, note 15.

8. C. Gilligan, J. Kohlberg, M. Lerner, and M. Belenky, *Moral reasoning about sexual dilemmas. Technical report of the U.S. Commission on Obscenity and Pornography, VI* (Washington, D.C.: Government Printing Office, 1971), pp. 141–174.

9. See R. Gailbraith and T. Jones, *Moral reasoning* (Minneapolis: Greenhaven Press, 1976); R. Hersch, D. Paolitto, and J. Reimer, *Developmental moral education: Kohlberg's theory in practice* (New York: Longman, 1978).

10. For a complete review of the research on this point see J. Rest, Morality, in *Carmichael's manual of child psychology*, 4th ed., J. Flavell and E. Markman (New York: Wiley, 1981).

11. *The Ethical Quest Project* (Tacoma Public Schools, P.O. Box 1357, Tacoma, Wash. 98401; 1980).

12. *The Carnegie-Mellon Civic Education English Curriculum* (Pittsburgh: Carnegie-Mellon University, 1976).

13. This film series was produced by the Learning Corporation of America, available from Krasker Memorial Film Library, Boston University, Boston, Mass. 02115.

14. S. McNamee, Moral behavior, moral development and motivation, *Journal of Moral Education* 7, 1(1977):27–31. For a more complete review detailing the relationship of moral judgment and actual behavior, see R. C. Sprinthall and

N. A. Sprinthall, *Educational psychology: A developmental approach*, 3rd ed. (Reading, Mass.: Addison-Wesley, 1981), chap. 9.

15. J. Rest, *Development in judging moral issues* (Minneapolis: University of Minnesota Press, 1979).

CHAPTER 7

Family Relations
and Influences

INTRODUCTION

The family has been called "the crucible of identity." The sense of personal integration and coherence that Erikson saw as the major achievement of adolescence depends in large part on the social, intellectual, and emotional development that is fostered within family relationships.

In this chapter we examine the nature and influence of family relations in adolescence. Many of the important influences begin well before the adolescent years themselves, though. The emotional atmosphere of the family, the way in which parents train and teach their children, the opportunities and difficulties that family life presents for normal development—all are present from early life and merely continue their influence in adolescence. Consequently, the first question we will address is, "How do family environments in childhood shape the later characteristics of adolescents?"

The way families meet the special circumstances and problems of adolescence itself is also important, however. The transition from childhood to adulthood presents some special challenges. The sheer rapidity of the primary changes—physical, cognitive, and social—puts demands on families that adolescents sometimes feel very keenly. For example, 15-year-old Paul commented of his parents: "Sometimes I can't believe how much I've changed in just a few days and they can't see it." At 16, Deanne complained that "they don't tell you they know you're growing up. They always remember you as you were when you were five." In addition, parents change over the years, and the changes and stresses they experience often affect their responses to the changes in their adolescents. So we will also discuss these parallel changes in this chapter. Finally, we will address several important areas of family influence that seem particularly central to the formation of identity in adolescence.

Beginning with this chapter on family relations and influences, we turn our attention to the major *settings* of adolescent development and to the aspects of individual growth and change that appear especially important in the second decade of life. In Chapter 1 we characterized family as the first of three major settings, or contexts, within which the primary physical, cognitive, and social changes of adolescence occur. As we saw in Chapters 3–6, school and peer contexts influence these developing characteristics as well. Our goal in this book is to show how the changing adolescent encounters, and is influenced by, people and situations in the course of growth toward adulthood.

FAMILY ENVIRONMENTS

Families provide both our initial social relationships and the settings for most of our early learning about persons, situations, and skills. This early learning is highly influential. Later experiences may affect us powerfully, too, of course. But if in adolescence we changed behavior patterns, attitudes, and values drastically, we would have to undergo considerable unlearning of old patterns and painstaking learning of new ones. This *discontinuity* of learning would make adolescence far more difficult than it appears to be for most young people. Perhaps the formative influence of early learning explains why families seem to affect so many of the relationships and tasks of adolescence and adulthood. As we will see in this chapter and later chapters, school achievement, vocational aspiration and success, and marital and family adjustment all are tied to some degree to childhood experiences in the family.

What aspects of family life account for these far-reaching effects? Often family effects actually reflect social and economic conditions. Less affluent families, living in crowded urban environments, share many problems in rearing their children that are different from the problems of affluent suburban families [1]. Nevertheless, many approaches to rearing children transcend social and economic circumstances. In recent years some important differences between families in the socialization of their children have been identified. These differences, which we will examine in this section, tell us a great deal about how adolescents from those families adjust to the changes and new demands of adolescence.

**Parents'
Child-Rearing
Styles**

It is difficult to say what characterizes a complex social system like a family. However, in 1965 psychologist Diana Baumrind attempted to describe differences in families through extensive observations of children and

The family is a complex social system encompassing several generations and a variety of personalities
Photograph from William Gladstone/Anthro-Photo

through tests and interviews with their parents [2]. She asked a straightforward question: What reliable connections can we see between parents' attitudes and behaviors in the family and what their children are like?

Baumrind explored these issues in a longitudinal study of 110 middle-class children and their parents. The results of her first experiences with them, when the children were four years old, showed an intriguing relationship between characteristics of the children and their family backgrounds. Baumrind found that some of the children were self-reliant, self-controlled, explorative, and content; others were discontent, withdrawn, distrustful, and low in self-control and self-reliance. She also found three distinct clusters of parents who differed from each other in how they made and enforced demands on their children and how warm and accepting they were toward them: authoritarian, permissive, and authoritative. Let's look now at these family types.

In *authoritarian* families parents are strict and controlling. They attempt to teach children absolute standards of behavior and "favor punitive, forceful measures to curb self-will at points where the child's actions or beliefs conflict with what they think is right conduct" [3]. The emphasis is on *preventing* children from behaving unacceptably, as the parents define that term, and on teaching them respect for authority. The emotional tone of the family is often cold and rejecting (although not always so). Youth researcher Gisela Konopka quotes a 15-year-old girl's description of her authoritarian father:

"I'm really scared, I'm afraid of what he's going to say. I've done it a couple of times, not very many times, but I just can't go up and say 'Hi, let's talk.' Because when I say that, I'm so afraid of what he will say.

"Well, when I do it, he will say, 'Well, look, I don't want to talk to you,' or 'There's no way we can get along; you mess up too much; you don't understand the rules around here,' and stuff like that. Or sometimes he will say, 'Well, what do you have to say?' And that's when I get scared, and I will just say, 'Well, let's kind of reason,' or I will just say, 'I'm sorry,' just to get him to start going along. And then he will say, 'Okay, I'll forgive you, but you know I'm right,' or 'Next time, you will know better,' and it's just a short conversation." [4]

Permissive families, by contrast, make few demands and rarely use force or power to achieve their child-rearing goals. Instead, they tend to favor reason and persuasion in their interactions with children.

The third type of family, the *authoritative* family, shares some characteristics with the other two types, but the blend has a quite different tone. Authoritative parents have firm boundaries and expectations for their children's behavior. However, they attempt to provide guidelines through the use of reason and rules. And they judiciously use rewards and punishments that are clearly related to the child's behavior. Such parents recognize their responsibilities to be authority figures, but they are also responsive to the special needs and interests of their children. The atmosphere in authoritative families is generally warm and accepting.

Konopka reports two similar reactions to authoritative parents among the thousands of adolescent girls she interviewed. The first was that of a 15-year-old girl:

"My father always checks on us at night. He checks our lessons and what we have been doing in the day and where we have been and so forth. But I do not mind this because he is interested in us." [5]

The second comment came from a 17-year-old girl:

"He never does try to tell us what to do, but if he thinks it's gonna be wrong and hurt us, he tries to talk us out of it. And he usually wins . . . because I agree with my father mostly." [6]

In both cases the family relationship was characterized by mutual respect and the father's attempting to draw out, monitor, and teach his daughter.

When Baumrind correlated parents' characteristics with the categories of children she had studied, she found that the self-reliant, self-controlled, explorative, and content children came mostly from authoritative families. In contrast, children of authoritarian parents were submissive, dependent, and not very responsible or achievement-oriented. The children of permissive parents were self-reliant and independent at age four, but they were less socially responsible and achievement-oriented than the children of authoritative parents [7].

Baumrind was obviously looking for early indications of mature behavior: independence, social responsibility, and achievement orientation. And her preliminary reports indicate that the differences she observed on these characteristics in early childhood have continued into adolescence [8]. Thus Baumrind has shown some long-term connection between mature behavior and the family environments of adolescents.

Parental Styles and Adolescent Behavior

Parents who vary in the way Baumrind described probably react very differently to the changes of adolescence. What are the implications of these differences for their relationships with their adolescent children? This question was the topic of a large-scale study of more than seven thousand junior high and senior high school students [9]. In this study the adolescents' descriptions of their parents were categorized as *autocratic* (similar to Baumrind's authoritarian parents), *democratic* (similar to authoritative parents), or *permissive*.

The study's author, Glen Elder, believed the most important difference between autocratic and democratic parents was the way in which they exercise their power in the family. In democratic families, parents legitimate their power by encouraging adolescents to "participate in discussing issues relevant to their behavior, although the final decision is always made or approved by the parent" [10]. In autocratic families, parents do not "allow the adolescent to express his views on subjects regarding his behavior nor permit him to regulate his own behavior in any way" [11]. In short, the democratic parent teaches and explains while showing respect for the adolescent; the autocratic parent coerces and disregards the child's opinions and feelings.

Elder's results showed that adolescents from democratic families were more self-confident and independent than those from autocratic families. Furthermore, the more parents respected adolescents' opinions and sought to involve them in discussions and explanations of decisions, the more the adolescents felt that their parents were people they would "want to be like" and the more they chose friends and activities of which their parents would approve [12]. A striking example of the benefits of a democratic family style comes from a 16-year-old girl's comment about her father:

> I'd like to be able to work as hard as he does. He really tries, shows me a lot of ways like when I totally disagree with him, he has taught one how to argue out the responses and kind of debate things [13].

Like Baumrind's 4-year-olds, the adolescents Elder studied showed the effects of the family style in which they had been reared.

SPECIAL TOPIC
Different Family Atmospheres: Implications for Practice

Baumrind's and Elder's works give substantial support to the notion that family atmospheres generally fall into one of three categories: (1) autocratic, (2) permissive, and (3) authoritative-democratic. You may believe that it is helpful at a very general level to understand that teenagers come from different family backgrounds, but beyond that, what's the point?

There is one very important point, especially if you are directly involved with adolescents. At a conscious and an emotional level adolescents develop implicit expectations about how they will be treated from the interpersonal atmosphere created by their parents. Thus with a teenager from an autocratic family, there may be evidence of obedience, expectations of close monitoring, and perhaps some rather subtle resentment that may or may not be verbalized. In contrast, teenagers from a permissive family atmosphere will generally expect limits to be always negotiable, rules to be very relativistic, and the general environment to be benignly neglectful. Those teenagers from an authoritative-democratic atmosphere will have had substantial experience in gradual independence training and will show some inner-directedness and self-reliance. Thus in terms of today's vernacular "knowing where someone is coming from" often involves understanding the different family atmospheres.

Even more important, however, is what such information may tell you about your own role. How the teenager may perceive you can depend on his or her own present and past experiences at home. This perception has two elements. First, in spite of your best efforts to establish an authoritative-democratic level, some teenagers may insist on translating your approach to their experience. They may not be able to distinguish between authoritative and authoritarian behavior. This result is often seen in student teaching. Students in training say they are against autocratic teaching (maybe because they were raised that way or taught that way). As a reaction the beginning teacher then refuses to employ almost any structure or direction to the lessons. The teacher sees such activity as authoritarian and says, "Kids need to be free to develop at their own rate. I'm a resource and will teach at their request." The problem, of course, is that such a view confuses being an authority with acting authoritarian. Thus one element of importance is how the teenagers' family atmospheres generally influence their current perceptions.

A second element is what is called the *transition problem:* What happens when an adult deliberately changes the atmosphere? A classic study by Kurt Lewin, Ronald Lippett, and Ralph White examined just such a problem [1]. A group of early adolescents were taught how to build model airplanes under the three conditions authoritarian-dictatorial, authoritative-democratic, and permissive-laissez faire (from French, meaning "to leave alone"). The pupils who experienced the greatest difficulty adjusting to the task were those taught in the authoritarian condition first and who then moved to the democratic. The transition from a highly structured, adult-dominated group, in which no questions were permitted and every aspect was directed, to a more democratic group was the most difficult. The group members had trouble responding to requests for suggestions and group discussions for planning. In other words, their expectations of leadership style and their experience in the first condition created dissonance when the atmosphere changed.

Since this study was an experiment, the group leaders were not permitted to comment to the pupils. In common practice, however, there is every reason to talk about your own expectations as a teacher, counselor, or youth worker. If you suspect that some of the teenagers you're working with come from an authoritarian atmosphere (or from a laissez faire atmosphere), you should clearly state how you plan to interact. This technique is called setting norms, or setting expectations of participation—what you will (and won't) negotiate on, how much self-direction and independence you except, and so on. It provides teenagers with a reasonable definition of your boundaries, particularly if your goal is to achieve the authoritative-democratic condition.

But note that setting expectations is only the first step in handling the transition. Some adolescents will need substantial help from you to develop the kind of independence you may want from them. Teenagers reared under strict authoritarian methods will require your patience and direction in setting a series of small steps to help them move gradually to greater self-direction.

In the 1960s, to cite an example, many well-meaning white, middle-class college students went into the inner-city schools absolutely committed to democratic-participatory methods of teaching. The children for the most part had experienced extremely directive, authoritarian teaching prior to the arrival of the new teachers. The veteran teachers employed corporal punishment (caning); the children sat in straight rows and recited only on call. But the new teachers did not attend to the transition problem; instead, they immediately restructured the classrooms along the lines of a town meeting. The results were disastrous for all. The new teachers experienced chaos in the classrooms, the old teachers were extremely resentful, and the adolescents were totally confused. In these situations transitions are extremely important and require careful planning and a sequencing of experiences to help pupils move to a more complex level of functioning.

REFERENCE

1. K. Lewin, R. Lippitt, and R. K. White, Patterns of aggressive behavior in experimentally created social climates, *Journal of Social Psychology* 10(1939):271–299.

ADOLESCENT CHANGES AND FAMILY CHANGES

The different family atmospheres that Baumrind and Elder studied indicate that the general ways in which parents exercise their authority during childhood influence the social and emotional skills of their children. These parental styles rarely change in character as children move into adolescence; the general methods of child rearing usually stay the same in a family as a child moves from one age to another [14]. Other changes do occur as the children of the family move into adolescence, however—changes not in general family style but in specific patterns of interaction among family members. There are also important changes in the lives of individual family members—parents as well as children—that influence how family life proceeds. In this section we discuss both the impact of changes in adolescents on their family relationships and the influence of more subtle changes that parents of adolescents are often experiencing at the same time.

Changes in Family Interactions

We begin with a brief consideration of changes in the interactions between parents and their children as the children move into adolescence. As we indicated in Chapter 3, adolescents' physical changes alone may create new expectations and demands on the part of parents as well as other adults. These expectations and demands can alter the way in which parents and children get along together. One example has been described by Laurence Steinberg [15]. By examining the problem-solving discussions of parents and their adolescent sons over a period of time, Steinberg was able to document the ways in which family interaction changed as the son showed the changes of puberty.

Steinberg gave the families imaginary but realistic problems to solve—for example, where to go on a family vacation. He instructed them to reach common agreement on a solution to the problem. Steinberg observed the family discussions at three points in the son's development: before pubertal changes had begun, at midpubescence, and after puberty. He found that the family's interactions changed as the son matured physically.

At midpubescence, boys deferred to their mothers less often in discussion than they had before pubescence. They interrupted frequently, and mothers interrupted their sons frequently in return. Both boys and their mothers offered fewer explanations and justifications for their opinions and statements than they had before pubertal changes began. As a result, family interaction became more contentious and rigid. Family members responded less and less to the different opinions each of them expressed. Fathers often served to balance and correct the interactional difficulties between mothers and sons. For example, at midpubescence fathers asserted themselves more in discussions, and adolescent boys continued to defer to them.

After puberty, family interactions generally became more flexible and responsive, however. Mothers interrupted their sons less often, and sons offered more explanations to support their positions in the family discussions. At the same time the sons' relative influence on the final outcome of the family's decision making increased. Before puberty the two parents' opinions had dominated decisions; but after puberty the son's influence was typically greater than the mother's, although noticeably less than the father's.

Although these results may be applicable only to middle-class families with sons, the pattern of changes in family interaction seems to mirror the experiences of many families as their children enter adolescence. The parallel between family interactions and the physical changes of puberty suggests that adolescents may change their expectations about how they should be treated in family interactions as they mature. These changing expectations probably also reflect new social experiences and demands that teenagers experience with peers and other adults outside the family. For example, adolescents can usually be more assertive with their friends and schoolmates than they can be at home. At first adolescents may be unable to judge properly the conditions under which assertiveness is appropriate in family discussion and the ways in which one can constructively express contrary opinions and arguments. As time passes, though, both they and their parents are likely to devise new ways of reaching decisions that are appropriate to the increasing physical and social maturity that pubertal changes signify.

Changing patterns of interaction and influence in family decision making can be described as part of a series of *transformations* in family relationships that occur as children mature. Let us now consider several aspects of adolescent development—and changes in parents—that affect transformations in parent-child relationships.

Social Cognitive Change and Parent-Child Relations

One factor in changing family relations may be adolescents' developing abilities for comprehending the nature of parent-child relationships. In Chapter 5 we saw evidence that adolescence is a time of marked changes in abilities for understanding the relation of oneself to important other persons. Selman, for example, described levels of interpersonal understanding. Recently, Selman also applied these levels to the understanding of relationships between self and parents [16].

As shown in Table 7.1, Selman outlines five levels in the understanding of parent-child relations. These five levels parallel the four general levels of interpersonal understanding described in Chapter 5.

During the period of egotistic understanding (level 0), children understand parents simply as adults who meet specific and immediate needs—for example, "Who will make my dinner?" Selman refers to this interaction as an understanding of the parent as boss, the child as servant. In the

TABLE 7.1   Selman's levels of conceptions of parent-child relations

Level	Parent-child relation
0	Parent as boss
1	Parent as caretaker and helper for child
2	Parent as guidance counselor and need satisfier
3	Parent and child mutually show tolerance and respect
4	Parent-child relations change as circumstances, abilities, and needs of each change

young child's eyes the parent role is defined in terms of the child's immediate needs.

Later, at the subjective level of interpersonal understanding (level 1), children begin to conceive of parents as caretaker-helpers. Rather than emphasizing the physical constraints that parents exercise or the physical needs they meet, children are able to conceive of parents in terms of their characteristics and intentions toward the child.

In the reciprocal period (level 2) young persons become aware that the parent-child relationship depends on both the child and the parent. Children may be satisfying and gratifying to an adult, just as an adult is able to meet particular needs of children. As shown in Table 7.1, Selman calls this level the "guidance counselor–need satisfier" level. The child is showing an awareness that the child needs parental advice and guidance and that parents, in turn, need to be able to experience pleasure from observing their child's growth and happiness. At this level conflicts are understood to be caused by genuine differences of opinion between parents and children rather than simply by mistake or error on the part of either party. In summary, understanding of parent-child relationships has become relative rather than absolute, as it was in levels 0 and 1. In level 2 the main focus is on the quality of emotional ties between parents and children.

At level 3 the changing cognitive capacities of adolescents enable them to view parent-child relationships in terms of tolerance and respect. This level of thinking about parent-child relations emphasizes the mutuality of such relationships. Understanding involves recognizing that parents have psychological needs, just as children do. At this level adolescents understand that conflicts are naturally likely to occur because they and their parents have an unequal relationship and different needs and expectations. As Selman says:

> Getting along is not characterized by absolute agreement, but by respect for the others' position. For instance, the parental demand for obedience is understood to be related to the adults' need to be respected and acknowl-

Young adolescents may think of parents as sources of guidance and need satisfaction, services they give in return for the gratifications of parenthood

Photograph from Strix Pix

edged as the source of authority in the family system. Conflicts between obedience to parents and the need of growing children for autonomy and independence are also articulated at Level 3. [17]

Understanding at this level obviously involves the perspectivistic-thinking skills that emerge in adolescence.

Selman found it difficult to specify the details of thinking at level 4, the societal-symbolic level described in Chapter 5. However, he speculates that one important aspect of thought at this level is the recognition that parent-child relations are a system that changes from time to time as the characteristics of individuals change. This recognition of the family as a system, or set of relationships, may underlie the relative ease with which some families seem to negotiate the adolescent years. As we can see from Selman's descriptions of earlier levels, however, this advanced level of understanding probably comes only gradually. In the course of change and growth, adolescents may pass through several levels of comprehending the nature of their relationships to their parents [18].

Changes in Parents: Family Development

At the same time that adolescents are changing physically and cognitively, parents are also changing. In fact, it has been suggested that not only in adolescence but also in other life periods as well we should think in terms of *family* development [19]. That is, family relations in adolescence refer to the changes that take place as the result not only of adolescent changes but also of the changing relationships, expectations, and tasks faced by the family during the same period of time.

To give you a feeling for what we mean by family development, we will look at a description of characteristic periods in the history of many families. The stages are outlined in Table 7.2. As you can see from the description for each stage, the successive periods encompass family life from the time the parents are married to the time children have grown up and left home and the parents are alone again. Although this scheme assumes that *family* refers only to a pair of parents and their children (a nuclear family), it is also possible to outline the stages for a single-parent family progressing from stage 1, when the single-parent family was established, through the growing up of children, to the point at which a parent rearing children alone is living alone again as a single person without children.

Whether we are talking about a nuclear family or a single-parent family, however, the period of interest to us is the one that involves the change from a heavy emphasis on child rearing in parents' lives to the point where child rearing becomes less and less central to the way they spend their time. Thus we are most interested in stage 3, the stable stage, and stage 4, the contracting stage, which parents of adolescents are often anticipating.

During these two stages children in most families are reaching adolescence, and at the same time parents are often undergoing changes in their own occupational experience, personal goals, or hopes for the future. The age period of many parents with adolescents is popularly known as the time of *midlife crisis,* a time when questioning often takes place about how the middle and later adult years should be spent. In addition, adolescence often corresponds to a time of increasing pressure on parents who are

TABLE 7.2 Stages of family development

Stage	Label of stage	Description of stage
1	Establishment stage	Time of marriage
2	Expanding stage	Addition of first child to arrival of last child
3	Stable stage	Period of child rearing until first child leaves home
4	Contracting stage	Period of children's leaving home until last child has gone
5	Couple-alone stage	

Adapted from J. Aldous, *Family careers: Developmental change in families* (New York: Wiley, 1978), p. 84.

employed, particularly for those who are attempting to get ahead in their careers. Very heavy demands on their time and energies at work may increase the difficulty of adjusting to the problems of adolescents. And for women who were not pursuing careers while their children were young, adolescence presents a time when it is necessary to think about what they will do when there are no longer children at home. In short, while adolescents are undergoing a period of identity formation for their own future adult roles, their parents may also be questioning the bases on which their early adult lives were founded. Thus parents as well as adolescents may be facing identity issues at the same time, but in different ways [20].

Family development scholars make the point that we need to think not only about how families influence adolescents but also about how the changes associated with adolescence can be handled by families. If parents are facing economic pressures, occupational stresses, and serious doubts about the future, they may simply be unable to respond to adolescent changes as flexibly and constructively as is needed. Or adolescents may feel their parents' strain in other ways that complicate the transitions they are experiencing physically and socially.

In the remainder of the chapter we turn to several areas of family influence in adolescence. We will see how the ways that families differ in their child-rearing practices and how the circumstances of the parents' own lives may affect the course of adolescent development.

THE FAMILY AND IDENTITY FORMATION

Families help—or fail to help—their children achieve the tasks of adolescence in many ways. One important positive family function clearly is to help provide continuities between childhood learning and the new demands of adolescence and adulthood. As part of that function, the roles and behaviors learned in childhood must be merged into anticipated adult roles and behaviors. As we noted in Chapter 2, this integration of past and future roles is part of the challenge to a sense of identity in adolescence. Robert Enright and his co-workers have recently shown a strong association between parenting styles and the extent to which seventh and eleventh grade adolescents had reached a relatively mature identity [21]. They found that adolescents from democratic and permissive families were more likely to show mature identities than were adolescents from autocratic families.

Elder and Baumrind discovered several ways in which family experiences prepare adolescents for achieving mature identities [22]. Authoritative, democratic parents set the stage in childhood and adolescence for assuming responsible adult roles later on. These parents themselves demonstrate responsible attitudes by monitoring their children's behavior and

showing respect for their opinions. At the same time they provide opportunities to practice responsibility within broad guidelines, and they use
explanations and clear responses to their children's behavior to teach about
mature behavior. Furthermore, the warmth, acceptance, and respect that
these parents characteristically show toward their children encourage mutually respectful relationships that help make parents effective teachers
and models during adolescence.

The families described by Elder and Baumrind show how much families in our society vary in their reactions to adolescence. This diversity
especially influences how families fulfill two functions that have traditionally been linked to the family: (1) helping once-dependent individuals prepare for autonomy and (2) preparing adolescents to assume adult roles,
including social, relationship, and work roles. Both are important to
achieving a healthy sense of self as adolescents look forward to adulthood.
In the remaining sections of the chapter we examine families' influences on
independence and on vocational and social sex roles.

INDEPENDENCE: DISRUPTION OR TRANSFORMATION?

As we noted in Chapter 1, many people think adolescence is a time of
wholesale rebellion and rejection of parents and their values. The transition to adulthood may, of course, sometimes bring turbulence to all social
relationships, not only relationships with parents. But as a general characteristic of adolescence, rebelliousness and rejection of adult values do not
appear to be as common as people often think.

For example, research findings available today indicate that adolescents generally feel positive about their parents [23]. Indeed, their attitudes
become increasingly more positive over the course of adolescence. And
when adolescents' values seem different from their parents', it is mostly a
difference in extremity of opinions and not a difference in content [24]. For
example, in the 1960s young people often seemed to hold liberal political
views, while their parents held conservative views. Actually, though, the
content of the values on which adolescent views were based were usually
quite consistent with their parents'. Adolescents typically advocated more
extreme solutions to problems than their parents did, however, and were
activist in supporting them [25].

Thus the reality is much more complex than we might guess from the
simplistic, popular myth of rebelliousness and rejection. At the same time
it is true that both parents and their adolescent children tend to *overestimate*
the differences between them. Each side is also likely to *underestimate* the
amount of positive regard the other has for them.

The same conclusion is true for the popular view of breaking away

Independence does not usually mean emotional distance between parents and adolescent or adult children

Photograph from George W. Gardner/Stock, Boston

from the family during adolescence. At the simplest level *independence* means having the ability to meet one's own basic needs—the needs that have been met in early life by parents or others on whom one has been *dependent.* But consider the families you know in which some of the children have moved out of the family home. In most cases those children continue to maintain and appreciate family relationships. They join other members of the family on special occasions, keep in touch by phone or letter writing between times, and often receive and offer advice and support from family members. Although disruptions in these emotional ties can and do occur, the majority of young persons probably achieve independence largely by physically separating themselves from family and assuming responsibility for their own affairs, but *not* by rejecting their families or severing the emotional ties to them. In fact, some writers have suggested that the process of becoming independent is a *transformation* rather than a disruption or a deterioration of relationships [26]. Other transformations in family relations take place throughout life—in the transition from infancy to toddlerhood, for example, or in the transition in which some elderly parents become dependent on their adult children for basic needs. Adolescents' striving for independence, then, is a part of the natural flow of human development. In most cases it is not the aberrant, traumatic experience implied by popular myth [27].

This view of independence includes two important points about the role of the family. First, independence involves adjusting not one but

SPECIAL TOPIC
Adolescent Abuse

A social problem that currently gets great attention in our society is child abuse. But while it is recognized that adolescents are subject to emotional, physical, and sexual abuse, less attention is given to this age group than to younger children, who are seen as particularly vulnerable. Although we cannot say how many of the estimated 1.5 million children abused annually are adolescents, many cases clearly do exist, with serious costs to the families and individuals involved.

Witness the following letter to Ann Landers:

Dear Ann:

My husband abused our four children and me. In my ignorance, I took the frustrations of my unhappy marriage out on the kids.

When the boys got big enough to flatten out their father, they did. The girls escaped as soon as possible by getting jobs after school and on weekends.

Today, they are all married and have children. We are not welcome in their homes. The only knowledge I have about my grandchildren is what I hear from relatives. I am grateful when they bring snapshots so I can see how much the kids have grown.

I beg all parents to keep in mind that your actions today may have a big impact on what happens tomorrow.

—Mellowed Too Late [1]

several aspects of behavior and feelings—physical and economic independence and also autonomy in values and judgments. Second, independence is defined partly in terms of what a culture or community expects. In other cultures and subcultures within our own society, independent family members follow their culture's norms and values regarding ties to their families [28]. For example, the tradition that family members spend certain holidays together is one example of a cultural pattern that helps define the transformed family relationships of adulthood. Thus, as we saw in Chapter 1, many of the changes of adolescence depend on societal and cultural expectations about the second decade of life. In this section we will examine more closely these two aspects of the family's role in encouraging—or not encouraging—independence in adolescents.

There is no way to know how typical these consequences of parental abuse are. And since we have a record only of the parents' guilt and regret, there is no way to estimate the damaging effects on the children. However, we see in this letter several aspects of the aftereffects of abuse that we can identify.

It is clear that the letter writer is referring to physical abuse. Defining abuse is sometimes difficult, because it is not clear how broadly the term *abuse* should be applied. Although most people agree that many instances of abuse are emotional rather than physical, instances of emotional abuse are difficult to substantiate because physical evidence of abuse is often demanded in legal proceedings. Consequently, most definitions of child abuse employ a physical criterion. Further, community norms are used to help solve the definitional problem. Thus we have the following definition: An abused child or adolescent is one "who receives nonaccidental physical injury (or injuries) as a result of acts (or omissions) on the part of his parents or guardians that violate the community standards concerning the treatment of children" [2]. Although this definition is not inclusive enough for many, its specificity probably enables social service providers, policymakers, and legal authorities to act in cases of abuse.

At this time the most stable and general findings about abuse are these: (1) abusive parents themselves often experienced a good deal of harsh physical treatment in childhood; and (2) their abuse of their own children is often associated with stress in their lives [3]. As the writer to Ann Landers pointed out, marital dissatisfaction may be one source of stress. Unemployment, inadequate and crowded living conditions, large families, and lack of commu-

(Continued)

Training for Independence

Cultural differences—and as we pointed out earlier in this chapter, *family* differences—affect the transition to independence in one particularly important way: They govern how much preparation children are given for the independent behavior that is expected of adolescents and adults. Expectations about mature behavior vary from one family or community to another, however. For adolescents the problem is how much *continuity* there is within their own lives. As we saw in Chapter 1, discontinuity—changes in demands and expectations—increases the emotional difficulties of adolescence. If training and interactions in the family increase continuity of socialization from one life period to another, transition to adult independence should be relatively easier than it will be if family backgrounds create discontinuities in what adolescents are expected to know and do.

SPECIAL TOPIC (Continued)

nity supports for dealing with stress have also been found to be significant factors in abuse. Although we must be guarded about so complex a problem, it now seems reasonable to suggest that adolescents are at risk for abuse if their parents were physically mistreated themselves. Under conditions of stress these peremptory reactions become even more likely.

Another aspect of abuse is that abused children and adolescents are somewhat more likely than children in the population at large to be difficult in some way. In infancy the difficulties often come from low birth weight, which is typically associated with a number of health and development problems that place heavy demands on parents. Among older children and adolescents there may be other characteristics to which parents react negatively. One such characteristic is the physical attractiveness of the child. Several studies indicate that attractiveness may affect an adult's treatment of adolescents. For instance, Karen Dion gave female adults the opportunity to set penalties for the same levels of performance on a picture-matching task by an unattractive child and an attractive child [4]. Adults gave significantly harsher penalties to unattractive children than they gave to attractive children. In another study activity level similarly affected adults, who tended to react more negatively to high-activity behaviors [5]. Adults were asked to select punishments for the same misbehavior in videotaped children who were generally underactive, overactive, or about average in activity. They chose harsher punishments for the overactive child than for the two less active children.

These studies involve adults punishing children they have not seen before. Adolescents who ordinarily elicit relatively harsh reactions from emotionally uninvolved outsiders would probably arouse excessive punitiveness in a parent who is under stress and who is especially likely to resort to physical methods in dealing with frustration.

A comparison of two cultures Independence allegedly did not trouble adolescents and their families in Margaret Mead's Samoa of 60 years ago (see Chapter 1) [29]. From their early years children were trained to be socially responsible and to contribute economically. In the extended families of the villagers, adolescents often simply moved in with an uncle or other relative without fanfare. In short, both physical and economic independence from parents was a part of the system in which Samoan adolescents were reared, according to Mead's famous report.

Industrialized Western societies in general cannot match the flexible social arrangements of Samoa. But different Western societies vary in how much they prepare children and adolescents for independence. Psycholo-

This point about excessive punishment may be particularly true for adolescents. In the transition from childhood they often become more assertive and behave more autonomously. These characteristics may set the stage for abusive reactions in families for whom abuse is already a pattern. Perhaps adolescent abuse could be reduced by helping families understand the predictable changes in behavior as their child enters adolescence.

Physical abuse of adolescents in families is a social problem that needs further research. Although we know relatively little about the long-term effects of child abuse, abusiveness probably contributes to such antisocial patterns as delinquency. Given the usual history of abusing parents themselves, we might at least expect that an abused child or adolescent becomes a parent who helps perpetuate the endless repetition of this tragic and wasteful phenomenon: "Abuse begets abuse."

REFERENCES

1. Ann Landers, Field Newspaper Syndicate, *Minneapolis Tribune,* August 28, 1980.

2. R. Parke and C. Collmer, Child abuse: An interdisciplinary analysis, in *Review of Child Development Research,* vol. 5, ed. E. M. Hetherington (Chicago: University of Chicago Press, 1975), p. 513; see also C. Kempe and R. Helfer, *Helping the battered child and his family* (Philadelphia: Lippincott, 1972).

3. Parke and Collmer, pp. 509–590.

4. K. Dion, Children's physical attractiveness and sex as determinants of adult punitiveness, *Developmental Psychology* 10(1974):772–778.

5. J. Stevens-Long, The effect of behavioral context on some aspects of adults' disciplinary practice and affect, *Child Development* 44(1973):476–484.

gists Denise Kandel and Gerald Lesser addressed this issue in a large-scale study of adolescents and their families in Denmark and in the United States [30]. They wanted to discover some of the sources of family conflict during the second decade of life; naturally, many of their questions concerned independence. They gave detailed questionnaires to 1141 adolescents (average age of 16) and their mothers and fathers in the United States and 977 such pairs (average age of 15) in Denmark. The adolescents attended high schools in both urban and rural areas in the two countries.

Lesser and Kandel found that Danish families are predominantly democratic, while American families are predominantly authoritarian, a pattern that is infrequent in Denmark. Thus, overall, Danish adolescents and their parents both reported significantly more discussion and explanations about decisions involving adolescents than did American adolescents. American parents had more specific rules and gave fewer explanations than Danish parents. Perhaps this result explains why more Danish adolescents than American adolescents reported that they *felt* independent. Danish youth felt that they were treated as adults by their parents, that they had sufficient freedom, and that they would—if their opinions differed from their parents' views—feel free to disregard their parents' opinions. At the same time, however, compared with American adolescents, Danish youth showed a high proportion of conformity to parents' wishes, even when the parents did not make specific rules about an issue. American youth conformed best when rules were clear and specific.

To summarize, Danish parents exercised less tight controls over their adolescents' behavior, but parents did involve adolescents in discussions about their actions and about decisions involving them. As a result, Danish youth appear to behave according to internalized standards, which are generally very much in accord with their parents' expectations. American youth appear to be less internally controlled; they respond best to specific rules, which their parents often seem to impose without discussion and explanation.

These results contradict a number of popular ideas in American society about what is required for adolescents to become independent. For example, even though the United States is widely considered to be permissive toward youth—a child-rearing tactic that is considered to work against independence and respect for parents—middle-class parents in the United States actually appear to give their adolescents *less* autonomy, not more, than parents in some other Western countries give. Furthermore, in Denmark, at least, granting autonomy is not necessarily associated with rebellion and emotional distance from parents. Instead, the greater feelings of autonomy expressed by Danish youth appear to be associated with more internalized standards of behavior and closer, more respectful, and affectionate feelings toward parents. The Danish findings indicate that it is when parents frequently engage in discussions and explanations that adolescents seem to feel greater, not less, satisfaction with the amount of freedom and independence granted [31]. The lesson for American parents may be that willingness to engage in discussions about decisions with their teenagers, while showing respect for their opinions, is at least as important in independence training as is the outright granting of freedom.

One result that is not so surprising, when we remember the studies by Elder and Baumrind, is that adolescents from democratic families seem to achieve independence most smoothly. In Danish society, families tend to emphasize training for independence from early childhood. Consequently, during adolescence they find it less necessary to restrict independent behavior; their sons and daughters have been prepared to be autonomous and to follow internalized standards rather than external constraints. By contrast, American families seem obliged to exercise more control over adolescents. Their authoritarian approach, furthermore, provides fewer opportunities for *teaching* independence through explanations and inculcation of principles and guidelines. What apparently happens in authoritarian families illustrates a well-established principle of behavioral development: Relying on external constraints leads to behavior that is more dependent on external controls than on internal standards [32].

Subcultural differences within the United States   The differences among families in training for independence result in some striking contrasts among United States adolescents in their perceptions of independence. For instance, sociologist George Psathas surveyed tenth grade boys in the high schools of New Haven, Connecticut, to learn whether and how their parents granted independence [33]. Boys from a variety of social class and ethnic backgrounds were included in the study. Psathas first asked the boys about how independent they were in a large number of specific activities, such as whether they account to parents for how they spend their money, whether they are asked where they are going on dates and with whom, whether parents check to see that homework is done, and whether they were included in family discussions. He then used a statistical technique to determine whether situations clustered in ways that revealed differences in how families dealt with independence.

Psathas found four types of activities that were especially important for New Haven adolescents. As Table 7.3 shows, they felt that their parents were relatively permissive with them about their activities outside the

TABLE 7.3   Average rating of how much independence boys felt they had (by social class)

Social class	Outside activities	Status activities	Age-related activities	Parental regard for judgment
I and II (highest)	90	102	86	121
III	98	104	92	112
IV	100	97	103	91
V (lowest)	108	104	118	94

Adapted from G. Psathas, Ethnicity, social class, and adolescent independence from parental control, *American Sociological Review* 22(1957):422.

Note: The numbers shown in the table refer to average ratings of perceived independence on scales composed of a large number of different specific questions. The higher the scale score, the more independent the boys perceived themselves to be.

family (e.g., where to go with friends, how to spend their own money); their activities that had implications for reputation or status (e.g., what occupation sons chose, who they dated); and age-related responsibilities (e.g., for buying their own clothes, for making their doctor's appointments). In addition, some sons thought their parents showed regard for their opinions by including them in discussions about decisions, taking care to explain rules, and so forth; others thought their opinions were considered unimportant. In short, Psathas found that adolescents do not think of independence simply as freedom to do as they please. Their feelings of independence also reflect the sense that their parents have regard for their opinions.

How adolescent sons perceived their independence depended partly on the social class background of the family, as defined by father's occupation, education level, and the family's area of residence. Table 7.3 also shows the pattern of relationships between perceived independence and social class. At the lower economic, occupational, and educational levels, boys felt parents permitted more independence in outside activities and age-related responsibilities than boys from higher-status families did. By contrast, sons in the higher social statuses felt that their parents showed more regard for adolescents' opinions than lower-status sons did. Families were equally guarded about activities that might affect their sons' reputations.

What do these contrasting patterns tell us about the role of family in the transition to independence? In some families adolescents are readily given autonomy in what they do outside the home, but inside the home they are expected simply to comply with parents' wishes. In others autonomy is restricted outside the family, but considerable attention is given to adolescents' opinions, judgments, and expectations within the family. Psathas suggests that the fundamental difference among these patterns concerns training for independence. Parents who show regard for their children's opinions, while monitoring their autonomy in activities outside the home, have the opportunity for explicit training of standards and values. They can also gauge their children's readiness for independence in different activities. Parents who are permissive in outside activities, but who rarely engage in discussions about their children's decisions and activities, have fewer opportunities for this kind of instruction. As with authoritarian parents, their major influence over their children comes from coercion.

Dependency—The Failure of Independence Training in the Family

Ironically, parents who do not train for independence but rely on asserting their power to influence their children often reap the opposite of control over their children's behavior. Adolescents in such families are obliged to rely on the dictates of parents; as adolescents and adults they are often most comfortable when they can depend on others. Consequently, they are likely to be unusually *dependent*—on peers, on spouses, on authority figures.

The tie between authoritarian family experiences and dependency in adulthood shows up especially clearly in a 40-year longitudinal study of parents and children conducted at Fels Research Institute in Ohio [34]. Measures were taken of parents and of their children in early childhood and at ages 18 and 26. Across these ages young people whose parents had been demanding but also rejecting, cold, and repressive—the classic authoritarian pattern—were, at adolescence, highly conforming to parents and low in self-esteem. As young adults they were quite likely to behave as they believed others wanted them to. As young adults they were not autonomous, perhaps because as children and adolescents conforming was the way to earn their parents' approval. Since their parents had stressed the need for social approval, but had made it tenuous and difficult to obtain, these young adults were especially anxious to assure themselves of approval from others.

Besides being highly susceptible to the expectations of others, young adults from authoritarian families also tend to believe that they have little control over what happens to them. This belief, which is known as *external locus of control*, seems to be associated with a perception that parents have controlled one's life. Belief in the ability to control one's own outcomes, called *internal locus of control*, is lowest when parents are perceived as dominating, rejecting, and very critical. Internal locus of control is highest when parents are warm but have high expectations for achievement and provide predictable standards for behavior [35]. Like Baumrind's authoritative parents, families that urge high standards and are supportive toward their children are likely to be successful in encouraging one important aspect of independence: the sense that one has the necessary skills and competence to produce, most of the time, the outcomes one desires.

Value Autonomy

Adolescents may gain physical and economic independence with relative case, but they may find it more difficult to achieve another aspect of autonomy: *value autonomy*. Value autonomy means that adolescents make judgments and hold opinions as a result of independent reasoning. If teenagers merely adopt the opinions and values of others, they are remaining dependent in a way that is especially important for many adult roles [36].

By the term *value autonomy* we do not mean that one's values must be different from the values of friends and family. Rather, as Erikson has pointed out, we mean that commitments to specific values—whatever they are—have been reached through individual reasoning and judgments. Otherwise, as we saw in Chapter 2, identity will not be truly achieved but will simply be the result of foreclosure, or adoption of others' values and roles.

SPECIAL TOPIC
Pathogenic Family Dynamics

Most people recognize that abuse may be psychologically damaging to children and adolescents. But children's experiences in families aren't always easy to characterize as potentially negative. This point is particularly true of one category of family problems that has been especially identified with adolescence: families in which adolescent children have marked psychological or behavioral problems, ranging from delinquent to schizophrenic symptoms and excessive aggressiveness. Over the past twenty-five years comparisons of such families with families of adolescents who have not displayed these characteristics show some striking differences.

Most of the studies have focused on the ways in which family members behave toward each other during the discussion of some assigned topic or problem-solving task in the laboratory. Two major differences have emerged.

First, in disturbed or problem families negative emotions are frequently expressed. In most studies these emotional messages are directed toward the adolescent with problems; there tend to be fewer directed toward other children in the family [1].

The question of whether negative expressions of affect are the *cause* of problem behavior is a difficult one, of course. Most studies of family relationships are *retrospective*; they look back at family history after problems have developed to see if differences can be identified. One obvious problem with this method is that a researcher can't tell whether family differences preceded ad-

The problem of value dependence may cause potentially serious discontinuities in later adult roles. For example, consider the case of young adults whose college or work experiences bring them into contact with peers (or superiors) who hold different values from those of their parents. If they lack autonomy in values, these individuals probably will be either rigidly defensive of beliefs adopted from parents or especially susceptible to new values espoused by others, since they have been socialized to accept the influence of others with little deliberation about values and principles. By contrast, someone whose family background encouraged discussion and reasoning about decisions should be more truly autonomous—less susceptible to simple adoption of new values and open to reexamination of beliefs.

Like other aspects of independence, then, independent reasoning

olescent problems—and therefore might be among the causes of them—or whether the differences resulted from having a problem adolescent as a part of the family system.

Nevertheless, one possibility is that adolescents' problems are at least maintained, if not aggravated, when negative emotion is expressed toward them in their families. There may be a self-fulfilling prophecy at work, in which adolescents confirm the negative labels their parents attach to them during family interactions by showing unacceptable behavior in other settings. For example, James Alexander found, in a study of apparently similar white middle-class families, that sons' aggressiveness in school tended to be greater when their parents were relatively critical, threatening, or punitive toward them in family interaction [2]. Rare is the person who can survive high levels of critical, demeaning, and rejecting language without showing negative effects.

A second characteristic of families with problem adolescents can be summarized as *uncertain responsiveness*. This term means that the family's communication and its organization are unpredictable; children cannot count on reasonably consistent reactions and outcomes for their own behavior. For example, in many studies of families with problem adolescents, discipline has been found to be highly inconsistent; children are sometimes punished and sometimes rewarded for what they do [3].

There also tends to be a great deal of discord and disharmony in such families. Children are often drawn into parents' battles when one parent enlists their support against the other parent. Such coalitions exploit children in ways over which they have little control [4].

(Continued)

about values requires training. Parents provide such training by encouraging adolescents to express their opinions and by stimulating them to consider additional aspects or alternative viewpoints. Furthermore, the parents of the most independent and mature adolescents tend to be warm and supportive. They show respect for their children's opinions and take care to involve them in constructive discussions of issues. This positive emotional atmosphere is probably the reason that many parents continue to influence their children in adolescence, in spite of the variety and number of forces outside the family that might detract from their influence.

This point, as we will see, is an important principle of family relations in adolescence. The positive relationship some parents foster in their families makes it more likely that adolescents will rely on them for information and as models of behavior. Furthermore, whatever training the parents

SPECIAL TOPIC (Continued)

Families of disturbed adolescents also tend to be considerably less clear in their messages to each other than do comparison normal families. One viewpoint on this difference has been that lack of clarity in and of itself often creates a double bind in which conflicting messages to the child must be reconciled through psychotic behavior [5]. Recent evidence suggests, though, that this hypothesis does not fit the majority of cases of unclear communication and family dysfunction. Instead, families in which communication is typically unclear may affect adolescents because unclear messages make family interactions unpredictable as a basis for action [6].

One factor in communication difficulties may be the patterns that adolescents themselves have developed for participating in family interactions. For example, Mavis Hetherington and her colleagues compared the discussions of families in which there were delinquent children whose antisocial activities varied in type and severity with those of matched nondelinquent families [7]. The most dramatic finding was the difference among these families in adolescents' expressions of disagreement during the discussions. In nondelinquent families sons and daughters asserted themselves in discussions and were active at arriving at solutions in collaboration with other family members. In the families with delinquent adolescents, disagreements were handled differently: Delinquent daughters tended to be excessively assertive and belligerent in taking a viewpoint; sons tended to be passive, but unyielding, in disagreements.

The differences that distinguish families of problem adolescents from other families give us some interesting suggestions, but we still cannot describe exactly *how* families contribute to adolescent problem behavior. For example, we need to determine whether family behavior causes adolescent problems or whether—and how—having a problem adolescent distorts and

provide probably becomes more effective because of the positive feelings between parent and child. Like most learning, becoming independent proceeds most effectively when teacher and student mutually respect one another.

We now turn to a second aspect of learning in the family that affects adolescent development: learning of social roles.

SOCIAL ROLES: IDENTIFICATION AND IDENTITY

Every person develops as a member of several—perhaps many—social groups; in each of them the person plays particular roles. Some roles continue from one age to another, of course. Kinship roles—being someone's

disrupts family functioning. Furthermore, most of our current information comes from laboratory discussion measures that may only give us surface indicators of more fundamental family processes that we cannot fully comprehend from an analysis of verbal communication. Whether symptom or active agent, however, differences in the verbal interactions of parents and their adolescent children reveal once again how significant—though subtle and complex—the effects of families on adolescents are.

REFERENCES

1. J. Doane, Family interaction and communication deviance in disturbed and normal families: A review of research, *Family Process* 17(1978):357–376.

2. J. Alexander, Defensive and supportive communication in family systems, *Journal of Marriage and the Family* 35(1973):613–617.

3. A. Bandura and R. Walters, *Adolescent aggression* (New York: Ronald Press, 1959); S. Glueck and E. Glueck, *Family environment and delinquency* (Boston: Houghton Mifflin, 1962).

4. Doane, p. 361.

5. J. Haley, An interactional description of schizophrenia, *Psychiatry* 22(1959):321–332.

6. T. Jacob, Family interaction in disturbed and normal families: A methodological and substantive review, *Psychological Bulletin* 82(1975):33–65; J. Riskin and E. Faunce, An evaluative review of family interaction research, *Family Process* 55, 4(1972):365–453.

7. E. Hetherington, R. Stouwie, and E. Ridberg, Patterns of family interaction and child-rearing: Attitudes related to three dimensions of juvenile delinquency, *Journal of Abnormal Psychology* 78(1971):160–176.

offspring, brother, or sister—remain similar for most individuals from childhood to adulthood, although they may take on different qualities as the role occupants change in age or status. Other roles, or at least significant aspects of them, do change more or less drastically from childhood to adulthood. For example, many aspects of sexual behavior are infrequent and are disapproved of for children and adolescents, but they are considered normal and desirable in adults. Similarly, training for a vocation is reserved for young adulthood in Western industrialized society; childhood is reserved largely for play. In short, partly as a function of culture, Western adolescents are subjected to major discontinuities in the basic roles required of adults [37]. (In Chapter 1 we outlined some of the factors of discontinuity and noted its implication for adolescent development.)

Achieving autonomy requires opportunities to arrive at one's own values through independent reasoning and judgment
Photograph from Charles Gatewood

In spite of cultural patterns that require different roles for children and adults, families *can* increase the continuity from childhood to adolescence to adulthood. For example, even though sexual behavior is generally disapproved of before adulthood, families can influence basic gender role development and attitudes toward sexuality that make the transition to adult sexuality less difficult. Also, even though vocational *choices* are delayed until adulthood, families can influence adolescents' personal characteristics and orientations that affect later vocational preferences and job success [38].

Before discussing family influences on gender and vocational role development, however, we will examine adolescents' identification with their parents as a basic psychological process for learning the roles required by a mature identity. *Identification* involves knowing or wanting to learn about another person's behaviors, values, and expectations. As a stepping-stone to identity, identification with parents has important advantages. Adolescents can draw on models with which they are already familiar—from whom they have been learning since infancy—to help them meet the new demands of impending adulthood. Identification with parents provides continuity in development, because the learning and relationships of childhood lead directly to the learning and relationships of adolescence.

It is often difficult to know exactly what people mean when they say an adolescent *identifies* with parents, a teacher, an older brother or sister, a friend, or a hero figure. Psychologists now believe that a simple photocopy notion, in which adolescents imitate others in a wholesale fashion, is too narrow a view of identification. Instead, they feel that identification probably involves two components: a *cognitive* component, or knowledge about others' behaviors, attitudes, values, and expectations; and a *motivational* component, or the desire to emulate others' characteristics in one's own behavior. Identification with parents, then, occurs when adolescents both know how their parents usually behave in a situation and adopt the parents' behavior when faced with similar circumstances.

Of course, adolescents may sometimes know their parents' behavior, but because of negative feelings about them or because they know the behavior is inappropriate, they may adopt other courses of action. In Baumrind's and Elder's research parents who were generally warm and accepting toward children were most likely to be seen as desirable role models. Their sons and daughters not only wanted to be like them but also tended to follow their advice in choosing their friends. The enhancing effect of nurturance and warmth on identification is a well-known psychological principle [39]. In most cases continuity is greatest from childhood to adulthood when adolescents are firmly identified with warm, nuturant parents who provide competent models for adult roles.

The effects of identification are not always positive, however. In extreme cases identification can work against effective identity formation. As we saw in Chapter 2, the adoption of parents' opinions and commitments can result in identity foreclosure. Adolescents may become mindless copies of their parents, without having determined for themselves their own individually derived beliefs and commitments. Consequently, adolescents may have difficulty when faced with new situations and demands for which adoption of their parents' beliefs and roles had not prepared them [40].

Identification may also create problems when parents' attitudes, values, and behaviors are inappropriate for adolescents' roles and responsibilities. For example, confrontational or physically abusive approaches to conflicts may have been characteristic of a person's family background, but such tactics may work against successful adjustments when brought into school, work, or personal relationships. Of course, seeing inappropriate behavior in the family may teach adolescents how *not* to behave—but probably only if there are opportunities to learn alternative ways of dealing with problems.

Identification affects adolescents at many levels, both specific and general. Mannerisms and personal styles are relatively specific characteristics that are often—and obviously—affected by identification. For instance, take the case of the budding tennis player who insisted on carrying his tennis gear in an airline bag because that's what his tennis-playing father did. Other identifications, like social roles, are more general and fundamental to psychological adjustment.

We now turn to two cases of social role development in which identification with parents plays an important part. First, we consider the effect of identification on gender roles—being male and female not in a biological but in a social sense. Then, we turn to the effect of identification on vocational roles. Both topics will also be discussed in greater detail in later chapters.

Identification and Gender Roles

Gender roles refer to the roles males and females are generally expected to take in a society or social group. In our society in the 1980s there is a range of possibilities for acceptable male and female behavior. However, a distinction described by sociologist Talcott Parsons probably still applies to the general expectations in Western societies [41]. Parsons points out that males are expected to be relatively *instrumental,* or oriented to reaching goals and producing outcomes, while females are expected to be primarily *expressive,* or concerned for interpersonal relationships. These gender role expectations may no longer be as rigid and extreme as they once were. Still, indications are that males are expected to be competitive, dominant, and independent, while females are expected to be dependent, sensitive, and socially nurturant. These stereotypes affect not only adults' reactions to each other but also, for example, the way parents hold and talk to newborn infants [42].

Despite its pervasiveness, however, the instrumental/expressive distinction mostly reflects cultural definitions of social roles. In other cultures gender roles are less different and sometimes are even reversed [43]. Learning cultural expectations, then, is an important component of learning gender roles. In addition, learning to use and apply these cultural expectations in relationships with others is also important. This process will be discussed in this section and in our examination of gender roles and sexuality in Chapter 9.

For adolescents the transition to adulthood is most continuous when there are opportunities to learn and apply gender roles in childhood that will meet adult gender role expectations. And rightly or wrongly, the family has always been assumed to have major responsibility for gender role development. Although other forces like the mass media, teachers, and the peer group also play a role, it is in the family where the most intensive opportunities for learning the rudiments of maleness and femaleness occur. Thus the question is probably not *whether* the family is influential in this aspect of development but *which* family experiences are important and *how* they affect development.

As with other aspects of identification, the family characteristics that affect gender role learning most are the parents' nurturance and warmth. In particular, boys who perceive their fathers as nurturant and supportive and girls who have similar perceptions about their mothers are likely to match the cultural expectations about male and female behavior relatively well [44]. Although gender role learning shows sometimes quite different patterns for males and females, the father's role seems to be pivotal in gender role learning for both. For example, Mavis Hetherington found that boys develop a masculine gender role most effectively when fathers are perceived as strong, decisive individuals who take an active role in the socialization of their sons [45]. Masculine gender role development is least effective when fathers are passive and mothers are dominant. For girls, Hetherington discovered, feminine role development also reflects the father's role; girls are most likely to fit the feminine stereotype when fathers conform to masculine role expectations, view the mother as a positive model for the daughter, and reward daughters' feminine activities [46]. It is *not* that the mother has no influence on either boys' or girls' gender role development; rather, the father's influence seems to help sharpen the distinctions among children who best fit the cultural stereotypes and those who match them less well.

Miriam Johnson has suggested that a *principle of contrast* determines how parents influence their children's gender role development [47]. In this view fathers and mothers who manifest the culturally approved gender role characteristics in turn demonstrate their own gender roles and show the contrast between that role and the other parent's role. Thus in the case of females, fathers reward daughters for feminine activities and for their emulating the mothers' gender role characteristics. Fathers also demonstrate the contrasts between male and female behavior.

The contrast principle probably does pertain to many families, particularly those in which both parents are present. However, many adolescents live in families where one parent, most often the father, is absent. In families in which the father is not present, either because of death or because of divorce or desertion, we might expect some problems in sex typing. For example, in one study Hetherington compared the play behaviors of father-absent 9–12-year-old boys with the behaviors of a similar group from father-present homes [48]. The father-absent boys were less oriented to contact sports, were less competitive, and were more dependent on other adults than father-present boys were. Furthermore, the effect was more pronounced the longer fathers had been absent from the home. But not all boys in mother-only families have problems in gender role learning. For example, when there are other sources of male influence or when the mother herself specifically encourages and rewards her son's masculine activities, there are few differences between father-present and

MAVIS HETHERINGTON (1926–)

Mavis Hetherington came to psychology by a circuitous route through literature, poetry, and the theater. Her work as a psychologist is distinctive not only for its style and elegance but also for its relevance to the everyday experiences of children, adolescents, and their families.

Hetherington started out as a clinical psychologist. In fact, after she received a master's degree from the University of British Columbia, she worked for four years in a child guidance clinic in western Canada. Says Hetherington: "We were really doing community mental health before it had a name. We would fly in unpressurized planes into remote areas of caribou country. Some of the cities had 300 souls, counting the dogs and the day's catch of fish" [1]. Later, she returned to graduate school, the University of California at Berkeley, to earn a Ph.D. in psychology. While there, she decided to devote her career to research rather than to clinical practice.

Nevertheless, Hetherington's four books and more than seventy articles have always dealt with the real problems of people. Although on the surface her research interests appear diverse—she has studied sex role identity, learning, humor, father absence, and divorce—one theme has always been dominant: families and the children and adolescents who are part of them. Her work on children in families from which fathers are absent is the most important body of research on this problem. In recent years she has been conducting influential research on the effects of divorce and of stepparents.

Besides her extensive research involvement, Hetherington is active in the profession of psychology. She has served as president of developmental psychology organizations and as editor of journals in the field. In addition, she has served as chairman of the Department of Psychology at the University of Virginia, where she has taught since 1972. How does she do it? "I work an 80 hour week. I usually get to work about 8:30, but if I really want to get things done, I'll get up at 5:00" [2]. One of her colleagues calls her a "running dynamo."

father-absent boys. By adolescence the majority of father-absent boys have probably found alternative ways to learn the basic elements of the masculine gender role—from peers, other adults, and the mass media [49]. Indications are that differences between father-absent and father-present boys are not very pronounced in adolescence in any case. In other words, while childhood gender role learning may be somewhat retarded when the father

*Mavis Hetherington
(1926–)*

Photograph from University
of Virginia, Graphic Com-
munications Services

Hetherington practices her beliefs about the importance of family.
She and her husband, a corporation-law professor, have three sons.
"Life would have been very empty without my children," Hetherington
says. "They have been the most satisfying part of my life. If I tried to
stay home and be a 24-hour-a-day, in the house mother, I would have
been miserable. The combination of a career and children, has been
wonderful" [3].

REFERENCE

1. R. McCall, Mavis Hetherington, *APA Monitor*, May 1981.
2. *Ibid.*
3. *Ibid.*

is absent, most boys find compensatory learning possibilities by the time
they reach adolescence [50].

The contrast principle may apply more to girls than to boys. In contrast
to boys, girls primarily show the effects of father absence in adolescence
and afterward. The effects are particularly apparent in girls' relationships
to males—just the area in which Johnson predicted the father was espe-

cially important. For example, Hetherington reported that father-absent adolescent girls were either inappropriately reserved or inappropriately assertive with males. In a follow-up study she found that these girls' marital relationships were less happy than the marriages of father-present girls [51]. Thus while family effects on gender role development may well occur before adolescence, for girls, at least, gender role learning affects one significant aspect of adolescence and adulthood: interactions with the opposite sex.

In summary, although we need to know a great deal more about how parents influence gender role development in adolescence, we can say that the continuity adolescents are likely to experience in the transition from childhood to adulthood partly comes from family effects on gender roles.

We now turn to a second aspect of role development affected by family relations in adolescence: vocational roles.

Identification and Vocational Roles Sigmund Freud's most famous observation about adult identity was that the well-adjusted person has two fundamental needs: to love and to work. Choosing an adult work role and accomplishing it successfully are two of the changes that adults expect of adolescents. We will discuss career choices in detail in Chapter 13. In this section we focus on family influences on vocational preferences and success in them. As in the other aspects of adult role learning we have discussed, continuity between socialization in the family and the demands of adult vocational roles helps determine how difficult identity achievement will be in adolescence.

Vocational preferences The general types of vocations adolescents prefer often reflect their degree of identification with their parents. Identification is measured by the amount of similarity adolescents perceive between their parents and themselves. For example, in one study male college students' perceived similarity to both their fathers and their mothers was assessed and compared with the students' profiles on a widely used test of vocational aptitude, the Strong Vocational Interest Blank [52]. Several links between identification and vocational aptitude were found, some of which also show the strong effects of gender role stereotypes in our society. For example, males who strongly identified with their fathers were especially well suited to technical occupations; those who strongly identified with their mothers showed marked aptitude in linguistic-verbal occupational categories. Mixed-sex identifications, in which the young men strongly identified with both mother and father, produced a blend of technical and verbal-linguistic vocational aptitudes—a pattern that is well suited to the social sciences and social service professions.

There was also a *general* effect of parent identification. Relatively few students who showed strong identifications with one or both parents reported difficulties in choosing a vocation. In contrast, students who weakly identified with parents, especially fathers, had more often experienced vocational difficulties, to the point of seeking counseling help. Identification with parents may influence particular vocational preferences and also may underlie a sense of identity and direction in making vocational decisions.

Vocational satisfaction and success Identification with parents in adolescence also affects vocational success once a choice has been made. For example, Alan Bell's 10-year longitudinal study—in which 14-year-old boys' identification with parents and their occupational satisfaction and success at age 25 were examined—showed the importance of positive identification with parents [53]. Boys who, at age 14, had considered their fathers to be positive role models were more satisfied and successful in their occupations at age 25 than were boys whose attitudes toward their fathers had been neutral or negative in adolescence. Interestingly, however, occupationally satisfied, successful young adults reported that their *current* role model was not a family member but a person in their professions. Perhaps positive identification with father in adolescence serves as a model of the *kind* of relationship, such as identification with a successful employer or coworker, it is possible to achieve in adult roles.

The effect of identification on females' vocational development has been studied far less than effects on males. However, in recent years the effect of maternal employment on the attitudes of both adolescent boys and girls toward female work roles has become an important topic. In general, both daughters and sons of working mothers have more favorable attitudes toward female employment and hold higher educational and vocational aspirations for themselves than do children of nonworking mothers [54].

Some information about the effects on females comes from a study by Grace Baruch, who interviewed college women to discover their own attitudes toward working women and toward dual careers (in which both husband and wife in a family pursue an out-of-home vocation) and their general beliefs about the competence of women [55]. She found that daughters whose mothers had worked during two or more years of the daughters' lives had more positive attitudes toward working women and dual-career families. This was especially true, as we might expect, when women perceived their own mothers' attitudes to be positive. Baruch also found that daughters of working women attributed more competence to women and relatively less to men than did daughters of nonworking mothers.

These different attitudes may not necessarily be the result of identification, of course. That is, daughters of working women may simply have had

SPECIAL TOPIC
Television and Teenagers—Pastime or a Window on Reality?

Television is a common part of life in most families in the United States and in other Western countries. Thus there can be little doubt that television plays a role in the socialization of most young people. But television probably plays different roles for adolescents and for children. So we can ask the question, what is the role of television in adolescents' lives?

Although the television set is a fixture of the lives of teenagers, all of our available information shows that teenagers watch less television than children and adults do. The amount of television watching tends to increase from early childhood to late childhood, but around ages 12 and 13 it drops off dramatically. This pattern depends partly on family background, of course. Adolescents from lower social and economic status families watch television considerably more than adolescents from middle-class and upper-class families. Also, regardless of social class, families tend to use television for different reasons. For example, some families—called socio-oriented viewers—use television as background for social interaction in the family, as a punctuator or regulator of conversation, as a center of discussion and attention, or as a reason to avoid talking to one another. By contrast, concept-oriented families tend to use television as a source of information or specific entertainment. In other words, family social class and communication and viewing habits influence the amount and kind of television viewing that adolescents in those families do [1].

Nevertheless, adolescents who watch a good deal of television are as likely to be influenced by what they see as younger viewers are, even though teenagers are expected to be more knowledgeable and sophisticated than younger children about the fuctional nature of television. Surveys indicate that half or more teenagers believe that television "shows life as it really is" and that television characters are "realistic and true to life" [2]. Teenage girls who are heavy viewers of violence are more likely than light viewers to say that violence is an effective and desirable solution to problems; and they are more likely to say that they would use violence themselves [3].

Naturally, these reactions to television shows are not simply the result of watching during adolescence. Since most of these young people have grown up with television, their past television viewing, along with other aspects of their developmental histories, affects their responses to the television shows they watch as teenagers. For example, one study found that a reputation for aggressiveness at age 18 was more closely related to the kinds of television programs young people preferred to watch at age 8 than to the kinds of programs they watched currently [4]. In other words, patterns of television watching in middle childhood influenced later patterns of social behavior.

These results raise the possibility that for young people who watch a great deal of television, the programs they see help define a view of reality. In other words, television programs may not only influence particular behavior patterns by demonstrating alternative ways of reacting to different situations. Television programs may also influence the way particular situations are perceived and interpreted.

This idea is a relatively new but influential one in the study of the mass media. And it may be an important lead to understanding the impact of television on teenagers in particular [5]. For example, while television does not appear to influence purchasing decisions of teenagers to the extent that it influences younger children's or adults' consumer behavior, television advertisements may nevertheless have an impact on teenagers. The emphasis on appearance and heterosexual success in advertisements directed toward teenagers may be combined with their natural concerns about physical and social matters to create unrealistic, unreasonable expectations about social life and their own development.

In other words, television may offer a distorted "window on the world" for teenagers. For most this possibility is somewhat offset by the greater amount of time they spend away from television and, probably, spend with their friends or engaging in activities that are newly available to them. For many adolescents, however, television appears to define a reality that may not always be beneficial or reassuring for them.

REFERENCES

1. J. Murray and S. Kippax, From the early window to the late night show: International trends in the study of television's impact on children and adults, in *Advances in experimental social psychology*, vol. 12, ed. L. Berkowitz (New York: Academic Press, 1979), pp. 253–320.

2. A. Dorr, Controlling TV's impact, *The Interpreter*, July–August 1977, pp. 2–7.

3. B. Greenberg and T. Gordon, Social class and racial differences in children's perceptions of television violence, in *Television and social behavior*, vol. 5, ed. G. Comstock, E. Rubinstein, and J. Murray (Washington, D.C.: Government Printing Office, 1972), pp. 185–210.

4. L. Eron, L. R. Huesmann, M. Lefkowitz, and L. Walder, Does television violence cause aggression? *American Psychologist* 27(1972):253–263.

5. W. A. Collins and N. Korać, Recent progress in the study of the effects of television viewing on social development, *International Journal of Behavioral Development*, in press.

TV's influence on teenagers is often determined by their families' TV-viewing practices and interaction styles

Photograph from National Education Association, Joe DiDio

more information about the nature of women's career experiences and successful instances of merging work and family roles than others did. As with many other instances of parental effects, the models' influence may come from the information the models supply—the cognitive aspect of identification—rather than from the degree to which adolescents actually imitate parents.

The Myth of Similarity

When we think about parents' influences on adolescents, we often think in terms of how similar children and parents are. For example, we usually rely on some measure of similarity or perceived similarity between parents and children to indicate the degree of parents' influence over adolescents. Similarity is a tricky criterion, however. For one thing, similarity might result from a number of different processes by which parents affect children, not just identification. For example, adolescents may be similar to their parents because of genetic, rather than social, influences. Similar activity levels and similar likings for stimulation may be transmitted through heredity—and both of these characteristics affect adult roles, such as the type of occupation to which one is attracted. Similarity may also result from the environments that parents and children share.

While similarity indicates something very important about family influences, lack of similarity does not necessarily indicate that parents do not influence their children. Consider the findings of Harold Grotevant, Sandra Scarr, and Richard Weinberg [56]. These researchers compared similarity in interests between parents and their biological or adopted children. The correspondence was noticeably closer for biologically related parents and children than for adopted pairs. While this finding may attest to the importance of partly genetic dispositions in interests, it does *not* indicate that adopted parents do not influence interests. That is, parents of adopted children probably encourage the children to follow their own interests, whether or not they conform to the directions that the parents had chosen for themselves. These parents' influence over their children's interests may not make the children more *similar* to the parents but, rather, may help the children reach their own full potential, whatever their interests are.

In short, similarity is not always a good indicator of parental influence. We must make a distinction between our assumptions about the *outcomes* of parental influence on identity development and the *processes* by which such outcomes may be brought about. When we focus on similarity, we are examining one possible outcome. But we must not overlook the numerous ways in which parents influence adolescent development that do not lead to similarity.

SUMMARY

The influences of the family on adolescent development begin well before the adolescent years; but they are particularly important during the second decade of life. Moreover, family relations are influenced by the changes of adolescence and, in turn, may help to ease the transitions for teenagers or may make them more difficult.

In this chapter we discussed Baumrind's distinctions among authoritarian, authoritative, and permissive parents. Authoritative parents demand socially responsible, independent behavior within broad guidelines. They teach their children by offering explanations for rules and decisions; they also respect their children's opinions. Children of authoritative parents tend to rank higher on social responsibility and independence than children of authoritarian or permissive parents. Elder's research on family communication patterns indicates that democratic families provide opportunities for the training of mature behavior and also foster warm, nurturant parent-child relationships that enable parents to continue to be influential during the adolescent years.

Family relations often change as children enter adolescence. Three factors may contribute to these transformations in interactions: (1) Adolescents change physically and socially and may base their own expectations about their family roles on perceptions of their more adultlike status; (2) adolescents develop more mature reciprocal concepts of parent-child relationships; and (3) parents themselves often experience a period of stress and questioning—a midlife crisis—at the time that their offspring are experiencing adolescent identity struggles. We introduced the notion of family development as a basis for understanding the changing family context in which adolescent development takes place.

Finally, we discussed two areas of adolescent development in which families are especially influential. One area is the development of independence; as we saw, families vary in the effectiveness with which they train for independent behavior. We discussed the problems of excessive dependence in adolescence and adulthood, which are often tied to authoritarian family backgrounds. The second area involves family influence through identification with parents. Learning about behavior patterns and desiring to adopt them are two components of identification that may influence adolescent development. Particularly important is the effect of identification on two aspects of the development of identity: gender role identity and vocational choice and success. We noted, however, that being similar to parents is not the only evidence that parents have influenced adolescents in their development toward adulthood. Family influences may also involve encouraging adolescents to recognize and act on their individual strengths and interests, whether or not they are the same as the parents'.

KEY POINTS AND NAMES

Family environments

Discontinuity and continuity

Diana Baumrind

Child-rearing styles
    Authoritative (democratic) parents
    Authoritarian (autocratic) parents
    Permissive parents

Gisela Konopka

Glen Elder

Family changes

Laurence Steinberg

Transformations

Selman's levels of parent-child concepts

Family development

Parents' midlife crisis

Family influences
    Independence, dependence
    Cultural differences
    Locus of control
    Value autonomy

Social roles
    Identification
    Gender roles
    Principle of contrast
    Vocational roles
    Similarity

REFERENCES

1. M. Kohn, Social class and parental values, *American Journal of Sociology* 64(1959):337–351.

2. D. Baumrind, Child care practices anteceding three patterns of preschool behavior, *Genetic Psychology Monographs* 75(1967):43–88.

3. D. Baumrind, Authoritarian vs. authoritative parental control, *Adolescence* 3(1968):255–272.

4. G. Konopka, *Young girls: A portrait of adolescence* (Englewood Cliffs, N.J.: Prentice-Hall, 1976), p. 68.

5. *Ibid.*, p. 69.

6. *Ibid.*, p. 69.

7. Baumrind, Child care practices, p. 61.

8. D. Baumrind, Personal communication, 1980.

9. G. H. Elder, Jr., Parental power legitimation and its effect on the adolescent, *Sociometry* 26(1963):50–65.

10. *Ibid.*, p. 50.

11. *Ibid.*

12. *Ibid.*, p. 57.

13. Konopka, p. 68.

14. G. Roberts, J. H. Block, and J. Block, Continuity and change in parents' child rearing practices (Paper presented at the Society for Research in Child Development, Boston, Mass., April 1981).

15. L. Steinberg, Transformations in family relations at puberty, *Developmental Psychology* 17, 6(1981):833–840.

16. R. Selman, *The development of interpersonal understanding* (New York: Academic Press, 1980), pp. 147–151.

17. *Ibid.*, p. 150.

18. *Ibid.*, pp. 147–151.

19. J. Aldous, *Family careers: Developmental changes in families* (New York: Wiley, 1978), pp. 84–85, R. Hill and P. Mattesich, Family development theory and life-span development, in *Life-Span development and behavior*, vol. 2, ed. P. Baltes and O. Brim, Jr. (New York: Academic Press, 1979), pp. 162–204.

20. J. Conger, A world they never knew: The family and social change, *Daedalus* 100(1971):1105–1138.

21. R. Enright, D. Lapsley, A. Drivas, and L. Fehr, Parental influences on the development of adolescent autonomy and identity, *Journal of Youth and Adolescence* 9(1980):529–545.

22. Elder, pp. 50–65; Baumrind, Authoritarian vs. authoritative, pp. 255–272.

23. R. Hess and I. Goldblatt, The status of adolescents in American society: A problem in social identity, *Child Development* 28(1957):459–468.

24. R. Lerner, M. Karson, M. Meisels, and J. Knapp, Actual and perceived attitudes of late adolescents and their parents: The phenomenon of the generation gap, *Journal of Genetic Psychology* 126(1975):195–207; R. Lerner and J. Knapp, Actual and perceived intrafamilial attitudes of late adolescents and their parents, *Journal of Youth and Adolescence* 4(1975):17–36.

25. Hess and Goldblatt, pp. 459–468.

26. J. Hill, The family, in *Toward adolescence: The middle school years* (*NSSE yearbook*), ed. L. Steinberg (Chicago: University of Chicago Press, 1980), pp. 32–55.

27. *Ibid.*; A. Bandura, The stormy decade: Fact or fiction? *Psychology in the Schools* 1(1964):224–231.

28. J. Hill and L. Steinberg, The development of autonomy during adolescence (Paper prepared for the Symposium on Research on Youth Problems Today, Fundacion Orbegoza Eizaguirre, Madrid, Spain, April 26–30, 1976).

29. M. Mead, *Coming of age in Samoa* (New York: Dell, 1928).

30. D. Kandel and G. Lesser, *Youth in two worlds* (San Francisco: Jossey-Bass, 1972).

31. *Ibid.*, pp. 168–185.

32. M. Hoffman, Moral development, in *Carmichael's manual of child psychology,* 3rd ed., ed. P. Mussen (New York: Wiley, 1970), pp. 261–359.

33. G. Psathas, Ethnicity, social class, and adolescent independence, *American Sociological Review* 22(1957):415–423.

34. J. Allaman, C. Joyce, and V. Crandall, The antecedents of social desirability response tendencies of children and young adults, *Child Development* 43(1972):1135–1160.

35. W. Katkovsky, V. Crandall, and S. Good, Parental antecedents of children's beliefs in internal-external control of reinforcement in intellectual achievement situations, *Child Development* 38(1967):765–776.

36. E. Douvan and J. Adelson, *The adolescent experience* (New York: Wiley, 1966), pp. 131–132.

37. R. Benedict, Continuities and discontinuities in cultural conditioning, in *Readings in child development*, ed. W. Martin and C. Stendler (New York: Harcourt Brace Jovanovich, 1954), pp. 142–148.

38. H. Grotevant, S. Scarr and R. Weinberg, Patterns of interest similarity in adoptive and biological families, *Journal of Personality and Social Psychology* 35(1977):667–676.

39. A. Bandura and A. Huston, Identification as a process of incidental learning, *Journal of Abnormal and Social Psychology* 63(1961):311–318; P. S. Sears, Child rearing factors related to playing of sex-typed roles, *American Psychologist* 38(1953):431 (abstract).

40. J. Marcia, Development and validation of ego identity status, *Journal of Personality and Social Psychology* 3(1966):551–558.

41. T. Parsons, Family structure and the socialization of the child, in *Family socialization and interaction process*, ed. T. Parsons and R. Bales (Glencoe, Ill.: Free Press, 1955), pp. 35–131.

42. D. Best, J. Williams, J. Cloud, S. Davis, L. Robertson, J. Edwards, H. Giles, and J. Fowles, Development of sex-trait stereotypes among young children in the United States, England, and Ireland, *Child Development* 48(1977):1375–1384; R. Parke and D. Sawin, The family in early infancy: Social interactional and attitudinal analysis (Paper presented at the Society for Research in Child Development, New Orleans, March 1977).

43. M. Mead, *Sex and temperament in three primitive societies* (New York: Morrow, 1935).

44. P. Mussen and L. Distler, Masculinity identity and father-son relationships, *Journal of Abnormal and Social Psychology* 59(1959):350–356; P. Mussen and L. Distler, Child rearing antecedents of masculine identity and kindergarten boys, *Child Development* 31(1960):89–100.

45. E. M. Hetherington, The effects of familial variables on sex-typing, on parent-child similarity, and on imitation in children, in *Minnesota Symposia on Child Psychology*, vol. 1, ed. J. Hill (Minneapolis: University of Minnesota Press, 1969), pp. 82–107.

46. Hetherington, Effects of familial variables; M. Johnson, Sex role learning in the nuclear family, *Child Development* 34, 3(1963):319–333.

47. Johnson, pp. 319–333.

48. E. M. Hetherington, Effects of paternal absence on sex-typed behaviors in Negro and white preadolescent males, *Journal of Personality and Social Psychology* 4(1966):87–91.

49. H. Biller and R. Bahm, Father-absence, perceived maternal behavior and masculinity of self-concept among junior high school boys, *Developmental Psychology* 4(1971):178–181; E. M. Hetherington and J. Deur, The effects of father absence on child development, *Young Children* 26(1971):233–248.

50. Hetherington and Deur, pp. 233–248.

51. E. M. Hetherington, Effects of father absence on personality development in adolescent daughters, *Developmental Psychology* 7(1972):313–325.

52. J. Crites, Parental identification in relation to vocational interest development, *Journal of Educational Psychology* 53(1962):262–270.

53. A. Bell, Role modeling of fathers in adolescence and young adulthood, *Journal of Counseling Psychology* 16(1969):30–35.

54. C. Etaugh, Effects of maternal employment on children: A review of recent research, *Merrill-Palmer Quarterly of Behavior and Development* 20, 2(1974):71–98; L. W. Hoffman, Maternal employment, 1979: An updated look at the effects of maternal employment on child development (Paper presented at the

meeting of the Society for Research in Child Development, San Francisco, March 1979).

55. G. K. Baruch, Maternal influences upon college women's attitudes toward women and work, *Developmental Psychology* 6(1972):32–37.

56. Grotevant, Scarr, and Weinberg, pp. 667–676.

CHAPTER 8

Peer Relations and Influences in Adolescence

INTRODUCTION

The term *peers* is almost synonymous with *teenagers* in popular impressions of adolescence. Think of the terms you commonly hear: "peer pressure," "peer culture," or in the words of one inarticulate celebrity father, "peer stuff." More often than not, terms like these are meant to be negative. Many people assume that the increasing association with peers means that families lose influence over their adolescents to other teenagers with attitudes and values different from their own. When 11-year-old Carrie wants to wear jeans everywhere because her friends do, it doesn't seem the same as her father's concern about dressing to convey the proper conformity to his co-workers' style preference. In spite of the fact that people of all ages have peers—and peer pressures—adolescence is thought to be the period when conflicts between peers and families are greatest.

There are elements of truth in this impression, of course. But it is also true that peers contribute positively to the development of adolescents in ways that the family cannot. As we noted in Chapter 1, peer relationships, along with family and school, are major settings in which adolescents develop the personal and social characteristics they will need as adults. Perhaps that is why adults often feel almost as concerned about teenagers who seem isolated from others of their own age as they do about young people who appear to be overly influenced by peers.

Adolescents' peer relationships give us a number of clues to psychological and social development. Naturally, like all human relationships, adolescents' friendships and group involvements are complex. They depend heavily on the personalities of individuals. But there are some general patterns and psychological principles that help us understand adolescent peer relationships. In this chapter we focus on these patterns and principles and on the role of peers generally in adolescent development. First, we will examine changes in the qualities of peer relationships from childhood to adolescence, and we will review the development of cognitive and emotional characteristics of adolescents that affect their relationships with others. Next, we will discuss the characteristics of adolescents that make them more or less likely to be accepted by their peers, and we will consider the nature of adolescent groups and the effects of these groups on the development of individuals. Finally, we will address an issue that comes up repeatedly in discussions of adolescence: conflict between parent and peer influences and the conditions under which *cross-pressures* between these two important sources of influence may occur.

PEER RELATIONS DURING ADOLESCENCE

Adolescents spend more time with people of their own age than children do. Although children interact with peers, of course, they do so less often and in less mature ways than adolescents do. Most of their interactions involve adults. By contrast, adolescents' contacts with peers make up a large proportion of their social experiences [1]. In this section we will examine the quality of peer interactions and adolescents' concepts of peers and others.

Adolescent Friendships

Even more important than the sheer amount of time spent with peers are the changes in the nature of relationships in adolescence. The *qualities* of their relationships set adolescents' experiences with peers apart from the experiences of younger boys and girls. Take, for example, the differences in preadolescents' and adolescents' comments about friendship. The term *friendship* means close personal relationships in which both parties identify the other as being liked and valued. Before adolescence, friendships typically center around activities. For instance, at age 8 Cammie described her current best friend as "the girl I like to play dolls with." But at age 13 her best friend is "someone who understands me. We think alike about a lot of things, like school and teachers and other kinds of stuff like that." Cammie's different descriptions reflect the change in adolescence toward thinking of friends as persons with whom one shares common thoughts and feelings.

Thus sharing is the basis for the emotional interdependence that adolescents typically expect from friendships. In other words, the personalities of friends and the ways in which they respond to each other become the central themes of friendship. The emphasis is on loyalty, trustworthiness, and respect for confidence [2]. This change in the nature of friendship may be one reason why childhood playmates seem to grow apart during adolescence. When the personal characteristics of the other person become more central to the relationship, former playmates often have less in common than they did when friendship simply depended on liking to play the same games.

Changes in the qualities of relationships with friends during adolescence are especially pronounced for girls. Boys, even in the adolescent years, continue to focus on common activities more than on interpersonal commitments. These differences are, of course, consistent with the typical socialization of males and females in our society. Remember Parsons's distinction from Chapter 7: Masculine roles reflect an instrumental, goal-directed orientation, and female roles have an interpersonal-expressive orientation. This contrast matches very closely some common differences between friendships of boys and of girls in adolescence [3].

The deeper friendships of adolescence present difficulties as well as rewards, however. Adolescent friendships, far more than the relationships of childhood, involve adolescents in interpersonal experiences that can be both intense and rewarding but that also can make both parties potentially vulnerable. This vulnerability was captured in a cartoon picturing a woman standing in her psychiatrist's office holding a gun. Pointing the weapon at him, she said, "You've done me a world of good, Doctor, but you know too much." Adolescent friends assume a high degree of loyalty, trustworthiness, and respect for confidence from each other. As a result, they often feel very vulnerable to betrayal.

Concepts of Others and Peer Relationships

One of the reasons adolescents' friendships change in quality is that adolescents think in complex and mature ways about other persons, themselves, and the kinds of relationships that are possible between two people. In our discussion of Selman's theory of interpersonal perspective taking in Chapter 5, we pointed out that young children have very egocentric, or self-centered, conceptions of individuals and their actions. But as they move toward adolescence, children develop more complex concepts of themselves in relation to other people. They no longer see themselves as having the same view of situations and experiences that everyone else has. Instead, adolescents recognize that their particular point of view may be unique and that others also have unique perspectives. Furthermore, adolescents have the ability to recognize that two people can conceive of themselves as part of a relationship. They can understand that both parties have the ability to step outside themselves and see themselves as someone who influences others and is influenced by others at the same time. Table 8.1 outlines Selman's application of interpersonal perspective-taking skills to the understanding of friendships.

TABLE 8.1 Selman's levels in conceptions of friendship

Level	Label	Description
0	Egocentric perspective taking	Close friendship as momentary physical interaction: Friends are individuals who are close enough physically to play together and who engage in play without hurting people or things.
1	Subjective perspective taking	Close friendship as one-way assistance: Friends are people who do things the other person wants done.
2	Reciprocal perspective taking	Close friendship as fair-weather cooperation: Friends meet personal needs for companionship and being liked, but these needs are thought of in terms of specific incidents or issues rather than an underlying system.
3	Mutual perspective taking	Close friendship as intimate and mutual sharing: Friendship is a relationship for two rather than for each individual separately; basis of the relationship involves sharing intimate personal concerns and the efforts of each party to maintain the relationship.
4	Societal-symbolic perspective taking	Close friendships as autonomous interdependence: Friendships are seen as being in a constant process of formation and transformation, within which each individual is changing and growing. Thus friendships partly serve the function of providing individuals with a sense of personal identity. The relationship depends on each person's understanding of this basic autonomy of two individuals, whose personalities are compatible but who may grow out of the relationship as further personal changes occur.

Developed from R. Selman, *The development of interpersonal understanding* (New York: Academic Press, 1980), pp. 136–142.

The new understandings that Selman describes probably underlie statements like these from adolescent girls:

"I think [a friend is] somebody that is loyal. Somebody that would stay on your side no matter what anybody—well, if somebody started a rumor and everyone believed it, somebody that wouldn't believe it. Or somebody that, if they knew you did it, they wouldn't say, 'ah, you did it' just to be like everybody else."

"[A friend is] someone who . . . when you really need them, they will come, someone who sticks close and is truthful, and, you know, I won't really have to worry about them goin' out and telling your business or something like that." [4]

In seeking friendships teenagers look for common personal feelings and goals as well as common activities

And finally:

> "All of my friends are a lot like me. You know, none of them are carbon copies, but enough like me so that they can understand me and I can understand them. I think understanding is really important to a relationship cuz if you don't have it, then you spend too much time explaining things and you never get around to really helping each other or being more personal and deep. They have a lot of the same attitudes that I do, so that really affects your reactions. So, I don't ever have to worry about them doing something I am not going to do or me doing something that they would disapprove of. So when you go out, you know you are not going to be embarrassed by them, or vice versa. We would enjoy the same types of things." [5]

Not all adolescents can express themselves so articulately about friendship. But statements like these are common enough—and different enough from the types of statements children make about other children—that they tell us something distinctive about peer relations in the second decade of life.

SOCIAL ACCEPTANCE AND REJECTION

The development of cognitive concepts that appear necessary for adultlike relationships is only one ingredient for a successful social life, however. In adolescence, as in other periods of life, some individuals enjoy social acceptance, while others frequently experience rejection by peers.

What determines whether an adolescent will get along well with peers or will be rejected by them? The answer is vague at best, although for adolescents it is relatively easy to predict which characteristics will lead to acceptance by peers. Adolescents seem to follow fairly consistently an implicit set of norms for who will make a good companion or group member. Children also use these norms, but less consistently. Although we can't fully chart the norms, social acceptance usually involves physical attractiveness and a pattern of friendly, prosocial, competent behaviors. Devious, negative behaviors usually lead to social rejection. But in neither childhood, adolescence, nor adulthood do we find that one single characteristic of a person guarantees social acceptance or rejection. Even intelligence and achievement, both of which seem to contribute to good relationships with peers, by no means guarantee social success [6].

The difficulty of defining the standards for social acceptance—or for rejection—comes through in one writer's description of her own group in the midwestern, middle-class community where she grew up:

> If I couldn't be a member of the Society Six, I was delighted to be accepted into the next group on the social scale, a larger and more fluid one, ten or fifteen girls, democratic enough at least to be nameless. . . . The other girls in this group were from various backgrounds, some with faculty parents, others with fathers who included an insurance salesman, a banker, a plumber, an oil-company representative who toured the state for Mobil. What your father did wasn't important, though you needed to have a house where you could bring friends home without embarrassment.
>
> Most of us attended the nearby Presbyterian, Methodist, or Baptist churches, but by ninth grade, when parochial schools ended, we had two Catholic friends, as well. I'm not sure on what grounds we admitted others as friends, how we made up the guest lists for our slumber parties or Valentines or birthdays, how we knew whom to call to go to the movies. Most of us went on to college, but we certainly didn't base our friendship on intellectual merit. Most of us were moderately attractive, but one or two of us didn't date at all for years. Most of us were "popular," but I don't know exactly why. Perhaps we merely defined ourselves in relation to the Society Six and to all the other girls below us, the loners, the stupid ones, the fat ones. We had absorbed already by sixth grade a set of careful and cruel distinctions. [7]

ADOLESCENTS IN GROUPS

Confusing as the status rules may be, membership in one or more adolescent groups is a normal and probably significant part of social experiences. And some of the principles of adolescent group life are now less puzzling than they once were. For example, it is now clear that adolescent groups are better defined and more structured than the loose arrangement of groups during childhood. Whereas childhood groups are formed for the purpose of play or the activity of the moment, usually in neighborhoods or in some temporary gathering, adolescent groups are formed on more stable bases [8].

Furthermore, groups in adolescence quickly take on an obvious structure in which there are certain rules for achieving status and certain expected behaviors for remaining a part of the group. For example, James Coleman studied several junior high schools and found social systems that included a number of rules for who attained status and how status was maintained [9]. In Coleman's analysis this adolescent social system was based, for boys, on participation in athletics and, for girls, on being attractive and wearing nice clothes. Academic achievement was not important in determining status in the school's social system. Physical attractiveness, of both face and body, often seems to be an important determinant of adolescent social status, as we saw in Chapter 3.

In early adolescence, groups often become almost tyrannical about obedience to the rules for appropriate behavior set by members of the group. For instance, in Herman Raucher's novel *Summer of '42*, the small group of adolescent boys who were the central characters voted that one of their members had to have the name "Hermie" stitched into the jacket that was to be worn as a part of their informal club. When he removed the *ie* to have the more adult-sounding "Herm," the group ostracized him for going against their edict [10].

At every age, of course, groups become closed and establish implicit rules for in-group and out-group behavior. Young children and adults, as well as adolescents, participate in social groups with clear status and membership rules. But the structure of peer groups in adolescence—especially early adolescence—is more pronounced and rigid than that of the social groups of childhood [11].

What are some of the characteristics of adolescent groups? Ritch Savin-Williams has documented the formation of groups in a 5-week summer camp for boys in the north central United States [12]. More than 200 boys between the ages of 10 and 16 attended the camp, and Savin-Williams singled out one group of 6-, 12-, and 13-year-old boys to study intensively over a 5-week camping period. All the boys were Caucasian, Protestant, and upper middle class; none of them had mental, physical, or emotional problems. Besides observing all of the boys very carefully himself, Savin-Williams asked the boys in the group to rank each other on "toughness" and to nominate members of the group whose characteristics best fit a group of adjectives describing social behavior (e.g., meanest, follower, most handsome, smiler). He also gave the boys tests of cognitive ability and personality, and he measured their physical development. Finally, he used his extensive observations of the boys' behavior to rank-order how dominant they were in their groups.

Savin-Williams found that by the third day of camp a very clearly established dominance hierarchy had emerged. Among the adolescent boys in the group it was apparent who had most status and enjoyed most prerogatives among the members of the group. When the group members ranked the toughness of the boys in the group, they came up with a hierarchy very similar to Savin-Williams's observations.

The dominance hierarchy affected the groups' activities in many ways. For example, the most dominant boys slept closest to the camp counselor's bed in the cabin. They also took the lead on hikes. Near the end of the 5-week camping period, they were rated highest on athletic ability, physical fitness, and popularity. However, the most dominant boys were not necessarily the most popular during the first weeks of camp, nor were they the most intelligent or the biggest. Both the most and the least dominant boys in the group were well liked by the other boys, but they were quite different in style. For example:

> Overall [the most dominant boy] appeared to be the all-American boy; athletic, witty, popular, intelligent, handsome, and possessing an aura that breeds confidence and authority. On the other hand [the least dominant boy] was an individual who blended into the surroundings. Many times during the camp, he would be missing and no one noticed. [13]

Thus within a very short period of time, this group of adolescent boys had formed a stable social structure for their group—a structure that lasted throughout the 5 weeks together in summer camp.

In many adolescent social systems, indications of popularity, such as being elected cheerleader, guarantee high status

Photograph from Jim Anderson/Stock, Boston

Undoubtedly, adolescent girls' groups develop in a similar way. For example, studies of girls just about to enter adolescence show that their groups are often extraordinarily closed to newcomers [14]. Like boys, pre-adolescent girls are especially aware of their group identity and eager to preserve it. Of course, other groups at other age levels establish themselves in this way as well. But adults working with adolescents should be especially sensitive to evolving group structures that the young people themselves may not even recognize.

PEER INFLUENCES AND INDIVIDUAL DEVELOPMENT

Whether in groups or in the one-on-one encounters of friendship, peers are very important to the normal development of adolescents. A poignant, personal statement of the importance of being part of a group appears in Carson McCullers's novel *The Member of the Wedding*, in which she describes a young teenager who feels she has no group to belong to:

> The long hundred miles did not make her sadder and make her feel more far away than the knowing that they were there and both together and she was only her and parted from them, by herself. And as she sickened with this feeling, a thought and explanation suddenly came to her, so that she knew and almost said aloud: *"They are the we of me."* Yesterday, and all the 12 years of her life, she had only been Frankie. She was an *I* person who had to walk around and do things by herself. All other people had a *we* to claim, all others except her. . . . all members of clubs have a *we* to belong to and talk about. The soldiers in the Army can say, *"we"* and even the criminals in the chain gang. But the old Frankie had had no *we* to claim, unless it would be the terrible summer *we* of her and John Henry and Berenice—and that was the last *we* in the world she wanted. [15]

A sense of belonging is an easily understood reason for seeking and succeeding in peer relations. But the importance of peer relations may go beyond the sense of being part of a group. Many research findings indicate that the quality of peer relations in childhood and adolescence is one early forerunner of successful adjustment in adulthood. For example, delinquency among adolescents and young adults has been shown to be closely associated with poor peer relations in childhood. Poor peer relations have also been found to predict a wide range of adult problems, including behavioral difficulties, occupational problems, and marital and sexual problems. Indeed, in one large-scale study of community mental health, the best predictor of mental health in adulthood was the rating that individuals received from their peers in middle childhood. Adults who were listed in the mental health registers in this study were more than $2\frac{1}{2}$ times as likely to have been viewed negatively by their peers in the third grade than those who did not appear in the mental health registers [16].

Of course, it may be that poor peer relations do not *cause* later unsatisfactory adjustment. Instead, poor peer relations may be an early symptom of many other problems that actually cause later difficulties. However, unsatisfactory peer relations in childhood and adolescence almost surely contribute to behavior patterns that cause problems in adulthood. In fact, peer relations make unique contributions to the growth of individuals. For example, the capacity for relating to others, the development of social control, and the acquisition of social values all depend on interactions with peers.

One of the reasons the peer group so strongly influences these aspects of development is that peer relationships are *horizontal*; that is, the differences in power between teenage friends are usually relatively small compared to the differences in power between children or adolescents and adults. These horizontal relationships enable adolescents to work out problems together rather than merely giving in to more powerful individuals like parents and teachers. Such relationships also enable them to explore problems with each other, without feeling threatened by punishment [17].

Erik Erikson saw group relations as an essential part of the process of identity formation [18]. From Erikson's viewpoint it was necessary to undergo a period of *psychosocial moratorium*, a period of distance from adult roles and commitments during which a number of different roles can be attempted and a number of different kinds of relationships tried. Erikson saw the peer group as especially important for this moratorium period, because in the peer group adolescents could find a source of support and an arena for experimentation that the mainstream adult culture would not permit. Thus in Erikson's view the peer group, as a set of horizontal rather than vertical social relationships, constituted a necessary arena of identity formation. And as we will see in Chapter 9, in one area that is especially important to adolescent development, sexuality, peers appear to be essential—if not always the most informed or capable—teachers.

TWO PROCESSES OF PEER INFLUENCE

How do peers exert influence over individuals? With this question we are not simply referring to aspects of development that are particularly likely to be affected by friends and associates. Instead, by asking *how* peers exert influence, we are raising a question about the psychological *processes* that explain the peer group effects. When we focus on processes, we want to know not what happened but how it happened. In this section we will discuss some possible explanations for the impact of peers on adolescent development.

Several explanations for the impact of peers have been suggested through the years. It is helpful, first, though, to recognize that peer influences may be of two types: informational influence and normative influ-ence. In *informational influence* peers serve as sources of knowledge about behavioral patterns, attitudes, and values and their consequences in differ-ent situations. In *normative influence* peers exert social pressure on adoles-cents to behave as others around them behave [19]. Thus when Hilary notices the kinds of clothes worn by the members of the elite group in her school, she is experiencing informational influence. When she is noticed by members of that group for wearing the right kind of clothes—or ostracized by them for not dressing correctly—she experiences normative influence.

Different processes seem to be involved in these two types of influ-ence, but both play important roles in the development of a sense of oneself as a member of a social group, which is basic to achieving a sense of identity. Two social psychological processes seem especially important for understanding the influence of peers on adolescents: social comparison and conformity. The two processes are related, but there are important differences in them as well. Since both contribute to the normative and informational influences of peers, we will discuss them in detail.

Social Comparison

Peers provide opportunities for adolescents to compare their own behavior and skills with those of others of similar age and social standing. This process is called *social comparison:* using others' behavior and skills as a standard against which to evaluate oneself. Social comparison is a funda-mental social psychological process; adults and quite young children, as well as adolescents, engage in social comparison [20]. But social compari-son seems to have an especially powerful impact in adolescence. Here is one description of the importance of friends as sources of social compari-son:

> Girlfriends were as essential as mothers. . . . A set of girlfriends provided a sense of security, as belonging to any group does. . . . having a best friend was more complicated: using a friend as a mirror or as a model, ex-panding your own knowledge through someone else's, painfully acquiring social skills. What little we learned about living with another person in an equal relationship, outside our own families, we learned from our girl-friends. It certainly wasn't a full preparation for marriage, but it was the only one some of us ever got. [21]

Awareness of self and others and the social systems within which one lives and works is relatively new during adolescence, as we saw in Chapter 5. In fact, social comparison in adolescence shows the effects of cognitive and social differences between adolescence and childhood [22]. But new sensitivity to social comparisons and to information about the kinds of outcomes and circumstances others enjoy can have both positive and nega-tive implications for adolescents. Consider Will, for example. Will had

SPECIAL TOPIC
Cheating on a Test: A Case of Social Comparison?

Social comparison is a process of using information about others' behavior and the outcomes of their actions to evaluate one's own behavior, opinions, or abilities. In our achievement-oriented society social comparison seems to be especially important as a way of assessing how well we perform. Instead of having absolute standards for our achievements, we often use the achievements of others similar to ourselves to determine whether we are measuring up.

The importance of social comparison in achievement situations is dramatically illustrated in a study of high school students' willingness to falsify their scores on a vocabulary test after receiving information about the relative success or failure of other students [1]. The authors, Jev Shelton and John Hill, worked with both tenth and eleventh grade males and females. Two sessions were included in the study.

In the first session the high school students were asked to do a simple vocabulary test, which they were told measured creativity, not intelligence. Afterward, they also took an achievement anxiety test, which showed whether they were high, medium, or low in their fear of failing on achievement tasks.

In the second session the students were assigned to one of three groups. Students in the first group, the *success* group, were told that their scores on the word task were 5–7 words above the performance of a fictitious comparison group. In other words, the researchers had made up the feedback without regard to students' actual performance on the test. Students in the second group, the *failure* group, were told that their scores were 5–7 words below the fictitious comparison group. Students in the third group, the control group, got no feedback about their relative performance.

always felt inferior to his classmates, but at 15 he recognized that he was actually fairly attractive and competent in comparison with those peers. Once he recognized his own characteristics, his self-esteem rose; his confidence in himself was buoyed. As a result, he became a class leader and more socially active. Students like Will who move into leadership roles for the first time in high school are examples of adolescents for whom the social comparison process has salutary effects.

Then in all three groups individual students got their own papers back and were asked to help score them. The authors were interested in what percentage of the students cheated in each condition by falsifying the scores they reported for themselves. They suspected that because of the power of social comparison, most cheating would occur for the students who were told that, on the average, their group's performance had been 5–7 words below the other group's performance.

That suspicion turned out to be correct—but only in that the failure group students were very likely to falsify their scores. What surprised Shelton and Hill is that the success group falsified their scores to about the same extent that the failure group did. Both groups were much more likely to falsify their scores than the control group students, who had not received any feedback about their relative performance.

Why would both success and failure groups cheat? Given what we know about social comparison, one guess is that simply being reminded about the possibility of comparison with peers induced enough anxiety among the students that they were willing to falsify their scores. This explanation makes sense. The increase in cheating was not apparent for low–achievement anxiety students in the study, even when they had been told that they had done more poorly than other students that age. The effects of feedback about peer performance was very pronounced, however, among the students who had scored high on the achievement anxiety test given in the first session of the study. It may very well be that Shelton and Hill's study illustrates a case where students have been socialized to be competitive or to compare favorably with their peers. Thus having information about the performance of others affected their representation of their own performance. Considering the general prohibition against cheating in our society, this influence for social comparison is all the more dramatic.

REFERENCE

1. J. Shelton and J. Hill, Effects on cheating of achievement anxiety and knowledge of peer performance, *Developmental Psychology* 1(1969):449–456.

Social comparison can also have negative effects, as we mentioned above. Consider the case of Jane. An unhappy home life with authoritarian parents made Jane especially susceptible to peers as a source of information about appropriate behavior. (This dependence on peers is not uncommon among the children of highly authoritarian parents, as we saw in Chapter 7). In Jane's case comparison with peers led her to believe that the reason she lacked the peer group status she craved was that she was not sexually active, as other members of her peer group claimed to be. As a result, Jane changed her behavior in accordance with the group's norms. She became sexually active, and she was rewarded by in-group status. Jane was emotionally unprepared to handle some of the complex feelings associated with her sexual experiences, however, and she suffered severe psychological problems as a result [23]. The normative influence from social comparison processes involved this adolescent in a set of circumstances that was potentially damaging to her development.

It is important to keep in mind that social comparison is a neutral process that can lead either to beneficial or negative effects. The outcome depends not only on the process of social comparison per se but also on the actions taken on the basis of social comparisons. One thing is clear, though: Measuring up or looking good in comparison with peers is personally important for most adolescents. Positive social comparisons can be a source of improved self-image; at the very least they may lead to social rewards. In working with adolescents, you should know what types of social comparisons may be especially rewarding to a young person and how he or she may use information from social comparison processes to change or direct behavior and to reach some self-definition. The accompanying special topic on the role of social comparison in cheating on an academic exercise illustrates some of the potential negative effects of social comparison processes.

Conformity

Perhaps the most commonly noticed result of the information derived from social comparison processes is *conformity*, the process of adopting the same behavior or attitudes others have adopted. By contrast, social comparison leads not only to adoption of particular actions but also to changes in self-esteem and self-image, persistence at tasks and activities, and other personal and social effects. Conformity need not always involve social comparison, however. Adolescents may show the same behavior as others around them because they have previously been taught to behave in that way, or they may be specifically encouraged in those behaviors through rewards and punishments from peers or adults.

Everyone conforms in some ways, of course. So the questions of interest for adolescent psychology are these: Do adolescents rely less on their own individual judgments and adopt the opinions of others more frequently than people of other ages do? And what characteristics of teenagers make them more likely to conform? One stereotype of adolescents surely is that they are especially susceptible to the influence of others. Objective information about the truthfulness of the stereotype is difficult to come by, however, partly because the similarity between any two people's opinions or judgments may result from unrelated causes. We now turn to some evidence that adolescence is a time of especially strong tendencies to conform.

Through social comparison teenagers seek self-definition in the context of peers
Photograph from Donald Dietz/Stock, Boston

Age trends in conformity: The Costanzo study   To study conformity tendencies as objectively as possible, conformity researchers focus on judgments of the perceptual characteristics of physical objects. For example, Philip Costanzo used a method originally devised by the social psychologist Solomon Asch. In Costanzo's study four adolescents sat in booths arranged in a semicircle [24]. Each faced a screen on which a series of slides, each with four straight lines, were shown. In each picture one straight line was identified as the standard; the other three were comparison lines: one longer, one shorter, and one the same as the standard. The adolescents were asked to choose the line that was the same as the comparison line. They were to push a button corresponding to the number beside the line that was a correct match for the set.

None of the adolescents could see the other adolescents who were being tested at the same time, but they all were told that they would be able to tell which lines the other three adolescents had chosen by watching the panel of indicator lights in the booth. Thus participants 2, 3, and 4 would know what participant 1's answer was, just as participant 1 would know theirs. Actually, the lights on each person's panel were controlled by the experimenter, who made it appear as though the other three participants had chosen the wrong answer on 15 of the 20 trials. Since participants could easily choose the correct answer on the task when they were answering alone, any errors they made in the booth could be attributed to the influence of the other group members' answers.

Costanzo tested 590 males ranging in age from 7 to 21 to see if the tendency to conform to group judgment was greater at some ages than others. As Fig. 8.1 shows, the highest percentages of conformity occurred for adolescents. Both elementary school children (ages 7–8) and young adults (ages 19–21) conformed less often to erroneous judgments than did 12–13-year-olds or 16–17-year-olds. This same pattern has been found in many other research studies using a similar kind of task to the one Costanzo used.

Why do young adolescents conform so strongly to the judgments of others, even when they know they are wrong? Perhaps their responses are affected by the changes in reasoning and thinking about oneself and others that we described in Chapter 5. For example, David Elkind talked about young adolescents' unusual misperceptions about the reactions of others toward them, a pattern he called the imaginary audience (see Chapter 5). In Costanzo's perspective judgment study young adolescents' sense of others' attention to their behavior may have caused them to conform to the erroneous judgments of others to avoid standing out. At younger ages the cognitive skills necessary for imaginary audience thinking have not yet developed, so individuals at those ages are more likely to follow their own judgments than the judgments of others. And at older ages the additional cognitive achievements that overcome the imaginary audience enable one to discount the judgments of others and to rely on one's own judgment instead. These speculations have not yet been tested in research. But in any case, Costanzo's information gives some credibility to the assumption that adolescents are particularly susceptible to the influence of others.

Individual factors in conformity   Costanzo also found that some individuals are more conformist than others, even in adolescence. He measured the willingness of each adolescent to take blame for accidents described in a series of hypothetical stories. Costanzo divided the adolescents into high–, medium–, and low–self-blame categories on the basis of their answers. At each age the adolescents who were most likely to blame themselves for accidents were also the ones who were most likely to conform to erroneous judgments. Those medium in self-blame tendencies were also medium in conformity. The tendency to blame oneself for events apparently means that individuals are likely to be especially anxious not to deviate from the way most others are behaving. Although Costanzo does not say so, self-blame seems similar to what we commonly call low self-confidence or low self-esteem [25].

Other differences among adolescents also make conformity more or less likely. For example, beliefs about their own lack of competence to do a particular task may affect how much adolescents' conform to the behavior of others. If an adolescent feels especially incompetent in particular situations, that adolescent may be especially likely to follow others' lead.

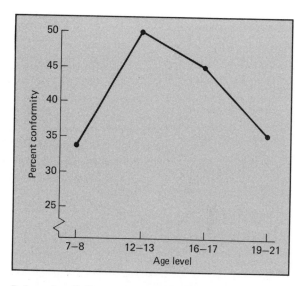

FIG. 8.1 Percentage of conformity at various age levels (n = 36 per age level)

Redrawn from P. Costanzo, Conformity development as a function of self-blame, *Journal of Personality and Social Psychology* 14(1970):370. Reprinted by permission.

Status in the peer group also affects the extent of conformity. For instance, several studies have involved adolescents from the same school whose statuses in social groups were determined [26]. The persons most likely to conform were middle-status persons. The leaders of the groups, the high-status individuals, were the least likely to conform. And the low-status group members were almost as unlikely to conform as the high-status members. Why this unusual pattern? Perhaps high-status teens are not motivated to conform to others' behavior because of the self-confidence that comes from their leadership positions. Low-status adolescents may be insensitive to the group standards or to the possible gains from conforming. Middle-status adolescents, however, are likely to be the ones who perceive the value of conforming to the group and anticipate that their status may improve if they conform. Undoubtedly, adolescents' inferences about the implications and outcomes of conforming affect whether or not they conform to others' behavior.

Social cognitive abilities, including the perception of other people's characteristics relative to their own characteristics, affect adolescents' conformity to others'. The cognitive abilities needed to make the sorts of moral judgments described by Kohlberg (see Chapter 6) are also related to adolescents' tendencies to conform to the judgments of others. For example, in one study adolescents were first tested on their moral judgment ability;

then they were asked to participate in a perceptual judgment task like the one in Costanzo's research [27]. The researchers wanted to find out if cognitive abilities, as reflected in Kohlberg's moral judgment scheme, affected the tendency to conform. The results demonstrated a significant link between moral judgments and conformity.

The adolescents most likely to conform were those with moral judgments at stage 3 in Kohlberg's scheme. They are the ones who are most oriented to approval from others. Their cognitive abilities enabled them to be acutely atuned not simply to the demands of authority figures or to their own wishes but to others' reactions to them and their actions. The least conformist adolescents were those who had reached stages 4 and 5 in Kohlberg's system; at both of these levels cognitive abilities permit an orientation to more general social principles than simply approval from others. As shown in Fig. 8.2, adolescents with moral judgment abilities at Kohlberg's stages 1 and 2 were intermediate in conformity between the stage 3 group and the stages 4 and 5 group. While we cannot argue that advanced moral judgment abilities ensure independent thinking and action, there does appear to be a connection between cognitive skills that facilitate adolescents' understanding of self and others and the tendency to conform to erroneous judgments from peers.

Conformity and identity   We suggested earlier that processes like social comparison and conformity are important to adolescents because they contribute to the formation of identity. If so, then conformity should be especially likely among individuals who show signs of grappling with fundamental identity issues. Psychologists Nancy Toder and James Marcia studied this question in a group of college women who varied in the degree to which they showed identity achievement [28]. Within the group were women who fell into each one of Marcia's four identity statuses: achievement, foreclosure, moratorium, and diffusion (see Chapter 2). When these young women participated in perceptual judgment tasks like those described earlier, the greatest conformity was seen in the unstable identity group. Young women who were in moratorium or diffusion were more likely to conform to erroneous judgments of their peers than those who were in achievement or foreclosure statuses. Since individuals who have achieved an identity or have accepted a self-definition through foreclosure presumably have less need to use the behavior of others in order to define themselves, this group may have felt less uncomfortable about not conforming.

Information about the behavior of others may be an important source of information for adolescents seeking to define themselves. But in Erikson's view bringing oneself into accord with the social group is only one part of the complex process involved in identity achievement. In addi-

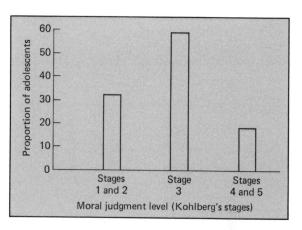

FIG. 8.2 Proportion of adolescents at each of three moral judgment levels who conformed to wrong answers on the Asch conformity task

Data from H. Saltzstein, M. Diamond, and M. Belenky, Moral judgment level and conformity behavior, *Developmental Psychology* 7(1972): p. 333.

tion to finding constructive and essential similarities with members of the social group, true identity achievement involves being comfortable with *differences* between oneself and the social group. Individuals in unstable statuses like moratorium and diffusion may use the social group to define themselves because they lack internally held standards or an adequate sense of self.

THE EFFECTS OF SIMILARITY BETWEEN FRIENDS: SOCIAL COMPARISON AND CONFORMITY IN ACTION

In the laboratory studies that we have used to demonstrate the principles of social comparison and conformity, the effects on adolescents were clear and striking. But can we see the principles at work in the complex real life friendships and group affiliations of teenagers? Let's turn to a case in which these processes appear to be involved—the widely discussed social problem of marijuana use.

We might expect marijuana use to be affected by similarity between friends. It is well known that, at all ages, friends tend to be similar in age, sex, and economic and racial backgrounds. But even if they are similar to begin with, friends may further influence each other through social comparison and conformity so that they become even more similar the longer they are friends. Thus friends may reinforce each other's involvement with drugs like marijuana.

This idea was the basis of a longitudinal study of similarity and influence in peer relations. Sociologist Denise Kandel contacted 1879 adoles-

SPECIAL TOPIC
Improving Moral Judgment Abilities—Starting with the Basic Equipment

The idea that social reasoning and thinking may develop in a predictable, stagewise sequence has led to a number of attempts to improve the social competence of children and adolescents. In most cases such efforts have involved at least two assumptions: (1) All mental functioning is governed by the complexity of certain basic cognitive *structures*, or abstract patterns of thought; (2) these abstract patterns, once available, can be applied to a variety of different intellectual problems, including social reasoning. For example, Kohlberg has argued that each of his stages of moral judgment depend on a certain level of cognitive capabilities, such as the skills described by Piaget. He has further suggested that moral thinking and reasoning depend on a certain level of social perspective-taking skills, like those described by Selman. He contends that once these underlying skills are available, training in moral reasoning will make it possible for students to achieve higher levels of moral judgments than they had previously demonstrated.

Kohlberg's arguments have recently been supported in a striking study by Lawrence Walker [1]. Walker's study can be divided into two main parts. First, he tested Kohlberg's contention that general cognitive abilities and social perspective-taking skills were prerequisite for moral judgments. Second, Walker tested the idea that if cognitive and social perspective-taking skills had

cents in New York suburban and small town schools and requested them to fill out questionnaires, which asked them, among other things, to give the name of their best friend in school [29]. Kandel was then able to match the questionnaires of people who were best friends in school and could examine the ways in which friends were similar to and different from each other. Predictably, she found that friends were most similar on grade in school, sex, race, and age. Similarity on such characteristics as religion and socioeconomic background (e.g., how much education their parents had) was much less important, however. Surprisingly, pairs of friends were not as much like each other as we might expect on activities and attitudes such as time spent on homework, academic performance, attitudes toward parents, occupational values, or political preferences. But friends were similar in the degree to which they used marijuana and certain other illicit drugs.

One important question is, Do the similarities that Kandel found result from friendships, or do they explain how friendships come to be formed in

been achieved, a corresponding level of moral judgment could be reached through training in moral reasoning.

In the first phase of his study Walker tested a group of fourth, fifth, sixth, and seventh grade children on cognitive, social perspective-taking, and moral judgment tasks. He reasoned that children who had reached the prerequisite level of cognitive skills or social perspective-taking skills might or might not show the corresponding levels of moral judgment skills. The correspondences among these three types of thinking and reasoning problems are shown in the accompanying table (p. 280). For example, Walker thought that students who had achieved beginning formal operations and stage 3 in perspective taking might also show moral judgment at stage 3. Or they might be functioning only at stage 2 on moral judgment. In no case, however, did he expect to find children who were functioning at stage 3 on moral judgment but at the concrete level on cognitive skills or at stage 2 on perspective taking.

These predictions, which come directly from Kohlberg's theory of the cognitive abilities necessary for moral judgments, were supported strongly in Walker's study. In cognitive level all children were more advanced than, or at the same level as, they were in perspective taking. Only one out of sixty-four children was more advanced in moral judgment than in perspective-taking skills. No child was more advanced in moral judgments than in cognitive functioning, as measured by Piaget's tasks. In other words, the sequence of skills that Kohlberg suggested were necessary for mature moral judgments appeared to be the case for the children that Walker studied.

(Continued)

the first place? This question is a common one in attempts to understand the nature and effects of peer relationships. Kandel was able to find some information relevant to the question by following her friendship pairs over a period of one full school year. At the end of the year she had three groups of friends to examine more closely: (1) pairs who remained friends throughout the school year, (2) pairs who dissolved their friendship during the year, and (3) individuals who were not friends at the beginning of the year but who formed friendships by the end of the study.

In general, Kandel's comparisons showed that friends influence each other as time goes by. The pairs that remained friends throughout the year were more similar to each other at the end of the year than they had been at the beginning of the year. Furthermore, individuals who became friends during the year were more similar to each other at the end of the year than they had been at the beginning of the year, when they were not yet friends.

SPECIAL TOPIC (Continued)

Parallel stages in cognitive, perspective-taking, and moral development

Cognitive stage	Perspective-taking stage	Moral stage
Preoperations: The "symbolic function" appears but thinking is marked by centration and irreversibility	*Stage 1 (subjectivity):* There is an understanding of the subjectivity of persons but no realization that persons can consider each other as subjects	*Stage 1 (heteronomy):* The physical consequences of an action and the dictates of authorities define right and wrong
Concrete operations: The objective characteristics of an object are separated from action relating to it; and classification, seriation, and conservation skills develop	*Stage 2 (self-reflection):* There is a sequential understanding that the other can view the self as a subject just as the self can view the other as subject	*Stage 2 (exchange):* Right is defined as serving one's own interests and desires, and cooperative interaction is based on terms of simple exchange
Beginning formal operations: There is development of the coordination of reciprocity with inversion, and propositional logic can be handled	*Stage 3 (mutual perspectives):* It is realized that the self and the other can view each other as perspective-taking subjects (a generalized perspective)	*Stage 3 (expectations):* Emphasis is on good-person stereotypes and a concern for approval
Early basic formal operations: The hypothetico-deductive approach emerges, involving abilities to develop possible relations among variables and to organize experimental analyses	*Stage 4 (social and conventional system):* There is a realization that each self can consider the shared point of view of the generalized other (the social system)	*Stage 4 (social system and conscience):* Focus is on the maintenance of the social order by obeying the law and doing one's duty
Consolidated basic formal operations: Operations are now completely exhaustive and systematic	*Stage 5 (symbolic interaction):* A social system perspective can be understood from a beyond-society point of view	*Stage 5 (social contract):* Right is defined by mutual standards that have been agreed upon by the whole society

From L. Walker, Cognitive and perspective-taking prerequisites for moral development, *Child Development* 51(1980):132. Published by University of Chicago Press. Reprinted by permission.

In the second phase of Walker's research, in which he tried to change children's moral judgment, Kohlberg's second contention was supported. In other words, Walker found it easiest to change the moral judgments of children who had achieved the prerequisite levels of cognitive functioning and social perspective-taking skills. His intervention was as follows: Two adults engaged in role play with children who had reached beginning formal operations and stage 3 in social perspective-taking skills but had not yet reached stage 3 in moral reasoning. In this role playing the adults acted out the reasoning that was appropriate for the higher level of moral judgment. In other words, the two adults demonstrated for the child the sort of reasoning that was required at the moral judgment level above the one in which the child had typically been functioning.

These role-playing sessions were carried on for several weeks, and then children were tested after a delay of eight days on their moral judgment. The children who had achieved beginning formal operations and stage 3 in perspective taking but not stage 3 in moral reasoning before the intervention were the only ones who really benefited from the role-playing sessions. Of this group 62% made moral judgments at stage 3 after the intervention, whereas only 25% had made moral judgments at this level before the intervention. If children had achieved cognitive but not perspective-taking skills at the required level for stage 3 of moral judgment, or if neither their cognitive nor perspective-taking skills were at the appropriate level, the interventions did not appear to help them. Separate groups of children who were not trained on role playing did not show the kind of improvement that the most successful group did when they were tested again after a period of several weeks.

Walker's study shows the importance of cognitive and social perspective-taking skills in the processes of making moral judgments. It also demonstrates that the most effective training for adolescents whose moral judgments are at a low level involves carefully matching moral-reasoning training to the level of cognitive and social perspective-taking skills at which the adolescent is functioning.

REFERENCE

1. L. Walker, Cognitive and perspective-taking prerequisites for moral development, *Child Development* 51(1980):131–139.

With regard to adolescent drug use, which is a special concern of Kandel's, the general patterns of friendship formation and consolidation were manifested in activities like the use of marijuana. In some of the pairs of teenagers she studied, marijuana use had become an integral part of the friendships. Figure 8.3 shows Kandel's findings about the association between drug use and friendship. Note that the number of times adolescents reported having used marijuana themselves was strongly associated with the number of times their best friends had used it. This correspondence may indicate that marijuana use sometimes serves as a powerful behavioral device for defining oneself in comparison with someone else. Adolescent friendships are natural occasions for the workings of social comparison and conformity processes in connection with such attempts at self-definition.

PARENT-PEER CROSS-PRESSURES: DO ADOLESCENTS REJECT PARENTS?

The influence of peers has, not surprisingly, helped to create a popular impression that adolescents characteristically reject the values of their parents in favor of the values and behaviors of peers. Is this a fair appraisal of the way adolescents make decisions and govern their behavior? Both the question and the answer are more complex than they may appear. But there are certainly anguished parents who believe they have been rejected by their teenage children. The following letter to Ann Landers gives an example:

Dear Ann:

What has happened between parents and children in the last 15 years? The Bible says, "Raise up a child in the way he should go and he will not depart from it." Do you believe it? I don't.

Our own children are living proof. We have four. I stayed home and took care of them. We always went to church together. They had plenty of love, responsibility, and discipline. Everything was fine until they started high school and went to college. Within 6 months they fell in with friends who could twist and turn them any which way. Peer pressure, they call it. Well, whatever it is, I don't understand how it could have negated all the years of love and good training.

Our sons and daughters look like bums. They have no interest in decent clothes. They tell us they are agnostics. Three are college graduates, yet they can't find jobs they like. They think it is hypocritical to do work that isn't "rewarding, exciting, and stimulating." Don't they realize that life isn't all fun and pleasure?

Ann, you can do a lot of good by printing this letter and letting our children know that we as parents are fed up with their scraggly appearance, foul language, and total disrespect for authority.

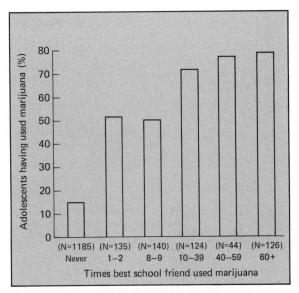

FIG. 8.3 Adolescent marijuana use correlated with self-reported marijuana use of best school friend

Note: Dyads comprise students and best school friends in five schools in the fall of 1971; N = number reporting. Redrawn from D. Kandel, Adolescent marijuana use: Role of parents and peers, *Science* 181(1973):1068. Reprinted by permission.

My husband is in his early fifties, and he is a broken man. We cry for each other, and for thousands of other parents who feel they have failed. We did our best and can't figure out what went wrong.

Yes, we know many children go the right way, but this letter is for parents like ourselves who are sick at heart because we raised a generation of messed up misfits. What can you say to us?

—Failures [30]

This mother was writing about *parent-peer cross-pressures,* the conflict between the values and wishes of parents and those of peers. Such cross-pressures certainly exist in the lives of almost all American adolescents. Not surprisingly, the conflict reaches its peak for most young people in early adolescence, when the recognition and increased salience of peers force attention to them and their wishes [31].

In a recent interview study Thomas Berndt asked children and adolescents to respond to some hypothetical situations in which conflicting pressures from parents and peers were described [32]. Increasing conflict was expressed in the interview responses of early adolescents. One reason for the increased cross-pressures at this age may be that adolescents' emerging cognitive abilities permit them to see peer and parent influences as separate social systems, governed by separate sets of values. Thus it is probably accurate to say that adolescents feel parent-peer cross-pressures keenly. These feelings of conflict represent one of the distinctive problems young people face during this period.

However, adolescents are not merely captives of conflicting pressures. In many instances they make judgments about issues on their own, even though they may be aware that their parents or friends favor one position or another. We can see the autonomy of adolescents' judgments when adolescents are presented with hypothetical issues about which their parents and peers have conflicting views. For example, sociologist Clay Brittain presented a group of hypothetical situations to girls in grades 9–11 [33]. The stories were presented twice, once with peers advocating certain alternatives and once with parents advocating those same alternatives. Brittain wanted to see if the *source* of the judgments—parents or peers—affected the girls' judgments about the situation. For example, he wanted to know if a girl would change her opinion about which boy to go steady with, how to get selected for a school honor, or how to dress for a football game or party, depending on whether an alternative was favored by parent or by peer.

Brittain found that the girls in his study were neither unusually oriented toward peers nor unusually submissive to parents. Indeed, many of them were not influenced by either parents or peers but made their own independent judgments. Those who were influenced by parent or peer tended to use parents and peers in different areas of judgment. For example, peer influence was strongest on problems relevant to status in the peer group, while parents were more influential on life decisions, ethical and value judgments, and issues that were relevant to the reputation and status of the girls and the family in the community.

In short, adolescents are not mindless victims of others' influences, as popular stereotypes sometimes suggest. Rather, in most cases they use information from different sources in a discriminating fashion. Furthermore, parents and peers often influence adolescents in the same direction. In fact, generally speaking, parent-peer cross-pressures are probably far less common than parent-peer concordance.

Now we turn to a specific example of cross-pressures. Then we will examine how cross-pressures can be resolved.

An Example: The Case of Cigarette Smoking

If we want to examine the influences of parents and peers on adolescents in real life, we can examine behavior patterns like cigarette smoking that often begin during the teen years. The factors that cause adolescents to begin and to keep on smoking should give us interesting information about the role of social influence in adolescent behavior.

In recent years a number of studies on smoking have been conducted because of the health risks associated with tobacco use. Many of these

To many adults, teenagers' conformity to fads is a sign that the adolescents are rejecting parental influence in favor of peer group influence
Photograph from Charles Gatewood

studies have focused on adolescent smoking. In one of them psychologists John Krosnick and Charles Judd surveyed 847 junior high students, 11- and 14-year-olds, about their own smoking habits and the smoking habits and attitudes of their parents and friends [34]. For example, the participants were asked how often they smoked and, specifically, if they had smoked a cigarette "in the last month," "in the last week," and "yesterday." They were also asked how many of their "really good friends" smoked and whether and how often each of their parents smoked. Finally, they were asked what instructions parents had given them about smoking and what their parents' attitudes would be if the teenager smoked. Krosnik and Judd then tried to determine the effect of peer smoking or parental smoking and attitudes on teen and preteen smoking.

Both 11-year-olds' and 14-year-olds' smoking was affected by their parents' own smoking behavior and attitudes. If parents smoked or expressed relatively positive attitudes toward smoking, there was a greater likelihood that their child would smoke, too. Peer influence was weak in determining whether 11-year-olds smoked, but it became significantly more important among 14-year-olds. This result does not indicate that parents' influence decreased from one age group to the next, however. Instead, peer influence on smoking was greater, *relative to parental influence,* among 14-year-olds. In other words, in the case of smoking, peer influence does seem to grow during adolescence, but parental influence does not drop. Parents remain powerful influences on adolescent behavior, but peers become powerful as well. Thus if you wanted to affect the smoking practices of teenagers, you could not rely on family education programs alone. You would have to affect peer group practices as well.

Resolving Cross-Pressures

Even though cross-pressures may not be as dramatic as the popular stereotype suggests, adolescents often do encounter values and behaviors that conflict with those they have learned in their families. Consequently, an important question is how adolescents resolve cross-pressures when they exist. An interesting example of the problem was documented fifty years ago in a study of students at Bennington College in Vermont [35]. The women students of the college came from predominantly upper-income, urban families whose political and social attitudes tended to be conservative. The college itself, which was newly opened at the time of the study (1935 to 1939), was staffed mostly with liberal, socially concerned teachers. Would the attitudes of the students be affected primarily by their family background or by the college environment? Attitudes were measured when the women entered the college as freshmen and each year thereafter until they graduated.

Over the course of four years there was a general trend for the women to be conservative as freshmen and liberal as seniors. Thus for most of the students there was clearly some influence from the college environment; their attitudes changed both from the time they entered college and from the attitudes their families typically held.

But not all of the women changed. Some stayed the same, and others actually became more conservative. And an important difference between those who changed and those who did not was the *quality* of the relationships between the girls and their families, on the one hand, and the college community on the other. The liberal seniors were motivated to achieve independence from the family and to achieve leadership and prestige in the college community. For them college teachers and friends had become the primary *reference group,* and they wanted to conform to its norms and values. The conservative seniors, in contrast, tended to be defensive and to withdraw from the community. They actively resisted the community's influence in order to maintain their family ties. For them the family was the important reference group; thus the women adhered to family norms and values. Since the two groups of women had similar potential experiences in the college, the identity of their primary reference group seemed to play an important role in how and why their opinions changed. When two reference groups clashed, the group in which membership was most important to the person had stronger influence over attitudes and values.

For adolescents, membership in the family group and in the peer group may sometimes conflict, producing the parent-peer cross-pressures we have been discussing. One way of resolving membership group conflicts was illustrated by Brittain's study: using the two membership groups as reference groups under different circumstances. However, emotional involvement with the family as a membership group probably plays an especially important role in resolution of parent-peer cross-pressures. If relationships with parents are warm and supportive, adolescents may be more likely to resolve parent-peer cross-pressure in favor of family wishes. If relationships with parents are strained or unsatisfactory, peer influence may become *relatively* more attractive as a source of influence than that of the family.

The importance of the quality of family relationships in resolving parent-peer cross-pressures is apparent in a large-scale study conducted by Lyle Larson [36]. Larson interviewed more than 1500 students in grades 7, 9, and 12. He asked them to rate their parents, their best friends, and others on four characteristics: how understanding they were, their openness of communication, their helpfulness with problems, and the amount of control they exerted in the adolescent's life. He also specifically asked the participants about their feelings toward their parents: how much they enjoyed family activities, how warm their feelings toward their parents were, and so forth. As in other studies, a high proportion of the participants (75%) felt that parents were more important influences on them than peers, or they saw no differences between parents and friends as a source of influence. Only 25% said that their peers were most salient for them.

Larson then questioned *why* peer-oriented adolescents preferred the influence of other adolescents over their parents'. One clue came from the measure of feelings toward parents—how positive or negative adolescents perceived their relationships to their parents to be. Figure 8.4 shows that the more positive the feelings toward parents, the more salient parents are as a reference group. Friends are correspondingly less influential under these circumstances. But when family feelings are not very positive, friends become much more salient and potentially have more influence than parents.

Judging from Larson's findings, this pattern becomes more pronounced over the course of adolescence. For adolescents in the seventh grade, positive feelings for parents were less related to parents' degree of influence than they were for adolescents in ninth and twelfth grades. At these older ages adolescents with low positive feelings for parents said peers were considerably more influential than parents, but adolescents

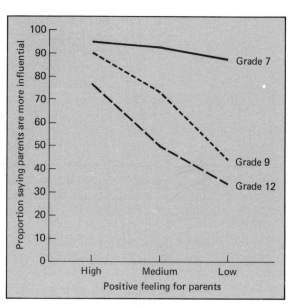

FIG. 8.4 Average proportion of adolescents at each grade for whom parents were more salient than, or as salient as, peers as a source of influence

Redrawn from L. Larson, The relative influence of parent-adolescent affect in predicting the salience hierarchy among youth, *Pacific Sociological Review* 15(1972):100.

with high positive feelings for their parents said parents were more influential than peers. Perhaps, then, true parent-peer cross-pressures exist when peer influences increase and family relations are less positive than the adolescent would like.

Larson's study has interesting implications for work with adolescents for whom parent-peer cross-pressures are a problem. Although it is unlikely that the problems of unsatisfactory parent-child relationships can be turned around overnight, it might be possible for a concerned youth worker or teacher to help unhappy adolescents find constructive sources of influence and guidance to fill in the gap they perceive—rightly or wrongly—in family relationships.

On balance, the problem of cross-pressures has become part of the myth of adolescence, and like most myths, it is somewhat exaggerated. More than likely, popular impressions represent an overgeneralization from instances where parent-peer conflicts are obvious and attention getting [37]. At the same time we must recognize that some aspects of adolescents' development—including cognitive growth, changing expectations about social roles and privileges, and a whole range of new social relationships—make some conflict between adolescents and their parents almost inevitable. In some families, conflict may be more extensive and more traumatic than in others. When cross-pressures do occur, resolving them usually depends on the qualities of the relationships that adolescents and their parents have developed in the years leading up to the transformations of adolescence.

SUMMARY

Peer relationships provide a major setting in which adolescents develop personal characteristics for adulthood. Although peers have often been considered to be in conflict with family and other adult influences, we have argued in this chapter that peers play a complementary role in adolescent development. Many of the influences of peers could not be successfully duplicated by family members alone.

One of the major changes in adolescent peer relations is that adolescents form relationships on the basis of common feelings and interests rather than common activities alone. Although in childhood doing things with others seems to be the main basis for friendship, adolescents are likely to seek friends with whom they can share thoughts and feelings. Undoubtedly, this new basis for friendship is partly the result of cognitive changes that permit adolescents to understand the true nature of mutuality and sharing.

The bases of social acceptance include physical attractiveness, normative behaviors, intelligence, and achievement; however, no single characteristic guarantees social acceptance in the adolescent society. Adolescent groups, like groups at other age levels, follow certain patterns of formation and operation. For example, in groups studied under real life conditions the members highest in dominance function as leaders of the group and enjoy special privileges within the group. Once groups are formed, they tend to remain relatively closed to newcomers. Erikson has argued that adolescent groups serve an important function in the achievement of identity by offering members protective covering for experimentation with adult roles.

Indeed, peer relations in general have emerged as important predictors for successful adult adjustment. Poor peer relations in childhood and adolescence are often associated with a range of adult problems, including behavioral difficulties, occupational problems, and marital and sexual problems. Individuals who have satisfactory peer relations in middle childhood, by contrast, are often well-adjusted adults. Successful peer relations may have these long-term effects because they provide opportunities to make social comparisons, through which adolescents measure their own behavior against that of others, and to resist conformity pressures, in which adolescents are influenced to adopt others' behavior and values.

Conformity seems to be especially high in early adolescence, perhaps because awareness of others' perspectives is dominant in the thinking of young people at this period of development. And heightened conformity to peers is often seen as a problem, particularly when peer behavior conflicts with parental standards. For the most part, however, parent-peer conflict seems to be much less likely than agreement between parents and peers. Recent research indicates that parents and peers tend to influence adolescents in different areas of activity. Furthermore, parents tend to be the favored source of influence for most activities, especially when family relationships have been positive. When adolescents feel less positive toward their families, however, the salience of peers as sources of social influence often increases. In Chapter 9 we will examine the relative influence of parents and peers in the area of sexuality.

KEY POINTS AND NAMES

Peer relationships	Conformity
Friendship	Philip Costanzo
Sex differences in friendship	Age trends in conformity
Selman's levels of friendship concepts	Factors in conformity
	Conformity and identity
Social acceptance and rejection	Denise Kandel
Adolescent groups	Effects of similarity in friends
James Coleman	Parent-peer cross-pressures
Similarity	Thomas Berndt
Ritch Savin-Williams	Clay Brittain
Functions of peer relations	Jon Krosnik and Charles Judd
Horizontal relationships	Cigarette-smoking study
Psychosocial moratorium	Bennington College study
Informational influence and normative influence	Reference group
	Lyle Larson
Social comparison	

REFERENCES

1. W. W. Hartup, Peer relations. in *Carmichael's manual of child psychology*, 4th ed., ed. P. Mussen and E. M. Hetherington (New York: Wiley, forthcoming); E. Medrich, J. Roisen, V. Rubin, and S. Vuckley, *The serious business of growing up: A study of children's lives outside school* (Berkeley: University of California Press, 1982), pp. 230–239.

2. E. Douvan and J. Adelson, *The adolescent experience* (New York: Wiley, 1966), pp. 186–197.

3. T. Parsons, Family structure and the socialization of the child. in *Family socialization and interaction process,* ed. T. Parsons and R. Bales (Glencoe, Ill.: Free Press, 1955), pp. 35–131.

4. G. Konopka, *Young girls* (Englewood Cliffs, N.J.: Prentice-Hall, 1976), p. 84.

5. *Ibid.,* p. 86.

6. Hartup.

7. S. A. Toth, *Blooming: A small-town girlhood* (Boston: Little, Brown, 1981), pp. 62–63.

8. Hartup.

9. J. S. Coleman, *The adolescent society* (New York: Free Press, 1961), pp. 11–172.

10. H. Raucher, *Summer of '42* (New York: Dell, 1971), pp. 219–221.

11. Hartup.

12. R. Savin-Williams, An ethological study of dominance formation and maintenance in a group of human adolescents, *Child Development* 47(1976):972–979.

13. *Ibid.,* p. 977.

14. G. Sones and N. Feshbach, Sex differences in adolescent reactions toward newcomers, *Developmental Psychology* 4(1971):381–386.

15. C. McCullers, *The member of the wedding* (New York: Houghton Mifflin, 1946), p. 39.

16. E. L. Cowen, A. Pederson, H. Babigan, L. D. Izzo, and M. A. Trost, Long-term follow up of early detected vulnerable children, *Journal of Consulting and Clinical Psychology* 41(1973):438–446.

17. Hartup.

18. E. Erikson, *Identity: Youth and crisis* (New York: Norton, 1968), pp. 45–53.

19. M. Deutsch and H. Gerard, A study of normative and informational social influences upon individual judgment, *Journal of Abnormal and Social Psychology* 51(1955):629–636.

20. Hartup.

21. Toth, p. 60.

22. D. Ruble, A. K. Boggiano, N. S. Feldman, and H. J. Loebl, Developmental analysis of the role of social comparison in self evaluation, *Developmental Psychology* 12(1976):192–197.

23. G. W. Goethals and D. S. Klos, *Experiencing youth* (Boston: Little, Brown, 1970), pp. 24–31.

24. P. Costanzo, Conformity development as a function of self-blame, *Journal of Personality and Social Psychology* 14(1970):366–374.

25. *Ibid.,* pp. 366–367.

26. J. Landsbaum and R. Willis, Conformity in early and late adolescence, *Devel-*

opmental Psychology 4, 3(1971):334–337; O. Harvey and C. Consalvi, Status and conformity to pressures in informal groups, *Journal of Abnormal and Social Psychology* 60(1960):182–187.

27. H. Saltzstein, M. Diamond, and M. Belenky, Moral judgment level and conformity behavior, *Developmental Psychology* 7(1972):327–335.

28. N. L. Toder and J. E. Marcia, Ego identity status and response to conformity pressure in college women, *Journal of Personality and Social Psychology* 26, 2(1973):287–294.

29. D. Kandel, Homophily, selection, and socialization in adolescent friendships, *American Journal of Sociology* 84(1978):427–436; D. Kandel, Similarity in real-life adolescent friendship pairs, *Journal of Personality and Social Psychology* 36(1978):302–312.

30. Ann Landers, Field Newspaper Syndicate, *Minneapolis Tribune*, August 30, 1974.

31. V. E. Bixenstine, M. DeCorte, and B. A. Bixenstine, Conformity to peer-sponsored misconduct among junior-high school boys, *Developmental Psychology* 4, 2(1971):178–181; W. Emmerich, K. Goldman, and R. Shore, Differentiation and development of social norms, *Journal of Personality and Social Psychology* 18, 3(1971):323–353.

32. T. Berndt, Developmental changes in conformity to peers and parents, *Developmental Psychology* 15, 6(1979):608–616.

33. C. V. Brittain, Adolescent choices and parent-peer cross-pressures, *American Sociological Review* 28(1963):358–391.

34. J. Krosnick and C. Judd, Transitions in social influence at adolescence: Who induces cigarette smoking? *Developmental Psychology* 18(1982):359–368.

35. T. Newcomb, *Personality and social change: Attitude formation in a student community* (New York: Dryden Press, 1943).

36. L. Larson, The relative influence of parent-adolescent affect in predicting the salience hierarchy among youth, *Pacific Sociological Review* 15(1972):83–102.

37. A. Bandura, The stormy decade: Fact or fiction? *Psychology in the Schools* 1(1964):224–231.

CHAPTER 9

Adolescent Sexuality

INTRODUCTION

Becoming a mature sexual being involves some of the primary biological changes of adolescence, of course, but that obvious fact makes the emergence of sexuality seem far simpler than it really is. When an adolescent boy or girl becomes capable of reproduction, only one aspect of being sexual is involved. *Sexuality* more generally means the emotions, behaviors, and attitudes that are associated not only with being able to procreate but also with the social and personal patterns that accompany intimate physical relationships in a person's life.

In this chapter we discuss the many facets of the sexuality that emerges during the second decade of life. First, we discuss the nature of sexual pressures that adolescents are supposed to feel so keenly. Then we deal with what appears to be current patterns of sexual behavior among young adolescents in the United States and with some of the problems associated with adolescent sexuality—problems for adolescents themselves, for parents, and for society. Finally, we examine sexuality and sex education from a developmental view.

THE BIOLOGICAL BASES FOR ADOLESCENT SEXUALITY

In Chapter 3 we discussed the main primary and secondary changes in sexual characteristics during pubescence. The most obvious changes, secondary sex characteristics, are also the most dramatic signs of becoming an adult physically. Interestingly, however, as far as the basic physiological aspects of sexuality are concerned, changes at adolescence are mostly external and relatively superficial.

The fundamental sexual apparatus—and the basis for physiological sexual responses—is present either before or immediately after birth. Hormones like the androgens and progesterones are present and active even in prenatal development. The androgens determine both the physical morphology, or shape, of the genitals and—apparently—the organization of the nervous system that underlies different responses by males and females. For example, in studies with animals typical male and female sexual responses in adulthood can be altered by changing the balance of hormones very early in life [1]. Female rats can be made to show male behaviors, like mounting and genital-pelvic thrusts, by an increase in the proportion of androgens in their systems immediately after birth. Similarly, male rats are more likely to show typical female responses to mounting and thrusting if the proportion of androgen in their systems has been reduced postnatally. Furthermore, it appears that thresholds of responses, which are generally lower in males than in females, and differences in perceptual distractibility during sexual pursuit and consummation may be linked to hormone balances in the system considerably in advance of puberty. Thus it appears that there is an early critical period for the effect of hormones on the basic organization of the nervous system that controls sexual responses in adults [2].

What, then, happens at puberty? For one thing, the absolute level of androgens increases in both males and females, affecting the frequency and intensity of sexual arousal. However, the hormone is the same for both males and females, so this pubertal change tells us little about the different patterns of sexuality shown by males and females. The other major pubertal change, besides the appearance of reproductive capacity, is that the male becomes capable of ejaculation. Of course, these changes in adolescents are important. In fact, much of what attracts attention to adolescent sexuality is the increase in frequency and intensity of arousal that takes place after puberty. However, changes in the absolute level of androgens and in ejaculatory capacity in males explain only a small part of what we observe about the emergence of sexuality among adolescents of different sexes, among members of different social groups in our own society, or from culture to culture. Thus to understand these differences, we need to go far beyond the biological bases of sexual response.

SOCIAL PSYCHOLOGICAL BASES OF ADOLESCENT SEXUALITY

Like adolescence itself, then, sexuality may begin in biology but end in culture. And as with understanding the nature of adolescence, the difficulty in understanding adolescent sexuality is to get a sense of how much the sexual nature of adolescents is determined by the changes at puberty and how much reflects social and cultural expectations, or learned patterns of behavior.

When social scientists face such questions, they often turn to two sources of differences among individuals in their search for answers: differences between males and females, and differences across societies and cultures. For example, as we saw in Chapter 1, Margaret Mead found that Samoan adolescents experienced the second decade of life as a relatively calm, trouble-free, and pleasant period. Therefore, it was no longer reasonable to conclude that the apparent difficulties of adolescents in Western industrialized nations indicate that adolescence is inherently difficult. So what do such comparisons tell us about sexuality?

Two psychologists, Clellan Ford and Frank Beach, have carefully examined information about patterns of sexual behavior in cultures throughout the world [3]. Their research question was very similar to Mead's: Do adolescents, in other cultures besides our own, adopt quite different patterns of sexual behavior as they mature? If so, then sexuality is clearly not all biological. Rather, in one or several ways basic sexual impulses and responses are channeled by culturally dictated patterns and expectations.

Ford and Beach did indeed find variation from culture to culture that would lead one to conclude that social and cultural factors are an important part of emerging sexuality in adolescence. For example, in some cultures sexual activity is permitted—even encouraged—throughout the life cycle. Some African and Asian groups believe that individuals will not be able to beget children unless they exercise their sexual capacities early. In other groups, by contrast, sexual play before marriage is strictly forbidden, even to the point of keeping information about sex entirely secret until the last stages of the marriage ceremony. In our own culture there has traditionally been disapproval of sexual knowledge and activity before marriage, particularly for females. The well-known double standard has allowed more freedom in males following puberty—although generally not before.

Anthropologists John Whiting and Irvin Child argue that these differences in cultural attitudes toward sexual patterns result in psychological differences as well [4]. For example, in societies where sex is forbidden or is highly restricted before marriage, guilt is thought to be a more common psychological phenomenon than it is in societies with somewhat more permissive attitudes toward sexual expression. From this point of view, then, what adolescents experience in the emergence of sexuality is only partly determined by the increased frequency and intensity of arousal associated with hormonal changes at puberty. The variety of sexual behavior patterns and psychological states associated with sexuality suggests many important influences from outside as well. In the following sections we discuss one view of social influences on sexuality, including influences

The development of sexuality involves learning patterns of behavior and role expectations
Photograph from Charles Gatewood

on sex differences and subcultural differences in sexual attitudes and behavior.

The Social Scripting of Sexuality: Simon and Gagnon's View

The importance of the social system in which adolescents come of age sexually leads psychologists William Simon and John Gagnon to suggest that sex is a *socially scripted* activity [5]. By this term Simon and Gagnon mean that for most adolescents the expression of sexuality is governed less by biological impulses per se than by the expectations and social significance associated with certain patterns of sexual activity. These patterns must be learned and actively reinforced by the individuals around an adolescent, although the learning and reinforcement may take place very subtly.

One dramatic example of social scripting is found in the research on sexually aggressive males done by Eugene Kanin [6]. By *sexually aggressive* we mean young men who have pursued sexual intercourse to the point that the female partner has become very upset and resistant (e.g., crying, screaming, pleading); we are not referring to rapes but to situations in dating that reach the point of sexual aggressiveness by the male. Kanin interviewed a large number of males in a major midwestern university and identified 87 who reported that they had engaged in sexually aggressive behavior. These men were compared with 244 men who were similar to them in background but who could be considered nonaggressive. On the average, the aggressive men had had more sexual contact than the nonaggressive males, but they reported greater dissatisfaction with the amount of sexual experience they were having than the nonaggressive males did.

They also reported that they believed it would take a larger number of orgasms per week to satisfy them than the nonaggressive males did.

When the social environment of these two groups was compared, one contrast was especially remarkable: The sexually aggressive males were involved with peer groups that placed high value on sexual experiences and granted status to members who claimed such experiences. Consequently, these men typically claimed to feel pressure from peers to be sexually active. By contrast, a higher proportion of nonaggressive men claimed they would feel no pressure from their friends with regard to premarital sexual experience. Unlike the aggressive males, these nonaggressive males felt there would be no particular loss of status to them if they had to admit to being virgins. What is important in these findings is not the question of whether the males were accurate in their perceptions of their peer groups' standards and values but the fact that their perceptions varied so greatly.

While the sexually aggressive males that Kanin studied may be an extreme example, the differences in behavior between them and the nonaggressive group are consistent with the social-scripting notion. Aggressiveness is often construed to be a part of the masculine sex role, as is the notion of strong sexual drive. Thus combining—or confusing—the two characteristics is not difficult to understand. And males would be likely to act on this stereotyped concept of masculinity particularly when there is strong, immediate reinforcement from the peer group. Thus the difference between the aggressive and the relatively nonaggressive groups may actually reflect a difference in the conception of the male sex role and a difference in the way sex role learning is integrated with sexual behavior expectations for these late adolescents.

Scripting and Sex Differences

Research indicates that there are notable differences between the early sexual experiences of males and females that parallel several subtle aspects of differences between the sexes. Adolescents, like adults, enter their sexual lives under the constraints of the social roles and expectations that are part of our culture. For example, the typical pattern for males is to begin sexual expression in solitary masturbation and only later to merge sexual expression with social relationships. The majority of males report their first sexual experiences to have been solitary. Furthermore, when they do begin heterosexual activities, it is often not fully integrated with social and emotional involvement. For example, most males report relatively few contacts with the person with whom they first had sexual intercourse. Thus early heterosexual experiences for males rarely occur in an interpersonal context with prospects for lasting emotional involvement.

By contrast, females are most likely to have their first sexual experiences in the context of an emotional relationship. Masturbation, which is relatively less common for females than for males, in general, is more likely to follow rather than precede heterosexual experiences for girls. In addition, females are likely to report a relatively large number of sexual contacts with the first person with whom a sexual relationship is experienced. Thus in comparison with boys, girls may be more likely to experience sexuality in an interpersonal, emotionally committed context.

In many ways these different patterns for males and females parallel fundamental differences in the gender roles, as discussed in Chapter 7. Males' sexual behavior tends to be relatively instrumental or goal-directed, the goal being achievement of sexual activity. On the other hand, females are more likely to subordinate sexual activity to their goals of expressiveness and sensitivity, which characterize the female sex role [7]. In fact, Simon and Gagnon have suggested that sexual activity for males is initiated primarily by the biological events that permit them to ejaculate; for females the initiating event is the female's perceiving herself to be at an age with a certain proximity to marriage. Whatever the initiating event, however, it is very clear that the males' pattern of emerging sexuality is from sexuality to sociosexuality; the reverse pattern is true for females. To quote Simon and Gagnon:

> The female appears to be trained in precisely that area for which males during adolescence are the least trained and for which they are least expected to display a capacity: intense, affect-latent relationships and a rhetoric of romantic love. When sexual arousal is reported by females during this period, it is more often reported as a response to representations of romantic love than as a response to erotic representations. . . .

> The movement into later adolescence and the concomitant increase in opportunities for sociosexual activity can be described as the situation in which males — committed to sexuality and relatively untrained in the rhetoric of romantic love—interact with the females who are committed to romantic love and relatively untrained in sexuality. Dating and courtship may well be considered processes with which persons of one sex train members of the opposite sex in the meaning and content of their respective commitments. [8]

Table 9.1 outlines the successive phases of sexual maturing. For each age period the major *agents*, or influences, are shown. In the third column the *assemblies*, or aspects of personal and social identity that must be integrated for mature sexuality, are described.

Scripting and Subcultural Differences

Within our own culture there is considerable variation in adolescents' early sexual experiences. For example, lower-class black adolescents experience sexual intercourse much earlier than white adolescents in the same age group [9]. Black males show a higher level of heterosexual interaction at ages 12–13 than white males do. Furthermore, their attitudes are similar to

TABLE 9.1 Outline of a sexual career

	Stage and ages	Agents	Assemblies
Gender identity	1. Infancy, ages 0–2½–3	Mother to family	Formation of base for conventional gender identity package
	2. Childhood, ages 3–11	Family to peers, increasing media	Consolidation of conventional gender identity package; modesty-shame learning; nonsexually motivated sex play; learning of sex words without content; learning of sex activities without naming; learning of general moral categories; mass media through commercials and programming content reinforcing conventional gender, sex, and family roles; media also preparing for participation in youth culture
Sexual identity	3. Early adolescence, ages 11–15	Family, same-sex peers, media	First societal identification as a conventional sexual performer; first overt physical sexual activity with self or others; development of fantasy materials; beginnings of male/female divergence in overt sexual activity; application of gender package to sexual acts; application of moral values to emergent sexual behavior; privitization of sexual activities; same-sex peers reinforce homosocial values; family begins to lose moral control; media reinforces conventional adult content of gender roles; media attaches consumer practices to gender success; basic attachment to youth culture formed
	4. Later adolescence, ages 15–18	Same-sex peers, cross-sex peers increasing, media, family reducing	Increased practice of integrating of sexual acts with nonsexual social relations; movement to heterosocial values; increased frequency of sexual activity; declining family controls; continuing media reinforcement of sexual-gender roles and consumer and youth culture values; sexual experience with wider range of peers; common completion of sexual fantasy content; consolidation of gender differences in sexual roles and activity; good girl/bad girl–maternal/erotic distinctions completed
Family formation	5. Early adulthood, ages 18–23	Same-sex and cross-sex peers, media, minimum family of origin	Mate selection, narrowing of mate choice; increased amount of sexual practice; commitment to love by male, sex by female; linkage of passion to love; dyadic regression; insulation from family judgment and peer judgment; increasing pressure to marry; relief from same-sex competition by stabilization of cross-sex contacts; legitimization of sexual activity by peers and romantic code; media reinforces youth culture values of romance and virtues of marriage; experience with falling in and out of love; termination of protected school/student statuses

TABLE 9.1   (Continued)

	Stage and ages	Agents	Assemblies
Family formation	6. Final mate selec-tion–early mar-riage, ages 20–27	Fiancé(e), spouse, same-sex peers, family of origin increases	Regularizes and legitimizes sexual activity; stable rates of sex activity; variation in kinds of sexual behavior; children born in most cases; increasing sexual anxiety about children; family values reinforced by children and family of origin; declining eroticism, increased maternalism; culmination of purchasing/consumer values in wedding gifts or buying new products; routinization of sexual behavior; decreased contact with cross-sex peers unless they are married; interaction in multiple dyads; sexual activities restricted by pregnancy, children, work
Reproduction	7. Middle marriage, ages 28–45	Spouse, same-sex peers, family of origin, married peers	Declining sexual activity in marriage; some extramarital sexual experimentation; maturing children; conflict of erotic with material; emergence of sexual dissatisfactions; increase in occupational commitments; declines in physical energy and physical beauty; fantasy competition by youth culture; continual multiple dyadic interactions and insulation from cross-sex peers; marriage moving to nonsexual basis for stability and continuity
	8. Post-young chil-dren, ages 45+	Spouse, same-sex peers, married peers	Further decline in sexual activity; some extramarital sexual experimentation; substitution of nonsexual commitments other than children as basis of marriage; further decline in physical strength and beauty; further desexualization of gender identity; movement out of public sexual arena.

From J. Gagnon and W. Simon, *Sexual conduct* (Chicago: Aldine, 1973), pp. 61–62. Reprinted by permission.

the attitudes of black females in this age group, although the actual level of heterosexual activity is higher for males than for females. Apparently, black adolescents experience sexual intercourse earlier than their white age-mates and also tend to continue activity at a higher level than that of white adolescents, particularly in the lower class.

Among adolescents in general, lower-class males tend to follow a pattern that reflects markedly different social scripts both from lower-class females and from males and females in other groups. Among lower-class males, engaging in sexual activity earns one special status in the male peer group. Heterosexual involvement is reinforced through social status recognition [10]. This motivational pattern has interesting implications for later sexual patterns. Lower-class males tend to marry earlier, and the reported frequency of intercourse in their marriages tends to drop off more dramatically as the years pass than it does for marriages in other social classes. One suggestion that has been offered for this result is that the source of reinforcement for heterosexual activity disappears when the marriage takes place. Thus the lower-class male, dependent on social scripting that involves reinforcement from male peers, begins to lose interest in sex in marriage. If this interpretation is correct, it is another piece of evidence for the role of society and culture in determining the social scripts out of which sexual expression arises throughout the life span.

The implication of a social-scripting view of sexuality is that adolescents' experiences as they come of age sexually are not entirely based in the pubertal changes to which we give so much attention when we talk about this age period. Instead, we need to consider adolescent sexuality in the context of a very wide range of social learning experiences, expectations, and social roles with which adolescents come in contact as they move toward adulthood. The pressures of sexuality that adolescents experience are as much social pressures as biological ones.

LEARNING ABOUT SEX AND SEXUALITY

Some of the social pressures that adolescents feel surely must arise from the kinds of learning opportunities the society provides for them. The contrasts that Ford and Beach saw across cultures in the way sexuality is introduced indicate that learning about gender role is one of the important sources of social scripts that later affects adults' social sexual behavior. Who teaches American adolescents about sex? What do they learn, and how do they learn it?

The best available evidence suggests that adolescents learn surprisingly little and that their sources of information are not the most reliable sources potentially available to them. For example, the editor of *Teen Magazine* reported that many questions about sex are written into the magazine from teenagers who appear appallingly ignorant of basic facts [11]. One such letter read as follows:

> I am 13 and have a terrible problem! I have HAIR on my private parts. Help me before I die of embarrassment! School starts in two weeks and I will be in junior high and will have to change for gym in front of the other girls. Help! [12]

In addition to letters of this sort, many more conventional questions come into the magazine that reveal ignorance of many basic items of information about sexuality and sexual function. For example:

> What is masturbation? Is it really wrong?

How do you know when a boy is just using you?

When is a girl most likely to get pregnant?

Can you get pregnant if you have sex standing up?

I am 14 and haven't started my period yet. Am I normal?

Why are boys so pushy about sex?

I think about sex more and more. I have these feelings and dreams . . . Is something wrong with me?

If two girls love each other, does it mean they're lesbians?

Is it possible to get pregnant without actual intercourse?

What are the symptoms of VD and can you get it in other ways than sexual intercourse?

At what age are boys capable of making girls pregnant?

I don't feel ready to have sex. How can I say 'no' to my boyfriend without losing him? [13]

Magazines such as *Teen* obviously serve an important function for adolescents in providing answers to questions like these, but they probably reach only a small proportion of the adolescent population. Where do the others get their information, and why must even *Teen* readers resort to an impersonal source like the magazine for the knowledge they need? In this section we will look at two important sources of sex information: parents and peers.

Learning from Parents

Recent surveys of adolescents have found that fewer than 30% of the adolescents report that they and their parents "talk pretty freely" about sex. Two-thirds or more of American adolescents report that their parents have never discussed with them such important topics as masturbation, venereal disease, and contraceptive methods [14].

Parents also report much the same kind of distance between themselves and their children. Recently, a major survey was conducted in Cleveland, Ohio, of more than fourteen hundred parents from many different social backgrounds, occupational statuses, and types of families. The parents filled out a questionnaire that tapped their attitudes and family practices regarding sex education. A smaller number of parents were interviewed intensively to determine in more detail how most American families teach their youngsters about sex. The authors concluded:

> Most parents are uncertain about what their children already know, what they want them to know, and how to tell them. Parents experience conflict

over how to find the balance between what they believe and what they want their children to believe. Parents' uncertainty or lack of clarity about their own belief in this area certainly contributes to a communication problem. [15]

Perhaps the most important reason parents communicate so infrequently with their children and adolescents about sex is their own sense of discomfort and shame about it. For example, one girl reported:

"Mother talked to me about menstruation like it was something on the moon. She was looking up at the ceiling. I won't forget that as long as I live. Boy, I knew everything she was talking about, and I was saying to myself, this is too late now. . . . I don't want my child to grow up that way." [16]

When parents do feel a responsibility for communicating with their children, it tends to be directed toward their daughters rather than their sons. And most feel that the responsibility falls on mothers rather than fathers. Furthermore, fathers are no more likely to talk with their sons than with their daughters. Indeed, parents frequently reported that their son "asked no one" in the family about sex. When fathers are concerned about their children's sexuality, they tend to be more concerned about their son's masturbation—"fearing that it will lead to homosexuality"—and their daughter's premarital sexual activities, because of the implications for her reputation and that of the family [17].

Most parents believe that their adolescents learn about sex from other sources—from television, from older siblings or peers, and so forth. Few of them believe that adolescents turn to other adults to get information—and, indeed, adolescents themselves report that adults are very minor sources of information about sex. Parents' intuition that peers and the mass media are major sources of information is correct.

Learning from Peers

A large majority of adolescents indicate that they get most of their information about sex from members of their peer group. This finding is not so surprising. Peers are less threatening than adults as a source of information about a topic that is widely treated in our culture as having elements of shame and guilt associated with it. Perhaps it is natural that young people should avoid recognition of the topic to their parents by avoiding discussions with them about it.

The difficulty with learning from peers, of course, is that adolescents in general are so poorly informed about sex that they are scarcely competent teachers for each other about the topic. But because peers are involved in heterosexual relationships at the same level and within the same context as adolescents, their credibility is enhanced, even if the level of information they present is inadequate.

SPECIAL TOPIC
Effects of Father Absence on Girls

Fathers seem to figure importantly in the sex role learning of both boys and girls. But by the adolescent years the absence of a father from the family shows up more in the social behavior of girls than that of boys. Mavis Hetherington examined the aspects of girls' behavior that showed effects of father absence by studying 13–17-year-old girls from three types of families: intact, or father-present, families; families of widowed mothers; and families of divorced mothers [1]. All were firstborn children. The groups were similar in age and education of the subjects; occupation, education, or age of the parent(s); how many of the mothers worked outside the home; religious affiliation; and number of younger siblings. None of the father-absent families had had males living in the home since the father had been gone.

Using trained observers, Hetherington gathered information about these girls' behavior while they carried on their usual activities in a neighborhood recreation center and while they were being interviewed by two of Hetherington's assistants, a male and a female. In the recreation center she recorded such things as dependence on adult and same-age males and females; seeking praise, encouragement, and attention; how often they sought contact and nearness to males and females; amount of verbal aggression toward males and toward females. In the interviews she noted whether they chose a seat near, far from, or at a medium distance from the interviewer; their posture in the chair (e.g., whether they sat straight or leaned backward, the position of feet and legs); how much they talked; and how often they made eye contact. The girls were interviewed about their relationships with family and male and female friends; their mothers' warmth and restrictiveness and the closeness of their relationship to her; their attitudes about or memories toward their fathers; and other information about family experiences. Their mothers were interviewed on similar topics. Both mothers and daughters completed several standardized personality tests, including mea-

What is this peer context for heterosexual relations like? A picture of it is given to us by sociologist Dexter Dunphy [18]. Dunphy charted the relationship among groups of adolescents in an urban setting. He notes that in early adolescence the social scene tends to be composed of isolated cliques of either boys or girls that are parallel to each other. Gradually, these unisexual cliques come together in group-to-group interaction to

sures of sex role identification, amount of control they felt they had over the environment, and amount of anxiety.

The observational measures from the recreation center and the interviews showed striking differences in the behavior of the girls from the father-present, the divorced, and the widowed family groups. Daughters of divorcées sought more attention from adult males and more often put themselves in proximity and physical contact with male peers than did the father-present or widowed girls. They also spent more time in areas of the recreation center typically frequented by males, whereas daughters of widows tended to avoid these areas and prefer areas more typical of females. And in the interviews girls in the three groups behaved very differently toward the male interviewer. Here is Hetherington's description:

> Subjects in the divorced group . . . tended to assume a rather sprawling open posture, often leaning slightly forward with one or both arms hooked over the back of the chair. In contrast, subjects in the widowed group sat stiffly upright or leaned backward with their back often slightly turned to the male interviewer, their hands folded or lying in their laps and their legs together. Compared to girls in any other group, daughters of widows with a male interviewer showed more shoulder orientation away from the interviewer, more backward lean, less arm openness, less sideways lean, and less eye contact during silence or when the interviewer was speaking. In contrast, daughters of divorcées . . . showed more forward lean, more arm and leg openness, more eye contact when the interviewer was speaking and during silence than did any other group of subjects. They also smiled more than did the other two groups with a male interviewer. Daughters of widows smiled less with a male than a female interviewer. It should be noted that there were no differences between average scores of these groups with a female interviewer. [2]

These patterns seemed to be somewhat intensified if the father had left the home before the child reached age 5.

These apparently contrasting ways of relating to males seem especially reasonable in light of differences among the groups of girls on their interview responses. Both father-absent groups reported more insecurity around

(Continued)

form heterosexual crowds. Within these crowds the upper-status individuals begin to interact as couples, forming a heterosexual clique. This high-status group within the crowd serves as role models for lower-status members of the group who have not yet begun to form heterosexual relationships. Finally, in late adolescence the crowd takes on the character of a loosely associated group of couples. Thus the peer group serves as a

SPECIAL TOPIC (Continued)

males—adults and peers—than the father-present group did. But divorced family girls reported less positive attitudes toward their fathers, less warmth from the father, lower estimates of the father's competence, more conflict with the father, and lower self-esteem than the other groups of girls did. They also reported more involvement in heterosexual activity than either widowed family girls or father-present girls. However, all the girls had equally feminine attitudes and interest.

It is difficult to say exactly why father absence plays so important a role in girls' relationships with males. Hetherington noticed that family relationships had previously been, and continued to be, more difficult in the divorced mother family than in the other two types of families. Daughters reported more conflict with their mothers in this group. The divorced mothers themselves "appear to have had a negative attitude toward their ex-spouses, themselves, and life in general. Their lives and marriages had not been gratifying, and they were concerned about their adequacy as mothers" [3]. Nevertheless, they felt positive toward their daughters, and they seemed no less affectionate or different in their disciplinary habits than did the mothers from the other types of families. What difficulties they reported seemed to be a result of the daughter's behavior *after* she reached adolescence, particularly her behavior toward males. It could be that the family stress pattern generally explains the behavior of the girls whose fathers were absent because of divorce. Another possibility is that when fathers are absent, learning the appropriate behaviors for interacting with males is more difficult. The different ways in which the mothers in the two types of father-absent families protected their daughters before adolescence and the attitudes about men and marriage they conveyed may account for the different ways these two groups of girls dealt with male-female relationships.

REFERENCES

1. E. M. Hetherington, Effects of father absence on personality development in adolescent daughters, *Development Psychology* 7(1972):313–326.
2. *Ibid.*, pp. 318–320.
3. *Ibid.*, p. 321.

vehicle for the transition to sexuality that makes possible mature adult relationships. Once we see this role of the peer group in heterosexual development, it becomes easier to understand why peers are such an important source of sexual information for most adolescents.

Heterosexual interactions in adolescent groups provide a safe setting for learning about many aspects of male-female relationships

Photograph from Barbara Alper/Stock, Boston

Sullivan's View of Intimacy and Sexuality

The pattern of peer relationships described by Dunphy may also provide important psychological transitions from childhood to adolescence in the emergence of sexuality. Psychiatrist Harry Stack Sullivan, for instance, viewed peer relationships, particularly same-sex friendships, as vital to the development of healthy heterosexual relations [19].

According to Sullivan, adolescence is a time when two particularly strong needs must be merged, intimacy and lust. Intimacy involves overcoming loneliness, which Sullivan thought was common to every person's experience. By overcoming loneliness through close friendships with same-sex peers before adolescence, Sullivan believed, individuals form a basic pattern of achieving intimacy as a part of their psychological makeup. He called this period the *chum stage*. In a sense, in preadolescence, individuals develop psychologically by sharing thoughts and feelings with a person similar to themselves—much in the way that Elkind thought comparison of oneself with someone else helped overcome adolescent egocentrism.

But with the advent of puberty the need for intimacy is complicated by a set of sexual needs, or lust. The task of adolescence is to integrate the two needs—intimacy and lust—in order to experience the satisfaction of sexuality within a healthy, intimate interpersonal relationship. In Sullivan's view, if intimacy in the chum stage is not experienced before the enormous pressure of lust appears in adolescence, integration will be a very difficult psychological task.

Friendship with peers is a major arena for psychological growth that makes mature heterosexual relationships possible. The capacity for intimacy develops in such relationships. Even with the cushioning provided by the peer group, however, the achievement of intimacy and lust together in adolescence presents enormous threats to personal security, in Sullivan's view. Among other things, adolescence involves transferring intimacy needs from same-sex to opposite-sex peers so that intimacy and lust needs may be met within the same relationships.

In short, in Sullivan's view adolescents who have not successfully met intimacy needs in childhood are unlikely to be successful in coping with lust needs in adolescence and adulthood. Since childhood intimacy is the basis for later successful sexual relationships, if childhood intimacy is not achieved, mature heterosexuality will not be achieved, either.

ADOLESCENT SEXUAL BEHAVIOR

As we have seen, both biological factors and social scripting contribute to the social pressures and urges for greater involvement in sexual activity that adolescents feel. Exactly what are the patterns of sexual involvement for today's adolescents? And do those patterns constitute what is widely called a "sexual revolution," in which today's adolescents show far different and presumably more liberal patterns of behavior than adolescents did in earlier generations? In this section we will present current information about these issues.

The Developmental Pattern: Increasing Age, Increasing Activity

Sexual intercourse is by no means the only aspect of sexuality that is significant for adolescents or for a consideration of developing adolescent sexuality. But it is certainly the aspect that has the most direct implications, for the simple reason that coitus can—and often does—lead to premarital pregnancy. Despite popular impressions, however, there is little evidence that the incidence of coitus in early adolescence *before* age 15 or ninth grade has increased in recent years. The most reliable study of the past decade indicates that about one in ten adolescents in this age group has experienced sexual intercourse, although that figure may be substantially higher in certain disadvantaged groups of adolescents. However, studies of 15-year-olds show that by this age sexual activity is increasing dramatically. For example, recent studies have found that as many as 38% of the males and 24% of the females in the 15-year-old age group have already experienced coitus [20]. It would not be surprising to find that those percentages have increased over the decade of the 1970s.

By late adolescence, involvement in sexual activities increases substantially. As many as half of the twelfth grade boys and girls in many American cities have reportedly experienced sexual intercourse [21]. And among college students a clear majority of both males and females have been found to have engaged in sexual intercourse by their fourth year in school [22]. Estimates do vary, though. One study found that over 80% of both males and females were sexually active. Other studies indicate that while more than half of the college males had engaged in sexual intercourse, substantially fewer females had done so [23]. Undoubtedly, the results of such studies depend on the colleges and universities sampled, since institutions of higher education vary greatly in the particular types of students they attract and the particular codes of behavior enforced on campuses.

Little is known about noncollege youth in late adolescence, since virtually all of the information available to us comes from studies with college and university students.

Social Norms and Standards: A Revolution?

A general circumstance that is relevant to adolescents' involvement in sexual behavior at earlier ages is a historical change in the conditions under which premarital sexual behavior is approved of by most young persons [24]. In recent decades females in particular have increasingly endorsed premarital sexual activity when the two partners feel affection and commitment toward each other, even if that commitment does not include marriage. Males today are also more likely to state an affectionate relationship as a condition for engaging in premarital sex than they were some years ago. However, it still appears that there is a double standard—at least in the sense that males feel less need to be romantically involved with their sexual partners than females do. Consistent with this result are findings that although males and females report similar degrees of sexual activity in the 1970s, boys continue to report more different partners than girls do [25].

Nevertheless, it has been suggested that we are moving toward a single standard for the two sexes in which affection is the determining criterion for whether sexual relations are approved or disapproved. This standard has been labeled "permissiveness with affection" [26]. Whether it has actually been accepted by today's society as a standard for approval of premarital sexual activity will be shown by whether similar judgments are made in the future about sexual activity for males and females—the basis for the double standard that has prevailed throughout most of history.

If it is indeed reasonable to apply the term *sexual revolution* to adolescents' sexual behavior in recent decades, it is appropriate on two counts: First, there has been an increase in premarital sexual activity for females. Thus today in our country, by age 16 females are as likely to have had premarital sex as males are. In previous generations males were far more likely to have engaged in premarital sex than females were. Second, a sexual revolution might be inferred from the change from the double standard to the single standard that many see emerging. In both cases, however, it is far from clear that *revolution* is the right term to apply to the changes that have taken place in the past fifty years. At least one author has suggested that *evolution* is a more appropriate term [27].

Contraception and Pregnancy

One factor is quite apparent in the changed pattern of sexual activity over the past fifty years: Birth control devices are more readily available and more frequently used today than they previously were. However, that fact by no means indicates that a sizable proportion of sexually active adolescents are protecting themselves against pregnancy. For example, one study found that 77% of both black and white adolescents had never used contraceptives or only sometimes used them [28]. Among black females only 50% began to use birth control devices at the age at which they became sexually active; among whites only 64% used contraception from the beginning of sexual activity.

It is difficult to explain the reluctant and infrequent use of contraceptive devices by sexually active adolescents. A number of possibilities have been suggested, of which misinformation is the most frequent. For instance, recent studies indicate that 42% of the white females and only 18% of the black females, aged 15–19 years, have a generally correct understanding of when the danger of pregnancy is greatest [29]. The most common misunderstanding for both blacks and whites is that the risk of pregnancy is uniform throughout the entire month.

Some writers, such as Baizerman, suggest that adolescents often lack the cognitive maturity to understand the implications of failing to practice contraception [30]. In this view something like Elkind's personal fable, in which the adolescent sees herself exempt from the risk of getting pregnant, figures prominently. But at this time there are no reliable data on the interpretations adolescents make of the risks involved in unprotected intercourse. Other reasons that have been suggested include a desire on the part of adolescent girls to get pregnant for economic or emotional reasons and the conviction on the part of adolescent males that their partners should accept responsibility for protection against pregnancy. Until we better understand the motivations involved in what often appears to be outright resistance to the practice of contraception, it will be difficult to get a clear picture of the personal and social circumstances that lead to adolescent pregnancy.

Not surprisingly—given the generally higher rate of premarital intercourse, the earlier age at which active sex lives are beginning, the lack of information about the biological aspects of sex and pregnancy, and the low rate of use of contraceptives—the rate of teenage pregnancy has increased dramatically over the past decade. This increase has been particularly true among black females. One-fifth of all never-married black females between the ages of 15 and 19 have experienced pregnancy, a figure almost ten times the proportion of whites in the same age group who have ever been pregnant [31]. Recent available figures indicate the following:

> About 10% of U.S. adolescents get pregnant and 6% give birth each year. One-third of all adolescent births are out of wedlock and another one-third of adolescent births following marriages are conceived before marriage; thus, only one-third of the first births to adolescents are conceived after marriage has taken place [32].

In recent years younger adolescents have delivered more, not fewer, babies. The Guttmacher Institute, a major center for the study of population characteristics, has reported that out-of-wedlock births increased by 25% among younger adolescents and by 33% among 18–19-year-olds in the decade of the 1970s [33]. According to a recent review, United States adolescent child-bearing rates are among the world's highest, higher than those of many developing countries [34]. The result is that in 1973 one in eight babies born in the United States was born to unmarried adolescent parents; by 1980 the estimate was one in six [35].

The potential results of unmarried parenthood in adolescence are serious, both for the unmarried teenage mother—since it is females who are most often faced with the responsibilities of out-of-wedlock pregnancy—and for the child of that mother. Death rates for babies born to mothers under age 15 are greater than death rates for those born to 15–19-year-olds and more than twice the rates for babies born to mothers aged 20–34. Even when babies survive, children born to mothers under age 20 show a higher rate of mental retardation, birth defects, epilepsy, and birth injuries. Young mothers themselves are more likely than older women to have difficult pregnancies and deliveries, with higher rates of toxemia and related complications, anemia, irregular size or position of infant to the pelvic structure of the mother, and prolonged labor [36].

The psychological consequences of unmarried teenage parenthood are severe as well. The number of teenage mothers who attempt suicide is seven times greater than the number of teenage girls without children who attempt suicide. Furthermore, less than half of the females who become mothers between the ages of 13 and 15 complete their high school education. One study indicated that 80% drop out [37]. The special topic on unplanned pregnancies deals with further psychological consequences of teenage parenthood.

In short, adolescent pregnancy, perhaps resulting from distortions or inadequacies in the social scripting provided to adolescents as they become physiologically mature, has important developmental implications for the adolescent and for the offspring of teenage pregnancies. The question remains: How can society more effectively and adequately convey social scripts that lead to responsible expression of normal sexuality in American youth?

SPECIAL TOPIC
Unplanned Pregnancies: Uncalculated Risks?

The large number of unplanned pregnancies among teenagers in the United States is a social problem of great concern. It may be tempting to dismiss teenage pregnancies as a function of moral decline or just dumb luck or both. But in the case of individual teenagers the problem of unplanned pregnancy may be at least partly related to the young person's sense of control over her own life and capability for making rational decisions about sexual activity.

This possibility has recently been studied by psychologist Barbara Steinlauf [1]. Steinlauf worked with a group of pregnant, unmarried women between the ages of 15 and 25. These women either had contacted an abortion clinic, seeking a first-trimester abortion, or were attending a clinic for a checkup. Of the sample, 52% were white, and 47% were black. Steinlauf questioned the women about the number of times they had been pregnant. Next, she asked them to participate in several measures of cognitive ability (see Chapter 4). In addition, she gave each of them measures of *locus of control*. Recall from our discussion in Chapter 7 that locus of control refers to one's sense of whether one has control over the things that happen to one. Internal locus of control refers to the sense of personal control; external locus of control, or chance control, refers to a feeling that others or chance determines outcomes. Naturally, a young woman with external locus of control has little faith in her own ability to determine the effects of her actions, including, perhaps, the results of sexual intercourse.

Steinlauf reasoned that young women who had frequently become pregnant would be lower in internal locus of control and lower in the cognitive

Diana Baumrind, a specialist on child development and family relations, suggests that it is time for our country to face this issue directly [38]. While the birth rate among teenagers has declined over the past decade, the decline for teenagers is smaller than the decline for older women. Thus teenage women are still producing a relatively large number of children each year, yet fewer are marrying. Further, as the number of illegitimate children increases, the increase is not uniform across social and economic class. In fact, Baumrind points out that there is a decrease in the number of children born of unmarried mothers among those with more education and with greater affluence. She argues that this pattern will eventually result in "a new caste system" in which the children of adolescent mothers will be trapped in poverty and social disadvantage. Her recommendation is for "a

skills required for problem solving. In particular, she was interested in abilities for reasoning from means to ends, or the recognition that certain kinds of actions lead to certain kinds of consequences. She also suspected that individuals who had a history of multiple pregnancies would be high on the scale of chance control.

Her predictions were strongly supported among the young unmarried women she studied. For example, the more pregnancies a young woman reported having had, the lower she was likely to be on internal locus of control. These same young women were likely to be high on chance control. Furthermore, young women who had frequently been pregnant were especially likely to have poor skills for reasoning from means to ends. In short, both a sense of control and cognitive problem-solving skills were related to the likelihood that young women would take the risk of not using contraceptives during sexual intercourse.

Most likely, the complex problem of teenage pregnancies goes far beyond notions of locus of control and cognitive problem solving, of course. Social class and economic variables have proven to be important factors, for instance. However, recent increases in the incidence of teenage pregnancy cut across social and economic levels. And among the characteristics of individuals that affect the incidence of pregnancy may very well be the capacities for understanding the complexities of sexual relationships, sexual activity, and the long-range implications of children having children.

REFERENCE

1. B. Steinlauf, Problem-solving skills, locus of control, and the contraceptive effectiveness of young women, *Child Development* 50(1979):268–271.

less permissive type of sex eduction in our schools and an increase in the social sanctions for irresponsible parenthood" [39].

In the remaining sections of the chapter we will discuss a developmental approach to sex education that draws on the social psychological view of adolescent sexuality that we have just presented.

THE NEED FOR EFFECTIVE EDUCATIONAL PROGRAMS

The problem of adolescent sexuality can be viewed from a developmental perspective. As we have noted, the problem is complex. Sexuality begins in biology and long before the onset of actual puberty, but it is obvious that cultural scripting plays an enormously important role in determining how sexuality is expressed. In this country we have not so far really addressed the problem of sex education. As we noted earlier in the chapter, these issues generate so much conflict that parents and schools either close their eyes and turn their backs or provide brief and totally inadequate information. Adults in all probability fear that sex information may encourage sexual activity. Perhaps they feel that by not discussing the issues and making it clear that sexual activity is wrong—by encouraging ignorance—the problem will simply go away.

However, as the statistics point out, ignorance is neither blissful nor a barrier to sexual activity by adolescents. Nor is it a reality. No matter how we as adults may feel about it, sexuality is present in every way in this society, both in healthy and unhealthy forms. Popular songs, movies, television, books, billboards—in short, almost every conceivable aspect of media constantly presents sex in almost every possible form. Complicating this universal presence of sexuality is a change in the way the presentation of sex is viewed. Legal definitions of pornography have changed drastically in the past fifty years. The movies and books that were banned as recently as the 1940s and early 1950s seem mild compared with the common fare today. The *Scarlet Letter,* Nathaniel Hawthorne's novel of nineteenth-century puritan New England, had more in common with attitudes toward sex as recently as 1950 (a 200-year span) than with current attitudes. Thus adults who work with teenagers cannot hope to maintain the current attitude of silence or assume that somehow the problem will go away.

SEX EDUCATION AND DEVELOPMENT

Since a major theme of this book is the developmental perspective, it is appropriate to examine the understanding of sexual processes from that view. How adolescents come to understand the nature of sexuality and how they make decisions or judgments about these issues fit into a developmental sequence. Different levels of psychological maturity determine how individuals understand their sexuality and interaction.

The developmental view is unusually complex in the domain of sexuality. This strand of development reaches across a series of areas simultaneously. That is, how a person thinks and acts on sexual issues will depend on the level of cognitive maturity (Piaget's theory, Chapter 4), the level of identity formation (Erikson's theory, Chapter 2), the level of interpersonal and self-development (Selman's and Loevinger's theories, Chapter 5), and the level of general value judgment (Kohlberg's theory, Chapter 6). These multiple perspectives mean we need to approach the questions of sexuality and sex education according to the levels of maturity of the teenagers rather than, as is now the case, according to age. As we have noted, at present the approaches are either a no-information method or a facts-and-rational-explanations, relativistic method. In both instances the common methods simply ignore the possibility that adolescents may be at dramatically different levels of maturity and therefore reach completely different interpretations. And from our view it is the interpretation and judgments the teenager reaches that may make major differences in actual behavior choices.

To illustrate our point, we refer to a recent TV special, which presented a series of interviews with unwed mothers. The females had all received a strict religious upbringing. They indicated that the church and their parents made it very clear that sexual activity was wrong. But in each instance the women choose *not* to use contraceptives when they decided to participate in sexual activity and go against the dictates of adult authorities. Their reasoning level is most important in their somewhat contradictory decision. "I really wanted to become active, but if I used contraception then it would look like I planned it. This way I did get pregnant, but I could say it was just an accident." The logic is contorted: "I didn't want it to look like I deliberately planned to go against my parents." The results were an unwanted child and a psychologically immature single mother. From this example, then, we see that it is most important to understand the individual's level or stage of development in order to present information that will improve the individual's ability to make wise choices. The choices in such cases are extremely complicated: The individual's welfare, the possibility of a child, the parents, society at large, and the prospective partner—all are factors in making a choice. In addition, both the short- and the long-term consequences—today's pleasure versus tomorrow's responsibility—must be considered.

From Erik Erikson's work we would say that an individual could not make a complex and fully informed decision such as outlined above until late adolescence. Sexual activity with another person is, by definition, an extremely close and deep emotional experience. Such genuine intimacy is possible only *after* the process of identity formation is completed. In other words, the person's sense of individuality and self-direction, the final step in identity formation, precedes true sexual intimacy.

It is important to remember that Erikson is defining intimacy in a special way—the act of sharing major emotional experiences and commitments, a process of equality and mutuality. Neither partner exploits the other for his or her own sake. Rather, each considers the issue for the benefit of all concerned. In Selman's view intimacy would include the ability to place oneself in the other's shoes. That is, the person's level of emotional maturity must allow for the simultaneous processing of deep feelings of the self and the other.

*Group discussion of sex-
uality issues may be
helpful for mature adolescents*
Photograph from Paul S.
Conklin

With these ideas in mind, in the sections that follow we examine
primary developmental periods in the emergence of sexuality, beginning
with the mature ideal.

**Late Adolescence:
Formal,
Integrated Level**

We refer to a mature level of development as the *formal, integrated level*—a
level through which a person can process information and the emotional
components of sexuality autonomously. At this level the individual reasons abstractly, can process emotions accurately in self and others, and has
a firm sense of self-identity and individuality. Social role-taking ability is
complex, and mutuality is evident, with both long- and short-term consequences considered. This level is generally achieved in late adolescence or
early adulthood.

A person who functions at this level can be presented with a variety of
information concerning sexuality since the person is basically at mature
level in all of the domains noted. The person is clearly capable of reaching
thoughtful and considerate decisions to engage or not in sexual activity. A
youth worker or teacher providing information on these issues with such a
person can function nondirectively—more or less as a sounding board—
and make open-ended suggestions. Appropriate readings might be recommended in any area where the person seems to lack information. In fact, an
evenhanded approach is highly recommended since overt attempts to influence would be resisted. It is perhaps an overgeneralization, but in our

view most of the publicly available material on sexuality, such as found in regular bookstores, is genuinely helpful for psychologically mature persons. Issues of personal responsibility and commitment are clearly understood by such individuals. The person at this stage is capable of what Erikson calls, for want of a better phrase, "real intimacy" with the opposite sex, a deep friendship of love and inspiration.

Middle Adolescence: Early Formal, Identity-Forming Level

At the next lower level, involving *early formal thought* processes, adolescents have begun to reason abstractly. However, some egocentric thinking persists, and role taking and empathy are not necessarily consistent. Persons at this level, generally adolescents in high school, show major inconsistencies in thought and action. The individuals may be functioning quite maturely in some areas, such as academic work, sports clubs, and relations with adults. Yet in heterosexual areas the persons may not really understand the emotions of a potential partner. Erikson notes that during this identity-forming period individuals may shy away from intimacy, recognizing their own lack of readiness.

Another characteristic of this stage is the endless conversation, usually over the telephone, with lengthy discussions about one's own feelings, the changing nature of emotions, one's plans, aspirations, hopes, and goals. Such talk is not just wasting time, as it may seem to adults. These conversations, along with becoming aware of the meaning of love songs and poems, watching soaps, and reading love stories, are tryouts, preparations for the next stage of integration. Adolescents in the early formal stage need these seemingly circular discussions and reflections in order to work through, at both the intellectual and the emotional level, the meaning of interpersonal attraction.

During this period adult society—and adults specifically—can make a major mistake if any attempt is made to push the person into forming a relationship. In fact, conservatism is probably appropriate at this point. Teenagers of both sexes need implicit and explicit reassurance that it is not necessary to participate in sexual intercourse in order to achieve an adult identity. In fact, it is just the reverse: Intimacy *follows* identity formation. Erikson notes, "Unfortunately many young people marry under such circumstances, hoping to find themselves in finding one another . . . the condition of a true twoness is that one must first become oneself" [40].

Adults, then, need to help teenagers realize that neither sexual conquest nor submission is a necessary goal. In fact, early intimacy can have a growth-retarding effect. Lacking a sure sense of identity, the person has little ability to integrate the intense emotions that may accompany sexual activity. The experience may be a developmental mismatch and may generate dissonance.

The evidence for this view is drawn largely from clinical observations

*Sexual intimacy before
partners have reached a
mature psychological
level may be damaging to
personal development*
Photograph from Bryan E.
Robinson

by psychologists and psychiatrists particularly sensitive to adolescence,
such as Erikson. Some empirical research also supports this view, though.
As noted in a previous section, studies of lower-class males who were
sexually active in early adolescence reported that these males experienced
a marked decrease in sexual activity after marriage. (As another example,
Jackie Cooper, a child movie star of the 1930s, reported the terrific difficulties he had in achieving personal maturity, partly because adults provided
him daily with starlets, with whom he could have intercourse between
movie scenes, when he was 13!) Thus premature adulthood can lead to
interpersonal isolation.

In sex education at this stage we cannot assume that a simple, relativistic presentation of sex information will promote the development of greater
insight and maturity. This point poses something of a dilemma for the
teacher, counselor, or youth worker. Being objective or nondirective and
supplying the teenager with a carefully balanced list of pros and cons about
sexual activity unfortunately misses the point. It is far too easy for a teenager to interpret a relativistic presentation as permission or support for
sexual activity. The nonprescriptive method is usually understood to mean
that "sex is all right, as long as I'm careful." This is not the intention of the
message, but it is often the interpretation.

It is more helpful at this stage to present teenagers with counterpropa-
ganda. In other words, adults can help teenagers reason through the pro-

totypical come-ons they will experience, the scenarios an aggressive male or female may use to try to convince a reluctant partner that it is time for sex. Such role playing can be done most effectively in small groups, probably with the sexes separated at first. Discussions can focus on the persuasive lines most often used and then on a careful analysis of the possible consequences. These discussions can be followed by practice in polite but firm refusals. Since personal reputation is a major part of middle adolescence, it is important to explore these effects. Adults may wish to emphasize consequences such as an unwanted baby, but that result will seem more remote to a teenager than the consequence of a damaged reputation.

Thus it is important to discuss the *issue* (How far shall I go?) that all teenagers face. However, it is equally important to do more than just act as a sounding board. A group discussion leader needs to go beyond the adolescents' present level of reasoning in the manner outlined in Chapter 6. This exercise will help teenagers develop greater ability to resist peer group pressure. The research by Kohlberg and by Gilligan (see Chapter 6) indicates quite clearly that high school pupils tend to reason about sexual activity at a lower level than they reason about other, less personal issues. High school students are more apt to process such questions only from their own perspective. The role of the educator, then, is to promote their growth by helping them realize that their own needs are not the only ones to be considered.

Early Adolescence: Transitional Level

We now shift to the junior high, or *transition level*, which typically occurs at the onset of adolescence. At this stage a major discontinuity in reasoning becomes apparent. Excessive egocentrism is evident, and concrete facts become easily confused with myths and magical thoughts. At this period adolescents are in the initial stages of identity formation, which may lead them to extremes in self-definition. Furthermore, role-taking ability is extremely low, but peer pressure is strong.

The problems of sex education are most difficult at this level, because the range of developmental differences is greater during this period than during any other in the growth cycle. As we noted in Chapter 3, the developmental differences between the sexes are the greatest at this stage. Biology and physiology essentially create two groups, a bimodal distribution of maturity, with females on the average reaching their growth spurt at approximately 12 years and boys reaching theirs two years later at 14 years. Thus girls enter junior high (grade 7) at the peak of their growth spurt, while boys enter at a far less mature level.

As Fig. 9.1 shows, the range of differences by sex in overall physical maturity is substantial. Girls at $12\frac{3}{4}$ years can range from adultlike to childlike. Boys show the same range but at $14\frac{3}{4}$ years, two years later. Most boys at $12\frac{3}{4}$ years would look like the late-maturing $14\frac{3}{4}$, while most girls at that

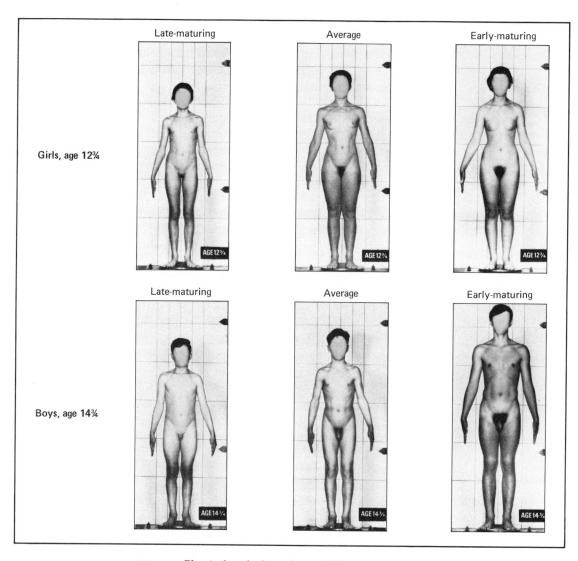

FIG. 9.1 Physical and physiological differences for junior high boys and girls

Adapted from J. M. Tanner, Growth and endocrinology of the adolescent, in *Endocrine and genetic diseases of childhood,* 2nd ed., ed. J. Gardner (Philadelphia: Saunders, 1975), p. 238. Reprinted by permission.

age would look like the average picture [41]. By grade 9, though, the boys begin to catch up across the board—in weight gain, height, both primary and secondary sexual characteristics, reproductive organs, facial hair, voice change. Nevertheless, the sequence of change is nearly complete for girls well before it is complete for boys.

These diversities in developmental timing create general difficulties in working with early adolescents, but in the domain of sexuality the difficulties are monumental for both sexes. The difficulties could be minimized if schools were organized according to developmental principles, with separate general education (not just sex education) according to gender during this period. However, there is little chance that school systems will adopt separate schools by gender for grades 6 to 8. So it is important that youth workers, teachers, and counselors working with mixed sex groups during early adolescence understand the developmental problems at this stage. One is attempting to deal with two populations, each at a point of major difference on levels of maturity. Girls, especially those who have matured early (before the average age of $12\frac{3}{4}$), feel out of place and may experience major psychological upset. And nearly all boys at $12\frac{3}{4}$ can plainly see how similar they still are to fourth and fifth grade boys and how different they are from their female age cohorts.

The educational problem at this stage, then, is how to minimize the difficulties created by such major discontinuities between the sexes. When the human body changes so much in such a short period, it is inevitable that body image will be the major preoccupation of this stage. So sex education at this level is really helping both sexes, but separately, understand the changes they experience and the meaning and implications of such changes. But do not expect rationality to reign. On the contrary, the wilder the misinformation, the greater is the chance of it fitting into the magical thoughts and secret myths of early adolescents. All the mental processing Elkind outlines (see Chapter 5) is operating fully on questions of sexual development. Hence facts are easily misunderstood. And almost any mention of sex can bring classroom confusion. Thus discussing problems of relating to the opposite sex at this point is clearly ahead of the question. But both boys and girls need the reassurance that the changes they experience are a major part of their individuality, the beginning of an adult self. Each group needs time and space to reflect on these changes before they can really consider interpersonal questions. The inner person needs integration first.

There are many common fears that each sex experiences during the transition stage. Those worries are really the agenda for sex education.

For girls, sex education programs can begin as early as grade 6, since their changes start that early. The programs need to focus on issues of menstruation, uneven development of breasts, fertility cycle, pubic hair appearance, height and weight, and other aspects of bodily changes. For example, many seventh grade girls are horrified by the growth spurt effect on their shoe size; it seems to them that their feet are like those of an elephant. They need to understand that the general growth cycle is from head to foot during early childhood and the reverse during adolescence. So their feet reach maximum length before other body parts reach adult size.

SPECIAL TOPIC
Homosexuality

Although we usually think of sexuality in terms of relationships between people of the opposite sex, sexual feelings and behaviors can and do exist between persons of the same gender. Unfortunately, we know relatively little about homosexual preferences, including how such preferences come to be a part of an individual's personality. Nevertheless, as a manifestation of sexuality, homosexuality is clearly a concern to many adolescents, both males and females.

Homosexuality is relatively rare among adolescents. Surveys indicate that fewer than 5% of college students consider themselves to be exclusively interested in members of the same sex. However, perhaps 20% or more of young people have one or more homosexual experience sometime during their late childhood or early adolescent years [1]. Thus homosexual *contacts* seem to be somewhat more common than true homosexual *preferences*, in which only persons of the same sex are seen as possible affectional partners. Indeed, it has been suggested that homosexual contacts among both adolescent boys and girls are quite common but have no lasting implications for normal sexual development. In fact, we might think of typical same-sex contacts in early adolescence as mutual masturbation rather than as the acting out of a true homosexual preference. In other words, boys, or girls, as couples are involved in exploring sexual feelings rather than in expressing their attraction to one another. A difficulty often arises, however: Adolescents themselves assume that because they found such experiences pleasurable, they may be homosexuals. As in many other instances, how we label or explain our experiences is often more important than the experiences themselves.

Explaining the causes of development of homosexuality in adulthood remains very difficult. But two possibilities have been given the most attention in past research.

Also, girls at this age need help in learning to cope with their advanced maturity (the teasing, the sexual comments of older males and females).

The question of individual differences must also be addressed. On the average, most girls mature much earlier than boys, but there are still some important ranges. Menarche, for example, can vary between 10 and 17 years. Breast development (unfortunately referred to as "buds") can start as early as 8 and as late as 13 years. And genital maturity usually, but not always, precedes the appearance of pubic hair. Finally, the beginning of

One possibility that has been explored is a biological explanation. In such research cellular or hormonal differences between homosexuals and heterosexuals have been sought. To date, no real hormonal or other biological differences between homosexuals and heterosexuals have been identified, however. In several studies hormonal conditions, such as adrenogenital syndrome in girls, have been found to affect sex-typed interests such as career versus marriage and attraction to children, but the hormonal condition does not seem to be related to affectional preference.

The second possible explanation involves social factors, and various types have been examined in an effort to explain the differences between homosexuals and heterosexuals. Most attention has been given to the nature of parent-child relationships. In a number of such studies the results have indicated that homosexual males felt less attached to their fathers and more closely identified with their mothers than heterosexual males did [2]. However, causality is very difficult to establish. Homosexual males also state that they felt less comfortable in stereotyped masculine activities as children. It may be that their poorer relations with their father were partly related to the lesser extent to which they showed typical masculine sex typing, rather than the other way around. Indeed, in the most recent published study of homosexuality, no characteristic pattern of parent-child relationships or of other childhood experiences could be found to distinguish homosexuals from heterosexuals [3]. The authors of this study concluded that *if* there is a single factor that explains the differences between these two groups, it is likely to be subtle and something that occurs very early in development or even prenatally.

By contrast, a social-scripting view of sexuality, such as we have outlined in this chapter, suggests that a primarily homosexual orientation is likely *not* to be the result of a single factor or experience. Rather, sexual preference for one's own gender is likely to come from a biological disposition plus experiences that result in feelings of inadequacy or inappropriateness for heterosexual relationships or for the male or female role. Perhaps such experiences are

(Continued)

menstruation does not indicate the stabilization of the fertility cycle. In fact, there is such wide variation in the length of the cycle and the actual release of the unfertilized egg that sex educators have adapted a motto for early adolescence: "There is no safe period for intercourse at this age."

For boys, sex education can start later than it does for girls since both sexes do not face similar issues concurrently. The programs should focus on the time differences between boys and girls, since boys need to understand that they will catch up to girls. Boys also need to understand about

SPECIAL TOPIC (Continued)

often accompanied by positive homosexual or homosocial experiences, such as close identifications with others of the same sex in a social group. That is, homosexual preference is probably only one manifestation of a pattern of social and personal functioning that extends far beyond sexuality per se.

Obviously, we need more information than we now have about the nature and sources of homosexual orientation. But we do have enough information to date to suggest that a better appreciation for the different influences on sexuality and the range of ways in which sexual feelings can be aroused could help adolescents and adults alike sort out the meaning of experiences that are sometimes very troubling.

Most important, from the standpoint of the youth worker, is the understanding that same-sex preference is not an index of psychopathology. After analyzing the debates and carefully reexamining all the research evidence, both the American Psychological Association and the American Psychiatric Association revised their prior official policies. They now conclude that homosexuality, defined as a major affectional preference for the same sex, is not an indicator of psychological disturbance [4]. The combination of biological predispositions interacting with cultural scripting seems to be the likely set of conditions that produce a predominant heterosexual or homosexual orientation. Sensitive understanding of these issues is particularly important for the youth worker who is counseling homosexually oriented adolescents.

REFERENCES

1. J. Bieber, *Homosexuality: A psychoanalytic study of male homosexuals* (New York: Vintage Books, 1962), pp. 20–33; R. Sorenson, *Adolescent sexuality in contemporary America* (New York: World, 1973), pp. 85–96.

2. N. Thompson and B. McCandless, The homosexual orientation and its antecedents, in *Child personality and psychopathology: Current topics,* vol. 3, ed. A. Davids (New York: Wiley, 1976), pp. 57–82.

3. A. Bell, M. Weinberg, and S. Hammersmith, *Sexual preference: Its development in men and women* (Bloomington: Indiana University Press, 1981).

4. J. Marmor, ed., *Homosexual behavior: A modern reappraisal* (New York: Basic Books, 1980).

the growth of primary and secondary characteristics—genitals, pubic hair, nocturnal emissions, voice changes, height and weight changes, and the apparent lack of smooth bodily changes. For example, at one point facial and chest hair may start to appear—a blessing, just in time. Then closer examination may indicate that the boy's breast has also increased. During the glandular shifts, including a major increase in sweat glands, it is not unusual for a boy's nipple (subareola) to enlarge (estimates vary between 20 and 30% of boys) or, perhaps, to become very sensitive. In either case, these characteristics disappear by late adolescence. During onset, however, it is most important to convey to boys the temporary nature of such changes.

Also, as with girls, the range of individual differences must be addressed, especially for late-maturing boys. The height spurt in boys, for instance, ranges between 10 and 17 years. Genital growth varies from 9.5 to 17 years, and pubic hair may appear anywhere from 12 to 16 years. General muscular maturation has a similar broad range. Thus it is quite possible for a male as late as the junior year in high school to still *not* have experienced adolescent physiological development. The sex educator at this point needs to provide a combination of facts and psychological support to such pupils. The goal is the understanding of self as an important prior step to considerations of general heterosexual activity.

SUMMARY

In this chapter we reviewed basic issues in the emergence of sexuality during adolescence. Although physiological maturing is obviously fundamental to adolescent sexuality, the main issues of sexual development in the second decade of life are not biological ones but social ones. For example, most of the fundamental biological differences between male and female sexuality are determined either before or immediately after birth. The changes of puberty mainly affect the frequency and intensity of sexual arousal in both sexes. Even the capacity for sexual arousal, however, results from a complex exposure to social roles, behaviors, mores, and values. The form of sexual expressiveness is influenced more by these factors than by strong biological impulses—to which adolescent sexuality is often reduced in popular thinking.

The role of social influence in sexual development has been attributed to social scripting. This term refers to learned expectations and the social significance associated with certain patterns of sexual activity. Both male-female differences in sexuality and subcultural variations in expressions of sexuality can be attributed to different social scripts. In adolescence the appearance of social scripts seems to involve the integration, or assembly, of aspects of personal and social identity needed for mature heterosexual relationships.

Because the development of sexuality involves basic learning and reinforcement processes, we reviewed the common sources of information about sex available to teenagers: parents, media, and peers. For most teenagers, parents are relatively minor sources of information about sex, often because the parents themselves are uncertain or ashamed. Peers are a much more widely used source of information, although the information they provide is often incorrect. Teenagers probably rely on their friends for information, however, because the peer group is an important context for development of heterosexual relations generally. Sociologist Dexter Dunphy has described a common process in which high-status members of male and female peer groups form couples and thus serve as role models for lower-status members of the groups. This role model function gives peers a special credibility as a source of information about sexual behavior.

Integration of personal, social, and biological issues as a part of the development of sexuality was described in detail by Harry Stack Sullivan. Sullivan envisioned adolescent changes as involving the integration of intimacy needs—the capacity to be close to others—and lust, or sexual desire. In Sullivan's view healthy development requires a sound basis for intimate relationships before the unusual sexual pressures associated with puberty begin. Consequently, preadolescents' peer relationships are essential to the development of psychological capabilities for intimacy that permit mature sexuality in adolescence and adulthood.

Despite popular impressions adolescent sexual behavior in the 1970s and 1980s does not appear to indicate that a sexual revolution has taken place. Two major historical changes have occurred, however: (1) A larger proportion of both males and females express approval of premarital intercourse when it occurs in the context of an affectionate relationship; and (2) a larger proportion of females are engaging in sexual activity during the midteen years than had done so in past decades. However, the changes are occurring gradually enough that to describe them, the term *evolution* seems more appropriate than the term *revolution*.

A major difficulty associated with any increase in sexual activity among teenagers is the incidence of pregnancy. This incidence has increased significantly in the 1970s and 1980s, especially among black adolescents. Two associated factors appear to be reluctance to use contraceptive devices and widespread misunderstanding of the basic facts of conception. These results have led many observers to suggest that more detailed programs in sex education are needed as a part of public school programs.

In the final section of the chapter we outlined a program of sex education differentiated according to developmental maturity. Three developmental periods were described. During late adolescence and early adulthood, programs for personal and sexual development should focus on genuine intimacy, commitments, and mutuality. In middle adolescence, the formal thought, identity-forming period, sex education should focus on discussions, role playing, scenarios, and similar (not real) experiences to help teenagers formulate their own identities and interpersonal relations. In early adolescence, a transitional period, sex education should focus on intrapersonal issues, including the understanding and implications of the physical and physiological changes of puberty. This latter group (roughly grades 6–8) should be divided by gender for sex education programs. The range of differences between the sexes at this period is simply too great for mixed-group discussions of sexuality to be effective.

In the next chapter we turn to a consideration of some of the developmental problems that are often encountered in adolescence.

KEY POINTS AND NAMES

Biological bases of sexuality

Social bases of sexuality

Clellan Ford and Frank Beach: cultural variations

William Simon and John Gagnon

Social scripting
  Sex differences
  Subcultural differences

Information sources for sex education
  Parents
  Peers: Dexter Dunphy

Harry Stack Sullivan: the chum stage

Developmental behavior patterns: age and activity

Sexual revolution or evolution

Contraception and pregnancy

Diana Baumrind

Sex education from a developmental view
  Late adolescence: formal, integrated stage
  Middle adolescence: early formal, identity-forming stage
  Early adolescence: transition stage

REFERENCES

1. H. Katchadourian, *The biology of adolescence* (San Francisco: Freeman, 1977), pp. 27–34; J. Money and R. Clopper, Jr., Psychosocial and psychosexual aspects of errors of pubertal onset and development, *Human Biology* 46(1974):173–181.

2. Money and Clopper, pp. 173–181.

3. C. Ford and F. Beach, *Patterns of sexual behavior* (New York: Harper & Row, 1951), pp. 167–198.

4. J. Whiting and I. Child, *Child training and personality: A cross-cultural study* (New Haven: Yale University Press, 1953), p. 256.

5. W. Simon and J. Gagnon, On psychosexual development, in *Handbook of socialization theory and research*, ed. D. Goslin (New York: Rand McNally, 1969), pp. 733–752.

6. E. Kanin, An examination of sexual aggression as a response to sexual frustration, *Journal of Marriage and the Family* 29(1967):428–433.

7. T. Parsons, *Social structure and personality* (New York: Free Press, 1964), p. 59.

8. Simon and Gagnon, p. 746.

9. C. Broderick, Social heterosexual development among urban negroes and whites, *Journal of Marriage and the Family* 27(1965):200–203.

10. Simon and Gagnon, p. 749.

11. K. McCoy, What *Teen* readers are asking about sex . . . and what we're telling them: A study in evolution, *Journal of Child Clinical Psychology* 3(1974):34–36.

12. *Ibid.*, p. 34.

13. *Ibid.*, p. 34.

14. R. Sorenson, *Adolescent sexuality in contemporary America* (New York: World, 1973), p. 47.

15. E. Roberts, D. Kline, and J. Gagnon, *Family life and sexual learning: A study of the role of parents in the sexual learning of children* (Cambridge, Mass.: Population Education, 1978), p. 51.

16. *Ibid.*, p. 49.

17. *Ibid.*, p. 80.

18. D. C. Dunphy, The social structure of urban adolescent peer groups, *Sociometry* 26(1963):230–246.

19. H. S. Sullivan, *The interpersonal theory of psychiatry* (New York: Norton, 1963), pp. 227–310.

20. P. Miller and W. Simon, The development of sexuality in adolescence, in *Handbook of adolescent psychology*, ed. J. Adelson (New York: Wiley, 1980), pp. 397–398.

21. A. Vener and C. Stewart, Adolescent sexual behavior in middle America revisited: 1970–1973, *Journal of Marriage and the Family* 36(1974):728–735.

22. S. L. Jessor and R. Jessor, Transition from virginity to nonvirginity among youth: A social-psychological study over time, *Developmental Psychology* 11(1975):473–484. At least one longitudinal study of adolescent sexual behavior by these authors suggests that involvement in sexual activity goes along with a pattern of relatively heavy influence from peers, involvement in problem social behaviors such as drinking and drug use, and parent and family systems in which relatively liberal social and political values are expressed. At the same time sexually active adolescents, in the Jessors' study, tended to be less involved in religion and to be less achievement-oriented. It is impossible to tell from this study whether there are causal connections between sexual activity and these other aspects of adolescent experience or whether there is merely coincidental association between them. However, Jessor and Jessor did report that of the adolescents who became sexually active over the four-year period of the study, the majority displayed these other characteristics in addition to sexual involvement. By contrast, the group that did not become sexually active did not show the characteristics generally found to be associated with sexual involvement.

23. R. Lewis and W. Burr, Premarital coitus and commitment among college students, *Archives of Sexual Behavior* 4(1975):73–79.

24. Miller and Simon, pp. 401–405.

25. Vener and Stewart, pp. 732–733.

26. I. Reiss, The sexual renaissance: A summary and analysis, *Journal of Social Issues* 22(1966):125.

27. J. Diepold and R. Young, Empirical studies of adolescent sexual behavior: A critical review, *Adolescence* 14(1979):62.

28. J. Kantner and M. Zelnik, Sexuality, contraception, and pregnancy among preadult females in the United States, in *Demographic and social aspects of population growth*, ed. C. Westoff and R. Parke, Jr. (Washington, D.C.: Commission on Population Growth and the American Future, 1972), pp. 335–360.

29. *Ibid.*, p. 351.

30. M. Baizerman, Can the first pregnancy of a young adolescent be prevented? *Journal of Youth and Adolescence* 6(1977):343–351.

31. Kantner and Zelnick, p. 353.

32. *Ibid.*, p. 354.

33. Alan Guttmacher Institute, *Data and a analyses for 1976 revision of DHEW five-year plan for family planning services* (New York: 1976).

34. Allan Guttmacher Institute, *Teenage pregnancy: The problem that hasn't gone away* (New York: 1981).

35. United States Census figures: 1973, 1975, 1980.

36. P. McKenry, L. Walters, and C. Johnson, Adolescent pregnancy: A review of the literature, *Family Coordinator* 28(1979):23–24.

37. *Ibid.*, pp. 24–25; I. Nye, *School-age parenthood*, Extension Bulletin 667 (Pullman: Cooperative Extension Service, Washington State University, 1977), p. 5.

38. D. Baumrind, New directions in socialization research, *American Psychologist* 35(1980):641.

39. D. Baumrind, Clarification concerning birthrate among teenagers, *American Psychologist* 36(1981):529.

40. E. Erikson, *Identity and the life cycle* (New York: International University Press, 1959), p. 95. This material was written originally in the late 1940s, but the insight is still valid today. Social mores, however, have changed, so living together is now an acceptable alternative to marriage. Such a practice will not hasten identity formation, though, since identity always precedes intimacy.

41. J. M. Tanner, *Fetus into man* (Cambridge, Mass.: Harvard University Press, 1978, pp. 60–86.

CHAPTER 10

Juvenile Delinquency

INTRODUCTION

Throughout history juvenile delinquency has been almost synonomous with adolescence. In fact, too often, to the adult on the street any act by an adolescent—except, perhaps, abject obedience—might be regarded as an index of delinquency. Thus we are caught in a complex web when we try to focus on the topic of adolescence and delinquency.

Much emotion is aroused in the adult society at any mention of non-conformist behavior by adolescents. In the 1960s two leading authorities on the topic both requested that the term *delinquency* be discarded. The concept of delinquency had been so overgeneralized and the term had become such a dangerous and pejorative label that Robert MacIver, an authority from New York, and William Kvaraceus, an authority from Massachusetts, both urged that the term be dropped from the literature. They argued that it caused a negative conditioned reflex response. From newspaper head-lines, video news, and sensationalism, in general, the public had learned to associate delinquency with serious criminality. MacIver noted: "In the popular mind, the juvenile delinquent more often connotes a gang killer or acute thief than a child who is truant or disobedient to his parents" [1]. Similarly, Kvaraceus said that the term is a nontechnical label whose mean-ing is so imprecise that it covers everything under the sun [2].

Unfortunately, hopes for the creation of an exact set of designators for adolescent behavior that is aggressive and antisocial have not been realized in the subsequent years. Books, articles, research, academic courses, and the popular media still use—and, perhaps, overuse—the concept of juvenile delinquency so much that a text in adolescence must focus on the issue, as imprecise as the term may be.

In this chapter we will provide a new approach to the definition of delinquency as well as a review of classical and contemporary studies of the causes and consequences of delinquency. We will also distinguish between delinquency as it pertains to boys and as it pertains to girls, and we will examine the question of cultural differences. Then we will review current programs aimed at prevention and treatment. Unfortunately, as we will see, there is an urgent need to create new and more effective treatment methods. While there are some effective methods, as we note, much work is still needed to build programs designed to promote healthy psychological development.

THE DEFINITION PROBLEM

Given the controversy generated by the concept, it is small wonder that adequate definitions of delinquency are hard to come by. One of the major factors in the definition problem concerns the question of social class subjectivity. Behavioral sciences like psychology have difficulty in being completely objective. And no matter how well trained a psychologist may be, some level of nonscientific subjectivity may creep in. Thus as long as one set of humans studies another set of humans, there are limits to objectivity, even in relatively noncontroversial and nonemotional areas.

In the arena of the general public there is even less objectivity than in the behavioral sciences. So to a very great degree, delinquency exists or not depending on the social and economic class of the teenager. Adult authority figures (police, judges, juvenile officers) unconsciously rely on social class bias in deciding who is and who is not labeled a delinquent. For example, a 20-year study conducted in an upper-middle-class community (Garden City) between 1940 and 1960 showed no recorded arrests of juveniles for delinquency. The record was spotless—not a single case [3]. In contrast, a study in a different location (Kansas City) indicated that as much as 16% of the teenage population was considered "adjudicated delinquents"—in other words, were arrested—3128 arrests from a teenage population of 20,000 city youth [4]. The rate in suburban Garden City was 0% for 20 years, and the rate in Kansas City was 16% in one year. Can there possibly be that much difference in the makeup of the teenagers?

Closer inspection of these studies strongly suggests that a social class bias was operating. That is, almost precisely the same behavior could be evaluated differently according to social class background. For instance, in an urban environment car theft would be seen as a criminal act, and in a suburban community it would be seen as an adolescent prank. Working-class and minority teenagers are arrested, and police records made, while

Is delinquency a generic problem or a passing phase?
Photograph from Jean Boughton

engaged in the same activities for which middle- and upper-middle-class children are driven home by the police officer and given a talk by their parents. Thus it has been estimated from a variety of studies that up to 90% of teenagers actually commit acts for which they could be adjudicated—if they were caught *and* if they were arrested [5]. Two big *if*s, as the figures show.

Is there no generic delinquency, then? Sociologist Howard Becker has suggested that labeling teenagers as delinquent is simply an adult cover-up to throw the burden of their own mistakes on the children [6]. In his view there are no delinquent children but, rather, delinquent parents—or police or juvenile officers, or judges. Becker suggests that we should study the motives and values of the adults who label the teenager rather than those of the delinquents themselves. This view leads us to the question of the causes of delinquency and the question of incidence.

INCIDENCE AND DEFINITION

As an attempt to clarify the definition and incidence of delinquency, apart from the inherent social bias in how delinquency is labeled, two researchers, Ruth Cavan and Theodore Ferdinand, have created a continuum that hypothetically defines the activities considered delinquent regardless of whether the activity is reported. Their continuum is shown in Fig. 10.1.

The researchers created the continuum by analyzing the incidence from numerous studies reported over the past decade. Obviously, the overwhelming majority of adolescents fall into the middle range, in catego-

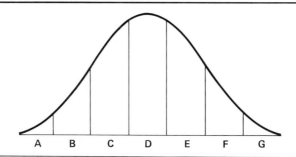

	A Contraculture (delinquent)	B Extreme underconformity	C Minor under- conformity	D Normal conformity	E Minor overcon- formity	F Extreme overconformity	G Contraculture (extreme goodness)
Public attitude	Condemnation; "hard core"	Disapproval	Toleration without approval	Tolerance with approval	A sissy by peers; valued by adults	Extreme over-conformity; a real "goody two shoes"	Extreme goodness; seen as saintly
Public reaction	Rejection; school expulsion; commitment to correctional school	Police warnings; school suspension; referrals to social agencies	Disciplinary action by parents or school	Indifference; acceptance; mild reproofs	Some isolation by peers; positive regard by adults	Major social isolation by peers; adults are somewhat uncomfortable	Total isolation by peers; too good to be true by adults
Child's attitude toward public	Rejects values of D	Wavers between acceptance and rejection of D values	Accepts values of D; feels guilt	Accepts values of D; feels no guilt	Anxious to please	Extremely anxious to please adults; avoids own age group	Avoids all contacts with peers
Child's attitude toward self	Self-concept of delinquent	Confused self-concept; marginal to D and A	Views self as a misbehaving nondelinquent	Conforming nondelinquent	Anxious and somewhat tense	Never really enjoys anything; living means working hard	Pretends to be an adult; a nonadolescent
Examples	Indiscriminate murder	Manslaughter in fight	Negligent homicide	Somewhat carless but no danger to others	Avoids misbehaving Too conscientious Excessive worry over any mistakes	A teacher's pet; assignments always perfect; attendance always perfect; one error is regarded as a catastrophe; upset by an A-grade	Avoids all wordly pleasures May join an isolating religious cult
	Armed robbery; burglary	Larceny of valuables	"Borrowing" to use; pilfering	Minor pilfering			
	Rape; serious sex deviations; promiscuity; prostitution	Promiscuity; minor sex deviations	Extensive normal sex relations	Occasional normal sex relations			
	Drug addiction	Occasional use of drugs	Smoking marijuana only	Smoke tobacco only			

FIG. 10.1 Delinquency: An hypothetical continuum of different behaviors

Adaptation of Figure 2.1, "Hypothetical formulation of a behavior continuum," from *Juvenile delinquency*, fourth edition, by Ruth S. Cavan and Theodore N. Ferdinand. Copyright © 1981 by Harper & Row Publishers, Inc. Reprinted by permission of Harper & Row Publishers, Inc.

ries C, D, and E, identified as minor underconformity to societal expectations, normal conformity, and minor overconformity. These three categories account for two-thirds of the population of juveniles. Under category B, extreme underconformity, they estimate 13%, and under A, 3%. In these two areas the juvenile engages in generally serious antisocial acts that, under almost anyone's definition, would be considered significant deviations from the range of normal behaviors. It is probably in the C and D ranges where social class makes such a big difference in the reported incidence of delinquency.

It is also noteworthy that Cavan and Ferdinand list the other extremes on their continuum. By doing so, they suggest that from 13 to 16% of teenagers are overconformists, goody-goodies and teacher's pets. Such behavior in the short run is not seen as a major problem by society. On the other hand, it may be a real though somewhat unobtrusive index of a failure to develop a sense of individuality and independence.

In any case, the continuum does provide a framework that defines delinquency in a broad yet nonlegal sense and avoids the social class bias. The authors note:

> Several conclusions and observations can be made. The more serious a misbehavior is regarded by the public, the fewer are the children who indulge in that behavior. The younger the child the more likely it is that his [sic] behavior will fall into D and C rather than A. Adolescents may spread out over the entire continuum in decreasing numbers from D to A but they make up most of the delinquents in area A. [7]

The Cavan and Ferdinand framework also gets us out of the trap of needing to decide whether delinquency is on a rampant increase. That is, we can view the dramatic increases announced publicly every so often as a result of a change in reporting or, for the seventies, at least, of the proportional increase in the teenage population.

RESEARCH INTO CAUSES

As we have noted, the Cavan and Ferdinand continuum suggests that approximately 13 to 16% of the youth population engages in serious antisocial acts and that as the seriousness increases, the proportion of teenagers decreases. But experts in delinquency like to point out that such behavior is not limited to the twentieth century. Hammurabi's code of 2200 B.C. specified penalties for teenage misbehavior, as did the code of the early Roman republic of 200 B.C. In England in A.D. 900, just prior to the Norman conquest, there were explicit laws punishing delinquent acts by minors. Even in the nineteenth century, as Charles Dickens so dramatically pointed out, juvenile misbehavior not only was a serious national concern but also was dealt with severely and cruelly. Both in Rome in the seventeenth century and in England in the early 1800s, the forerunners of today's detention homes were in place. The Hospital of Saint Michael in Rome was for "the correction and instruction of profligate youth, that they who when idle were injurious, may when taught become useful to the state." In England the Kingswood Reformatory was established to detain "hordes of unruly children who infested the streets of the new industrial town [and] . . . that the crimes committed by the youthful offenders are often the worse description" [8].

Naturally, any obvious human behavior such as delinquency, which is both long-standing and visible, prompts adults to search for theoretical explanations. This has been true throughout history, and some of the early psychological theories not only are interesting from a historical perspective but also relate to some of today's misconceptions. Mental retardation, arrested physical development, chromosomal deficiency—all have been suggested as causes of delinquency. And all these explanations have a similar orientation—that delinquents are born, not made.

Henry Goddard, one of our country's early psychologists, who believed firmly that intelligence was inherited, tried for many years to show that delinquency resulted from low intelligence. A feebleminded person had poor judgment and was set on the path of crime from the time of birth. His classic doctrine was, "Every feebleminded person is a potential criminal" [9].

This view, of course, had serious consequences, because it supported such approaches to treatment as incarceration and sterilization on the basis of some rather thin evidence. Goddard unfortunately did not change his theory in spite of his own studies. In testing offenders (and remember that the tests in those days were extremely crude and contained culturally biased items), he found the full range of tested intelligence among the inmates. In other words, adult criminals demonstrated a wide range of intelligence. That line of inquiry having failed, he switched his focus. He then attempted to examine the family histories of the feebleminded boys and girls at his school to identify criminal families. If he couldn't find that adult criminals were retarded, he hoped to find that families producing feebleminded children were themselves criminally oriented. As one researcher today noted, even by loading his results in his own favor, he found that only 10% of the families and 1% of the individuals were criminals [10].

The so-called bad seed theory was thus refuted, and looking for mental retardation as a cause of delinquency ended up in a blind alley. However, that result did not deter other researchers from seeking other kinds of bad seeds. If one couldn't find the cause in the brain, then one should look at the body, they said. Physical characteristics would show that delinquency was inherited—or so thought Ernest Hooton [11]. The theory was simple. Theorists such as Italian doctor Cesare Lombroso and (unfortunately) our own G. Stanley Hall suggested that criminals were really evolutionary throwbacks, early savages, criminallike persons of incomplete development—a child born centuries too late. Thus a delinquent was an untamed beast and subnormal on the evolutionary scale. The physical characteristics included the following:

- forehead, narrow and long

- ears, outstanding and large

- jaws, large

- cheekbones, large

- lips, thin

- skin, hairy and wrinkled

- arms, long

- handedness, predominantly left-handed

If these characteristics were not enough to help identify delinquents, a final characteristic was a "ferocious squint."

On the basis of these ideas Hooton set out to confirm the hypotheses by actually measuring and recording the physical characteristics of over seventeen thousand males. Hooton's data indicated no statistically significant differences between the criminals and noncriminals. So physical characteristics could not identify criminals as throwbacks. Nonetheless (suffering apparently from the same kind of myopia as Goddard), Hooton concluded that the theory was sound and that criminals should be either eliminated or at least segregated permanently from the rest of society on the basis of their physical characteristics. A more recent version of this approach is Sheldon's research on body type: ectomorphs, mesomorphs, and endomorphs. He claimed significance for his findings. However, reanalysis of the data indicated no statistically significant differences of the 200 subjects by body type [12].

Not too long ago another aspect of the bad seed hypothesis was suggested in the form of a chromosomal deficit. Early research in this area had led to studies of brain dissections of criminals but could unearth no differences. With more sophisticated techniques it was possible to examine chromosomes. Most males have the familiar XY sex chromosome designation. However, some researchers, in investigating criminals accused of extremely serious and violent crimes, found an extra chromosome; they called the phenomenon the XYY syndrome. There are apparently some significant probabilities: Serious offenders are twenty times more likely to have the pattern than males in the general population. However, as an explanation for delinquency in general, the overall occurrence is too rare. Only 2% of those adults judged violently, criminally insane have the extra chromosome.

It seems clear that there is no convenient, single inherited characteristic that predetermines delinquent behavior. Thus delinquents are not born—but are they made? That is, are there interacting conditions that may stimulate delinquency? A classic study by Sheldon and Eleanor Glueck sheds light on this question, at least for boys who are judged delinquent. It is to that study we now turn. Later in the chapter we will present the findings from another classic study by Gisela Konopka that focused on females.*

The Gluecks Study Male Delinquency

Sheldon and Eleanor Glueck set a new course for research in delinquency when in the 1930s they embarked on a longitudinal study on a large scale with 1000 boys [13]. Rather than test out preconceived hypotheses (Goddard, for example, wanted to prove that retardation caused delinquency, and Hooton sought to confirm his theory of arrested development), the Gluecks wanted to explore all possible facets in seeking causes. They picked 500 boys from Massachusetts who had been adjudicated and committed to detention for serious antisocial acts. A control group of 500 boys was also created. They carefully matched the groups on intelligence, age, nationality, and place of residence. They even stratified the control group membership according to the base rates of delinquency from given neighborhoods. So, as far as possible, they had two groups of boys from similar social and economic backgrounds who were similar in age, intelligence, and ethnicity but who differed on presence or absence of delinquent behavior. At the time of the initial study the average age was 15, placing them in midadolescence. Also, the parental occupations of both groups were working-class semiskilled to unskilled jobs—essentially blue collar.

A major difference emerged from the comparative study: The quality of the home environment consistently distinguished between the two groups. Figure 10.2 describes the differences in terms of the relationships of the sons to fathers and to mothers and in terms of the general conduct standards of the parents. As we might expect, there was some overlap in each of the aspects between delinquent and nondelinquent groups. How-

---

* There are, of course, many additional theories of delinquency, from social conditioning, a kind of Marxist view that blames everything on society, to a wide range of psychoanalytic views, which search for symbolic difficulties between father and sons, as exemplified by James Dean in the movie *Rebel Without a Cause*. But we will restrict our discussion to the views described above.

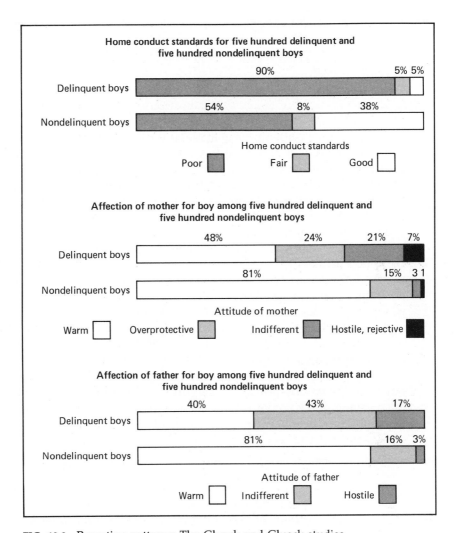

FIG. 10.2 Parenting patterns: The Glueck and Glueck studies

From S. Glueck and E. Glueck, *Unraveling juvenile delinquency* (Cambridge, Mass: Harvard University Press, 1950) p. 129. Reprinted by permission.

ever, there were also noticeable differences in the quality of the at-home interaction. The largest differences were as follows:

- In conduct standards: 90% of the delinquent boys versus 54% of the nondelinquents came from homes judged as poor on conduct. A home was rated poor if there was strong evidence of drunkenness, criminality, immorality, and "unwholesome ideals."

SPECIAL TOPIC
Treating Juvenile Delinquency: "Just Scare the Pants Off Them"

In 1977 a dramatic attempt was made to treat delinquency [1]. A number of teenagers (both boys and girls) took part in a special study. They had been classified as delinquent and were randomly assigned to a treatment or a control group. Delinquents in the treatment group were taken to an adult prison in Rahway, New Jersey; there, hard-core adult lifers verbally confronted them with the error of their ways. The adult criminals yelled at, bullied, and threatened the delinquents. They related the unvarnished truth about prison life, such as the brutality, the homosexual rapes, the degradation, and the lack of personal freedom.

A film was made of the program for national television. The publicity became enormous, especially after preliminary findings revealed that from 80 to 90% of the treated teenagers had reversed their behavior. It suddenly seemed as if all the problems of delinquency could be solved: Send the teenagers to an adult prison for a visit and a verbal shock treatment. This dramatic glimpse of their likely future would immunize them from a life of crime.

When the follow-up results were carefully and objectively examined, however, the mighty promise of the project was undone. In fact, the findings, shown in the accompanying table, indicated that the program was worse than no treatment at all. The control groups had fewer subsequent arrests than the treatment group.

- For affection of father: 40% of the delinquents versus 81% of the nondelinquents indicated warm relationships to the father.

- For affection of mother: 48% of the delinquents versus 81% of the nondelinquents indicated a warm relationship to the mother. In addition, only 22% of the delinquents versus 71% of the nondelinquents felt that their mothers were substantially concerned about their welfare.

From these findings the Gluecks constructed their prediction tables as an index of delinquency-prone families. Since no single variable by itself could perfectly distinguish between the two groups, the Gluecks devised a method of weighting a series of factors into a predictive index to identify

Outcomes of Rahway Prison experiment

Group	Outcome 6 months later	
	No arrests	Arrests
"Scared straight" (N = 46)	27	19
Control (N = 35)	31	4

Thus in spite of the promise and the wide publicity, the program did not work. The failure was not a result of a lack of effort. The forty adult lifers in the prison were committed to the idea that they might prevent delinquency-prone teenagers from becoming what they had become. Also, judges and juvenile officers were very supportive of the program. However, it appears that a one-shot confrontation will not solve a problem as complex as delinquency. In fact, and quite unfortunately, in one high school, visiting the prison became a status symbol. Some 400 of the 1200 students at Ridgefield High School (New Jersey) were sent to Rahway, and the students began to feel that something was wrong if they didn't get selected.

REFERENCE

1. J. O. Finkenauer and L. Kuhmerker, Scared straight, *Moral Educational Forum* 4, 3(1979):1–7.

proneness toward delinquency. They combined five specific factors in order of importance; Table 10.1 outlines the elements. The weights indicate that lack of cohesiveness is the most important factor in predicting delinquency, followed by two aspects of mother-son relationships and then two father-son elements. These results indicate that even though the delinquent was an adolescent, the quality of the relationship with the mother was more important than that with the father.

A test of predictive accuracy was made in the 1950s. Since almost all the delinquents in the original study had engaged in some antisocial acts in elementary schools, the system was applied to a sample of elementary school boys, who were then followed up ten years later. Table 10.2 presents the results. Overall, of the 220 predictions, 209 were accurate over

TABLE 10.1   Predicting delinquency-prone families with Glueck's social
prediction method

Social factors	Weighted score[a]	Rank order
1. Discipline of boy by father		
Overstrict or erratic	72.5	5
Lax	59.8	
Firm but kindly	9.3	
2. Supervision of boy by mother		
Unsuitable	83.2	3
Fair	57.5	
Suitable	9.9	
3. Affection of father for son		
Indifferent or hostile	75.9	4
Warm (including overprotective)	33.8	
4. Affection of mother for boy		
Indifferent or hostile	86.2	2
Warm (including overprotective)	43.1	
5. Cohesiveness of family		
Unintegrated	96.9	1
Some elements of cohesion	61.3	
Cohesive	20.6	

From S. Glueck and E. Glueck, Early detection of future delinquents, *Journal of Criminal Law, Criminology and Police Science*, Northwestern University School of Law, 47(1956):175.

[a] The weights were determined by the proportion of boys who were delinquent in each social factor.

the decade. The mistakes are boxed in the table—7 were predicted to be nondelinquent who did not turn out that way; similarly, 4 were predicted to become delinquent who remained nondelinquent.

Long-Term Follow-Up

Follow-up studies have been conducted for the Glueck index. The question researchers used was, "Does delinquency lead to adult criminality?"

The follow-up study of the original matched group of 500 boys was conducted over a 16-year span [14]. The average age at follow-up was 31, well into adulthood. By that time 438 delinquents and 442 nondelinquents remained in the sample. In general, there was a major difference between the groups. Only 3.6% of the nondelinquents had been arrested and convicted, that is, 16 of the 442. By contrast, for the delinquents 51.3%, or more than half, had been arrested and convicted. However, when the severity of the behavior involved in the crime was examined, that percentage dropped to 28.9% of the delinquents.

This result indicates that the majority of delinquents adapted to society and had decreased activity in serious crime. When we remember that all of

TABLE 10.2 Predictions of delinquency-proneness: *Gluecks' three-factor table* (total = 220 boys)

	Outcome	
Prediction	Delinquency	Nondelinquency
Delinquency	23	4
Nondelinquency	7	186

Adapted from M. Craig and S. Glick, Ten years' experience with the Glueck social prediction table, *Crime and Delinquency* 9(1963):255.

Note: In the study in New York City, many of the boys came from families without fathers, so the index was composed of (1) integration, (2) mother's affection, and (3) mother's supervision. Also, there were 19 boys in the sample whose scores on the index placed them in the middle range, so no prediction was made. Essentially, those 19 had an even chance (50:50). Follow-up indicated 9 were delinquent and 10 were not—just about 50:50.

the delinquents were in reform schools for at least a year, this follow-up finding seems to be a tribute to some kind of adaptability in spite of their detention. As we will note in Chapter 12, studies have consistently shown that reform schools, or juvenile correctional institutions, do not give corrective education. That is, instead of learning to become better citizens, the inmates learn to become better criminals. Thus the delinquents in the Glueck study appear to have fared better than most in adulthood.

However, in terms of actual numbers the findings indicate little real optimism. Less than one-third of the adolescent boys could be classified as genuinely criminal at follow-up—but that figure still means 127 individuals of the 438 persisted in criminal behavior. Also, as shown in Table 10.3, the high school dropout rate for the delinquent group was enormous when compared with that for the control. Approximately all the delinquents had dropped out of secondary school, whereas only about one-half of the control group had dropped out. Thus the delinquents' formal education ended early in secondary school—not an optimistic note for future development.

TABLE 10.3 School dropouts in the Glueck study

	Delinquents (N = 438)	Nondelinquents (N = 441)
Dropouts prior to age 16	62.3%	12.2%
Dropouts at age 16	34.3%	39.7%
Total	96.6%	51.9%

Developed from S. Glueck and E. Glueck, *Unraveling juvenile delinquency* (Cambridge, Mass.: Harvard University Press, 1950), p. 132.

The study had—and still has—a number of important implications concerning the causes of serious antisocial behavior of teenagers:

- Delinquent behavior starts prior to adolescence. During adolescence the antisocial acts increase in seriousness and frequency.

- The home environment—especially the quality of the mother-son relationship—is a major causative factor.

- The actual economic status of delinquency-prone families is lower than that of nondelinquent families, even though there is no difference in the level of parental employment.

- There is virtually a 100% rate of school dropout for the delinquents.

- Follow-up studies indicate that in adulthood almost one-third of the delinquents engage in serious crimes.

We must also underscore the limitations of the follow-up study. All generalizations must be limited to white working-class children and to parents at semiskilled to unskilled occupational levels. Also, the generalizations must be limited to male delinquents. Finally, there are some unknown factors. Cavan and Ferdinand wisely note:

> Within a family, proneness to delinquency differs from one child to another. Each child has his personal relationship with his parents. One child in a family may be loved, another rejected; one child may be favored by the mother, another by the father. [15]

Nevertheless, the study does indicate the seriousness of the problem, in spite of the possibility of individual differences. The family home environment certainly appears to be a major causative factor in predetermining adolescent delinquency. The implications of this result from a developmental view will be examined in a later section of this chapter.

Cultural Differences: A Complex Question

There is little substantial information on delinquency and cultural differences among, for example, blacks or Mexican-Americans. These groups have not been studied in detail, so it is not possible, as yet, to isolate the effects of racial and ethnic bias from the adult society, family influence, and economic circumstances as causes. As we note in Chapter 13, minority groups have high rates of unemployment and school dropout. Thus the information on the incidence of delinquency by itself cannot be taken as information on causation. For example, in the 1970s, black adolescents made up about 24% of the total juvenile arrests while only accounting for approximately 12% of the population [16].

Given the general lack of opportunity for minorities, the poor quality of urban schools, and the persistent prejudice of the majority, antisocial acts of minority group youth and of white delinquents in the previous studies may come from a different set of causes. We do not mean to say that some minority youth may turn to delinquency for entirely different reasons from those described above. Indeed, a proportion of minority group teenagers may come from homes highly similar to the pattern outlined by the Gluecks. However, since the structure of the family may be quite different in white and in minority cultures, it would be dangerous to generalize. Also, as sociologist David Matza has noted, much of the so-called minority group adolescent delinquency may be a genuine adverse reaction to the social environment [17]. This observation finds expression in the high incidence of suicide among black males in our society.

However, we do not take the position that minority group adolescent delinquency is a myth created by white authority figures to justify oppression or that it is exclusively caused by adverse social conditions. At the moment we simply do not know enough about it to make definitive statements. Probably, minority youth delinquency results from a highly complex set of elements, some similar to those found for white teenagers, some unique to intrafamily cultural differences, and some due to the prejudice and racism of the majority society. But at the most obvious level we can say that as long as such relatively huge numbers of minority group adolescents do not have access either to adequate schooling or reasonable economic

Unraveling the causes and consequences of delinquency is a complex pattern
Photograph from Hazel Hankin/Stock, Boston

opportunities, urban environments will continue to be breeding grounds for delinquent gangs and antisocial acts.

Female Delinquency: Girls in Conflict

As in other areas in psychology, attention to the question of sex differences in delinquency is relatively recent. In the past researchers felt that there was little reason to study female teenage delinquents. They were viewed as mindless followers of boys whose only problem was sexual promiscuity. Thus their behavior was seen as a morals problem more than anything else: The teenage delinquent girl simply needed lectures on the importance of chastity. This sexist view—the double standard—clearly undervalued the importance of female teenagers and their behavior.

Gisela Konopka (see the accompanying biography) changed all that. She conducted an intensive study of over 180 females, aged 14–18 years, who were adjudicated delinquent and placed in reform schools [18]. Her research method was unique. Since there was little theory to follow and were almost no prior studies, she spent hours interviewing each girl, using an open-ended semistructured technique. Whether a researcher develops significant information with this approach depends almost entirely on interviewing skill; so much is dependent on a trustful relationship that the procedure is rarely used. Also, it requires a considerable commitment of time. Konopka, though, had the requisite talent to establish trust, to convey genuine empathy and understanding so that she could gain both the confidence of the girls and an accurate picture of their world. She carefully and respectfully introduced herself to each girl through an official letter and requested their cooperation right from the outset. A copy of her letter is shown below; it will give you some sense of the genuineness of her interest and caring.*

September 4, 1962

Dear Friend:

Perhaps you have met me before, when I visited The School. I am teaching at the University of Minnesota. I have worked a lot with young people who have had some difficulties in their lives. I have found increasingly that we know very little about girls. We adults talk much about them, but we seldom have an opportunity to hear really what the girl herself thinks.

All girls have their dreams and wishes, their likes and dislikes. They usually talk about all this among themselves. I have been very fortunate to have the opportunity to take one year away from my job and spend some time at The School just to listen to you. I hope you can consider me as your friend. Nothing you say will go into your records. I come only to listen and

---

* From the book, *The Adolescent Girl in Conflict* by Gisela Konopka © 1966 by Prentice-Hall, Inc. Published by Prentice-Hall, Inc., Englewood Cliffs, N.J. 07632.

to learn. I will be at The School every Monday and Tuesday from September to the end of December.

I may not be able to listen to all of you, but I look forward to talking to some of you. I will appreciate your help. Thank you and best wishes.

Sincerely,
(Mrs.) Gisela Konopka, D.S.W. [19]

From this intensive method she was able to draw out the major themes, or parameters, of female delinquency. She listened to the girls, relistened to tape recordings, and poured over the transcripts. Gradually, a cluster of salient themes or elements emerged from her interviews. In a sense this procedure is similar to a clinical factor analysis, where the researcher gradually can list commonalities from the words used by the subject. Konopka correctly decided that one of the major problems in studying female delinquency involved the girls themselves. For understandable reasons the girls were extremely mistrustful of adults. They were very reluctant to volunteer information concerning their innermost thoughts, feelings, hopes, and fears. However, because of Konopka's unusual background, she was able to convince the girls to trust her with their private and deeply personal concerns.

The girls in Konopka's study were adjudicated by the courts for three general categories of offenses: (1) criminal offenses, (2) morals offenses, and (3) status offenses. The last category involves acts that are considered violations only if committed by an adolescent; that is, they would not be offenses if committed by an adult. For example, the adolescent's status as a juvenile determines that such acts as running away from home, being declared a stubborn child, or being unwed and pregnant are violations of the law.

Since the study was done in Minnesota, the great majority of the girls were white from working-class (semiskilled and unskilled) backgrounds. There was a small proportion of black and Native-American girls. Thus the generalizations had to be limited to girls from similar backgrounds, predominantly white working class.

Four major elements made up the pattern of psychological needs of the girls. These elements are presented below in the approximate order of importance as causations of delinquency.

Unfulfilled dependency needs Konopka found that a major theme from all the girls in her study related to their desire to be dependent. Since they were between 14 and 18 years old, the girls felt they were too old to be dependent on their parents, yet the desire for dependency was usually strong. They all related stories about their fears of leaving childhood and a

GISELA KONOPKA (1910–)

If there is one theme that has permeated Gisela Konopka's entire life, it is the dual theme of despair and hope. She is truly a child of the twentieth century. She personally experienced the worst and most inhumane aspects of Europe in the 1930s, for nine long and fateful years. But both before and afterward, in Germany in the 1920s and in this country in the 1950s and onward, she continues to live a life of hope.

Her early childhood was spent as part of a close-knit family. Her parents had emigrated from Poland, and they ran a small grocery store in Berlin. Her father fought in the German army, even though he was not in sympathy with the kaiser, being a Social Democrat. During the twenties with the flourishing of the Weimer Republic, Gisela grew through adolescence with a spirit of equality, personhood, and justice. She joined a youth group of adolescents and young adults, a common thing to do at the time. These idealistic young people spent weekends camping and discussing the great issues of the day and worked during the week for social reform for a truly democratic Germany. They passed out leaflets against facism as it took hold in Italy; they helped organize workers into democratic trade unions. They helped get out the vote, all the while participating in intense philosophical discussions that helped Gisela formulate her own ideology.

She moved to Hamburg in 1929, and while working in a factory to support herself, she enrolled for the equivalent of our academic doctorate at the university there. It was at this point that the hope of the 1920s vanished. Chaos, unemployment, inflation, and a host of factors strangled the young republic. In a paroxysm of fear the German people turned to the man on horseback, Adolf Hitler. For Gisela the change couldn't have been worse. She was a socialist committed to world peace, and she had Jewish parents. In 1933 she was sitting for her final examinations for the doctorate when Hitler came to power. The storm troopers appeared in her class and removed her examination papers. A short time later she was sent to a concentration camp—deprived of her fam-

wish to return to elementary school age. They hoped, somehow, to be able to go back to a safer and less complex time in their lives where they might be able to cope better and have an adult they could really depend on; leaving the safety of childhood created a major void of loneliness and despair. During the onset of adolescence they felt vulnerable and unprotected, an "outspoken ache," in Konopka's words.

Gisela Konopka (1910–)

ily, her intended spouse, her degree, and her identity. The new laws declared that she was no longer a German citizen.

By 1937 she had escaped, and until 1941 she was on the run, first to Austria and then to France. Each time the German army was not far behind. She supported herself with a variety of jobs, child care, nurse, laborer, housecleaner—anything to earn enough to live and yet allow her to be ready to move without notice when the storm troopers arrived.

(Continued)

The changes from the physical maturation, without exception, were seen as too much to handle. The girls were overwhelmed by the transition from childhood to adulthood. Puberty was viewed as fearful and brought into high relief their desires to regress in order to avoid the implications of adulthood. They all had feelings of unfulfilled longing.

At the same time their desire for dependency, in opposition to their physical maturity, was further complicated by mother-daughter competi-

GISELA KONOPKA (Continued)

She said later that it was this entire dreadful experience that sensitized her to the legitimate needs of all humans, the needs for caring, empathy, and respect. She was also horrified by the treatment she received from bureaucrats, officials of the establishment (even so-called friendly ones) who cared more for their rules than for people. Even in 1941, when she successfully emigrated from southern France to this country, she found that our officials required each refugee to possess money in order to pass through immigration. She literally had nothing but her clothes. Fortunately, one in her group had a $5 gold piece, which was passed back and forth to each new candidate for entrance.

In the United States she soon found work with slum children in Pittsburgh, and she simultaneously studied for a master's degree in social work, which was completed in 1943. Her true gifts in human relationships became apparent, both through her actions and through her writing. A succession of academic appointments followed, first at the University of Pittsburgh, then at Carnegie, and, in 1947, a professorship at the University of Minnesota. Also, once in the United States, she finally was rejoined by the man with whom she had fallen in love in the early 1930s, her beloved Paul. They were married in 1941, but Paul soon left to continue the fight against nazism. He had fought with the French army and joined the American army shortly after immigrating.

At Minnesota Konopka soon established herself as a major theorist on the nature of adolescent development, with a particular sensitivitiy for those who might be labeled delinquent females, as we note in the text. She also has served on innumerable national commissions, has created a truly unique interdisciplinary center for research and program development, and has managed a large number of research grants. In 1978 she officially retired from the University. Her work, however, continues, and her impact on humanizing reeducation for girls in conflict has become a national goal.

In the middle 1950s Konopka received a sabbatical leave and officially completed her doctorate at Columbia University. There were no storm troopers to confiscate her examination papers this time.

tion. Fathers were important, as will be noted in the next theme, but mothers were seen as the primary parent. Yet they were viewed as competition. Thus the girls' feelings were complex. They wished to return to a safer world in a somewhat desperate hope that the mother would provide them with a dependable and loving relationship. Arrayed against that desire was the reality of physical change and deep feelings of hostility and competition toward the mother. This reaction is similar to, yet more complicated than, the frustration-aggression syndrome. The girls dependency needs during childhood had not been adequately met by the mothers, a factor that is related to the subsequent competition with mother as the primary parent.

In all cases the pleas by the girls for support and understanding were graphic:

Loneliness in an Anonymous World

I wish I were a child! People don't understand. Adults forget. I was twelve years old when I got into trouble. . . . I ran away ten times; I was homesick. Nothing keeps me when I am homesick. . . . Oh, *I wish I were a child!*

Each generation is really not so different from another. It is only that adults sometimes forget that. . . . One doesn't talk much with parents. Perhaps people never did, *but today one expects it more.* One should be able to.

Have you ever been lonely? When I was in the foster home I could not see my sister or my brother. I felt so lonely. I wanted to hang around other kids.

I am just terribly lonesome. I don't think I was even in love. I just wanted to get close because I was so lonesome. I wouldn't marry him. I was aware I could have a child.

I wish I could get help. If I could go to a club where there are real friends! Real friends understand you. It all revolves around friendship. I would like to have an older friend. I have one and she is a woman who works, but my mother doesn't like me to go to her. But I need friends.

I like to meet new people, but I haven't many friends. I thought the girls were my friends, but they really are my enemies. They talk behind your back. I want friends so badly that I always push myself on others. [20]

Negative image of adults This negative image was composed of three major elements, a kind of tragic trilogy: (1) men as brutal, (2) women as ineffectual, and (3) authority as anonymous and uncaring. In fact, the most difficult-to-read, yet most revealing, aspects of Konopka's study were the experiences of those girls with the adult world. The physical brutality was stark: rape by fathers, physical beatings, extensive corporal punishment for minor misdemeanors, and drunken rages by adults. In addition to the picture of violence in the homes, she found the situation not much better with regard to adult authority figures. Physical brutality, to be sure, was much lower, but adult judges, social workers, teachers, attendants, and counselors were singularly unsuccessful in responding to the girls' needs.

The adult world that these girls came into contact with was harsh;

justice was rarely, if ever, constrained by mercy. The negative expectations of authority figures presented a clear message to the girls. The adults were watchful, distrusting, on their guard—forever "formidable and frightening" to the girls as "massive walls but no faces." Konopka concludes:

> Most of the teachers, social workers, judges, church representatives, policemen, do not live in their neighborhood, do not experience the noise, the smell, the fighting, the deprivation, the confusion . . . they are strangers with power. [21]

Thus the second theme in their lives focused on past and current brutality from parents and on continuing interaction with a faceless set of authority figures who continued to reinforce the negative perception the girls had vis-à-vis adults in general. This alienation was far deeper than the somewhat superficial estrangement of the hippie flower children of middle-class America in the 1960s, whose mantra was, "You can't trust adults over 30." These girls genuinely felt they couldn't trust any adult—and with reason.

Social segregation and prejudice   The third element included experiences of social segregation and prejudice. These feelings, of course, were most intensely experienced by the black and Native-American girls in the study, yet they were also quite common for all. Konopka calls this terrible sickness of our society the "stigma of prejudice." Each girl could relate incidents, almost indelibly burned into their psyches, of being shunned, stared at, rejected, and made to feel unworthy. The blatant racism and the more subtle segregation by social class had the effect of increasing the sense of isolation from the mainstream of society. Thus their unfulfilled dependency needs from childhood, which left intense feelings of loneliness, were increased by the failure of the general society to affirm their identity as worthy humans. Instead of being acknowledged, they were rebuffed.

The Cinderella fantasy   The fourth theme came from what Konopka called the Cinderella fantasy. Essentially, this element was the girls' coping mechanism. As a result of loneliness, desire for dependency, realistic fears of brutality in the family, and a not-so-benign neglect by authority figures—a negative constellation of forces—the girls' own aspirations were fantasies rather than realistic possibilities.

This result, however, negatively affected their self-development. They dreamed of a Hollywood-like marriage as a way out of their predicament. But this romantic dream as a solution had the effect of preventing them from seeing schooling or preparation for a career as worthy of serious interest, especially since their family traditions did not value education. So classes were seen as irrelevant. As a result, the dropout rate for the female delinquents was almost as high as it was for the males in the Glueck studies: almost 100%.

The levels of upset in the home, in the neighborhoods, and in the schools themselves were also barriers to achievement. The girls had not been socialized to accept the middle-class values of work and study. And they did not view school achievement as a necessary stepping-stone to career. In fact, they saw the world of work not in terms of the skilled and professional occupations held by middle-class career women but, rather, in terms of the jobs held by their mothers and the neighborhood women. These women were housecleaners, maids, washerwomen, and unskilled factory laborers, working long hours at physically demanding jobs. So here was the Cinderella fantasy played out in real life: "As I scrub floors, some day my prince will arrive and spirit me away."

Fantasies, of course, can be dangerous crutches, yet they provided, apparently, the only hope in these girls' lives; fantasies gave them the motivation to keep existing and enduring. It was particularly ironic to Konopka's trained eye that many of the girls had, through experience, developed great natural empathy and would have made excellent contributions in the helping professions, such as caring for the elderly or for young children. Yet it was clear that their school failure would bar entry to such fields. It comes as no surprise, then, to find that the delinquent girls had increasingly lowered self-esteem, which took the form of alternating cycles of passive withdrawal and acting out.

Summarizing the causes From Konopka's study a discouraging outline of causes emerge. As in the Glueck study, the home environment was of poor quality and prior to adolescence failed to provide the girls with adequate psychological care. This condition resulted in major unfulfilled dependency needs and the ache of loneliness. The girls were not prepared to handle the changes of physical maturation. Their experience with adults was largely negative: physically brutal fathers and ineffectual yet competitive mothers. The defect in the mother-daughter relationship was particularly crucial. Other adult authority figures were viewed as faceless and uncaring. To make matters worse, the girls suffered prejudice directed either at their race or at their social class, since they were all from working-class (semiskilled to unskilled) backgrounds. School work and self-direction were viewed as alien goals, replaced instead by the fantasy of a romantic marriage as the solution to their problems.

Underneath the entire syndrome, however, was the wish that somehow it could have been different. Rather than find themselves locked away in a correctional facility, victimized by the complexities of home, community, and school, the girls did wish, poignantly, that their lives could have been different:

"I want to be back at age eleven and start all over again. I want to go to school. I want to finish and to be somebody. I want to have a good name and be a nice girl.

"I wish there were somebody to help!"

This was a message from a 16-year-old. Her friend put it more simply, "I just want to be like any other girls!" [22]

TREATMENT AND PREVENTION

In general, one of the major failures of our society has been the inability of the socializing institutions in the country to treat delinquency effectively. It is depressing to review the literature on treatment programs, since so few have worked. Part of this failure may be due to a general inadequacy to understand the causes of delinquency as a basis to tailor treatment. Without an understanding of causes, treatment may have little direction. Also, there is a general ambivalence on the part of the adult society to face the problem and provide enough money for effective remediation. In other words, it simply seems easier to let the police catch the delinquents and remove them to a geographically isolated detention home.

Thus in our view there has been a failure to commit resources to create, try out, and evaluate new methods for treatment. Past history reveals a grab bag of techniques, some borrowed from other contexts, some based on little more than intuition, and some grounded in passing fads. No wonder, then, that the treatment outcome has been so consistently poor. In this section the methods and outcomes of the past will be reviewed briefly to give you some background for the treatment problem today.

Effects of Traditional Therapy: Individual and Group Approaches

A major study, the Cambridge-Somerville Youth Study, was carried out in Massachusetts in the late 1930s [23]. The study identified a large group of preadolescent boys (N = 325) for whom future delinquent behavior was highly likely. A matched control group of boys was created for whom similar predictions were made. The boys in the study received individual counseling and tutoring; the controls did not receive any special treatment. The project was carried on for 5 years. The results indicated no substantial difference between the two groups in number of subsequent adult criminal convictions. A second, smaller study in New York with a treatment group of 21 predelinquent boys and a matched control group also showed no differences at follow-up in criminal activity over a 10-year period [24].

These discouraging findings seemed to indicate that regular individual counseling even of an intensive nature was not powerful enough to alter the course of subsequent delinquent behavior. Because of these findings, individual treatment was largely abandoned, and group therapy was tried. According to Cavan and Ferdinand, group therapy became almost a fad after World War II and was eagerly seized as the method of choice [25]. The nondirective balanced group technique of Slavson was most popular. Unfortunately, in spite of its promise intensive group therapy proved no more successful than individual treatment for delinquents.

To some degree, the general research on individual and group therapy has indicated that both can be successful, but usually only for relatively well-adjusted individuals who are verbal, intelligent, and basically introspective. This circumstance is sometimes called the YAVIS syndrome—young, attractive, verbal, intelligent, and successful. Thus a treatment technique that has moderately successful results with middle-class clients from the majority group culture will not be successful when transferred to delinquent boys and girls. As the information from both the Gluecks' studies and Konopka's work would suggest, the delinquents' psychological needs are beyond the reach of traditional individual or group work.

Institutional Treatment

The most traditional approach to treatment has been, as it's variously called, the detention center, correctional facility, reform school, or, more quaintly, home for wayward boys or girls. Each state, from the turn of the century on, has erected large-sized facilities, usually in geographically remote places, as a means of treating delinquency. In a study of 79 such institutions over a 22-year period following World War II, the results of treatment were negative [26]. There was no reduction in subsequent criminal activity (called the rate of recidivism). Thus so-called correctional facilities simply didn't correct; they were merely temporary way stations for teenagers. As a result, beginning in the 1970s states have been closing these large-scale residential treatment programs.

Given the range and complexity of the present marginal psychological adjustment of delinquents and their past histories, it is no wonder that grouping them in large numbers in such institutions did not prove to have positive results. Konopka, in her visits to such facilities, found them sterile at best and more often humiliating. The programs were unimaginative and the staffs often well-meaning yet inadequate to the task. In her view such large institutions should continue to be closed. She is convinced, for example, that the incidence of lesbianism among delinquent girls is in direct response to their institutionalization and loneliness and does not represent their primary sexual identification [27]. The institutions are, quite simply, unhealthy environments.

Because the traditional approaches to treatment of delinquency did not work, we are now in a period of transition. But solutions to the problem are hard to develop.

SPECIAL TOPIC
Teenage Prostitution: The Unhappy Hooker

Although teenage prostitution has been a long-term problem for centuries, recent publicity of the infamous Minnesota Connection has refocused attention on the causes of adolescents' selling sex. Many of the nation's magazines and some leading newspapers such as *The New York Times* carried stories describing the recruitment of blond, blue-eyed, female Minnesotans for transport to the Big Apple for work on the streets. Of course, the problem is not unique to Minnesota families nor to New York City. The publicity, however, did increase the national awareness of the problem. Why would teenage girls become attracted to such activity? Was it simply a case of being oversexed? Or was it a desire for easy money that led teenage females into prostitution?

Mike Baizerman and colleagues of the Center for Youth Development and Research at the University of Minnesota recently investigated the causative factors in teenage prostitution [1]. Using a variety of methods, including training teenagers themselves as researchers, they were able to uncover both the myths and the realities. They found that prostitution by teenagers is never a fully examined rational decision.

After interviewing over three hundred young prostitutes during a three-year period, the researchers found the following picture emerge. The basic recruitment technique used by the pimps (the males for whom the girls work) is the love approach. The girls themselves, for a variety of reasons, are most vulnerable to the pimp's role as an adult caretaker. The girls generally have a poor self-image, lack confidence, and are usually in the process of running away from home.Their family relations had almost always been poor, and the pattern of disruption increased. The home atmospheres were often similar to Konopka's portraits—angry fights, brutality, instability. Their own needs for care and support during childhood had not been adequately met. Thus the girls are lonely and seeking dependency. The pimp, being a kind of streetwise psychologist, knowingly and expertly exploits and manipulates them. In most cases he starts dating the girl and then gradually, through flashy gifts, clothes, parties, and dinners, convinces her that he can provide the care, security, and love she needs. Once their attachment is formed, the rest follows inexorably. She wishes to please him, and after being taught how to perform sex acts with him, she is soon willing to work for him. She sees herself as part of a family and gets to know the other girls in the stable. The pimp skillfully convinces his group that he really does care for each of them. The girls all hope to earn the ultimate status and become his "main woman." He does, after all, provide for them. They turn over their profits to him; he buys the

Teenage prostitution is often the result of unfulfilled needs for love and attachment
Photograph from David Burnett/Stock, Boston

food, clothes, liquor, and drugs. The overall picture is tragic and poignant. In the researchers' words:

> When asked to interpret what love means to them, young prostitutes have used such phrases as "feeling secure; feeling cared for; and being paid attention to." What we understand from these responses is that for some girls "prostitution" is not a reality. For them what is real is that they are the pimp's "lady" or "woman"; this is what love means. [2]

In other words, teenage prostitution does not derive from a simple desire for sexual thrills or for easy money. And it is not a carefully considered decision. In most cases the adolescent female is conned into prostitution by a street-wise adult. The male pimp understands all too well the psychological needs of the girl. With utmost skill he manipulates that basic human need for love and attachment. Baizerman notes, "This is puppy-love twisted and mauled for money and social status." [3]

REFERENCES

1. M. Baizerman, J. Thompson, K. Stafford-White, and "An Old Young Friend," Adolescent prostitution, *Children Today*, September–October 1979, pp. 20–24.

2. *Ibid.*, p. 23.

3. *Ibid.*, p. 24.

A houselike atmosphere provides delinquent teenagers with needed understanding
Photograph from United Press International

Massimo's Boys: A Technique That Worked

An example of what it may take to deal effectively with a problem as difficult as delinquency is provided by a small pilot project undertaken by Joseph Massimo in the 1960s [28]. He gave extremely intensive treatment to a small sample (N = 12) of predelinquents. Essentially, he became an adult mentor to each boy. He found employment for each, took them on recreational activities, provided academic help (taught some to read, others to do math, etc.) to improve their job skills, and provided some, though not much, talk therapy. He used the job as the basic tool to help the boys become successful, making sure that they got to work on time, learned to get along with co-workers, and so on. He also, quite skillfully, found jobs where the boss might have been in trouble when he was a teenager. The results were positive when the treatment group was compared with the matched controls. Massimo's boys, as they became known, were much less likely to continue delinquent behavior on follow-up.

It took a great personal and professional commitment by one unusually skillful professional to effect such a change. Massimo remarked that he really became a surrogate father to most. He was a perfect identification figure for the boys. He had grown up in a working-class background and was in superb physical condition as a gymnast—all in addition to his professional training as a counseling psychologist. This somewhat unique approach, by an unusually gifted person, provides some insight about what it may take to treat delinquent behavior. But it is clear that such an intensive approach is unique and probably could not be undertaken for society, in general.

Current Methods of Treatment: Diversion Techniques

At the moment we are witnessing an explosion of trial-and-error techniques to replace traditional therapy and large-scale institutionalization. Programs run the full range: Forestry camps, outward bound programs, walk-abouts, special summer camps, halfway houses, group homes, and alternative schools are just some of the current diversion techniques being tried. Some, such as forestry camps, have long histories, while others, such as halfway houses and group homes, are quite new.

Obviously, we are still in an exploratory stage in treating delinquency. So we cannot yet identify the particular range of treatment ingredients that will help adolescents. Certainly, some intensive work with parents is necessary, as Roger Barker's Re Ed Program has shown [29]. His workers spent substantial time working with the parents before the delinquent was allowed to return home, which greatly aided their reentry. Also, it is clear that delinquents need a special and continuous relationship with helping adults, which, in turn, means that the adult helpers must have a high level of professional competency.

Finding an effective treatment program is certainly not easy. For example, in the 1960s during the height of the development of juvenile gangs (popularized in *West Side Story*), social workers were trained to work with the gangs on their own turf rather than in formal treatment facilities. Unfortunately, such an approach did not work. Somewhat ironically, an unusual study found that when detached workers actually attempted to reduce the solidarity of the gang, undermine the power of the leader, and reduce the rate of recruitment (these are usually not the objectives of a gang worker), the crime rate was reduced [30]. Such a reduction, of course, does not cure gang delinquency. Rather, reversing the general disintegration of the urban environments would be a first step in undermining the attractiveness of such gangs.

DELINQUENCY: A DEVELOPMENTAL VIEW

As a means for understanding and increasing the likelihood of creating effective treatment approaches, we now outline a developmental framework for delinquency. This framework is a synthesis of some of the research studies outlined previously as well as information from some more recent work.

Robert Wirt provided the first major step in the developmental view. Employing Erikson's theory, he did not find evidence in general that would support juvenile delinquency as a result of psychopathology. This

SPECIAL TOPIC
Role-Taking Training and Delinquency: Chandler's Study

The commonsense hypothesis that better social understanding paves the way to better social relations constantly shadows the study of social cognitive development. Consequently, research on children's inferences and judgments about others has often been followed rapidly by attempts to use research findings to change behavior.

For example, psychologist Michael Chandler built on his own research interests in role-taking and communication skills to devise a program for adolescent delinquents [1]. He reasoned that chronic delinquency may result partly from an egocentric tendency to "misread societal expectations, to misinterpret the actions and intentions of others, and to act in ways which were judged to be callous and disrespectful of the rights of others" [2]. If role-taking skills could be improved, these antisocial tendencies might be reduced.

Chandler first identified 45 adolescent males—15 each at 11, 12, and 13 years of age—who had lengthy police and court records and had committed one or more crimes that would have been considered felonies had they been committed by adults. They came from poor families in inner-city neighborhoods that were characterized by high crime and delinquency rates.

Were they poorer at social perspective taking than boys who were not identified as delinquents? For comparison purposes he selected 45 nondelinquent males at the same ages as the delinquent participants. At each age 5 of the nondelinquents were selected from the same inner-city neighborhoods as the delinquent boys, and they had similar socioeconomic, racial, and ethnic backgrounds. Ten additional comparison subjects at each age were from white middle-class families.

conclusion doesn't mean that there are not individual cases of a delinquent bordering on psychosis, but such individuals would be rare. Wirt found that most male delinquents were not yet at Erikson's stage of identity formation. Instead, they were functioning at a lower stage, acting in ways appropriate only to younger children. Wirt noted: "These boys are superficial, sensual, and selfish. Their relations with others are casual and their chief interests are self-indulgent and characterized by needs for excitement and changes" [31].

If we recall the outline of Loevinger's strategy of personal social (ego)

Chandler tested both groups with a measure of social-reasoning skills. The task consists of ten cartoon stories that the subject retells from the viewpoint of a late-arriving bystander. If he lets the information that he has as a result of hearing the whole story intrude on his description of what the late arriver knows, he gets a higher egocentrism score than if he distinguishes the other perspective from his own. Chandler found that, indeed, delinquent boys' egocentrism scores were several times greater than the comparison boys' scores, even when differences in verbal ability were statistically controlled.

At this point Chandler instituted an intervention program designed to improve the role-taking skills of the delinquent boys. (The comparison group subjects did not participate further in the project.) Thirty of the 45 boys in the delinquent group came to a storefront workshop weekly for a 10-week period. Divided into two groups of 15 each, and meeting in groups of 5, they made videotapes with the assistance of Chandler's staff.

Three of the 5-member teams in the first group of 15 (the role-taking training group) wrote and acted brief skits about persons their own age doing "real-life things." They could choose their own topics, but they were required to write enough parts for all group members and to redo the skit five times so that every group member played every part in the skit. Afterward, the videotapes of each performance were reviewed to find ways of improving them. The idea was to help the adolescents see themselves from the perspectives of others and to help them appreciate the perspectives of others as well.

The second group of 15 who came to the weekly sessions also worked with audiovisual equipment to make animated cartoon sequences. They were a placebo group whose involvement in weekly planned activities with interesting equipment resembled the role-taking group's experience but did not provide an opportunity for role-taking practice.

The third group of 15 delinquent boys, randomly selected from the origi-

(Continued)

development from Chapter 5, we can locate Wirt's delinquent boys somewhere in the delta and impulsive stages. At these stages the primary orientation is to the present. There is little understanding of long-term consequences; planning, when used at all, is toward short-term objectives. Running away from home is common, and there are preoccupations with bodily impulses (Wirt's syndrome of superficial, sensual, and selfish). Also, there is much self-protectiveness, which leads to opportunism, deception, and stealing. The main point is that it is not only all right but also stage-appropriate for young children to behave in these modes. But gradu-

SPECIAL TOPIC (Continued)

nal 45-person group, did not participate in any kind of training program. They served as a control group against which the effects of training could be measured.

At the end of the 10-week period Chandler and his associates again tested all 45 delinquent boys on the social egocentrism task, using five cartoons that had not been used in the first testing. As a result of the role-taking training, the delinquent boys showed an average of 56% less social egocentrism on Chandler's measure than they had 10 weeks earlier. The placebo group showed only a 30% reduction; the control group showed only a 22% average reduction in social egocentrism. In short, Chandler's training program had improved social cognition skills.

But did these changed social role-taking skills affect the boys' behavior? Chandler has some evidence that they did—at least in the sense of reducing the likelihood that they would get into trouble with the law. He followed their careers by watching police and court records over the next year and a half, and he found that boys in the role-taking training group were significantly less likely to commit delinquent offenses during this lengthy posttreatment period than were boys in the other two groups.

In this instance, at least, improving social cognitive skills appeared to affect behavior in a positive way. How it affected behavior and under what conditions this kind of effect should be expected are questions for further research.

REFERENCES

1. M. J. Chandler, Egocentrism and antisocial behavior: The assessment and training of social perspective-taking skills, *Developmental Psychology* 9(1973):326–332.

2. *Ibid.*, p. 327.

ally, through effective parenting, young children move to the more complex, higher stages, where they give up this less mature level of functioning. The stages of development, remember, represent a sequence of modes of functioning and processing through which individuals pass with appropriate adult and environmental support and challenge. The findings of Wirt strongly suggest that the delinquent boys are, in fact, functioning at a stage of development that is appropriate for much younger children (preschool and elementary age).

We can also see that Konopka's girls might have been at a similar early stage of development. They wished to go back to childhood, had strong beliefs in fantasy as solutions to problems, and were hostile and protective. Other researchers have found similar patterns of evidence that supports the concept of delinquency as an immature stage of psychological development. For instance, Selman found a distinctive deficit in the interpersonal stages of development between delinquents and adolescents of similar ages [32]. The delinquents were much less able to place themselves in someone else's shoes, to understand thoughts and feelings in other persons. Paralleling Selman's work, Henry Dupont, another developmental researcher, found that predelinquent boys were lower on their stage of emotional development than the comparison group [33]. They were more "heteronomous," a Piagetian phrase connecting fearfulness of adults and an infantile emotional dependency. Also, Kohlberg (Chapter 6) found that delinquents were clustered around stage 2 as their primary mode of value functioning. In short, teenage delinquents operate at the level of a con man, attempting to get something for nothing, with a sharp eye ready to better themselves at someone else's expense.

We can say, then, that many research studies point to delinquency as a product of immature psychological development. Somewhere during the preschool and elementary years, the child who becomes a teenage delinquent halts in development. This is not a deliberate act on the child's part. As we pointed out at the beginning of this book, development depends on a positive interaction between the person and the environment. A person is not born a delinquent, nor does a person become a delinquent exclusively through circumstances and conditioning. Rather, the delinquent's potential for continued growth is prevented by the interaction between the person's stage and the response by the environment. The lack of appropriate stimulators prevents the child from growing through the impulsive and delta (self-protective) stages. Thus delinquency is neither genetically inborn nor shaped but, rather, developed.

Are the parents to blame for their child's delinquency, then? We can say that they are only if we also accept the idea that delinquency-prone parents themselves are at immature levels of development. As Konopka points out, these parents have great and usually unfulfilled psychological needs themselves. So they may be doing the best they can, however inadequate their efforts may be. Thus while they can be blamed for providing poor home environments, we must also remember that they themselves may have experienced conditions that did not stimulate their own development.

A recent study by Patricia Bielke provided some evidence about the parent-child interaction [34]. She studied a relatively large sample (N = 220) of unwed teenage mothers from working-class backgrounds; most were white. She found some differences in the stage of psychological (ego) development on Loevinger's system among the adolescent mothers, al-

Most male delinquents do not show psychotic behavior but, rather, behavior that is characterized by a need for excitement and change

Photograph from Schwartz/Editorial Photocolor Archives

though the differences were not large. However, there was a difference in the quality of parenting the mother provided. The mothers at stage 3 were able to parent with some sensitivity and effectiveness. And the mothers at the lower stages (delta) were all right when the baby was 6 months old, but by the time the baby reached 12 and 18 months, the mothers' functioning had deteriorated. They tended to see the baby as a doll or an object. When the baby's individuality began to emerge, the mothers became harsh, impatient, and neglectful. As the complexity of the task increased, then, the lower-stage mothers were less able to manage.

From our discussion we see in somewhat stark terms how complex the problems of delinquency are. When children are not aided in the process of psychological growth and, instead, receive negative personal development, they grow up physically and physiologically as adults but remain at an immature psychological level. And such immaturity may have particularly unfortunate effects for the subsequent generation.

SUMMARY

The term *delinquency* has been so misused that some experts have called for a new term. However, no new designator has as yet appeared.

To provide more precision in discussing the concept of delinquency, we adopted the hypothetical continuum of Cavan and Ferdinand, which defines delinquency on a normal curve. Since over 80% of all teenagers at one time or another engage in mildly antisocial acts, it seems appropriate to use the term *delinquent* only for those who engage in serious antisocial behavior. Otherwise, the incidence of delinquency is confounded by differential arrests and convictions according to local community and social class expectations. Under these restrictions it is estimated that approximately 15% of adolescents engage in repeatedly serious antisocial acts, and one-third of that number engage in serious adult criminality.

In this chapter we examined the research into causes of delinquency. It seems highly probable that a combination of family and environmental factors create delinquency. Both the Gluecks' study of males and Konopka's study of females indicated a pattern of delinquency-prone families prior to adolescence. The quality of the relationship between preadolescents and their parents was shown to be a major predictive factor. Such factors may halt the adolescents' process of normal stage growth at a level appropriate for early elementary school students. With the onset of puberty the adolescents' inadequate level of psychological maturity results in hostile, antisocial activity, a lack of self-direction, and a deficit in the process of identity formation.

The Gluecks' work and Konopka's work have supplied important information on family patterns. However, as we noted, their generalizations must be limited. The causes and consequences of delinquency for culturally different or minority group adolescents are not well understood. As a result, there is a need for basic research on cross-cultural differences.

We also discussed the problems of prevention and treatment. Traditional treatment methods, such as intensive individual counseling and psychotherapy, have produced few positive results. Nor has institutionalization been successful. Detention schools do detain, but these correctional facilities do not reform or reeducate delinquents. As a result, we are now in a state of flux. Evidence shows what does *not* work, but only a few new methods have achieved positive outcomes. However, Massimo's intensive work-related treatment indicates that success is possible. Also, some new models of treatment, such as diversion programs, halfway house, group homes, camps, and probation, are steps in a positive direction. But these methods all treat delinquency after the fact. We still need techniques that will prevent delinquency from developing.

We concluded the chapter by presenting a developmental framework for delinquency based on Robert Wirt's study. If this work is cross-validated, it will indicate that adolescent delinquents may be functioning at preadolescent stages of psychological development. Prevention in this case would start during the elementary school years and could result in a higher level of maturity prior to the onset of puberty.

KEY POINTS AND NAMES

Delinquency

Ruth Cavan and Theodore Ferdinand

Behavior continuum

Incidence of delinquency

Research in causes of delinquency

Henry Goddard: feeblemindedness

Ernest Hooton: physical characteristics

Chromosomal deficit

Sheldon and Eleanor Glueck
  Male delinquents
  Home environment
  Delinquency-prone families

Cultural differences

Gisela Konopka
  Female delinquents
  Four themes in psychological needs

Traditional treatment
  Therapy
  Institutionalization

Joseph Massimo: intensive treatment

Current methods of treatment

Developmental view of delinquency

Robert Wirt

REFERENCES

1. R. MacIver, *Report of the New York City Delinquency Evaluation Project* (New York: Board of Education, 1960).

2. W. C. Kvaraceus, *Dynamics of delinquency* (Columbus, Ohio: Merrill, 1966).

3. D. Robinson, Scraps from teacher's notebook, *Phi Delta Kappan* 49(1967):160.

4. W. Ahlstrom and R. Havighurst, *400 Losers* (San Francisco: Jossey-Bass, 1971).

5. H. D. Thornburg, *Development in adolescents* (Monterey, Calif.: Wadsworth, 1975).

6. H. Becker, *Outsiders* (New York: Free Press, 1963).

7. R. Cavan and T. Ferdinand, *Juvenile delinquency*, 3rd ed. (Philadelphia: Lippincott, 1975), p. 32.

8. *Ibid.*, p. 5.

9. H. Goddard, *Feeble-mindedness, it's causes and consequences* (New York: Macmillan, 1914).

10. Cavan and Ferdinand, p. 178.

11. E. Hooton, *Crime and the man* (Cambridge, Mass.: Harvard University Press, 1939).

12. E. Sutherland, Critique of Sheldon's varieties of delinquent youth, *American Sociological Review* 16(1951):10–13.

13. S. Glueck and E. Glueck, *Unraveling juvenile delinquency* (Cambridge, Mass.: Harvard University Press, 1950).

14. S. Glueck and E. Glueck *Delinquents and nondelinquents in perspective* (Cambridge, Mass.: Harvard University Press, 1968).

15. Cavan and Ferdinand, p. 213.

16. FBI statistics, 1974.

17. D. Matza, *Delinquency and drift* (New York: Wiley, 1964), chap. 3.

18. G. Konopka, *The adolescent girl in conflict* (Englewood Cliffs, N.J.: Prentice-Hall, 1966).

19. *Ibid.*, p. 11.

20. *Ibid.*, p. 40.

21. *Ibid.*, p. 56.

22. *Ibid.*, p. 86.

23. J. McCord and W. McCord, A follow-up report on the Cambridge-Somerville Youth Study, *Annals of American Academy of Political and Social Science* 322(1959):89–96.

24. J. Toby, An evaluation of early identification and intensive treatment programs for delinquents, *Social Problems* 13(1965):168.

25. Cavan and Ferdinand, p. 291.

26. R. Martinson, What works, questions and answers about prison reform, *Public Interest* 35(1974):25–33.

27. Konopka, p. 103.

28. J. Massimo and M. Shore, Comprehensive vocationally oriented psychotherapy: A new treatment technique for lower-class adolescent delinquent boys, *Psychiatry* 30(1967):229–236.

29. R. Barker, *Ecological psychology* (Stanford, Calif.: Stanford University Press, 1968).

30. M. Klein, *Street gangs and street workers* (Englewood Cliffs, N.J.: Prentice-Hall, 1971).

31. R. Wirt and P. Briggs, Personality and environmental factors in the development of delinquency, *Psychological Monographs* 73(1959):41.

32. R. Selman, *The development of interpersonal understanding* (New York: Academic Press, 1980).

33. H. Dupont, Meeting the emotional-social needs of students in a mainstreamed environment, *Counseling and Human Development* 10(1978):1–11.

34. P. Bielke, The relationship of maternal ego development to parenting behavior and attitude (Ph.D. thesis, University of Minnesota, 1979).

CHAPTER 11

Psychological Disturbance and Alienation

INTRODUCTION

Like other aspects of adolescence as a stage of development, the problem of psychological disturbance involves complicated issues. For example, the storm-and-stress theory we discussed earlier strongly suggested that virtually all adolescents go through a period of severe psychological disturbance. The onset of puberty, the physical changes, the expectations of society, the pressures from peers—all these forces combine to overwhelm the adolescent. In psychoanalytic terms the *id,* a seething caldron of unconscious, instinctual drives for sex and aggression, reaches its peak of strength during adolescence. As a result, each teenager can be considered on the verge of chaos at any moment—or during the entire period. As we noted in Chapter 1, both Freud and G. Stanley Hall considered the storm-and-stress view a major feature of adolescence. Thus there is a major definition problem in denoting and classifying adolescent behavior. Obviously, we can't simply diagnose all teenagers as pathological. Nor can we assume that all adolescent behaviors are just manifestations of normal behavior for that age group.

In this chapter we will present a system for analyzing the problems according to (1) mild to moderate psychological disturbances and (2) serious difficulties. Then we will describe a general problem that almost all adolescents experience at some point in their development, alienation. To be accurate, though, alienation is not actually a type of disturbance but, rather, a response that is almost synonymous with adolescence itself.

Before we present the framework for classifying psychological problems, however, we will discuss the question of incidence, some special characteristics of adolescent disturbance, and sex differences.

INCIDENCE DURING ADOLESCENCE

Part of the difficulty in identifying the amount of disturbance during adolescence, of course, depends on how we define normal and abnormal behaviors. Where do we set the dividing lines or the parameters? If our definition is too broad, then, like Hall, we include all behaviors; if our definition is too narrow, we may omit a significant proportion of abnormal behavior. Furthermore, we can't solve the problem by simply turning to the records of psychiatric clinics and hospitals. While psychology and psychiatry have elaborate procedures for differential diagnosis of children and adults, that system breaks down when applied to adolescents. Clinics employ interviews, observation techniques, and a battery of psychological tests to identify patterns of disturbance common to children or adults; the results of these assessments are the basis for classification and treatment. But when it comes to adolescents, most clinics classify nearly all their teenage patients as having "adolescent adjustment reaction," a catchall. Thus to gain some accuracy about incidence, we must examine quite carefully the records and procedures that studies have employed in order to identify how common psychological disturbance is.

Some useful perspective can be obtained from studies done in western Europe and in this country. For example, Michael Rutter, an English child psychiatrist, conducted a comprehensive study on a small island off the

Alcohol abuse is a continuing
problem for some adolescents
Photograph from Paul S. Conklin

coast of England [1]. With careful screening of over 2000 randomly selected teenagers, he estimated that about 10–15% of the adolescents exhibited genuinely recognizable and significant disturbance. This figure has been consistently reported in other studies from other countries. For instance, an Australian study by Henderson, in which all 2000 inhabitants of a town were interviewed, estimated from 10 to 20% as disturbed [2]. Similarly, Lavik, in a Norwegian study in Oslo, set the incidence at about the same level [3]. And a variety of studies in this country have come to approximately the same estimation, whether based on interviews from longitudinal growth studies, such as the Berkeley and the Fels Institute [4], or from huge survey studies such as the famous Minnesota Stark Hathaway Survey [5]. The Hathaway study used the Minnesota Multiphasic Personality Index (MMPI) with over 11,000 teenagers. Hathaway estimated that between 10 and 20% were disturbed. Thus the conclusion seems quite firm: Less than one-fifth of the teenagers exhibit behavior that can be accurately classified as representing significant psychological disturbance.

These studies indicate, then, that the storm-and-stress hypothesis, which suggests that virtually all teenagers are in acute turmoil, does not hold. We do not mean to conclude, though, that adolescence is stressfree. On the contrary, there *are* difficult problems and stresses that all teenagers face. The overwhelming majority, however, are capable of handling these difficulties, although their own perceptions of these problems may be quite different. As we noted earlier, during the phase of egocentric thought, adolescents may feel that their conflict is gigantic in size and galactic in scope. But more objective study indicates the most of these problems, though real, are not manifestations of major interferences in psychological functioning.

TYPES OF DISORDERS COMMON TO ADOLESCENTS

Are there specific psychological disorders common to adolescence that are also different from those experienced by children or by adults? If adolescence, as we have stressed, is a unique stage of development, then we would expect to find significant differences in the types of psychological problems met in this stage when compared with either the preceding or the following stage. But if this is not the case, then the continuity hypothesis would hold, which suggests that adolescence is simply a continuation of childhood—or, in more elegant language, a recapitulation of the earlier stages of growth.

To answer the continuity versus discontinuity question, we must again refer to a variety of studies from this country and from other industrialized nations. This technique provides a broad picture of adolescence and helps to cross-validate findings from any one particular study. The massive compilation by Michael Rutter is again most helpful as a general information source [6]. The various studies Rutter summarizes indicate that there are three major disorders that increase significantly during adolescence: (1) depression, (2) alcoholism/drug dependency, and (3) anorexia nervosa, or severe dieting and extreme weight loss. Paralleling the increase in these areas is an increase in a fourth area, attempted suicide.

Actual suicide is virtually unknown during childhood, but it dramatically increases during adolescence. However, suicide does not peak during this stage but, rather, continues to increase through adulthood. What is unique to adolescence is that attempts at suicide reach their zenith during this stage. This phenomenon has been called *parasuicide*, an attempt at ending one's life that failed. Thus parasuicide is a major indicator during adolescence of psychological disturbance. Suicide, on the other hand, represents a discontinuity with the previous stage, childhood, but a continuity with the succeeding stages of adulthood.

It may be somewhat comforting to note that actual suicide during adolescence is still relatively rare. A study in England found the rate to be 18 per 100,000; a French study set the rate at 10 per 100,000; and a United States study reported a rate of 7 per 100,000 [7]. In other words, the actual occurrence is quite rare, less than one-tenth of 1%.

Finally, the studies indicate that severe disturbances such as psychosis (schizophrenia) do occur during adolescence, but they are not unique to the stage since the onset of such severe disturbances increases through adulthood. Psychosis during adolescence appears at a rate of approximately one per 1000 teenagers [8].

Thus the psychological disturbances that are greatest during adolescence are depression, chemical dependency, anorexia, and attempted suicide. Other indices that increase during adolescence but continue to an even greater degree during adulthood are actual suicide and psychosis. Also, the adolescent disturbances are much more common during middle adolescence (high school age) and late adolescence (college age) than during early adolescence (junior high) age.

The four common problem areas distinctive of adolescence are themselves not entirely separate entities. Obviously, depression and deep moods of despair are associated with excessive chemical dependency, and certainly, both are associated with attempts at suicide. Also, it may be that anorexia—a condition in which individuals, usually females, literally starve themselves to the point of death—is similarly connected to the emotions of depression and negative self-worth. Thus it is the overall configuration that may be most important for study rather than each area as a separate problem.

By midadolescence, then, there is an increase in the incidence of significant psychological disturbances in four related areas. Table 11.1 lists the

TABLE 11.1 Psychological disturbances during adolescence

Problem area	Incidence
Depression	17 per 1000
Chemical dependency	
Marijuana	100 per 1000
Alcohol	50 per 1000
Other	20 per 1000
Anorexia nervosa (females)	4 per 1000
Attempted suicide (parasuicide)	
Females	6 per 1000
Males	2.5 per 1000

Note: Estimates are combined from numerous studies.

disorders and their approximate base rates. These rates are estimates combined from numerous studies and represent educated guesses. Obviously, in areas as sensitive as psychological disturbance, accuracy in reporting is somewhat problematic. Adolescent suicide and attempts at suicide may be underreported or reported as accidents. Also, not all teenagers respond accurately to questionnaires or interviews concerning their problems.

A comprehensive documentation of chemical dependency is given in Table 11.2. The table, based on surveys taken each year from 1975 to 1981, indicates some important trends. For example, the percent using marijuana on at least a monthly basis peaked with the high school class of 1978 and has declined from 37.1% in that year to 31.6% in 1981. Although the decline in percentage is encouraging, there still are a large number of adolescents using marijuana apparently without much regard for adverse personal and psychological consequences.

Table 11.2 also indicates that the percentage of adolescents using stronger drugs has remained fairly constant over the time period under study, with two exceptions. The first exception is in the use of stimulants, which appears to have increased from 8.5 to 15.8%. The University of Michigan researchers, however, caution that this finding may have been the result of a sharp exaggeration by adolescents who included nonamphetamine look-alike and sound-alike diet and stay-awake pills in their answers. The second exception is the small but fairly constant increase in cocaine use, from 1.9% in 1975 to 5.8% in 1981, certainly an alarming trend. Overall, then, the survey provides a mixture of findings: a decline in marijuana use, a steady rate of use for other drugs in general, and an increase in cocaine use.

Since adolescent use of drugs is a pervasive problem, those who work with adolescents should be aware of the dangers of drug abuse. Drugs do

TABLE 11.2   Trends in drug use over a one-month period

	Percent who used in last thirty days							
Drug Approx. N =	Class of 1975 (9400)	Class of 1976 (15,400)	Class of 1977 (17,100)	Class of 1978 (17,800)	Class of 1979 (15,500)	Class of 1980 (15,900)	Class of 1981 (17,500)	1980–1981 change
Marijuana/hashish	27.1	32.2	35.4	37.1	36.5	33.7	31.6	−2.1s
Inhalants	NA	0.9	1.3	1.5	1.7	1.4	1.5	+0.1
Inhalants adjusted[a]	NA	NA	NA	NA	3.1	2.7	2.3	−0.4
Amyl and butyl nitrites[b]	NA	NA	NA	NA	2.4	1.8	1.4	−0.4
Hallucinogens	4.7	3.4	4.1	3.9	4.0	3.7	3.7	0.0
Hallucinogens adjusted[c]	NA	NA	NA	NA	5.5	4.4	4.4	0.0
LSD	2.3	1.9	2.1	2.1	2.4	2.3	2.5	+0.2
PCP[b]	NA	NA	NA	NA	2.4	1.4	1.4	0.0
Cocaine	1.9	2.0	2.9	3.9	5.7	5.2	5.8	+0.6
Heroin	0.4	0.2	0.3	0.3	0.2	0.2	0.2	0.0
Other opiates[d]	2.1	2.0	2.8	2.1	2.4	2.4	2.1	−0.3
Stimulants[d]	8.5	7.7	8.8	8.7	9.9	12.1	15.8	+3.7sss
Sedatives[d]	5.4	4.5	5.1	4.2	4.4	4.8	4.6	−0.2
Barbiturates[d]	4.7	3.9	4.3	3.2	3.2	2.9	2.6	−0.3
Methaqualone[d]	2.1	1.6	2.3	1.9	2.3	3.3	3.1	−0.2
Tranquilizers[d]	4.1	4.0	4.6	3.4	3.7	3.1	2.7	−0.4
Alcohol	68.2	68.3	71.2	72.1	71.8	72.0	70.7	−1.3
Cigarettes	36.7	38.8	38.4	36.7	34.4	30.5	29.4	−1.1

From L. D. Johnston, J. G. Bachman, and P. M. O'Malley, Student drug use in America 1975–1981 (National Institute on Drug Abuse) U.S. Government Printing Office, 1981. Reprinted by permission.

Note: Level of significance of difference between the two most recent classes: s = 0.05, ss = 0.01, sss = 0.001. NA indicates data not available.

[a] Adjusted for underreporting of amyl and butyl nitrites.

[b] Data based on a single questionnaire form; N is one-fifth of N indicated.

[c] Adjusted for underreporting of PCP.

[d] Only drug use that was not under a doctor's orders is included here.

not really solve people's problems. The relief is temporary; the rush of good feelings declines, and the problems of daily living continue. Furthermore, over the long run drug abuse can lead to serious health problems, possibly even death, as the descriptions in Table 11.3 show. And there is no evidence that drug use provides humans with new insights. Any claims that drug use promotes an increase in creative problem solving or in energizing one's human potential are unsubstantiated.

TABLE 11.3 A primer on drug use and effect

Drug group	Examples	Medical use	Physically additive?	Psycho-logically habit-forming?	Long-term effects of abuse	Additional information
Narcotics: drugs made from opium (an extract from the seeds of poppies). Narcotics depress the central nervous system	Heroin (white powder); usually injected, can be inhaled	None (illegal)	Yes	Yes	Addiction, malnutrition caused by loss of appetite, risk of overdose, hepatitis from dirty needles, withdrawal symptoms—sweats, shakes, nausea, diarrhea, painful stomach and muscle cramps (people following doctors' instructions for use of prescription medicines will not experience these effects)	Heroin reduces hunger, thirst, and sex drives. While at first it brings on a euphoric high, the feeling disappears with increased use. Junkies shoot up not to get happy but simply to avoid the pain of withdrawal. Heroin is sometimes cut (diluted) with quinine, deadly if injected in high amounts. Babies of mothers using narcotics during pregnancy are addicted and go through painful withdrawal. Deadly if mixed with alcohol or barbiturates.
	Codeine (tablet or liquid)	To ease cough and relieve pain (by prescription only)	Yes	Yes		
	Morphine (white powder, liquid, or tablet); swallowed or injected	Pain relief (by prescription only)	Yes	Yes		
	Paregoric (liquid)	To treat diarrhea (by prescription only)	Yes	Yes		
	Demerol (tablet); synthetic (laboratory-made)	Pain relief (by prescription only)	Yes	Yes		
	Methadone (tablet); synthetic	Relief of heroin withdrawal symptoms (by prescription only)	Yes	Yes		
Hallucinogens (also called psychedelics): work on the central nervous system to alter perceptions and information processing	LSD (D-Lysergic Acid Diethylamide)	Experimental research	No	Possibly	Possible damage to chromosomes, distortion of senses, panic reactions; may intensify existing mental disorder, frightening bad trips, possible flashbacks (recurrence of symptoms months or weeks later); accidents caused by drug-induced feelings of invulnerability	Mescaline and psilocybin are milder hallucinogens with similar effects on sense perception. What street dealers say is mescaline or psilocybin can often be LSD.
Inhalants: fumes of various solvents, which are sniffed	Glue, gasoline, paint thinner, hydrocarbons (propellants in products like hair spray)	None	Possibly	Possibly	Possible death by suffocation (victims put plastic bags over their heads to concentrate fumes, then pass out and suffocate); permanent damage to brain, kidney and liver	
	Amyl nitrite	To relieve chest pains	Possibly	Possibly	Possible addiction; nausea, dizziness, and headache; dangerous for people with asthma, hepatitis, or circulatory problems.	
	Isobutyl nitrite (marketed as Rush, Locker Room, Bullet; nicknamed "poppers")	None	Possibly	Possibly		
Stimulants: speed up the central nervous system; create sense of alertness, well-being, and euphoria: increase the heart rate and blood pressure	Cocaine (white powder from leaves of the South American coca plant); inhaled or injected	Formerly local anesthetic; now none	No	Yes	Weight loss, depression, severe damage to nasal passages	You can't always know what you're getting when you buy cocaine on the street. It may be cut with PCP, codeine, or benzocaine (an anesthetic).

TABLE 11.3 (Continued)

Drug group	Examples	Medical use	Physically addictive?	Psychologically habit-forming?	Long-term effects of abuse	Additional information
	Amphetamines [synthetic drugs like methedrine (speed), benzedrine, dexedrine] in tablet, capsule, liquid, or powder form; swallowed or injected	Relief of depression; appetite control	Possibly	Possibly	Exhaustion, severe depression, hallucination, toxic psychosis (mental disorder brought on by drug use)	
	Nicotine (found in tobacco)	None	Possibly	Yes	Lung cancer, heart disease, emphysema, chronic bronchitis	
Marijuana: drugs derived from the hemp plant	Marijuana (leaves of the hemp plant) and hashish (flowers of the hemp plant); smoked or swallowed	To reduce pressure on eye in glaucoma; ease nausea that accompanies chemotherapy treatments for cancer	No	Possibly	Possible lung defects, eye inflammation	Researchers are now studying the effects of marijuana on fertility and unborn babies, on its connection to lung cancer and heart problems, on possible pot-induced damage to the body's immune defense system, and psychological effects of long-term use. "People who consider smoking marijuana should be aware of possible hazards," says Larry Schott, national director of the National Organization for the Reform of Marijuana Laws.
Sedatives or depressants: slow down the central nervous system	Alcohol	None	Yes	Yes	Addiction, brain damage, toxic psychosis, cirrhosis of liver, withdrawal symptoms—tremors, vomiting, sweating, muscle cramps	Deadly if mixed with narcotics, tranquilizers, barbiturates, and anticoagulants used by heart patients. Alcohol doesn't have to be consumed in large quantity to adversely affect a user's physical and emotional health.
	Barbiturates (drugs like Nembutal, Seconal, Amytal, Phenobarbital)	Sedation, control of high blood pressure and epilepsy	Yes	Yes	Addiction, possibility of overdose; irritability; bruises and cigarette burns from accidents while intoxicated; withdrawal symptoms including possible convulsions and hallucinations	Deadly if mixed with alcohol.
	Sedative hypnotics [drugs like Quaaludes (methaqualone)]	To induce sleep	Yes, if abused	Yes	Addiction; liver problems; withdrawal symptoms similar to those for barbiturates	
	Tranquilizers (drugs like Valium, Librium, Miltown, Placidyl)	To reduce anxiety	Yes	Yes	Addiction; withdrawal symptoms similar to those for alcohol and barbiturates	Deadly if mixed with alcohol.
	PCP (phencyclidine), an animal tranquilizer known as Angel Dust (powder)	Illegal for human use	Possibly	Yes	Numbness in arms and legs; can cause violent psychotic episodes; increasing paranoia; overdose can be lethal	Many experts agree that PCP is the most dangerous drug on this list. It is often incorrectly called a hallucinogen.

Toking up—but the effects may not be benign

Photograph from Sacks/Editorial Photocolor Archives

SEX DIFFERENCES AND PSYCHOLOGICAL DISTURBANCES

There are differences between the sexes in areas of disturbance. Females are more likely to have problems of depression and attempted suicide, and they almost exclusively make up the population of anorexia nervosa. Males, on the other hand, are somewhat more likely to abuse alcohol and drugs. There is also a difference in the completed suicide rate: Males exceed females by ratios of from 4:1 to 7:1 in completed suicides, even though, as Table 11.1 indicates, females attempt suicide at least twice as frequently as males.

Although there are a variety of explanations for the observed sex differences in disturbances, which range from genetic influence to social conditioning, we tend to agree with Rutter's analysis. He suggests that the differences are due to the disadvantaged social status women are moving into as they traverse adolescence [9]. We would interpret this observation within the interactive hypothesis of development, as follows.

As we pointed out in the discussions of the work of Erik Erikson and of Robert Selman, the process of forming a personal social identity during adolescence depends on the quality of interaction between the person and the environment. And as females emerge from childhood, a period in which their interactions are largely positive with a broad range of acceptable behaviors, the interactions change. They become aware of their unequal status and their unequal opportunities, created, by and large, by the

SPECIAL TOPIC
The Effects of Marijuana: Keep off the Grass

Adult society has too often sent a mixed message concerning the effects of marijuana use. In the 1960s during the initial increase in use, there was either massive overreaction or indifference. In order to prevent the spread, authorities circulated horror stories through gossip and newspapers. In one particularly unfortunate story, which many newspapers headlined, some teenagers in Pennsylvania allegedly went blind from using drugs. When a suspicious reporter finally checked on the story, he found that a well-intentioned adult had made the whole thing up in order to prevent drug use from spreading. Also, there were unsubstantiated reports of chromosome damage from using marijuana and a whole array of undocumented long-term dangers. The only thing that was true in these stories was the reported lack of research.

This scare tactic provoked an understandable but unfortunate reaction. Some people pointed out that marijuana seemed quite mild, at least in comparison with hard drugs. Cultural relativists turned to history in an attempt to legitimize its use: Many famous historical figures such as Jefferson were noted smoking "hemp," an earlier version of grass. Thus the problem seemed only one of a choice of values. The heavy-handed use of propaganda backfired. Soon adolescents learned to answer the objections with a combination of cynicism and relativism: "Who are you to lecture me about the dangers of grass with your cigarette in one hand and your cocktail in the other? For me, I feel good with grass and don't have a hangover the next day!"

traditional expectations of the adult and largely male-dominated world. Two negative factors are operating here. First, marriage serves as a positive and protective factor for men but not for women. Being a married female ranks lowest of the four categories—married males, single females, single males, married females—in terms of self-fulfillment. Second, being a working female is not as positive as being a working male. Males tend to have higher status, higher pay, and easier working conditions than females. Thus the situation of facing a future in which females will have less opportunity to develop as persons in their own right—the subservient role in marriage and/or in employment—creates interactive conditions encouraging depression for females.

Martin Seligman has suggested that such negative interaction during the process of identity formation leads to a further component of depression, namely, *learned helplessness* [10]. Learned helplessness represents a

Fortunately, research has now cleared away much of the ambiguity surrounding marijuana. For instance, the active ingredient has been isolated, THC (tetrahydrocannabinol). The amount of THC varies according to where the grass was grown and the strain cultivated. Thus it is, or was, possible to smoke grass that had only small amounts of THC and hence suffer few effects. In fact, a study done in the late 1930s under the direction of New York's Mayor La Guardia concluded that there seemed to be no lasting harmful effects.*

Recent research, however, comes to quite different conclusions. With the active ingredient now identified (and with growers deliberately increasing the amount of it through their procedures), the results of marijuana use are clearer. The following trends have been noted and replicated: In males there is a reduction in the testosterone levels, which may (1) delay the onset of puberty and/or (2) reduce the sperm count. In females (in this case rhesus monkeys) there are notable effects on pregnancy, such as abortion, stillbirth, and low birth weight. In both sexes there are adverse effects on the respiratory system, effects more toxic than those of tobacco and including (in studies of mice) stimulating the growth of tumors and lesions in the lungs. There are, in addition, negative consequences to the immunizing system and the central nervous system and some possibility of negative effects on DNA synthesis (the so-called building blocks of life). Apparently, because THC is soluble only in fatty tissue rather than in water (as is the case for alcohol), the active ingredient remains in the body for extended time periods; its half-life is from five to seven days. THC collects in areas such as the brain, adrenal glands, ovaries, and testes [1].

(Continued)

pattern of giving up on self-direction, autonomy, and independence. Such a syndrome is common to minority groups in this country who have been systematically shortchanged by the majority group culture in terms of education, jobs, and social status. And it is possible that adolescent women—a huge population of one-half of all teenagers—are in a position similar to that of minority persons.

For example, in the past, women have often been denied access to equal education and employment opportunities. In addition, women have been taught by the culture to accept less significant roles. These lowered expectations and aspirations then became incorporated into the belief sys-

* This view was quite common in psychiatric circles as recently as the early 1960s. One author's training supervisor strongly maintained that grass itself had no effect; it was all simply a social invention.

SPECIAL TOPIC (Continued)

Naturally, such evidence by itself does not solve the problem of use and abuse. For adults in the educational and helping professions, for parents, and for concerned teenagers, however, the information about marijuana is no longer so controversial. As a result, there is a much firmer basis for educational programs. Information, by itself, though, will not deter teenagers—nor anyone else—from self-defeating behavior. Pressure from friends, curiosity, the attractiveness of forbidden fruit, the belief in individual autonomy ("It's my body!"), all are powerful motives for drug use. So, too, are accumulations of negative experiences in school and at home. In our view it is the extent of alienation among adolescents that probably accounts for continued drug use with substances like grass. Thus programs designed to rechannel adolescent behavior away from drugs need components of imagination and innovation in order to be successful and to promote development. Stimulating healthy development is the first line of defense against drug abuse.

REFERENCE

1. This synthesis of recent research findings is derived from Robert Margolis and Nancy Popkin, Marijuana: A review of medical research with implications for adolescents, *Personnel Guidance Journal* 59, 1(1980):7–14.

---

tems of the women themselves, a version of the self-fulfilling prophecy. Matina Horner's research (see Chapter 13) has defined this syndrome as a fear of success. In other words, women can become afraid to achieve in accordance with their potential and learn helplessness instead. The pattern, then, may be similar both for minority groups and for female adolescents, with depression the result.

RESPONSE PATTERNS BY ADOLESCENTS: PSYCHOLOGICAL DEFENSES

Anna Freud, after many years of clinical experience with adolescents, created a highly useful framework that classifies the systems of psychological defenses most common to this stage [11]. A *psychological defense* is a method of responding to the demands of the environment in a manner that protects the individual. The problem is that the protective system distorts reality. In other words, the person's response is not true to reality and therefore is not based on an accurate reading of the environment. How much reality becomes distorted depends on how many defenses a person employs and how often.

As Freud points out, all humans use psychological defenses to cope with the demands of reality. The important question is the choice of defense and how often one employs it. According to classical psychoanalytic theory, a person's choice of defense is determined by the particular neurosis. For adolescents, however, that is not the case. During adolescence, as opposed to adulthood, an individual's defense cannot be accurately classified in specific adult neurotic patterns. Thus defenses in the traditional sense are not crystallized. A teenager may use any one of a number of systems in order to accommodate to reality.

We note here that use of a psychological defense does not mean that a person is seriously disturbed. But if an individual uses a wide variety of defenses or uses only a few defenses but uses them much of the time, then that person is most likely experiencing substantial psychological difficulty. For example, if a teenager has had a particularly dominating, authoritarian father and has never been able to express and work through the feelings of resentment and hostility, then the teenager may occasionally flare up at other authority figures. This response would be an intermittent and not neurotic use of a defense. If the teenager reacted with hostility and aggression to all authority figures, however, then the response would constitute a definite sign of maladjustment. Thus the key to disturbance is how much reality is distorted and how often. Defenses are a bit like reflexes in that the person employs a defense without much planning or reflection, and defenses are not, by themselves, indicators of psychological disturbance.

Anna Freud listed the most common defense systems in a rough approximation of their use. In this section we follow Freud's order in discussing the defense systems.

Displacement

In displacement a person transfers feelings and needs from one situation or person to another object. For example, teenagers may begin to feel attached to their parents, especially the parent of the opposite sex, and defend against this attachment by becoming overly attached to other adults. Teenage crushes on movie stars, rock singers, and attractive school teachers are common examples. Displacement also is often accompanied by substantial acting up and heightened emotional expressiveness.

Displacement is the most common defense system used during adolescence, especially at the junior high school level. Its signs are not hard to miss since the emotions are usually overdone. In displacement teenage girls are attracted to a sympathetic adult male (a teacher, counselor, youth worker), and teenage boys are attracted to an understanding adult female. It requires great tact by the adult to avoid either extreme of playing into the fantasy or ridiculing the teenager. Playing into the fantasy is inappropriate since pupils at this age perceive sexual connotations in practically everything in the world anyway. If the adult becomes coy and seductive in response to an adolescent crush, then the adult simply exacerbates the teenager's problems. The teenager's nonverbal signs will be readily apparent: amorous looks, excessive volunteering of help, and putting down immature classmates. But ridicule of these first stirrings of feelings of closeness and attraction, is also inappropriate, since the pupil may be genuinely shamed. And probably the least appropriate response by an adult is silence, because ambiguity actually increases projection and fantasy thinking on the part of a teenager.

Thus the way adults respond to the displacement defense is a crucial element. Adults need to help the adolescent understand that it may be quite normal and natural to have strong feelings of liking for a person just a bit older. These feelings mean that the teenager is in the process of growing up. At the same time, however, adults need to help the teenager realize that it would be quite inappropriate for the adult to play favorites and that eventually the teenager will find someone closer in age. These are very sensitive moments for adolescents as they develop their initial impulses for tenderness and caring.

Of course, displacement can work with feelings of anger and hostility as well as with those of tenderness. There may be instances where well-intentioned adults suddenly find themselves on the receiving end of bitterness and negativity. Teenagers may have very negative feelings toward one or both parents or someone very close to them. And they may transfer these feelings to other adults (teacher, counselor, youth leader).

How do you as a youth worker handle that situation? First, you should review the overall interactions: how the teenager has reacted in the past and how you have tended to react. If the current hostility is clearly not in the usual pattern and if your own honest appraisal of your behavior indicates that you are not provoking the situation, then you can be pretty sure that some kind of displacement is going on. In response, you should understand that the teenager is upset, and you should try to find a way for both of you to get along. Probably the least helpful response is a response in kind, making a test of strength out of the confrontation. Unfortunately, all too often such displacement is handled in just that way: Anger is met with anger, hostility with hostility. In that situation both you and the teenager lose.

What happens in the home itself? We have outlined how teenagers' feelings toward parents may be displaced to other adults, but what does this displacement mean to the parents themselves? Generally within the home the adolescent's feelings are only partially displaced, in the sense of being divided. Especially during early and middle adolescence the positive emotions are usually attached to the opposite-sex parent and the negative emotions to the same-sex parent. The situation is analogous to sibling rivalry during childhood, when children in the same family compete with each other. During adolescence the same-sex dyad of teenager and parent becomes the arena for negative, hostile, and aggressive competition, almost as if they were sibling rivals. Thus the father-son or the mother-daughter dyads are usually the scenes of the most bitterness, at least in families where emotions are permitted expression. In families where they are not, the feelings remain intense but hidden. In either case the feelings tend to be displaced through division, positive toward opposite sex and negative toward same sex.

Unfortunately, parents may be as unaware as the teenager of this set and interact in ways that make it worse. One parent tends to receive all the negative reaction and responds in kind, both verbally and physically. The other parent receives all the positive reaction and bends over backward in being accepting and understanding. Interactions become reduced to the simple and the concrete, the good and the bad, with one parent overvalued and the other undervalued. However, it would be far easier on all parties if parents were more aware of displacement and division of affects during adolescence. Rather than play into the defense, the parents should accept it as part of the identity formation process and work together as a team in responding to it. As in the case of handling displacement by itself, great tact and diplomacy are required. Parents need to affirm the teenager's developing adulthood. At the same time they need to provide a coordinated and steady response—no easy task, to be sure, yet a critical one since these conflicts are so common, indeed, almost endemic, to parent-teenager relationships.

To summarize, then, displacement is by far the most common defense system used during adolescence. In most cases it is not a sign of deep psychological disturbance but, rather, of an attempt to deal with legitimate but strong emotions, especially love, on the one hand, and hostility, on the other. An adult, such as a teacher, counselor, or youth worker, may recognize the pattern by a change in relationship that is out of proportion with reality. Parents may recognize the pattern by noting increased conflicts between the teenager and the same-sex parent, with all the positive responses directed toward the opposite-sex parent. In all cases it will require maturity and tact on the adults' part to not escalate the difficulties but, rather, to recognize and work through the interaction. In the long run, and with steadiness, these difficulties can be worked out. In fact, we often hear parents and their college or postcollege-age children reviewing these past conflicts with new found objectivity and mutual compassion.

Reversal of Affect   In reversal of affect needs and feelings are turned inside out. It occurs when teenagers suddenly change the manifestation of feelings from one extreme to the other. Thus instead of showing anger, the teenager may display an exaggerated coolness. The desire for closeness may be demonstrated by withdrawal, alienation, and hiding in one's room. Feelings of curiosity and needs for excitement may become inverted and appear as expressions of boredom.

The defense of reversal is also quite common to all adolescents. If displacement comes about because of the teenager's increased feelings of love and hostility, then reversal may be thought of as a result of the newly emergent personal identity. Consider that the prior stage during elementary school comes to a close with a reasonably firm identity as a female or as a male child. Parent and school expectations are clear. Ambiguity is low, and roles are differentiated. In this stage almost everybody—adults, boys, and girls—is on solid ground. As a result, all participants in the interactions can freely express themselves. If upper-age elementary school children are happy, delighted, and ecstatic at school, home, or in the neighborhood, they will express it directly. As we noted in both Chapters 2 and 5, they are in a position of psychological integration and are not terribly concerned over who they are or where they fit. But as we have seen, all this changes with the onset of puberty. The new modes of thought and the increasing importance of interpersonal relations during adolescence mean that childhood integration must give way. Teenagers find the resultant egocentrism a barrier to direct expression. Thus feelings tend to become inverted.

Teenagers become easily embarrassed by adults, especially parents. They may be highly animated and expressive with each other, especially in groups, yet in the presence of adults they are withdrawn. The withdrawal sometimes appears to be a kind of aloofness. It is as if they were not yet integrated enough as persons to express themselves without excessive self-censoring. Almost anything can become a cause for embarrassment. A family name that is different, the parents' appearance, the house, the car, the furniture, the job—literally anything about the parents that does not fit some mythical, middle-class image of the all-American home. Parents who themselves immigrated to this country are often stung by their junior high school teenager who renounces all interest in family heritage or anything to do with the old country. Family vacations are similarly devalued. It is simply unacceptable to have an enjoyable time with one's parents. Thus feelings are reversed. Misery more often than joy is the message sent.

Probably the best response to this defense is to wait it out. Endless debating over, say, the authenticity of a parent's particular life-style and values will probably not solve anything. The differences are symptoms of an underlying disagreement. Yet we do not mean that adults should passively retreat. In fact, it is important that adults make clear that they do not agree with the teenager's views and explain their reasons. But adults should not expect to win any such debate.

In school the reversal of affect and embarrassment also have trouble-some components for adults. This defense is related directly to the inability to tolerate differences in classmates. As we have seen, peer pressure and social conformity peak during early and middle adolescence. Thus prejudice and stereotyped thinking are also greatest during this time. Taste-less ethnic jokes, negative rumors about racial ancestry, and, even more disconcerting, direct expressions and behaviors steeped in prejudice are common.

Such prejudicial thinking is a form of egocentrism. The teenager emotionally desires to be like the leading crowd of the school, as both the Coleman and Goodlad studies have shown (Chapter 13), with the emphasis on good looks, clothes, athletics, and dates. Anything different is to be shunned and avoided. A study by social psychologist Cody Wilson some years ago found that the range of prejudicial thinking by teenagers was the greatest in the age grouping 15–16 years [12]. During that period the amount of variance, or spread, in ethnic prejudice was far greater than at 13–14 or 17–18 years. In other words, ninth and tenth graders were more open to prejudice than either younger or older adolescents. In this study the prejudice found was toward Jews and blacks. Although research has yet to be done, there is every reason to infer that this result would also hold for sexism by males and antifeminism by females. Accepting individual differences and tolerating teenagers from other social classes and ethnic or racial backgrounds reaches its low point during the transition from early to middle adolescence. Thus the bravado and coolness are symptoms of an intense egocentrism and a need to be like everyone else.

Such a defense presents schools with major difficulties, especially in social studies and English classes where curriculum materials in other cultures directly confront prejudice. Since social role taking in the Selman sense is low at this point, it is hard to believe that such material has its intended positive impact. It would appear that a slow-paced introduction to contributions from other cultures and to the advantages of individual differences in our country is necessary.

It is clear that adults cannot affect the reversal defense overnight. Instead, a long, slow, and painful process of gradually helping teenagers move beyond excessive social conformity is needed in order to promote genuine growth. With growth the ability to accept differences develops. As toleration develops, teenagers are often shocked at their own earlier actions, the cruelty and the meanness of their own group toward outsiders, a theme so vividly depicted in the first part of the movie *Carrie*. Adults, then, should provide extra support and encouragement to teenagers who are the objects of prejudice while simultaneously working gradually to reduce such immature thinking in those adolescents who display it.

SPECIAL TOPIC
Diagnosing Adolescents: Never Mind the Psychologists; Is It Good for the Children?

In this chapter, as far as possible, we avoid using traditional categories of psychological disturbance. Instead, we attempt to discuss common problems of adolescence by giving descriptions of how teenagers respond, descriptions largely taken from the work of Anna Freud. Why have we chosen this course? After all, the American Psychiatric Association recently published a complete listing (taxonomy) of mental disorders in its *Diagnostic and Statistical Manual (DSM) III*. Why not simply use the APA categories of mental illness as a basis for diagnosing adolescent disturbance? Well, it is not quite that simple—in fact, just the opposite. The category system is so broad in scope that virtually all aspects of adolescent behavior that deviates in any way from the normative can be labeled as mental disease.

Norman Garmezy, a clinical psychologist whose major work has focused on childhood emotional problems, recently provided a comprehensive critique of DSMIII. He feels that psychiatry made a fatal and overreaching error in labeling as disorders those deficits and disabilities during childhood and adolescence that "are *not* mental disorders." He cites one listing of such diseases as an example of his concern:

> . . . *Specific Reading Disorder* (i.e., Specific Reading [Mental] Disorder), *Specific Arithmetical Disorder, Developmental Language Disorder, Developmental Articulation Disorder, Enuresis, Attention Deficit Disorders, Separation Anxiety Disorder, Shyness Disorder*(!!), *Overanxious Disorder, Introverted Disorder of Childhood, Oppositional Disorder, Academic Underachievement Disorder, Emancipation Disorder of Adolescence or Early Adult Life, Identity Disorder, Specific Academic or Work Inhibition.* If you place the word "mental" before the word "disorder" in each of the "conditions" above you will rapidly understand. . . . [1]

What DSMIII does, then, is take a rather common difficulty in adolescence—academic underachievement, for example—and transform the problem into a form of mental illness. And then following diagnosis comes a treatment recommendation—referral to a medically trained psychiatrist. When we realize that academic underachievement for high school males is extremely common (estimates have run as high as 30 to 40%), then we see that DSMIII has turned a common phenomenon of adolescence into a psychiatrically defined illness, complete with label, code number, and treatment recommendation. The same situation holds in many other areas designated as mental illness. For example, shyness is also labeled as an illness. As Garmezy points

Garmezy (1918–)

out, according to the criteria, literally millions of shy children will be labeled as disturbed, when, in fact, their difficulties are well within broad normal parameters [2].

Indeed, the proliferation of labels is the most disturbing aspect of psychological diagnosis. Garmezy found that the original manual published in 1952 contained 60 disorders. That number has now grown to 230, even though there has been no major increase in the knowledge base for mental illness in the intervening years. In short, he suggests that the psychiatric establishment has created a self-serving classification system without realizing the negative effects on the general population of children and adolescents. Thus he advocates use of a *No Mental Disorder* category until there is firm scientific evidence of the existence of a disease state [3].

Especially during adolescence, when so much change is occurring, invalid labeling may have extremely negative consequences. And a conservative approach to diagnosis is always the rule during times of rapid change and growth. Such an approach "would help a large portion of our young citizenry who should not carry the burdens of mental disorders they do not have" [4].

REFERENCES

1. N. Garmezy, DSMIII Never mind the psychologists: Is it good for the children? *American Psychologist* (forthcoming).

2. *Ibid.*

3. *Ibid.*

4. *Ibid.*

Uncompromising

Individuals who are uncompromising rigidly adhere to a narrow, prescriptive ideology. This defense is, by definition, an attempt to avoid accepting the complexities of life, the shades of grey, including compromise and cooperation. All issues become dichotomized into right and wrong, and dogmatic positions abound.

The uncompromising defense is related to reversal of affect, but it is of increasing seriousness. More of reality becomes distorted with this defense. Teenagers become increasingly positive that their own views are correct. Tolerance for other views is practically absent. The adoption of neonazism is probably the best example of this defense. A small neonazi group, complete with secret meetings, cross burnings, and swastikas painted on lockers, can suddenly emerge in almost any high school in the country. Fortunately, the attraction of such extremist philosophies is not widespread during adolescence. However, it is still cause for concern. For those who are attracted to such antidemocratic views, the adoption of uncompromising zealotry can have serious consequences. The amount of reality distorted can increase to dangerous proportions. The tragedy in Jonestown, Guiana, was an extreme case, to be sure, but it does indicate the power and attraction of an uncompromising leader skillfully employing a kind of charismatic pseudoreligion. Choice was removed; no compromise was possible. And 800 adults, adolescents, and children mindlessly obeyed.

For the teenager steeped in the uncompromising defense, professional treatment is probably the wisest choice. However, any sign of an inability to compromise is not necessarily grounds for referral. At times all adolescents will use the uncompromising attitude as a defense. That is a normal expectation. But if the defense is so overused that the teenager begins to distort large portions of reality on a consistent basis, then a need for professional help is indicated.

Regression

In regression individuals wish to return to an earlier stage. This defense is quite simply an attempt to remain a child and to avoid growing up. Boys and girls, especially at the onset of obvious signs of puberty, may attempt to deny the changes and to dress and play as if they were still in elementary school.

The use of regression can be temporary or extended. In the latter case professional referral is almost always indicated.

The most extreme sign of the regression defense is anorexia nervosa. We noted in an earlier section that there was a major increase in this problem during adolescence, especially for females. Anorexia involves an extended starvation diet; there is noticeable major weight loss. And just the appearance of food is enough to make the individuals sick. They have reached the point where they cannot stand the thought of food, and none of the usual inducements will work. As in other defenses, the crucial element is duration of the defense. It is obviously not uncommon for teenage girls (especially) to go on crash diets in the desire to become thin. In fact, a major problem in adolescent health is the teenager's belief that smoking reduces food craving and enhances one's figure. But anorexia is a much more extreme reaction.

Anorexia is usually associated with perfectionism in the home. A researcher in this area, Hilda Bruch, has found that the parents of adolescents suffering from anorexia are unusually demanding; hence academic overachievement is a common symptom [13]. The teenager is excessively worried about school performance and constantly strives for achievement at all costs. There is little balance in life-style and a constant need to please parents. Fortunately, treatment programs are relatively successful. Community mental health facilities usually employ some combination of individual work with the teenager and some work with the family. They help the parents reduce their demands to a more manageable level and attempt to increase the teenager's ability for self-direction. Without effective treatment anorexia can become severe enough to cause death. In fact, Bruch estimates that without treatment, as many as 10% of anorexic teenagers do starve themselves to death.

A somewhat milder form of regression during adolescence is the school phobia syndrome. This difficulty occurs at two developmental points: at the onset of formal schooling in kindergarten and again during adolescence. Both are examples of a desire to halt the process of growth. The fear of growing up, of accepting new challenges, and of going through the discomfort that always accompanies a transition is expressed through a fear of the school itself. Thus school phobia may have nothing to do with school. The teenager simply fears growing up, and that fear is transferred to the school as the object. The school becomes too big, too far away, and too impersonal, with unkind teachers and mean teenage gangs.

Once again, it is important to distinguish between reality and a defense. There may be real fears common to adolescents such as gangs that intimidate and extort money. Also, the school phobic is different from the truant, who usually finds school a distasteful reality of poor grades, much detention, and even hidden messages to drop out. The fears of the school phobic, in contrast, are clearly out of proportion with reality.

The school phobic shows substantial dependency at home. The phobic essentially wants to remain there, because it is safe. And treatment investigation usually reveals that the dependency involves teenager and parents [14]. One or both parents usually wish to keep the teenager dependent. Thus the striving for independence, so common at this stage, is frustrated by adults. Rather than help the teenager overcome the normal fears that accompany moving into a new stage, the parents escalate those fears.

As in the case of anorexia, school phobia is amenable to treatment and usually requires a combined approach, working with the teenager and the parents. Both need help in separating their own dependency needs and in stimulating growth toward self-direction.

Asceticism

In asceticism individuals deny pleasure. Some adolescents attempt to deny the development of pleasurable feelings by becoming ascetic. The increase in the depth and the range of emotions is checked (metaphorically, at least) by rejecting food, sleep, and normal comforts. Shaving the head and dressing in monastic robes are other manifestations.

Asceticism is a defense that, when carried out consistently, distorts significant sections of reality. The person is increasingly out of touch with normal interactions. Thus benign or even innocuous behavior by adults can be easily misconstrued. The reasoning process of the ascetic is nearly impervious to logic or objective reality. So it is extremely difficult for anyone, even the most skillfully trained professional, to deal effectively with a teenager entrenched in this defense. Almost anything a person says or does will be misconstrued. The ascetic is like someone who has been brainwashed. The belief system is almost totally closed.

This defense in adolescents tends to provoke an extremist response from adults, such as the use of deprogrammers. For example, ascetic teenagers will join a cult, give away all their possessions to the leader, shave their heads, learn to chant, often experiment with strange drugs, and beg at airports. They will also renounce any further family connection (e.g., "My name is now East Wind. I serve my master. I am no longer Joan Anderson. That person is now dead."). Parents, in their grief, can easily turn to an equally uncompromising solution. They hire a deprogrammer, who literally kidnaps the teenager and takes the person away to an isolated location. Then the deprogrammer directly confronts the teenager through long hours of counterbrainwashing in order to free the person from the power of the cult. This technique is obviously highly controversial ethically and has problematic outcomes.

The most important response by adults, as difficult as it may seem, is to maintain some kind of contact. The door must be left open so that when the teenager does begin to question the extremism of ascetism, there will be someplace to return to. A professional intermediary such as a counselor, psychologist, or psychiatrist can often be most helpful at this point to both parents and teenager. The professional can arrange for a return and even negotiate solutions to issues that might otherwise ignite new conflict. These times can be, without question, among the most difficult times in both a teenager's and an adult's life. The biblical story concerning the return of the prodigal son perhaps reminds us that such issues are not new.

Withdrawal

In withdrawal individuals hide psychologically. This defense is a more extreme defense than the others in the sense that teenagers begin to more actively separate themselves from both adults and peers. There is a greater use of fantasies.

The extreme use of withdrawal is usually an indicator of what is called borderline psychosis or of actual psychosis. In using the term *psychosis*, we are following Rutter's view [15]. Adolescent psychosis, or preschizophrenia, represents a pattern of extreme disturbance. Actual schizophrenia generally does not fully emerge until adulthood, although the differences between the symptoms of preschizophrenia during adolescence and of adult schizophrenia may be quite small. In these conditions individuals maintain little contact with reality. Magical voices can direct them to engage in genuinely psychotic acts, such as unpremeditated murder, arson, gross sexual abuse, or dismemberment. Individuals in these states are subject to "ideas of reference," a psychiatric term indicating that the individuals can no longer rationally process events or understand consequences. Thus such individuals will actually believe, for example, that the world is full of people whose only mission in life is to poison them. Psychotic behavior is clearly out of control.

Diagnosing psychosis during adolescence, however, is a difficult task. It requires careful examination by expert psychologists and psychiatrists. Diagnosis is difficult partly because of the nature of adolescence and partly because of the incomplete scientific knowledge base. We will discuss each of these factors in turn.

It is much more difficult to accurately assess psychosis during adolescence than during adulthood or childhood. There are so many physical, physiological, and psychological changes occurring simultaneously in adolescence that an untrained person can easily mistake some developmentally normal though upsetting behavior as an indication of extreme pathology. It is especially difficult to diagnose borderline psychoses, since the individuals literally move back and forth between fantasy and reality. Thus it is most important to check out extreme psychoticlike behavior with experts in that field. Lay persons, or even professionals who are not experienced in dealing with pathology, should restrict themselves to identifying or noting bizarre behavior. That is, a teenager who continuously presents genuinely bizarre ideas, is seriously withdrawn, and seems to live totally within the self is presenting symptoms usually associated with schizophrenia. Identifying such symptoms would be the first step in the referral process for expert diagnosis.

The second difficulty in diagnosing psychosis is that the scientific knowledge base is not yet complete. Psychosis itself at any stage has been a puzzlement because it seems to result from a peculiar combination of heredity and environment. As opposed to the milder, neurotic psychological problems, psychosis has a substantial, though not clearly understood, inherited component. Studies of identical twins indicate that if one twin is psychotic, the chances are 50%, or 1 out of 2, that the other twin will also be extremely disturbed. The proportion for fraternal twins is only 12% [16]. Further, studies of children born to schizophrenic parents indicate that the genetic causation is strong. Such children, even those reared in adopted normal homes, were far more likely to become schizophrenic during adulthood than other adopted children. Norman Garmezy, an expert in the field, notes that there is a strong tendency for such children to inherit a vulnerability to psychosis [17]—which, however, does not mean that psychosis is entirely due to heredity. Fortunately, there are children who may inherit the predisposition yet do not develop the disturbance.

In addition to the genetic component of psychosis, there is an environmental component—how the person is reared—that contributes either to exaggerating the vulnerable personality characteristics or to enhancing healthy development. Thus in addition to examining heritability, the diagnosis expert must also review the quality of the home and community environment. If one or both of the teenager's parents have histories of psychosis, that teenager would be much more vulnerable. A moderately unhealthy environment (and, of course, an extremely unhealthy one) would increase the likelihood of psychosis. And even in a healthy environment there is still some possibility that the person might develop schizophrenia, but the probability is much less.

Prognosis   Unfortunately, the prognosis for adolescent psychosis—or, as it is sometimes called, preschizophrenia—is not particularly good—that is, the chances for recovery are modest. In general areas of psychological disturbance, such as cases of mild upset, problems like depression, drug use, school phobia, and anorexia, and other areas involving mild to moderate defense mechanisms, the prognoses are relatively positive. With good treatment and positive interactions with parents, teachers, and adults in general, adolescents can recover, outgrow their difficulties, and become adequately functioning adults. For psychosis, in contrast, similar to what we have seen for genuine delinquency, the recovery rates leave much to be desired. For such teenagers who are hospitalized (which means that the data base is incomplete since some psychotic adolescents are not hospitalized), the recovery rate is only 25%. The second 25% will recover marginally, and the remaining one-half will show little or no change. Thus adolescent psychosis or preschizophrenia is rare, with estimates of less than one per 1000, but the prognosis is poor. Only one-fourth of those hospitalized recover sufficiently to pursue relatively normal adult lives [18]. This is the current picture.

The hope for new techniques   There is always hope that with new techniques, including chemotherapy, the recovery rate can be improved. Also, with increased awareness of the role of environmental stress, there is hope that new approaches to family treatment may be developed that will increase positive outcomes. The problem is unusually complex: how to make up for or control for the genetic defect that leaves a person unusually vulnerable to the stresses of daily living, on the one hand, and how to improve the quality of the environment to reduce the overall incidence, on the other. Research continues on both fronts, and the near future may see some improvement in the recovery rates.

Summary of Defenses

Anna Freud provided a comprehensive description of the psychological defenses common to adolescents. The first two defenses, displacement and reversal, are employed to a greater or lesser degree by virtually all teenagers. Consequently, we have outlined preferred methods for adult response that will serve to de-escalate their use. Such defenses will not disappear. Yet adults do not need to become enmeshed in the defenses to the point of overreacting themselves.

The uncompromising, asceticism, and regression defenses are more serious than displacement and reversal since with their use greater sectors of reality become distorted. Procedures to help adults tolerate such defenses and professional help for both parents and teenagers are two important components in treatment.

Finally, we have noted the difficulties of differential diagnosis in the case of the extreme defense of psychotic withdrawal as well as the poor prognosis. At the moment the treatment of both borderline psychosis and adolescent schizophrenia is, unfortunately, largely a holding action. New techniques and new theory are both needed to improve the treatment and the recovery rates.

TREATMENT TECHNIQUES

The range and the availability of treatment techniques have gradually increased in the past twenty years to the point where psychological help is now within the reach of most teenagers and their parents. Thankfully, the picture *has* changed. Not so many years ago there were few techniques available, and many people felt that psychologists and psychiatrists did not really choose to provide help. In fact, traditional modes of treatment were almost sure to increase defensiveness on the part of adolescents. Their growing spirit and need for independence was in direct confrontation with traditional methods that sought to make the patient dependent, using transference as a means to work through the authority figure problems.

With children, in play therapy, and with adults, through free association, the therapist as a blank screen could become the target for psychological projection. For teenagers, on the other hand, the ambiguity of such a therapeutic role was often confusing and contradictory. The result was high resistance and high dropout rates.

More recently, however, the range of techniques permits much more therapeutic activity by the professional helper [19]. School counselors, social workers, and psychologists, together with community-based psychologists and psychiatrists, can provide a variety of helping procedures. There are short- and long-term counseling on an individual and a group basis, community halfway houses, teenage clinics, special topic groups such as alateen (teenagers with alcoholic parents), and a variety of groups focused on chemical dependency. There are also some highly active outdoor methods such as Outward Bound that are designed to provide an experiential education (e.g., a 24-hour, sole-survivor experience).

It is clear that no single technique is the treatment of choice for all teenagers. However, it is also clear that the skill of the professional providing treatment is most important. Whether the helper is a counselor, social worker, psychologist, or psychiatrist, the major ingredient in effective treatment is the helper's own professional experience in dealing with teenagers. Helpers who may be extremely good with children or adults are not necessarily effective with adolescents. It takes a blend of flexibility, the ability to set limits, and the ability to send messages of unconditional and positive regard to reach adolescents. To find such individuals, one should check with people in the community for names of helpers who have good therapeutic reputations with teenagers. Local medical doctors, clergy, school teachers, and community leaders are sources for information. If the community has its own mental health center, it is another place to check for specialists in working with adolescents.

Of course, knowledge of mental health resources is only a first step in treatment. Thus in this section we will discuss common signs indicating a need for referral and some techniques to help a teenager accept a referral.

Signs Indicating a Need for Referral

Common signs indicating the need for help are usually any noticeable changes for the worse in behavior. In most cases one would look for some noticeable pattern of change over time. The only exception to this guide is a suicide attempt. An immediate referral is always indicated in that case. Any talk of suicide, notes about it, or even comments made in passing should always be taken seriously. Other, somewhat obvious indicators of psychological trouble are excessive drug use, alcohol abuse, running away, out-of-control tantrums, and similar types of acting out.

As is the case with children, it is much easier to spot the aggressive, overt, and acting-out behavior of adolescents. But remember that quiet, shy, and withdrawn behavior may also be a definite indicator of a need for help. In the novel *The Bell Jar,* by the late Sylvia Plath, the author gives a vivid description of her plight during college, which led to a suicide attempt. The signs were subtle and the plea for help muted. Nevertheless, her message was clear: "Somebody, help me, please!"

Methods of Referral

Suppose an adolescent is giving signs of needing professional help, and it seems that a referral is in order. How do you go about it? You may feel very uncomfortable about the prospect of confronting a teenager with his or her psychological problems. That is a common reaction; almost any adult experiences discomfort concerning referral. But it is neither necessary nor appropriate to directly confront an adolescent. Instead, it is much more appropriate to offer your own help without specifically labeling the problem or even having the teenager admit to a problem. Thus the approach is not to confront the person but, rather, to offer assistance. Let's say you are a teacher and you notice that one of your star pupils has been increasingly quiet, withdrawn, and sad for the past three months. You might say, "I don't know how it is with you, but some people your age have many feelings of being down all the time. There are some professionals I know who can help in situations like that. I could give you a name and call for an appointment."

The objective is to assist the teenager in seeking help without offering your own diagnosis or label as mentally disturbed. That is not your job. Your role is to make it possible for the individual to feel comfortable about seeking help. And there is almost always some resistance to such a pros-

Group treatment techniques often attempt to reestablish a sense of relatedness
Photograph from O'Neill/Editorial Photocolor Archives

SPECIAL TOPIC
Treatment for Shizophrenia: *The Bell Jar* and *I Never Promised You a Rose Garden*

Sylvia Plath, the author of *The Bell Jar*, and Hannah Green (pen name of Joanne Greenberg), the author of *I Never Promised You a Rose Garden*, were similar in many striking ways. Their adolescence was extraordinarily painful. Their academic brilliance was matched by periods of deep depression and, most of all, by a desire to withdraw almost totally from encounters with reality.

Plath's psychological scars are dramatically exposed in her autobiography, *Bell Jar*, complete with a chilling description of her unsuccessful attempt at suicide while a twenty-year-old college student. Her subsequent recovery provides a picture of marginal functioning [1]. The specter of death and a preoccupation with morbidity unmistakably dominate her final work, a cluster of poems entitled *Ariel*, written just before she committed suicide at the age of 31 [2].

Hannah Green, in contrast, gives us a glimpse of hope in her novel *Rose Garden*, in which she describes her slow climb out of the depths of psychological disturbance with the help of an enormously gifted therapist [3]. The point should not be missed: Treatment can work even with severely disturbed and withdrawn adolescents. Green was fortunate. She received intensive treatment (in the novel) from a Dr. Fried, who in reality was Dr. Frieda Fromm-Reichmann, one of the giants of psychotherapy. Her work *Principles of Intensive Psychotherapy* was long considered the authoritative handbook for

pect; any one of us might respond, "You mean you think I need a shrink?" So the idea is to make the referral as palatable as possible. Thus to the question, "Do you think I'm crazy?" You might answer, "It isn't a question of being crazy or not. All humans have problems at one time or another. When a person is going through a time when things just don't seem to be going well, there are a lot of feelings of being depressed. Then it usually makes sense to talk with someone who is trained to help." Or "I know you may be feeling uncomfortable, but there are professionals trained specifically to help people your age. It is not a question of being crazy. But there are times when we all may need someone to talk things over with." Or "You know, adolescence is a time when an awful lot of changes are taking place. It helps to talk these things through. Sometimes you may need a professional to help you for a short time."

professional training [4]. Plath, tragically, was not as fortunate as Green.

In her novel Green describes the long, slow, and often tortuous path she followed. She massively resisted efforts to leave her own special world of fantasy. The real world was too cruel, too harsh, too untrustworthy. Fromm-Reichmann all the time worked quietly and patiently to build trust, to form a relationship, and to help Green begin to believe in herself.

Adolescent psychosis is not untreatable. In reading Green's novel, however, we get a firsthand glimpse of the complexity of adolescent schizophrenia. There was one critical turning point as Green began to recover. She started to come out of her cocoonlike fantasy world she called "The Kingdom of Yr." But during the transition the psychological pain was enormous, and she often wished to retreat. The real world does have pain, disappointment, loneliness. As this realization grows, there is often an intense desire for retreat, to go back to the comforts of fantasy and psychological illness. Fromm-Reichmann, sensing this retreat in Green, offers her hope: "We will work hard, together, and we will understand." Also, the doctor admits that reality can be upsetting; after all, she says, "I never promised you a rose garden!" She did promise her life, instead.

REFERENCES

1. S. Plath, *The bell jar* (New York: Bantam Books, 1972).
2. S. Plath, *Ariel* (New York: Harper & Row, 1965).
3. H. Green, *I never promised you a rose garden* (New York: Signet Books, 1964).
4. F. Fromm-Reichmann, *Principles of intensive psychotherapy* (Chicago: University of Chicago Press, 1958).

Finally, you will want to assure the teenager that it is not a sign of weakness to ask for help. Rather, emphasize that talking with a professional is usually a good sign. It means that one is starting to take charge of one's own life, to sort things out, to clarify one's thoughts and feelings, and to better understand oneself as a growing, developing human being. This last point is probably the most important single message you can convey.

PSYCHOLOGICAL ALIENATION: A MALADY OF ADOLESCENCE

Alienation has been called the most common adjustment reaction during adolescence. In this sense it cannot be considered pathological; rather, it is expected behavior. In fact, Anna Freud has commented that the only adolescent behavior pattern that is abnormal is showing no change at all. In other words, the person who retains essentially an elementary school psychological identity is in all probability a major candidate for psychological distress. Such psychological immaturity will not provide the teenager with enough psychological strength to handle the more complex interactions met in adolescence. Periods of alienation, on the other hand, are indicators that the person is, in fact, experiencing the growth process. Teenagers put it more simply: "It's when you start thinking about things you never thought of before." In this section we will discuss the concept of alienation, provide some examples from recent research, and discuss roles that secondary schools may play in reducing the incidence of alienation.

Piaget said that a child was a natural philosopher in the sense that, without prompting, a young child will ask questions on the nature of time, space, and causality. For example: Why do things in the physical world work the way they do? How does electricity work? What is gravity? Why does the water swirl going down the drain? The child seeks explanations for physical causation.

During adolescence, though, with the increased complexity of thought, teenagers shift the inquiry focus to themselves. Adolescence, as a result, has been called a period when the person becomes a natural psychologist. The teenager becomes introspective. There is an increased awareness of the subjective nature of experience. As Selman's work has shown (see Chapter 5), the increase in role-taking capacity, especially after the initial egocentrism of early adolescence fades, means that by middle adolescence individuals can simultaneously process their own experience and that of others. This capability opens up a new line of inquiry to understand one's own behavior, both objectively and subjectively. As the American Psychological Association survey graphically demonstrated (see Chapter 12), teenagers want to examine, question, and understand more about the nature of their own existence as persons. A quality of existential psychology appears as a major strand in their questioning: What is the meaning and purpose of life, and, most importantly, where do I fit in? And such inquiry is necessary in order for the person to fashion a new and more complex personal identity, as Erikson's theory has dramatically demonstrated. But it is in this process of questioning that alienation occurs.

Alienation as Separation

By *alienation* we mean a sense of despair and separateness. It is this latter feeling that is unusually strong, the sense of being separated and removed. It is the feeling of being outside one's own experience, as if one were watching oneself in a movie. A more literal translation means simply that the person feels like an alien, a stranger in a foreign land, without connections or roots. During such periods there is a strong sense that nothing is really very important. Since reality is subjective, each person's experience is different; each person is unique. So there is really no point at all in meeting other persons' expectations and rules. Thus a teenager might say, "Well, what's the point?"

During the discontinuity between childhood and adulthood, then, periods of psychological alienation represent a normal response, an inquiry into the subjective aspects of being human and where each person fits into society's broad framework. We will concentrate here on alienation as it affects secondary school pupils. We present the concept with regard to college youth in Chapter 14. And during the junior high years psychological alienation is relatively rare. A few students at that age might exhibit signs consistent with alienation. In all probability, however, such symptoms are indicators of psychological immaturity rather than alienation. For example, the Chisholm study discussed in Chapter 2, which illustrated the differences in levels of psychological maturity in junior high pupils, found students who appeared to be alienated but who actually were giving evidence of a failure to move from their elementary level of psychological development.

At the high school level, then, alienation is an indicator of active questioning rather than passive withdrawal or a desire to go back to an earlier stage. Also, the signs of this stage are obvious. During periods of alienation teenagers wear more unique (and perhaps bizarre) clothing and hairstyles and exhibit more unique behavior in general. They are less willing to go along with the general expectations of school and parents. Their music, which may seem obnoxious to adults, is perhaps the most obvious example of their desire to be different and to have the difference noticed. On an individual level, a teenager may suddenly appear with a new friend. The parents quickly realize that all the values of the new friend seem to be in opposition to their own. Their own teenager may then begin to lecture them on the value of relativity: "But father, just because you value achievement does not mean that all of us must conform to that view. Relationship is more important to me." Such dialogues take different forms, of course, but underneath the message is the same. The teenager, at least momentarily, is questioning many of the assumptions of the adult society. Whereas the elementary school and, for the most part, the junior high pupils accept the adult world as it stands, the teenager will question almost anything and everything as part of the alienation process.

Other indicators of alienation are such acts as mindless vandalism of schools and community parks, extended school absenteeism, careless schoolwork, and a refusal to participate in practically all school and community activities. Melvin Seeman, an expert in this area, has summed up the problem of alienation [20]. He sees it as involving a sequence of overlapping psychological processes during adolescence that lead to a sense of the following:

- powerlessness

- meaninglessness

- normlessness

- cultural estrangement

- self-estrangement

- social isolation

Fred Newmann, a major theorist-practitioner in secondary school social studies at the University of Wisconsin, comments that each of these elements reflects a lack of integration or any meaningful connection with values, people, tasks, and authority [21]. The alienated adolescent is adrift.

Alienation: Some Recent Research   Although there is not much empirical research on alienation, some current work is beginning to shed light on its possible factors. James Mackey of the University of Minnesota has for the past five years been engaged in creating a means of assessment, which gives promise as a necessary first step in research [22]. He found that most of the measures currently available were inappropriate. Some tests were normed only on abnormal populations or on adults, and some were too brief to have reliability and validity. So working with an expert in measurement, Andrew Ahlgren, he systematically field-tested a large number of items and piloted the resulting questionnaire with a variety of groups of normal adolescent populations. Employing some of Seeman's constructs and a process called factor analysis, he ended up with three major factors on his scale: (1) personality incapacity, (2) cultural estrangement, and (3) guidelessness. Table 11.4 illustrates some of the items in each cluster.

The overall test met the standards of measurement. The factor analysis technique the researchers used was a means of confirming the number of elements that they thought made up the concept of alienation. For example, test designers may start with a scale they think is composed of, say, five elements. But when the scale is administered, the respondents may indicate that there are fewer elements or factors. In this case the test designers thought that there were five factors (from Seeman's list), but the adolescents who took the test only perceived three elements in the entire scale. Individual items clustered, or gathered, around those three dimensions. Measures of internal consistency then were applied and indicated that the factors were reliable and could be replicated (repeated) in additional testing.

TABLE 11.4 Sample items from alienation scale of Mackey and Ahlgren

Personal incapacity (15 items)

19. The problems of life are sometimes too big for me.
25. It is hard to think clearly about most issues because the world is changing so fast.
34. More and more I feel helpless in the face of what is happening in the world today.

Guidelessness (12 items)

 6. Cheating in school is all right if you don't get caught.
20. There's little use for me to vote, since one vote doesn't count for very much anyway.
21. It is all right to get around the law if you don't actually break it.

Cultural estrangement (14 items)

 2. It is important to act and dress for the occasion.
 8. The school is more important as a place to build social relationships.
17. I am not interested in adjusting to American society.
29. I'm not much interested in TV, movies, or magazines that most people like.
37. I'm not hung up on money or success.
39. I could easily live in another country.

Note: Agreement indicates alienation except for 2 and 8, which are reverse-scored.

From J. Mackey and A. Ahlgren, Community and sex differences on three dimensions of adolescent alienation (Minneapolis: University of Minnesota, 1981) p. 16. Reprinted by permission.

With these three clusters, or elements, of alienation the scale was then administered to numerous groups of teenagers, boys and girls, according to four different types of schools: (1) suburban, (2) working-class, (3) inner-city, and (4) rural. The schools were selected as representing the major socioeconomic clusters of public secondary schools. The main results were as follows:

1. Overall, males had higher scores on guidelessness than females. For example, males tended to feel it was all right to cheat or break the law as long as they didn't get caught. Females were less likely to agree. Part of guidelessness for males, then, would be manifested by stage 2 values in the Kohlberg sense, values for materialism and taking advantage of opportunities even if it means going against the values of the adult society.

2. On cultural estrangement the differences came from community backgrounds. The students, both males and females, who felt most distance from society's mainstream were from the working-class school. The rural students felt closest to (least alienated from) and most accepting of values for dress codes, conformity, and adjusting to adult society. Inner-city and suburban pupils were in the middle range. In Kohlbergian terms the rural students were most accepting of stage 3 values for social conformity.

3. On personal incapacity the differences followed precisely the income-level distributions of the community. This element was lowest for suburban students; working-class and inner-city students were in the middle range; rural students scored highest. Thus rural students were more likely to see the world as too complex and the problems of life as too hard to handle—a kind of fatalism—than the other groups. Self-direction and autonomy were low for this group.

These results are summarized in Fig. 11.1.

Mackey and Ahlgren's work demonstrates that the elements of alienation are different according to the social class makeup of the school community. Thus we cannot generalize and say all adolescents in secondary schools are alienated. Instead, we need to specify that alienation takes different forms, and these forms do not always follow general expectations. But how feelings of alienation are expressed follows certain lines in general.

For example, males are more likely than females to adopt a me-first posture, with a greater willingness to break laws and act out. This result is highly consistent with the findings from juvenile delinquency research (see Chapter 10). Also, males are much more likely to engage in mild to moderate antisocial acts than females, although the great majority of males are certainly not hard-core delinquents.

Students from working-class schools are likely to express their feelings of alienation in materialistic terms. They feel that their clothes and their

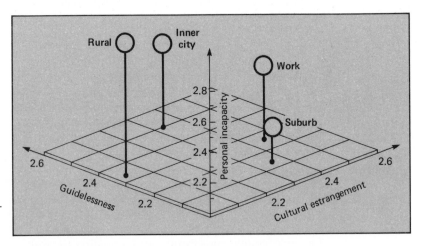

FIG. 11.1 Profiles of alienation for secondary school students

Based on research data from J. Mackey and A. Ahlgren, Community and sex differences on three dimensions of adolescent alienation (Minneapolis: University of Minnesota, 1981) p. 16. Reprinted by permission.

place in society puts them at a disadvantage. Mackey and Ahlgren speculate that the Archie Bunker stereotype of the past ten years has produced a kind of bitterness and cynicism among the blue-collar segments of the population. They see the material advantages of the wealthier surrounding suburban districts, and they are envious of the cars, the homes, the vacations, and the clothes this group has. Simultaneously, they perceive that the inner-city communities are favored by government spending programs and special breaks. The accuracy of such perceptions is not the issue here. What is important is the belief of these students that they are caught in the middle and that nobody cares about them.

The main component of alienation for rural students is the lack of a sense of personal mastery. Although these students feel that they fit into the mainstream and wish to adjust to adult society, social conformity does not carry with it a sense of self-direction. The rural students are more apt to feel out of place, to feel that they cannot compete with their more sophisticated peers from the cities. Lack of confidence, then, is a major element in the alienated feelings of rural students.

Do these results mean that there are no alienated students in either the suburbs or the inner city? Obviously not. The pattern for these groups, however, is less distinctive. Overall, the scores in all the elements indicated a substantial degree of alienation for both suburban and inner-city pupils. For example, the average scores on personal incapacity, cultural estrangement, and guidelessness for both groups were well above the minimum possible scores for each scale. Thus among these students there is greater variability in feelings of alienation than there is among the other groups, but alienation does appear as a common attribute.

To summarize, then, there is a relatively high incidence during adolescence of psychological depression, mild to moderate delinquent behavior, attempts at suicide, and chemical dependency and abuse, all of which occur with increasing frequency. These for the most part are symptoms and expressions of alienation. As we have noted, major psychological disturbance during adolescence is significant but limited to about 10 to 15% of the population. Adolescence is not a time of major storm and stress for most teenagers, then. Instead, for the great majority it is a time of alienation, of feeling separated, of not being sure, of lacking self-confidence, of unhappy and depressed feelings. These feelings are perhaps best exemplified by a hauntingly poignant song of a few years back by Janis Ian, "At Seventeen":

At Seventeen

I learned the truth at seventeen—that love was meant for beauty queens and high school girls with clear skinned smiles who married young and then returned.

The valentines I never knew, the Friday night charades of youth were spent on one more beautiful.

At seventeen I learned the truth.

And those of us with ravaged faces, lacking in the social graces, desperately remained at home inventing lovers on the phone who called to say— "Come dance with me" and murmured vague obscenities. It isn't all it seems—at seventeen.*

Now that we have examined the problem, we must consider the question of what can be done. In our view a good deal of the personal anguish and misery documented in these studies is a result of the structure of secondary schools. (This point will be developed in more detail in the next chapter.) School personnel need to take the results of alienation studies seriously. Thus it seems possible for schools to offer more personally rewarding learning experiences than they now do. Current programs rarely come to grips with the teenagers' normal concerns about self and relationships. To be sure, a small percentage of adolescents in secondary school excel in activities, athletics, and even occasionally in their academic programs. But these students are those in the leading crowds, perhaps representing only one-quarter, at most, of the secondary school pupils. Most students, unfortunately, drift through school, not really understanding the point of the curriculum, not grasping the concepts in the courses, and not having the requisite skills to succeed in extracurricular activities. It is small wonder that the Flanagan survey, which is reviewed in detail in Chapter 12, indicated that the great majority, over two-thirds, of the teenagers sampled twelve years after high school regarded the experience as irrelevant.

SUMMARY

In this chapter we reviewed both the incidence of psychological disturbance during adolescence and the most common types of disorders. We distinguished between difficulties common to earlier stages of development and problems that increase substantially during the onset of adolescence. Also, we outlined, largely from Anna Freud's work, the most common defense mechanisms adolescents may employ. These mechanisms were presented in the order of the seriousness of the difficulty, from normal defenses, which are those generally used by almost all teenagers at one

---

* Words and music by Janis Ian. Copyright © 1975 Mine Music, Ltd. Reprinted by permission.

time or another, to extreme defenses, which are usually symptoms of major disturbances.

We also outlined some of the issues concerned with referral and treatment methods for extreme problems. However, we make the point that for most teenagers the adolescent period is not a time of extreme storm and stress. In fact, the concept of alienation has been defined as a period of questioning and separation common to the majority of teenagers, a period that is often accompanied by psychological depression. Such relatively mild behaviors associated with alienation should not be classed as major adjustment problems. In fact, as we will show in the next chapter, a rather substantial portion of alienation could be solved through more adequate school programs designed to enhance the growing sense of personal competence during this period.

KEY POINTS AND NAMES

Incidence of psychological disturbance

Michael Rutter

Types of disorders
Depression
Alcoholism/drug dependency
Anorexia nervosa
Parasuicide

Sex differences and disturbances

Martin Seligman

Learned helplessness

Anna Freud

Psychological defenses
Displacement
Reversal of affect
Uncompromising
Regression
Asceticism
Withdrawal

Treatment techniques and referral

Alienation

Melvin Seeman

James Mackey and Andrew Ahlgren

REFERENCES

1. M. Rutter, *Changing youth in a changing society* (Cambridge, Mass.: Harvard University Press, 1980).

2. *Ibid.*, p. 46.

3. *Ibid.*, pp. 45–46.

4. J. Black, *Lives through time* (Berkeley, Calif.: Banecroft, 1971); J. Kagan and H. Moss, *Birth to maturity* (New York: Wiley, 1962).

5. S. Hathaway and E. Monachesi, *Adolescent personality and behavior* (Minneapolis: University of Minnesota Press, 1963).

6. Rutter, p. 43.

7. *Ibid.*, p. 131.

8. *Ibid.*, p. 130.

9. *Ibid.*, p. 206.

10. M. E. P. Seligman, *Helplessness* (San Francisco: Freeman, 1975).

11. A. Freud, Adolescence, *Psychoanalytic Study of the Child* 13(1958):255–276.

12. W. C. Wilson, The development of ethnic attitudes in adolescence, *Child Development* 34(1963):262–274.

13. H. Bruch, *Eating disorders* (New York: Basic Books, 1973).

14. I. B. Weiner, *Psychological disturbance in adolescence* (New York: Wiley, 1970).

15. Rutter, pp. 72, 76.

16. I. I. Gottesman and J. Shields, Contribution of twin studies to perspectives in schizophrenia, in *Progress in experimental personality research*, ed. B. A. Maher (New York: Academic Press, 1966), pp. 1–84.

17. N. Garmezy, Intervention with children at risk for behavior pathology, *Clinical Psychologist* 28(1975):12–14.

18. I. B. Weiner and D. Elkind, *Child Development: A core approach* (New York: Wiley, 1972).

19. Two very fine recent references to treatment methods are J. Meeks, *The fragile alliance* (Huntington, N.Y.: Krieger, 1980); Group for the Advancement of Psychiatry (GAP), *Power and authority in adolescence*, publication no. 101 (New York: GAP Publications, 1978).

20. M. Seeman, Alienation studies, in *Annual Review of Sociology, 1975*, (Palo Alto, Calif.: Annual Reviews).

21. F. Newmann, *Organizational factors and student alienation in high schools*, Final Report No. G79–0150 (Washington, D.C.: National Institute of Education, 1980).

22. J. Mackey and A. Ahlgren, Dimensions of adolescent alienation, *Applied Psychological Measurement* 1(1977):219–232.

CHAPTER 12

Adolescents and Secondary Schools

INTRODUCTION

In general, throughout this text we have stressed the concept of developmental interaction. The quality of the relationship between the person and the environment is a crucial factor in determining whether growth occurs. Such interaction is not benign. Rather, interaction can produce positive growth outcomes or growth-arresting results. For example, teenagers who are jailed for status offenses or adult crimes are usually placed in a so-called correctional facility. Yet what they learn in such an institution is not reform but new and more sophisticated techniques for crime [1].

Thus the environment with which the person interacts has an extremely important influence on the growth potential of the individual. For adolescence this influence is more significant than it is for any other period of development, except possibly the first 18 months. The reasons for such vulnerability to influence have been detailed in the previous chapters. And since, as we have noted, adolescence is, by definition, a time when previous identities are shed and overall change is so rapid, it is hardly any wonder that general environmental influences are so strong. Even newborns have a greater ability than adolescents to resist the impact of the environment; children in the first few days of life can turn away from unpleasant and unhealthy influences. Adolescents, on the other hand, seem to be seized by almost any experience or influence that comes along.

Two major influences on adolescents are the junior and senior high schools they attend. Unfortunately, their impact is not always positive. In this chapter we will present a brief history of secondary schools to give some historical background on how such institutions grew both in scope and size. Then we provide a review of a number of research studies over the past thirty years, studies that yield important information on the negative impact schooling in general has had on adolescents. Research from the 1950s, 1960s, and 1970s has consistently shown that the majority of adolescents are not aided in the process of growth either intellectually or psychologically. Finally, we point out some studies and recommendations that indicate that positive reform is possible. Secondary schools could provide a more balanced set of learning experiences designed to promote development.

THE COMMON SCHOOL

Secondary schools (particularly high schools, grades 9–12) were the prominent socializing institution for teenagers at the turn of the twentieth century. Then in the 1920s junior high schools were developed as an intermediate institution, taking grades 7 and 8 from the old grammar schools and grade 9 from the senior highs. Thus by the 1930s the two major institutions for adolescents were in place: junior high for early adolescence (ages 12–14) and senior high for middle adolescence (ages 15–17). Of course, not all teenagers attended these institutions. Yet by the mid 1970s, as shown in Table 12.1, almost three-fourths (75%) of all teenagers were completing secondary school [2].

Today almost 90% of all teenagers in the country attend a public secondary school. Thus the concept of the public school as a common school has been realized. Schools are open to all pupils without direct costs. This achievement is, of course, the democratic vision of the foundation for a free society: that all persons be provided with a free educational opportunity in order to develop their intellectual and human potential to become informed and judicious citizens.

Before we examine the current situation, however, there are a number of historical trends that need to be considered. In this section we will look at the growth of secondary schools and the changes effected by industrialization.

TABLE 12.1   Adolescents completing high schools

Year	Percentage completing
1870	5
1920	17
1975	75

Secondary schooling in America has grown enormously in the past fifty years
Photograph from Joe Di Dio/National Education Association

**The Growth of
Secondary
Schools**

In addition to an increase in the number of teenagers attending and completing high school, there are other noteworthy historical trends. In the past one hundred years the time spent in school at the secondary level has increased by 50 days per year, from 130 to 180 days. The size of the schools has also changed. Prior to 1959 most high schools in this country were relatively small, composed of five hundred or so pupils [3]. Since that time small school districts have consolidated in order to offer a broad curriculum. Also, after World War II the explosion of suburban communities ringing each major city resulted in huge campus-style schools of up to five thousand pupils. These two trends, consolidated rural schools and new suburban schools, have radically altered the context of secondary education. Thus, in general, most teenagers of both sexes are now clustered in large schools, for longer periods, and within a relatively narrow age range.

This result is in stark contrast to the situation of the last century, when, as shown in Table 12.1, only 5% graduated from high school. These graduates were almost exclusively males who attended school for only part of the year (mostly during the winter); they were grouped in relatively small schools with a very broad age range. In fact, it is quite revealing of the times to note that there was very little age-grade distinction. The ages might range from 12 to 20, with only a cursory label dividing lads from large boys on the basis of physical size. Females generally did not attend secondary schools. They were placed out of the home either as domestic workers or as factory labor. Their education, with the exception of a few who became teachers and of even fewer from the upper social classes, ended with grammar school.

The Impact of Industrialization

In a larger sense these changes in school structure came about from massive societal changes. That is, schools were not transformed by themselves or as the result of specific educational policies. Rather, school change was a derivative of social change. The decline of farming and the increase in industrialization were, of course, two major changes affecting the schools. Also, a huge wave of immigration at the turn of the twentieth century added to clustered urbanization. Finally, with the advent of political leaders like Teddy Roosevelt and Woodrow Wilson, a new active social role was carved out for the federal government. Child labor laws resulted, forcing adolescents out of the factories and back to the schools.

The net result of these historical forces has been the establishment of large-size educational institutions, which house almost all the adolescents of the country in an age-segregated environment, for long periods of time, and separated from the balance of the society. These trends added together helped to create a special subculture that James Coleman labeled "the adolescent society" [4].

The goal of the common school is to be this country's agent for education and democracy. A careful examination of the impact of secondary schools, however, reveals a major gap between theory and reality. Coleman's study provided a searching criticism of the actual effects of secondary schools on teenagers. It is to that report that we now turn.

THE COLEMAN REPORT: *THE ADOLESCENT SOCIETY*

Although the Coleman report, titled *The Adolescent Society*, was published in the early 1960s, the results of the study are still applicable today. As we will note later in the chapter, a recent study conducted in the 1980s by John Goodlad at UCLA unfortunately demonstrates that little has changed over the past twenty years in terms of the general impact of secondary schools on the pupils [5].

In his study sociologist James Coleman surveyed a large number of secondary school pupils, grades 9 to 12, from a variety of schools [6]. The schools represented a cross section of the country, including rural, urban, and suburban districts as well as the major social and economic classes.

The survey provided a massive photograph of what the schools were like from the pupil's point of view. In other words, Coleman did not assess the formal curriculum—the official list of school courses, the teacher qualifications, and the educational objectives as spelled out in school board policy statements. Instead, he assessed the informal curriculum, or, as it is sometimes called, the hidden agenda, of secondary schools. In other words how do the students themselves make sense of their daily experience? The school board may announce that the goal is to educate students for participation in a democratic society. But does that goal become a reality in the eyes of the pupils?

To give you some flavor for the main findings of the report, we will present in this section tabulations from the study across a few major dimensions.

Dominant Source of Values: The Leading Crowd

In all the schools studied Coleman found that the dominant source for values was an elite subgroup, the leading crowd. For both boys and girls the leading crowd in each school was well known and easily identified. However, the most important result is not the existence of such a clique but, rather, the values represented by the clique. To get this information, Coleman asked questions about the main career goals and personal values of all the students. The answers to these questions are presented in Table 12.2.

TABLE 12.2 Personal values and career goals in Coleman's adolescent society

Values or goals	Boys		Girls
"If you could be any of these things you wanted, which would you want to be?"			
Jet pilot	31.3%	Actress/artist	19.2%
Nationally famous athlete	36.9%	Nurse	26.0%
Atomic scientist	25.9%	Model	33.5%
Missionary	5.9%	Teacher	20.6%
	(N = 3746)		(N = 3922)
"How would you want to be remembered?"			
Most popular	23.4%		34.2%
Star athlete (boys)	45.1%		—
Leader in activities (girls)	—		37.8%
Brilliant student	31.5%		27.9%
	(N = 3690)		(N = 3876)

Data from J. S. Coleman, *The adolescent society* (New York: Free Press, 1961), pp. 27–36.

The table indicates that for both boys and girls the main career objective was to be nationally famous, either as an athlete (boys) or as a fashion model (girls). Similarly, the way the teenagers wished to be remembered, a kind of adolescent epitaph, was either as a star athlete (boys) or as an activity leader (girls). For both sexes being a brilliant student was far less significant when compared with the athlete and activity categories. These two elements, then, formed the main value network of the school. Intellectual activity and learning, the actual goals of the school, received little support.

However, within each school the most prized goal was to be in the leading crowd itself. In other words, the group that most teenagers wanted to be with and to be like was the leading crowd. Coleman called the leading crowd students the social elites. They were the dominant social force in all the schools. He found that the leading crowd had an even lower value for being a good student than the entire school body had. That crowd in each school had the lowest value for intellectual activity. Coleman noted: "The social elites are less willing to see themselves as engaging in intellectual activity, and found the idea . . . more repugnant than those who are outside the leading crowd" [7]. Quite surprisingly, Coleman found that nearly all the leading crowds in all the schools valued the same things. Table 12.3 describes the main characteristics of the elites. From the table we see that the rank order of significance for boys was based on an attractive personality, reputation, looks, and athletic ability, with good grades a distant fifth in rank. For girls there was even greater emphasis on personal characteristics such as personality and reputation along with physical elements such as looks and clothes. For girls good grades were even lower in rank than they were for boys.

Given these values emphasizing externals such as looks and clothes and activities such as athletics and modeling, it is small wonder that

TABLE 12.3   Characteristics of members of the leading crowd (rank order; Coleman survey)

Boys		Girls	
Personality	1	Personality	1
Good reputation	2	Good looks	2
Be an athlete	3	Good clothes	3
Good looks	4	Good reputation	4
Good grades	5	Be neat	5
Other (car, money, neighborhood, etc.)	6	Other	6

Data from J. S. Coleman, *The adolescent society* (New York: Free Press, 1961), pp. 28–37.

Note: Coleman's question was, "What does it take to get into the leading crowd in this school?"

Coleman found that over 20% of all boys and girls wanted to *be* someone else. He asked the pupils if they would trade places with someone else. This question relates directly to the issue of adolescent identity formation. A core requirement for a healthy personality in developmental terms is to accept one's self and to build in positive directions from that core. The finding that more than a fifth of both boys and girls wanted to be someone else is probably related to the power of the leading crowd and its emphasis on social attractiveness and external appearances.

Finally, Coleman found that these values of the social elites increased in all schools between grades 9 and 11. The ninth graders were more tolerant of individual differences than were the students two grades ahead of them in school.

School Differences

The differences across schools were not important. That is, most of the schools showed similar results. In fact, quite surprisingly, in one of the suburban schools noted for its college preparation curriculum and large number of graduates who went to four-year colleges, the leading crowd was by far the group least interested in learning. In the school Coleman named Executive Heights, to reflect the predominant social class of the neighborhood, less than 10% of the boys and less than 1% of the girls who made up the leading crowd wanted to be remembered as a brilliant student.

Sex Differences

Since the survey was conducted prior to the start of the feminist movement, the results on the issue of sex differences may no longer be accurate. Somewhat ironically, Coleman found that in every school surveyed girls did better academically than boys. Regardless of location, school size, or socioeconomic makeup, the results were always the same—the girls studied more and achieved academically at a higher level. Girls averaged about a B to B− in grades, while boys averaged C+ to C. The irony was that many of the brightest girls, at least on standard intelligence tests, managed to hide their intellectual competence, "leaving somewhat less bright girls to be named as best scholars." In view of this strange finding Coleman concluded that the high school female (in the 1950s) "is pushed toward doing well in school by her allegiance to her parents and teachers, but she wants dates and popularity" [8].

The School's Role: Accepting the Values of the Leading Crowd?

Given this rather dismal picture of an adolescent subculture that dominates the value orientation of secondary schools, what was the actual role of the school and the teachers? Did the teachers and the curriculum offer alternative experiences to counteract the superficial values of the leading crowd? In Coleman's view the answer was, apparently not at all.

SPECIAL TOPIC
15,000 Hours: British School Study Shows That Quality, Not Quantity, Is Important

Adolescents spend a major part of their lives in school. But up to now little has been known about what characteristics of school make those hours profitable for adolescents—profitable in terms of academic achievement and involvement in the school environment.

A few years ago, British child psychiatrist Michael Rutter conducted the most comprehensive study of school influences ever undertaken [1]. He studied the students in twelve secondary schools in an inner-city neighborhood in London. The title of the study was *15,000 Hours,* which is the amount of time a British student spends in school in order to complete a secondary education. The main objective was to determine whether the school students attended made a difference in their performance on the national achievement tests that are given to all British students when they complete secondary school. Like many achievement tests, the British tests were designed to measure how much students had learned in different school subjects.

The problem Rutter studied is not an easy one. In the first place, there are often sizeable differences between schools in the caliber of students when they enter school. That is, one school may serve a neighborhood in which many of the families are relatively well-to-do and their children relatively advantaged, educationally and culturally. Another school might have a very different level of cultural and educational advantage. To deal with this problem,

Adolescents, as we have shown, increase their capacities in physical, emotional, social, and intellectual arenas, and they are increasingly less willing to accept passive obedience to adults. How did the schools seek to channel, co-opt, or even guide this capacity for activity? The general school response was to prescribe extremely traditional textbook exercises, homework assignments, and tests. In examining these learning activities, Coleman found the work generally required "not creativity, but conformity, not originality, and deviation, but attention and obedience" [9]. He found exceptions to be sure. Some teachers were able to create interesting and challenging projects that effectively channeled adolescent energy into learning activities. In general, however, these few were exceptions to the general rule of rather dull, listless, and passive classroom routines.

Thus Coleman sees the need for massive reform of secondary education. Schools as presently organized are simply no contest for adolescent

Rutter got careful measures of the characteristics of students in each of the twelve schools he studied before they entered school. These preentry measures he referred to as *in-take measures*. He also carefully monitored attendance records at the various schools, and he observed their operation over a period of $2\frac{1}{2}$ years. Furthermore, for each of the schools he had information about the students' records of delinquency from police files. With all of this information Rutter was able to determine, better than anyone else ever has been, whether the school itself affected students' performance at the time they were ready to leave the school.

What school characteristics might be expected to have particular effects on student achievement? Rutter examined the physical features of the school, its student composition, the typical social interactions between students and staff members, community variables, and abilities of students who attended the school. Rutter found a strong correlation between academic achievements of the students in the twelve schools and particular characteristics of the schools themselves. In other words, he found strong evidence that certain school characteristics are associated with higher academic achievement.

What are these characteristics? Here is a brief summary of Rutter's findings:

1. The degree of academic emphasis in the school was correlated with high achievement. By *emphasis* Rutter did not mean the content of the school's curriculum but the fact that academic work was emphasized over other types of school activities. The expectation that academic work would come first was clearly evident in some schools but not in others.

(Continued)

commitment to learning. Intrinsic interest in learning—that is, learning as a self-rewarding activity—declined between grades 9 and 12. In other words, the longer the teenagers remained in school, the less they became interested in learning activities. Coleman concluded with a pessimistic prediction: "If intellectual activities remain passive exercises, while the excitement of *doing, exploring, creating,* and *meeting a challenge* is left to the athletic field, the yearbook office, and the back seat of a car, then interest in academic directions will certainly decline" [10].

SCHOOLING IN THE SIXTIES

At the surface level it seemed that massive changes in secondary education were occurring during the revolutionary atmosphere of the 1960s. Experimentation was visible: storefront schools, alternative communal schools in

SPECIAL TOPIC (Continued)

2. In schools in which students did better academically, there were clear, understandable guidelines for behavior, and rewards rather than punishment were frequently used. These schools had not only better academic achievement but also less behavioral disruptions in the classrooms and a generally better attendance record.

3. The cleanliness and orderliness of the school's interior was higher for schools that produced high academic achievement. By *condition* Rutter did not mean the age of the school; some of the schools whose students performed least well were new, but the interior conditions were, nevertheless, dreary.

4. The amount of responsibility students had and the degree of their participation both in school activities and in their own respective school programs correlated with high academic achievement.

5. Schools in which the staff was highly organized and engaged in a great deal of group planning of school programs generally had more successful students. Organization does not mean regimentation; rather, organization refers to the degree to which the staff seemed to be operating in consonance with each other and with some generally agreed on goals for the school. Rutter refers to this variable and other school atmosphere variables as the school *ethos*.

6. Finally,—and surprisingly, to many formal and informal observers—the nature of the school's peer group was not strongly related to academic achievement. That is, the proportion of students in a school who had previously been identified as behavior problems and delinquent youth was not associated with academic achievement of students in that school. Furthermore, the proportion

the mountains of Vermont and upper New York State, national curriculum committees bent on breathing new life into secondary school courses, and a plethora of new programs—new math, science, and social studies and some entirely new and quite radical strategies such as confluent education and gestalt learning. With national funding a deliberate attempt was made to sponsor innovation.

However, as a Rand Commission study recently pointed out, very little real change occurred. Too often the experimental programs were temporary efforts, spearheaded by university-based innovators. The experimental programs rarely were incorporated into the mainstream; nearby districts almost totally ignored the new programs, however exciting they might have been [11]. Thus no matter what school changes were attempted, the conclusion was that very little of substance was altered. The

of ethnic minorities in a school was not related to achievement. However, the proportion of high–verbal ability students in a school population was related to the degree of academic achievement that the students showed overall.

Many of Rutter's findings are easy to accept, but many of them are surprising. For example, although we usually assume that the individual performance of teachers is the all-important factor in the school setting, Rutter's results indicate that the degree of cohesiveness and faculty cooperation may be a very important school characteristic as well. Furthermore, while we tend to assume that the social and economic characteristics of students with whom a young person is associated in school are likely to affect what that person can be expected to achieve, Rutter's study indicates that it is more likely to be the abilities of such students rather than their demographic characteristics that influence academic outcomes.

Rutter's findings come from correlational research; thus we can only conclude that certain school characteristics are associated with a certain level of performance by a school student. We *cannot* conclude that these characteristics of school *cause* higher academic performance. However, Rutter showed us that even when the characteristics of students at the time they enter school are taken into account, there are patterns of relationships between a school's characteristics and what its students achieve academically.

REFERENCE

1. M. Rutter, B. Maughn, P. Mortimore, J. Ouston, and A. Smith, *Fifteen thousand hours: Secondary schools and their effect on children* (London: Open Books, 1979).

unplanned and often chaotic alternative schools of the 1960s prompted Coleman to remark, scathingly, "A school composed of corridors of wandering souls . . . have taught anew the lesson that there was no simple solution in educational reform. 'Grooving' and 'self-actualization' will not make a school" [12]. There is a French expression that sums up the efforts to revitalize and restructure secondary schools: *La plus change, la plus c'est le meme chose* ("the more things change, the more they remain the same").

So the secondary schools of our country entered the 1960s with a curriculum that could only be described as passive and routine and with a classroom organization that did little to engage adolescent interest in learning. The 1960s, of course, was a decade of enormous social unrest in this country, witnessing multiple upheavals. The question we are interested in is this: Did the schools interact any more successfully with adolescents during this period than they had during the previous period that Coleman investigated? Was there any evidence that the power of the adolescent society had declined or, perhaps, had been redirected? Several studies indicate that, unfortunately, little of substance changed during this period; Coleman's original findings remained valid [13]. There were some differences due to changing times, but the overall results were quite consistent. A few highlights from one investigation, *Studies of Adolescents in the Secondary Schools* (SASS), will be enumerated in this section to illustrate the point.

The SASS Research

Norman Sprinthall and Ralph Mosher selected two public schools for intensive investigation [14]. The two were chosen as prototypes of the two major models of secondary schools: One was a suburban, predominantly middle-class, college preparation school; the other was a predominantly working-class school. Over one hundred pupils were randomly selected from the eleventh grade, divided equally by sex. Testing and interviews required seven or eight hours per student. The objective was to view the school experience as completely as possible from the pupil's point of view. How did the students make sense of their daily experience in school? The study was subtitled "Voices from the Back of the Classroom." In other words, how did the pupils really feel about school? In their own terms, what were they learning?

The findings indicated that in neither school was learning perceived as a significant activity. In individual interviews and tests boys and girls in both schools rated learning as the least significant. In the survey questionnaire it was rated last in rank order; on a Q-sort learning was rated as least important; and on a semiprojective test (somewhat ambiguous pictures of students in school) a favorable reaction to school learning was mentioned in only 72 of 1068 essays, about 6% of the time.

Motivation for Schooling

The major motivation for schooling was extrinsic in both schools. The students saw little purpose in learning for its own sake; they did not view learning as exciting discovery or even as interesting. Instead, the motivation for studying and attending school was preparation for college (75% in the suburban school) or for a job (70% in the urban school). In other words, the content of the motives varied according to the social class background of the school, but in both schools the major motive was preparation.

The researchers next examined how the students really felt about their experience in the school atmosphere. It was here that major differences between the two schools showed up. The students in the suburban school were the most hostile and negative. The following comments were common in a factor analysis of responses:

"School is boring."

"I study only for tests."

"I never remain after classes."

"Classes don't interest me."

"I can't wait for the bell to ring."

"I can hardly wait to leave here."

Similar responses were presented in the interviews and the semiprojective tests. Both boys and girls seemed to feel quite antagonistic to the general program, even though, on the average, they spent two or three hours per night on their homework. Their attitude came somewhat as a surprise. One of the original expectations was that the working-class pupils would see little relevance in schooling and would be hostile to required attendance. Instead, the suburban students seemed to feel that way. These students were under a good deal of pressure from their parents and teachers, who constantly reminded them of the need for good grades and hard study. The students did not rebel openly. They did study, but they felt negative and sullenly hostile to the demands.

The working-class students, on the other hand, seemed more fatalistic and accepting in their motivation feelings. Their responses were much less hostile and negative; they seemed to be much more willing to go along with the school program. Their comments were as follows:

"It's important to follow advice."

"You shouldn't disagree with a teacher."

"It's important to learn facts."

"You just have to put up with school."

"I'll pay my dues now for the future."

Thus among the working-class students there was a noticeably greater passive acceptance and obedience to the school, yet their acceptance was not related to the ostensible purpose of the school, learning. In fact, one of the ironies most apparent to the observers was that the curriculum of the school was, in secondary school parlance, a general program—not college prep and not vocational. Thus the students were getting a watered-down version of the standard curriculum—English, history, social studies, and general science—a program that would prepare them neither for college nor for the world of work. Yet the students fully believed and accepted the need to get a diploma in order to get a job, even though the program itself was irrelevant to their goals.

The Leading Crowd and Popularity

The study also indicated that the pupils from both schools in the 1969 survey were similar to the pupils in the original Coleman sample. Almost 70% of the pupils wanted to be remembered as either a star athlete or a

TABLE 12.4 Elements of popularity (rank order)

Boys		Girls	
Good reputation	1	Good reputation	1
Good dancer and dresser	2	Good dancer/dresser	2
Stir up excitement	3	Be a good student	3
Be a good student	4	Be a leader in activities	4

Data from N. A. Sprinthall and R. L. Mosher, *Studies of adolescents in the secondary schools* (Cambridge, Mass.: Harvard Graduate School of Education, 1969), p. 73.

Note: The researchers' question was, "Among the crowd you go around with, which of the things below are important in order to be popular in the group . . . ?

popular student leader, results just about the same as those in the Coleman report. The elements making up what it meant to be popular were also similar, as Table 12.4 shows. Thus in the 1960s popularity in the adolescent society continued to focus on looks and personality and rarely included academic achievement.

As further evidence of this trend, the researchers asked each student whether they were in with the leading crowd, and if not, whether they would like to be. To some degree, this question provides a rough measure of personal congruence and self-satisfaction. The responses are shown in Table 12.5. The table indicates that in the random sample of eleventh graders, about 75% of the boys and 85% of the girls considered themselves outside the leading crowd. The researchers also asked, "If you are not in the leading crowd in your school, would you like to be?" A yes response was given by 40 boys (out of 46) and 40 girls (out of 50). This last result is perhaps the most poignant, suggesting quite clearly that a large majority of both sexes wish to be in with (but are not) the dominant subgroup in the school. Thus the social power and values of the adolescent society are known by all and desired by most.

TABLE 12.5 Membership in the leading crowd (both schools combined)

Membership	Boys	Girls
In with the crowd	13 (26%)	9 (15%)
Outside	46 (74%)	50 (85%)
Total	59	59

Data from N. A. Sprinthall and R. L. Mosher, *Studies of adolescents in the secondary schools* (Cambridge, Mass.: Harvard Graduate School of Education, 1969), p. 87.

SECONDARY SCHOOLS IN THE 1980s: THE GOODLAD STUDY

John Goodlad, dean of education at UCLA, and his associates recently conducted yet another national survey of secondary schools [15]. The researchers used a combined approach including (1) almost 1000 actual classroom obervations, (2) questionnaire data from almost 15,000 pupils, (3) interviews with over 800 teachers, and (4) over 6000 parent questionnaires. Using a stratified sample approach, they surveyed seven major regions with different socioeconomic and racial-ethnic backgrounds. Hence the researchers attempted to gain an accurate national picture of the public schools. In this section we will look at some of the results of the Goodlad study.

The Leading Crowd Revisited

In terms of the goals of schooling, all the secondary school pupils agreed that schools should provide an equal balance across four areas: (1) intellectual, (2) social, (3) personal, and (4) vocational development. In other words, the general view of schooling as important in developing the whole person was held in high regard. However, when the pupils were asked what the one best thing about their school was, quite a different picture emerged. As Table 12.6 indicates, peers and sports were runaway favorites. Ironically, "nothing" was rated higher than "the classes I'm taking."

Thus there is a major discrepancy between the stated goals of schooling and the students' perceptions of those goals. A second question on the survey concerning popularity gave further evidence of the discrepancy. The students were asked about the sources of popularity; the results are presented in Table 12.7. This table shows that good looks and athletics are by far the major values of secondary school pupils. However, there is a noticeable difference between junior and senior high. Being smart sinks from 13 to 7%, while looks and athletics increase, from 60% to almost 80%.

TABLE 12.6 One best thing about this school (secondary students; N = 11,767)

Value	Percentage	Rank order
My friend	34.9	1
Sports	13.4	2
Good attitudes	11.3	3
Nothing	8.0	4
The classes I'm taking	7.0	5
Other (teachers, principal, buildings, fair rules, etc.)	25.3	—

Data from J. Goodlad, A study of schooling, *Phi Delta Kappan* (1979, 1980; reprints of four articles).

TABLE 12.7 Most popular students in this school (N = 13,700)

Most popular	Junior high school	Senior high school
Good looking	37%	} 78.6%
Athletic	23%	
Smart	13%	7%
Other	26%	14%

Data from J. Goodlad, A study of schooling, *Phi Delta Kappan* (1979, 1980; reprints of four articles). Reprinted by permission.

The goal of balanced development, then, seems a long way from the reality of actual school experience. It is small wonder that Goodlad also found that student self-concept declines between junior and senior high. After all, not many students fit the Madison Avenue image of good looks. How many teenage movie stars can there be walking the halls of our high schools? And how many can make it as outstanding athletes? In a sense this finding is similar to the Coleman finding on the leading crowd. It becomes more difficult to be in the leading group in high school since the definition of the leading crowd becomes more narrow. If looks and athletics are the predominant values, it is no wonder that the positive perception of self—personal self-concept—becomes increasingly negative. And it's not hard to tell if you fit in or not by the time you reach secondary school: The popularity values are so painfully clear.

Curriculum Content and Teaching Strategy

The Goodlad data indicate that the general Coleman study results still hold: The secondary school values from the student's view are still primarily extrinsic. But what of the curriculum itself? What are the content and strategies of classroom interaction? Are schools and teachers doing their best to promote balanced development? Are methods and materials up to date? Or are adolescents so caught up with their own personal preoccupation that balanced growth cannot proceed? These questions, of course, are complex, but they must be asked before possible remedies can be explored.

The Goodlad data on actual classroom observation of teaching provide some answers. What did his associates find when they sat in the back of the classroom? The English/language arts curriculum was selected for an in-depth study since that area was common to all secondary schools in the study. The observers and the survey data both agreed that by far the predominant mode of instruction and material employed was traditional—a textbook, a work sheet, and rote memory recitation. In fact, in over half the secondary schools these were the *only* methods and materials used. Thus these students were not exposed to even one different medium or method of instruction—no films, no slides, no television, no simulations, no tapes, no teaching machines, no learning kits. Of the remaining schools, the reported use of nontraditional materials varied from 40 to 3%.

Hence in spite of the major changes in providing multimedia material in English over the past decade, these innovative materials have not been incorporated into the classrooms. In addition, the observers found that the use of teacher praise, encouragement, correction with guidance, and positive interaction declined sharply when compared with earlier grades. Elementary school teachers apparently are much more likely to use innovative materials, praise their pupils, and open up their classrooms than are secondary school teachers. Positive classroom interaction between teachers and pupils in secondary schools dropped 50%. So formal teaching methods, at least in English, have remained almost unchanged over the past decades. And one of the most powerful teaching strategies, positive classroom interaction, declines in use in the secondary schools.

Before we conclude that the difficulty in secondary education is a problem because of student preoccupation with self and sports, then, we need to reexamine curriculum methods and teaching strategies. Methods conducive to learning and balanced development are quite different from the existing pattern of textbook recitation and absence of teacher encouragement. Unfortunately, though, both the teachers and the parents surveyed were highly satisfied with the curriculum in use (teachers rated 75% and parents 80% satisfaction). Also, the teacher alone had the major voice in determining curriculum content and method. Apparently, the image of the teacher-directed, self-contained classroom reaches its peak in secondary schools.

An obvious question of major importance is one that we can't really address: Why, after twenty or so years of developing imaginative material and methods, has so little of this innovation actually reached the secondary school classroom? Of course, this question is one of organizational change. How can innovative practice be transmitted to schools? How can schools be changed to more adequately meet the needs of the variety of adolescents in the classrooms? The overall conclusion from Goodlad's massive study is not optimistic:

> In light of the data presented here, I don't see any actions, planned or taking place that offer any real prospect of addressing what I conclude to be, at best, a poor academic and intellectual atmosphere in many of our secondary schools. Instead the recent pre-occupations with proficiency examinations, behavioral objectives, and simplistic pedagogical formulas appear to me to be puny responses to an institutional problem of great social significance and complexity. [16]

Whether secondary schools can, in fact, change may be a moot point. However, what is clear is the kind of changes that could be made in order for the school to positively aid in the process of adolescent growth.

SPECIAL TOPIC
Dropouts and Push-Outs: The Unsolved Problem

Traditionally, those who do not finish formal schooling are called dropouts, suggesting that the individuals, acting on their own behalf, have chosen to leave school. Additionally, earlier investigations had indicated that the typical school dropout was only marginal academic material, with below-average (85 or lower) intelligence scores. Also, since there was a pattern of high rates of school suspension among those who eventually dropped out, it appeared that they were very unhappy in school anyway. Thus it seemed that the choice was a good one for all concerned.

Recent investigations into the dropout question have revealed quite a different picture. Dropping out is not the act of a single individual's conscious choice. And among adolescents, even the level of intelligence is not a major factor. By lumping together both elementary and secondary school dropouts, earlier studies had blurred the differences. At the secondary level, dropouts have average IQ scores. So the intellectual deficit theory for teenage dropouts does not hold up. Instead, there appear to be social, economic, ethnic, and school procedural and policy questions that combine in a way to produce the dropout. There are three elements involved:

1. The dropout rate is strongly associated with socioeconomic class and ethnic background. In upper-class majority group homes the rate is 2%. In lower-class minority group homes the rate is 50% [1].

2. Dropouts have histories of underachievement and academic failure. On the average, those who eventually drop out are two years or more behind on grade level performance, particularly in the basic skills of reading and math [2].

PROPOSALS FOR CHANGE: *THE EIGHT YEAR STUDY*

Before reviewing some of the current proposals for change in secondary schools, we present in this section a summary of a highly successful program carried out in the 1930s that went a long way to solve many of the seemingly insoluble problems of today. A team of educators and psychologists put together an interesting approach to reform the secondary curriculum [17]. The program, called *The Eight Year Study*, attempted to deliberately shift the learning atmosphere.

3. Dropouts have very high rates of school suspension and delinquency. Almost all the male delinquents in the Gluecks' studies and the female delinquents in Konopka's work (see Chapter 10) had significant patterns of school suspension prior to dropping out. After being adjudicated (legally defined) as a delinquent, the dropout rate was 100%.

These elements, then, describe a problem of negatively interacting factors. Low–social class and non–majority group families generally do not value the conventional educational programs. In fact, the parents themselves had usually had major difficulties during their own schooling. Educational attainment is not viewed as a ladder to a better life, as Konopka has shown. Thus the home atmosphere is not positive or supportive.

In a similar manner, the picture in school is not much more favorable for the eventual dropout. We will not go into all the details, but studies have shown that teachers in general have significantly lower educational expectations for pupils from lower-class and/or minority group backgrounds. These lowered expectations, sometimes called the self-fulfilling prophecy, result in lowered academic achievement. Two major researchers in this area, Jere Brophy and Thomas Good, concluded:

> Thus to put it baldy, in some school systems a student's career is somewhat determined as of the day he/she enters the school, simply on the basis of clothing, appearance, and other factors related to the family SES, but not necessarily to his/her ability or potential. [3]

The atmosphere and expectations in the classroom are negative for the potential dropout, and so is the experience with the principal (or, more likely, the assistant principal). The rate of school suspension, as we have noted, is high, but it is also class-linked. A recent Children's Defense Fund study indicated that minority group and/or lower-class children were *three* times more likely to be suspended than majority group white children [4]. Further inves-

(Continued)

The Activity-Based Curriculum	Wherever possible, the formal curriculum was shifted from the passive and traditional textbook recitation, work sheet, and quiz orientation to what the reformers called an "activity orientation." The goal was to teach problem solving, inquiry, and active learning through a kind of project method. A number of high schools, both public and private, agreed to participate and soon came to be known as the "activity schools."

The approach stressed an interdisciplinary study. The teachers were urged to employ a variety of methods, downplaying lectures and recitation

SPECIAL TOPIC (Continued)

tigation revealed that the so-called offenses were hardly crimes of violence. Truancy and tardiness were common problems, as was fighting with other pupils. As many as 2 million pupils (mostly adolescents) are suspended from school each year for relatively minor transgressions. Ironically, the punishment for truancy, tardiness, and dodging classes, as well as other school-related misdemeanors, is to keep such pupils out of school.

Thus the dropout problem is probably a symptom rather than a cause, a result rather than a conscious and wise choice. As we note in Chapter 13, the unemployment rate among dropouts is enormous. Indeed, the long-term career prospects for unskilled dropouts are not optimistic. The difficulty, then, is that genuine solutions seem remote.

Certainly, community education programs for families are needed in order to encourage facilitating home atmospheres. By itself, however, that would not be sufficient. Secondary schools, particularly, need to take seriously the self-fulfilling prophecy and the need for more broadly based, innovative learning experiences. Alternative schools, flexible scheduling, work-study programs, time-out rooms for in-school suspension, token economies, outward bound or upward bound programs, and a broader array of curriculum experiences are some of the changes needed.

Innovative programs, however, must be staffed by adults who value their pupils. Of all the factors, genuine human caring is probably the major ingredient in helping pupils currently on the dropout road. We do not mean a simplified form of caring—accepting and approving everything the potential dropout does. Love is not enough if the youth worker, teacher, or counselor

and increasing the use of small groups, cooperative learning, simulation, and field trips. In addition, the pupils were helped to assume increasing amounts of responsibility and active participation. For example, instead of memorizing the facts in a social studies unit on local government, the students designed a survey instrument, carried out the project, and presented their findings. Similarly, a unit on consumer education involved comparative shopping in different areas of a city and writing up and presenting the results to a panel of students and teachers.

It would require too much space for a complete description of this project-based, interdisciplinary approach. The main point is that thirty secondary schools were willing to put aside their standard textbook curriculum and their lecture-recitation teaching method and be deliberately innovative, encouraging full participation of the pupils.

does not also impose requirements and demands. The problem for any worker is to create a balance between supportive, positive regard and challenge, to side with the teenager but also to set up a structure of expectations and tasks for the teenager to accomplish.

Students in this group are probably the most difficult of all to help. Grossman's vivid account in *Nine Rotten Lousy Kids* will give you a firsthand glimpse of the difficulties [5]. So inexperienced or untrained adult volunteer helpers will almost always end up in bitterness and frustration. Thus careful training is requisite. These adolescents have learned to survive in any unfriendly and hostile world. It requires expertise on the adult workers' part to restructure learning experiences for such adolescents from negative to positive coping skills.

REFERENCES

1. H. L. Voss, A. Wendling, and D. Elliott, Some types of high school dropouts, *Journal of Educational Research* 59(1966):363–368.

2. J. S. Coleman, *Youth: Transition to adulthood* (Chicago: University of Chicago Press, 1974), p. 68.

3. J. Brophy and T. Good, *Teacher-student relationships: Causes and consequences* (New York: Holt, Rinehart and Winston, 1974), p. 9.

4. Children's Defense Fund, *School suspensions: Are they helping?* (Cambridge, Mass.: 1975).

5. H. Grossman, *Nine rotten lousy kids* (New York: Holt, Rinehart and Winston, 1972).

The Effects of Activity Schools

Since the study had involved some of the most eminent educators of the day, such as Ralph Tyler and Arthur Jersild, there was insistence on careful evaluation of outcomes. To meet this criterion, the researchers compared a large group of the activity school graduates who went on to college with a matched group from traditional high schools who also went on to college. The groups were equated on the variables known to affect academic performance, such as age, sex, socioeconomic status, and intelligence test score. The students from the activity schools, however, were admitted to college on the basis of the school's recommendations, without regard to their Scholastic Aptitude Test scores. The colleges agreed to set aside their usual admission criteria and allow each high school in the study to recommend admission on the basis of the student's actual performance in the activity curriculum. If the high school felt that the student was ready for college, he or she was admitted. The colleges admitted the students from the matched control group independently.

The results of the comparison are shown in the list below. That is, in college the activity school students showed the following behaviors:

1. Earned a slightly higher total grade average.
2. Earned higher grade averages in all subject fields except foreign language.
3. Specialized in the same academic fields as did the comparison students.
4. Did not differ from the comparison group in the number of times they were placed on probation.
5. Received slightly more academic honors in each year.
6. Were more often judged to possess a high degree of intellectual curiosity and drive.
7. Were more often judged to be precise, systematic, and objective in their thinking.
8. Were more often judged to have developed clear or well-formulated ideas concerning the meaning of education—especially in the first two years in college.
9. More often demonstrated a high degree of resourcefulness in meeting new situations.
10. Did not differ from the comparison group in ability to plan their time effectively.
11. Had about the same problems of adjustment as the comparison group, but approached their solutions with greater effectiveness.
12. Participated somewhat more frequently, and more often enjoyed, appreciative experiences in the arts.
13. Participated more in all organized student groups except religious and "service" activities.
14. Earned in each college year a higher percentage of nonacademic honors (officership in organizations, election to managerial societies, athletic insignia, leading roles in dramatic and musical presentations).
15. Did not differ from the comparison group in the quality of adjustment to their contemporaries.
16. Differed only slightly from the comparison group in the kinds of judgments about their schooling.
17. Had a somewhat better orientation toward the choice of a vocation.
18. Demonstrated a more active concern for what was going on in the world. [18]

The individual differences were not great if taken one at a time, but the cumulative differences were quite substantial. In other words, across the board, whether it was in academic work, college leadership, general problem solving, extracurricular activities, or a general concern for society at large, the differences favored the pupils, 1475 of them, who graduated from one of the thirty high schools with the experimental curriculum.

Why, then, in view of these results, have the high schools in this country not been more innovative in the past thirty years? *The Eight Year Study* certainly provided a solid research base to attest to the differences a curriculum can make. The one major factor that the study could not contend with, though, was history. The results were published in 1942, just as the country was entering World War II. The war, the subsequent flooding of schools and colleges with returning veterans and postwar-boom babies, the Cold War, and the competition with Russia for leadership in science in the intervening years were some of the main elements that obscured both the need for secondary school reform and the major blueprint for change outlined by the *Eight Year Study.* The nation became occupied and preoccupied with other issues of postwar recovery, issues that appeared most pressing in the short run. In the long run, of course, the secondary school as an institution suffered a major setback. As the Coleman study, the Sprinthall-Mosher research, and the Goodlad investigation have clearly shown, in the interim nothing much has changed in secondary education.

RECENT POLICY INITIATIVES FOR SECONDARY SCHOOL REFORM

In the 1970s several national commissions called for change in secondary schools. The National Association of Secondary School Principals (NASSP), the National Commission on Resources for Youth (NCRY), the National Panel on High Schools, the National Commission on the Re-

The leading crowd produces conformity to extrinsic values

Photograph from Bruce Anderson Photography

formed Secondary Education, and the Report of the Panel on Youth of the President's Science Advisory Committee all studied the problem and reached similar conclusions: "The barrier between youth and the larger society could be reduced by increasing their participation in the 'real' world outside the school" [19].

The President's Science Advisory Committee report, authored by James Coleman of the *Adolescent Society*, suggested, along with the other commissions, that the so-called problems of adolescent growth and development were in large part attributable to how schools were organized. These commissions have all recommended that schools be organized into smaller units of from five hundred to one thousand pupils, with greater choice by students and more role diversity, including the possible alternative of work and study. The recommendations, particularly Coleman's, called for an activity curriculum (similar to that of the *Eight Year Study*) emphasizing especially the learning of responsibility for others. They cited the very promising findings from a series of "action learning" programs as examples of effective curriculum change. Since the midseventies there have been an increased number of studies supporting the importance of such programs in high schools. It is to these studies that we now turn.

Action-Learning Programs: Hope for the 1980s

The current experimental programs have two major characteristics. The first component is actual real world experience—hence the phrase *action learning*, or, as it used to be called, learning by doing. Action learning means participating in the topic under study, not passively observing, listening, or taking notes. The pupils actually do the activity. This technique is sometimes called role-taking learning as distinguished from role playing, which is usually a simulation rather than the real thing. The basic objective is simple and direct. If one wishes a person to learn a sense of responsibility, the person must be placed in a role where responsibility is required. So learning from experience is one major element.

However, there is no guarantee that a person will learn anything through experience by itself. Each of us can think of times when we have not really learned anything at all from an experience. We are certainly capable, for example, of repeating our mistakes.

Thus a second component is essential in order for action learning to have a positive effect—namely, that the students think about, or process, the experience. Guided reflection and rigorous intellectual examination of experience are as important as the experience itself. The programs, then, have a time period each week for the students in action learning to reflect about their experiences, to read, and to write about their experiences in their own journals. Similarly, discussions in class focus on the similarities and differences of the experiences the pupils are going through. The atmosphere in these discussions is similar to that in a seminar: The teacher's role is questioner, facilitator, and discussion guide rather than lecturer.

Experience and guided reflection are the general components of action learning. The specific components may vary. Some programs involve high school students as tutors for younger children; others involve them as community interns. The list below presents a few of the roles currently encouraged in action learning:

- tutors: reading, spelling, physical education, and so on

- teachers of almost any subject

- child care workers

- cross-age counselors

- cross-age teachers

- companions to the elderly

- community survey workers

- community service workers

- field-visit directors

- medical assistants (emergency room)

- bilingual day-care helpers

- aids to handicapped children

The intellectual or reflection component matches the form of the activity. Thus in a program of peer counseling, teenagers will read about approaches to counseling, the psychology of helping, and techniques of verbal and nonverbal communication. A syllabus for readings will provide perspective on their own role as peer counselor. Similarly, readings on child development would accompany the program for teenagers working as child care workers. Each class, then, would have its own action focus and intellectual focus. Either one by itself would miss the mark.

A national study was recently conducted on the impact of such programs [20]. The investigators wished to find out if such programs actively help the learning development of the helpees as well as the helpers. Certainly we can imagine a situation in which groups of teenagers might help first graders to read, but do the teenagers also learn? The study found that the tutees—that is, the children who receive teaching or tutoring by teenagers—do benefit. Their skills increase in whatever area they are being helped, reading, math, social studies, or other subjects. That result really isn't surprising. However, what is both surprising and encouraging is that the high school students also benefit, and in two ways: academically and psychologically.

SPECIAL TOPIC
Exceptional Adolescents: The Challenge of Mainstreaming for Secondary Schools

Until recently, children and adolescents classified with any one of the ten or so major handicapping conditions had been largely segregated from their peers. States and local communities followed a variety of policies, variously referred to as separation, deviate status placement, or even warehousing, in carrying out programs for different children. The most typical scenario included a special residential school located in a rural area where such children were educated. Many remained at such institutions for their entire lives.

A series of landmark legal cases, culminating in the passage of Public Law 94–142 in 1975, has changed all that. The major provision of the act was simple and direct: A free appropriate public education must be provided for all handicapped children in the *least restrictive environment.* Thus schools must do everything possible to include, rather than exclude, handicapped children from regular classrooms. The intent of the legislation was to guarantee, in so far as possible, that public schools were for all students. As a result, school policies now provide a variety of programs. Some previously excluded handicapped children can now spend full time in regular classrooms that have some modifications (alterations of the physical environment to reduce barriers, inclusion of person trained in sign language for hearing-impaired, new reading materials for the visually impaired, more individualized tutoring for mildly retarded, etc.). Children and adolescents with other handicapping conditions now spend part of their time in regular classes, supplemented with special classes for the balance of the day.

From a developmental point of view, a major rationale for such change comes from the interaction concept. Positive interaction with the environment stimulates development from less complex stages to more complex. The reverse is also true: Reduced interaction, isolation, and the lack of stimulation arrests growth.

A series of recent studies summarized by Henry Dupont has shown that these results are especially true during adolescence [1]. Under the previous policies of exclusion, teenagers with a wide variety of handicaps actually fell further and further behind in psychosocial development. For example, in studies of groups of mildly to moderately retarded, hearing-impaired, and visually impaired students, all three groups demonstrated increased levels of social and emotional disturbance during adolescence when compared with their adjustment in elementary school. A study of mildly retarded adolescents found a pattern of increased social isolation, and what friendships existed were with children between five and six years younger. A study of physically handicapped adolescents with spina bifida demonstrated extreme isolation patterns. Some teenagers with this condition (over half of a sample of 59) had no contact with a nonhandicapped peer over periods exceeding one month [2]. A study of hearing-impaired children showed similar results, though not quite as extreme patterns of isolation. The most unfortunate consequence of this lack of positive interaction is that such pupils experience declines in their level of development, particularly in interpersonal and social growth.

Thus youth workers, teachers, counselors, administrators, and caring adults must encourage schools to genuinely support (not just with lip service) the concept of mainstreaming. And the requisite changes must include the psychological environment as well as the physical environment. Jack Birch has summarized a series of studies of successful mainstreaming by schools and has found that positive attitudes were extremely important [3]. These attitudes include the following:

- Belief in the right to education for all children.

- Readiness of special-education and regular class teachers to cooperate with each other.

- Willingness to share competencies as a team in behalf of pupils.

- Openess to include parents as well as other professional colleagues in planning for and working with children.

- Flexibility with respect to class size and teaching assignments.

- Recognition that social and personal development can be taught and that they are equally as important as academic achievement. [4]

Birch also noted that in the school districts that successfully mainstreamed, at both the elementary and secondary levels and across disciplines, three factors stood out:

1. There was genuine appreciation of the team work with the special-education teachers, particularly the help the regular classroom teachers received with the children already in their rooms.

2. Regular classroom teachers found that special-education pupils were usually no more difficult to include in their classes than some children who were already there.

(Continued)

SPECIAL TOPIC (Continued)

3. The school spirit that "all the children are in the same school system" was expressed time after time. [5]

Clearly, the psychological agenda on an issue such as mainstreaming is critical. As one rather discerning adolescent noted, "It's bad enough being a teenager, but being in a wheel-chair too. . . . I get the feeling from some adults that I have the plague and I am a welfare cheater at the same time." Unfortunately, there is a heavy element of the self-fulfilling prophecy in our treatment of the handicapped. If we are convinced that handicapped adolescents are not capable of learning and growing, then that attitude is conveyed, even if we attempt to mask our real feelings. A study at Kansas State University by Parish and Copeland demonstrated that teachers did have significantly more negative expectations of handicapped pupils than the pupils did themselves. The teachers expected such children to have negative self-images (a low self-concept) [6].

A junior high school shop teacher recently experienced a different outcome. In a story he related to one author, he told of a 13-year-old boy (EMR), mainstreamed for the first time, who appeared in his woodworking class [7]. The teacher had taken some courses as part of his in-service training to develop his skill in relating to a broad variety of pupils. Also, he had attempted to use a greater variety of teaching strategies, including learning to recognize the legitimate feelings teenagers experience. As a result, he was quick to spot both a high level of anxiety and a hesitation to try anything when the 13-year-old entered his class. Gradually, as the teacher individualized his lesson plans, he was able to get the boy going on a task, making bookends. Using positive reinforcement, the teacher soon saw the young man take a genuine interest. Each day he would appear earlier and earlier at the door. He worked

From an academic standpoint studies have shown that high school students who teach reading, for example, to younger children also improve their own reading skills. In fact, in one study the teenage tutors showed greater gains in reading than the tutees [21]. Similarly, in a peer-counseling program the teenage counselors showed major improvement in their own communication skills. In a cross-age teaching class high school students, as small-group discussion teachers in a junior high school, improved their own ability to reason and critically analyze dilemma situations [22]. These are important results. They show that the teenagers in action learning are not simply being exploited. In fact, they achieve significant

furiously, cutting, gluing, and sanding. Finally, the project was finished, just as the term ended. (The bookends, said the teacher later, weren't exactly straight but were they smooth.)

That evening the teacher received a phone call from the boy's mother. She said, "I just wanted to thank you for your work with my son." She continued, "You know we had some qualms about this mainstreaming, but no longer. Today, after school, he appeared and rang the doorbell at the front door. It was a shock. Usually he would sort of sneak home from the special class and go right to his room, in silence, and stay there until supper. Not today. Today he appeared at the front door. I opened it and there he stood, at least ten feet tall, holding up these tippy bookends. 'Look,' he said. 'Look what I can do.' "

As the teacher related the story to me, he said, "Look, what we can do!"

REFERENCES

1. H. Dupont, Meeting the emotional-social needs of students in a mainstreamed environment, *Counseling and Human Development* 10, 9(1978):1–11.

2. S. Dorner, The relationship of physical handicap to stress in families with an adolescent with spina bifida, *Developmental Medical Child Neurology* 17(1975):765–776.

3. J. Birch, *Mainstreaming* (Reston, Va.: Council for Exceptional Children, 1974).

4. *Ibid.*, p. 94.

5. *Ibid.*

6. T. S. Parish and T. F. Copeland, Teachers' and students' attitudes in mainstreamed classrooms, *Psychological Reports* 43(1978):54.

7. The case study of the junior high school boy was related by Victor Hauck, a teacher at Northview Junior High School, Osseo, Minnesota.

intellectual and academic gains as a result of the responsibility involved in helping younger children.

From the standpoint of this text, of course, we would hardly be content with programs that produce only academic gains. What of the psychological effects? What happens to the level of psychological maturity of the teenager? We have stressed throughout this book the importance of psychological growth. In this chapter we have presented findings that indicate quite clearly that the general program in most secondary schools has uncertain psychological effects on adolescents. Too often they remain in the grips of the adolescent society that emphasizes the extrinsic values of

Effective learning can occur through experience and reflection
Photograph from Elizabeth Hamlin

looks, clothes, and athletics. Decision making not based on the values of the leading crowd and intrinsic interest in learning are rare in the usual atmosphere of secondary schools. The results of the action-learning programs, on the other hand, have produced positive effects specifically in the area of psychological maturity.

In a study directed by Dan Conrad with a national sample of over six hundred students from nine different school systems, the results were quite clear [23]. He compared students in action-learning classes with students in control classes from the same schools. The experimental class students demonstrated gains in the following areas:*

- self-esteem

- social problem solving: personal efficiency

- social and personal responsibility

- empathy: altruism

- career exploration

- moral/value development

- ego development

---

* A variety of scales were employed, including Rosenberg's, Janis-Field's, Kohlberg-Rest's, and Loevinger's, as estimates of the various psychological domains.

Conrad's findings show a definite balance in favor of the action-learning classes. In every instance the experimental class students showed gains exceeding those of the control groups from a variety of estimates of psychological maturity. This result indicates that classes can be organized in a manner that provides both intellectual and psychological growth during adolescence.

It is also interesting to note which characteristics the teenagers themselves cite as making a positive difference. The following list gives the results of a multiple regression analysis (a sophisticated multivariate statistical technique) that rank-orders the elements considered most important by the students:

1. Had adult responsibilities.

2. Made important decisions.

3. Did things myself instead of observing.

4. Had freedom to develop and use my own ideas.

5. Felt I made a contribution.

6. Had freedom to explore my own interests.

7. Discussed my experiences with teachers.

8. Discussed my experiences with family and friends.

9. I was given clear direction.

10. Adults at site took personal interest in me.

11. Was appreciated when I did a good job.

Compare what these teenagers said about their learning experience with the results of the Coleman, Sprinthall-Mosher, or Goodlad surveys. In all those studies students ranked learning at the bottom of the scale.

Toward a Balanced Curriculum

The overall message seems quite clear: Students in secondary school can engage in effective learning experiences. It is also clear that for most of them the traditional curriculum and the usual method of instruction leaves much to be desired. The standard program of most schools is, at best, a weak competitor for adolescent energy and commitment. Yet it doesn't have to be. The classic *Eight Year Study* demonstrated that an activity and interdisciplinary curriculum can make a difference, especially for students who wish to go to college. The Conrad survey, involving college prep, working-class, and urban ghetto schools, showed that all students can develop under conditions of responsibility and action learning. Thus the effective curriculum needs a careful balance of real world experience and active reflection. Learning must always address the personal and psychological aspects of the individual as well as the intellectual aspects. The advantages of action learning, when it works, is its balance between learning information about other people and learning about one's self. At no time is the need for this balance greater than during adolescence.

The American Psychological Association conducted a survey of some four thousand teenagers, and the message they gave was clear [24]. The survey asked teenagers what topics from psychology they would be most interested in studying. The list of possibilities was massive, encompassing practically every known aspect of behavior, both human and animal. Unhesitatingly, the teenagers voted for the following topics as central to their concerns:

1. Love, pleasure, joy, humor, entertainment (relationship to emotions, love, humor, novelty).

2. Emotions (causes, effects, and methods of control).

3. States of consciousness (waking, consciousness, sleep, dreaming, meditation, and biofeedback).

4. Depression (types, origins, and treatment).

As we have noted, adolescents are in the process of growing, changing, asking, and seeking. The secondary school has for the most part either neglected or eschewed any focus on the teenager as a person. Unfortunately, as long as the schools remain entrenched in this view—a separation of academic learning from psychological development—then findings similar to those of *The Adolescent Society* will emerge. Alternatives are possible. Yet until an active curriculum becomes widespread, at least a major part of the adolescent problem will reside not in the teenagers but in the institutions they attend.

DEVELOPMENTAL GOALS FOR SCHOOLING

We have strongly suggested that promoting developmental growth is an important concern during adolescence. By developmental growth we mean growth in a wide variety of developmental sectors or domains. In Chapter 4 we explained the importance of interaction in classroom activities across the entire scope of the academic curriculum. Cognitive development in this sense results from the role of active learning rather than from the passive role of a listener. Modifying teacher methods and curriculum materials could result in intellectual development for all pupils, not, as it stands now, for only a small proportion.

From a developmental view, however, we are not content to settle for an exclusive focus on intellectual growth. Other domains of growth are of equal significance. For example, Erikson includes the goal of identity formation, a firm sense of one's own individuality. Selman and Loevinger argue for the importance of interpersonal and ego development. They feel that during adolescence the major task is to move from social conformity—mindlessly following the dictates of a leading crowd—toward conscientious individuality. Part of that goal is the need to achieve interpersonal empathy, to place oneself in someone else's shoes. Kohlberg thinks that development during adolescence includes a major shift in perspective about the basic source of value choices and moral judgment decisions. Whether any of these changes take place depends on the quality of the formal and informal educational experience.

We noted in Chapter 1 that development is not automatic. In fact, in the domains of cognition, identity, interpersonal/ego development, and moral judgment, there is apparently a very substantial leveling out during middle to late adolescence. Estimates indicate that only a third of adults achieve formal operations fully, and the estimates in the other areas are not more optimistic. The results given in Chapter 6 indicate the stability of stage 3 reasoning well into adulthood. From this view, then, it is most important for schools to take these issues seriously—that is, to promote growth within each domain. Table 12.8 depicts the areas, the domain content, and the goals that may be possible.

We have also indicated in various sections of this text that there is an important functional relationship between one's current stage and one's behavior. We have shown, for example, that persons at relatively low stages of ego development have difficulty in dealing positively with others. Selman (see Chapter 5) has shown that emotional disturbance during early adolescence is linked to the level of interpersonal development, and Bielke's study (Chapter 5) of unwed mothers demonstrated a similar effect. A series of studies related scores on the Loevinger system to antisocial and delinquent behavior (Chapter 10). The Chandler study (Chapter 10) dem-

TABLE 12.8 Developmental goals for secondary schools

	Cognitive intellectual	Personal identity	Moral value	Interpersonal	Ego stage	Decision making
Theorist	Piaget	Erikson	Kohlberg	Selman	Loevinger	Miller-Tiedeman
From	Concrete	Identity foreclosure and/or identity diffusion	Social conformity	Sequential role taking (concrete)	Conformist	Impulsive/fatalistic
To	Formal I (abstract) and formal II	Identity moratorium and identity achievement	Inner-directed legalistic	Simultaneous mutual role taking (abstract)	Self-directed conscientious	Rational planner

onstrated that an increase in social role-taking capacity reduced the incidence of delinquent behavior. Also, we showed in Chapter 6 that there are important links between the stage of moral reasoning and how humans behave, especially in stressful situations. In addition, in Chapter 2 we indicated the relationship between the level of identity formation and performance in a complex task such as teaching: Those teachers in identity diffusion were ineffective in the classroom. We have not reviewed all the studied detailing these relationships since the purpose of this book is not to provide a comprehensive research review. But there is considerable evidence to support our view [25].

In short, we have attempted to make three related points. First, there is a strong functional relationship between a person's stage of development and how the person thinks and acts. Second, there is a potential for growth from less complex to more complex stages of development. Third, the secondary schools can, but do not now, provide educational programs designed to promote stage growth. By neglecting to create the needed effective programs, the schools promote stabilization in development at levels below potential in the variety of domains we have noted.

SUMMARY

In this chapter we provided information on the historical development of secondary schools in this country. Industrialization during the late nineteenth century, combined with urbanization, created the need for a better-educated population. We showed how these trends aided in creating today's large-scale and comprehensive schools for nearly all teenagers.

However, the main goal of this chapter was to review a series of studies detailing the effects of the secondary school experience on the adolescents. The results of the now-classic work of James Coleman in the 1950s provided a significant, but not positive, picture of how the school's adolescent society shapes and molds the values and aspirations of a great majority of the students. Unfortunately, it is the content of these values that is the problem. Two recent studies of the impact of schooling cross-validate Coleman's earlier work. The schools are still dominated by anti-intellectual values that seek to promote conformity, superficiality, and an excessive concern for good clothes, good looks, and fast cars.

We also provided information on how schools can be organized to promote development. The classic *Eight Year Study* and some very recent research on action-learning programs indicate that what is, is not what has to be. In other words, there are teaching methods combined with experiential-learning activities that may promote growth toward higher stages of psychological maturity for a much greater proportion of secondary school pupils than is now the case. We concluded the chapter with a discussion outlining possible developmental goals for schooling across a variety of stage domains.

KEY POINTS AND NAMES

Common school

The adolescent society

James Coleman

Leading crowd

Schooling in the sixties

Norman Sprinthall and Ralph Mosher

Goodlad study

John Goodlad

Activity schools: *The Eight Year Study*

Action learning in the 1980s

Dan Conrad

Developmental goals for schools

REFERENCES

1. T. Newcomb, Youth in colleges and correction, *American Psychologist* 33(1978):114–124.

2. J. S. Coleman, *Youth: Transition to adulthood* (Chicago: University of Chicago Press, 1974),p. 80.

3. J. S. Coleman, *The adolescent society* (New York: Free Press, 1961), p. 14.

4. *Ibid.*

5. J. Goodlad, A study of schooling, *Phi Delta Kappan* (1979, 1980; reprints of four articles).

6. Coleman, *Adolescent society.*

7. *Ibid.*, p. 245.

8. *Ibid.*, p. 255.

9. *Ibid.*, p. 315.

10. *Ibid.*, p. 292.

11. D. Mann, The politics of training teachers in schools, *Teachers College Record* 77(1976):3.

12. Coleman, *Youth*, p. 87.

13. E. Z. Friedenberg, *The vanishing adolescent* (Boston: Beacon Press, 1959); C. Silberman, *Crisis in the classroom* (New York: Random House, 1970).

14. N. A. Sprinthall and R. L. Mosher, *Studies of adolescents in the secondary schools* (Cambridge, Mass.: Harvard Graduate School of Education, 1969).

15. Goodlad.

16. *Ibid.*, p. 40.

17. D. Chamberlain, *Did they succeed in college?* vol. 4 (New York: Harper and Brothers, 1942).

18. Wilford Margaret Aikin, The story of the eight year study, Vol. I (New York: Harper & Row, 1942). Reprinted by permission from The story of the eight year study, Vol. I of *Adventure in American Education* by Aikin. © 1942 by McGraw Hill, Inc. pp. 111–112.

19. Coleman, *Youth*, pp. 145–173.

20. D. Conrad and D. Hedin, *Action learning in Minnesota* (St. Paul, Minn.: Center for Youth Development and Research, undated monograph).

21. A. Gartner, M. Kohler, and F. Riessman, *Children teach children* (New York: Harper & Row, 1971).

22. N. A. Sprinthall, Psychology for secondary schools: The saber-tooth curriculum revisited? *American Psychologist* 35(1980):336–347.

23. D. Conrad, The differential impact of experiential learning programs on secondary school students (Ph.D. thesis, University of Minnesota, 1980). Also see D. E. Conrad and D. P. Hedin, How to learn from nonclassroom experiences, *Synergist* 5, 3(1976):20–23.

24. Human Behavior Curriculum Projects, *Ratings of module topics by high school psychology teachers and students* (Washington, D.C.: APA Clearinghouse on Pre-College Psychology, 1977).

25. For a comprehensive review of studies that validate the relationship between stage of development and actual behavior, see N.A. Sprinthall and L. Thies-Sprinthall, The teacher as an adult learner, in *National Society for the Study of Education yearbook*, ed. G. Griffin (Chicago: University of Chicago Press, 1983). For a review focused exclusively on the relationship between moral development stage and behavior, see J. R. Rest, Morality, in *Carmichael's manual of child psychology*, 4th ed., vol. 1, ed. J. Flavell, E. Markman, and P. Mussen (New York: Wiley, forthcoming). The references just in the area of moral development now exceed five thousand entries, and Rest's review is probably the most comprehensive and concise.

CHAPTER 13

Career Development During Adolescence

INTRODUCTION

In Oscar Lewis's novel *La Vida*, a young girl, Catin, is discussing her career plans. In the midst of a background of abject poverty as a school dropout (or push-out) and with a large number of siblings, all existing on the very edge of survival, she brightly announces that she will provide her disorganized family with money. "That's why when I grow up, I want to be a doctor or a chambermaid" [1].

This statement typifies the problem of career choice during adolescence. The correlates of realism are often low. An understanding of the relationship between what an adolescent is now accomplishing and future career choice is often lacking or ignored. Yet decision making and planning for the future are extremely important if an adolescent is to keep options open. The situation presents a paradox: premature closure on job choice versus no choice because of aimless diffusion.

Adolescents, of course, would like to have a clear and specific career objective. But early choice may be unwise or premature in the sense that abilities, competences, and values are not fixed by adolescence. On the other hand, we know that purposeless behavior or unplanned and impulsive choice without goals can lend to circular meandering—hence the paradox. Adolescence as a stage of development is synonymous with significant change in a variety of domains. During such a period of change early choice may be based on highly inaccurate assessments of competence. Yet keeping career options open when so many other areas of a teenager's life are also unfocused may only add more confusion and instability to the teenager's life.

In this chapter we will examine a framework that describes the process of decision making in relation to developmental stage concepts. We will also review some recent research identifying the most common systems teenagers actually employ. Then we will describe educational programs designed to improve the teenager's ability to explore and examine the issues of career choice. The I-Power program, the career value dilemma approach, and the Born Free project illustrate some of the newer approaches to career education. We conclude the chapter with a discussion of career choice, developmental maturity, achievement motivation, and the significance of sex differences, as a means of highlighting the long-range goals of effective programs.

PIAGET: A FRAMEWORK

Piaget has pointed out that a major difference between the child and the adolescent is the ability of the latter to "think beyond the present," particularly in reference to the occupational world. In fact, in spite of many cultural differences and different societal norms, the process of entry into a productive occupational role is literally synonymous with the beginning of adulthood and the end of adolescence. According to Piaget, there are two important aspects to this process: (1) the decline of egocentric thought and (2) the emergence of commitment. Both Piaget and Elkind have commented on the relation between the emergence of formal operations (the step forward) and the parallel growth in egocentric thought (the step backward). And occupational choice can be the major arena for the decline of egocentric thinking and the increase in *decentered cognition*. Decentered formal operations, by definition, permit a person to understand the subjective nature of possibilities and probabilities, time perspective, and, indeed, the paradox of choice and commitment. Thus Piaget and Inhelder note:

> The focal point of the decentering process is the entrance into the occupational world or the beginning of serious professional training. The adolescent becomes an adult when he undertakes a real job. It is then he is transformed from an idealistic reformer into an achiever. [2]

However, entering the occupational world or making a professional-training commitment does not ensure that decentering actually results. Piaget suggests formal and decentered thought as a possibility, not a guaranteed outcome, of job entry. In other words, the process of interaction between the adolescent and career choice can foster developmental cognitive growth within the stage of formal operations. Such growth, as we have noted, is referred to as filling in the "horizontal decalage" since the change is to a more adequate process within the same stage. However, remember that growth is not automatic. The quality of the interaction and the learning atmospheres determines whether the choice will function to decenter the adolescent's thought patterns about careers.

CAREER DECISION MAKING

In the past career education theory and practice were in the same trap as the general secondary school curriculum in this country. Career education assumed that children and adolescents could and would process career choice at a rational, logical level. Career materials were thus based on the assumption that if teenagers wished to reach a career goal, all they had to do was calculate the precise steps they must take to reach it. This model is called the probability model. For example, with this model, if a 16-year-old wished to be a doctor, the teenager would collect information on the academic achievement records of students admitted to medical school, their college majors, their high school rank, and so on. Then the student's present high school program, grade point average, and so on would be compared with the data collected and the probability of success computed. If the teenager were currently in, say, the middle range of the high school grade point average, the probability of success would be 1 out of 10,000 or so. So the implications were clear and direct: If the teenager really wanted to be a doctor, then that person must work very hard.

The assumption that was so obvious in the past we now know is incorrect. Information by itself will rarely change human behavior. In fact,

In making a career choice, are teenagers self-directed or simply following along?
Photograph from Joe Di Dio/ National Education Association

information is usually forgotten almost as quickly as it's presented. Thus the procedures stressing rational decision making as a means of stimulating career choice have yielded negative results. And as one recent national survey showed, the pupils themselves felt betrayed. In a survey of high school graduates some ten years after graduation, a huge proportion (85% of over one thousand persons) indicated that they felt almost totally unprepared for the process of career choice [3]. Guidance information was viewed as superficial, narrow, and inadequate.

In this section we will examine some of the issues surrounding career decision making, such as changing one's mind, levels of decision making, and strategies and stages of development.

Changing One's Mind

A study involving some two hundred secondary school pupils indicated that at least part of the decision-making problem was the short-term nature of career choice [4]. This research study found that the content of career choice shifted rapidly; in a one-year span in high school only 26% of the students maintained their career choice. When these pupils were studied over a three-year period (grades 9–12), only 17% retained their original choice. Thus one conclusion is obvious: Using specific career goals as either the only or the major component of career development during secondary schools impacts from between 25 and 17% of the pupils. The normal pattern is for one to change one's mind many times about the career one wants to have as an adult. Studies of adult career development reveal similar shifts. Estimates run as high as from four to six major career changes during the period of a lifetime [5]. That finding does not include job change within the same field but only changes across major occupational categories—that is, changing one's career not just changing one's job.

Levels of Decision Making

We have seen that the content of career objectives is volatile. Now we will turn to the decision-making process itself. That is, what system are the teenagers actually employing as they ponder their goals?

This question has not been subjected to numerous investigations, unfortunately. But we do have the results of one major study in this area. This research was conducted in secondary schools representing two different socioeconomic classes, working class and middle class [6]. Equal numbers of males and females were randomly selected from the total population of eleventh graders. To assess the decision-making process, the researchers conducted individual interviews with each pupil. Students were asked to describe how they were presently approaching vocational and/or college choice. The interviewers, all experienced counseling psychologists, asked the students to elaborate and clarify whatever process they were using. In other words, the researchers did not impose their view of how teenagers should or ought to proceed. Instead, with substantial nondirective questioning, the staff probed for the reasons, feelings, and methods the students were actually employing as they confronted job and career decisions at the end of the eleventh grade.

The students' decision styles gradually formed into a cluster of approaches. With these clusters a scoring manual was created by using student excerpts as illustrations of the different styles. Then the researchers interviewed a second larger sample of pupils whose responses were scored blind according to the decision style clusters.

After the study was completed, it became apparent not only that the decision styles could be clustered into logical groupings but also that the decision styles formed a developmental hierarchy. In other words, with the benefit of reanalysis it was obvious that adolescent decision styles concerning career choice formed a system of stages, shown in Table 13.1. The stage categories are denoted according to levels of complexity. The amount of use within and across each category is also presented in the table. This data gives an initial picture of the most common, or modal, systems the teenagers employ. From the table it is readily apparent how infrequently teenagers conform to the expectations, discussed previously—that is, carefully weighing objective information and choosing a career on the basis of logical probabilities.

Overall, there were negligible sex differences, as the data in Table 13.1 show. Males and females tended to produce highly similar styles. The distribution of strategies, then, was independent of sex classification.

TABLE 13.1 Decision-making strategies (public high school juniors)

Stage	Description	Males	Females	Total choices	Percentage
I	Impulsive or leave it to fate	47	54	101	31
II	Compliant, other-directed	28	35	95	29
	Exploration leads to confusion and/or paralysis	13	19		
III	Rational planning or a deliberate moratorium	57	57	114	35
	Analytical and creative	7	11	18	5
	Total			328	100%

SPECIAL TOPIC
Professor Jones and Occ-U-Sort: Helping Teenagers Learn About Careers

The problem of career choice has been as troublesome to the expert as it has been to teenagers themselves. A basic difficulty has been how to help adolescents understand the different nature of a variety of careers. There is obviously an information deficit that seems insurmountable when we think of some twenty thousand careers. With that many job possibilities, how can anyone really know enough at the outset to make wise choices?

Psychologists in the past have tried to help students make choices by creating a series of tests, or inventories. The idea is simple. The student takes the test, and the examiner then interprets the meaning of the responses. This approach, however, has some fundamental problems. It is very difficult for a student to understand why profiles of interests (such as the Strong-Campbell Interest Inventory or the Kuder Preference Record) relate to job choice. "What does answering a lot of questions about whether I like to go to a play or read a book have to do with being a banker or a salesperson or an engineer?" And it is just that problem that is a fundamental weakness of such tests. It requires an expert examiner to explain and reexplain the meaning of the profiles. Even then the pupil may not get the point. The student may confuse interest with aptitude and view the test as some kind of magical predictor.

Approximately 60% of the sample responses could be classified as either impulsive or other-directed (stages I and II in Table 13.1). Thus almost two-thirds of the teenagers did not employ rational planning, that is, thinking through consequences or weighing alternatives in decision making. Instead, they tended either to choose blindly and impulsively or leave it to fate (stage I) or to seek advice from others (stage II).

For those seeking advice, however, there is little evidence that such information was weighed and considered. Instead, the teenagers seemed to uncritically accept and follow directions from adults. This stage took two forms. In one form the teenagers merely complied with others' wishes. In the second form the teenagers seemed to go through a kind of pseudoexploration. These students understood that decision making involves exploring and weighing alternatives and so, in a sense, they dutifully went through the motions of exploration. However, they appeared to become lost or confused by the process. The students apparently were not self-

Into this breach stepped Larry Jones from North Carolina State University [1]. He reasoned that the main object is to provide direct help to adolescents so that they will begin to learn about themselves in relation to possible careers. Rather than place an expert between the pupil and the process, he created a process the students can use themselves. He eliminated the need for the expert and, as well, eliminated the gap between taking the test and interpreting the findings.

Jones borrowed a technique from Stephenson (the Q-sort method) and built on some earlier pioneering work of Leona Tyler. After many tryouts, he created a self-administered career choice instrument called an occupational card sort. With it users explore their occupational preferences by sorting, into different piles, cards that contain the names of occupations. These cards are then resorted in helpful ways. His next step was critical. He constructed different sets of materials so that adolescents at junior high, senior high, and college levels could test themselves and interpret the findings. This step required much skill and patience, since experts can easily overestimate or underestimate the abilities of adolescents at different levels of maturity. Jones, after much effort, produced understandable versions.

His final problem, after getting the materials straight, was the actual content of the Q-sort. Since there were 20,000 occupations, if he used one per card, it could take a year to administer the test. On the other hand, if he collapsed the list too much, choice would be overly restricted, even though testing time would be brief. So he needed some kind of a category system where

(Continued)

directed enough to actually establish priorities in the process. Thus these strategies of compliant and confused or paralyzed exploration are different aspects of the same stage—like a Kohlberg stage 3, social conformity without self-direction.

The students in the third category primarily employed a rational-planning model. They could sort through a variety of alternatives and think in probability terms concerning career decisions. This process is similar to a process educator John Dewey termed *scientific decision making*. These components include (1) open-ended exploration, (2) assessment of short- and long-term consequences, (3) evaluation of self, and (4) closure on the most likely choice. In other words, a rational problem solving or task analysis approach is applied to career and personal choice. However, only 35% of the high school juniors actually employed this method.

A very small proportion (5%) used a somewhat unique system. These students seemed to be both rational and intuitive—using a combination of

SPECIAL TOPIC (Continued)

jobs could be clustered, with a few representing many. This process also required much field testing to ensure that the final selection was, indeed, still
representative. He settled on a set of 60 cards, each one describing the basic
elements of a particular job, which represented the six vocational interest categories of John Holland [2] (10 cards for each group).

The process of career choice does not stop with sorting the cards,
though. Jones carefully added a series of follow-up steps, all of which can be
accomplished by the pupil.

The evaluations conducted thus far are positive at all levels, junior high
through college. The students find Jones's system helpful. It reduces the mystery of career choice and makes the process seem much less formidable and
intimidating. Perhaps that is its greatest contribution—a structure that students themselves can use as an initial step to informed career self-development.

REFERENCES

1. L. K. Jones, *Occ-u-sort* (Monterey, Calif.: Publishers Test Service, 1981).

2. Holland's system includes six broad categories: (1) realistic, (2) investigative, (3)
   artistic, (4) social, (5) enterprising, and (6) conventional. These categories also
   match Roe's categories, almost one for one, so the Jones system probably represents an adequate synthesis of the two most well-known occupational classifications. For further discussion on this point, see R. Rehberg and L. Hotchkiss, Career counseling in contemporary U.S. high schools, in *Review of research in
   education,* ed. D. C. Berliner (Washington, D.C.: American Educational Research
   Association, 1979), pp. 92–147.

planning and open-ended creativity. But since there were so few in this
mode, conclusions must be extremely tentative. It is possible, though, that
this mode may be an index of a significantly higher stage of decision making. Such a process may be a synthesis of the rational and the emotional.
The person may be able to review carefully all the objective information as
well as make a personal or subjective assessment of assets and liabilities.
When career-decision-making theory in the Piagetian sense mentions the
concept of commitment, this aspect may be the focus. The process of
personal choice and commitment may be more comprehensive and complex than the process of rational planning. We do not mean, however, that
this creative process is therefore irrational. Instead, the implication is that
after a weighing of alternatives, objectively and scientifically, the subjective

or self component of intuition may add an important dimension to the choice—a personal commitment. Such an intrinsic element may in the long run distinguish between a logical and a creative career choice. There is a need for longitudinal research to document and validate whether this creative/analytical mode is an indication of the next stage up on the developmental sequence of decision making. We can say now, however, that this small trend does indicate that decision-making stages do not necessarily stop at the rational-planning mode.

Cicourel and Kitsuse: Who Makes the Decision?

Given the findings reported above—namely, that almost two-thirds of the teenagers in the study approached career decision making in a rather haphazard manner—we now ask, Who does, in fact, make the decisions? Some years ago two sociologists studied that question. Aaron Cicourel and John Kitsuse carefully investigated the decisions teenagers made and found that adults were the actual decision makers [7]. They discovered that school counselors played an extremely important, although low-profile, role. Without being overly obvious, the counselors were sorting the teenagers into certain tracks.

The counselors made the placements, unfortunately, according to superficial social and economic stereotypes. For instance, middle-class and upper-middle-class students were urged to attend college and consider professional careers, reinforcing parental wishes. Thus the counselors and parents formed a kind of unwritten alliance and were the decision makers. Because of the system of decision making that the majority of teenagers actually employ (unplanned, leave it to fate, impulsive, follow the crowd), we see that it would not be overly difficult for adults to take over the process in that way.

For teenagers from working-class and lower-class backgrounds, the counselors also played an important role, but in a different direction. Cicourel and Kitsuse found that these teenagers were systematically persuaded away from higher career aspirations and directed toward manual training and low-wage service occupations. To make matters even worse from the standpoint of human development, other studies have shown that counselors spend a disproportionate amount of their time helping middle-class students [8]. The working-class students receive very little of the counselors' time and effort, and the help they do receive is of rather dubious quality.

Neither group of students is really being helped in a developmental sense—to learn how to make informed decisions themselves. There is an old story that perhaps sums up the situation. During World War I after the French army had suffered innumerable defeats, the direct result of incompetent military leadership, the head of the civilian government, Georges Clemenceau, announced that war was too important to be left to generals.

After that the civilian government took over the decision making. Similarly, perhaps the question of career choice is too important to be left to teenagers to resolve; adults must make the choices for them. Yet if adults do make their decisions, how will the teenagers learn the process? The work of Anna Miller-Tiedeman and David Tiedeman points in a new and positive direction for possible answers.

Strategies and Stages of Development

Anna Miller-Tiedeman and David Tiedeman combined the results from decision-making strategies and stages of development to study the issue of career choice [9]. Employing a framework from ego development theory based on Jane Loevinger's work, the Tiedemans constructed a framework that charts development from the perspective of career choice. Table 13.2 presents the Loevinger stages of general personality development along with the Tiedemans' model for career decision making.

In other words, according to the Tiedemans, one important manifestation of career decision making is derived from the individual's stage of ego development. Other theorists have referred to this result as career selection being determined by and as a by-product of a person's self-concept. Career choice as the implementation of a self-concept is another way of stating the idea. The stages of career choice, then, line up with particular stages of ego development, as Table 13.2 illustrates. And the stages of ego development, as we have seen, provide a clear chart of qualitative milestones in a sense that parallels the stages in other domains.

In addition to ego/personality stage, there are other factors that affect the career decision process. The Tiedemans refer to those elements as "influences and determiners." Since no individual will always use the same strategy in every situation, there must be dynamic factors affecting the process in addition to the general stage relationships, factors such as physical condition, current emotional processing, constraints of time, number of important concurrent decisions, general motivational level, and satisfaction with current interpersonal relationships. Thus we cannot examine decision making in isolation. We must also review the surrounding life space and the specific focus of a particular decision. Of course, at more complex stages the individual has an increasing capacity to take into account many of these life space considerations. But the Tiedemens inject a note of caution: Career decision making does fit a stage sequence in general. The relationship, however, is not precisely one for one—individualistic dynamic factors also influence both the specific choice and the implementation.

Implications

Probably the most important, immediate implication of career decision-making research is that teenagers actually employ a very immature method, and that system parallels the outcomes in the other development

TABLE 13.2 Decision strategy and Loevinger stages of ego development

Stage	Loevinger code	Description	Decision strategy
Presocial	I–1		Impulsive: "Act now; think later or not at all."
Symbiotic			
Impulsive	I–2	Impulsive, fear of retaliation	Aimless-delaying: "I don't care and don't want to be bothered."
Self-protective		Fear of being caught, externalizing blame, opportunistic	Fixed: "What will be, will be." "It's who you know, not what." "Watch out for number one."
Conformist	I–3	Conformity to external rules, shame, guilt for breaking rules	Compliant: "If it's OK with you, it's OK with me." "I started to explore but it was too much of a hassle." "Tell me what the tests tell me to do and I'll do it."
Conscientious	I–4	Self-evaluated standards, self-criticism, guilt for consequences, long-term goals and ideals	Planned: "I'll set some goals and plan steps to get there." "Sometimes after looking at all the alternatives, I decide to wait." "I'm enough of a self-starter that I can rely on myself."
Autonomous	I–5	*Add:* Coping with conflicting inner needs, toleration	Analytical/creative: "I look at the facts, the theories—and let my imagination wander around too—before I decide." "After looking at my thoughts and feelings both in the short and long run, I'm ready to decide and commit myself or not—."
Integrated	I–6	*Add:* Reconciling inner conflicts, renunciation or unattainable	

Note: "*Add*" means in addition to the description applying to the previous level.

domains. As we have noted in the areas of social cognition (personal relationships) and value judgments, teenagers are heavily dependent on external direction. Thus it comes as no surprise in the sociological study of teenage decision making that the teenagers themselves tended *not* to make their own decisions and that, instead, parents and school personnel made the decisions for them.

Presenting findings of what is, however, is not the same as suggesting what might be. But the need for effective career education is obvious from the studies. In a recent survey over one thousand randomly selected adults 30 years of age were asked about their high school experience [10]. The most common response was that high school as a whole had been "irrelevant." The adults were generally satisfied with their current life-styles and careers. However, they all singled out career guidance as the one aspect of high school that they considered a failure. The adults felt totally unprepared to make effective decisions. Less than 17% of the national sample reported that the secondary school experience had helped them learn how to make their own decisions with regard to career selection. The random, impulse, and other-directed decision-making methods teenagers employ do not promote growth or development. Thus programs are needed that start where the teenager currently is as a decision maker and then promote growth to a slightly more complex level.

At the outset of this chapter we noted Piaget's suggestion that career choice with commitment is perhaps *the* critical element in transforming the egocentric thought of the adolescent to the decentered world of adulthood. However, we realize that such a transformation is not automatic. Programs are necessary to aid in the transition from other-directed decision making to the beginning of self-generated decision making. An excerpt from a counseling dialogue illustrates the problem. A college sophomore, who has always dutifully followed directions from others, begins to discern his own lack of inner direction as a result of comments from a girl friend:

College student: I used to have a girl friend who told me that I never made my own decisions, and just let my parents make them for me, and that was bad because eventually some day I would have to make my own decisions. And I kept telling her that maybe I liked it this way. I wasn't sure, because I had never tried the other way. She seemed to be doing pretty well with her method. She said that I ought to start making my own decisions, and I said that I liked the way I lived. I liked to have my decisions made for me. I guess she was there all along; she thought it was a good idea. And now after I've seen both sides of it, of course, to a degree, not very much, now I like the other way more than ever. Having it really set up; slide down the chute instead of . . .

Counselor: Go alone.

College student: Yeah. Just follow the path that's laid down, rather than try to find my own path in the wilderness. Seems good. [11]

The student is obviously struggling with the question of moving from a compliant, other-directed stage of decision making toward the beginning of a more self-directed system. Such a transition is not smooth, however. In this case, the student has experienced some eighteen years in which the major decisions were made for him. Giving up this system inevitably creates dissonance. In his words:

College student: And if I decide to make decisions, I am going to have to do that all the time. That seems like a pretty crummy alternative to the other.

Yet that's the sort of thing I'm worried about. If I thought . . . or chose to remain on the path [where other people make my decisions for me], I might become instead of more flexible, sort of ossified. Which is fine, for that path; and what if she comes along, or someone like her and says . . . and then if I'm really in that way of life and somebody opens my eyes again and brings me back into the world of decisions, it would really throw me for a loop. [12]

Career development is an uncertain process during adolescence

Photograph from Joe Di Dio/ National Education Association

Perceiving the alternatives intellectually and emotionally does represent a beginning step in the growth process. In the case above the student is confronting, perhaps for the first time, an awareness of his present mode and its inadequacies. However, change to inner direction will require time, and he will have to work through the implications of the change. At the moment the current exploration and comparison of his old strategy (one path) with a new one seems to him like a choice between security and chaos.

EDUCATIONAL CAREER-DECISION-MAKING PROGRAMS

A number of programs to aid adolescents in the difficult process of developing more complex decision-making strategies are now available. In this section we will present information on a few of these programs, which have been selected as illustrating a developmental approach.

I-Power

The system most directly related to a developmental stage system is one constructed by the Tiedemans [13]. They use the phrase "I-power" to denote the major focus. Since most teenagers are in the compliant, other-directed decision stage, the major objective of the program is obvious, namely, to engender an increase in self-direction.

In the Tiedeman model a major focus is on the current system that teenagers actually use. The Tiedemans found that nearly all of the high school students defined the concept of responsibility in other-directed terms—that is, that responsibility is a process of meeting the expectations of other people, as shown in Table 13.3. There is almost no evidence of self-defined responsibility. So the Tiedeman program starts where the learner is and avoids the trap of assuming, but not promoting, development. Thus a major portion of I-power focuses on an intense examination of the present personal strategies; in this sense it is similar to the individual

TABLE 13.3 Responses to the assignment "Define the concept of responsibility." (juniors and seniors in public high school)

Responses	Number of students
"Doing what I'm told to do"; "Doing what I'm expected to do" (and similar comments indicating that responsibility is primarily accepting directions from others).	128
"It is to make decisions on my own, thinking about what's right for me and others. . . ."	2

counseling dialogue—a genuine and comprehensive review of the present system. The program also includes a lengthy personal discussion of how teenagers maintain their current system. Thus they are taught to identify their current stage method. Generally, this technique allows groups of secondary pupils to review the issues of conformity, going along with others' decisions, and making sweeping generalizations, issues that are consistent with decision making at this stage.

I-power emphasizes the transition to self-awareness and the conscientious stage of Loevinger's ego development system. The introduction of self-direction and planning is specifically oriented to the learners' current system and the next stage up, as illustrated in the listing of the I-power steps below:

1. Become more conscious of self in a dynamic sense. Future plans are not fixed.

2. Become aware of the relationship between present activities and future consequences.

3. Awareness of difference between self-directed plans and other-directed plans.

4. Awareness of attractiveness of current "drifting."

5. Learning to process anxiety that accompanies open-endedness.

6. Recognizing "old ways" of processing and the use of projecting the blame on others:

   "I can't," or "I don't want to."
   "It's impossible," or "I'm afraid to try."
   "I know it won't work out," or "I'm afraid to start."
   "I'm too busy," or "I'm choosing not to make it important." [14]

A second point of significance in the Tiedeman approach is that it requires a substantial time commitment, as do all genuinely developmental programs. The Piagetian concepts of disequilibrium, accommodation, and assimilation mean that it takes considerable intellectual and personal experience at each stage to manage the transition. The I-power program, then, requires a one- or two-term course rather than a one- or two-week career unit to actually impact the decision-making strategy.

The students in the program may examine decisions in their own realm and in works of literature in order to obtain an expanded context. Excerpts from stories such as "He" by Katherine Anne Porter or *Lord of the Flies* by William Golding, or even excerpts from Julius Caesar, are employed as an external focus. Here is an example of a technique that might be used:

The short story "He" concerns a family living in extreme poverty. The family consists of Mr. and Mrs. Whipple and their three children, Adam, Eve, and "He," a retarded ten-year-old. When "He" takes sick and the doctor can do no more for him, the doctor recommends that "He" be taken to the county hospital. The Whipples face a hard decision: It would be difficult for them to care for "He" at home, yet to send him away to the county hospital seems like a rejection.

1. Read the story and list the different factors, or influencers, that persuade the Whipples to send their son to the hospital.

2. What influencer(s) seem(s) the most important in determining the final decision? Give reasons to justify your answer.

3. How would you describe the strategy or strategies that the Whipples use?

4. Faced with the Whipples' dilemma, what would you have done? Why?

5. Can you think of any other similar dilemmas (real or fictional) that people have faced? [15]

Of course, a discussion of literature will fall flat unless the discussion leader has a reasonably firm understanding of the nature of fiction—characters, plot, setting, theme, and points of view. However, with an experienced leader the pupils can develop an understanding of the pros and cons, the balance of forces that influence a personally demanding decision.

Students in the program also review some of their own current decision-making strategies as a means of identifying the decision influencers they experience. This dual focus from works of literature and from one's own current life stage gradually encourages students to employ a slightly more complex and self-directed process.

The research results indicate that such a program does affect the general level of ego development. For example, Miller-Tiedeman found the following differences between an experimental and a control class:

1. Increase in ego development scores from compliant (stage 3) to conscientious (stage 4).

2. Increase in use of planned and analytical decision-making strategies.

3. Decrease in impulsive strategies.

4. Increase in tests of critical thinking.

5. Decrease in aimless-delaying strategy. [16]

The author concluded that an educational program like I-power is a keystone for career guidance both for secondary schools and for colleges. Otherwise, students will not have the capability to engage in the career-planning process. In other words, without the ability to use strategies at or near stage 4 (conscientious), the pupils will be at a loss. "Only with an adequate level of ego development are the large quantities of educational and occupational information, ordinarily used in the career guidance phase of career education, likely to have a noticeable effect in career development" [17].

The Career Dilemma Approach and Stages of Work Values

A strategy similar to I-power has been created by Sharon Strom and Wes Tennyson; it focuses on value dilemmas in work-related areas [18]. This approach allows adolescents to reflect on occupational value questions they may encounter in the near future. In this program the students clarify what they consider to be the major considerations in a possible job conflict situation. In a sense the format is similar to the moral and value judgment discussion strategy outlined in Chapter 6. In this case, however, the content is appropriate to career and job-related issues.

In aiding students to clarify their values, the teacher employs open-ended questioning and does *not* prejudge the different levels of reasoning the pupils employ. The following excerpt from a classroom discussion presented in the Strom-Tennyson book illustrates the clarifying process the teacher used and the different stage levels of reasoning exhibited by the students.

Mr. Marlowe, an instructor of accounting in a high school business class, uses a class discussion of dilemmas related to career involvement. He encourages a student, Dennis, to share his thinking about an accounting career with the class:

Dennis: I find myself asking whether the job is important. I know it's important to people who deal in financial transactions, who have to be accountable. It's important to businesses and banks, even to those who are managing a personal estate. (Pause.) But I'm not out saving the world, rescuing the environment or anything like that. It's importance to society . . . (a long pause)? Not too important, I think. Necessary perhaps, to the economy. Probably most of you in this class don't share my views. (Laughs.)

Mr. Marlowe: Perhaps others *are* asking similar questions of themselves. In raising questions about the value of accounting, are you possibly questioning your personal investment in this field—the degree of commitment you can give to it?

John: The importance of accounting for me is having the technical experience in a field where complexity increases each year. Quite frankly, I like the power this gives me.

SPECIAL TOPIC
The Classic Workaholic, by Ellen Goodman*

He worked himself to death finally and precisely at 3 A.M. Sunday morning.

The obituary didn't say that, of course. It said that he died of a coronary thrombosis. I think that was it, but every one of his friends and acquaintances knew it instantly. He was a perfect Type A, a workaholic, a classic, they said to each other and shook their heads, and thought for five or ten minutes about the ways they lived.

This man who worked himself to death finally and precisely at 3 A.M. Sunday morning—on his day off—was 51 years old and he was a vice president. He was, however, one of six vice presidents, and one of three who might conceivably—if the president died or retired soon enough—have moved to the top spot. Phil knew that.

He worked six days a week, five of them until 8 or 9 at night, during a time when his own company had begun talking about the four day week for everyone but the executives. He worked like the Important People who are listed in this week's *New York* magazine along with their obsessive hours quotas: Gerald Lefcort, lawyer, 90 hours; Milton Greene, photographer, 81 hours; Robert Abrams, Borough President, 102 hours, per week. He had no outside "extracurricular" interests, unless, of course, you think about a monthly golf

Kathy:	I agree with John. Accounting is an act of creation; it has form, a kind of beauty which has to do with structure. The accountant sees that all the bits and pieces come together to form a good structure. That can be very pleasurable.
Jerry:	For me, helping management make financial decisions is contributing to the social good by increasing the efficiency and effectiveness of society's use of natural resources.
Mr. Marlowe:	Each of you, then, attribute different meanings and importance to accounting. Dennis, the position Jerry takes apparently disagrees with your position; he feels that accounting does help conserve the environment.
Dennis:	He has an interesting point of view; I never looked at it that way before.

game that way. To Phil, it was work. He always ate egg salad sandwiches at his desk. He was, of course, overweight by 20 or 25 pounds. He thought it was okay though because he didn't smoke.

On Saturdays Phil wore a sports jacket to the office instead of a suit, because it was the weekend.

He had a lot of people working for him, maybe 60, and most of them liked him most of the time. Three of them will be seriously considered for his job. The obituary didn't mention that.

But it did list his "survivors," quite accurately. He is survived by his wife, Helen, 48 years old, a good woman of no particular marketable skills who worked in an office before marrying and mothering.

She had, according to her daughter, given up trying to compete with his work years ago when the children were small. A company friend said, "I know how much you will miss him," and she answered to no one in particular, "I already have."

In "missing him" all these years she must have given up the part of herself which had cared too much for the man. She would be "well taken care of."

His "dearly beloved" eldest of the "dearly beloved" children was a hard-working young executive in a manufacturing firm down South. In the day and a half before the funeral he went around the neighborhood researching his father, asking the neighbors what he was like. They were embarrassed.

(Continued)

Mr. Marlowe:	Let's come back to this in a moment. For now, how do you see all this relating to the issue of commitment?
Dennis:	What I've found out is that I have to be pretty clear about my values, and that may require getting more information and thinking about what it is I really mean when I say I value this or that.
Kathy:	I guess what I'm getting from the discussion is that one's commitment to a career doesn't rest on one value alone, but one has to look at the whole picture, weigh many values.*

The Strom-Tennyson system classifies the levels of career reasoning according to the following stages:

---

* From S. M. Strom and W. W. Tennyson, *Influencing the development of work values*, unpublished monograph (Minneapolis: University of Minnesota, copyright pending, 1981). Reprinted by permission.

SPECIAL TOPIC (Continued)

Phil's second child was a girl who is now 24 and newly married. She lives near her mother and they are close, but whenever she was alone with her father, in a car driving somewhere, they had nothing to say to each other.

The youngest is 20, a boy, a high school graduate who has spent the last couple of years, like a lot of his friends, doing enough odd jobs to stay in grass and food. He was the one who tried to grab at his father and tried to mean enough to him to keep the man at home. He was his father's favorite and over the last two years Phil stayed up nights worrying about the boy.

The boy once said, "My father and I only board here."

At the funeral, the 60-year-old company president told the 48-year-old widow that the 51-year-old deceased meant much to the company and would be missed and would be hard to replace. The widow didn't look him in the eye. She was afraid he would read her bitterness and, after all, she would need him to help her straighten out the finances, the stock options and all that.

Phil was overweight and nervous and worked too hard. If he wasn't at the office, he was worrying about it. Phil was a Type A, a heart attack natural. You could have picked him out in a minute, out of a line-up.

So he finally worked himself to death at precisely 3 A.M. Sunday morning. No one was really surprised.

By 5 P.M. on the afternoon of the funeral, the company president had begun, discreetly, of course, with care and taste, to make inquiries about his replacement. One of three men. He asked around: Who's been working the hardest?

Stage 1: Work-related choices are determined according to immediate wants and desires with little awareness or understanding of one's real needs or the work conditions that influence one's behavior. Choices do not reflect an understanding of the norms and expectations of others (e.g., supervisor, co-workers, management, spouse), and behavior is guided by the pleasure-pain principle. Such individuals do not actively seek information; they tend to act impulsively and to employ "past patterns of reacting" to problems that arise. There is little critical thinking (e.g., exploring alternatives) in resolving conflict.

Stage 2: Work choices are based on narrow self-interest, although the person at this stage reasons more complexly than someone at stage 1.

"What's in it for me" in the short run is the major determinant. The fast-talking salesperson pushing used cars or land in undeveloped areas and the carnival booth operator are examples of people at this level. Cheating is condoned by someone at this stage as long as the person doesn't get caught. *Caveat emptor* ("let the buyer beware") is the slogan; the world of business runs on dollars and cents, not compassion and empathy.

Stage 3: Work-related choices are determined by others' wishes with little regard for the long-range implications of one's own behavior. Thus information search is generally restricted to one point of view. There is concern for following work rules and obeying and conforming to others' norms and expectations. The person does what the boss says. Corporate "yes persons" or workers who always obey the union are prototypes. Value issues are polarized; consequences are rated as good or bad, right or wrong, satisfying or unsatisfying, tolerable or intolerable, according to what the superiors say. Value judgments tend to be absolutistic. Identification and clarification of work values are just beginning at this level.

Stage 4: Work-related choices show an understanding of personal values and some integration of these values with facts. In other words, the person shows greater maturity and complexity in valuation. There are attempts to examine alternatives critically and to generate consequences of different valence (attractiveness) and from more than one perspective. Individuals at this level are increasingly able to assess the facts for accuracy and relevance. They will question arbitrary authority, stand up for their own convictions, and accept responsibility for outcomes. While they are independent in performing tasks, they show increasing awareness of others' feelings and experience. Concern for mutuality and interpersonal harmony may be emphasized in conflict situations. Empathy is just beginning at this level.

Stage 5: Work-related choices reflect a meaningful integration of personal values and relevant tasks, an understanding of others' points of view, and consideration of the impact of one's behavior on others. At this level individuals maintain a balance between task and interpersonal relationships; they are independent in thinking and interdependent in relationships with colleagues. They set priorities and exercise influence in adapting the work environment to their own and others' needs. They are able to generate many conceptions of a problem situation and use a process for solving problems that is both rational and humane.

Thus in accounting class example above, Dennis illustrates the emergence of a stage 4 process—questioning some of the more obvious stereotypes of accounting almost in a Charles Dickens sense. "There is more to life than a balance sheet," he seems to be saying. John, on the other hand, may be attracted to the field at the stage 2 level—power and manipulation of others. And Kathy may be exhibiting a very high level of intrinsic value, accounting as an art form, unless she is repeating what she has been told by others. If she is merely repeating, she is at stage 3. In any case, the class discussion demonstrates the variety of reasoning levels reflected in occupational planning and choice, with the differences in complexity readily apparent.

During the initial phase of the Strom-Tennyson program, students are aided in learning to identify career value elements. They also learn how to distinguish between significant value issues and issues of less moment (e.g., personal preferences or superficial characteristics). Then students are ready for the next step, analyzing issues in conflict situations.

In the accounting class example above the students were in the first phase. Mr. Marlowe was asking the pupils to state their own views on why they did or did not value accounting as a career. There were different levels of complexity apparent, but essentially very little dissonance was created since no action choices were involved. During the second phase, however, the career value content becomes more complex. Conflict and dilemmas are now added to the content of the discussions. There are no easy solutions for the pupils to puzzle their way through. This process is illustrated in another case study from Strom and Tennyson, the case of Ken the carpenter:

CASE

Ken B.

Occupation: Carpenter

Dilemma: It's something we all do. You might say we compromise with the material, that's all. Of course I never feel completely comfortable about it. Like recently, we finished this apartment complex. Well, not quite; there's still some inside finishing to be done. Cedar siding, that's the material we used. But geeze it can be a headache; those knots just fall out. One hit with the hammer and you're looking through a knothole. So we just tack those knots back in. With the price of wood today, what can you expect! It's real nice lumber. You cut a six-foot piece off a ten-foot board. Whatcha gonna do with that four feet? Splice it? Throw it? Burn it? Take it home and use it? After all, it took a long time to grow that. Of course some supervisors complain that we should have planned

better, but you've got to use what's there. We are expected to work fast. You're thinking about this all the
time. You compromise!

Categories of   Job performance
Dilemma: Ecological relationships

Value Issues: Quantity vs. quality
                         Responsibility vs. responsibleness
                         Conservation vs. exploitation

Possible Underlying
Values: *Prudential*

- conservation of time
- economic wisdom
- efficiency

Moral

- honesty—consideration of others' rights
- conservation of world resources

Aesthetic

- preservation and creation of beauty*

Or examine the issues from the case of Carole, an advertising writer
who is confronted by the question of deliberate deception:

CASE

Carole H.

Occupation: Commercial Advertiser

Dilemma: Sometimes my job makes me sick. Like last week, I had
                         to write a trade publication ad for this client who was
                         providing additives to food preparations. Here we were
                         meeting with these company executives who were out to
                         provide a service to meat packers so they can cheat the

(Continued)

---

* From S. M. Strom and W. W. Tennyson, *Influencing the development of work values,* unpublished monograph (Minneapolis: University of Minnesota, copyright pending, 1981). Reprinted by permission.

CASE (Continued)

government inspectors of their sausage products. I ask, "Why are we doing this ad for mustard?" They say, "Mustard acts as a binder." In other words, it holds together the fat that's going into these sausages. So I make a living selling mustard because the guy wants to substitute fat for meat protein, and the public ends up cheated. These execs don't even see it as cheating, but it sure gets to me.

Categories of Dilemma:	Job performance Occupational colleagueship
Value Issues:	Quantity vs. quality Egocentric behavior vs. social justice
Possible Underlying Values:	

Prudential

- creating something that has utility and meaning
- making a living

Moral
- human welfare—health of others
- trust—obligation not to cheat the public
- consideration of others' rights
- personal integrity

Intellectual
- truth in advertising*

In a discussion of such work-related dilemmas the instructional format is similar to the value dilemma approach outlined in Chapter 6. The group leader needs to clarify the different levels for the pupils and, most importantly, help the students listen to each other's views. Can the carpenter, for example, simply continue to turn his back on shoddy work simply because the boss says he must? What are possible long-term consequences to the building contractor if the nails loosen and the knots fall out? What happens to the advertising agency if an investigative newspaper runs a story on the

---

* From S. M. Strom and W. W. Tennyson, *Influencing the development of work values*, unpublished monograph (Minneapolis: University of Minnesota, copyright pending, 1981). Reprinted by permission.

substitution of fat for protein? Obviously, the pressure on the people in these work dilemmas is enormous. And the short-run benefits of conformity may seem almost overwhelming to most teenagers. But the Strom-Tennyson materials help to correct the balance by providing for other views and longer-term consequences.

CAREER DEVELOPMENT AND SOCIAL CONDITIONING

The Miller-Tiedeman materials and the Strom-Tennyson procedures have been shown to promote development in secondary pupils. But these approaches represent only one side of the coin—materials and classroom strategies. What about the teachers, counselors, and principals themselves? Or is it enough to produce materials that show that growth can be stimulated?

Obviously, people are important too. The adults that teenagers come into contact with may be a significant source of influence. We can all think of instances during our own adolescence when even unintentionally an adult had an extremely powerful effect. The so-called hidden agenda of schools—how teachers, counselors, or advisors really feel about the pupils—exerts a major effect on their expectations, aspirations, and goals. Study after study has shown that self-fulfilling prophecies are a most important influence. Thus an eighth grade girl may get an unmistakable message that a career in math or engineering is really not for her through the voice tone, facial expression, and informal comments of the adult advisor. A tenth grade ghetto youth may receive a message in kind: "College is a possibility for you, Juan, but there are some really exciting manual training programs. After all, you are gifted with your hands."

Unfortunately, it is abundantly clear from many sociological studies that most adults advise pupils according to social, economic, and cultural stereotypes. Such thinking freezes career development into a caste system. Thus if a teenager's parents are blue-collar factory workers, then that's what their sons and daughters are cut out to be. Similarly, ghetto blacks, Chicanos, or American Indians can be stereotyped as individuals who do not respect school learning and consequently channeled into physical labor or dead-end jobs such as car wash attendants. The class-linked nature of job and status thus becomes perpetuated by self-fulfilling prophecies.

A classic study of the relation between social class and occupation gives us a picture of the real life situation [19]. The study found that there were five job levels in a typical manufacturing company, and there was almost no mobility between the levels. Figure 13.1 details the five levels and the two major substructures, which act as a barrier preventing mobility. Thus for a person once hired at a particular level, mobility ceased. In addition, the most important break was between blue-denim and white-

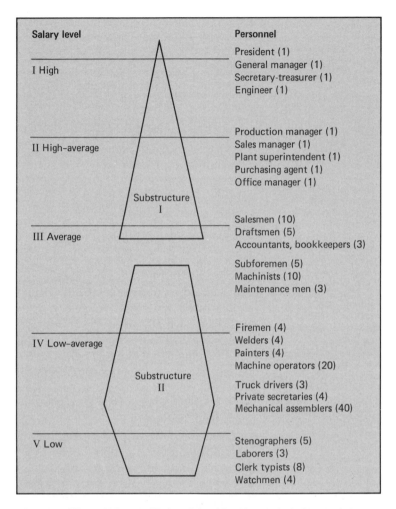

FIG. 13.1 Class structure differences in a midwestern industry

Adaptation of Figure 11.2, page 459, from *Industrial sociology*, 2nd ed. (New York: Harper & Row, 1964), p. 459. Copyright © 1964 by Delbert C. Miller and William H. Form. Reprinted by permission of Harper & Row, Publishers, Inc.

collar workers, levels III and IV in Fig. 13.1. The differences were clearly marked not only by dress but also by obvious perquisites ("perks") such as salaries (versus wages), parking privileges, extended vacations, and clean and quiet working conditions.

Vance Packard has noted:

I would say that the class structure of the United States is more like a jungle gym than a ladder. Or to be more precise, in view of the gulf developing between the diploma elite and supporting classes, it is like two jungle gyms. One jungle gym is on the ground floor of a building. The other, directly above it, is on the second floor. To move from the lower jungle gym to the higher one, you must go outside and climb up the fire escape of higher education [20].

The following news story was nationally syndicated. It represents a case illustration of the social and psychological costs of unemployment. The complexity of the unemployment problem is clear, as is its devastating impact on single individuals.

"Staying Alive"/the Ghetto's Vicious Circle

Eddie Morris, 19, drank cheap wine and smoked marijuana recently in an abandoned building on Jones Street in St. Louis's slums and told a visitor: "I've been to the employment office and they've got jobs there only in the suburbs and I don't have a car. It wouldn't be worth my time to pay bus fare, taxes, lunch and stuff for a job way out in the suburbs that pays $2.65 an hour."

Morris lives with his mother and admits to just enough petty thievery "to stay alive."

If he is caught and jailed, says Ernest Green, an assistant secretary of labor, "it will cost an average of $20,000 a year" to keep him behind bars "but it would only cost $5,000 to pay a year's tuition for an average private college."

Crime is part of the Catch-22 of black youth unemployment. Without employment, the youths drift into crime, making future employment even more difficult to obtain. The middle class abandons the crime-ridden area, taking away businesses that had provided some employment. They take away, in addition, the community's tax base.*

Thus when pupils from nonmajority group backgrounds are intentionally or unintentionally channeled into the lower job entry levels, their chances for growth and change are severely limited. Their job is almost a permanent assignment. There are always a few, of course, who can overcome the most severe hardships, denials, and personal defeats. However, to hold up the exceptions—Helen Keller, George Washington Carver, Dick Gregory, Daniel Patrick Moynahan—as models for all is both unrealistic and hypocritical.

The jungle gyms of which Packard speaks have a bottom line, namely, no job at all. As Fig. 13.2 shows, among black youth, age 16–19, unemployment may reach epidemic proportions. For example, for black youth the rate has varied from 25% to almost 40% in the decade of the seventies.

---

* © 1979 by the New York Times Company. Reprinted by permission.

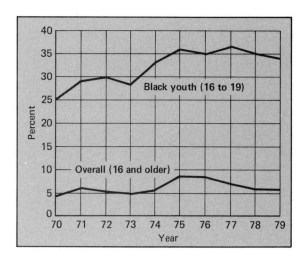

FIG. 13.2 Unemploy-
ment and
black youth

Redrawn from Bureau of Labor Statistics, U.S. Department of Labor (Washington, D.C.: May 1979).

Thus almost one-half million teenagers are simply floating, merely staying
alive from day to day. For a variety of reasons such youth have either
dropped out or been pushed out of school; they have no steady job, no
career plans, and, perhaps, no hope. Their rate of unemployment has risen
dramatically. In 1954 the unemployment rate for black youth in the same
age bracket, 16–19, was 16.5%. Now it is more than double that figure. The
social cost of such a vast pool of untapped human resources is a problem
not only for the teenagers themselves but also for the nation. Incarceration
is both expensive and nonproductive, as the excerpt about Eddie Morris
points out.

CHANGING THE PROCESS OF CAREER DEVELOPMENT: PROJECT BORN FREE

Because adolescence as a stage of development is, by definition, a time of
unsureness, exploration, and tentativeness, teenagers need extra support
and encouragement. For teenagers who are the first in the family to consider further education as a means to a more complex career, the need for
encouragement is even greater. There is no natural support group of peers
who are continuing to higher education; neither is there a visible support
group of adults who are already in a profession. For example, How many
black, Indian, or Chicano pilots do you see at air terminals? How many are
medical doctors (as opposed to orderlies)? How many use executive parking spaces in major companies?

Thus there are at least two built-in psychological barriers to career development, friends and adults, in addition to all of the most obvious forms of systematic discrimination that act as deterrents to career aspirations. As a result, Sunny Hansen has created a special educational program, Project Born Free, designed to impact the career education of teenagers through adult teachers, counselors, school principles, and advisors [21]. She suggests that boys and girls enter this world free of stereotypes about who they are and what they can do with their lives. Echoing the phrase of French philosopher Jean Jacques Rousseau, Hansen says that such children are "born free." Each baby has a set of capacities that under positive educational and parental influences can lead to successful actualization without regard to race, creed, or social status. The human potential for career success is spread across all children. Biology is not destiny; inherited genes are not an internal guidance system directing middle-class and upper-middle-class majority group teenagers into higher education while directing minority group adolescents into jobs as day laborers, at-home garment workers, or migrant farmers. But her research demonstrates clearly that just such stereotypes abound in the structure and process of schooling. For example, schools and their programs are often organized by adults in modes that perpetuate stereotypes by sex.

Hansen's work notes that teenagers themselves are particularly susceptible to such stereotyping. In other words, many adolescents are ready to believe that biology *is* destiny. From a developmental view their entry into formal abstract reasoning is still extremely tentative vis-à-vis their own career choice. Their ready acceptance of culturally determined stereotypes

Project Born Free helps in reducing stereotypes and promoting female development
Photograph from Allen Ruid

makes the problem all the more difficult. Thus Hansen's program makes the important point that the responsibility to break the career determinism for culturally different teenagers belongs to all teachers, counselors, and advisors—in short, all those who have significant influence over teenagers. Her program for those working with teenagers includes a variety of educational resource materials such as readings, videotapes, and simulations. The focus of her curriculum is to help adults confront their own hidden agendas, stereotypes, and self-fulfilling prophecies. As Hansen notes:

> By making teachers, professors, counselors, administration and parents more aware of the ways in which they consciously and unconsciously *inhibit* or *facilitate* career decisions of youth and adults, it is expected that educational systems will be more supportive of expanded options based on individual needs and talents [22].

ISSUES OF CAREER DEVELOPMENT

There are a number of important general issues involved in career development questions. Teenagers faced with the problem of career choice may find themselves asking questions like these: How can I finally select a single career from so many alternatives? What are the basic values of work in relation to the larger questions of living? Related to such larger questions are issues of career maturity, abstract thinking, the nature of achievement motivation, and, certainly, the important contemporary issue of sex differences in occupational choice. The final set of issues we consider in this section focuses on the interrelationship between career development for men and women and the overall question of personal competence as a goal for all individuals.

Career Choice and Basic Values

William James, the originator of psychology as a field of study in this country, wrote to a friend concerning his own career choice. After studying art, chemistry, comparative anatomy, physiology, medicine, and anthropology (the latter included an extensive field trip up the Amazon River), he simply could not decide. "I have at least four alternatives," he wrote. "Natural history, Medicine, Printing and Beggary." Some six years later, after receiving an M.D. degree, he chose to enter teaching, or, as it was known in those days, pedagogy.

Certainly, the content choice of career is as bewildering to an adolescent today as it was to even so distinguished a thinker as William James. The sheer number of occupations is overwhelming. The *Dictionary of Occupational Titles* is as fat as a New York City telephone book. And even when jobs are classified into groupings and choice is narrowed, the scope is broadened. It's no wonder that teenagers may get confused and then simply avoid the issue.

One helpful system that provides some framework for content choice is to view the underlying work values. In an oversimplified sense these values can be split into two broad world views: "I work in order to live," or the obverse, "I live in order to work." In other words, general career values are defined by instrumental needs.

In the first category of working to live, the person wishes to earn money in order to have, say, a big house with a pool, lots of cars and clothes, and membership in a country club. The major requirement of the job or career is extrinsic. Thus high pay is the priority for someone who wants to live in a high style. Similarly, at the other extreme, a person might wish to live simply and might have few materialistic needs; this person might desire only a homemade log cabin in the wilderness. Again, the job is selected as simply a means to meet those needs: "I'll work in the country store three mornings a week. That will give me enough money for food and clothes." In both cases the major work orientation is for a job as a means to live according to a particular life-style. The job itself—its content—is secondary.

In the category of living to work, of course, are a totally different set of concerns. The person's life *is* work. The intrinsic personal satisfaction from the job itself is the most important life value. The job represents the major commitment of energy, both physically and personally. All else is secondary, such as family, friends, recreation, or volunteer activities. The person and the job are literally synonymous. Throwing oneself into a job, of course, can happen in a variety of fields. The industrial manager, the stock market tycoon, and the lonely billionaire are stereotypes. Yet as the special topic about the workaholic illustrates, devotion to a job is not reserved just for the so-called captains of industry; those just below the top may be the most tragic victims.

Of course, the professions have their quota of persons who live in order to work. In a recent study of lives of psychiatrists it was noted that well over one-half of a large national sample were so committed to their work that they found their patients more interesting than their own family [23]. Their family relationships and relationships with friends were more distant, impersonal, and less significant than their professional relationships with patients.

Career Development Maturity: Donald Super's Findings

A longitudinal study of career development was conducted by Donald Super [24]. Employing a variety of sophisticated assessment procedures, he and his associates tested and then followed, over a ten-year period, a sample of young males from high school age through young adulthood (age 25). The Career Pattern Study produced two major findings.

First, only one-half of the sample of males had been pursuing stable career goals since leaving high school. Thus one-half of the men at age 25

SPECIAL TOPIC
Female Career Aspiration: Fear of Success?

A number of studies have underscored the importance of Sunny Hansen's Born Free program, especially in relation to females. In the first major study of its kind, Esther Matthews and David Tiedeman found that there was a massive shift in career orientation between junior and senior high school females [1]. During junior high most were actively considering career choice and occupational questions, including a great variety of alternatives. By the end of senior high, though, there was a noticeable and dramatic shift in aspiration from career choice to selecting a marriage partner. In other words, the senior high school females gave up active pursuit of career choice based on their own potential interests and abilities and, instead, viewed their future role mostly in terms of marriage and homemaking. Essentially, as Hansen would point out, the females were accepting the old cultural stereotype that the woman's main role is in the home, even though actual employment statistics indicate that more than half of the entire adult female population will work outside the home for most of their lives.

To shed light on possible psychological factors involved in this cooling off of female career aspirations, Matina Horner, now president of Radcliffe College, conducted a highly original study [2]. She found that college-age women, as opposed to men, seemed to fear the prospect of being successful in careers. In other words, while males (especially in the working and middle class) aspire to becoming a president or an executive in industry, following in Horatio Alger's footsteps, women not only have different goals but actually fear the prospect of being successful in careers dominated by males. Horner found that in her sample two-thirds of the women (60 out of 90) feared success while only one-tenth of the males (9 out of 88) had similar fears.

From the work of David McClelland (see the text), a crucial psychological variable in determining successful career performance is the need for achievement, or N.Ach. This factor involves three components: (1) moderate risk taking, (2) the use of feedback to modify performance, and (3) performing according to standards of excellence. The women in Horner's sample would be

were still in an exploratory stage, although their exploration was not goal-directed. Rather, many of the young men were unsure of their career plans and were following more or less random patterns. If we recall the study of actual decision-making patterns used in high school (see pp. 446–447), it considered quite low on the first two elements—fearing success they would have difficulty taking risks as well as positively employing feedback.

Recent studies using the same techniques that Horner used have produced somewhat more equivocal results, indicating that college women may be less ambivalent concerning career success. Numerous factors could account for such a shift. Perhaps the most obvious factor is the major new orientation on the part of women to see themselves as capable of success. In the last decade the female consciousness and career aspirations may have been raised. On the other hand, Hansen's data, as well as other recent survey data, indicate that in the years since the Horner study, women have entered previously male-dominated careers, but only in very small numbers. From a proportional standpoint, then, we would still have to accept the basic finding that women may still fear success and avoid competition with males.

Two other researchers have produced findings highly similar to Horner's, although they used different techniques. Eleanor Maccoby and Carol Jacklin found that college women, as opposed to younger women and to men in general, have less self-confidence on task achievement, have less sense of agency and less self-direction, and define themselves according to social roles rather than career roles [23]. Thus there is certainly a strong need to continue the process of breaking down cultural stereotypes in order to promote female potential and male potential. Equity according to sex is, of course, a problem not only for women but also for men.

Unfortunately, it appears that one of the main concepts women have learned from our male-dominated society is a sense of inferiority. And ironically, if the recent soundings on the Equal Rights Amendment are accurate, more females than males believe that women are inferior. The lesson of fearing success has been so well taught that it will not disappear quickly.

REFERENCES

1. E. Matthews and D. Tiedeman, Attitudes toward careers and marriage and the development of life style in young women, *Journal of Counseling Psychology* 11(1964):375–384.
2. M. Horner, Toward an understanding of achievement related conflicts in women, *Journal of Social Issues* 28(1972):157–176.

would seem that not very much development had taken place between high school age and the age of 25.

The second finding, of particular significance to this text, was that an index of career development maturity in high school was an important predictor of occupational success. We noted in Chapter 12 that levels of psychological maturity were relevant predictors of actual behavior. This observation is also true for levels of career development maturity, an index composed of the following factors: (1) planfulness, (2) goal-directed exploration, (3) accurate self-knowledge, (4) mature decision making, and (5) a reality orientation. The high school students who demonstrated a rational-planning competence with those elements demonstrated successful career patterns ten years later.

These results indicate that effective career development in high school is a process of deliberate exploration rather than closure on a specific job. In fact, in a study that paralleled Super's in many ways, Warren Gribbons and Paul Lohnes found that exploration was a key element [25]. The individuals who changed their choices during high school demonstrated greater vocational maturity than those who did not change their goals. This finding also fits well with Erikson's concept of identity formation—that is, exploration is critical in order to test out information about self and career. Premature closure of exploration during adolescence can lead to identity foreclosure and inadequate vocational maturity as well. Thus career development maturity does make a difference in actual behavior after high school.

Formal Operations

In addition to the relationship between career exploration and identity formation, career development has a functional connection to Piaget and formal operations. Super's research demonstrates that pupils need to understand and use probabilistic thinking. That is, each person possesses a variety of job competencies (ability, interest, value) that can fit into a variety of careers. So there is no single choice, once and for all. Rather, each person needs to consider the question of probabilities of success in a variety of careers.

Also, since there are numerous possible career paths, a person needs to view options in a balanced and somewhat relativistic mode. Piaget's formal operations stage allows an individual to weigh and balance alternatives, maintain a future time perspective, understand long-term consequences, and consider a host of as-if possibilities. Note that those elements of formal thought are similar to Super's elements of career maturity.

This issue reminds us of the central theme in all these domains, the need to promote rather than assume development. As we noted at the outset of this chapter, most current career education curriculum material implicitly assumes the ability to process at a formal level. But research has shown that we need to follow approaches and methods such as those of the Tiedemans, Strom-Tennyson, and Hansen, which seek to promote growth. And still another method has been devised to promote development in the form of education for achievement, a method to which we now turn.

The Achievement Motive: McClelland and Alschuler's View

While Super stressed the importance of promoting decision-making strategies and productive exploration for career development, two researchers from Harvard have focused on the question of motivation. David McClelland and Al Alschuler reasoned that career development and motivation could be stimulated through direct instruction [26].

In a complex industrial and competitive society such as ours, one major element that distinguishes between successful and unsuccessful adults in careers is what the authors denote as N.Ach, or need for achievement. Their research shows that the motive to achieve is actually composed of three linked factors:

1. performance to a standard of excellence

2. moderate risk taking

3. constructive use of feedback

These three elements make an important difference in a variety of complex tasks. And successful persons use all three elements in combination.

There is a drive to personal competence according to McClelland and Alschuler. In other words, we are all born with the need to master the environment, sometimes referred to as personal efficacy or effectence. We are not passive, inert, and empty boxes; rather, we have innate drives to develop competence. The actual form of competence, however, is partly determined by the culture. In the case of an industrialized society that values individuality, competence often takes the form of N.Ach. Persons who can set competent goals for the task at hand (whether it's organizing a group to put on a play, building an industrial plant, or creating a university) and then take moderate risks, constantly adjusting their plans according to an accurate reading of feedback—such individuals manifest the achievement motive. On the other hand, persons who have slapdash performance goals, take either wild risks or none at all, and avoid adjusting plans according to feedback are the ones who do not succeed. In schools and colleges that syndrome is called underachievement; on the job that syndrome is called the ticket to unemployment, or underemployment.

Achievement behavior shows strong elements of making rational plans, setting priorities, making reality-oriented choices, and modifying plans as one goes along. Can anything be done to stimulate this achievement behavior during adolescence? McClelland and Alschuler tried out a number of different educational programs and concluded that it is, indeed, possible to stimulate N.Ach. Examples of the programs can be found in Alschuler's book and will not be described here. From a developmental viewpoint the programs stress growth from being other-directed toward being self-directed. In Loevinger's and Kohlberg's scheme this growth is movement from stage 3 to stage 4. The individual develops the ability to make decisions on the basis of internally directed processes, an ability

(a)

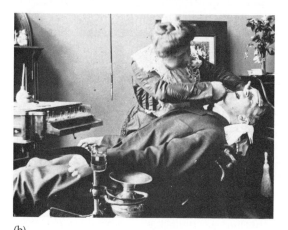

(b)

(c)

Historical evidence shows that a woman's place was not always in the home

Photograph from: (a) Lee Bros./Minnesota Historical Society, (b) Albert Munson/Minnesota Historical Society, and (c) Historical Pictures Services, Chicago

often referred to as *personal agency*, that is, the individual acting as his or her own agent. Compliance or conformity to the superficial dictates of the leading crowd fades as the individual develops more self-reliance.

Thus the N.Ach program has been designed to stimulate development from one common adolescent stage (stage 3) toward the next highest stage (stage 4) and the beginning of self-directed and conscientious cognitive processing. As the special topic about the fear of success notes, though, creating effective N.Ach runs directly into some cultural stereotypes when it comes to the question of an achievement motive for women.

Sex Differences

Career development, like other domains, has only recently focused on the question of women. As a result, the information base is quite tentative. But some issues are obvious. As Hansen's material demonstrated, women have been systematically cooled out, rechanneled, redirected—or whatever phrase we want to use to describe the process of cultural sex stereotyping. This redirection has severely limited their career options. But the accompanying photographs, from a collection by Andrea Hinding, show quite clearly that in reality women have been involved in almost every conceivable career that this culture offers [27]. And certainly, as any anthropologist can point out, such is the case across most cultures. Women can and do participate in all work roles. Yet for reasons of culture, our society in particular has limited the options except in times of national need, such as war. Also, at least in the past, most women have accepted such unequal treatment without protest. At the end of both major wars the male culture convinced females to give up their "masculine jobs" as part of the debt of a grateful nation. The boys returned to work; the women went home.*

Certainly, a major issue for the 1980s is the need for a theoretical framework that will explain and facilitate the process of female career development. As larger and larger numbers of females attend professional graduate schools, the old stereotypes will fade. And the recognition that females are capable of self-directed choice creates the need for new theory. For example, previous studies have shown that occupational choice was a primary determinant of successful identity formation—but for boys only. Now, however, females face more choices than before; in addition, they face built-in conflicts between traditional homemaker roles and employment outside the home. In developmental terms women must accomplish a formidable task; to find a balance between self-directed achievement motivation for job success and motivation for caretaking of children. There are also implications for males: finding a new balance between being a breadwinner and being a nurturing parent for the children.

Long-Range Goals

We have stressed throughout this text the importance of developmental goals for adolescence. In all of the major domains we have referred to the significance of promoting the emergence of individuality during this period. To reach formal operations, to achieve a firm sense of personal identity, to reach a self-directed conscientious ego and moral stage, to acquire

---

* A case in point: In going through some old family papers at the time of his mother's death, one author found information that his mother (a schoolteacher during World War I) had worked overtime and on Saturdays as a machine tool operator in a munitions plant—a fact never mentioned during her subsequent 50 years.

the ability to empathize and to role-take, to exercise achievement motiva-tion—all these aspects of the shift from stage 3 to stage 4 denote the stimulation of a full-fledged self. Now we face the question "What next?" And it is the emergence of female career development that has created that question.

It appears that we are confronting a paradox. That is, if women pro-gress in development as men do—for example, become stage 4 achievers—then what happens to the importance of relationships and of caring for others? David Bakan refers to this problem as one of agency versus com-munion [28]. Agency, as we have noted, refers to self-direction, the recog-nition that one has a separate self as an identity. Communion refers to the opposite: a sense of connectedness, of belonging, of relating and support-ing. It is like the difference between the story of Hercules, the mythic hero who held up the world all by himself (the highest point on anyone's N.Ach), and *The Gift of the Magi*, O'Henry's famous story emphasizing relationship. In developmental terms, is it possible to fuse the best aspects of stage 3, an empathic sense, with the positive aspects of stage 4, individ-uality and self-direction?

This question is probably the most important question currently facing those involved in creating theory for adult career development. In other words, *resolution* is the problem for the next stage up, stage 5 in the Kohlberg, Loevinger, and Selman schemes and the committed relativist stage in Perry's system. In Erikson's terms it is the dual question of inti-macy and generativity. Only at the next highest stage on the developmen-tal sequence are the characteristics complex enough to provide a synthesis of individuality and relationship based on mutuality. In other words, true interdependence between adults is possible only when both are able to process experience at a very complex stage of development.

In Chapter 2 we noted that Levinson's study, *The Season of a Man's Life*, underscored the significance, to men in particular, of the need to develop genuine intimacy and relationship. Levinson calls the question one of in-complete development, what males miss in the course of growth [29]. Similarly, Mead, in her remarkable concluding chapter from *Coming of Age in Samoa*, commented on the needs of women in a complex society. By contrast, she said that a primitive culture such as Samoa knows only one way of life and instills that singular pattern upon the children. In our society we stress choice, individuality, and the need to teach our children how to think, not what to think. For women in the process of career development, learning to make wise choices is difficult indeed. She notes: "They must be taught that many ways are open to them, no one sanc-tioned above its alternative, and that upon them and upon them alone lies the burden of choice . . . they must come clear-eyed to the choices which lie before them" [30].

MATINA S. HORNER (1939–)

Matina Horner (1939–)
Photograph from Harvard
University News Office

Matina Horner has had a career little short of meteoric. She received her bachelor's degree in 1961 from Bryn Mawr, her master's degree in 1963, and her doctorate in 1968, both from the University of Michigan. With honors in psychology and an election to Phi Beta Kappa, she demonstrated early promise. She was appointed a lecturer and assistant professor at Harvard in 1968–1969 with the department of social relations.

Her research focus gained almost immediate attention, not because of the topical nature of her investigation but because of the careful examination she performed and the significance of the findings themselves. Her work provided a breakthrough in understanding the paradox and the dilemma of female development.

It is for educators, of course, that the implications of her work are most far-reaching. Her theory, which indicates how societal expectations shape and mold the motivational systems for females, forces educators to revise practically all their assumptions concerning male and female differences. She has shown that such differences in motivational patterns are a result of social conditioning or social inventions. Thus educators need to revise their ideas, practices, and policies concerning young women in schools and colleges. They need to promote full development for all, regardless of gender. Horner's work forms the basis for these needed changes.

To indicate her own versatility and her willingness to meet the major educational challenges of the 1970s, Horner moved in 1972 from an assistant professorship at Harvard to the presidency of Radcliffe College, at age 34. A model of achievement motivation, scholarship, and administrative talent, she sets a high standard for others to follow.

Career and competence

Career education and occupational choice are bound to remain confusing and bewildering experiences for adolescents. The occupational world is not fixed, at least not to the extent to which adults are capable of breaking down the artificial, nondemocratic barriers. There are different jobs within occupational families as well as different levels and different groupings, and theoretically, at least, a person can choose from among those families and levels. Simultaneously, given the nature of adolescence, the person is not at a fixed point either. Thus we have two dynamic systems interacting concurrently.

Here the paradox emerges. How do we teach teenagers to make decisions and choices so that they do not artificially foreclose on their future? Commitment and openness are not exactly compatible concepts. Yet, in essence, they are the objects of career development: to make fully informed decisions and commit oneself to investing wholeheartedly in bringing about successful implementation, and to remain open to new information, to changing times, and to new careers as obsolescence inevitably arrives. Thus the problem is to help teenagers understand the paradox. The commitment to career that Piaget notes as the key in the transition from adolescence to adulthood is not closure on a single job. Rather, it is the investment of self into a significant work experience that serves self as well as others.

Holden Caulfield, the prototypical adolescent, was struggling with the questions of choice and commitment throughout Salinger's novel *Catcher in the Rye*. At one point Holden, with a combination of envy and hopelessness, mused over the question of career. He recalled observing a performance at Radio City Music Hall during the Christmas holidays. He and his brother Allie were awestruck by the kettle drum player, the best they had ever seen. They got seats as close to the stage as possible in order to watch the drummer, who was constantly tuning, arranging, and getting ready to bang the drums, even though he performed only a few times during the piece. But the drummer never looked bored; he was always at attention. And when he struck the drums, his whole body was involved.

The envy and awe Holden experienced were not for the drummer's talent and technique but for the sense of personal competence that he portrayed so well. Thus at a surface level career choice may always involve a confusing and often contradictory set of alternatives. But at a deeper level it may involve a process of personal competence and commitment, less obvious but far more significant concerns. Lawrence K. Frank, a developmental theorist, commented on the larger issues:

> A free society must keep open not only the possibility but the obligation to make choices and decisions predicated upon the values and aspirations we cherish and must continually strive to attain. [31]

SUMMARY

In this chapter we outlined the issues in career choice from a developmental point of view. Studies have shown that the critical strategies that secondary school students employ tend to be inadequate—largely either impulsive/fatalistic or compliant/other-directed. We described some original work that helps students cope with this problem, such as the I-power approach of Anna Miller-Tiedeman and David Tiedeman. This approach also connects to the earlier work of Jane Loevinger relating stages of ego development to decision methods. I-power programs enhance the students' ability for self-directed choice. The career dilemma discussion programs of Strom and Tennyson were also presented as another means of stimulating growth. Sunny Hansen's Born Free program was next reviewed; her program illustrates the need to provide both males and females, regardless of social class background, with equal opportunities.

We followed the program descriptions with a section outlining some of the major issues involved in career development. A basic value issue was discussed in terms of the conflict between working to live and living to work. Then we examined the implications of Super's longitudinal study of male career development and the primary finding that most men well into their middle to late twenties were still exploring career choices. We also noted the relation between effective career choice and formal operations in the Piagetian sense.

The research of McClelland and Alschuler was shown to be pertinent to the career success question. These researchers were able to elaborate the dimensions of the need for achievement and make some programmatic suggestions. This research led us into a discussion of women's career development interacting with men's development. It was suggested that in the long run a developmental synthesis may be possible, including mutuality and interdependence. We concluded the chapter with a view relating career development to general human competence.

KEY POINTS AND NAMES

Piaget and decentered cognition

Career decision making

Levels of decision making
    Impulsive/fatalistic
    Compliant/other-directed
    Rational planning
    Creative/analytical

Aaron Cicourel and John Kitsuse

Adults as decision makers for adolescents

Anna Miller-Tiedeman and David Tiedeman

Ego Stages and Decision Strategies

I-power

Sharon Strom and Wes Tennyson

Career dilemma approach

Stages of career reasoning

Social class and occupational limits

Sunny Hansen

Project Born Free

Donald Super

Career development and formal operations

Career development maturity

David McClelland and Al Alschuler

Achievement motive

Sex differences

Career development: long-range goals

Stage 5 and adult development

REFERENCES

1. O. Lewis, *La Vida* (New York: Random House, 1966), p. 246.

2. J. Piaget and B. Inhelder, *The growth of logical thinking from childhood to adolescence* (New York: Basic Books, 1958), p. 346.

3. J. Flanagan, Education: How and for what, *American Psychologist* 28(1973):551–556.

4. W. Cooley and P. Lohnes, Functions and designs for a computer-measurement system for guidance (Paper presented at the American Personnel and Guidance Association National Convention, Washington, D.C., April 1966).

5. L. K. Jones, *Occ-u-sort* (Monterey, Calif.: Publishers Test Service, 1981), p. 1.

6. N. A. Sprinthall and R. L. Mosher, *Studies of adolescents in the secondary schools* (Cambridge, Mass.: Harvard Graduate School of Education, 1969), chap. 7.

7. A. Cicourel and J. Kitsuse, *The educational decision-makers* (Indianapolis: Bobbs-Merrill, 1963).

8. R. Rehberg and L. Hotchkiss, Career counseling in contemporary U.S. high schools, in *Review of research in education,* ed. D. C. Berliner (Washington, D.C.: American Educational Research Association, 1979), p. 137.

9. A. Miller-Tiedeman and D. V. Tiedeman, Decision-making for the 70's, *Focus on Guidance* 1(1972):1–15; D. V. Tiedeman and A. Miller-Tiedeman, An "I" power primer, *Focus in Guidance* 9(1977):1–16.

10. J. Flanagan, Educations contribution to the quality of life of a national sample of 30 year-olds, *Educational Researcher* 4, 6(1975):10.

11. N. A. Sprinthall, *Guidance for human growth* (New York: Van Nostrand, 1971), p. 90.

12. *Ibid.,* p. 95.

13. Miller-Tiedeman and Tiedeman, Decision making, pp. 1–15; Tiedeman and Miller Tiedeman, "I" power, pp. 1–16.

14. Tiedeman and Miller-Tiedeman, "I" power, pp. 1–16.

15. A. Miller-Tiedeman, Structuring responsibility in adolescents: Actualizing "I" power, *Pupil Personnel Services Journal* 6, 1(1977):157.

16. *Ibid.*, p. 163.

17. *Ibid.*, p. 164.

18. S. Strom and W. W. Tennyson, *Influencing the development of work values,* monograph (Minneapolis: University of Minnesota, 1981).

19. D. C. Miller and W. H. Form, *Industrial sociology,* 2nd ed. (New York: Harper and Row, 1964), pp. 459.

20. V. Packard, *The status seekers* (New York: McKay, 1957), p. 56.

21. L. S. Hansen, *Project Born Free,* University of Minnesota Monograph Series (Minneapolis, October 1978). Born Free materials are now available from the Educational Development Corporation, 55 Chapel Street, Newton, MA 02160.

22. L. S. Hansen, B. Mills-Novoa, and T. Hatfield, Born Free: Concepts, process and materials for sex-fair career development, *Journal of Career Education* 5(1978):97.

23. W. Henry, J. Sims, and S. Spray, *Public and private lives of psychotherapists* (San Francisco: Jossey-Bass, 1973).

24. D. E. Super, *Measuring vocational maturity for counseling and evaluation* (Washington, D.C.: National Vocational Guidance Association, 1974).

25. W. D. Gribbons and P. R. Lohnes, *Emerging careers* (New York: Teachers College Press, 1968).

26. D. C. McCelland, Toward a theory of motive acquisition, *American Psychologist* 20(1965)321–333; A. S. Alschuler, *Teaching achievement motivation* (Middletown, Conn.: Education Ventures, 1970).

27. A. Hinding, Invisible women, *Research* (University of Minnesota), Fall 1980, pp. 21–29.

28. D. Bakan, *The duality of human existence* (Chicago: Rand McNally, 1966).

29. D. Levinson, *The seasons of a man's life* (New York: Ballantine Books, 1978).

30. M. Mead, *Coming of age in Samoa* (New York: Mentor Books, 1949), p. 144.

31. L. K. Frank, Centralization and decentralization. Toward the year 2000: Work in progress, in *Daedalus,* ed. D. Bell, (Boston: Houghton Mifflin, 1968), p. 181.

CHAPTER 14

College Students: A New Phase of Adolescence?

INTRODUCTION

The increasing numbers of teenagers in this country attending college have created the possibility of a new stage of development, a stage between the end of adolescence and the beginning of adulthood. Since this shift has occurred relatively recently, it may be premature to announce, in definitive terms, that student development in college is an established new stage, much like adolescence itself at the turn of this century. However, many theorists feel that such a stage is emerging.

As we noted in the first chapter, adolescence as a stage of development was a product of both physiology and culture. It was brought about in large part by industrialization in the late nineteenth and early twentieth centuries, which caused massive changes in family structure, career opportunities, and urbanization. As a result, teenagers no longer moved directly from childhood to adulthood. Instead, they moved into an intermediate stage of growth, a stage we now call adolescence.

Today, in the era of postindustrialization, it is possible that similar psychological and cultural changes are occurring. In this chapter we will outline some of these changes and the reasons that support the emergence of a new phase of adolescence for the college years. We will also describe a number of domains of development for this age span, roughly 17–21, to illustrate different facets of growth.

The major figure in what might be called the discovery of this new stage has been Kenneth Keniston. We begin our discussion with a description of his theory.

KENISTON: A STAGE CALLED YOUTH

In very broad strokes Keniston has outlined some of the major factors in support of his thesis that college-age students are neither adults nor adolescents in the usual meaning of that concept [1]. Instead, he refers to such students as "youth."

In the first half of the twentieth century, Keniston notes, there was a massive shift in secondary school attendance. In 1900 approximately 6% of teenagers completed high school; today approximately 80% complete it. This huge population of teenagers staying in high school and out of the work force—238,000 in 1900, 7 million in 1970, and 10 million in 1980—created the basis for James Coleman's classic concept of an adolescent society.

Since the 1960s a second shift has occurred. Its roots can be traced to the post–World War II years when college attendance through the GI Bill opened up the possibility of a college education for many. Since that time there has been a steady increase in college attendance. Today almost 50% of all teenagers attend higher education programs. Keniston suggests that this large number of 17- and 18-year-olds delaying formal entry into the adult world of work creates a new concept, a stage of youth, an intermediary stage between adolescence and adulthood.

We do not mean to say, however, that the college youth stage is simply an extension of adolescence or a moratorium—although years ago it used to be said that college, for boys, was simply a four-year hiatus between mother and wife. Certainly, as recently as the late 1930s there was no such thing as major demand for college attendance. The selective admission policies of today's prestigious colleges did not exist. For example, the class of 1938 at Harvard College had approximately 1200 applicants for 1175 openings; today there may be as many as 10 qualified applicants for each opening. And what is true for selective private colleges is also true for major public universities, although on a reduced scale. The point, however, remains. Large numbers of teenagers are extending preparation time prior to job entry. In addition, as Kenniston points out, the college experience itself has given rise to a new set of psychological and sociological issues that go hand in hand with the period.

PSYCHOLOGICAL AND SOCIOLOGICAL THEMES IN YOUTH

At the most obvious level, one characteristic that distinguishes college youth from adolescence is the major reduction of contact between youth and their parents. That is, the influence of a high school subculture is strong but always moderated to a great degree by daily contact with parents, at the dinner table, if nowhere else. However, the amount and kind of contact with one's own parents is greatly reduced during the higher education years. Thus an atmosphere is created for new issues and new tasks demanding resolution.

Keniston proposes three major themes of development that distinguish the youth phase from secondary school adolescence:

1. tension and ambivalence between self and society

2. enstrangement and omnipotentiality

3. refusal of socialization and acculturation

A number of characteristics are symbolic of these major themes, including youth-specific identities and the value of change and abhorrence of stasis. In other words, the three major issues are worked out in the context of a youthful counterculture as the object of personal identification and the increased valuation of change in movement, of being in process or on the road. The counterculture becomes attractive to college youth for a major psychological reason: Our culture so highly values change and growth.

In the area of tension and ambivalence between self and society, the college youth faces deep questions of transformation. The questions are larger than a close-to-home confrontation with one's parents over time curfews, friendships, and responsibility for immediate planning. Rather, society in general replaces the family as the source of conflict. That is, in any complex industrial society there are obvious social ills. However, during the youth phase, the perceptions and awareness of such societal weaknesses are greatly heightened. This heightened awareness increases the ambivalence about joining the adult society. Also, it may lead to temporary or (unfortunately) even long-lasting personal alienation. The youth may decide to withdraw in estrangement. Thus what Keniston calls the "wary probe" of college youth involves a careful examination of the question "How do I become an effective adult in society and honor my sense of personal integrity?"

The outcome of such a probe can lead, in a positive sense, to judicious commitments both during and after college. However, it can also lead to frustration and alienation. This outcome is perhaps best portrayed by the fictionalized account in *Catch 22* of American airmen during the Italian campaign in World War II [2]. The hero, a youthful officer, Yossarian, becomes acutely aware of the deception, fraud, and manipulation practiced by his superior officers. The commanders juggle the rules, fatten their own wallets through black market sales, and are immune to the deep personal issues of anguish experienced by the pilots. The number of missions required before rotation is increased. The pilots and crews appear totally powerless; psychological breakdown becomes epidemic. The rule says that psychological disturbance is a legitimate cause for relief. However, if an airman requests such leave, then that means he is really sane.

Many college students are attracted to a counterculture

Photograph from Anderson/ Editorial Photocolor Archives

Only an insane person would continue to fly missions without challenging authority. Permission denied! Catch 22. As a result, personal alienation and estrangement set in. Yossarian, on an off-duty day, sees a fellow pilot crack up psychologically and throw a person out a window.

Some college students experience a similar sense of bewilderment and estrangement at how our imperfect adult society distributes its resources and enforces our rules and laws. Keniston notes:

> The estrangement of youth entails feelings of resolution, unreality, absurdity and disconnectedness from the interpersonal, social and phenomenological world. Such feelings are probably more intense during youth than in any other period in life. [3]

Thus the general tension between self and society carries along with it the theme of estrangement and the theme of a refusal of socialization and acculturation. Instead of making careful and judicious commitments, of becoming acculturated, the youth may join the counterculture. The exact form of the counterculture may vary according to the times. Thus during the Vietnam era the counterculture involved the peace movement, flower children, communes, and a high degree of student activism. More recently, during the era of inflation and uncertain economic outlooks, the counterculture has taken the form of nonactivism—a counterculture whose hallmark is apathy. In either case, the counterculture serves the same function: It is an inherently temporary life space specific to youth.

Inevitably, though, the counterculture fades; the students age. Their status changes even though a few may maintain their allegiance well into their thirties. For most, however, the period of youth ends with the completion of the exploratory stage in higher education.

Even though both the emergence of the youth stage and its identification are recent, there is evidence that it has specific domains of development. We have shown that during early and late adolescence, in junior and senior high school, psychological functioning can be examined from a variety of related yet separate domains. In the same way, investigations of college youth are providing evidence about the structural changes that occur during these last years before adulthood. There are two domains of immediate significance: (1) the intellectual and (2) the moral value. We will now examine some of the most recent theory and research in these domains.

INTELLECTUAL DEVELOPMENT FOR COLLEGE YOUTH

In a longitudinal study William G. Perry identified a number of discrete stages of intellectual development [4]. Perry and his staff interviewed college students over a period of more than a decade. From these open-ended reports he created a system of levels according to the structure of thinking the students employed.

Perry was specifically interested in how the students understood what they were being asked to do in the process of studying for and taking examinations. In other words, what does a college education look like not according to the catalogue, the faculty reports, or the president's speeches, but according to the students' point of view? How do the consumers of a college program understand what they are going through? The answer is most enlightening. The way the pupils view their experience is almost totally determined by their level of development, and that level is highly independent of grade point average and the usual measures of scholastic aptitude. Within even a highly selective college student body, there are vastly different experiences and understandings. There are almost different "colleges" of students; all are taking the same courses yet they perceive those courses in widely varying ways.

Perry identified three major levels of development during the college years according to how the student understands the learning process:

1. dualism

2. relativism

3. commitment in relativism

We will discuss each of these levels in turn.

Dualism

The student at the dualism level perceives the world of learning as consisting of facts that are either true or false; there are no grey areas. In all the disciplines there are only right answers or wrong answers. Thinking is absolutistic. Knowledge is handed down from authority figures; it is not to be questioned. The student as learner must memorize the bits and pieces of knowledge and repeat them to the professors. Knowledge is perceived as a fixed and unchanging truth.

Students in the dualistic position approach studying as a process of rote memorization. In lectures they copy down everything the teacher presents without distinguishing between major and minor points or alternative theories—in fact, there is no differentiation at all. There are no priorities; everything the teacher says is relevant. Every chapter of every book is of equal value. Learning is the process of piling on facts, like building pyramids, one fact at a time. The student is a passive agent, absorbing the information. Thinking tends toward the concrete.

Relativism

At a higher level of development, students at the relativity stage perceive knowledge as abstractions and concepts. Instead of blindly accepting information as factual truth, students weigh and compare alternative points of view. Learning involves examining facts, theories, and which theories explain phenomena most adequately. Theories are understood as sets of ideas that help explain and predict areas of human existence. Thus concepts replace facts and theories replace bits and pieces of unorganized knowledge at this level.

In a developmental sense the shift from dualism to relativism represents a major change in stage. The learner is now able to understand more clearly what the tasks of college are all about. Studying becomes more selective. The student can distinguish between the important and the trivial. Thinking on the basis of concepts, the student can set priorities, learn the significant generalizations, and avoid cluttering up the mind with meaningless trivia.

To illustrate the difference between the two stages, let's imagine a freshman college class called Civilization and Literature. The first hour exam presents the following essay question:

> Compare the conception of a tragic hero in the *Iliad* and *Death of a Salesman*. (45 minutes)

A dualist would perceive the question this way: "I'm supposed to put down everything I can remember about Achilles, the central person in the *Iliad*. Then I'll list all attributes of Willie Loman, the central character in *Death of a Salesman*. Finally, I'll show how these two characters are different." After discussing the plan of attack, the dualist writes an essay in the following manner:

A Dualist Essay

The hero of the *Iliad,* wirtten by Homer, is Achilles. He leads a large number of different armies against Troy. As the general in charge, he is the best fighter, the most coura-geous, and time after time he saves his forces through brilliant strategy and enormous strength. He is most famous for his speed since he was given extra superhuman strength at birth by the gods. Also, he seems to have a real temper. When his best friend Patroclus is killed, he sulked in his tent for a long time and almost refused to continue fighting. At the end, though, he does continue and his side wins. Troy falls. Hector, the Trojan leader, is defeated. The victors sack and burn the city and thank Achilles for being such a great general.

Now for Willie Loman. He is much different from Achilles. In fact, I can't really say they are alike at all. Willie is not very successful as a salesman. He spends an awful lot of time on the road, taking trains through western Massachusetts—small towns like Chicopee, West Springfield, North Adams. He's al-ways hopeful, but when the story begins he is near the end of his life. His sales record is going downhill. He seems to be having lots of trouble with his family. His wife doesn't seem to understand him and gets into arguments with his son, Biff. Both father and son seem disap-pointed in each other. In the end he dies, very unhappy.

Thus Achilles and Willie were just about entirely different. Achilles was great and Willie was a nobody. I don't really see how you can com-pare them since they were so dif-ferent.

Student Comments to Self

Remember to put down everything I memorized about the story. Homer wrote it—or told it. Achilles is the main character. Say a lot about what a good fighter he is and also about the time when he nearly quits. Re-member to say how the war comes out.

Remember to put in all the stuff about his traveling—names of towns. It will show that I did read it.

Also show how much different Willie was from Achilles—I don't even think Achilles had a family.

Remember to summarize—a con-clusion that they are really very dif-ferent.

Instructor grade and comment: "Grade D—see me. You don't seem to understand the question."

Student comment to self: "I sure don't understand what the teacher means."

In contrast, the relativist writes an essay in the following manner:

A Relativist Essay

Homer and Arthur Miller have an entirely different world view on the nature of a tragic hero. For Homer, a product of his time and cultural tradition, the hero had to be godlike, a human endowed with qualities no mere mortal could have. Achilles exemplified this Homeric view to the nth degree—he saved his forces time after time with 11th hour interventions. By force of his physical and psychological strength, he leads, others followed. From Homer's view the *Iliad* became a literary vehicle to educate the future generations, as the story was told and retold, on the nature of humanity, the role of leaders and followers, and particularly how gods really do control destiny.

Arthur Miller takes almost a totally opposite view of humanity. For him the hero is everyman, the common, the everyday person. Willie could be anyone's neighbor—trying to live, to support his family, to eke out an existence that may have some meaning. He epitomized the phrase "living out a life in quiet desperation." Thus Miller paints a careful portrait of Willie's struggling, seeking yet never really achieving significant human contact. He's isolated and estranged from family, desperately hoping for the next sale. Each day he goes forth with a smile, a handshake, and a promise. He returns defeated and discouraged. His death comes almost as a relief.

Student Comments to Self

What in the world is this guy after with a question like this? We've read about 20 different assignments and he's picked out the *Iliad* and *Death of a Salesman*—Wait a minute. He's asking for a comparison of the authors, not the protagonists. So how do the authors differ on their assumptions—and that means I don't have to try and remember a lot of dates or Homeric book numbers.

So Homer sees the world in elite terms with gods interfering, while Miller is democratic, the hero as the person next door, struggling and feeling.

For Homer and Miller, then, the meaning of life is very different. Heroes are either superhuman and successful or quietly and desperately living out their lives in slow tragedy. Each hero represents a different world view symbolic of the author's conception.

Well, let's see—that about does it. I didn't forget to be balanced. Each is described according to the assumptions. The end summarizes the differences.

Instructor grade and comment: "A−/B+. An interesting essay catching the essence. Perhaps you could have a bit more depth in cross-comparison. Would Miller believe that the present day gods had forsaken Willie and that caused his trouble? Would Homer believe that the masses are only capable of following?"

Student comment to self: "Well, that's not bad at all. As for his other comments—comparisons can be made ad infinitum. Someday I'd like to grade him and tell him, "But what about yet another point of view!"

The differences between the two essays are perhaps obvious. In the first example, the dualist misreads the question. The exam asks for a comparison of the conception of a tragic hero. What does each author think about heroism and tragedy?—not What is the difference between Achilles and Willie? By missing the point of the question at the outset, the dualist is

Shifting from dualism to relativism is sometimes a lonely struggle

Photograph from Thad R. Wiseheart

doomed from the beginning. Since the dualistic thought process is so concrete, it is difficult for the dualist to step back and reread the question. Also affecting the student, of course, is the great pressure that almost all students feel in an exam situation. Under conditions of stress, perceptions narrow and students are apt to miss obvious clues. The first moments just before and during the handing out of exam questions are usually filled with great body movement—coughs, blank stares, and nervous twitches. Thus the Dualist grabs for the most convenient framework—"I'll give 'em the facts. Then the instructor will know I read the stuff."

The relativist, on the other hand, quickly spots the point of the essay, namely, to compare the authors' world views on the nature of persons. The relativistic thought process is abstract, focusing on the differing interpretations and concepts. Thus the relativist's essay does not compare the concrete facts or descriptions but, rather, analyzes the theories of the authors. The relativist compares the two theories, very carefully spelling out the divergent set of assumptions. Also, note that the relativistic essayist seems more comprehensive than the dualist's. And true to the stage, the relativist sees underlying issues as "relative"; issues depend on time and circumstances.

Essentially, then, the relativistic stage represents an advance over dualism, since the thought process is abstract and theoretical. However, relativism does have drawbacks. To understand these drawbacks more clearly, we move to Perry's third major stage.

Commitment in Relativism

At the committed relativist stage the student is capable of abstract thinking, as in relativism, but is also able to take a stand or value position. Thus the process is not simply abstract theorizing. Instead, after a careful weighing of alternative points of view, the committed relativist eventually arrives at a conclusion and value judgment.

The concept of commitment in relativism may strike you as a paradox. How can you be committed to one view and be relative at the same time? And if you've been asking yourself this question, you're right. Perry gets out of this apparent paradox by noting that the process of knowing is one of successive approximation. Today's theories, which seem adequate and airtight, gradually give way to tomorrow's views, which may be more adequate and more comprehensive—"better" theories. The committed relativist, as a result, can take a stand, reach closure, and make informed judgments. Simultaneously, the person at this stage also can remain open to new information, to new theories, and to new ideas. There is, in Gordon Allport's phrase, a whole-heartedness and a half-sureness [5]. Perry calls it the process of making a commitment yet remaining open to new views.

Perhaps the easiest way of making this point is to take a brief look at some of our older theories in view of today's information and theories. In American history, for example, most of the textbooks written prior to 1950 were based on a theory explaining that expansion was due to a process of manifest destiny. This theory was used to justify the subjection of the Indians, the exploitation of the environment by profiteers, and much of what we now call power politics. The committed relativist in the 1930s would have adopted this view, since that was the only theory around. At the same time such a theorist would have remained open to additional analysis and synthesis, so that today that person would be able to understand why Native Americans celebrate Thanksgiving as a day of shame and why we are paying a fearful price for the damage done to forests and streams. If we were to analyze other disciplines, we would find many similar examples. For instance, in psychology the theory of intelligence as fixed at birth, the theory that personality type is determined by body build, and the theory that adolescence is an age of stress and storm are just a few examples of previously held "true" theories.

At Perry's highest stage, then, individuals can synthesize and analyze the best of what they now know. Concurrently, such persons realize the limits. This dual attitude prevents the knowledge base from becoming absolute. Thus the intellectual process of policy or theoretical analysis at this level of thought provides individuals with a good ability in problem solving and inquiry. Ultimately, of course, all human knowledge is limited, as Allport says, by our own cerebral cortex.

Let's return to our essay question on Achilles and Willie Loman for a moment. The committed relativist would write the first part of the essay probably in a manner similar to that of the relativist. At some point, however, the committed relativist would go beyond the relativist:

A Committed Relativist Essay	Student Comments to Self
In my view neither Homer nor Miller quite captures the full potential or complexity of the nature of humans. Homer felt only a few preordained could reach heroism. This is elitist. Most of humanity is relegated to less human roles: robotlike, actions determined, futures controlled by the few godlike heroes. Miller, more egalitarian, still views the hero, as Aristotle would, "A person essentially good with a flaw—."	This is really going to be a struggle. I don't really agree with each view, so I'll have to develop and defend my own. Be careful, now, because I'm starting to stick my neck way out.

(Continued)

A Committed Relativist Essay	Student Comments to Self
Both assumptions appear incomplete. Humans may be capable of more, of learning from victories *and* defeats (small and large), of recorrecting and redirecting. Perhaps the real heroes are those persons (common or great) who can halt an inevitable process, who can admit error and not worry about "face," and who can at least question concepts such as honor. There is certainly a preponderance of evidence in favor of the tragic view—the Holocaust, My Lai—yet can't we hold a nobler view of human potential? Humans learning and growing rather than doomed to run out their tragic string could become a more complex view of the human condition.	I'm not sure what the professor thought about the issue. Well, that's it. Let's see if the professor agrees with me!

Instructor grade and comment: "Grade A—You've done a very fine job. Although I don't happen to agree (I'm a tragic viewer and suggest you read Freud's *Civilization,* etc.), you do make a good case for your alternative. I hope your idealism can stand up against all the onslaught coming down the road."

Student comment to self: "Well at least our differences are seen as thoughtful alternatives. I wonder what it would take to convince her that her view is really too limited."

As the essay shows, the atmosphere is vastly different at this level. The student and teacher have reached a point in their dialogue approaching colleagueship. The student perceives the teacher as a resource person, knowledgeable yet not infallible. The subjectivity of theory is ultimately tested by the logical persuasiveness each musters on behalf of his or her own views. The student's position is grounded in the context and moves gradually to divergence from the relativist's answer. The willingness to take risks may be one of the most obvious differences between this stage and the previous one.

TRANSITION STAGES

In presenting the three major stages found to varying degrees among college students, we have not mentioned perhaps the most interesting aspect of this framework. How do students shift from one level to the next?

What happens during the transitions? Since developmental stages are neither static nor permanent classifications, these aspects of change and transition are extremely important. We will consider the two major shifts in sequence: (1) the change from dualism to relativism and (2) the shift from relativism to committed relativism.

Transition One: From Dualism to Relativism

In moving from dualism to relativism, students experience a major discontinuity in their world views. The dualist is wholeheartedly convinced that facts are important and theories are too abstract. There is a strong emotional allegiance to authority. A professor must always be right.

It is hard for an adolescent to give up this view about learning, since memorizing and repeating answers by rote has paid off in the past. In fact, research studies in secondary and elementary schools have shown that questions and tests at those levels often call for dualism. "Don't think, just repeat what I've told you" is often the message sent. Students who obey this lesson receive rewards, good grades, good recommendations, and admission to college. Thus there is a strong drive to make the old system work: It's worked before.

This transition is particularly painful. At first the dualist learns a kind of pseudorelativism: "I'll find out which theory the professor wants and memorize that one." Indeed, sometimes, as Perry points out, such a method can reach almost a high art form. A dualist in transition can carefully memorize all of the professor's clichés, asides, and quibbles. By studying the teacher, the dualist in transition learns the game approach to writing essays. Perry notes:

> The pros and cons, the glib presentation of several points of view, the summary which judiciously selects one position to be in favor of, "all things considered"—these become the stock armamentarium of the gamesman—[who] would always find ways of imitating, of holding before the tired eyes of the professor the image of his fondest hope, all done up in his favorite words, his pet references and his treasured qualifications. [6]

Underneath, of course, the dualist in transition is still hopeful of finding the single right answer. In fact, the individual may experience some level of irritation during the transition. Gradually, however, the dualist in transition does move toward relativism. Having learned the form of abstract thought, of the existence of competing theories, students can shift to both the form and the structure of more complex thought. However, such a change is not necessarily automatic. The quality of the interaction, in a developmental sense, will determine whether or not positive growth occurs. But when positive growth does occur, students gradually give up on the hunt for the equivalent of the "Holy Grail" or the "Rosetta Stone," the key to unlock all the mysteries. Instead, there is a gradual acceptance of the basic relativistic view. In academic disciplines there are a series of compet-

SPECIAL TOPIC
The Uncommitted: Walker Percy's *Moviegoer* Confronted by Aunt Emily

Both Perry and Keniston have made a particular point that one of the greatest difficulties confronting students as they finish college is the question of commitment. After 16 or so years of education as preparation for commencement, the problem of choice and commitment is a major task. There is every reason to resist commitment since it implies closure. And much of college education, in particular, opens up new areas of thought to explore, new points of view to consider, new possibilities to examine. Thus there is a major discontinuity in shifting from open exploration to choice and closure. Perceiving commitment in the Perry sense is complex and difficult. Keniston suggests that it is so difficult a step that the usual response by college students is to remain uncommitted.

In the novel *The Moviegoer*, which was awarded the National Book Citation, Walker Percy depicts just such an uncommitted person, Binx Bolling [1]. A graduate of a fine private secondary school in New England, Binx goes through the motions as a college student. He does graduate, but only barely, and after a short stint in the Army he spends the next eight years of his life drifting. He does work, after a fashion, as a stock and bond salesman, but his major activities include driving his MG, attending practically every movie ever made, chasing women, and spending weekends at his country lodge. His only commitment is to live in the present and to avoid change. His favor-

ing theoretical explanations. My job as a student is to learn to understand the structure of each theory and the assumptions. This adds up to what is sometimes called a frame of reference, or a cluster of assumptions. Thus Thanksgiving as a national holiday may be appropriate given a particular frame of reference—from the European immigrant's point of view. Similarly, in the Achilles–Willie Loman question, the answer could compare the two different frames of reference, elitism and common-person democracy.

Once the student catches on to this level of processing, the experience of college changes markedly. As the student moves through the transition, a lot of the past fog disappears. The student, for example, may recall, with a combination of humor and chagrin, previous episodes in college—"Like

ite mental exercise is what he calls "successful repetition"—the reenactment of past experience just as it was. He uses this exercise to prove to himself that nothing of consequence has happened to him in the intervening years, a satisfying reminder that all is as it once was, with no growth, no change.

His interpersonal relationships are similarly shallow. In visiting a wartime buddy who saved his life, Binx said, "We must meet and greet, wish good luck and bid farewell." All in twenty minutes.

His family background might indicate a different world view. His father, a successful doctor, joined the RCAF in 1940, the year before this country entered World War II in order to fight totalitarianism. His Aunt Emily worked in a Chicago settlement house in the 1930s and later as a Red Cross volunteer in the Spanish Civil War. She returned to help guide Binx after his father died a hero's death. The family tradition, then, was one of service to others, to ideals, and to responsibility. Binx, in contrast, seemed to go out of his way to avoid anything that resembled these traditions. Near the end of the novel, with his usual thoughtlessness, he takes off on an impulse to visit Chicago. He brings with him a woman, Kate, who twelve hours earlier had made a serious suicide attempt. He stood by as she took the drugs.

Aunt Emily is beside herself, not so much with rage but with total disbelief that one human could be so callous as to completely disregard the welfare of a woman like Kate who was in such genuine distress. In a memorable scene Emily confronts Binx:

> "First, is it not true that in all of past history people who found themselves in difficult situations behaved in certain familiar ways, well or badly, courageously

(Continued)

the time I waited for the philo teacher after class and said—I've just finished the Republic—now whose definition of justice am I supposed to learn?" Or a discussion with the poly-sci professor—"Why do you keep saying that Rousseau had the feeling but not the theory behind the French Revolution?"

One final point: As we emphasized above, this transition occurs gradually, usually starting in one particular discipline and gradually spreading to others. However, the change from dualism to relativism may not always be complete. For example, it is common in graduate school for extremely well-versed abstract thinkers, who can conceptualize multiple theories with the speed of light, to come a cropper when they are forced to take courses outside their disciplines. A required course or two in statistics, for example, may find such a high-level conceptualizer in education or psy-

SPECIAL TOPIC (Continued)

or cowardly, with distinction or mediocrity, with honor or dishonor. They are recognizable. They display courage, pity, fear, embarrassment, joy, sorrow, and so on. Such anyhow has been the funded experience of the race for two or three thousand years, has it not? Your discovery, as best as I can determine, is that there is an alternative which no one has hit upon. It is that one finding oneself in one of life's critical situations need not after all respond in one of the traditional ways. No. One may simply default. Pass. Do as one pleases, shrug, turn on one's heel and leave. Exit. Why after all need one act humanly? Like all great discoveries, it is breathtakingly simple." [2]

Without commitment, then, one simply passes time, watches movies, enshrines mediocrity, and finesses life. So the major psychological task for young adults is to explore and examine alternatives. Premature closure, to be sure, must be avoided. Also, an endless moratorium must be confronted.

In the novel the starkness of Binx's extreme lack of humanity apparently is enough to shake him from his passivity. At age 30 he marries and enters medical school. But it is troublesome to see just how close Binx was from not learning anything at all from his, perhaps, penultimate escapade. After Emily's upbraiding, his first response is to call his secretary, Sharon, for an assignation. When he finds that Sharon is not available, something finally clicks. He learns that he cannot continually recreate past experience, that to live means growth and, above all, commitment.

REFERENCES

1. From *The moviegoer*, by Walker Percy. © 1960, 1961 by Walker Percy. Reprinted by permission of Alfred A. Knopf, Inc.

2. *Ibid.*, p. 174.

chology suddenly reverting to dualism. "I don't care about the derivations for analysis of variance, I just memorized that random, fixed, and mixed stuff."

Transition Two: From Relativism to Committed Relativism

The second transition phase is in many ways more complex and less sure than the first phase. This transition involves the shift from perceiving teaching and learning as abstract and relativistic to making a commitment in relativism. But in many instances high school students, college students, and even graduate students who reach Perry's second major stage, relativism, find it highly satisfying. It certainly is personally and intellectually safe to understand that abstractions and theories are just that, theories—

not carved in stone and not eternal truths. Thus some students may adopt relativism as a way of life.

In a sense this coming of age represents a breakthrough. The student feels liberated; at last things are clear. The answer to everything is, "It depends." Context and situation determine the answer; it is all a matter of opinion. The relief comes from the sense of finally being in on the game. The professor is no longer the authority figure but simply someone trained in one school of thought. There are other schools of thought, just as correct, elegant, and even aesthetically pleasing.

However, some students may also use the ability to understand academic problems from a variety of points of view in the service of cynicism. The logic proceeds in a linear form. A student may say, "If a theory is simply a set of temporary assumptions, and there are a series of competing theories, then it's all really a matter of opinion." That is, the accuracy and comprehensiveness of a position depend on accepting the assumptions that go along with that view; all views are equally valid. The cynicism takes the form of a decision to respond to relativism with relativism. For example, Perry cites what he calls the classic misuse of discovering cultural diversity. The student says, "Since it's all right for the Trobriand Islanders to do thus and so, you've no right to make me feel guilty about what I do sexually. It's purely a matter of individual decision." So students in this transition stage learn to muster evidence in support of whatever view they may have a temporary affinity for.

In a sense the genuine difficulty with this transition is the amount of academic success such a view can collect. Consider a college student majoring in political science. One professor demonstrates the advantages of government socialism, another teacher demonstrates the advantages of world federalism, and still another demonstrates the advantages of nationalism and power politics. In this situation the student can simply adopt whatever theory is being proposed, learn to analyze the problem from that point of view, and avoid the really difficult intellectual task of weighing, judging, and choosing. It's much less risky to keep the views in different compartments, each marked "the world according to Professor X." The same obviously holds true for other disciplines, psychology included. Consider the different essays a student at this point would write to the question of personality theory definition, if the professor was an avowed Skinnerian, Rogerian, or Freudian. Relativism can be a safe and effective stage for students.

The problematic aspect of this transition is the fact that even temporary closure is never achieved. Also, the longer a person remains in this style of processing, the more likely it is that cynicism will increase. That is, the student may feel that the world of learning is simply one great mass of conflicting opinion.

SPECIAL TOPIC
Raskolnikov: Kohlberg's Stage $4\frac{1}{2}$

"Is it a crime to have killed some vile vermin, an old usurer that was obnoxious to all, a vampire living on the life of the poor?"

"Brother, how can you talk like that? Aren't you guilty of shedding blood?"

"Suppose I am. And doesn't everybody do so? —I only wanted to make myself an independent position, to assure my entrance into life, to find the means, for then success would have been certain. —If I had carried my point, the victor's wreath would have been mine."

"But I cannot conceive in how far it is more glorious to shell some besieged town, then to destroy by the blows of an axe. The fears of aestheticism are the surest signs of impotence." [1]

"Perhaps the influence of his desires made him believe that he was a man to whom more was revealed than any other, and, therefore, more was permitted." [2]

Kohlberg's research with Kramer indicates that approximately 20% of his sample of college students adopted the stage $4\frac{1}{2}$ transition stage as they moved from stage 4 toward stage 5 [3]. In other words, almost one-quarter of his college subjects shifted to an extremely egocentric and self-centered relativistic moral judgment scheme. In fact, one college student who had been the most respected, outstanding leader in his class, and a straight stage 4 on the tests, suddenly became a thief, although his crime wasn't as devastating as Raskolnikov's. He stole a watch from a friend at work because, he said, his

Eventually, though, given enough positive interaction in different academic disciplines, the student may leave the safe haven of relativism. As we have noted, the movement toward committed relativism is complex. Yet if students begin to puzzle through the process, they may come to the point of temporary closure. "After considering a variety of points of view and multiple theories, I think that Theory X seems to hang together." At this point students begin to see that one can judge and evaluate the significance of alternatives and choose. Relativism and the process of evaluating become the basis for informed choice.

If the student does not make this shift, then there is the possibility of relativistic thought shifting from cynicism to a more active and revolutionary ethic. To understand this point more clearly, we will move to another

friend "was just too good, too Christ-like, too trusting and he wanted to teach him what the world was like." He felt no guilt about the stealing.

However, upon retesting the longitudinal subjects, Kohlberg and Kramer reported that by age 25 every single one of the students who had shifted to the stage $4\frac{1}{2}$ transition had subsequently moved to a principled level of moral judgment. All of the "regressors" reached stage 5 upon reassessment. Also, there were no further reports or incidents of egocentric criminal behavior. "Moral relativism and nihilism, no matter how extensive, seemed to be a transitional attitude in the movement from conventional to principled morality" [4].

There is an intriguing question in these results for adult development in general. Do some adults with histories of respect, leadership, and straight stage 4 judgment, who suddenly engage in activities totally out of character, represent a parallel shift to a stage $4\frac{1}{2}$ transition? The unfortunate case of Homer Smith may be such an example. An all-American at Princeton and student head of the honor code, Smith later as an adult resigned as college football coach for irregular recruiting practices.

REFERENCES

1. F. Dostoevski, *Crime and punishment* (New York: International Collectors Library, 1953), pp. 347–348.

2. *Ibid.*, p. 403.

3. L. Kohlberg and R. Kramer, Continuities and discontinuities in childhood and adult moral development, *Human Development* 12(1969):93–120.

4. *Ibid.*, p. 101.

domain and reexamine Kohlberg's scheme. This analysis should help to clarify the nature of the transition stage between relativism and committed relativism as well as clarify the overall development of value judgments.

Kohlberg's Value Judgment Transition: Stage $4\frac{1}{2}$

As we noted in Chapter 6, in Kohlberg's scheme students develop through a sequence of stages in the domain of value judgments. Generally, college students experience two major modes of judgment in their initial years in college, stages 3 and 4. Stage 3, value judgments based on pleasing others and social conformity, begins to decline in college. A stage 4 system of judgment based on an understanding of an abstraction like law, the system of civil governance, begins to increase. As we noted, the stage 4 system is superior to the prior stage, since it is more democratic, abstract, and consistent as a manifestation of justice. However, the stage 4 system does have certain drawbacks. What do we do when the laws in a democratic society conflict? What happens when the law is silent or, even worse, obviously biased? What happens when social injustice seems to florish apparently protected by law? What happens when those who make the law use their position to break the law?

If individuals have reached the point where they can think through such questions of value judgments and understand the inadequacy of Kohlberg's stage 4, then they may move into a value judgment transition stage, called stage $4\frac{1}{2}$. It is highly similar to Perry's relativism, or, as it is sometimes called, relativism-run-rampant, transition. In this stage the student uses loopholes in the law as a basis for value or moral judgment. Thus in this transition values are relative too. "I can't rely on laws as a firm basis for choice anymore," the student says. "There are too many inconsistencies, too many examples of inequality—look at how the laws protect the rich and guard the establishment!"

This new perception represents a change in value development. The student can reject stage 4 reasoning and decide that value judgments (like academic theories) are a matter of opinion. Kohlberg calls this level the Raskolnikov stage, named after the protagonist in Dostoevski's *Crime and Punishment*. Raskolnikov felt that since the laws were simply an expression of the ruling class at the time, a matter of personal preference or opinion, then he had the right to decide for himself what was just or unjust [7]. Taking human life would enable him to confront a deep and vivid personal growth experience. Such growth was enough to justify the act, especially since it would test his abilities to the utmost to pull off the deception.

The hallmark of Kohlberg's transition stage is the ability of the person to use theory so that the ends always justify the means. The methods or procedures are incidental to the outcome. Usually, the outcome is perceived by the person in some noble context. In *Crime and Punishment* it is Raskolnikov's personal growth as a goal that justifies murdering the innocent old man. In more up-to-date and less fictionalized terms, the stage $4\frac{1}{2}$ transition was most obvious during the college campus riots in the late sixties and early seventies. Some of the student protesters used the transition system to justify their own acts. College buildings were ransacked and burned, files and memos republished, and innocent people held hostage. The justification was as follows: "The war in Vietnam and Cambodia is immoral, extralegal—and has led to the slaughter of innocent civilian populations. Therefore it is not only our duty as citizens to protest, but also it is our obligation to protest, using *any means at our disposal*."

Such rhetoric is (and was) powerful, exhilarating, and liberating. In this view the values of democratic society are no different than those of a totalitarian regime. All societies are run by money-grabbing, capitalist exploiters. Thus anything goes: All means are legitimate to root out such corruption. Some students during the "occupation" of college facilities at such universities as Harvard, Columbia, and Berkeley seriously suggested burning the buildings down. If faculty and administration were caught inside—"Tough luck, then the'll know how napalmed babies feel!" The appeal of such reasoning is great during crises, but even in less emotional times this reasoning can exert a powerful influence.

It is the ability to misuse abstract reasoning, especially the deliberate blurring of means-ends relationships, that represents the major flaw in this transition. For example, during the war protest in the 1960s many students, unfortunately, were caught up in the protest as a method of expressing their stage $4\frac{1}{2}$ reasoning. In contrast, other students protested by employing the next highest level, stage 5 in Kohlberg, similar to Perry's committed relativist. The stage 5 protesters were just as opposed to the war and the crimes committed against innocent civilian populations (the bombings and My Lai). However, the higher-stage reasoning did not justify corrupt protest methods through noble goals. Instead, those students firmly believed in their rights and responsibilities guaranteed by the Constitution—a peaceful demonstration to redress legitimate grievances. Civil disobedience in such a context carries with it *not* an immediate request for amnesty but, rather, a request for court action. In the democratic tradition of Mahatma Gandhi and Martin Luther King, Jr., the students at the higher stage deliberately disobeyed civilian rules and laws in order to challenge this country's participation in an undeclared war. Their willingness to use

Civil disobedience can take one of two forms: Seeking peaceful redress or mob violence

Photograph from
United Press International

legitimate means and risk arrest mark this stage as distinctly different from the transition stage. The students at stage $4\frac{1}{2}$ saw no relation between means and ends, between trashing buildings and demanding instant amnesty.

We can imagine the following dialogue between a student at stage $4\frac{1}{2}$ and either Gandhi or King.

Student

I'm against this country's participation in an immoral war.

Gandhi

I'm against the immoral colonialism of the British Empire.

King

I'm against the immoral white supremacy laws in this nation.

Student

I will occupy university buildings to symbolize my opposition. Then to show the establishment, I'll burn records, trash the computer, and destroy the dean's office furniture.

Gandhi

I will speak against the continued presence of British rule.

King

I will organize a boycott of businesses—I will peacefully demonstrate with the striking garbage collectors.

Student

If I'm arrested I'll demand amnesty— or even better, when the police come in the front door, I'll beat it out the back, mingle with the crowd, and let those other poor slobs get arrested.

Gandhi

I'll readily accept arrest and imprisonment as a means to test the justice of my cause versus the conscience of the British rulers.

King

I'll seek arrest and trial in order to confront injustice.

Student to Gandhi or King: "Why would anybody deliberately let themselves be arrested? The government is wrong, absolutely. I'm right, absolutely."

Gandhi or King to the student: "A democracy is founded on principles of respect for human personality and due process. You must use legitimate methods in pursuit of just ends. Civil disobedience and passive resistance are legitimate means—riot and anarchy are not."

Gradually, students (and adults) in the value relativity transition should move to the higher, more complex level of value judgment both in the Kohlberg scheme and in the Perry framework. In a sense this transition stage relates to Keniston's suggestion at the beginning of this chapter. College youth during this transition are easily attracted to a counterculture as a reinforcement for a sense of opposition to and cynical judgment against the mainstream of the adult society. However, if one examines the alternatives to a democratic society, as imperfect as it is, one will probably agree with Lincoln's judgment: Democracy is admittedly the worst possible form of government, yet it is better than all others that have been tried. D. W. Brogen comments:

> Authoritarian government is like a splendid ship, with all its sail set; it moves majestically on, then it hits a rock and sinks forever. Democracy is like a raft. It never sinks, but damn it, your feet are always in the water. [8]

PROGRAMS PROMOTING COLLEGE STUDENT DEVELOPMENT

Thus far we have described particular aspects of Keniston's college youth stage. We have also described growth changes that may occur during this period. And as we noted, developmental growth at any stage and in any domain depends on interaction. In this section we will review some recent findings about college learning environments and college student growth and development.

There is evidence that the college experience produces some changes in the students' personalities over a four-year period. For example, some of Jacob's studies over thirty years ago demonstrated general shifts in development resulting from college attendance [9]. However, in most cases these studies provided only the most general link between what goes on in college and the specific impact on the students.

Part of our lack of knowledge of the college experience is a result of the liberal arts tradition. In that tradition a liberal arts program was conceptualized at the highest level of abstraction—the pursuit of truth, an invitation to civilization, and other cosmic goals. Similarly, the educational process during college was often described in abstract terms—process goals of learning, inquiry, discovering the structure of academic disciplines. As a result, the overall learning experience in college was considered a process too difficult to pin down, to analyze, to examine. It was considered much like a metaphor from economics, Adam Smith's "Invisible Hand." That is, students sat in classes and libraries, engaged in informal bull sessions, studied for exams, wrote papers, and chatted informally with faculty. Such an overall experience—an invisible hand, or the combination of the formal and the informal curriculum—could not be quantified. We could look at some specific elements, but if we did, we would miss the gestalt—the whole picture was greater than the sum of the parts.

But now, as a result of new studies, we know that it is possible to begin to distinguish among elements of the college experience. We no longer need to view the problem in general terms. The psychological impact of various forms of formal and informal college instruction is beginning to emerge. From these studies a tentative picture can be drawn concerning growth-stimulating experiences and growth-inhibiting interactions. It is to these studies that we now turn.

Chickering and McCormick's Studies: Personality Development and the College Experience

Arthur Chickering and John McCormick have studied college environments in over a dozen small liberal arts colleges [10]. Thus their findings are limited to colleges of modest size (enrollments of about 1500), although they note that the findings are consistent with studies done at larger colleges and universities.

The researchers divided the college environment into three elements: (1) teaching practices, (2) studying methods, and (3) student-faculty contact. To measure the psychological impact of these activities, they used a personality test (the Omnibus Personality Inventory) focused on four factors. The results were presented according to each element in the college environment across the four factors.

Teaching practices associated with *increased* personal autonomy, cognitive complexity, and personal expressiveness are as follows:

1. Students participate in decisions about course content and procedures.

2. Students make statements in class.

3. Students question the instructor.

4. Students question each other.

5. Students think about the ideas presented.

Teaching practices associated with a *decrease* in autonomy, cognitive complexity, and personal expressiveness and with an *increase* in practical outlook are as follows:

1. Students listen and take notes.

2. Lectures follow the text.

3. The instructor outlines the lecture.

College student development includes participation, asking questions, and making statements

Photograph from Owen Franken/Stock, Boston

4. Students do not participate in course decisions, do not ask questions, and do not make statements in class.

5. Students do not think about ideas presented.

In other words, a clear picture emerges about the practices that are associated with an increase as well as a decrease in personality factors over a four-year period in college. Personal autonomy, self-direction, intellectual complexity, and personal expressiveness all increase with the teaching practices outlined above. Thus when instructors encourage class participation and questioning of themselves and other students and do not rely exclusively on the lecture method, the students develop personally and cognitively. Teaching practices that inhibit growth by stressing passivity in the classrooms result in an increase in practicality at the expense of autonomy, complexity, and expressiveness. These two clusters, then, appear as syndromes—groupings of associated factors that have positive or negative effects on the development of self-direction and individual inquiry.

To examine the different effects of these two approaches to college teaching, Chickering and McCormick investigated studying strategies. They found that the following mental activities were associated with increases in autonomy, complexity, and expressiveness: synthesizing, analyzing, and interpreting. The one activity positively associated with a *decrease* in autonomy, complexity, and expressiveness and an *increase* in practicality was studying for class tests by rote memory of facts.

These results begin to identify the different psychological effects that may result from different teaching strategies. However, note that the researchers did not examine the relationship of these teaching strategies to grade point average but, rather, to personality factors associated with development. In other words, they examined the level of psychological development of college students over a four-year period. Also, we note that these results held for both males and females in the samples. Sex differences did not appear to have any effect on one's ability to develop autonomy, cognitive complexity, or personal expressiveness, in a positive sense, nor to increase practicality.

We should not conclude from these results that the lecture method is necessarily a poor educational technique. But exclusive reliance on the lecture method apparently does decrease psychological growth. The degree of passivity in the lecture method may account for such an outcome. Certainly, a great number of research studies on teaching effectiveness at the elementary and secondary school levels support Chickering and McCormick's basic finding. As we pointed out in Chapter 12, all too often teachers employ only one model of instruction. Exclusive reliance on only one technique will almost always have negative psychological impacts. Human beings apparently need diversity, change of pace, and a large repertoire of teaching methods.

Widick, Knefelkamp, and Parker: Teaching to Promote Inquiry

Perry's studies on college student development have given impetus to a series of programs designed to promote growth. In the first study of its kind two graduate students, Lee Knefelkamp and Carol Widick, under the direction of their advisor Clyde Parker, created special courses for undergraduates [11]. The instructors arranged the course content and the teaching strategies to match the developmental level of the college students. For example, using the Perry scheme, they identified two major subgroups of undergraduates in a humanities class: a group of dualists and a group of relativists. They then set up different teaching strategies in accord with these two developmental levels. At the outset the dualists received clear, highly structured reading and writing assignments. The relativists received more open-ended assignments, less direction, and diverse and conflicting content. The model is detailed in Table 14.1.

In the Dualist mode the instructor at the outset planned the entire course content and set specific assignments, deadlines, study guides, and expectations. Ambiguity was low. However, within this framework the instructor gradually introduced increasing relativism. Thus rather than immediately confronting the dualists' desire for certainty with ambiguity, the instructor gradually began to raise questions concerning other points of view. Accordingly, in the first week or so a dualist might ask, concerning a reading from *Zorba the Greek*, "But which view of human life is correct?" The instructor would not say, "Well that depends—which do you think is right?" Such open-ended teaching usually does not work with students

TABLE 14.1 Widick, Knefelkamp, and Parker model

Instructional model

Dualistic students	Relativistic students	Content	Goals
1. Moderated relativism, a focus on conflicting content and analytic skills	1. Implicit relativism, a focus on intellectual personal commitment	Subject matter reflective of important psychosocial issues of life stage of learner	1. Development through intellectual and ethical stages
2. Direct experiencing emphasized	2. Indirect experiencing emphasized		2. Subject matter mastery
3. Limited degrees of freedom provided; high structure	3. Extensive degrees of freedom provided; low structure		3. Student satisfaction
4. Personal atmosphere in classroom	4. Personal atmosphere in classroom		

Adapted from C. Widick and D. Simpson, Developmental concepts in college instruction, in *Encouraging development in college students*, ed. C. Parker (Minneapolis: University of Minnesota Press, 1978), p. 37. Reprinted by permission.

who need high structure at the outset. Instead, the instructor would ask the student to pick out one of the main characters, such as Zorba, and list his values concerning what it means to be human. This discussion could be followed by a shift to relativism: "Now, are there other ways to view these assumptions? Does anyone else in the story view it differently? What are the main elements? Which are the same and which are different?"

As the students became more comfortable with such differences, in-class debates were formed. Small groups were created to detail the major assumptions by different novelists on the human condition. Also, the students were asked to play the role of particular character in one of the readings and then play the role of a character with the most totally opposite personality.

In the relativist mode the atmosphere was totally different. Very few class guidelines were set by this instructor, and all these were negotiable. Self-reflective journal writing was required, but the amount of writing, the content focus, and the due dates were left to the students. The instructor attempted to raise questions that required choice and commitment amidst relativism. For example, after reviewing a number of novels and psychological theories, the students were asked to synthesize and defend one view as most adequate and comprehensive. How they justified such a selection forced the issue of choice and commitment. The instructor did not allow them to remain relativistic and say (in essence), "It depends." At another point the students were asked to boil down the message (salient theme) of a novel to one line and then justify the choice. For example, for *Moby Dick* a student boiled down the novel to the following: "Obsession, pursuit, and 'You can't fool Mother Nature.' " As a result of these techniques, there was a discussion toward higher-order abstraction as a means of weighing, selecting, and choosing from among alternative points of view.

The results of this experimental program were highly interesting, though mixed. The students in the first group, the dualists, all indicated positive developmental growth. They were able to process questions abstractly rather than concretely. They stopped the search for one right answer. They became comfortable with different points of view and could analyze theory on the human condition detailing different sets of assumptions. The process goals of open-ended problem solving were also evident, as was a greater reliance on their own thinking rather then trying to guess the instructor's thoughts.

Unfortunately, these positive findings were not matched by similar growth in the second group, the students who were already in the relativistic mode. Apparently, the course was not significant enough to stimulate growth to the most advanced stage in the Perry system, committed relativism. The students remained essentially relativistic and did not perceive any need to move toward the more complex system. As we noted earlier, the goals of committed relativism are both paradoxical and highly complex. It may well be a process that can occur only over a very long time period where the conflict over choice and commitment is genuine and personal rather than vicarious. That is, a college course is not parallel to the general responsibilities of adulthood and thus may not be able to promote growth to the complex committed relativist stage.

In any case, the experiment did indicate that students entering college in a dualist mode can be aided in their development through deliberate instruction. We do not have to leave it to random forces to determine whether or not a student catches on to the hidden agenda in college courses. Teaching pupils how to learn in more complex systems can be accomplished directly in the classes themselves, at least for those starting in a dualist mode. And when we realize that a major causal factor in college attrition is the lack of attention to this necessary transition, such a finding becomes quite important. Dualists who continue to attempt to memorize facts, find the single right answer, and keep straight the content differences in four or five courses each term often feel bewildered, discouraged, and almost without hope. The language system and sets of assumptions about learning that they use are different and set them apart from the rest of the college. There is both some poignancy and painful confusion for the dualist. One of Perry's freshmen exclaimed:

And, actually, as I look at it, I'm on the wrong side of the fence here because it seems to me that, to its great distinction, I don't know from this college or from other schools, is that this college gets away from straight facts and puts an emphasis on reading between the lines and interpretation. And I can't do that. That's the thing that bothered me all the time too that, it seems to me around here that's what they want mostly, and I can't do it. Now I don't know, it must be me because everybody else seems to be able to do it. But, just grin and bear it, that's all. [12]

Moral Judgment Instruction: The Sierra Project

Colleges are fond of dividing education into two categories: formal instruction (classes, lectures, readings, exams, and papers) and informal instruction (extracurricular activities). Generally, the expectation has been that if a student doesn't catch on to the formal instructional goals, then the atmosphere in the informal curriculum will educate the student in psychological development. The first systematic attempt to attain this second objective was recently conducted at a major university in California; the program was called the Sierra Project [13]. The guiding principle was to set up undergraduate student dormitories along the lines of a Kohlberg stage 5 system. In other words, the dormitories would operate on participatory democratic principles. The laws governing the dormitory regulations would be set by the entire dorm community: students, dorm resident assistants, and housing and activity directors. Democratic participation would replace the usual system of regulation handed down from the central administration and enforced by upper-class advisors. In the words of its chief architect John M. Whiteley:

> The Sierra Project is designed to facilitate and study dimensions of character development in college students. As a research project, the Sierra endeavor was to study the developmental status of college freshmen, and to assess the growth and development of those freshmen over the course of their undergraduate experience on such dimensions as moral reasoning, ego development, and sex role choices. As a curriculum development project, the goal of Sierra was to construct a replicable curriculum intended to facilitate the transition from high school to college life, stimulate psychological development from late adolescence to early adulthood, foster a consideration of future life-style choices and career decisions, and challenge the learner to apply his or her educational experiences to problems in the broader community through community service. [14]

The actual instruction took place in the dormitory setting through a series of formal lesson units as well as participation as a helper in a community service project. Thus the curriculum was composed of two basic elements: (1) discussions, readings, and laboratory experiences and (2) participation in outreach activities such as volunteer tutoring and counseling in nearby elementary and secondary schools. The lesson modules were organized into eleven elements, as follows:

- Unit 1, survival skills: teaching freshmen the learning skills that will help them succeed academically in the university; organizing their time, studying effectively, and preparing for taking examinations.

- Unit 2, social perspective taking: developing students' empathy— their ability to understand the point of view of another and to communicate that understanding, which involves basic listening and communication skills.

- Unit 3, community building: working together with students to create an atmosphere of openness, trust, and group support in an environment that encourages the resolution of conflict through democratic decision making.

- Unit 4, conceptions of life-style: helping students consider themselves and their life-style choices in relation to how other people have chosen to live, with particular reference to different value choices and perspectives on the world.

- Unit 5, sex role choices: helping students consider differing sex role expectations within society and the implications of these expectations for two-person relationships and for partnerships between men and women.

- Unit 6, assertion training: teaching students methods for identifying the personal rights involved in a conflict situation and for resolving that situation in a way that ensures one's own legitimate rights without violating those of others.

- Unit 7, career decision making: encouraging students to apply what they already know or can learn about themselves to formulating their educational and long-term career plans, with an emphasis on helping them identify career fields consistent with their values and abilities.

- Unit 8, community service: providing students with the opportunity to apply the skills they have been learning in Sierra to a social action setting in the community, which allows students to have positive contact with agencies outside the university community while still receiving support from the campus.

- Unit 9, life planning: giving students the challenge of planning their lives on paper, determining what kind of persons they would like to be and how they would like to live.

- Unit 10, conflict resolution in society: encouraging student participation in a commercially available simulation game in which students are given only a vaguely structured role and allowed to form their own society; the simulation emphasizes survival issues, personal goals, problems of power and authority, and consideration of the type of society that will provide the most good for the most people, using principles of fairness and justice as well as conflict resolution skills.

- Unit 11, Race role choices: helping students consider differing race role stereotypes in our society and their impact on interpersonal relationships, as well as the bases of racial prejudice and lack of mutual understanding.

In assessing the results, the investigators employed an overlapping measures design (i.e., they used a variety of outcome instruments). Since there is a variety of domains of development, a series of tests were used to estimate the impact of the project. Included were measures of moral judgment, self-esteem, ego development, alienation, and attitudes toward a sense of community and toward people in general. The results indicated that there were modest and statistically significant gains for the students who participated in the special project versus those in the random control group. The gains are summarized in Table 14.2.

Since the Sierra Project was the first major attempt to create such a special program and include a comprehensive research design, the results are suggestive but not definitive. In fact, the research information indicated that the project director had overestimated the initial levels of psychologi-

TABLE 14.2 Sierra Project results for college students (N = 240 approximately)

Measure of psychological development	Result
Value development (principled reasoning)	Gain
Self-esteem	Gain
Ego development (Loevinger's measure)	Gain (males only)
Sense of community	Gain
Sense of alienation	No difference
Positive attitudes toward people	No difference

Note: Because not all students took all the measures, the sample sizes varied somewhat. In general, there were approximately 120 (60 males and 60 females) in the Sierra group and an equal number in the control groups.

WILLIAM G. PERRY (1913–)

For years—indeed, for centuries—there have been discussions, writings, and arguments about the purpose of a liberal arts education. Usually, every new college president appoints an interdisciplinary committee of scholars who labor mightily, long into the night, over this question. The process is always tortuous. Soon it becomes obvious that there is little consensus, and after a requisite number of meetings the committee produces a document and then disbands in exhaustion, only to repeat the cycle with the next new president. The result is a highly abstract college mission statement, containing broad strokes of high-sounding rhetoric and quite often circular in reasoning.

Into this context came William G. (Bill) Perry. He took a rather novel approach. Instead of polling faculty and creating more committee meetings, he decided to listen to the college students themselves. With the adage The test of a pudding . . . in mind, he reasoned that whatever the faculty said or did collectively as a community of scholars, purpose should be discerned by the object of the curricular and extracurricular activities, namely, the pupils themselves. After all, what kind of a process could college possibly be if its conception and transmittal was so immaculate that it bypassed the students entirely? Of course, it can be a high-risk adventure to assess the objectives of a liberating education from the hearts and minds of the students. They might not agree with the official institutional line. Many vaunted objective has turned to trivia when examined from the consumer's view.

Perry's entire career had prepared him to tackle the task of defining the nature and impact of a liberal arts experience. He was a product of such an experience himself, graduating from a small New England private school that had an unusually heavy emphasis on the classical liberal arts study; he also received an A.B. in 1935 with honors in English and Greek and an M.A. in English in 1940. The program at the school was heavily prescribed, including the classics read in the original Greek and

cal development of the participants. The initial test scores showed that the entering students were essentially at stage 3 of the Kohlberg system (see Chapter 6) and at about the same level in the Loevinger system (see Chapter 5). Thus the students were still at a point where social conformity was extremely important, compliance was high, and sex role stereotyping was common. Also, individuality, self-direction, and the ability to perceive and appreciate individual differences were low. It may be that the curriculum

William G. Perry, Jr.
(1913–)

Latin. Disciplined inquiry verged on disciplined obedience. Among this
welter of literal translations and authoritarian teaching methods (similar
to those depicted by John Houseman in the *Paper Chase*), Perry began to
wonder how the students, his colleagues, processed the experience.
Some thrived, while others seemed dazed by the encounter. And apparently the administrators at Harvard College were beginning to wonder
about the same things. Some proportion of the undergraduates seemed
unable to cope with the regimen. Were they poorly prepared, incompetent, or what?

To answer those questions, Harvard Provost Paul Buck reached out

(Continued)

units were not carefully structured enough to help the students develop a
greater sense of individuality and psychological maturity. Thus Sierra
should be viewed as a debut, not a finale, on the question of college level
programs designed to promote growth.

In general, a fair conclusion at the moment is that studies like the
Chickering-McCormick survey and the Widick-Knefelkamp-Parker programs indicate that the type of general teaching method or instructional

WILLIAM G. PERRY (Continued)

to Williams College at the western edge of Massachusetts. Perry, who was by then an English instructor, was brought back to his college. The provost dumped the problem into Perry's lap: "Find out why the students are having trouble here, and do something about it!"

Because of a congenital hearing difficulty, Perry had been excused from active duty during World War II. Instead, he was assigned to teach navigation air cadets as part of this nation's effort to create an officer corps quickly. The experience made an indelible impression on him. He started teaching in the form he had experienced—directive lectures in an atmosphere of some intimidation. He transmitted the information, as he said, but it wasn't received or understood. Gradually, through instruction and experimentation he found that the air cadets could become educational resources for each other. He organized students into small groups; some students took on the responsibility to teach certain aspects of the topics. He soon found that student initiative increased and learning outcomes were more than satisfactory. Since the topic was air navigation, success was most important. Years later he remarked that he learned two things: (1) effective teaching was basically a nurturing of student initiative, and (2) the outcome of his method was most impressive—follow-up studies indicated that none of his navigators misdirected their airplanes in combat.

With this experience in mind he set out to evolve a similar solution to the Harvard College problem. Since he was a committed teacher, he created programs and simultaneously conducted research, avoiding the luxury of doing basic research without regard to application. His educational programs turned out to be a highly creative mix—a special reading course, students tutoring students, teaching instructors how to connect with student initiative, teaching students how to discern the meaning of examination questions, how to formulate essays, how to be-

strategies used can make a difference in the psychological impact on college students. Students can be aided in the transition from concrete, dualist, factual thought to abstract, relativist, theory concepts. Further research of the Sierra type may shed more light on possible living and learning arrangements in dormitories that may accomplish similar goals.

However, there remains one underlying question: Does promoting something as abstract as development in psychological stages mean anything in the real world?

come selective in assignments—all tasks done in the service of students taking over their own educational destinies. At the same time he listened to students. He and his staff provided intensive educational counseling, which was first and foremost a careful attention to student concerns. It was just this process that led to his scheme of the stages of college student development. The goal of college education also became more visible—bridging the gap of openness and commitment, as we describe in the text.

The process of discovery of these stages was a process of successive approximations. Perry and his staff, over a twenty-year period, listened to tapes of student interviews, read transcripts, discussed possible meanings, tried out several frameworks, and continually sought for objective verification (he would have as many as six "blind" judges evaluating his frameworks). This work finally yielded his book *Forms of Intellectual and Ethical Development During the College Years.* He did and does resist closure and constantly worries that educators may use the framework to label students. In fact, when the final draft of the book was edited and ready for shipment to the publishers, Perry started to waffle and call for further research. However, someone reminded him that at the highest stage on the scheme a person takes a stand on the best evidence then available, even while remaining open for further growth. At that point he began to think about the next edition of the book—and sent off the first.

In 1979 he officially retired from Harvard University, where he had served both as director of the counseling program (Harvard is fond of quaint titles—he was director of the Bureau of Study Counsel) and as professor in the Graduate School of Education. He has continued an active interest in programs for college student development. In fact, his workshops are so popular that he still looks forward to the time "when I can do all the things I planned when I retire."

Psychological Developmental Goals: Do They Mean Anything?	Ralph Mosher puts the question in the form of an analogy. During the Watergate investigations of the Nixon administration, one of the Senate panel, Howard Baker, noted that lawyers spend their professional lives "shoveling smoke." Mosher suggests that all this talk about ego, moral, personal, interpersonal, and social stages may give the same impression [15]. Psychologists dealing with complex ideas like character and moral judgment may be engaged in the same smoke-shoveling game. In other words, where is the reality in all this rhetoric? In the world of adulthood,

SPECIAL TOPIC
College Students in the Decade of the 1970s: Activism to Apathy

College campuses in the early 1970s were focal points for student activism on two fronts. The assassination of Martin Luther King, Jr., in the late 1960s had galvanized the drive for equal educational opportunity for minority students. Sit-ins, demonstrations, and protest rallies were common. Black leaders and the black community campaigned for affirmative action in admission and the creation of new academic programs and scholarships. Simultaneously, the colleges were also politicized by our massive armed intervention in Vietnam. Draft resisters organized. College students in large numbers demonstrated both on their own campuses and in the national capitol. Activism was everywhere. Faculty joined the student-led effort to force a change in our foreign policy. In the midst of this supercharged atmosphere college students at Kent State University in Ohio and Jackson State University in Mississippi were shot to death while protesting. These tragic events served to further escalate activism. Colleges held memorial services for the slain students. Concurrently, the names of some 25,000 servicemen killed in Vietnam were read, one at a time, to silent gatherings. To be a college student at that time was synonymous with being actively committed to seek justice. The nation became the classroom.

The decade of the seventies closed on a completely different note. With

after you've taken your last entrance test, completed your last multiple-choice exam, and finished your final term paper, does your level of psychological development relate to anything real?

The answer to this question is quite surprising. Numerous recent studies on the transition from college to adulthood indicate clearly that psychological development predicts success in life quite effectively—and, surprisingly, test scores of scholastic aptitude and an undergraduate grade point average do not. The studies provide conclusive evidence that indices of psychological maturity and stage development consistently predict success after college, while the more traditional measures of SAT score and grade point average do not.

However, before you decide to stop studying for exams, read on. Doing well academically in higher education programs was never designed to produce success in the complex world after graduation. The justification

the return of political conservatism nationally, and the beginning of economic hard times plus inflation, the memories of activism faded. Concern for social justice receded. A new generation of students wished to forget the past. Vietnam and the drive for black rights were only dim memories of their childhood. Instead, they viewed college in more conventional terms—a time for study, a time for pleasure, and a time to rejoice in apathy. The silent campus replaced the torchlight rallies. Student political leaders were viewed as egocentric campus pols interested in advancing their own careers.

In May 1970 students died at two campuses protesting on behalf of what they felt to be an unjust war.

In May 1979 less than 5% of the students at the University of Minnesota voted for a student president. The winner received 1158 votes from a student body of over 40,000. In second place with 971 write-in votes was a nonstudent, Bombo Rivera, a second-string outfielder for the hapless Minnesota Twins baseball team. According to an article in the Minneapolis Tribune:

> Rivera was supported by a group called the Committee for Student Apathy. The group said Rivera was the best candidate because his travel expenses would be paid by the Twins, not by student government. It also noted Rivera had no political experience thus making him qualified to run for student government. [1]

REFERENCE

1. *Minneapolis Tribune*, May 23, 1979.

for the academic course content and process is basically intrinsic—the idealistic goal of investigating the process of civilization. So as you read and digest the next set of studies, do not conclude that disciplined academic inquiry is a mindless exercise.

PREDICTORS OF SUCCESS: THE CASE FOR PSYCHOLOGICAL MATURITY

In the past decade several studies have examined the relationship between development during college and success after graduation. There is, of course, no ultimate measure of life success. In fact, the early Greek philosophers warned us to "count no person happy until death." However, it is still possible to use a variety of measures and judgments as a basis for evaluating college graduates who succeed in life and those who don't. The studies noted in this section generally employed a combined index that included some measure of occupational success, judgment by peers, listings in an association such as Who's Who, and evaluation of work performance by co-workers. There is, admittedly, some bias in any attempt to assess a criterion such as success in adult functioning. But with the use of multiple indices it is possible to reduce, though not eliminate, bias.

Do Grades Predict Success?

One series of studies summarized by David McClelland of Harvard University came to some surprising conclusions [16]. He found that actual job performance by adults had no relation to grade point average (GPA). Such a finding held no matter what level of job classification was studied: factory worker, bank teller, air traffic controller, or scientific researcher. In other words, whether the job required physical or mental skills, the GPA was not related to job success. For example, in the research category the top one-third of the sample, based on peer judgment, had undergraduate GPA's of 2.73, or about a B average. The GPA for the bottom one-third of the scientists was similar, 2.69, again about a B average.

Does Scholastic Aptitude Predict Success?

Longitudinal studies of scholastic aptitude have come to conclusions similar to McClelland's on GPA. In these studies the samples were selected during the college years and then followed up with retesting over a period of years after graduation. Instead of examining the relation between college grades and life success, however, these longitudinal investigations examined the relation between academic ability, as measured by the Scholastic Aptitude Test, and life success.

A major study at Brown University found that ratings of psychological maturity were highly related to success after college, while SAT scores were not [17]. High school principals and guidance counselors were far more accurate than the SAT in predicting success. The school personnel rated college admission applicants on traits such as self-direction, autonomy in thinking, problem-solving orientation, and maturity of judgment—all traits related to higher stages of psychological development. The highly rated students excelled not only in college but also in a follow-up 12 years after graduation. Many of these psychologically mature students had low SAT scores (about 150 points lower, on the average, than the comparison groups; or SAT verbal scores of 410 versus 566), yet they performed exceedingly well in college. At the time of the study these students were referred to as "high risk" applicants. Because of their success in college and postcollege, they became known as "Tom Sawyers."

Douglas Heath, a researcher at Haverford College, also conducted an intensive longitudinal study of predictors of life success [18]. He used over two hundred indices of successful adaptation to life after college. He studied college graduates not only from this county but also from other countries (Protestant, Jewish, Catholic, and Muslim countries). He found that there was general agreement among his judges from different cultures about the definition of adult maturity. Successful functioning as an adult in any of these cultures was composed of the following elements:

1. Symbolization and reflective intelligence.
2. Allocentrism, empathy, and altruism.
3. Integration, or the ability to combine a variety of views.
4. Stability.
5. Autonomy and self-direction according to broad humane values.

In other words, the definition of successful functioning among college graduates included all five areas. College students who were rated high on these traits were successful as adults. Students who rated low were not. Most surprisingly, Heath found, especially for the American students in his study, that there was no relation between aptitude and success. He notes:

> Adolescent scholastic aptitude as well as other measures of academic intelligence do not predict several hundred measures of adaptation and competence of men in their early thirties. In fact, scholastic aptitude was inversely related in this group to many measures of their adult psychological maturity, as well as their judged interpersonal competence. [19]

An inverse relationship means that higher SAT scores were related to less competent adult functioning in the sample. However, Heath is not arguing for a nonintellectual view. Rather, he takes the position, on the basis of his findings, of distinguishing between psychological maturation and intellectual development. Intelligence, at least as measured by tests, is not enough by itself. Instead, Heath's work suggests that a far broader conception is necessary—the college student as a thinking, feeling, relating person who considers viewpoints carefully and systematically, who can accurately understand and respond to emotions in others, who considers human relationships in accord with humane values, and who can trust and modify the method of judgment. Such traits he sees as being essential to balanced growth, or what he calls the process of personal integration. Thus the error we can too easily make as educators is to overvalue any single domain of functioning to the exclusion of the other areas.

To Heath—and we would certainly agree—the goal of college education should be to stimulate balanced psychological growth toward maturity. By promoting reflective judgment, allocentrism, empathy, altruism, personal autonomy, competence in interpersonal relationships, and integration, education can become humanly liberating.

Kohlberg's Studies: Childhood to Adulthood

The previous studies have examined the relationship between college performance and adult functioning. An extensive series of studies conducted by Lawrence Kohlberg has taken the next step and investigated possible childhood predictors of successful adult functioning [20]. These studies reach conclusions similar to those of the others.

Kohlberg measured adult success by career achievement, psychological ratings of life adjustment, absence of crime and mental illness, and other such measures. After reviewing literally hundreds of studies, he concluded that academic achievement made no independent predictive contribution to successful life adjustment. However, he also found that broad measures of psychological maturity and moral judgment were accurate predictors. In other samples of same-age children those rated as more psychologically mature and higher on measures of moral judgment were more successful as adults, according to his multiple criteria. Also, he found that the emotional treatment of children who demonstrated personal problems was neither better or worse than that of comparable control groups. He concluded:

> The best predictors of the absence of adult mental illness and maladjustment are the presence of various forms of competence and ego maturity in childhood and adolescence rather than the absence of problems and symptoms.
>
> Put bluntly there is no research evidence indicating that clinical treatment of emotional symptoms during childhood leads to predictions of adult adjustment. [21]

SUMMARY: TO EMPOWER AND ENNOBLE

In this chapter we have suggested that the college experience can be a significant one for the process of psychological development. In the Keniston sense, college can be a time for movement from noncommitment to choice and commitment. In Perry's terms the movement can be from dualism through relativism, with anticipations of commitment. From Kohlberg's perspective development can move beyond adherence to stage 4 moral judgment values through the stage $4\frac{1}{2}$ transition to stage 5, democratic principled values. College environments can aid in the process of this development. In Erikson's phrase, the plan for development is in place. It is possible for adults and college students to interact in humane and developmentally appropriate ways to ensure that the process of growth is not artificially halted.

The evidence reviewed in this chapter and the information presented in many of the earlier chapters suggest a broader point. Adolescence—early, middle, and late—is a critical period in human development. The theories we have presented provide a framework for understanding different aspects, such as personal, interpersonal, social, sexual, emotional, value, and intellectual development. This information reduces the mystery and increases an appreciation of the complexity of adolescent growth.

The developmental framework also includes direct implications for practice. At the outset we said that a major element that sets developmental theory apart from other conceptions is the concept of interaction. We have underscored the importance of stimulating human growth by starting where the learner is. Potentially, then, educational programs in a broad sense can interact with pupils in a growth-producing manner. The programs can be formal experiences in secondary school classrooms, such as action learning, or in colleges, such as Sierra-type living-and-learning experiences. Or the programs can be informal after-school activities in both school and community settings. In either case, the role of the leader (teacher, counselor, advisor, youth worker, parent) is critical in creating the conditions through which development may be enhanced. Certainly, the studies that searched for the predictors of successful functioning in life provide strong support for the goals of developmental growth. By promoting human growth, we empower and ennoble those we educate. John Dewey said it better when asked to describe the goals and methods of education for a democratic society:

> That meaning is to set free and to develop the capacities of human individuals, without respect to race, sex, class or economic status. . . . The test of their value is the extent to which they educate every individual into the full stature of his or her possibility. [22]

KEY POINTS AND NAMES

Kenneth Keniston

College youth stage

Themes in youth

William G. Perry

Intellectual development
  Dualism
  Relativism
  Committed relativism

Transition stages
  Dualism to relativism
  Relativism to committed relativism

Kohlberg's stage $4\frac{1}{2}$

Arthur Chickering and John McCormick

Effective college teaching

Carol Widick, Lee Knefelkamp, and Clyde Parker

Promoting inquiry

John M. Whiteley

Sierra Project

Psychological maturity and success in life

David McClelland

Douglas Heath

REFERENCES

1. K. Keniston, *The uncommitted: Alienated youth in American society* (New York: Harcourt, Brace & World, 1965).

2. J. Heller, *Catch 22* (New York: Simon & Schuster, 1961).

3. Keniston, p. 637.

4. W. G. Perry, *Forms of intellectual and ethical development during the college years* (New York: Holt, Rinehart and Winston, 1970).

5. G. Allport, *The person in psychology* (Boston: Beacon Press, 1968), p. 4.

6. Perry, *Forms*, p. 50.

7. L. Kohlberg and R. Kramer, Continuities and discontinuities in childhood and adult moral development, *Human Development* 12(1969):93–120.

8. D. W. Brogan, quoted by R. L. Mosher in *Value development . . . as the aim of education,* ed. N. A. Sprinthall and R. L. Mosher (Schenectady: Character Research Press, 1982), p. 69.

9. P. E. Jacob, *Changing values in college* (New York: Harper & Row, 1957).

10. A. Chickering and J. McCormick, Personality development and the college experience, *Research in Higher Education* 1(1973):43–70.

11. C. Widick, L. Knefelkamp, and C. Parker, The counselor as a developmental instructor, *Counselor Education and Supervision* 14(1975):286–296.

12. Perry, p. 76.

13. J. M. Whiteley, The Sierra Project: A character development program for college students, *Moral Education Forum* 3(1978):1–12; J. M. Whiteley, *Character development in college students* (Schnectady: Character Research Press, 1982).

14. Whiteley, Sierra Project, p. 1.

15. R. L. Mosher, *Adolescents' development and education* (Berkeley, Calif.: McCutchan, 1979), p. 103.

16. D. C. McClelland, Testing for competence rather than for "intelligence," *American Psychologist* 28(1973):1–14.

17. E. Nicholson, *Success and admission criteria for potentially successful risks, Project Report* (Providence: Brown University and the Ford Foundation, March 1970).

18. D. Heath, *Maturity and competence* (New York: Gardner Press, 1977).

19. *Ibid.,* pp. 177–178.

20. L. Kohlberg, J. LaCrosse, and D. Ricks, The predictability of adult mental health from childhood behavior, in *Handbook of child psychopathology,* ed. B. Wolman (New York: McGraw-Hill, 1971), pp. 1271–1284.

21. *Ibid.,* p. 1284.

22. J. Dewey, *Reconstruction in philosophy* (New York: American Library, 1950), p. 147.

A High School Course: Peer Counseling— A Curriculum Guide

INTRODUCTION

The first phase of the class begins with personal introductions by each participant. In previous classes we tried out a series of procedures for these introductions including structured exercises, games and simulations. We found that the development of listening skills, building the class as a group, and the creation of a collegial atmosphere between the pupils and the instructional staff could best occur without the use of such so-called simulation techniques. Instead we asked each person to take about 5 to 10 minutes to introduce him/herself, say something that would help us get acquainted and mention some significant learning experience in the past week or so. The class co-teachers would then respond to the introduction in a manner designed to indicate that they heard and understood both the content and some of the feelings that the person introducing him/herself was experiencing. There are some moments of awkwardness and self-consciousness in this procedure which the co-teachers acknowledge as well as a sense of relief when a person gets through his/her turn. To speak about "self" in front of 25 to 35 classmates and staff is a significant and difficult experience, yet the procedure is designed to provide a common experience base for the initial stages of the class as well as demonstration of difficulties of both sending and receiving communication messages. At the

From N. A. Sprinthall, Learning psychology by doing psychology, in *Developmental education*, ed. G. D. Miller (St. Paul: Minnesota Department of Education, 1976), pp. 27–33. Reprinted by permission.

conclusion of this phase we ask everyone to fill out a two page question guide on the introductions:

Please describe your *thoughts* and *feelings* as you introduced yourself.

How uncomfortable were you just prior to your turn?

Did you prepare something to say in your mind?

What were your feelings while you were talking?

Can you describe how you felt afterwards?

Did you have a sense that the class was listening to you? Were any specific individuals helpful with their questions?

Did you have difficulty at times listening to others?

Did you learn new ideas, more about your classmates, teachers, during the introductions? Any new thoughts and ideas about yourself?

We then summarize the comments for the pupils as a means of helping them understand that everyone in the class including the staff is somewhat uncomfortable, would like to say more about themselves, felt they were slightly incoherent, had difficulty in really listening to others, etc. Such information gleaned from their reflections upon the experience helps to promote an equalization and democraticizing of the classroom process. Also it is noteworthy how many times pupils comment that it's the first time they knew anything about many of their colleagues more than a name. The procedure also helps to begin to break down some of the previously formed teenage cliques.

TEACHING ACTIVE LISTENING SCALES

Immediately following the introductions we start direct teaching of the Active Listening Scale. We found that by modifying the original Rogerian Empathy Scale into two components, response to content and response to feeling, we could teach the skills more effectively. We could more easily focus on the particular domain that the pupils were having difficulty mastering by separating the dimensions. We described the scales briefly and handed out one page copies to each pupil.

Active Listening Scale

Response to Feelings—Emotions

5. Goes well beyond the person's expressed feelings. Provides the person with a major new view of the emotions he/she is experiencing.

Response to Content—Ideas

5. Goes well beyond the stated meaning. Provides new insight.

4. Goes to a slightly deeper feeling than expressed. Helps person understand his/her own feelings in more depth. Goes just beyond the emotions expressed.

3. An accurate understanding of feelings and/or emotions, expressed in your own words. An accurate reading of feelings.

2. A slight distortion of the feelings expressed—a near miss.

1. No awareness of feelings expressed, the wrong feelings— or a genuine put-down.

4. Goes slightly beyond the meaning stated. Provides some new insight. More concise. Helps the person understand his/her own ideas better.

3. An accurate understanding of the content—a restatement in your own words of what the person said.

2. A slight distortion of meaning—just misses what the person said.

1. Dead wrong—the opposite of what was said. A complete miss as to meaning or an active disinterest.

PRACTICING LISTENING SKILLS

Through practice such as writing down single responses to stated "role play" or actual concerns, the pupils gradually develop skill and comfort with the scales. It is a slow process to move from the artificial and somewhat "plastic" experience of writing single responses to the point of maintaining verbal dialogue with a role-play counselee and requires patience and support. The students' initial resistance to practicing the scales tends to be somewhat high. We found, however, that this structured approach seems to yield positive outcomes in skill learning. Also, we usually play audio tapes from some actual initial counseling interviews made by graduate students. By showing some of these first awkward interviews between real clients and graduate counselors in-training, the high school pupils see firsthand the difficulty in accurately identifying and responding to content and feelings. We emphasize the two stage nature of these learnings, (a) to accurately pick-up, hear, and identify content and feelings, and (b) to frame a response, "Using your own words which communicate to the role-play client that you do accurately understand the message." The pupils then learn to score responses both on the audio-tapes and on the single response in-class practice sessions. By teaching the pupils to "judge" their own as well as others' responses, learning the scale is hastened. The pupils become conscious of the dual process of identifying on one hand and responding on the other to understand and experience the process itself.

We have also used practice role play responses to video-taped excerpts as one further aspect of this skill training phase. We play an excerpt on video to the class, stop the tape, and ask them to write a response which captures both content and feeling. These excerpts can be "home-made" simply by asking pupils in a drama class to make up a problem that teenagers often experience and then tape a series of statements describing the problem. After showing the taped excerpts we then go over the responses in class usually listing on the blackboard all the content responses and then all the feeling responses to each excerpt. This particularly teaches a language for identifying emotions as we as a group then pick out from the list on the board the responses that seem most accurate. The pupils then rate their own responses on the two five-point scales. Thus the process teaches judging or rating skills and a language system for identifying emotions simultaneously.

ADDING NONVERBAL SKILLS

After the first three or four weeks on the active listening scales we introduce a third aspect of counseling and communication training—the nonverbal components. The summary below represents a framework around which we focus the questions of body-language. In the same way as the content-feeling dimensions are presented, we have the students learn to *identify* nonverbal messages and then after some practice sessions in class, we routinely assign a pupil the task of process observation of role play counseling sessions. Thus with the one page handout as a guide a pupil will jot down examples of body language "talk" observing the class practicing active listening responses. At the end of each exercise the process-observer will make a short presentation of his/her findings. This helps to illustrate the three major aspects of communication, content, feelings and the nonverbal aspects.

The Psychology of Counseling

1. *Nonverbal Cues: Body Language Signs*

	Quality	Quality
Voice	Harsh/Overly Sweet	Genuine
Facial Expression	Stone-face or disinterested	Interested
Posture	Leans away Tense, rigid or too casual	Leans toward-relaxed

Nonverbal Cues	Quality	Quality
Eye Contact	Avoidance of eye contact or excessive staring	Maintains reasonable eye contact
Touching	Avoids all contact or smothers (back-slapper)	Contact appropriate to situation
Gestures	Closed: guarded or overly jovial	Open, Flexible
Spatial Distance	Too far or too close	About "right" Comfortable

2. *General Congruence*

Similarity of verbal and nonverbal cues—how "together" is the talk and the body language.

Examples: "Oh, I'm not embarrassed." (Face reddens)
"I really enjoy lecturing to students." (Knuckles white)
"It's so nice to see you." (Voice tight)
"The test you gave us was a useful learning experience."
(Eyes like black darts)

3. *Three Areas of Communication: A Summary*

Verbal Content (5 pt. scale)	Feelings (5 pt. scale)	Nonverbal Cues Congruent/Dissonant

These three dimensions provide us with information on the *content* of what is being said, the *feelings* behind the content, and the *body* language. Sometimes the feelings and the nonverbal language are referred to as the "hidden agenda"—the messages just below the surface. If we learn to "see" and respond to these dimensions, we will tend to increase our own understanding of the complexities of "where the other person is coming from" or that we will become more accurate in "reading" of another person. Often when we say the "Medium is the message," we mean, *how* a message is communicated (the feelings and the body language) is more important than the content itself. Actions speak louder than words, feelings are more significant than rhetoric, are other ways of saying this same concept.

WRITING ASSIGNMENTS

Following these process learnings, we then handed out short reading assignments such as "Barriers and Gateways to Communication" by Carl Rogers (1952), and "Parent Child Communication Skills" by the National

Education Association (1971). We also showed the Gloria films ("Three Approaches to Psychotherapy") with counseling segments by Rogers, Ellis and Perls. We asked the students to prepare papers examining the communication issues. The format for one such writing assignment was as follows:

Writing Assignment (Sample A)

1. Read the Roger's article, "Barriers and Gateways to Communication."

2. Write a reaction paper, 2–3 pages, due next week. Hand in to your small group leader.

3. Almost any format will do since the purpose is for us to see how understandable and significant his comments are for you. If you wish, you can (1) *Describe his basic idea:* (how clearly does he state his position?, is his language too "academic?", does he explain his view adequately or is it too vague, too trivial, too Utopian?) (2) Put his ideas in your own words, e.g., this is like a level 3 response. How would you say what he says if you were talking with him? (3) Without being too judgmental, *how do you evaluate the significance* of his view for everyday life. (4) *Other comments:* Did he seem much different on "paper" than in the film? Does he make more sense in action with Gloria than in the paragraphs? Are his nonverbals and body language congruent (all together) with his words?

After completing the film of Perls and Ellis including Gloria's addendum, we hand out another writing assignment seeking to synthesize or integrate the three approaches to our overall goal of effective communication in all three modes. The writing format follows:

Writing Assignment (Sample B)

Write a reaction paper (2–3 pages) comparing Rogers, Perls and Ellis. Again, your paper may take almost any format that best fits your method of description and examination of the issues.

1. Gloria summed it up that Rogers responded to her emotions, Ellis to her mind, and Perls to her as a person. You might start by explaining in your own words what she meant by this.

2. Also, you could comment on your own reactions to her choice at the end—surprise, disbelief, dismay—that she chose Perls!

3. You also might comment on how complete are any of the single communication systems depicted in the films. For example, is it

complete just to focus on content (Ellis), feelings (Rogers), or body language (Perls)?

Is it possible to consider a "super-gestalt" of communicating in all three basic modes? Can a person learn to accurately identify content, feelings, and body language simultaneously (or is it like a three ring circus!). And further, can a person learn not only to *identify* in the three areas but also to respond accurately?

THE SHIFT FROM ROLE PLAYS

As we proceeded through the term we would follow the same overall format employing part of the class time on process skills and part on intellectual discussion and writing assignments. As the class proceeded the skill training aspect of the process work declined. Instead the pupils began to bring in their own "real life" concerns. The role play counseling shifted to actual problems, and the pupils started using their newly learned active listening skills on these genuine issues. The range of issues was substantial from one student expressing anger over being falsely accused by a teacher of stealing a book, another concerned over the loss of her dog, to yet another who had an over-protective mother and felt suffocated. Students had the opportunity to both counsel their peers and be counseled in turn by these same peers.

RECIPROCAL HELPING

At an experiential level, we were stressing the reciprocal nature of counseling and communication. We were not interested in creating a professional cadre of teenager counselors as one class of helpers with the balance of the school population as helpees. Instead we wanted the concepts of helping, caring, active listening to remain an essentially democratic responsibility. Pupils were asked to note the difference between this approach to counseling and communication and the regular professional approach with its univocal focus.

TRANSFER OF TRAINING ISSUES

As the class neared the end of the term, we then stressed the transfer of training problem. We examined the issues involved in moving from the context of the particular class into the "outside" world. We asked the pupils to make brief communication audio tapes with friends as a means of trying out their skills with nonclassmates—this provided for a significant discussion when the pupils realized both how much they had learned as well as how difficult it was to transfer such learning to different situations. As a final test of transfer we administered Counseling Skill tests to the class as a whole and reported those results at the final class.

Continuing issues that we stressed throughout this transfer of training phase concerned the questions of choice and the meaning of behavior in general. In the first instance we would focus on the responsibility that accompanies the use of active listening and helping others. As pupils learned to use these skills in the real world they often found themselves confronted with such difficult choice questions—"Should I respond to my friend now that I can hear the pain?" or "I'm not really sure that I like this at all. I was happier not listening to others" or "I was really surprised to find out how complicated the problem was, but now what?" We try to help the pupils understand that they can become effective helpers to each other, are genuine resources and can themselves be helped by their peers.

Also we point out that the process of active listening as helping provides all of us with an understanding of how complicated and multifaceted are problems of human behavior. In a sense the communication training becomes a means of teaching pupils that behavior is not the result of a single cause and effect sequence (we call that view the billiard-ball theory of human behavior). Instead the process becomes the road to multiple causation and what it means to say that human behavior is over-determined. Learning to explore and examine for meaning and the series of factors that are involved in almost any aspect human behavior becomes our way of teaching for nonstereotyped thinking about human behavior and its causes. The process of developing psychological and personal maturity on the part of teenagers is aided, in our view, by these learnings. To understand the complexities of behavior in ourselves and others is certainly a step toward the development of genuine empathy.

Index